The Opening of American Law

The Opening of American Law

Neoclassical Legal Thought, 1870–1970

HERBERT HOVENKAMP

OXFORD
UNIVERSITY PRESS

OXFORD
UNIVERSITY PRESS

Oxford University Press is a department of the University of Oxford.
It furthers the University's objective of excellence in research, scholarship,
and education by publishing worldwide.

Oxford New York
Auckland Cape Town Dar es Salaam Hong Kong Karachi
Kuala Lumpur Madrid Melbourne Mexico City Nairobi
New Delhi Shanghai Taipei Toronto

With offices in
Argentina Austria Brazil Chile Czech Republic France Greece
Guatemala Hungary Italy Japan Poland Portugal Singapore
South Korea Switzerland Thailand Turkey Ukraine Vietnam

Published in the United States of America by
Oxford University Press
198 Madison Avenue, New York, NY 10016

Library of Congress Cataloging-in-Publication Data
Hovenkamp, Herbert, 1948– author.
The opening of American law : neoclassical legal thought, 1870–1970 / Herbert Hovenkamp.
pages cm
ISBN 978–0–19–933130–7 (hardback : alk. paper) 1. Law—United States—Philosophy.
2. Law—United States—History. I. Title.
KF380.H68 2014
349.73—dc23
2014009690

To Christina

Contents

Introduction

TWO INTELLECTUAL REVOLUTIONS disrupted American legal thought in the late nineteenth century. First was the theory of evolution by natural selection, particularly Charles Darwin's argument in *The Descent of Man* (1871) that humanity is but another species going through the same evolutionary process as all others, and that cultural and social ideas are themselves a product of natural selection.[1] The second theory was the marginalist rational actor model in economics, which completely upended economics' theory of value, de-emphasized the role of history in policymaking, and initially provided powerful arguments for both wealth redistribution and greater public intervention in the economy.

Darwinism and marginalist economics both led to extremist views, and on both the political right and the left. Darwinism led to the laissez-faire of the Social Darwinists and the interventionist State of the Reform Darwinists. It also led to extreme views about genetic determinism and psychologists' discovery of the unconscious.[2] Moving historically in the opposite direction, marginalism led first to ideas that market failure is common and welfare would increase if wealth were more equal. Later, however, marginalism produced strongly laissez-faire ideas of market centrality and government failure. While many intellectuals, scientists and even a few jurists flirted with both extremes, mainstream views flowed to the middle.

Although contemporaries did not use the term, "classical" legal thought refers today to the dominant legal theory in the United States from the mid-nineteenth century until the 1920s or 1930s.[3] Just as classical political economy saw markets as largely self-executing, classical legal theory is characterized as a belief that the law largely tends itself, with ad hoc supervision by the State. When intervention did occur it was mainly through judges, who were umpires of both markets and the common law. Adam Smith's "invisible hand" of the market, which made order out of the chaos of individual trading, also guided the common law. Smith and William Blackstone, whose seminal works were written only a decade apart, shared a common vision about how society and markets work.[4] These ideas led to a powerful bias in favor of common law rules and against legislation.

The term "neoclassical" seems appropriate to describe the movement that gradually displaced classical legal thought. "Neoclassical" describes revolutions in economics, art, architecture, music, and other disciplines, referring to some period that is derivative of an earlier "classical" period. A neoclassical expression simultaneously recalls the earlier period's values and forms, but also contributes much that is new, often in revisionist ways that the classicists themselves would have rejected. That was certainly true of neoclassical economics, which sought to preserve most of classicism's faith in markets and even some of its more technical doctrines, but completely rejected its theory of value and decision-making. By contrast, Marxist economics, institutionalism, and Keynesianism departed more dramatically from classical values.[5] Neoclassical legal thought had much the same relationship with classical legal thought. Except at the far left, legal thinkers of this period believed that common law and capitalist legal institutions were worth preserving. At the same time, however, the new sciences of the Victorian era reshaped every legal discipline.

Neoclassical legal thought respected the common law and its history, but also called for more legislation and economic regulation. In the process tort, contract, and property rights were redefined but they hardly disappeared. Public policy in the United States has always avoided the extremes of libertarian laissez-faire and socialism, although each side certainly used these terms rhetorically against the other. For example, Grant Gilmore proclaimed the "death" of contract in 1974, but the great contract law institutions of the twentieth century, such as the Restatements, the Uniform Commercial Code, or Arthur Linton's Corbin's ground-shifting treatise, hardly killed contract law.[6] Rather, contract evolved into a broader amalgamation of views centered in the common law of voluntary exchange, but with greater government interference at the margins. Today legislation plays a much larger role in the legal system than it did in the nineteenth century. But legislation has hardly eliminated markets, substantial private ownership, or even the common law. Criminal law responded strongly to both Darwinian theories of inheritance and marginalist deterrence, but it never abandoned common law moralism and retribution.[7] One could go on with this list of truisms, but the point should be clear. The dominant legal thought that emerged in the late nineteenth century and across the twentieth was highly revisionist, but the roots of the old remained present and were often decisive.

Although Darwinism and marginalism offered radically different views about human nature and choice, legal thinkers harvested doctrine from both. A central theme of this book is that Darwinian ideas were gradually overtaken by economic ideas in which reasonable expectations became the focal point of policy analysis. In areas where the biological theory of evolution played a significant role, such as criminal law and race, Darwinian evolution remained an important factor in legal policymaking. In areas where the use of Darwin was more metaphorical, however, such as economic regulation and welfare policy, Darwinian analogies gave way to marginalist economics. This movement was often obscured by mid-twentieth century historians who continued to write about American economic policy in Darwinian terms. Although the rhetoric of modern legal-economic policy might embrace Darwinian metaphors, especially when used by critics, its motivating force has been economic. Marginalism had the distinct advantage of practicality: it offered policymakers from many legal disciplines a useful set of predictive and normative tools. This triumph of marginalism was most explicit in criminal law and business law, but it also reached to the common law, regulation, and even constitutional law.

One historical difference between Darwinism and marginalism is the way these two ideas worked their way into legal thought. Evolution theory was a part of political and legal philosophy before Darwin published *On the Origin of Species* in 1859. His ideas served to legitimate the views of social philosophers such as Herbert Spencer. Indeed, Sir Henry Maine's *Ancient Law* (1861), published two years after Darwin, had a well-developed theory of evolution of legal institutions even though Maine had probably not read Darwin.

Maine wrote at a time when elite legal thinking in Great Britain tended to be positivistic and utilitarian, with little regard for history. This was thanks mainly to the writings of Jeremy Bentham (1748–1832) and John Austin (1790–1859). Both viewed the law in utilitarian terms. By contrast, Maine believed that legal institutions were a product of customs that had evolved over many centuries and that sovereigns were largely powerless to change. Social and legal rules gradually evolved from domination by status to domination by contract. Legislation could move the law in modest ways or clarify its ambiguities but could never effect fundamental changes.[8] The past very largely determined the future.

Legal historians often speak of classical legal thought's successor as "progressive" legal thought.[9] However, the term "progressive" unnecessarily biases our characterization, creating an easy target for critics of twentieth century judicial doctrine.[10] Neoclassicism is much broader, embracing ideologies and movements that Progressives rejected. The term "progressive legal thought" also suggests that social and economic conservatives clung to an obsolete "classical" ideology, when in fact many were just as revisionist as the progressive legal thinkers whom they critiqued. Although most intellectuals in the early twentieth century embraced some form of Darwin's theory of evolution, it led them in different directions, from the radical antistatism of William Graham Sumner (Yale economist and social scientist) or James Coolidge Carter (lawyer and legal historian) to the equally radical agendas for social experimentation embraced by many Progressives, such as Lester Frank Ward, Edward A. Ross, Richard T. Ely, or Roscoe Pound.[11] The Progressives and New Deal thinkers whom we identify with progressive legal thought were nearly all marginalists, but not all marginalists were Progressives. Just as was true of Darwinism, marginalism was a big tent that fed different ideologies. For example, Oliver Wendell Holmes, Jr. was both Darwinian and marginalist, but he was just as certainly not "progressive." Indeed, he was deeply cynical about legislated reforms that were intended to make the world over.

Corporate finance and wage policy are areas where progressive and conservative lawyers flipped against each other. On the minimum wage, corporate interests generally clung to the classical and backward-looking wage fund theory, which found an absolute limit on wages based on historically accumulated capital. Progressives embraced a forward-looking marginal productivity theory. By contrast, in corporate finance the corporate interests generally rejected the established view that corporate value is determined by historical paid-in capital as reflected in "par" value of shares. Rather, stated corporate value should be based on reasonably anticipated performance, and this made the concept of par value obsolete. On the other hand, Progressives became the principal protagonists in the great "watered" stock scandals, defending the classical view.[12]

Another issue considered here relates to the balance of theory and interest group power in democratic policymaking. Intellectual historians tend to believe that ideas drive society's values and even its policy. Intellectual history is often regarded as more conservative than, say, social history because it relies mainly on published writings as source materials. Traditionally, people who publish have been overwhelmingly elite, educated, white, and male. These attributions are less true of the twentieth century than earlier periods, and intellectual history today embraces gender, ethnic, and cultural diversity much more than it did in the 1970s and earlier. In any event, intellectual history is an essential part of legal history, which in modern legal traditions is unavoidably a study of written words.

Today we are inclined to think that policy is driven by interest group pressure. Interest groups are motivated mainly by a search for wealth or status, although some are certainly driven by ideology as well. Within this model, ideas are often viewed as rationalizations for positions previously formed. Focusing on interest groups enables historians to account for policy changes without involving themselves too deeply in substance. If taken too far this approach trivializes our intellectual past and ignores many of its lessons. To be sure, the economic and social ideology of legal policy has always been affected by interest group pressure, but it also reflects belief systems that transcended interest group lines.

For example, sharply antagonistic interest groups claimed both Darwinian and marginalist thought as their own. On one side, marginalism led to progressivity in tax policy, and the idea that wages were limited only by the marginal contribution of each worker. Marginalism's strong environmentalism also led to greater egalitarianism in race policy, although that change was not well reflected among the Progressives themselves. Their economics was marginalist but their social theory reflected a racist brand of genetic determinism. On the other side, marginalism also led to a comprehensive revision of the theory of the large corporation, in which shareholders became largely irrelevant. It later gave us a renewed defense of the free market as well as public choice theory, with its deep distrust of government. The theory, developed by writers such as Mancur Olson and Buchanan and Tullock in the 1960s, was derived directly from the neoclassical economic theory of competition.[13] Marginalist thinking drove both the pro-legislative anti–common law reform missions of the Progressive Era and New Deal; and the pro-market, pro–common law, anti-legislative, and deregulatory counterreveolution that occurred later.

One thesis of this book is that the relative strength of interest group pressures depends on the robustness of the theory at hand. When theory is well defined and commands a broad consensus it tends to dominate over the wishes of disparate interest groups. This happened for many situations involving both regulation and common law rules about contract, property, or tort. By contrast, the theory underlying the proper scope and duration of intellectual property rights was never well developed. As a result that legislation has been acutely responsive to the interests of well-organized producers rather than poorly organized consumers.[14] This thesis places a premium on appreciation of the intellectual ideas behind legal movements. It also demands at least minimal commitment to the view that law can be more than a zero sum game played by competing interest groups.

An additional inquiry relevant to the history of legal thought concerns legal formalism, or the idea that judges came to think of the legal system as "closed," or that the important problems had been resolved. The case for a period of formalism in late nineteenth-century American law is greatly exaggerated. The influence of political economy on law is often misbranded as "formalism."[15] To the extent formalism of any kind exists, it has had two explanations, one in intellectual history and one that tends to dominate in social history. The intellectual history explanation, developed by such writers as Thomas Kuhn, Arthur Lovejoy, Joseph Schumpeter, Merle Curti, and Richard Hofstadter, sees formalism mainly as a defensive reaction to an intellectual "crisis."[16] A big idea has been developed and produced consensus but then is challenged from outside. Those supporting the status quo respond by building an intellectual wall that excludes or ignores ideas that do not fit the paradigm. This persists until the force of the new idea is so powerful that it eventually breaks through.

The other perspective sees formalism as what occurs when a dominant interest group achieves its political goals and then attempts to "freeze" them in place. Morton Horwitz's conclusion to *The Transformation of American Law*, entitled "The Rise of Legal Formalism," states this view very forcefully. The most powerful interests in American society were commercial ones frustrated by the precommercial state of the common law in the Federal period. They succeeded in transforming American law so as to make it less agrarian and to favor entrepreneurship. By 1850 "that transformation was largely complete." At that time

> If a flexible, instrumental conception of law was necessary to promote the transformation of the postrevolutionary American legal system, it was no longer needed once the major beneficiaries of that transformation had obtained the bulk of their objectives. There were, in short, major advantages in creating an intellectual system which gave common law rules the appearance of being self contained, apolitical, and inexorable, and which, by making "legal reasoning seem like mathematics," conveyed "an air . . . of . . . inevitability about legal decisions."[17]

The notion of formalism fits less well into the study of neoclassical economic or legal regimes. Classical economic thought was unified by a historical theory of value and a deep hostility toward State interference in private arrangements. Marx aside, classicism never developed a pronounced "left" and "right' wing. Classicists tended to debate about details, such as whether a high degree of economic and population development (England) or an undeveloped economy and an abundance of land (America) should affect policy. They agreed on most general principles. By contrast, marginalism has a forward-looking theory of value based on rational expectations, which is much less stable and breaks apart into radically different views about the State, the market, and other social institutions. As a result it has gyrated among political ideologies, all of which proved quite vulnerable to critique and change from within the neoclassical system. Neoclassicism has a right wing and a left wing that are both completely driven by marginalist assumptions. Indeed, some very prominent neoclassicists, such as Alfred Marshall, Arthur Cecil Pigou, and Joan Robinson in England, or Irving Fisher, Richard T. Ely, and John R. Commons in the United States, flirted with socialism. Classicism rarely embraced such diversity. Darwinian thought experienced similar extremes.

Another contribution of neoclassical legal thought is the expert. The neoclassical world was a vastly more complex place than its predecessor. Both Darwinian social science with its complex theories of human behavior and marginalism's incessant search for "equilibrium" invited the use of sophisticated techniques. Between the two, Darwin and marginalism introduced a legal universe in which the nonlawyer expert played an unprecedented role in legal policymaking and adjudication.

In the process, neoclassical legal thought became a far more interdisciplinary enterprise than the classical conception of law had ever acknowledged. In its formal conception, law for the classicists largely stood by itself. Its explicit sources were previously decided cases, statutes, and treatise writers. Today we know that this characterization of classical law is too narrow. Common law jurists were heavily involved in the making of policy. Economic, religious, customary, and historical ideas infected their thought. Increasingly in the twentieth century, however, law accommodated more pragmatic and technical issues rooted mainly in the social sciences and economics. Concerns that had been articulated in terms of natural law and morality were recast as problems of evolutionary social science and risk management. As a result it is impossible to write a history of neoclassical legal thought that draws its sources exclusively from formal law writing. Law became—and was acknowledged to be—a much more open and contingent enterprise.

Because we still live in an era that is predominantly neoclassical, the decade of the 1970s is a more-or-less arbitrary stopping point. It brings this book up to, but not that far into, the rise of modern law and economics, deregulation, and the civil rights movements. The 1960s is a watershed period because so many seminal, policy-shifting works were published then, including James Landis's *Report on Regulatory Agencies to the President Elect* (1960), Ronald Coase's "Problem of Social Cost" (1960), Alex Bickel's *The Least Dangerous Branch* (1962), Mancur Olson's *Logic of Collective Action* (1965), and Guido Calabresi's *Cost of Accidents* (1970), to mention a few. During the same period legislative policy saw the Great Society and the 1960s civil rights legislation. The first of these was the last gasp of New Deal social policy. The second represented the legal triumph of environmentalism over Darwinian genetic determinism.

This book traces these developments through several legal disciplines. Part One shows how Darwinian evolution and marginalist economics competed with each other to develop a scientific understanding of human nature (Chapter 1). The result was revisionist although often conflicting ideas about mental deficiency and criminal behavior (Chapter 2), as well as race relations (Chapter 3).

Part Two considers the crumbling institutions of classical law, whose conception of legal "science" as organization and arrangement gave way, first to Victorian biology and social science, but ultimately to economics. Chapter 4 describes a robust Gilded Age and Progressive Era law and economics movement whose ideology differed from the law and economics movement that developed after 1960. Then Chapter 5 turns to a methodological dispute in the sciences that quickly became a legal policy conflict as well—namely, whether "value" is a purely individual or a social concept. The most immediate implications were in tax policy, concerning both the income tax and the use of "Pigouvian" taxes as an alternative to direct regulation of economic harms. As Chapter 6 develops, the rise of institutionalism in economics provided a powerful Darwinian alternative to neoclassicism. Although mainstream economists rather quickly rejected institutionalism for its historicism and lack of analytic rigor, it remained a driving force in the work of the Legal Realists through the 1960s. Finally, marginalist economics in particular transformed the common law from its historical concern with redress for past harms to the management of ongoing risk and relationships (Chapter 7).

Part Three examines the "neoclassical" revolution in business policy, beginning with two chapters (8 and 9) on the nature of the business corporation and its financial dealings. Chapter 10 then considers why industrial economics never occupied the same place in innovation policy that it did in antitrust and corporate policy. Chapters 11 and 12 focus on competition policy—mainly, the "structuralist" revolution that dominated antitrust thinking from World War II through the 1970s, and the law of vertical control and franchising, a playground for special interest groups at every government level.

Finally, Part Four and the Epilogue consider neoclassical public law and the aftermath of the New Deal. The substantive due process U.S. Supreme Court gave us our first constitutional crisis of noninterpretivism, or decision-making that is not grounded in the Constitution's text. The doctrine was a heroic but ultimately unsuccessful effort to hold off the marginalist revolution that was infecting many aspects of legal thought. Even at the height of judicial anti-regulation bias, however, important exceptions were made for the regulation of health, safety, and morals (Chapter 13). These exceptions served as the opening wedge for a more secular theory of market failure that permitted broader rationales for regulation during the New Deal and after. Chapters 14 and 15 focus on the New Deal itself, particularly labor policy, the regulatory state, and the temporary suppression of federalism. Then the Eqilogue treats the very substantial rehabilitation of the market that occurred in the 1960s and after, mainly in the work of public choice theorists, the Coasean revolution that led to the modern law and economics movement, and deregulation.

Methodology and Sources

This book draws on a variety of legal and nonlegal primary sources, including books and journals in the social sciences, history, and economics. Interdisciplinary legal histories in areas such as science and race[18] or antitrust and regulatory law[19] also use nonlegal sources. Excellent examples include Charles Rosenberg's account of Gilded Age psychiatry in the 1881 trial of President James A. Garfield's assassin,[20] or David Rabban's study of the way legal writers turned to the discipline of history.[21]

Use of wide-ranging sources confronts one problem, however. Even doubters of the law's substantive or methodological autonomy must acknowledge that legal texts have *presented* the legal system as at least semiautonomous. The rhetoric of a closed legal system was historically regarded as central to law's legitimacy, proclaiming that law did not depend on the vagaries of shifting political or social views. That idea became institutionalized in seventeenth-century common law writings, lapsed during the first half of the nineteenth century, found new life after the Civil War, and lapsed again with the rise of Progressivism and Legal Realism. Nonetheless, a striking feature of formative legal texts even in the twentieth century is intellectual isolation. For example, while Hart and Sacks' *The Legal Process* (1958) displayed an acute awareness that law consists of policymaking with borrowed tools, its source material was predominately legal texts.[22]

Although judges prior to the New Deal cited nonlegal sources infrequently, elite legal intellectuals had good educations and many of them read widely. For example, Oliver W. Holmes, Jr., Francis Wharton, James C. Carter, John H. Wigmore, Roscoe Pound, and Jerome Frank all relied on nonlegal sources a great deal in their writings generally. Nonetheless, writing of that sort found little explicit recognition in the courts.

My methodology here is necessarily situational. I have relied on explicit references when they are available. I have also tried to support my arguments with biographical information or letters. Sometimes I offer little more than comparison with prevailing doctrine in other disciplines. For example, it is quite clear that contract law became more "neoclassical" or "relational" during the first half of the twentieth century, seeing the law more as a vehicle for managing ongoing relationships than for assessing discrete events in the past. However, one is hard pressed to find discussions of marginalism or citation to economic sources in the judicial opinions that embraced these changes. Whether I have overstepped in drawing these conclusions is for the reader to decide.

The most important sources for this book are primary legal materials from roughly 1870 through the 1960s, with some spillover in both directions, as well as many secondary sources. I did not read every decision, but rather consulted the vast treatise literature, which then led me to the case law. One effective way of tracing out legal developments in the courts is by looking at changes in the succeeding editions of legal treatises, which typically came out at four- or five-year intervals. The University of Iowa Law Library has one of the country's best collections of nineteenth- and early twentieth-century legal treatises, and many of these books are now also available in digital form. Another underutilized source of great value is the Briefs and Records of the Supreme Court, many of which have also been digitized. In addition, historical documents pertaining to the First and Second Restatement projects, including the American Law Institute's Annual Reports, proceedings, and newsletters, are available on HeinOnline. That is also a good source for Reports of the United States Attorneys General and many executive and legislative history documents. The other major set of sources is professional writings in the social sciences and economics. For journals I relied heavily on electronic databases such as JSTOR, whose coverage in this period is excellent. In addition I made full use of the University of Iowa's excellent period collection of books in these disciplines.

PART ONE

Human Nature and the Sources of Law

1

Scarcity, Biology, and the Rational Actor

> None of them knew the colour of the sky. Their eyes glanced level, and were fastened upon the waves that swept toward them. These waves were of the hue of slate, save for the tops, which were of foaming white, and all of the men knew the colours of the sea.
>
> STEPHEN CRANE, "The Open Boat," 1898

THE STARK OPENING lines of Crane's short story captured the human despair the Darwinian revolution had wrought. A decade later the American philosopher John Dewey agreed, although less eloquently. The thought of two thousand years had "rested on the assumption of the superiority of the fixed and final." The irony was that Charles Darwin's theory added so much to human understanding of nature, but also showed people how lacking in consequence they really were. Dewey was blunt. "Few words in our language foreshorten intellectual history as much as does the word species."[1]

Crane's story was of four men whose steamship *Commodore* had sunk off the Florida coast. The burly oiler, the unskilled cook, the correspondent who was ignorant of the sea, and the courageous but injured captain left the sinking ship in a dinghy after the last lifeboat had gone. The title "Open Boat" captured the human plight—too small to be noticed and fully exposed to an insentient fury that its occupants could not possibly control. The captain attempted to navigate and the others wielded the oars. Surrealistically, each thought more about the nature of the universe than his own immediate survival. Crane emphasized the crew's awareness that they were ignorant of ultimate questions. None of them knew the color of the sky. They knew nothing about final purpose or life plans, or about nature's unpredictable rules for determining who survives and who must perish. But each was intensely and painfully aware of the endless sea that surrounded them. Their greatest oppression was its disregard of their condition. Even the shark that nudged their boat ignored them, unaware of the bloody agony inside. "When it occurs to a man that nature does not regard him as important, and that she feels she would not maim the universe by disposing of him, he at first wishes to throw bricks at the temple," Crane lamented, "and he hates deeply the fact that there are no bricks and no temples."

Darwinism in biology and social science was one of the two most important scientific ideas of the nineteenth century. The other was marginalism in economics. That they could share the same intellectual turf is nearly incomprehensible. Darwinism is mainly an empirical concept. Darwin developed the theory of natural selection after years of scientific observation, and *On the Origin of Species* (1859) overwhelmed its readers with evidence. By contrast, economic marginalism is an analytic concept. We can observe choices but not states of mind. Both became starting points for the great social science revolution of the 1870s and later.

Darwinism's central principle was evolution by natural selection. Nature produces many more offspring than the environment can accommodate. Individuals must compete to survive. Those whose randomly inherited characteristics give them an advantage live long enough to have offspring. They pass these characteristics on to future generations, who continue the struggle. The human organism was produced by this process, shaped over many generations. Its choices were entirely dictated by surroundings and instinct.

Since the late eighteenth century radical biologists such as Erasmus Darwin and Jean Baptiste Lamarck had advocated theories of evolution to explain the differences between ancient fossils and living organisms. None of these theories made convincing science, in no small part because they required a divine component.[2] By contrast, natural selection provided an intuitively obvious relationship among scarce resources, the struggle for survival, evolutionary change, and even religion. All these ideas "seemed to lead somewhere—to some great generalization...," Henry Adams wrote in 1918 of the Darwinian revolution. To many philosophers "natural selection seemed a dogma, to be put in the place of the Athanasian Creed." It promised answers that stretched far beyond biology.[3] If it was so obvious that the strongest, the largest, the swiftest, or the smartest individuals survive, why not the same for social institutions? Darwinian physical and cultural anthropologists began to argue as much in the 1870s and 1880s. Compare two tribes struggling in a deficient environment. One tribe sacrifices all firstborn sons to the gods; the other does not. The former tribe would contain too large a proportion of females; it will have destroyed its best hunters and warriors. Eventually, tribes that sacrifice firstborn males will disappear.

Darwinism assumed that human beings are fundamentally bodies, instinctively committed to seek survival. The mind was one of its many organs. Indeed, the survival instinct did not even require a mind; it belonged to lower organisms and even plants. By contrast, marginalism saw the human being as a highly rational mind, controlling a body that would prosper or not from the mind's choices. Marginalism began with the same assumption of scarcity as Darwinism, but from it developed an intuitively powerful theory about human value and choice.

Early American social scientists such as Edward A. Ross were both Darwinian and marginalist, seeing them as complementary models of human behavior. Oliver Wendell Holmes, Jr., did largely the same thing. One might imagine a unified conception of human science in which evolutionary theory addressed issues about the formation of human instincts, and marginalist analysis determined how they are asserted as preferences. This occurred to some extent in the more practical sciences, such as criminology and risk management, whose concerns came to be stated as minimizing the social cost of crime or accidents.

But most areas experienced something far different. Darwinian scientists developed models in which human action was seen as nothing more than a consequence of evolution and instinctive response. They emphasized that the successful individuals in a particular environment have common characteristics and reactions. Variations were random and most led to an early death, although a few increased the odds of survival. With the development of Darwinian anthropology, these views were extended to individual choices, including social and sexual practices.[4] By the 1910s and 1920s behaviorists believed that the concepts of choice and even consciousness were scientifically meaningless. "The behaviorist is a strict determinist," John B. Watson wrote in 1924, "the child or adult has to do what he does do."[5] In a 1928 letter to Harold Laski, Oliver W. Holmes, Jr., described Watson as "so preoccupied with resolving all our conduct into reflex reactions to stimuli, that he almost denies that consciousness means anything and that memory is more than a useless and misleading word."[6]

Many Darwinian social scientists came to believe that so-called preferences were no more than reflections of an instinct to survive. The principal difference between human beings and lower organisms is that humans have the power to reflect about their choices, but the choices themselves result from instinct rather than free will. This model of human choice also led to the belief that the State could make "objective" welfare judgments based on criteria unrelated to mental state, such as the availability of food, shelter, health, or education. For the Reform Darwinists (as opposed to the Social Darwinists) this permitted Progressive Era economists to speak of "social" as well as individual wants.[7]

In sharp contrast, marginalist economists increasingly came to think that human preferences are autonomous, or at least that science could not uncover their origins and must treat them as autonomous. Increasingly after the 1920s, the enterprise of searching for a common biological or social structure that linked the preferences of different individuals was ostracized from economic science. Indeed, neoclassical ideas about choice became ever more stripped-down until their only qualities were that they can be asserted over the entire possible range and must be rational, or internally consistent.

From that point Darwinian social science and neoclassical economics adopted mutually exclusive methodologies, and each tended to regard the other's method as unscientific. Lurking behind was the nature-nurture controversy, in which Darwinism historically supported nature. Marginalists were really not interested in nature, but only in exerted choices. It became an important vehicle for nurture-based theories of social control.

Nevertheless, Darwinism and marginalism had a common starting point, which was scarcity in relation to the population. Confrontation of scarcity became the glue that bound many elements of twentieth-century policymaking—a proposition that historian Frederick Jackson Turner famously presented in 1894. The "Turner thesis" argued that American character and ideology had been uniquely shaped by the availability of unlimited land.[8] After nearly three centuries of land-based expansion, America was confronting its limits. Darwinism became the science of explaining how biology and culture were determined by an inadequate environment; marginalism became the science of ranking priorities when not every want can be satisfied. Both claimed the classical political economist Sir Thomas Malthus as an intellectual parent. Darwin's theory of survival was driven by the proposition that population growth outruns the growth of food supplies or other resources. The highly influential definition of economics offered by Lionel Robbins in the mid 1930s was that economics is "the science which describes human behaviour as a relationship between ends and scarce means which have alternative uses."[9]

In other respects Darwinism and marginalism were profoundly different. Most important were their differing views about social control. For Darwinists the human individual is largely what he is at birth; one can improve the species through selection, but not the individual. By contrast, marginalists believed that social control of behavior was always about governing incentives at the margin. For example, a Darwinist would address the problem of criminal behavior by seeking out genetic traits that signaled it and using sterilization or sexual isolation to prevent these individuals from reproducing. These views were readily extended to race, although in the United States they showed up not as mass sterilization but rather as advocacy of social segregation and prohibitions on interracial marriage. By contrast, marginalists attempted to create appropriate incentives by metering penalties or rewards to living individuals.

The Expansion of Biological Darwinism

Darwin's evolutionary ideas migrated quickly from biology into cultural, social, and economic thought. *The Descent of Man* (1871) sought to explain not merely humankind's physical characteristics in terms of natural selection, but also social, sexual, and religious practices. These views were developed further by the first Darwinian anthropologists, mainly Englishman Edward Tylor and American Lewis Henry Morgan. They were also picked up by legal scholars such as Holmes, whose *The Common Law* relied on Tylor's discussions of ancient legal institutions in explaining the development of common law rules.[10]

Most great ideas are fated to have mutually antagonistic followers. Darwinism engendered a right-wing ideology called Social Darwinism, which believed that the individual's struggle for survival was essential to the betterment of the human race. Attempts to interfere, such as State support for the poor, would retard the evolutionary process. But Darwinism also produced the Reform Darwinists on the left, who viewed social cultivation and planning as the key to a successful society. For the Social Darwinists the human environment was analogous to raw nature; for the Reform Darwinists it was analogous to a farmer's cultivated field.[11]

Social Darwiniam

The publication of Herbert Spencer's *Social Statics* in 1850 presaged the announcement of Darwin's theory, although Spencer hardly discovered natural selection before Darwin. The evolutionary theory he elaborated was heavily Lamarckian, with God an active participant in the process. By 1875, when Spencer revised *Social Statics* he had reconsidered his position. "Were I now to rewrite this chapter the theological implications of the argument would be avoided. But exclusion of these would leave the ethical doctrine unshaken." In the intervening years Spencer had read *On the Origin of Species*.[12]

Spencer was born in 1820 to dissenting Quaker parents in Derby, in central England. He had a thoroughly undisciplined education with little classical learning. He worked periodically as writer, teacher, civil engineer, inventor, sculptor, and social reformer. In 1859, nearly a decade after he had published *Social Statics*, Darwin's book so inspired Spencer that he undertook a complete revision of all science, applying the principles of natural selection. Until he died in 1903 Spencer wrote endlessly on psychology, ethics, biology, education, and sociology. However, *Social Statics* remained his most popular and influential work. It was widely used as a textbook in political economy classes in both England and America. Spencer's fate in England was much like that of John Dewey in the United States, however: revered and regarded as a leading intellectual during his lifetime, but largely forgotten after his death.[13]

For Spencer, the State's principal duty is to defend individual rights. For it "to take from a citizen more property than is needful for the efficient defense of that citizen's rights is to infringe his rights...." State creation of "what are commonly called public works, as lighthouses, harbours of refuge, etc., implying, as it does, the imposition of taxes for other purposes than maintaining men's rights against foreign and domestic foes, is as much forbidden by our definition of State-duty as is a system of national education, or a religious establishment." Spencer's *Principles of Sociology* discussed the evolution of private property. In many primitive cultures substantial property was held in common. As long as people subsisted on wild food and moved frequently they needed to use land jointly. Only cultivation made individual ownership of producing land feasible. Because private property was a product of evolution, Spencer found it superior to communal ownership. The right to exclude gave people an incentive to use property more efficiently and to protect its value. When the State transfers wealth it is reverting to an idea of communal property and retarding evolutionary development. "It seems hard that widows and orphans should be left to struggle for life or death," he admitted. "Nevertheless, when regarded... in connection with the interests of universal humanity, these harsh fatalities are seen to be full of the highest beneficence, the same beneficence which brings to early graves the children of diseased parents."[14]

Spencer's most notable advocate in the United States was William Graham Sumner, professor of sociology and political economy at Yale. In essays on legal rights, written just prior to 1900, Sumner argued that rights are created by political "in-groups." Within a particular society violence is wrong "because it lessens the power of the in-group for war with outsiders." Rather, conflicting property claims are settled by the gradual creation of taboos, laws, rules, and rights. The Lockean idea that rights are "natural"—that they come from a higher authority—was developed to justify legal rules and insure their permanence. Invariably, however, political power shifts, and losers protest by "expressing their pain in terms of violated rights." Such losers speak of rights "as if they floated in the atmosphere, and ought to come floating to [them] by a divine spirit." For Sumner, people have a right to participate in the struggle for existence, but not a right to succeed in it. For example, the individual right of property means that "each has a right to acquire and possess property if he can." It does not mean that every person "has a right to have some property."[15] Sumner conceded that "this will not produce equal results." However, "it is right just because it will produce unequal results—that is, results which will be proportioned to the merits of individuals."[16]

Reform Darwinism

Crane's world was filled with as many life and death struggles as Spencer's and Sumner's. "The Open Boat" is not only about an inhospitable and inadequate world, however, but also cooperation and survival. The wounded captain could do little physical labor, but he could navigate. The correspondent quickly learned to row and took turns with the oiler. By rowing and resting in turn the four prisoners of the open boat eventually approached shore and prepared to challenge the surf that was certain to swamp their tiny craft.

"The coldness of the water was sad; it was tragic," thought the correspondent as the capsizing boat threw him into the sea. "This fact was somehow so mixed and confused with his opinion of his own situation that it seemed almost a proper reason for tears." Almost immediately the oiler went out alone, swimming strongly. The cook, the captain, and the correspondent stayed together, the injured captain clinging to the overturned boat. The three shouted encouragement and instruction, and after some struggle they reached the shore. There they found the drowned body of the oiler, left face down in the sand by some accident that nature was not troubled to explain.

In Crane's indifferent world the strongest did not necessarily survive. Nature was much too careless for that, and "survival of the fittest" is only a rule of statistics. But cooperation can best nature at its own game. Granted that men are animals, they are nevertheless different from the world's other organisms. In sharp contrast to the Social Darwinists, "Reform" Darwinists jumped off with the observation that human beings, unlike the world's other organisms, *know* that they are evolving and are in a position to manage it. Confronting the environment need not be a zero sum game. By manipulating the environment one can improve upon nature's own processes. Reform Darwinists proved their point by looking at selective breeding. One of Darwin's most important contributions to evolutionary theory was his 1868 study of variation of species under domestication.[17] The book argued that the difference between natural and planned selection was the speed at which the process moved—the former taking millions of years to do what the latter did in a few generations.

The rhetoric of Social Darwinism pictured the human race as confronting a jungle; the rhetoric of Reform Darwinism pictured it as living on a self-cultivated field. Reform Darwinism led to the Progressive Reform agenda, which included control devices ranging from support for the poor to sterilization of the unfit in order to hasten human improvement. It dominated American social thought just as social science was being institutionalized in American universities and legal thought. Its protagonists included Albion Small and Edward A. Ross, perhaps the most prominent Progressive Era sociologist. In legal theory it also included Roscoe Pound.

The Reform Darwinist's American answer to Spencer was Lester Frank Ward, a trained botanist and lawyer whose interests merged into sociology. Ward was born in Joliet, Illinois, in 1841, the same year as Holmes, but raised in frontier Iowa as the youngest of ten children. His father was a laborer. Like Holmes, he fought in the Union Army. He was the first President of the American Sociological Association, which was founded in 1905, and spent most of his career working for the U.S. Geological Survey. He did not receive a permanent academic appointment until 1906, when he became professor of sociology at Brown University, seven years before his death. Richard Hofstadter called Ward's book *Dynamic Sociology* (1883)—whose title was intended to contrast with Spencer's *Social Statics*—"the first comprehensive sociological treatise written in the United States."[18]

Ward believed that Social Darwinism, which argued "that the natural processes of society be left undisturbed," ignored the fundamental differences between lower animals and man. "Nature acts on the assumption that her resources are inexhaustible, and no amount of expenditure is too great." The codfish must hatch one million young in order "that two may survive and the species not become extinct." Nature's "waste of reproductive power [is] enormous in proportion to the amount of life brought forth." This same inefficient process characterized primitive civilization, dominated by needless warfare, loss of human life, and waste of natural resources "with a wanton disregard of the future." All of this resulted from a lack of planning. People in competition with each other must always take today what is best. They compete in the slaughter of wild animals and make them extinct; they fight for jobs with the result that wages are low and populations are jammed into dense and dirty slums. Investors and laborers see themselves in competition, in spite of the fact that "their dependence upon each other is absolute." The result of laissez faire is that "all the functions of society are performed in a sort of random, chance manner, which is precisely the reverse of economical, but wholly analogous to the natural processes of the lower organic world."

Against this "biological economy" Ward proposed a "psychological economy" as the "method of rational man." Whereas organisms in nature are "pushed into existence by the pelting of atoms from behind, and thus become fortuitous or literally chance products, human creations are conceived in advance by the rational and foreseeing mind, designed with skill for definitive ends." The history of agriculture proved that men control evolution, not the other way around. Nature sows by leaving seeds "to the wind, the water, the birds and animals." But man "prepares the ground, clearing it of vegetable competitors, then he carefully plants the seeds at the proper intervals... and after they have sprouted he keeps off their enemies..., and supplies water if needed."

The great distinction between lower organisms and humanity is that "the environment transforms the animal while man transforms the environment." Ward praised Congress's 1845 appropriation to create the National Bureau of Statistics. Such information would "influence and direct" scientific legislation. He argued that "every movement of whatever nature going on in the country should be regularly reported to a central office, and all such facts should be there systematically elaborated and published in tables, charts, diagrams, etc., and regularly laid before Congress for its use in framing laws for the benefit of the general public."[19]

"I would rather have written Ward's *Dynamic Sociology* than any other book that has ever been produced in America," wrote Albion Small in 1910.[20] President William Rainey Harper had hired Small to found America's first department of sociology at the University of Chicago.[21] During the heyday of Progressivism, sociology was dominated by "big idea" people such as Ward and Small, who wrote broad arguments for social change and programs for legislation. Their work reflected an optimism that statistics could reform society. For people such as Ward, Small, Pound, and Woodrow Wilson during his academic career, the object of social science was to restructure human life, to make society better than nature could working alone. In the 1920s however, social science became obsessed with methodology, and the massive plans for social restructuring began to look premature. If Ward's ideas were too big for a later, more technical generation of sociologists, they were nevertheless influential on the people who consumed sociological data—social reformers, legislators, and liberal legal scholars such as Pound.[22]

Darwin in Legal Thought

Liberty of Contract

Liberty of contract is one of the most pervasive ideas in Anglo-American jurisprudence. Far more than a theory about contract law, liberty of contract was the raison d'etre of civil government for Locke, Hume, Blackstone, and Adam Smith—indeed, for the democratic ideal that government's legitimacy derives from the "consent" of the governed.[23] In *Ancient Law* (1861), the great British legal historian Sir Henry Maine identified modern law with the movement away from "status" and toward "contract" as the basis for social ordering. As a political idea, centrality of contract migrated from law to political economy and philosophy, rather than in the opposite direction. Indeed, only after the *legal* conception of contract arose, Maine argued, could classical political economy come into existence—for economics needed a set of market institutions to analyze.[24]

The heyday of liberty of contract in American public law grew out of the Jacksonian movement and ran its course during the substantive due process era, when the Supreme Court relied on a concept of contractual liberty to overturn many forms of government regulation.[25] Substantive due process has often been identified with Social Darwinism, particularly in intellectual, legal, and constitutional history written from the New Deal to the 1970s.[26] Economic theory was little more than a sideshow. For example, marginalist economics has no equivalent of Richard Hofstadter's *Social Darwinism in American Thought* (1944), one of the most influential books of U.S. intellectual history ever written. Evangelical clergy in the first half of the twentieth century did not preach sermons attacking marginalism the way they did Darwinism, even though marginalism produced significant threats to historical Christian principles. Of course, Darwinism obtained its notoriety from its idea that humankind descended from lower primates, a heresy that marginalism's hedonism could not match for the evangelical outrage it produced.[27]

Liberty of contract was never a Darwinian doctrine, however. The origins of substantive due process lay in classical political economy.[28] To be sure, Social Darwinism and liberty of contract both stated that people would be better off if the State declined to interfere with private choice. But the important similarities end there. Under natural selection, each person competed with his neighbor for the same niche, and the strongest prevailed. If the concept of "agreement" meant anything, it was that two organisms might cooperate for mutual advantage; but if one later defected there was no State to intervene. To be sure, Reform Darwinism offered a revitalized view of social cooperation for planning—but liberty of contract is hardly the doctrine of Reform Darwinism. Indeed, it was the Reform Darwinists' foil for a relentless critique of legal orthodoxy.[29]

Mainstream legal writing during this period has strikingly few references to Social Darwinism.[30] Holmes, who read widely, was a modest exception. In 1895 Holmes wrote of Herbert Spencer to Lady Pollock: "I doubt if any writer of English except Darwin has done so much to affect our whole way of thinking about the universe." His letters also contain several admiring references to Spencer.[31] In a professional career that stretched over sixty years, however, Holmes made only a few references to Darwin, mainly to his biology, and most are sufficiently ambiguous that people continue to dispute whether Holmes was a Social Darwinist.[32] Lester Frank Ward complained after *Lochner*, which struck down a legislative limit on workers' hours, that the name "Social Darwinism" did not fit the ideology it was used to describe. He found it "wholly inappropriate to characterize as social Darwinism the *laissez faire* doctrine of political economists."[33] There is a somewhat stronger case for tying Roscoe Pound to Reform Darwinism.[34]

To write about *Lochner* without being excessively ideological is difficult, and the scholarship has been heavily polarized.[35] For the legal historian, however, two observations stand out. First, Social Darwinism did not produce substantive due process, although it provided additional rhetoric, seldom referenced in judicial decisions, for views that had developed decades earlier.[36] Second, as Chapter 14 develops, *Lochner* was distinctly pre-marginalist in its economic conception, particularly where the labor contract was concerned.

The argument that substantive due process was legal Social Darwinism developed mainly in the 1940s, as constitutional historians conducted the first of many autopsies of *Lochner*, whose economic doctrine had ended in 1937. Edward S. Corwin, probably the most influential constitutional scholar of his generation, first analyzed substantive due process and claimed to discover Social Darwinism in 1941. Although the primary cause of substantive due process was classical political economy, for which Corwin referenced mainly John Stuart Mill, a secondary cause was Social Darwinism. He rather confusingly mixed the two, greatly exaggerating the degree to which Mill and Darwin occupied common ground. Corwin cited several substantive due process decisions as consistent with both classical political economy and Social Darwinism. But Corwin's evidence of Darwinism was sparse. Indeed, his explicit evidence was no more than Justice Holmes's tart *Lochner* dissent.[37]

The decisions of the Fuller Court, which gave us *Lochner*, also provide little basis for thinking that the Court was Social Darwinist. Although the majority's attitude toward state welfarism was consistent with Social Darwinism, the only explicit reference in the *United States Reports* is Justice Holmes's famous dissenting quip in *Lochner* that the Fourteenth Amendment "does not enact Mr. Herbert Spencer's Social Statics."[38] Beyond that, the evidence that Social Darwinism permeated Supreme Court thinking is extremely thin.[39] The most likely candidates for Social Darwinist were Holmes, as noted above, but he dissented in *Lochner* as well as other substantive due process decisions because they violated no "specific provisions" of the Constitution.[40] The second candidate is Justice George Sutherland, who also read Spencer. But even his Social Darwinism has been questioned. In any event, Justice Sutherland did not join the Court until President Harding appointed him in 1922, seventeen years after *Lochner*.[41]

Contractarian ideology on the Fuller Court almost certainly did not come from Social Darwinism. Superficially, Social Darwinism and contractualism both supported a minimalist state and abhorred forced redistribution of wealth. But Social Darwinism and contractualism arrived at that position from starkly different starting points. The social contract was based on a cooperative strategy inimical to Social Darwinism's idea that the human species and its institutions developed out of conflict. To be sure, the intellectualism of lawyers is often parasitic and superficial. Something in Social Darwinism may have reinforced their contractarian ideology, notwithstanding fundamental antinomies between the "social contract," in Lockean liberal terms, and "the struggle for existence," in the quite illiberal paradigm of Social Darwinism.

Social Darwinists believed that all human institutions, including the State, were the product of inter-individual struggle in which practices that enabled survival were perpetuated, while less successful ones were not. Nothing as rational and optimistic as a social compact ever emerged from this process. According to Spencer common property prevailed as long as people were wandering nomads, but gave way to private property as people became more settled and agrarian. Initially, political arrangements were determined by inherited hierarchies. Spencer believed that only relatively late in civilization did this "status" conception of social organization give way to more contractual ideas—an idea that he borrowed from Maine's *Ancient Law*.[42] But even this contractual conception was nothing more than a slowly evolving device for defining social and economic boundaries. From that point, Spencer developed his own theory of the State with no reference to a social compact.

By contrast, contractarianism assumes actors with free will, a well-formed set of preferences, and a desire to maximize their individual positions through cooperation. The social contract is an ahistorical act, undertaken before society commences, and creates institutions that are either permanent or else can be changed only by contractually adopted rules of social decision. This assumption could not be more contrary to the Spencer/Darwin view that human beings are bound by history and in perpetual conflict. For the Social Darwinist a social contract to explain human organization was no more rational than a "social contract" to explain the social organization observed among bees or beavers.[43]

Spencer discussed the idea of a social contract at some length in *The Man v. the State*, first published in 1884. The entire "hypothesis" of a social contract was "baseless," he concluded. Such a contract could never bind succeeding generations; the natural selection process might drive any subsequent social group to abrogate it. However, Spencer did consider what the State would be like if it were the product of an agreement produced by the unanimous consent of its citizens. He concluded that they would agree about very little, except perhaps the public defense and some principles of criminal law.[44]

Evolutionary historians such as Maine rejected social contract theory as inconsistent with the historical development of political institutions. Rather, it was an idea cooked up by lawyers to serve political ends. A central point of Maine's *Ancient Law* was that notions of legal obligation and rights evolved through a long period when legal relationships were based on status or birth family. Contract ideas of social obligation were a recent development in this historical evolution, and were used by philosophers to justify more sympathetic notions of the State. Thus, the Lockean social contract was "only the dress by which the ancient views were rendered more attractive to a particular generation of the moderns."[45] William Graham Sumner was even more skeptical of the social contract than Spencer and Maine. He regarded political theories as nothing more than a few of the many "folkways," or customs that have evolved slowly in organized human society.[46]

Darwinism and Historicism in Gilded Age Legal Thought

One prominent feature of Gilded Age thought was its historicism, or the view that at any given time the state of civilization is determined by its history. Historicism is an inherently conservative doctrine because pasts cannot be changed. Its champions in legal history were Maine and Friedrich Carl von Savigny from Germany.[47] The increasing popularity of historicism in late nineteenth-century American scholarship resulted at least partly because so many graduate students went to Germany to study in both social science and law.[48] Although the ideas of cultural evolution implicit in historicism antedated Darwin, historicists readily embraced natural selection as confirmation.[49] In the United States one can count among its protagonists both William Graham Sumner and lawyer and legal historian James Coolidge Carter. "Folkways are not Stateways," Sumner wrote. Ultimately States are powerless to change long-evolved social traditions and value systems, no matter how they try.[50] Carter's posthumous *Law, Its Origin Growth and Function* (1907), was intended to show that the customary practices reflected in the common law were an inexorable product of historical development that legislation was powerless to change. Carter's principal accomplishment was his campaign against codification in New York, which he attacked repeatedly in pamphlets and editorials as a reflection of "Benthamite" ideas about the superiority of legislation.[51]

Historicism affected not only theories about customary law, including the common law, but also the reasonable limits of constitutionalism—a theme that dominated the Gilded Age's public law treatise writers. For example Thomas M. Cooley, one of the great architects of substantive due process in the state courts, lamented the use of legislation to effect economic change because it "cast[] overboard the wisdom of experience" and substituted "the winds of mere speculative abstractions." In "nothing can the judgments of our ancestors be of more value than the matters of customary law, and in nothing can speculative reasoning be more at fault."[52] Cooley spoke of customary law as "springing from the nature of the people themselves" as an "outgrowth of their habits of thought and action."[53]

These ideas showed up repeatedly in arguments and judicial pronouncements such as the one that legislative land use regulation was appropriate only if it went no further than the common law of nuisance. They resurfaced with a vengeance in the aftermath of *Brown v. Board of Education*, when southern social scientists and political leaders argued that the Supreme Court was naive to think a judicial decree could destroy state-mandated segregation, an institution that had evolved over two centuries.[54] The historicist position had been institutionalized in *Plessy v. Ferguson*, which rejected the argument that separate but equal railway facilities violated the Constitution. As Justice Brown wrote for the Court, that argument:

> ...assumes that social prejudices may be overcome by legislation, and that equal rights cannot be secured... except by an enforced commingling of the two races. We cannot accept this proposition. If the two races are to meet upon terms of social equality, it must be the result of natural affinities, a mutual appreciation of each other's merits, and a voluntary consent of individuals. This end can neither be accomplished nor promoted by laws which conflict with the general sentiment of the community upon whom they are designed to operate.[55]

The important point for Sumner was that "folkways" were the product of long evolutionary development, not of government command.[56] Indeed, one common interpretation of the Supreme Court's "slowdown" in *Brown II*, ordering desegregation with "all deliberate speed," is that the Court realized the practical impossibility of turning a society so quickly on a deeply engrained social practice.[57]

The Rational Actor

Historicism as a doctrine of statecraft was fundamentally at odds with emergent marginalism, which was widely regarded as ahistorical. The very concept of forward-looking decision-making "at the margin" minimized the importance of the past, emphasizing expectations about the future. As a result the first generations of marginalists strongly favored legislation, including a great deal of legislation that conflicted with common law principles.

Marginalism equates value with the next choice to be made. A rational person chooses first what she wants most, then what she wants second-most, and so on. The analog of marginalism in philosophy is utilitarianism. In the late eighteenth century Jeremy Bentham had already written about declining marginal utility as a welfare measure: "[T]he quantity of happiness produced by a particle of wealth (each particle being of the same magnitude) will be less at every particle; the second will produce less than the first, the third than the second, and so on."[58] But classical political economists from Adam Smith, Bentham's older contemporary, through John Stuart Mill went about the study of economic value mainly by looking at historical averages. For example, the value of market goods was thought to be a function of the average cost of production. The value of wages equaled previous capital accumulation divided by the number of workers (the "wage fund" theory). Indeed, Mill himself managed to be utilitarian in his philosophical theory but classical in his economic theory. He began to see value in applying utilitarianism to economics only very late in his life.[59]

Although Bentham developed both the concepts of declining marginal utility and of marginal deterrence in criminal law,[60] he did not come close to developing a theory of cost or value based on marginalism. Before the theory of marginal utility could become useful for economics it had to be recast as a theory about how market prices are determined, and about the relationship between marginal utility (or value) and the amount of something that is produced. That is, utilitarianism had to migrate from ethics and political philosophy into a theory of exchange and market behavior.

Beginning in the 1870s, economists began to merge utilitarianism into economics by seeing value as based, not on cost, but rather on a person's willingness to pay for or produce the next unit. The protagonists were William Stanley Jevons (England), Carl Menger (Austria), and Leon Walras (Switzerland). By common belief they arrived at marginalism independently and roughly simultaneously.[61] The result of the marginalist revision of the concept of value was stunning, leading to the division between "classical" and "neoclassical," and also between the "political economy" of Adam Smith and his disciples, and the far more mathematical "economics" of the later period. Alfred Marshall and his wife Mary Paley Marshall, the first professional woman economist, popularized the term in the 1880s.[62] On a perspective line, the classicists and the marginalists stood back-to-back, the former equating value with averages taken from the past, the latter with rational expectations about the next thing.

Jevons' *Theory of Political Economy* (1871) broke sharply with the classical tradition by disputing the nearly sacred notion that value depended on cost, or the amount of labor that had gone into something. Rather, "value depends entirely on utility," a subjective notion unrelated to previous investment. "[W]e have only to trace out carefully the natural laws of the variation of utility... in order to arrive at a satisfactory theory of exchange," Jevons concluded. The more of something a person already has, the less she will be willing to pay for an additional unit. From this Jevons also developed the concept of equation of utilities—that a person buying numerous commodities will purchase each up to the point that he derives the same marginal utility from all. When someone is satisfied with exactly what he has, "it follows that... an increment of commodity would yield exactly as much utility in one use as in another.[63]

Carl Menger's *Principles of Economics* (1871) stood outside the British classical tradition. However, many young American economists studied in Germany and returned showing Menger's influence.[64] Among the earliest American marginalists were John Bates Clark (Columbia), Irving Fisher (Yale), Francis Amasa Walker (Yale), Simon Newcomb (Johns Hopkins, mathematics); and Charles Sanders Peirce (U.S. government, philosophy of science).[65]

Marginalism forced a shift in economics' methodology from the measure of *things* or the labor that went into making them, to the measure of human behavior based on presumed rationality. Alfred Marshall wrote in *Principles of Economics* (1890) that one could meaningfully speak of consumer demand only "as represented by the schedule of the prices at which he is willing to buy different amounts of" something.[66]

That marginalism overran Anglo-American economics when it did is not coincidental. The rise of railroads and large-scale industrial production called for a theory of value that incorporated long-run planning and entrepreneurial risk more realistically than the classicists did. Marginalism greatly facilitated the development of distinctions between investment (fixed) costs and operating (variable) costs, and of the effects of decisions over time. The new focus on industrial development is most explicit in Alfred Marshall, the most influential economist of his era. Marshall devoted his career to industrial economics. Nevertheless, once economists adopted marginalist analysis its influence appeared in every economic subdiscipline. It was the most important revolution in Western economic thought since Adam Smith.

A frustrating problem for classical political economists had been to explain why people and firms produce and consume particular mixtures of goods that have different values. Why is air cheap, even though survival depends on it? Why are diamonds expensive, even though they are luxuries? To illustrate the marginalist solution to these problems, consider the person whose favorite food is peas. Why does this person not purchase and consume tons of peas and nothing else? The classicists generally resorted to elaborate theories of objective value, or "primary" goods, or to the metaphysical explanation that people's nature requires them to consume what they do. These explanations were totally unhelpful in explaining the manifold differences one could observe in individual choices. Classical political economy generally concluded that the "value" of anything is a function of its cost. But that did not explain why different people place widely different values on one unit of a good, even though its cost is everywhere the same.

The marginalist answer appeared instantly to solve every problem about individual and social value. Even the person who says his favorite food is peas experiences declining marginal utility for them. The value of each additional pound decreases as he has more. He will buy peas until the utility from the next unit to be purchased has fallen to a level equal to his marginal utility for some other good, such as broccoli. For example, suppose he obtains twenty utils (an imaginary unit of satisfaction) from his first pound of peas, eighteen utils from the second, sixteen from the third, and so on in linear fashion. By contrast, he obtains seven utils from his first pound of broccoli, five from the second, and so on.

The classicists, not having the concept of marginal utility, observed only that the subject preferred peas to broccoli and were hard-pressed to explain why he purchased any broccoli at all. But on the above numbers the marginalist drew remarkably precise conclusions. Assume that peas cost $1.00 per pound, broccoli $1.00 per pound, and the subject had ten dollars to spend. Once he had seven pounds of peas the marginal utility for the next pound would be six utils. At that point an additional dollar spent on a pound of broccoli would give him seven utils of utility while another pound of peas would produce only six. A utility maximizer would buy a pound of broccoli. Then, with two dollars left he faced three options. He could buy two additional pounds of peas, which would produce six utils for the first and four utils for the second, or ten. He could buy two additional pounds of broccoli, which would give five utils and three utils, or eight. Or he could buy one of each, which would produce six utils and five utils, or eleven. He would buy one of each, giving him a total of eight pounds of peas and two pounds of broccoli. At this "equilibrium" point his utility from peas and broccoli is precisely equal.

Its politically destabilizing character notwithstanding, marginalism was in some ways ideally suited for American intellectual soil. It was forward-looking, emphasizing motion (both scientific and social), and symbolizing growth and change. It also appealed to the American penchant for science and technology. Marginalist analysis invited a focus on "equilibrium," or the imagined steady state toward which everything in motion continuously moves. Increasingly economists focused on identifying a market's movement toward equilibrium, or else in what was obstructing it—"chronic disequilibria," as Joseph Schumpeter put it in 1934.[67]

During the Gilded Age equilibrium was everywhere. It was a Golden Age for engineering, including such marvels as the Brooklyn Bridge and

Penn Station in New York, the Panama Canal and Great Britain's Anderton Boat Lift, described as the greatest waterway wonder of the late nineteenth century. The giant Corliss steam engine was a technological marvel, whose mile of drive shafts powered nearly every exhibit at the Centennial Exposition in 1876, symbolizing what Howard Mumford Jones called "the age of energy."[68]

Marginalist economists shared the obsession. "When two tanks containing fluid are joined by a pipe, the fluid, which is near the pipe in the tank with the higher level, will flow into the other," and "if several tanks are connected by pipes, the fluid in all will tend to the same level..."[69] The writing may sound like Newton's *Mechanics*, but it actually came from Alfred Marshall's *Principles of Economics* (1890). Marshall devoted three chapters to the "equilibrium" of demand and supply. He conceived the idea of "partial" equilibrium to account for demand and supply for a single commodity, which he compared to a closed vessel. He also developed a methodology of "comparative statics" to compare equilibria at two different times or under different assumptions.

Early American marginalist Irving Fisher defended his Yale doctoral dissertation on marginal utility by building a hydraulic machine with pumps and levers to illustrate how market prices flow toward an equilibrium. The dissertation, published in 1892 as *Mathematical Investigations in the Theory of Value and Prices*, is filled with figures of water reservoirs that Fisher called "utility cisterns," connected by tubes. They illustrated such propositions as "A given amount of commodity to be consumed by a market during a given period will be so distributed among the individuals that the marginal utilities measured in money will be equal." Fisher's dissertation committee found the machine so interesting that it was scheduled for display at the Columbian Exhibition in Chicago in 1893, but was unfortunately destroyed in transit.[70]

Justice Holmes also understood the concept. He wrote in a 1911 dissent that the price of a good depends on "the equilibrium of social desires,"[71] and used the phrase again that year in a letter to Harvard economics professor Frank Taussig, suggesting that prices "would express the equilibrium of social desire" in a socialist state just as much as in a capitalist state.[72] Three years later in the *International Harvester* decision he dismissed a state law indictment against firms accused of fixing the prices of agricultural machinery at higher than their "real value." Holmes observed that there was no evidence of what the "real value" was. Further, the evidence indicated that the buyers were also fixing prices and that the sellers' combination did "no more than restore an equilibrium that has been disturbed by a combination of buyers."[73]

Marginalist ideas produced several important corollaries. *First*, when people place value on goods they consider only the marginal value, not the total value. *Second*, when people produce or trade they equate utilities. In equilibrium, every person's stock of goods is such that her marginal values for each are identical. *Third*, business firms also equate marginal utilities, but these are measured in a constant currency. Suppose labor and machinery are alternative ways of making a product. Labor costs $5 per unit produced while machinery costs $4. The firm will invest in more machinery and less labor until the two are equalized. Likewise, in deciding how much of various products to produce, the firm produces each up to the point that marginal profit is equalized.

Fourth, if the rate of change in marginal value is constant, as in the example of the peas, the lines or "functions" that describe them are straight. Manipulating them is largely a matter of geometry. When the changes occur at differing rates, however, as they most often do, then the mathematics of marginalism becomes more difficult, requiring calculus and—in cases involving empirical observations—statistics. The result was to make neoclassical economics a far more technical enterprise than classical political economy. Marginalism provided economics with a general theory of consumer demand, a theory of value, a theory about production and consumption, and a theory of costs, all of which could be quantified with great apparent mathematical precision.

As a theory about how people exercise preferences, marginalism seemed very powerful. But some implications were controversial and produced considerable resistance. For example, marginalism indicated that the rate of wages is driven by the laborer's marginal contribution. If a laborer adds value of $1.00 per hour, then "at the margin" the employer will be willing to pay the worker $1.00. He may pay less if he can, but as soon as wages rise above $1.00 he will refuse to hire. This relatively simple notion displaced a century of classical theory that the rate of wages is a function of previously invested capital. For many Progressive Era policymakers, the observation that workers were earning less than their marginal contribution justified increased toleration for labor unions and even legislated minimum wage laws.[74]

Economics today is completely dominated by the mathematics of marginalism. In the 1920s and earlier, however, its future was uncertain. Marginalism was thoroughly embraced by some economists and thoroughly rejected by others.[75] For most, it was a useful tool but not the end-all of economic inquiry. Many of the older generation found its technical apparatus too daunting. Even Alfred Marshall kept most of the mathematics in the notes. His *Principles* apologized for the "diagrams" and "mathematical symbols" that would challenge readers. But, he assured, "there are many problems of pure theory, which no one who has once learnt to use diagrams will willingly handle in any other way."[76]

Straddling a Methodological Divide

Darwinian influences on scientific, social, and legal thought appeared mainly during Reconstruction.[77] Darwinism had a substantial head start over marginalism, and also the practical advantage that one could understand the fundamentals of natural selection without much technical knowledge. After 1900, however, both economic and legal thought were increasingly dominated by a mixture of Darwinian and marginalist principles, with marginalism taking on an increasing role.

Economics took a sharp rightward turn after the 1930s, when interpersonal comparisons of utility came to be regarded as outside the boundaries of economic science. The result, discussed in Chapter 6, significantly undermined the economic case for the social welfare state. In developing this position, however, economists largely divorced economics from Darwin. The only thing that counted was that people made choices; it did not matter very much that they were biological organisms with genetically produced needs. Mainstream economists increasingly denigrated queries about the biological or psychological sources of human preference as unscientific.

The result was the development of a great methodological divide. By removing the evolutionary sources of preference from economic inquiry, economists in the 1930s and later were able to develop mathematical models of markets and welfare with great analytic force. The other social sciences, with their insistence on more open-ended empirical inquiry, were not able to rival these models for elegance. Whether the methodological exclusivity that resulted was a good thing is open to dispute. Nevertheless, legal policy reflected a less purist attitude, often accommodating these two models of human behavior by ignoring their fundamental inconsistencies.

Darwinism and economic marginalism were hardly autonomous theories. They collected their premises from a variety of sources. Both rested on arguments developed over a century or more. Both became tools for political ends. Marginalist economics competed with the social sciences for a place in the policy writing of the early twentieth-century. American economists were not all on the same page. For example, the institutionalists largely preferred Darwinian models drawn from biology and psychology over the rational choice models of neoclassical economics. Soon after marginalism entered American economics, Thorstein Veblen criticized it for not being "evolutionary."[78] Veblen's position introduced an argument that persisted through the 1920s and, among the Legal Realists, long after: the neoclassical economists' vision of human choice was too narrow to provide a realistic accounting of human motivation and welfare. That view has been an important although diminishing component in public law ever since.

The marginalist revolution also had a powerful impact on the welfare agenda of the Progressive Era. In his *Theory of Legislation* Bentham outlined a general program of wealth redistribution based on the equation of marginal utilities: "Among participants of unequal fortunes, the more the distribution of new wealth tends to do away with that inequality, the greater will be the total mass of happiness."[79] From this, Bentham developed an important principle of both social and private insurance: "the greater the number of persons among whom a loss is shared, the less considerable will be the defalcation from the sum total of happiness." Between 1890 and 1930 marginalist arguments for forced redistribution and shared social risk were accepted in some form by prominent neoclassical economists such as Alfred Marshall and Arthur C. Pigou in England, and Irving Fisher, Richard T. Ely, Edwin R.A. Seligman, and John R. Commons in the United States. They continued to be used in legal policy analysis long after they were severely qualified by most mainstream economists.

Marginalism also produced theories of legal liability based on marginal deterrence. Once again, an important source was Jeremy Bentham, whose first rule of punishment was that "[t]he evil of the punishment must be made to exceed the advantage of the offense." Bentham's second rule was "[t]he more deficient in certainty a punishment is, the severer it should be." To cast the issue in more contemporary terms, the punishment must vary with the probability of detection. Further, "[w]here two offences are in conjunction, the greater offence ought to be subjected to severer punishment, in order that the delinquent may have a motive to stop at the lesser." As Bentham explained, a "highwayman may content himself with robbing, or he may begin with murder, and finish with robbery. The murder should be punished more severely than the robbery, in order to deter him from the greater offence."[80] Although the technical notation was absent, Bentham had developed a rather complete economic theory of crime and punishment.[81] For the marginalist, law's only relevant concern was external conduct, and penalties must be "metered" so as to provide appropriate sanctions for disapproved conduct, but not go so far as to discourage beneficial conduct. This was the essentially marginalist message of Holmes's *The Common Law* (1881), a book whose outlook on legal policy was far more marginalist than Darwinian.

Marginalism had a powerful impact on legal theories of value, divorcing it from historical cost and tying it to expected utility. The concept of value became more concerned with potential for growth than for previous commitment. Property came to be identified with the power to earn future profits, thus shifting its focus from land or physical objects to intangibles that could be appropriated. A significant element in such forward-looking valuation is risk, a concept that was never well formulated in classical analysis. During the first half of the twentieth century risk management would become a central focus of both common and statutory law.

Another principle that marginalists developed early on but later limited was that markets fail much more frequently than the classical political economists acknowledged. Further, markets differ greatly from one another, and different markets require different policy fixes. No doctrine of neoclassical economics did more than this one to limit the common law approach in favor of more market-specific statutory regulations.

Marginalism also separated the economic analysis of human behavior from that of business firms. Although people and firms are both rational actors, people maximize utility while firms maximize profits. Profits can be measured by a metric such as dollars, which is both "cardinal," in the sense that the measurement is constant ($10 buys ten times as much as $1), and comparable among actors, which means that a dollar held by one firm is worth the same as a dollar in the hands of another. These differences enabled industrial economists to derive strong theories about expected business behavior. For example, as Chapter 7 recounts, strongly objective theories of contract law as developed by Holmes and Samuel Williston had much greater impact on the law of commercial contracts than on personal contracts.

Marginalist theories relied on strong assumptions about rational choice. By contrast, the other social sciences assessed welfare by externally measurable survival characteristics such as health or productivity. If a Darwinian social scientist were asked to study the need for shelter she would do medical studies about the impact of inadequate shelter on the occurrence of illness, infant death, fatigue, labor efficiency, and the like. If the marginalist were asked the same question he would attempt to determine how individual actors ranked shelter among their preferences. The Darwinian generally asked "what do people need?" whereas the marginalist asked "what do people choose?" This difference in how the welfare question is posed was to have profound implications for legal thought.

2

Natural Selection, Deterrence, and Mental Defect

OVER HISTORY DEVIANCY and mental defect have been linked more or less closely. Thanks to the developing sciences of evolutionary biology and genetics, Progressives regarded the association as particularly strong. Darwinian science and marginalist environmentalism pulled in opposite directions, however, leading to radically different ideas about control. The theory of evolution suggested that people are not individually "responsible" for their criminal behavior. Rather, they inherited qualities that increased their propensity toward crime. The Darwinian remedy was to ensure that these "criminal types" could not reproduce, usually accomplished by either sterilization or sexual isolation. By contrast, marginalism saw criminal and other antisocial conduct mainly as a problem in metering sanctions. Closely related were theories that linked racial intermarriage to degredation, and in turn to an increased aptitude for dependency or criminal behavior. This chapter focuses mainly on mental defect and criminal law. The following chapter concerns race relations. These were the two areas of legal policy where Darwinian ideas about human nature were most explicit.

The criminal theory that emerged early in the century was a blend of biological determinism, marginal deterrence theory, and classical moralism. Some Progressives, such as Edward A. Ross, were both marginalist in their economics and Darwinian racists in their social theory. The racist models led to statutes forbidding practices such as interracial marriage that survived until the mid-1960s.[1] Biological models of criminal behavior showed up mainly in studies linking crime to physical or mental defect. In the 1940s environmentalism came to dominate in theories of both criminal behavior and race, although the influence of genetics hardly disappeared.[2]

The new theories of human behavior competed with a well-established classical orthodoxy. Traditionally crime was a moral issue, and retribution was the theory of punishment. Race was what it was, and God had intended for the races to be kept separate. Darwinian evolution was a difficult pill for many religious Americans to swallow, and until well after the Civil War this was true even for some scientists. For example, "polygenesis," or the view that the different races did not evolve but had distinct origins, was viable even in elite American universities. The principal protagonist of polygenesis in the United States was Louis Agassiz, paleontologist at Harvard University until the late 1860s.[3]

The story of Progressive social science and race is discomfiting today. Progressives could be quite interventionist in behalf of labor and the poor but also thoroughly racist in their views about crime, social segregation, interracial marriage, education, and restrictions on immigration.[4] Indeed, Progressive Era racism could be far worse than racism in a more laissez-faire society, because the racism was increasingly "managed" through the legal system, rather than mere acquiescence in private views. This was reflected in institutions such as racial residential zoning, discussed in the next chapter.

One of the Progressives' most important contributions to sociology was the concept of "social control"—or the idea that environmental and cultural rather than individual factors impose order on society, and that many of these factors can be manipulated through the legal system. Edward A. Ross, whose pioneering book *Social Control* was published in 1901, was also a student of marginalist economics.[5] As he envisioned it, social control was the use of social rules to change incentives at the margin. Ross's work helped shape a Progressive ideology that justified public intervention in order to improve humanity.

Nevertheless, Ross distinguished "social control," which influenced the behaviors of the current generation, from genetic control by forced selective breeding. Only the latter could produce long-term betterment of the race. "The way to create a short-clawed feline is not to trim the claws of successive generations of kittens, but to pick out the shortest-clawed cats and to breed from them," he wrote. "It is processes like these, affecting the relative birth-rates or death-rates of the social and the anti-social classes, which solve the problem of order in such a manner that it *stays* solved."[6]

By 1910 most scientists had rejected the Lamarckian evolutionary theory of inheritance of acquired characteristics.[7] Humanity could not be permanently improved by creating incentives for individual betterment, but only by identifying individuals who should be discouraged from producing offspring. Thus the great influence of eugenics. Nevertheless, the radical nature of State-directed limitations on breeding served to constrain their use. The policy consensus was that genetic intervention should be reserved for people on society's outer boundaries—criminals and the mentally defective. Beyond that, State policy should concentrate on the improvement of the individual. Sociologist Charles Horton Cooley spoke of "biological sociology" and "psychological sociology" to describe these Darwinian and marginalist strains.[8] Columbia University economist Simon Patten wrote of the "failure" of biological approaches to sociology. University of Pennsylvania sociologist and economist Franklin Henry Giddings argued that sociology should be driven by economic doctrines of marginal utility.[9]

His racism notwithstanding, Ross's theory of social control belonged in the marginalist, or "psychological," category. Ross believed that the most effective engine of social control was the law, whose principal purpose was marginal deterrence: "A scientific penology will graduate punishments primarily according to the harmfulness of the offence to society, and secondarily, according to the attractiveness of the offence to the criminal."[10] Nonetheless, during the first three decades of the twentieth century these views were very much in dispute, with the genetic theories gradually yielding to environmentalism or more blended theories.

The External Standard and the Rational Actor: Holmes's Marginalism

Oliver Wendell Holmes, Jr. was influenced by both Darwinian evolutionary theory and the work of the philosophical Pragmatists at Harvard in the 1870s.[11] *The Common Law* (1881) cites the Darwinian cultural anthropologist Edward Tylor several times for points about the cultural evolution of norms.[12] Holmes scholars have tended to emphasize the historical/evolutionary character of his work rather than its economics.[13] As David Rabban has suggested, however, whereas *The Common Law* presented itself as legal history, Holmes often subordinated historical accuracy to arguments about policy.[14]

The underlying framework of Holmes's legal theory was historical and Darwinian, but its policy content was utilitarian and marginalist, driven by concerns with deterrence and risk management. The mistakes of evolution were not a defense: If "a man is born hasty and awkward, is always having accidents and hurting himself or his neighbors, no doubt his congenital defects will be allowed for in the courts of Heaven, but his slips are no less troublesome to his neighbors than if they sprang from guilty neglect."[15] *The Common Law* contains numerous discussions of risk, in which minimization of expected losses is the central theme. "[T]he safest way to secure care is to throw the risk upon the person who decides what precautions shall be taken," he wrote in his chapter on trespass and negligence, giving several examples. The risk must be assigned to the one with superior control of the circumstances, he wrote in his introductory chapter on torts, speaking of the person who rides an unbroken horse on a crowded way. He defended aggressive rules for highly dangerous conduct that "throw the risk upon the party pursuing it." He famously argued that contracts should be viewed as "the taking of a risk" and a set of bets about the future. Consequential damages were not appropriate "unless the assumption of that risk is to be taken as having fairly entered into the contract."[16]

Holmes's marginalism is scattered across all of *The Common Law*, beginning with his development of the external standard.[17] Just as the neoclassical economists had merged utilitarianism into their theory of markets, Holmes merged it into a modern theory of deterrence as a unifying rationale for both criminal and common law rules. His thought followed the utilitarianism of Jeremy Bentham or John Austin far more than any Darwinian. Although he did not invariably agree with Austin, Holmes cited him more frequently than any evolutionist, including Henry Maine, twice as often as Blackstone, and more than any legal writer except the seventeenth-century English jurist Sir Edward Coke.

The external standard became a staple of elite jurisprudence in the first half of the twentieth century, producing such monuments as Samuel Williston's and Arthur L. Corbin's writing on contracts,[18] and the emergence of modern negligence theory.[19] The external standard begins with actors whose subjective state of mind can never be measured by an outside observer. Its purpose "is only to induce external conformity to rule," as Holmes said. Its "tests of liability are external, and independent of the degree of evil in the particular person's motives or intentions."[20] For both criminal and civil law, Holmes based liability on foresight, measured by an objective standard: "common" experience, rather than the experience of any individual.

Holmes's premise that we can never examine the internal workings of another's mind also became an essential component of behaviorist social science. His external standard purported to look at the "average man," considering "what would be blameworthy in the ... man of ordinary intelligence and prudence." Holmes never provided much detail about his "average" person, apparently believing that this person resembled someone with average height or weight. The difficulty inherent in identifying a "certain average of conduct" that applies to "temperament, intellect and education"[21] did not seem to trouble him, and he was generally content to leave that to the jury. Just as other Darwinians, Holmes did not assume radical indeterminacy of preferences. Rather, because human beings are the product of evolution by natural selection, their minds have roughly similar workings. As a class, they respond to incentives in similar ways. Holmes then considered how sanctions control conduct in order to minimize loss.

The external standard and the hypothesis of the "average man" turned even private law into a social control device, as Progressives would use that term. Noncomparability of mental states made Holmes's "average man" impossible to *find*; he had to be constructed by the legal system. This fact gave Holmes's approach to the common law an implicitly public character that Holmes himself never fully acknowledged. Harvard Law professor Warren Seavey, advisor to the first Restatement of Torts, argued in 1927 that the law never determines empirically what the standard of the "average person" is when measuring something such as negligence. Rather it invents the "average" person as the one who takes the amount of precaution that the legal policymaker believes to be appropriate. "The standard man evaluates interests in accordance with the valuation placed upon them by the community sentiment crystallized into law."[22] Judge Hand's cost-benefit test for negligence in the *Carroll Towing* case was purely objective in this way.[23] This was public policymaking disguised as private law.

By the time he wrote "The Path of the Law" in 1897, Holmes was much clearer that the point of this objective, external standard was marginal deterrence, and that economics was essential to its study. The whole purpose of damages was to give people a motive for good behavior, and law is nothing more than a prediction of what courts will do. This prediction theory served two purposes. One was the positive "study of this body of dogma" in order to determine its content. The other was guidance for someone who wanted to know what he could and could not do. For the "rational study of the law," Holmes wrote, "the man of the future is the man of statistics and the master of economics." He continued:

> I look forward to a time when the part played by history in the explanation of dogma shall be very small, and instead of ingenious research we shall spend our energy on a study of the ends sought to be attained and the reasons for desiring them. As a step toward that ideal it seems to me that every lawyer ought to seek an understanding of economics.

Holmes made this powerful argument for marginal deterrence as the goal of criminal punishment, categorically rejecting more Darwinian approaches:

> If the typical criminal is a degenerate, bound to swindle or to murder by as deep seated an organic necessity as that which makes the rattlesnake

> bite, it is idle to talk of deterring him by the classical method of imprisonment. He must be got rid of; he cannot be improved, or frightened out of his structural reaction. If, on the other hand, crime, like normal human conduct, is mainly a matter of imitation, punishment fairly may be expected to help to keep it out of fashion. The study of criminals has been thought by some well known men of science to sustain the former hypothesis.... But there is weighty authority for the belief that, however this may be, "not the nature of the crime, but the dangerousness of the criminal, constitutes the only reasonable legal criterion to guide the inevitable social reaction against the criminal."[24]

The same attitude guided Holmes's position on causation in tort law. As Chapter 7 develops, Holmes followed the lead of pragmatist Nicholas St. John Green in reducing the entire debate to a question of foreseeability, measured by an objective test. "If the intervening events are of such a kind that no foresight could have been expected to look out for them, the defendant is not to blame for having failed to do so," Holmes wrote in *The Common Law*.[25] The American Pragmatists, including Charles Peirce and William James, came to the same position.[26] The law must identify the harm to be avoided as a matter of policy, and then give people metered incentives to avoid it.

Arguments that Holmes accepted any form of Darwinism as a *political* philosophy are based on a few ambiguous statements, most of which are equally consistent with his cynicism about human nature. But Holmes's prescriptive thought represents a rather thoroughgoing although nontechnical marginalism, which shows up as (1) his broad-based willingness to jettison morality-based legal rationales for ones based on deterrence and risk management; (2) his stressing of negligence, externally measured, as the unifying principle of tort law; and (3) his identification of legally sufficient causation with objective foreseeability.

Marginalism is also implicit in Holmes's conclusion that the foundations of criminal and civil liability are fundamentally the same.[27] Both Holmes's theory of torts and his quest for a universal basis for liability in *The Common Law* seem quite inconsistent with the revulsion of unifying theories that American Pragmatism professed.[28] From the classical perspective criminal law deals with immorality and harms against the State; it is public law. By contrast, tort law is purely private and concerned only with harms to the individual. Nonetheless, both imprisonment and the payment of damages create incentives for behavior. Holmes identified "foresight" as the "common denominator" that cut across all forms of legal liability. A man "is bound to foresee whatever a prudent and intelligent man would have foreseen, and therefore he is liable for conduct from which such a man would have foreseen that harm was liable to follow.[29]

Holmes believed that evolution explained the development of the human species.[30] However, he refused to draw the broad implications for State policy that Social Darwinists gave it. Clearly he was not a Reform Darwinist, and the attempts to make him one failed miserably.[31] When Holmes made reference to evolutionary theory he was largely concerned with the descriptive question of how organisms or legal rules evolve, not with what evolution has to say about legal policymaking.[32]

Over his entire life Holmes expressed deep skepticism about statist attempts to improve the human race. In the early 1920s John H. Wigmore and Albert Kocourek edited a collection of essays entitled *Rational Basis of Legal Institutions*, concerned with the use of legislation as a social control device. Wigmore made the mistake of asking Holmes, now in his eighties, to write the introduction. Holmes complied by giving the book its first bad review:

> The subjects dealt with in this book are so interesting that it is hard to refrain from expressing one's own views upon some of them at least. But in one place or another I have said what I think about the foundations.... [E]ven the enlightened reformers that I hear or read seem to me not to have considered with accuracy the means at our disposal and to become rhetorical just where I want figures. The notion that we can secure an economic paradise by changes in property alone seems to me twaddle.[33]

Legal Realist Underhill Moore later condemned the book for confusing means and ends, and attacked the entire enterprise of searching for a single rationale for legal institutions. Upon reading Holmes's introduction he "sensed a spirit of weariness" in the old man's remarks. "Upon closing the book, [my] confidence is strengthened that this impression was correct."[34]

Deterrence and Determinism

In the late nineteenth century an outpouring of social science literature emphasized the role of law in regulating future behavior rather than punishing a previous wrong or compensating victims. The deterrence revolution in legal theory has been closely identified with the American philosophy of

Pragmatism and often characterized as Darwinian.[35] In fact, criminologists and other social scientists were deeply divided on the nature-nuture question. Within the Darwinian model individuals responded to the environment, but the consequences were changes in the likelihood of survival and production of offspring. So, for example, one might limit criminal behavior by sexual isolation or sterilization. By contrast, environmental models focused on behavior modification. Criminology responded by progressing from the study of the "criminal brain" in the late nineteenth century to the "criminal mind" in the 1920s.

The Gilded Age and Progressive Era's conception of legal social control included heavy elements of genetic determinism as well as marginal deterrence. Many Progressive policymakers tried to improve the world by ensuring that "defectives" would not reproduce. The science they relied on included an expansive form of physical anthropology, or "anthropometry," believed to predict human behavioral characteristics from skeletal features. Although the theories antedated *The Origin of Species*, they readily accommodated Darwinian evolution. Cesare Lombroso, an Italian physician and mental hospital director, performed autopsies on hundreds of deceased criminals, examining their skulls in particular. He concluded that criminal types bore certain "stigmata," including cranial and facial abnormalities. In 1887 Lombroso published the first broad summary of his findings, declaring that criminals had a high incidence of poorly developed wisdom teeth, small cranial capacity, flattening of the occipital, and retreating forehead.[36] A few years later he announced analogous differences between sexually promiscuous "criminal women," principally prostitutes, and normal women.[37]

Lombroso believed that many criminals were biological "throwbacks" ("*atavisme*"). Their primitive mental capacities made them unable to compete within the structure that society provided, so they resorted to crime. Criminals were evolution's inferior outcasts, not so deformed that they could not survive at all, but sufficiently defective that they could not live productive lives. Invariably, like all Darwinists, Lombroso had to deal with the role of the environment, as it determined the impact of an individual's inherited strengths and weaknesses. Lombroso found significant correlations between crime and poverty. A biologically inferior person who was poor was substantially more likely to commit a crime than one who was well off.

In 1900 August Drahms, a Lombroso student who was chaplain at San Quentin State Prison, published the results of extensive cranial and facial measurements he had conducted on two thousand inmates. Lombroso wrote the introduction. Many of these had been executed for capital crimes at a young age, and Drahms regarded them as "healthy" specimens whose features had not been degraded by disease. Drahms distinguished between the "instinctive criminal," who commited crimes no matter how favorable his environment, and the "habitual criminal," whose past included adverse circumstances. Drahms concluded that the primary causes of instinctive criminality were hereditary, whereas the chief causes of habitual criminality were environmental. He agreed with Lombroso that neither type was responsible for his acts. One was born without faculties that enabled others to survive within society's rules. The other was thrown into a life situation so adverse that only criminal behavior made survival possible. Drahms recommended that sanctions be addressed to reformation. His deterrence agenda included prohibition of alcohol, minimum wage laws, and indeterminate sentencing that would permit the early release of reformed criminals. "Change the environment and you inaugurate the process that will eventually render these conditions impossible and after-remedies unnecessary."[38]

Many of Drahms's contemporaries took more aggressively genetic approaches. In 1899 the vasectomy was developed by Indiana physician Harry C. Sharp as a reliable sterilization procedure without the debilitating effects of castration.[39] In 1903 Charles Ellinwood, chief surgeon at San Francisco Hospital, argued for vasectomy as a "means of diminishing crime and the number of criminals."[40] Several states began systematically sterilizing certain criminals, often with little legal process. Indiana began sterilization in 1899. In 1907 the legislature provided a statutory procedure in "An Act to Prevent Procreation of Confirmed Criminals, Idiots, Imbeciles, and Rapists." Under the authority of a state-created "Committee on Mental Defectives" hundreds of people were sterilized.[41] After it had been in use for fifteen years, the statute was struck down by the Indiana Supreme Court, mainly because it did not permit the accused to obtain expert testimony or even cross-examine the state's experts.[42]

By the mid-twenties twenty-three states had enacted sterilization laws.[43] Not all were limited to criminals. Many provided for the sterilization of those deemed mentally defective but without criminal convictions. For example, the Virginia statute upheld by the Supreme Court in *Buck v. Bell* (1927), provided for sterilization of any state inmate upon a finding that the subject was "afflicted with hereditary forms of insanity [or] imbecility." The opinion by Justice Holmes has often been used to quiet myths about his liberalism, for he uses some quite illiberal language. After quoting the lower court's conclusion that Carrie Buck "is the probable potential parent of socially inadequate offspring," he concluded that "three generations of imbeciles are enough."

For many Progressive Era reformers compulsory sterilization of defectives was an essential part of comprehensive planning. Sociologist Edward Ross supported them, and probably even Brandeis, who was a silent part of the *Buck* majority. Justice Butler, one of the most conservative members of the Court, dissented without opinion. He was Catholic, and the Catholic Church had come out strongly against sterilization as a social control device. Irving Fisher, a Yale economist who strongly argued for wealth distribution via progressive taxes, was also a founding member of the American Eugenics Society, and many Progressive Era economists shared his views.[44]

Sterilization of criminals and "defectives" was always controversial, however. From its inception it was attacked as both cruel and socially useless.[45] As one court observed about a statute compelling sterilization for rape of a child, the statute might be defensible as general deterrence to the extent that the children of rapists are more likely to commit rape, but it might have precisely the opposite effect as special deterrence because it removed one source of evidence that a rape had occurred. "It is easy to imagine that a brute guilty of rape, or who has a tendency to commit such a crime, might regard it rather an advantage than otherwise to be sterilized...."[46] The Superintendent of Central Howard Association, a Chicago halfway house for released prisoners, which was affiliated with Hull House, observed that sterilization of habitual criminals was unlikely to limit crime. Most such people did not reproduce in any event. "Only as it may apply to the rapist is there apparently any direct connection between the performance of this operation and the possible repetition of crime, and these degenerates constitute but one or two per cent of prisoners."[47]

Mandatory sterilization was designed to "deter" mainly by reducing the amount of criminal activity in the next generation. Strictly speaking, such policies could be implemented without any evidence of criminal behavior or promiscuity. Scientists such as Lombroso and Drahms believed they could recognize the "criminal type" on the basis of physical measurements alone. One need not wait for the commission of a criminal act. Indeed, statutes such as the one in *Buck v. Bell* were designed for this purpose, and Holmes did not object: "It is better for all the world, if instead of waiting to execute degenerate offspring for crime, or to let them starve for their imbecility, society can prevent those who are manifestly unfit from continuing their kind."[48]

The rhetoric supporting such legislation was often Social Darwinist. Albert E. Wiggam, director of the American Eugenics Society, argued that organized social safety nets were contributing to a "rising tide" of degeneracy. In a less protective society mental defectives would have died off or been isolated before they had a chance to reproduce.[49] Echoing Lombroso's work on sexually promiscuous women, Wiggam's popular 1924 book *The Fruit of the Family Tree* argued how important it was for men to select refined rather than degenerate women as partners.[50] State and county fairs sponsored "better babies" and "fitter families" contests to reward people for making good genetic choices in selecting partners. The winners received bronze medallions proclaiming their genetic fitness. A booth on eugenics at the Philadelphia Sesqui-Centennial Exhibition was entitled "Some people are born to be a burden on the rest."[51]

But there were also important dissenters. Lombroso's theories about the criminal brain were attacked by both anthropologists and psychologists, even as the science of genetics was coming of age.[52] Franklin H. Giddings, a Reform Darwinist and trained economist, had established sociology as a discipline at Columbia University in the 1890s. One of Giddings's proteges, Arthur Cleveland Hall, tried to find a correlation between social evolution and criminal behavior. For Hall, what was criminal at a particular time was defined by the state of society's ethical evolution. The ethical environment changed in exactly the same way that the physical environment did. Society evolved by continuously excluding its ethically "inferior" individuals. Hall argued that the production of crime and criminals was one of the "saving processes of nature." If nature had not induced "increasingly severe social selection and pressure toward the elevation of the individual and the improvement of the type," mankind would have resorted to inferior social devices favoring physical aggression. Criminals defined society's ever-increasing ethical standards by failing to meet them.[53]

Hall's criminology placed more of the blame for criminal behavior on the changing social environment. More complex explanations containing both Darwinian and environmental elements were heavily influenced by Sigmund Freud, whose earlier works had been translated into English by World War I. Freud believed that the unconscious so dominated explanation of human action that the key to most behavioral aberrations lay in some experience from the past, particularly early childhood.[54] Every aspect of a person's conscious mind, including his moral values, was part of a self-protection mechanism that the species had developed through natural selection. The amount of determinism was not less, but it came from environmental as well as genetic sources.

William A. White, one of America's foremost Freudian criminologists, argued in his 1923 book *Insanity and the Criminal Law* that social definitions of crime resulted from both natural selection and suppressed individual instincts.[55] White drew from sociologist William Graham Sumner the idea that the most powerful elements in social control were customs and instincts that evolved over countless generations.[56] The State, said Sumner, was generally powerless to change attitudes that had evolved into a part of "human nature." White located societal moral values exclusively in these shared customs and instincts that had enabled a particular social structure to survive and had therefore been appropriated by its members. The common law jury trial amounted to a "herd critique" of one person's behavior by his peers. The jurors came from the society "in which the alleged crime was committed, and their reaction to the crime was considered fairly to represent the state of the popular mind regarding it." White maintained that the "herd critique" was a primitive and irrational mechanism for judging human behavior. Every person's instincts inclined him toward selfish aggression and violence. The criminal became the "handy scapegoat" upon whom each member of society could transfer the guilt of his own harmful urges.[57]

"Based upon a deterministic psychology," White wrote, psychiatry "sees any given act of an individual as an end result determined and receiving its full explanation and meaning in the light of his personality make-up as affected by environmental circumstances." The treatment of crime contained two legitimate objectives: "first, to do away, so far as possible, with the conditions (mental defectiveness, insanity, and immoral social conditions, etc.) out of which crime grows; and second, the salvaging of the criminal for social usefulness."[58]

Sterilization had little place in White's framework. Earlier in his career he had been appointed chair of a Committee on Sterilization organized by the American Institute of Criminal Law and Criminology. The Institute, formed in Chicago in 1909, was composed of medical and legal professionals as well as law enforcers and prison wardens. Its organizers included John H. Wigmore, Dean of the Northwestern Law School; Roscoe Pound; and promnent trial lawyer Clarence Darrow. The membership was bitterly divided on the sterilization question, however. In the sterilization committee's 1917 *Report* White angrily concluded that there was "no common ground of agreement" among the committee. He recommended that some of its members be replaced by people "whose views on other topics do not incapacitate them for the study of a problem in public welfare."[59]

White obtained more consensus for his view that the scope of criminal jury decisions be limited to determining whether the defendant had committed the criminal act. Any questions about mental condition, diminished capacity, ameliorating social conditions, or punishment or treatment should be left to experts. In 1917 another Institute committee of lawyers and physicians incorporated many of these ideas into a model criminal responsibility statute. In order to be acquitted by reason of insanity, a defendant had to show that "by reason of... mental disease he did not have the particular state of mind that must accompany such act or omission in order to constitute the crime charged."[60] The proposal was a significant departure from the established position in most states. Although increasing the number of defendants who could take advantage of the insanity plea, it also increased the State's discretion to determine how such people should be treated, taking that issue away from juries.

The proposal also recognized different standards for persons of "diminished capacity," who could be considered only partially responsible. Since the mid-nineteenth century mental health reformers had been arguing that juries often improperly acquitted mentally ill defendants in capital cases. John Charles Bucknill, advisor to the British Chancellor on criminal conduct and mental illness, warned that juries in capital cases must be provided with "some middle way." Otherwise they "will continue to find verdicts of not guilty on the false plea of insanity."[61] Under the Institute's proposal, persons whose mental disorder was not enough to earn them an acquittal could instead be convicted of a lesser crime commensurate with the responsibility they were thought to have.

Most states still followed an "either-or" rule: the defendant was either sane and must be convicted of the crime with which he was originally charged, or else he was insane and entitled to acquittal. An 1883 Indiana Supreme Court decision held that there is "no middle ground between 'sanity' and 'insanity.'" The District of Columbia agreed. "There can be no recognition of the doctrine that a man is incapable of distinguishing between right and wrong so as to determine that the case is not a case of murder, and yet capable of distinguishing between right and wrong so as to be guilty of manslaughter."[62]

One dramatic example of the either-or rule is the case of Frank Willard, a chronic alcoholic from Mendocino, California, who had twice been committed to its hospital for the insane. He habitually told people that he had been hired by President Theodore Roosevelt to punish "evil doers," and threatened to kill anyone who interfered with his mission. Mendocino County sheriff J.H. Smith brought yet a third civil commitment action against Willard, and two psychiatrists testified at the hearing that Willard was homicidal and suffering from "insane delusions." Just as the judge was reading his commitment order from the bench, Willard jumped up, shouting that he would not return to a mental hospital, and ran from the courtroom. As Sheriff Smith went after him Willard drew a pistol from his pocket and shot Smith, who died immediately. Willard was tried and convicted of murder under a jury instruction that reflected California law: no degree of "mental impairment" could serve to mitigate his offense if he knew the difference between right and wrong. Willard was executed at San Quentin State Prison in June 1907.[63]

Increasingly in the 1920s, however, states became more receptive to White's view. New York developed four degrees of homicide depending on the defendant's mental state. Speaking of crimes induced by intoxication the new Criminal Code said: "Whenever the actual existence of any particular purpose, motive, or intent is a necessary element to constitute a particular specie or degree of crime, the jury may take into consideration the fact that the accused was intoxicated at the time, in determining the purpose, motive or intent with which he committed the act."[64]

White was a defense expert in the 1924 "trial of the century" of Nathan Leopold and Richard Loeb, two wealthy University of Chicago law students who kidnapped and murdered fourteen-year-old Bobby Franks in a senseless plot to commit the perfect crime. In fact, there was no trial at all but only a sentencing hearing. Knowing that a jury would almost certainly sentence them to hang, their attorney Clarence Darrow pled the boys guilty. This permitted him to make his sentence plea to the judge. Darrow himself had popularized criminal defense arguments based on determinism in his 1922 book *Crime: Its Causes and Treatment*. "Heredity has everything to do with making the machine strong and capable, or weak and useless; but when the machine is made and thrown on the world in its imperfect shape, environment has everything to do in determining what its fate shall be."[65] The hearing was dominated by expert psychiatric testimony and Darrow's own impassioned speech, arguing that the two young men were not acting out of free will but rather from mental illness and circumstance. "Science has been at work, humanity has been at work, scholarship has been at work, and intelligent people now know," spoke Darrow, "that every human being is the product of the endless heredity back of him and the infinite environment around him. He is made as he is and he is the sport of all that goes before him." Speaking of Loeb, "This terrible crime was inherent in his organism, and it came from some ancestor."[66]

White's psychiatric testimony was instrumental in getting the defendants a life sentence rather than the death penalty.[67] In a letter to Darrow he explained the case as reflecting the prosecutor's "lust for blood" more than the horror of the crime itself.[68] But White's testimony was too much for John H. Wigmore, the country's best known scholar of scientific criminal evidence.

He protested that White's position tended to "undermine the whole penal law" by turning it over to psychiatrists who believed that there is "no choice for us, because all human acts are predetermined."[69]

Morality, Responsibility, and Free Will

Determinist arguments against criminal liability hardly originated with the Progressives. But criminologists always rejected them, concluding that criminal law is a "practical" science where philosophical theories of determinism have no place. This robust traditional view was best articulated in *Wharton's Criminal Law*, one of the most widely cited American criminal law treatises of the nineteenth century.

Francis Wharton, an orthodox Episcopal priest, also wrote popular treatises on criminal law, medical jurisprudence, and negligence. In his sixties he became a law professor at George Washington University. The tenth edition of his criminal law treatise was edited by University of Pennsylvania Law Dean William Draper Lewis a few years after Wharton's death. The controversy over free will, he wrote, was simply "not a part of criminal theory." "From a speculative point of vision, all acts are necessitated. With this, however, jurisprudence, which is a practical science, has nothing to do." Further, "[n]o matter what may be our speculative views as to the existence of conscience, or of freedom of action, we are obliged, when we determine responsibility, to affirm both." Arguments from determinism must be set aside, not because the problems had been solved, but because they never could be and the law could not afford to address them.[70]

Even in the mid-1920s, during the heyday of instrumentalism and determinism in social science, many experts defended a position more or less like that of Wharton and Lewis. In 1924 Sheldon Glueck, a Harvard graduate student who became one of the foremost criminal psychologists of juvenile delinquency in the 1940s and 1950s, found that the discipline had deeply involved itself in a metaphysical debate about determinism and individual responsibility.[71] Glueck, another defense expert in the *Leopold and Loeb* case, concluded that "conservative law had shown herself much more sensible than her more impetuous sisters, the experimental sciences." While psychology and psychiatry had immersed themselves in broad questions about ultimate causation, law "takes the common sense view that this need not at all affect our practical belief in human freedom." Roscoe Pound summed it up in 1927: no matter what social science might indicate, criminal law "postulates a free agent confronted with a choice between doing right and doing wrong and choosing freely to do wrong."[72]

For people of Glueck's mind deterministic psychology had confused the absolute question of responsibility and free will with the much more pragmatic and relative "responsibility" that juries decide in criminal cases. Traced to their logical conclusion, behaviorist arguments such as those created by Lombroso, Drahms, and Freud and imported into the law by Darrow proved too much. As Wigmore had protested, they argued not merely that the mentally ill were not responsible for their acts, but that no one was responsible for anything. Law had to deal with the much more limited but also more manageable question of relative responsibility and deterrence of public harm. Glueck concluded:

> Our notion of moral responsibility is not necessarily dependent upon our views as to the metaphysical problems of human freedom.... Men condemn and forgive each other...not necessarily because of any belief in human freedom [but because] their intelligence and experience teaches them that most human beings have some capacity for purposive, creative activity.... When men fail to achieve the socially or legally acceptable minimum of required conduct, it is either because they deliberately chose such a result, or because, through native mental defect, mental disease, or the overwhelming pressure of the external world, they were actually unable to exercise their purposive-volitional capacity.[73]

Even if the human individual is a product of genetics and his environment, society might still be able to control the environment and modify behavior. Michigan law professor John Barker Waite concluded in 1925 that even the absolute determinist acknowledged that a controlled environment yielded controlled behavior. "By punishment of one person...there are created in other brains impressions which tend to prevent the translation of impulse into particular action.' "[74]

Psychiatry and behavioral psychology also had important limitations. Scientists could not examine human minds directly. The psychoanalyst's data were human actions, especially human language. Frequently, her only empirical evidence about human motivation was what her subjects told her. Many Freudians discounted the problem, believing that hypnosis and psychoanalysis could break down inhibitions so that a patient's words could be an accurate description of his state of mind. But that theory was itself unverifiable, for the psychiatrist could not get behind the words. Conservative Catholic psychologist Thomas Vernor Moore wrote: "It is impossible to investigate everything in our mental life by objective methods, for this inner experience is far richer than its manifestations by actions or reactions that can be the objects of an external observer's experience."[75]

The most expansive Progressive Era behavioralists thought they were replacing religion and myth with science. For jurists, however, there was no such easy dichotomy. Human behavior contained both a complexity and a moral content that social science ignored at its peril.

3

The Science and Law of Race

A TROUBLESOME LEGACY of the Progressive Era is its "managed" racism. No area of law was more affected by Darwinian science than race relations. Courts were influenced by scientific theories about race in two ways. First was the "background" scientific information that informed a judge's education and perception of the world.[1] Second, scientific or social science data were presented directly to the courts, often in briefs patterned after Justice Brandeis's famous one in *Muller v. Oregon*,[2] which used social science data to convince the Supreme Court that a state had the constitutional power to regulate the working hours of women even though it could not do so for men.

Racial Science and the Brandeis Brief

In the *Berea College* case (1908) the Supreme Court was confronted with social science data about race.[3] Berea College was an unfortunately situated product of the fervently evangelical antislavery movement of the 1830s. Its geographic setting, in one of the four slaveholding states that remained with the Union during the Civil War,[4] caused it difficulties that other religious institutions did not face. Berea entered the post-Reconstruction period as an ideological rarity: a school committed to the integrated education of white and black students, but isolated in a southern, formerly slaveholding state.

Berea College managed to withstand local opposition during and after Reconstruction—financial starvation, aggressive racial hostility, and occasional acts of violence against its faculty and students. Although today it is integrated once again, its interracial mission did not fare so well against the science and politics of the Gilded Age. Before the turn of the century, a large number of scientific studies warned against the dangers of racial mixing.[5] Both scientists and laypersons generally believed that Afro-Americans were permanently and inherently inferior, that they learned more slowly than white persons, and that their close association with whites could contaminate the white race. After the Civil War, the possibility of substantial racial mixing became more apparent, particularly in urban areas. The most feared prospect was "miscegenation," a term that referred to both interracial marriage and other interracial sexual contact. The way to prevent it was to keep the races separate, particularly in institutions such as schools, where young people's values and attractions were developed. In 1904 Kentucky prohibited the operation of "any college, school or institution where persons of the white and negro race are both received as pupils for instruction." At the time Berea was Kentucky's only integrated college.

The college argued that, although under *Plessy v. Ferguson* the Fourteenth Amendment did not prohibit states from forcing school segregation, Berea was a private school.[6] Nevertheless, the Kentucky court concluded that the legislature had simply recognized an obvious scientific truth—that "[t]he separation of the human family into races . . . is as certain as anything in nature." The "same power has been exercised to prohibit the intermarriage of the two races. The result of such marriage would be to destroy the purity of blood and identity of each." The Supreme Court affirmed, and law review writers generally agreed.[7]

Kentucky had relied on a "Brandeis Brief" of scientific data modeled after the one that Brandeis had used only three months earlier in *Muller*, citing an eclectic assortment of scientific studies, both new and outdated, as well as the rants of some notorious bigots. Kentucky Attorney General James Breathitt cited a study by Dr. Sanford B. Hunt, a U.S. surgeon and pioneer in the field of anthropometrics, or the study of the physical characteristics of the races of mankind.[8] Hunt had cited evidence that the average Afro-American's brain weighed five ounces less than the average white person's brain. He also found that the brain of the average mulatto was even smaller than that of the average black. Because it was generally assumed (incorrectly) that brain weight correlated with intelligence, Hunt concluded not only that blacks had less mental capacity than whites, but that racial intermarriage would produce offspring inferior even to the offspring of "pure-blooded" blacks.

Hunt came from a line of American anthropometrists that began with Samuel George Morton, a Philadelphia physician who compared human skulls in the 1820s. Morton filled crania with mustard seeds and found racial differences in cranial capacity similar to those Hunt observed later.[9] Morton also obtained the skulls of some three-thousand-year-old white Egyptians and their black slaves. He discovered approximately the same variations in cranial capacity. In three millennia blacks had come no closer to "catching up" with whites.[10]

Breathitt argued that this evidence demonstrated the commonwealth's interest in maintaining racial separation. A "mental gap" separated Africans and Caucasians that "is not the result of education, but is innate and God-given." Science had shown that "education, culture, refinement and civilization are the result of the polishing of the inborn and God-given faculty. Training, culture and education never produce faculty."[11]

Breathitt concluded his scientific argument by quoting an "eminent writer on natural selection"—namely William Benjamin Smith, a German-educated professor of mathematics at Tulane University whose hobby was eugenics. In 1905 Smith published an immensely popular book called *The Color Line*, which summarized what he believed to be the current anthropological and sociological information about Afro-Americans. Breathitt's brief quoted from Smith's conclusions that "social racial equality is...abhorrent alike to instinct and to reason." In fact, "[I]t is idle to talk of education and civilization and the like, as corrective or compensative agencies. All are weak and beggarly as over against the almightiness of heredity; the omnipotence of the transmitted germ plasma."[12]

Today it is easy to dismiss Kentucky's evidence as "pseudo-science."[13] In 1908, however, genetic racism was well within mainstream views. The traditional position was that racial characteristics were permanent—"innate and God-given," as Breathitt argued. God created the species and races "after their kind," and the distinguishing features of each group were permanent. In 1908 this view claimed many nonscientists, although it was being edged out of the mainstream scientific community.[14]

By 1908 most scientists were evolutionists and accepted the role of heredity in determining racial features. Genetic theory was just being developed, and scientific journals discussed the inheritance of physical and mental characteristics. These scientists believed that characteristics such as intelligence do "evolve," and some agreed that someday the Afro-American could develop intelligence equal to the Caucasian's. Because evolutionary processes are so slow, however, the intellectual differences between the races had to be regarded as practically permanent. Furthermore, race mixing was bad for two reasons. First, it could slow the evolutionary progress of the more advanced race. Second, interbreeding of dissimilar organisms increased the possibility of unhealthy offspring with disharmonic features, mental deficiency, weakness, and disease. These groups generally agreed that social integration of any kind was bad because race mixing would lead to miscegenation. As the Kentucky court said in *Berea*, "from social amalgamation it is but a step to illicit intercourse, and but another to intermarriage."

Another view of racial differences was held by a small number of scientists who had barely begun to be heard. They would not have a significant impact for almost a generation, and their views may have been unknown to Attorney General Breathitt. These scientists were also evolutionists, and they agreed with the genetic determinists that some human characteristics were hereditary and would take a long time to change by evolution—for example, skeletal or facial features. But other characteristics, such as behavior and intelligence are determined largely by outside influences that affect an individual during his developmental period. The only true intellectual difference between blacks and whites was that the latter had been denied the advantages of the white person's life situation, economic status, or education. More important, the genetic differences between the races were not nearly as great as the genetic determinists believed.[15] Racial differences were subvarietal. If one plotted all the world's organisms on a chart, the different races of humanity would be so close together that they would appear to be one. Most laypersons could not even distinguish two subvarieties of rabbits or mollusks. The environmentalists thus argued that, notwithstanding any negative social consequences, racial interbreeding was probably not biologically harmful.

An Integrated Past?

One myth of American racial practice is that at the time of the Civil War northern whites wanted to promote social integration, while southern whites wanted to avoid it. A closely related theory is that "Jim Crow" segregation in the postwar South was really a product of the late nineteenth century. According to this theory, there was little need for segregation before the Civil War because slavery created a caste system in which every black person knew his place. The relatively few Afro-Americans who were free posed no threat to white institutions. House slaves generally accompanied their masters everywhere. During Reconstruction, however, the South became occupied territory and northern racial values were imposed. Not until the 1880s, when southern state autonomy had been restored, did the offended whites inaugurate Jim Crow.[16]

In debating whether the antebellum and Reconstruction South practiced segregation or integration, many historians overlooked that the social practices of the day included a third and widely practiced alternative: exclusion. "Separate but equal" statutes such as the one upheld for railroad cars in *Plessy v. Ferguson* did not always abrogate statutory integration that had been imposed by Reconstruction governments, or de facto integration that had been part of the southern way of life. Often such statutes replaced laws or customs that allowed blacks no accommodations at all.[17] To that extent they may actually have served to increase rather than decrease access.

Before the Civil War most southern schools, hospitals, asylums, hotels, restaurants, and other public facilities excluded blacks unless they were working slaves attending their owners.[18] Many southern states had no public school systems, and education was provided only at private institutions. Slave states generally prohibited slaves to go to school at all.[19] North Carolina had the only statewide antebellum public school system, but it was open only to whites.[20] During the late 1860s and early 1870s, when Reconstruction was firmly established, the remaining southern public school systems were forced to educate blacks. Georgia, Arkansas, Texas, and Tennessee all established public schools while they were controlled by northern-imposed Reconstruction legislatures; these systems were segregated by statute.[21] The only exceptions were South Carolina and Louisiana.[22]

Most public places of amusement were operated exclusively for members of one race. The newspapers of Reconstruction Atlanta, Nashville, and Montgomery were filled with advertisements for "Negro barrooms," "Negro billiard parlors," or "colored skating rinks." Montgomery operated racially exclusive parks, and most privately owned theaters either excluded blacks or permitted them to sit only in designated sections of the galleries.[23] Since before the Civil War, Nashville had operated a streetcar system that excluded blacks. In 1867, under Union control, it began to operate separate cars for blacks. In New Orleans the operation of separate-but-equal streetcars replaced a custom of complete exclusion that predated the Civil War.[24]

Historians have offered different perspectives in large part because they looked at different source materials. C. Vann Woodward based his highly influential *Strange Career of Jim Crow* on the development of statutory law and on New Deal studies of American race relations. By contrast, Howard Rabinowitz additionally looked at many primary sources of social history: newspapers, letters, and other descriptive writing. A third set of valuable sources are the records of the many race accommodation cases that were litigated in various state and federal courts. For example, the trial transcript in *Hall v. Decuir*, which the Supreme Court decided at Reconstruction's end, contains a wealth of information about practices in southern public transportation systems.[25]

Interstate railroads and steamboats were common carriers regulated by federal common law, which required them to accept every paying customer.[26]

However, before the war and extending through Reconstruction, river steamboats maintained policies of fairly strict racial separation. In 1869 Louisiana's Reconstruction legislature passed a statute prohibiting common carriers from making any "discrimination on account of race or color" in accepting passengers.[27] The law did not clearly specify whether carriers had to integrate passengers or whether they could furnish them separate, equivalent accommodations. When the Louisiana statute was challenged under the U.S. Constitution's Commerce Clause, the defendant steamboat operator called a number of witnesses who testified about practices. Thomas P. Leathers, who had been steamboating for thirty-six years, testified that the "custom among steamboats . . . of keeping the white and colored passengers separate, has prevailed ever since I have been steamboating; I have never heard of any other." The record contains about thirty-five additional pages of testimony describing the segregation practices in the steamship industry. All the witnesses testified without contradiction that segregation was the rule of the day.[28]

In 1870 the Georgia legislature, controlled by Reconstruction Republicans, passed a separate-but-equal statute that mandated segregation in privately owned public facilities.[29] In 1881 Tennessee, still under a Republican governor, followed suit.[30] Even the Civil Rights Act of 1875, which was still in effect in 1881, did not dissuade southern states from passing segregation statutes.[31] An unlikely explanation is that these largely pro-Union Radical Republican legislatures believed that the federal Civil Rights Act would be declared unconstitutional, as it eventually was in 1883.[32] Even so, that would not explain their motive for segregation.

According to the reasoning the Supreme Court adopted in *Plessy v. Ferguson* in 1896, separate-but-equal facilities did in fact give Afro-Americans the "full and equal enjoyment" of public facilities.[33] Most Union Republicans did not want racial integration any more than southern whites did. The notion that the 1875 Civil Rights Act was an "integration" statute is the product of a century of hindsight. The Act guaranteed "the full and equal enjoyment of the accommodations, advantages, facilities, and privileges of inns, public conveyances on land or water, theatres, and other places of public amusement," and was "applicable alike to citizens of every race and color, regardless of any previous condition of servitude."[34] But in 1875 "equal enjoyment" did not mean "integrated access." In fact, the outcome in *Plessy* would have been the same even if the Supreme Court had upheld the Civil Rights Act of 1875. Northerners and southerners alike feared the consequences of close racial mixing, and even in the North most people would have been unprepared for fully integrated public facilities.

Between the Civil Rights Act's passage in 1875 and its demise in 1883, federal decisions uniformly concluded that "separate but equal" facilities were lawful under the statute. Even northern and Republican federal judges blanched at any suggestion that the Act mandated racial integration. One of the first northern decisions to apply the statute was *Newcomer*, which arose in abolitionist Pennsylvania. The federal court observed that prior to 1867 it was lawful in Pennsylvania "for innkeepers or carriers by land or water to discriminate against travelers of the colored race to such an extent as to exclude them from any part of the inns or public conveyances which was set apart for the exclusive accommodation of white travelers." During the Civil War Pennsylvania changed its law to require common carriers to admit black passengers, but "the law of the state was not changed as to inns." The court then charged a jury that the 1875 Act applied to an innkeeper who denied any accommodation to an Afro-American Baptist minister, even rejecting a request from a white guest who wanted to invite the minister to take a spare bed in his room.[35]

A month after the 1875 Act was passed federal judge Robert P. Dick, a Republican appointed by President Grant, explained the new statute to a North Carolina grand jury. The law, he said, merely declared what was already the law of common carriers in North Carolina—that an innkeeper must accept every paying customer regardless of her color. However, in doing this the innkeeper "may arrange his business to suit his own advantage," and the guest has "no right to select a particular apartment." The Federal Civil Rights Act was not "intended to confer any rights or privileges of social equality among men." After all, "the hope and expectation that there will ever be a nation on earth in which all men associate upon terms of social equality is a wild dream of fanaticism, which can never be realized." Under this rationale "innkeepers may have separate rooms and accommodations for colored men, but they must be equal in quality and convenience to those furnished white men."[36] A federal judge from Texas charged a jury in 1877 that it should acquit a railroad charged with violating the statute if it found that the railroad maintained racially exclusive cars that were "in all respects, equal."[37]

The five lower court decisions that were heard in the Supreme Court as the *Civil Rights Cases* concerned exclusion, not segregation. The Supreme Court heard arguments in four criminal cases and one civil case. They came from both northern and southern states, and each involved either absolute exclusion or the provision of facilities that were not equal. One was an indictment against a San Francisco theater for denying admission to "any part" of the building to a black man who had presented a ticket for the dress circle.

Another involved denial of access by a New York opera house. Two of the cases were convictions of restaurant or inn owners from Kansas and Missouri who had refused to admit blacks. In the fifth case, from Tennessee, a black woman had bought and paid for a first class train ticket but had been refused admission to the ladies' car. The petition emphasized that the alternative seating offered the plaintiff was dirty, unsanitary, and grossly inferior to the first class accommodations for which she had paid.[38] The railroad case also showed that the defendant railroad company did not operate "separate but equal" cars, but consistently relegated Afro-Americans to smoking cars, which were regarded as unsanitary. That would have been a violation of the federal statute no matter how it was construed. The brief filed by the United States in defense of the statute is cast entirely in terms of exclusion/inclusion, not segregation/integration: "The cases of Stanley and Nichols present indictments for refusing to admit colored persons into inns; that of Ryan is an information for refusing to admit a colored person to the parquette of a theater, and that of Hamilton—an indictment for excluding a colored person from the first-class cars of a railroad train."[39]

The same thing is true of Gilded Age litigation involving the Fourteenth Amendment's Equal Protection Clause and state-mandated segregation. Immediately after the Civil War Congress itself provided for segregated education in the Washington, DC public school system. The timing, 1866, is important because no Confederate states had been readmitted to the Union. The Congress that created the explicitly segregated system was run entirely by Union states.[40] An 1871 federal decision concluded that the Fourteenth Amendment did not bar Ohio from creating separate school districts for black children even though the districts were larger than those for white children, requiring many to travel further and effectively "debarring" some from attending any school at all.[41]

A preliminary version of the bill that became the 1875 Civil Rights Act prohibited the exclusion of black students from schools, but that provision was removed before passage.[42] In *Buntin*, an 1882 federal prosecution under both the Fourteenth Amendment and the 1875 Civil Rights Act, the federal court instructed the jury about an Ohio public school's exclusion of an Afro-American boy:

> [If] there was such a school in the district for the education of colored children, affording substantially the same educational advantages as were afforded by the school from which the prosecuting witness was excluded, and reasonably accessible, it was his duty to have gone there,

> and the defendant did him no wrong in the exclusion complained of. But if, as has been contended, you shall find that said colored school was so remote from the prosecuting witness' residence that he could not attend without going an unreasonable and oppressive distance; that he was thus placed at a material disadvantage with his white neighbors; that the school did not offer substantially the same facilities and educational advantages that were offered in the school established for the white children, and from which he had been excluded,—then and in that event he was entitled to admission.[43]

Much of the attention given to the "separate but equal" doctrine for state-mandated segregation has focused on *Plessy v. Ferguson* (1896), decided under the Fourteenth Amendment because the 1875 Civil Rights Act was no longer law. But consider a "separate but equal" case that came to the Supreme Court in 1890, six years earlier. In 1888 the state of Mississippi passed this statute:

> That all railroads carrying passengers in this State (other than street railroads) shall provide equal but separate accommodations for the white and colored races, by providing two or more passenger cars for each passenger train, or by dividing the passenger cars by a partition so as to secure separate accommodations.[44]

The Louisiana Act at issue in *Plessy* was passed two years later and copied the Mississippi act nearly verbatim:

> That all railway companies carrying passengers in their coaches in this State, shall provide equal but separate accommodations for the white and colored races, by providing two or more passenger coaches for each passenger train, or by dividing the passenger coaches by a partition so as to secure separate accommodations: *provided* that this section shall not be construed to apply to street railroads.[45]

The Louisville, New Orleans and Texas Railway violated the earlier statute and was represented in the Supreme Court by Wiley Pope Harris, former U.S. congressman and a leader of the Mississippi bar. In 1890 it did not even occur to Harris to argue that the separate-but-equal statute violated the Equal Protection Clause. He argued only that the Mississippi law was an unconstitutional state regulation of interstate commerce. In upholding the statute

Justice Brewer observed that Mississippi's own courts applied it only to intrastate travel. As a result, there was no impermissible interference with interstate commerce. The Court never mentioned the Fourteenth Amendment.

Justice John Marshall Harlan dissented, joined by Justice Joseph P. Bradley. Harlan believed that the nation's railway system was such an intrinsic part of interstate commerce that even an intrastate segregation rule was an impermissible burden.[46] Harlan's dissent would have been the perfect opportunity to object to the statute under the Fourteenth Amendment, but he never mentioned it either. Six years later Harlan used the Fourteenth Amendment as the basis for a passionate dissent in an identical case: *Plessy v. Ferguson*.[47]

When the Equal Protection argument was raised in *Plessy* it was an innovation—suggested by the railroad in a contrived case as a last resort, given that Commerce Clause arguments had failed. The defendant railroad in the 1890 case had argued that the statute would "greatly hinder, delay, and obstruct the defendant in making its interstate connections with other carriers of passengers."[48] In *Plessy* itself the railroad surreptitiously engaged the Citizens' Committee, a New Orleans civil rights organization, to plant the light-skinned Homer Plessy, who was seven-eighths white, on the train in order to create the dispute.[49]

Neither of these Supreme Court decisions discussed racial science as such. Justice Henry Billings Brown, a Republican from Michigan, wrote for the *Plessy* majority that the Fourteenth Amendment protected blacks politically but not socially.[50] That distinction long antedated the Civil War. For example, Thomas Jefferson was certainly sincere when he wrote that all men are created equal—but he also sincerely believed that blacks had inherently inferior intelligence and occupied a link in the Great Chain of Being above the lower animals but below the Caucasian.[51] To have political equality was to have the same basic human rights against the State that the white person has—the right to own property, to vote, to plead in court, and to share equally in the costs and benefits of government. Social equality, on the other hand, implied something completely different—namely, equality measured against other individuals. The Afro-American who wanted to vote was imposing on the State, but the Afro-American who wanted to ride in an integrated railroad car or attend an integrated school was imposing his presence on individuals who did not want him there. "Every man has a natural and inherent right of selecting his own associates," Judge Dick wrote in 1875, "and this natural right cannot be properly regulated by legislative action, but must always be under the control of individual taste and inclination."[52] Even Justice Bradley, a Fourteenth Amendment expansionist from New Jersey, believed that compelling close racial contact, such as the sharing of seats on a train, violated the white person's freedom of association. "To deprive white people of the right of choosing their own company would be to introduce another kind of slavery," he wrote in the mid-1870s.[53]

Post-Darwinian Science and the Race Problem

Anthropology became a science at a time when scientists were obsessed with new developments in biology.[54] Physical structure was the key to understanding humanity. America's first great contributor to the newborn science was Samuel George Morton, the Philadelphia physician with the mustard seeds. Morton developed a following of believers in broad and permanent differences among racial types.[55] Sanford Hunt, upon whom Kentucky's attorney general Breathitt had relied in the *Berea College* case, was heavily influenced by Morton's findings. When Hunt was working for the United States Sanitary Commission during the Civil War he prepared a report on the physical, emotional, and mental characteristics of the black soldier.[56] The problem of black intelligence troubled Hunt. He found intelligence testing unsatisfactory because the tests measured too many environmental influences, and most blacks were illiterate. Following the waning scientific theory of his day, Hunt decided that cranial capacity and brain weight were more accurate indicators of innate intelligence. He studied the results of 405 autopsies of white and black soldiers and reached the conclusions that Attorney General Breathitt cited in his brief. Much of the physical anthropology of the second half of the century was derived from similar experiments. Among these were anti-evolutionary anthropologist Joseph Barnard Davis, who agreed that brain weight was a permanent racial characteristic but also observed that humans with more advanced civilizations often had lighter brains than those from more primitive cultures. For example Neanderthal brain sizes were somewhat larger than those of modern Caucasians, whereas the ancient Egyptians at the height of their civilization had relatively small brains.[57]

By 1908, when *Berea College* was decided, the idea that one could measure intelligence by weighing brains had fallen into disrepute. However, psychologists were only beginning to realize that the separation of genetic and environmental factors in race development was very difficult. Unlike Morton and Davis, the physical anthropologists of the Gilded Age were largely evolutionists. The immediate effect of Darwin's work, however, was to confirm and strengthen long-established ideas about black inferiority. For Gilded Age

American evolutionary anthropologist Lewis Henry Morgan, the black man was inferior to the white and was falling farther behind every year.

Morgan, a New York lawyer who turned to ethnology, adapted Darwinian natural selection to a Spencerian idea of absolute cultural progress. He believed that the races were in different stages of physical and cultural evolution. In Morgan's view, "[t]he Aryan family represents the central stream of human progress, because it produced the highest type of mankind, and because it has proved its intrinsic superiority by gradually assuming the control of the earth."[58] Like Darwin, Morgan believed that species or varieties in close physical proximity compete with each other. Morgan applied this principle to cultural as well as physical development. He believed that the human races differed from the lower animals in that they no longer relied on brute strength but on intelligence and inventiveness to survive. The more advanced the culture, the more mental powers had replaced physical strength as the basic survival weapon. In this respect the Afro-American was outclassed. If the African had been left in isolation in his homeland, reasoned Morgan, his culture might have developed to a civilized maturity. However, when an inferior culture confronts a superior one the former must give way. Black culture and eventually the black race would disappear.

Frederick L. Hoffman, a professional statistician well known for his writings on public health, believed that emancipation had been the worst thing that ever happened to the Afro-American. The enslaved African had performed hard but simple labor, and in exchange he had been relieved from making complex social and economic decisions. Hoffman concluded that after the Civil War black mortality rates had increased, blacks had developed a much higher incidence of several diseases, and blacks' general standard of living had declined.[59]

The idea that the black race would eventually become extinct was actually quite popular at the end of the nineteenth century. For many American Anglo-Saxons a nation without blacks was thinkable, if not appealing. But interracial marriage destroyed the simplicity of the evolutionary idea. Although social scientists generally agreed about the characteristics of the "pure" African, the hybrid was a mystery and there was not much scientific agreement about her. Sanford Hunt believed that the mental capacity of the mulatto varied with the percentage of white blood.[60] Frederick Hoffman thought all mulattoes were inferior to members of either race. Nathaniel Southgate Shaler, a Harvard professor of paleontology and geology, believed that the mulatto was less healthy, shorter-lived, and less fertile than either blacks or whites. "From the white he inherits a refinement unfitting him for all work which has not a certain delicacy about it"; however, from his black parent the mulatto acquires "a laxity of morals which, whether it be the result of innate incapacity for certain forms of moral culture or the result of an utter want of training in this direction, is still unquestionably a negro characteristic." In short, the mulatto was an outcast in both worlds—too civilized to be comfortable with the black, but too primitive to live with the white without giving offense. Shaler became a strong advocate against interracial marriage.[61]

Although many opponents of interracial sexual relations were evolutionists, they cast the problem in a scientific model that was more Lamarckian than Darwinian. Jean Baptiste Lamarck's evolutionary theory was based on an idea of inheritance of acquired characteristics—for example, a cougar that develops strong legs from hard running could pass its superior muscles on to its offspring. "Neo-Lamarckianism" was a popular theory about race and marriage: any organism's "unconscious striving" naturally attracts it to the most superior mate. Thus in many species the males fight among each other, and the winner gets the best females, improving the species.[62] Progressive Era racial theorists used Lamarck to explain what to them seemed to be a universal phenomenon: the intense sexual attraction that black males had for white females. Any white person seeking out a mate would be naturally repelled by the thought of marriage to an inferior individual. The black, on the other hand, was instinctively striving to better his race and was naturally attracted to more superior types.[63]

Progressive Era Social Control and Race: "Miscegination" and Racial Zoning

How to combat the black male's urge for the white female was a question of social control. Self-help was one method, and lynchings of black males accused of sexual misconduct were relatively common in the New South, even through the New Deal era.[64] Several southern states passed statutes that increased the sentence for adultery if it was interracial. In 1882 the Supreme Court rejected a Fourteenth Amendment challenge to the Alabama statute. Justice Field wrote a two-page opinion that never cited a case. He noted only that the statute was nondiscriminatory because it applied equally to whites and blacks.[65] That decision was overruled in 1964 in *McLaughlin v. Florida*.[66]

Statutory prohibitions of interracial marriage were nearly universal in the South and relatively common in the North and the West. Louisiana prohibited them as early as 1810, North Carolina in 1830, and Arkansas in

1838.[67] After the war a few states relaxed these rules, but most did not. For example, North Carolina forbade interracial marriage, although its supreme court compelled recognition of such marriages performed in South Carolina, which permitted them.[68] State courts also held that the 1866 Civil Rights Act, which created an equal right to make contracts, did not offer protection for interracial marriage contracts.[69] During the Progressive Era eugenics movement more states banned them again, reaching a high of thirty-one states by 1940. States in both the North and the South tried to make miscegenation statutes more effective by providing for the punishment of any clergyman or public official who performed an illegal marriage. The presumption was that the official would know the law even if the illiterate bride and groom did not. The tide turned after World War II. A 1948 California supreme court decision struck down that state's prohibition under the federal Constitution's Equal Protection Clause.[70] Soon after, several states repealed their anti-miscegenation laws. No challenge reached the Supreme Court until *Loving v. Virginia* in 1967. At that time sixteen states still prohibited it.[71]

Another way to reduce interracial sexual contact was to force blacks and whites to live in different places. In 1910 Baltimore passed an ordinance that zoned separate residential districts for Afro-Americans and whites. Within six years more than a dozen southern cities followed suit. Most state courts struck these laws down, including the Baltimore ordinance, under a variety of theories.[72]

The Supreme Court agreed with these state decisions in *Buchanan v. Warley* (1917).[73] The Louisville, Kentucky, ordinance at issue prevented any black person from moving into "any house upon any block upon which a greater number of houses are occupied... by white people than are occupied... by colored people." The second section of the law made it unlawful for a white person to move onto a predominantly black block. White Robert Buchanan contracted to sell his home to black William Warley. At the time eight of the ten houses on Buchanan's block were occupied by whites. Under the new ordinance Warley could not occupy the house he had agreed to purchase. Warley refused to pay and Buchanan sued him. As a result the case came to the Kentucky court in a peculiar posture. Warley the black man argued that the racial zoning statute was constitutional and that he should be excused from performing his contract. Buchanan the white man argued that the statute was unconstitutional. Warley was the editor of the *Louisville News* and an active member of the NAACP, which immediately agreed to represent Buchanan against him.[74] The case had clearly been contrived so as to attract the Supreme Court, with its elevated concerns about liberty of contract.

Justice Holmes noted as much in the draft of an unpublished dissent, suggesting that the suit should not "be entertained without some evidence that it is not a manufactured case."[75]

Moorfield Storey, a prominent Boston attorney and the national president of the NAACP, argued the plaintiff's case on two days in April 1916. At oral argument Storey urged a position not presented in his brief: that racial mixing was essential to America's cultural vitality. Consistent with this position, he was forced to acknowledge that he believed statutes forbidding interracial marriage were also unreasonable and unconstitutional uses of State police power.

The Court held the case over for re-argument, probably because only seven justices were sitting the first round. This time Stuart Chevalier and Pendleton Beckley, who represented the City of Louisville, prepared a lengthy scientific brief in reply. The decision to use a "Brandeis brief" may have been strategic as well as scientific. Storey and Brandeis, who was now on the bench, were bitter political enemies. Storey had testified against Brandeis at the Supreme Court's Senate confirmation hearing only a few months earlier.[76] The brief offered one hundred pages of quotations designed to prove that amalgamation of the races was not in the best interests of either race. The sources included Henry W. Grady, editor of the *Atlanta Constitution*; Charles W. Eliot, former president of Harvard University; and Washington Gladden, a well-known liberal Protestant clergyman who was one of the leaders of the Social Gospel movement. The brief quoted these writers not because they had conducted any scientific studies, but because they revealed that America's intellectual leaders and even social liberals were opposed to the mixing of races. The Louisville brief also quoted some of the South's most notorious bigots—such as Nashville attorney and anti-women's suffrage activist John Vertrees, who had argued in 1913 that the Civil War Amendments to the Constitution were part of an Afro-American plot to destroy the purity of the white race.[77]

The Louisville brief also cited many scientific sources considered respectable at the time, including William Benjamin Smith's *The Color Line*. Smith in turn had drawn much of his evidence of mulatto degeneracy from Benjamin A. Gould, who had been employed as actuary to the United States Sanitary Commission. Gould had performed several anthropometric studies of the autopsy reports of black and white Civil War soldiers. He posited that the average lung capacity of a white soldier was 185 cubic inches, and of a black soldier 164 cubic inches. However, the average lung capacity of the mulatto was only 159 cubic inches.[78] Gould concluded that mulattoes were chronically unhealthy and unfit for hard labor. Because their hearts and respiratory systems had to work harder to keep them alive, they died much younger than either blacks or whites.

The Louisville brief also relied on the work of Oxford law professor and politician James Bryce, who would later become British Ambassador to the United States. Bryce had visited America in order to observe its race problem and concluded that when "similar" races, such as Caucasians and Chinese, intermarry the resulting stock can be quite healthy—as strong and intelligent as either parent. When "remote" races intermarry, however, they are so biologically different that genetic defects are sure to result. Bryce viewed the American South as populated by the two most different races.[79]

Chevalier and Beckley also cited evidence that interracial marriage was on the rise. Alexander Harvey Shannon, chaplain of the Mississippi State Penitentiary and an ethnologist, had found that at the time of the Civil War mulattoes composed 13.2 percent of the black population. By 1890, however, 15.2 percent of the black population was mulatto.[80] The figures were used to confirm Herbert Spencer's theory that intelligence and fertility were inversely related.[81] Shannon concluded that "[t]hese figures are sufficient to warrant whatever discrimination may be found necessary in controlling the situation."[82]

Finally, Chevalier and Beckley documented racial tension in the North. Race prejudice had been growing in northern cities at an alarming rate since the Civil War. They relied on a 1913 study by Frank U. Quillin, a sociologist from Knox College in Illinois, which concluded that northern racial prejudice was much stronger in 1910 than in 1865. Racial tensions seemed to grow as the proportion of black residents increased. Quillin concluded that in time northern racial attitudes would be no different from attitudes in the South.[83]

Justice Day's opinion striking down the zoning law never acknowledged the scientific evidence in the Louisville brief, and completely ignored the racial policy arguments. Rather, the unanimous Court held that the constitutionally protected right to own property "includes the right to acquire, use, and dispose of it." This was a property case, not a race case, just as the NAACP had strategized: "The right which the ordinance annulled was the civil right of a white man to dispose of his property... to a person of color, and of a colored person to make such disposition to a white person."[84]

Does the *Buchanan* Court's approach suggest that liberty of contract was a better vehicle for dealing with race discrimination than a more race conscious approach under the Equal Protection Clause?[85] *Buchanan*'s focus on liberty of contract occurred for an important strategic reason. Moorfield Storey understood that pursuing the Louisville ordinance on racial grounds would have required overturning *Plessy v. Ferguson*, something that could not have happened until after President Franklin D. Roosevelt remade the Court. In fact, it did not happen explicitly until *Brown*, nearly forty years after *Buchanan*.[86] Although nearly all state court decisions struck down racial zoning statutes, none relied on the Equal Protection Clause.

Tying the racial zoning provision to well-established liberty of contract doctrine was a brilliant legal strategy in the short run. It placed *Buchanan* squarely within *Plessy*'s well-established distinction between "political equality" and "social equality." Liberty of contract was a doctrine of political equality, whereas residential integration was a tool of social equality. This is borne out by the subsequent history. After *Buchanan* people wishing to perpetuate neighborhood segregation turned to private restrictive covenants rather than zoning ordinances. In *Corrigan v. Buckley* (1926), another case brought by the NAACP under Moorfield Storey's legal direction, the developer had created a twenty-five-lot subdivision covered by deed covenants excluding "any person of the negro race or blood." The Supreme Court unanimously upheld the covenants as private contracts. Subsequently most state courts enforced the covenants, including some that had struck down the racial zoning laws. A few states found them to be unlawful restraints on alienation.[87] *Corrigan* enabled continuation of residential segregation through widespread use of private racial restrictions, which were fully enforceable until the Supreme Court effectively overruled *Corrigan* in 1948.[88]

The Waning of Scientific Racism and the Legal Response

Supreme Court decisions on race policy have tended to track prevailing scientific opinion. Today we have a verbal formulation that defines the limits of explicit race discrimination by the State: it must be justified by a "compelling state interest."[89] However, identifying a compelling State interest may require the use of science. *Brown v. Board of Education* was a "social science" decision. Chief Justice Warren justified the action by citing sociological and psychological studies made by scientists who were thoroughly committed to environmentalism. Whether it was wise to base important fundamental rights doctrine on empirical scientific data has remained controversial.[90]

During the Gilded Age and perhaps even in 1920 most American scientists and social scientists believed that interracial propagation was socially and perhaps biologically harmful. The battle between environmentalists and hereditarians over racial characteristics placed American liberals in a difficult position. The effects of integrated education and interracial marriage would be irreversible. If the hereditarians were correct, a generation or two of unrestricted amalgamation could do broad and permanent harm to American society. In the near term these arguments did not subside. A year after the racial zoning decision Paul Popenoe, editor of the *Journal of Heredity*, and Roswell Hill Johnson, a professor at the University of Pittsburgh, published an enormously influential textbook, *Applied Eugenics*. The authors concluded that the Afro-American had certain hereditary shortcomings that made him unable to compete with whites in modern society. Miscegenation was dangerous because these characteristics would then infiltrate the white race as well.[91]

Even more devastating were the simultaneously published results of Army intelligence tests conducted during World War I. Robert M. Yerkes, Harvard University psychologist and president of the American Psychological Association, tested more than two million army recruits and published a detailed analysis of 160,000 of them. The analysts generally assumed that the tests measured innate intelligence, and the tests appeared to show that intelligence was correlated with the subject's percentage of white blood.[92] Of course, they were "white" tests—culturally biased in favor of the people who produced them.[93] From 1920 to the present, psychologists have debated which elements of intelligence are hereditary and which are environmental.[94] Nevertheless, within the biological paradigm of the day the test results seemed clear evidence of hereditary racial inferiority. They led some states to elaborate programs classifying residents by racial status, such as Virginia's Racial Integrity Act of 1924, which was not repealed until 1968. The law required the state's registrar of vital statistics to collect information from each resident and prepare a certificate showing the subject's "racial composition" as well as "in what generation such mixture occurred." Intentionally submitting false information for the certificate was a felony, carrying a prison sentence of one year.[95] The highly publicized New York case of *Rhinelander v. Rhinelander* (1927) considered whether grounds for divorce existed in the bride's alleged failure to tell her husband-to-be that she was of colored blood.[96] The issues were hardly limited to the South.

But scientific views about heredity and the environment were already changing. Most notable was anthropologist Franz Boas, who spent most of his academic career at Columbia University. By 1905 Boas was scoffing at the comparative method of physical anthropology that was so popular among the evolutionary hereditarians. In contrast to Boas's cultural relativism, Gilded Age anthropologists had defined the Caucasian as "superior" and then measured the inferiority of other races by their deviation. Boas attacked the general notion that there were discrete races.[97] The comparative method of Gilded Age anthropology had been based on the assumption that each race had evolved independently, radiating out from a primitive life form like the spokes of a wheel. Alternatively, as the followers of Samuel George Morton argued, the races were never genetically connected at all. In contrast, Boas argued that the human race had evolved as a single species and included a long history of interracial sexual contact.

Boas's revolution in anthropology was only one battle in the great war between hereditarians and environmentalists. In 1918 Edward Byron Reuter, a sociologist from the University of Iowa, published *The Mulatto in the United States*. Reuter did not commit himself on the wisdom of interracial marriage, but he concluded that most of the problems of mixed race persons were environmental, not hereditary. Because miscegenation was looked upon so unfavorably, he concluded, only the lowest class of white males took black wives or mistresses. The mulatto had many environmental difficulties that were not race-linked at all, but were simply a function of the intelligence and status of his parents. Following Boas, Reuter observed that in countries where multiple races are in close contact the concept of race became largely meaningless—there is "generally no sharp breach" between various mixtures of blood, but rather a gradation.[98]

The displacement of racist anthropology accelerated in the late 1920s. In 1928, Melville J. Herskovits, a student of Franz Boas, published *The American Negro*. It discredited many long-held scientific ideas about the physical and mental characteristics of the black American. For example, evolutionary anthropologists of the late nineteenth century had pointed to facial features associated with the lower intelligence blacks were presumed to have. Herskovits found that although statistically blacks did in fact have thicker lips and broader nostrils than whites, there was no correlation between these features and intelligence. In fact, highly intelligent, college-educated black women exhibited them just as prominently as did economically and socially disadvantaged black women from Harlem. Herskovits concluded that the real problem of the Afro-American was white values and stereotypes, not black features.[99]

Scientific racism waned considerably around World War II, partly in reaction to Hitler's racial policies, and partly with the publication of such consensus-creating documents as Gunnar Myrdal's *An American Dilemma* (1944).[100] When environmentalist science began to undermine the premises of genetic determinism, the social values of segregation became less apparent, and competing egalitarian values weighed more heavily in the scales.

The Supreme Court's 1948 decision in *Shelley v. Kraemer* reflected these views, declaring that judicial enforcement of private, racially exclusive real property covenants amounted to unconstitutional State action in violation of the Fourteenth Amendment.[101] The challengers' briefs quoted from the cultural relativists, particularly Herskovits and Myrdal. The Congress of Industrial Organizations (CIO), a leader in the labor movement's belated evolution toward racial equality, wrote an amicus brief arguing that the races of mankind are nothing more than "creations of the investigator, and creations with regard to which all the creators are by no means in agreement."[102] However, these creations "have been converted through ignorance and prejudice into rigid structures." Within the new environmentalist paradigm it was clear that "a court cannot permit itself to determine the rights and disabilities of individuals upon the basis of 'race.'" The petitioners' briefs cited nearly a dozen social science sources, all of which had been published after 1940. The United States submitted an amicus brief signed by Attorney General Tom Clark, whom President Harry S. Truman later placed on the Supreme Court. Clark's brief not only cited social science data concerning the need to remove limitations on residential integration, it also documented the heavy use of private racial restrictions to maintain segregation and raised concerns about the deteriorating quality of urban housing occupied by Afro-Americans.[103]

Scientific data to defend State-sanctioned segregation appeared again in the mid-1950s, in the debate over school segregation that culminated in *Brown v Board of Education*, and yet again in the Supreme Court's 1967 decision in *Loving v. Virginia*, which struck down state prohibitions on interracial marriage.[104] Coming when it did, the decision in *Shelley v. Kraemer* was nothing short of remarkable. In few areas of the law has the Court responded more quickly and decisively to a radical transformation in the sciences.

PART TWO

Neoclassical Legal Thought

4

Economics and Law in the Progressive Era

BEGINNING IN THE 1880s many American legal academics, economists, and public intellectuals began writing about the relationship between law and economics. This early law and economics "movement" was very broad, addressing many aspects of the legal system. It began first in a regulatory subject, the creation and administration of an interstate railroad system. Then it moved into the law of antitrust and trade restraints,[1] and later into criminal law, corporation law, taxation, property, and contract. Unlike the law and economics movement that developed in the 1960s and 1970s, however, these earlier writers were critical of the common law and much more supportive of legislation.

The later law and economics movement occurred after marginalist economic analysis had completely swept the field. In contrast, during the earlier period classical, marginalist, and Darwinian models competed vigorously for the attention of people who wrote about law. Many accepted more Darwinian ideas about value drawn from the social sciences, doubting that economic words such as "preference" had any scientific meaning. The idea of preference is a chimera that human beings' surplus brain power has created in order to rationalize survival instincts. This alternative view relied on "objective" welfare judgments, seeing questions about social well-being and the proper organization of society as presenting problems akin to self-managed cultivation. Farming seeks out the optimal combination of shelter, nutrition, and freedom from disease, measuring success by productivity. The farmer generally regards all the plants or animals of one species as having the same needs. Denial of nutrition or fertilizer does not provide "incentives" to try harder. Instead, organisms do their best if they are placed within a supportive environment. Whereas marginalism emphasized choice, welfare judgments drawn from Darwinian social science emphasized productivity. A distinctive feature of law and economics from the Gilded Age through the New Deal is that these two theories of value were very much in play.

The early law and economics movement was also driven by two developments within economics. One was an increased concern about wealth distribution and market imperfections and differences, two things that could be addressed through legal policy. Many Progressive Era economists broke with the classical tradition by asserting that laissez-faire, or "let things alone," was not the best policy choice. This necessarily invoked concerns about how government intervention in the market could be brought to bear.

The second development was professionalization. The forming of the American Economics Association in 1885 and the emergence of professional journals in the 1880s and 1890s largely ended the days when economists debated with clergy and business persons in the *North American Review* or *Princeton Review*, periodicals written for a nontechnical readership.[2] Serious work required more specialized forums. In addition, early marginalists were intensely aware that their new tool required the rethinking of fundamentals. Famous early essays in law and economics, such as Henry Carter Adams's *The Relation of the State to Industrial Action* (1887), began by considering whether human beings act rationally to maximize their individual interests, and whether these interests reliably coincide with those of society. Adams wove his theory from both Darwinian and marginalist threads, as did Edward A. Ross and later John R. Commons and John Maurice Clark.

Origins: Charles Francis Adams and Henry Carter Adams

The origins of American law and economics lay in American policy toward the railroads. Charles Francis Adams, a pioneer of American regulatory theory, argued as early as 1876 that railroad rates and expansion should be regulated by the State.[3] The railroads could not be made subject to the same laws of "competition and free trade" as other industries. Laissez-faire would yield "utter confusion within and without." Adams indulged in a long attack on classical economics for trying to generalize about all industries by hypothesizing a small number of invariable laws. The railroads were a powerful counterexample, where unregulated competition led to either monopoly or ruinous cutthroat competition. Adams believed the German Historical approach was more effective for developing distinctive economic rules for different industries. That idea—that markets differ from one another and require different fixes—became a distinctive feature of legal economic analysis in the first half of the twentieth century.

A decade later University of Michigan economist Henry Carter Adams agreed that the German Historical method was more suitable than British political economy for addressing legal questions.[4] Classical political economy failed to see legal phenomena in their historical and functional diversity. In his most important theoretical essay, "The Relation of the State to Industrial Action" (1887), Henry Carter Adams addressed the relationship between State industrial policy and economic theory. The "collapse of faith in the sufficiency of the philosophy of *laissez-faire*, has left the present generation without principles adequate for the guidance of public affairs." Laissez became dogma rather than science when it manifested as uncritical acceptance of the idea that unregulated competition should prevail in virtually all markets. Instead, legal policy toward business needed to make distinctions, because the optimal amount of competition varies from one industry to the next, and private firms will not settle on the correct amount themselves. Adams divided industries into three classes—"industries of constant returns, industries of diminishing returns, and industries of increasing returns."[5]

That simple observation moved Progressive regulatory theory forward substantially. Industries that displayed constant or decreasing returns to scale needed little or no state intervention. Competition worked well, because large firms had few advantages over smaller ones. Entry and mobility were easy, and there was little reason for thinking that one giant could eliminate smaller rivals.

Industries exhibiting increasing returns to scale were a different matter. Here the large firm had cost advantages over the new entrant. In such industries "it is easier for an established business to extend its facilities for satisfactorily meeting a new demand than for a new industry to spring into competitive existence." If increasing returns exist "with any degree of intensity, the principle of free competition is powerless to exercise a healthy regulating influence." Adams concluded that the "control of the state over industries should be co-extensive with the application of the law of increasing returns in industries." He cited the railroads as displaying increasing returns most obviously, although there were others. Such industries were "by nature, monopolies," and should be regulated accordingly.[6]

"The Relation of the State to Industrial Action" is an extraordinary piece of law and economics, written before Alfred Marshall's *Principles* (1890), before marginalism had much impact on American economics, and before American economists as a group turned their attention to monopolies and regulatory problems. Its perspective on regulation is thoroughly neoclassical in that it offered a compromise that avoided both socialism and classicism's absolute trust in the market, but made the case for significant deviations.

The Case for Legislation: Market Failure, Coercion, and Distribution

Within classical political economy and nineteenth-century policy markets were nearly all regarded as competitive except for a few with exclusive government grants. In the 1840s John Stuart Mill developed the concept of "natural" monopoly, or markets that operated most efficiently when they contained only one firm.[7] To be sure, land was a troublesome exception, which David Ricardo saw as fundamentally intractable in England. In the United States, however, land was available in such abundance that Americans did not see a monopoly problem, except perhaps in some far distant future.[8]

Neoclassical economics developed a far more complex picture of markets that evolved over the first half of the twentieth century. Most important, markets differed a great deal from one another. Under neoclassicism, markets worked more or less well depending on the number of sellers, the extent of fixed costs, and the degree of product differentiation. Economies of scale and high fixed costs often dictated a smaller number of sellers, entailing less competition. Within classical political economy entering a market was always assumed to be easy unless the government interfered with an exclusive grant or a license requirement. By contrast, many neoclassicists viewed new entry as "naturally" costly, requiring large amounts of capital, and full of risk. These ideas of market imperfection and diversity had profound implications for legal policy, including increased regulation and a switch from common law toward statutory management of economic relationships.

The progression of economics from the Gilded Age through the New Deal was steadily toward greater distrust of markets. Henry Carter Adams observed in the 1880s and Cambridge economist Arthur C. Pigou later elaborated that markets are subject to "costs of movement" that often prevent resources from flowing to better uses.[9] Still later, fellow Cambridge economist Joan Robinson concluded her influential *Economics of Imperfect Competition* (1933) by observing that we live in a "World of Monopolies." How far economics had come from Adam Smith's assumption of virtually universal competitiveness.[10] That same year Harvard professor Edward Chamberlin's influential *Theory of Monopolistic Competition*[11] presented a landscape in which manufacturers competed by differentiating their products rather than cutting prices to cost. For Chamberlin the result was that manufacturing and distribution markets performed poorly, with high prices and excessive product diversity.

A growing belief that markets were not free led both economists and legal thinkers to a conception of "coercion" that did not depend on explicit government regulation. The idea of coercion by private market forces actually entered policy discourse from two directions. In addition to the economic conception was the Darwinian conception of social control in sociology and psychology—an idea championed by Edward A. Ross, who had received his PhD in economics but spent most of his career writing in sociology. Ross's book on *Social Control* (1901) examined the way that social evolution produced institutions and values that limited and disciplined human behavior. Some economists tried to merge this idea into business economics as well—most notably John Maurice Clark in *Social Control of Business*, which was published in 1926.[12]

Methodological Disputes: Welfare and Mental State

The late nineteenth and early twentieth century saw an outpouring of economic writing on the distribution of wealth.[13] Marginalist economists typically saw economic value as having both a social and an individual dimension. Further, social value would increase as wealth was more nearly equal. The coarsest view was that aggregate welfare would be maximized when everyone had equal wealth. Few marginalists pushed the concept that far, but one impulse that proved very powerful was that the State could increase welfare by leveling wealth or income. The marginalists derived this notion from the concepts of diminishing returns, which suggested that a person obtained less pleasure from his tenth dollar than his first one, and the corollary that total utility would be greater as individual marginal utilities were more equal. As Alfred Marshall put it, "A pound's worth of satisfaction to an ordinary poor man is a much greater thing than a pound's worth of satisfaction to an ordinary rich man." In 1893 American economist John R. Commons stated similar views, which were held by other Americans through the 1930s: "To the poor man all the marginal increments may afford high satisfaction, because his supplies are limited; but to the rich man the marginal increments may give little satisfaction.[14]

This conception of welfare helps to explain the high degree of statism among many of the early marginalist economists. They believed that social welfare could be increased by minimum wage laws and labor unions, graduated income taxes, subsidized education, welfare payments to the poor, and taxes on monopoly profits. Health and safety regulations could also be justified as taxes on wealthy producers for the benefit of poorer workers, as could workers' compensation statutes.[15] None of this would result from free market exchange.

To the contrary, many Progressives saw markets and the legal rules that facilitated them as pushing resources in the opposite direction. For example, economies of scale gave cost advantages to large producers, enabling them to grow even larger at the expense of the smaller. These concepts permeated the writing of Progressive Era economists who wrote about the law. Notable examples were Richard T. Ely's *Property and Contract in Their Relations to the Distribution of Wealth* (1914) and Robert Hale's influential article "Coercion and Distribution in a Supposedly Noncoercive State" (1923). Ely argued that the very sort of free exchange facilitated by property and contract exacerbated the maldistribution of wealth. Even passive property rules are coercive to the extent that they give power to those who have property vis-à-vis those who do not. "Not only does the distribution of income depend on this mutual coercion; so also does the distribution of that power to exert further compulsion which accompanies the management of an industry."[16]

Just as economists were doing, other social scientists were also trying to achieve professional distinctiveness. Professional status required a defensible methodology, which initially was empiricism and later positivism. The ruling assumption for much of social science in the 1920s was behaviorism, or the view that scientists can study nothing more than observed human responses to stimuli. Mental state was a meaningless concept unless it could be equated with observed behavior. Particularly in psychology and sociology, social scientists rejected the view William James had championed a generation earlier that the psychologist must deal primarily in introspection.[17] Holmes anticipated these views in 1881 and applied them to legal policy. *The Common Law* argued that those who administer the laws are never bothered about subjective feeling as such, but only with external manifestations.[18]

John B. Watson and other early behaviorists believed that an important limit on scientific psychology is that one person cannot measure another person's thoughts or feelings. Behaviorism permitted a science of psychology even though thoughts are not interpersonally verifiable. Watson rejected introspection because it yielded "as many analyses as there are individual psychologists."[19] Behavioral psychology was thus much more "social" than introspective psychology. The behaviorist attempted to generalize about how large groups would respond to a given stimulus. Behaviorism gradually became more radical, culminating in Gilbert Ryle's conclusion in the late 1940s that as far as an outside observer knows, external acts and the mind's workings are exactly the same thing.[20]

Behaviorism also affected economics. The relevant stimulus was scarcity, and the response was individual ranking of priorities when not every want could be satisfied. Writing in 1927, economist John Maurice Clark found a growing obsession among economists for verification from external behavior.[21] Nevertheless, behaviorism in economics differed from the methodologies of other social sciences. Whereas psychology tended to distrust people's statements about how they felt, and looked for external indications, economics did precisely the opposite. It purported to measure "welfare" entirely by how individuals made market choices, not by how prosperous they appeared to be, or by whether they were educated, employed, housed, clothed, or even fed. In short, whereas psychology and the other social sciences adopted objective tests of adjustment, or welfare, capable of being generalized over large groups, economists came to rely on much more subjective and individualistic tests based on observed market choice.

In the 1920s these positions were hotly contested. Several economists argued that their discipline should rely more on external evidence for its conception of welfare. In 1920 Princeton's Frank Fetter urged economists to distinguish "price economics" from "welfare economics"—the former being based on subjective individual valuation, and the latter on objective standards of value drawn from observations of group behavior.[22] Fetter attributed the distinction to Alfred Marshall, who was obsessed with the problem of making economics speak to real human welfare while maintaining its status as an exact science. "Price economics applied to life" simplifies economic models and makes exactness possible, Fetter conceded, "but it does so by leaving out much (often all) that is of real importance to the individual life and to the social welfare." A few years later Wesley Clair Mitchell conceded that social welfare was a "rather vague" concept. However, "it is capable of being made objective and definite in reference to such matters as food, clothing, shelter, sanitation, education, fatigue, leisure."[23] Yale's Irving Fisher argued in 1927 that by using statistics one could construct averaged utility curves for families of different income levels, enabling Congress to construct an optimal progressive income tax.[24]

The policy consequences of these methodological choices are difficult to exaggerate. Permitting values to be aggregated across individuals threatened to lead economics into socialism. Already in 1894 Joseph Shield Nicholson,

Marshall's former student and President of the British Association for the Advancement of Science, warned economists that the emerging marginal utility school was socialistic and was undermining the individualism that had characterized economic classicism.[25] Prominent neoclassicists such as Marshall, Pigou, and Robinson gradually moved to the left as they grew older, finding an ever-increasing role for the State in the redistribution of wealth.[26] America's Progressive economists did much the same.

The Rise of Institutionism

Generalizing about the diverse group of renegade American economists who styled themselves "institutionalists" is difficult. Critics and supporters alike have disagreed about institutionalism's core beliefs, its membership, and the scope of its influence. Some define the movement broadly to include a wide range of marginalists who believed that market failure was common and that wealth distribution was an important economic issue.[27] The traditional definition views the institutionalists more narrowly, as dissenters from neoclassical economics who either denigrated marginalism or objected to mainstream economics' refusal to consider the evolutionary or behavioral sources of human choice. They also rejected neoclassical economics' assumption that resources move mainly through markets and generally without friction or cost.[28]

The discussion here favors this more traditional view, which seems more defensible historically and does not threaten the institutionalists with assimilation into emergent marginalism. Nevertheless, it bears emphasis that during the first three decades of the twentieth century American economics was a fractured discipline, with both individuals and university departments adopting various mixtures of marginalist rational actor assumptions, behavioral social science, and historicism. Many academics taught or wrote in two or more fields, combining economics with their other disciplines. This makes the boundary problem less important because, quite frankly, there were no clearly defined boundaries. It is also clear that the influence of institutionalism extended far beyond the relatively small group of self-identified institutionalists.

For most institutionalists the neoclassical idea of the "market" was too abstract to account for the wide variety of environments in which economic actors confront each other. As John Maurice Clark put it in a 1919 review of a book by his teacher Charles Horton Cooley, "price" is not merely the result of market transactions, but also "of many estimates of worth by different individuals and classes, formed under the influence of class prestige, tradition, fashion, and other forms of social and economic suggestion, expressed through legal and social institutions" The "effect of this view is to dethrone price as an ultimate measure of worth"[29]

Institutionalists believed that institutions differ a great deal and have their own working rules, which result from long evolutionary processes. Governments and legal systems were themselves institutions that affected all areas of human economic conduct. So it is hardly surprising that the institutionalists were heavily concerned with the interaction of the legal system with various institutions, including governments, corporations, unions, and families, as well as traditional markets.

Legal thinkers were drawn to the descriptively thick account of the economic world that the institutionalists provided. As Chapter 6 develops, the Legal Realists in particular clung to economic institutionalism long after mainstream economists had abandoned it. Marginalism provided only a shriveled image of the reality they observed, and they objected to its disparagement of history.

To be sure, the marginalists made a powerful point: one failure of classical political economy was its inability to explain how price, output, wages, or basic firm size are determined.[30] Price became a rough approximation of average cost, wages were determined by the amount of previously invested capital, and so on. By the early twentieth century marginalist analysis was starting to provide technical answers to these problems and more. Nevertheless, the required assumptions were strong and highly abstracted from reality. John Bates Clark, the leading early American marginalist, developed a static model in which "population neither increases nor diminishes, capital is fixed in amount,... the method of making goods does not change," and "the wants of consumers never vary in number, in kind, or intensity."[31] In the longer run, however, people switched from one thing to another whenever the marginal value of the shift was positive. They entered new businesses in response to high profits, immediately dropping what they were doing. Businesses immediately abandoned one production process or organizational structure when a more efficient one appeared.

Many institutionalists were not opposed to marginalism on principle. John R. Commons, one of the best known institutionalists, was an innovator in marginal utility theory.[32] But they did object to the lengths that marginal analysis was used to displace everything else. Institutionalism was dedicated to the proposition that commitments were more complex. History was important, disentanglement took time, and was often costly.[33] As a result the economist must consider an organization's prior commitments, its hierarchy, or other attributes of its structure. Marginalism assumes invariant profit or utility maximization. But if firm behavior reflects embedded history, structural inadequacies, or human irrationality, then marginalist models must either falter or become far more complex.

Historicism and Evolution of Legal Rules

In 1900 both economics and law contained strong strains of historicism. In the writing of legal history, historicism drove theories about how legal rules evolved over centuries out of customary social practice.[34] American writers linked this historical evolution to economic theory. Darwinian theory produced important followers in cultural anthropology[35] and soon in the other social sciences.[36] Many institutionalists emphasized that mainstream economics failed to account for these evolutionary aspects of social development that seemed obvious in the social sciences. Institutional rules tend to survive when they enable members of some group to maintain or increase their welfare.[37] Several legal writers in the 1910s applied the theory of evolution to legal rules as well.[38] Writing on "Law and Economics" in 1925, Commons identified the economic approach to the study of common law rules as Darwinian: "from the economist's approach, the common law is a special case of Darwin's 'artificial selection,' by the courts in this instance, of what are deemed to be good customs, and the rejection and penalization by the courts of what are deemed to be bad customs."[39]

The most important institutionalists in the Progressive Era law and economics movement were Thorstein Veblen, Richard T. Ely, and his student John R. Commons. All wrote important books and articles on law and economics. Each had an important impact on contemporary economics, although their influence waned in the 1930s and after.

Chapter 6 discusses the migration of institutionalist ideas into Legal Realism, just as institutionalism was being expunged from neoclassical economics.

Precursor: Thorstein Veblen

Unlike the Adams family, who were Boston and Harvard gentry, Thorstein Veblen was socially difficult and often alienated from the universities that employed him. He was raised on a Wisconsin farm by Norwegian immigrant parents, but managed to get a good education at Johns Hopkins and Yale. Too much a renegade to be accepted by mainstream economists, his academic life depended on the grace of a few benefactors. He enjoyed brief stints with faculty rank at the University of Chicago, Stanford, and the University of Missouri. Much of his life he was unemployed.[40] He wrote more as a critical, transcendent observer than as a participant in any group enterprise. Reading him today is frustrating, making it difficult to see why he was so influential. Although Veblen's best prose is brilliant, his discursive style often obscures his point. Nevertheless, Veblen's *The Theory of the Leisure Class* (1899) is a classic, widely read by economists and noneconomists alike. His reputation continues to be marred, however, by allegations that he was a sexual predator, and that he was disdainful of students.[41]

Veblen achieved notoriety in 1898 with a broadside entitled "Why Is Economics Not an Evolutionary Science?"[42] He argued that true science was "evolutionary" but neoclassical economics was not because it was "taxonomic" and "tautological." Because neoclassicism attempted to create a logical system whose rules never change, it was doomed to irrelevance. Veblen called for economics to become more historical, experimental, and empirical.

In *The Theory of Business Enterprise* (1904), Veblen addressed problems of both technology and natural rights, principally liberty of contract.[43] Business had developed a form of organization in which coordination and standardization were essential, but this was often frustrated by the law's elaborate protections for individual rights. The legal theory of individual rights, Veblen argued, antedated modern business enterprise, and grew out of a regime in which households were self-contained economic entities. Further, the legal theory treated people as equals, whereas a modern business organization required a hierarchy. While business efficiency required the hierarchical structure, legal doctrines such as liberty of contract, used to strike down wage-and-hour laws, effectively left the hierarchy unregulated. As a result the worker relinquished his freedom to private power, and State power was unavailable to assist him.

In *Absentee Ownership* (1923), published twenty years later, Veblen observed that the modern capitalist market was a forum in which goods could be exchanged even though they were located elsewhere or still to be produced.[44] Making such markets work required legal recognition of absentee ownership, or rights to property not in one's immediate physical control. This concept, Veblen argued, explained both the greatness and the weakness of the legal institutions that regulate capitalist production and finance. With the "transition to the machine industry and factory system," absentee ownership became the rule and owners became "investors" rather than managers. This led to both a lack of private accountability and social irresponsibility.

Although Veblen was too far outside the mainstream to have much immediate influence on American economics, his thought was seminal in the development of institutional economics in the 1920s, and he remained a darling of social and intellectual historians long after that. He had a modest influence on the judiciary. In his dissenting opinion in *Liggett v. Lee*, Justice Brandeis cited Veblen's *Absentee Ownership* together with Berle and Means's *The Modern Corporation and Private Property* for the proposition that ownership of the modern corporation had become separated from its control, reducing corporate accountability and justifying more elaborate regulation.[45]

Ely

As was true of many Progressive reformers, Richard T. Ely grew up in an evangelical Protestant family and found his orthodoxy shattered by a Darwinian liberal education. His evangelical zeal turned into social reform.[46] Graduate study in Heidelberg in the 1870s exposed him to the German Historical School. He became prominent in 1884 when he was an assistant professor at Johns Hopkins University, embarking on a generally difficult relationship with academic institutions.[47] Ely wrote a lengthy diatribe against British classical economics entitled "The Past and Present of Political Economy."[48] Simon Newcomb, his orthodox colleague, responded by identifying "two schools of political economy," and defending the older classical school.[49] Then began one of the most tempestuous debates in American academic economics, etching lines so clear that almost no American economist could straddle them.[50] The principal issue was whether belief in laissez-faire was a necessary credential to classify one as an economist. More technically, the debate revealed how much mathematics and the marginalist revolution were beginning to divide economists. One almost immediate result was the emergence of the American Economic Association in 1885 as an alternative to the British classical tradition.[51]

Ely devoted much of his career to examining the social role of private property and the legal rules protecting it. His work is characterized by a tension between the need for private ownership, which he believed necessary for prosperity, and the social need to prevent property from becoming a weapon of the strong against the weak. As Ely put it in 1894, the

> social theory of private property justifies a regulation of its use; but it must always be borne in mind that if this regulation is carried too

> far, the advantages of private property begin to disappear. When it becomes necessary to regulate private property minutely, we have a clear indication that private property should be replaced by public property.[52]

Ely's most ambitious venture into the economic analysis of law was his two-volume *Property and Contract in Their Relations to the Distribution of Wealth* (1914). He argued that the distribution of wealth in society was a product of previously created legal rules, and not merely of the natural laws of economics. Running through *Property and Contract* is a single theme: unregulated bargaining "tends to preserve advantages once secured." Contract "tends to keep the existing condition of things, or to allow existing currents to flow on.... The strong want unregulated contract; they are the economic conservatives. The reform forces must advocate regulation of contract." Ely objected to any notion that the law of contract is "natural" and thus justifies any economic inequality that might result. Rather, "*[t]he state itself is the source of contract.*"[53]

The belief that disparities in bargaining power required greater State intervention in contract became a prominent feature of institutionalist economics and later of Legal Realism. It eventually crept into the Restatement (Second) of Contracts and 1960s case law.[54] Judges typically used moral and not economic language to explain this substantial interference with liberty of contract. But historically judges were not inclined to use economic terminology. Even the later judges of the substantive due process era used essentially moral language to give effect to the policy views of the classical political economists when they struck down wage-and-hours legislation.[55] For Progressive economists such as Ely, however, such interference with liberty of contract was justified on economic grounds. Total welfare would increase, other things being equal, if wealth were distributed more evenly. The effect of bargaining power and unrestrained liberty of contract, however, was that wealth differences would become even greater. This powerful anti–common law theme later invigorated both Legal Realists and many others who would never have identified themselves as institutionalists.

Commons

John R. Commons was more scholarly than his teacher Ely and ultimately more influential. His writing over a lengthy career progressed from creative marginalist analysis to expansive work about the historical role of legal institutions in the economy. His most important book was *Legal Foundations of Capitalism* (1924), an economic classic that attempted to integrate the German Historical method into economic analysis of institutional behavior.[56] Commons developed the theory of the "going concern," which was both an economic institution and a legal one. The going concern had assets and liabilities as a single entity, just as an individual person did. In Commons's conception, the going concern was far broader than the business firm as a legal institution. Questions of resource use within each going concern were settled by that concern's unique "working rules," which could be quite different from the rules governing traditional markets. Markets were just one of many alternative mechanisms for clearing "transactions," or movements of resources from one person to another. Business firms, governments, families, and charitable and nonprofit organizations could all be going concerns. Every individual participated in many institutions, or going concerns, and the law itself was an institution with working rules for society.[57]

Legal Realists such as Wesley C. Mitchell, Walton Hamilton, and Karl Llewellyn carried these views into government policy, where institutionalism lasted long after it had gone out of fashion within mainstream economics.[58] The idea of the going concern drove Berle and Means's argument that corporations had deficient internal rules that divorced management from shareholders. Commons's work also strongly influenced the New Institutional Economics of the current day, particularly Oliver E. Williamson's influential union of institutionalism and the work of Ronald Coase.[59]

Although the concept of the going concern was not limited to business organizations, Commons devoted considerable attention to them. An important difference between the institutionalist view of the firm and the alternative presented by Coase's "Nature of the Firm" (1937) is methodological approach and strictness. For Coase, identifying the scope of the business firm was an exercise in pure marginalism, determined by comparing the costs of internal production against those of using the market.[60] By contrast, the institutionalists denied that economics alone could determine any institution's organization and decision-making. Firms make commitments to certain structures. Those commitments, once made, affect future decisions. Commons wrote that "[c]ustoms, practices, habits, precedents, methods of work, have been built up and handed down as working rules, which limit discretion in the present."[61]

Commons recognized "managerial transactions," or transactions within the going concern, as fundamentally different from "bargaining transactions," which were transactions between separate individuals or going concerns.

Managerial transactions required more legislative supervision than bargaining transactions, for managerial transactions were hierarchical, creating a potential for abuse. The law had always recognized this, Commons noted. For example, the common law of master and servant was more interventionist than the law of contracts generally, even though the relationship between employer and employee was contractual. The problem with the Supreme Court's decisions in *Lochner* and similar cases was that they treated managerial transactions as nothing but a species of contract. The result was that a "liberty" that presumed equality of bargaining position was applied inappropriately to a hierarchical relationship.[62]

Commons noted that even Adam Smith believed that institutions could distort value by suppressing market relationships. The market, "as Smith sorrowfully acknowledged, has been greatly interfered with by the collective power of political and industrial governments." As a result, Smith would have abolished "all corporations and associations."[63] Commons would not go that far, but believed that the corporation must be met with countervailing power. For example, he saw no basis for the legal distinction between the business firm as a single entity and the labor union as a *combination* of laborers.[64] Workers collectively sell added value to the production process, contributing just what the firm itself contributes in capital, machinery, and raw materials. Commons criticized American law for treating the incorporated business firm as a single "person," having both property rights and constitutional rights, including the right to contract. By contrast, labor unions were treated as associations of individuals. The business corporation "appears in court as a single individual," whereas "the union appears as a conspiracy of individuals…, merely inflicting damage on property by withholding the supply of labor until the terms of the contract can be agreed upon."[65] Commons approved of Justice Brandeis's conclusion in the *Hitchman Coal* case: "If it is coercion to threaten to strike unless plaintiff [employer] consents to a closed union shop, it is coercion also to threaten not to give one employment unless the applicant will consent to a nonunion shop."[66]

Commons argued that, although the modern business firm was a marvelous engine of efficiency, it used labor inefficiently because the costs could so easily be shifted away from the firm and to the laborers themselves. For example, steel manufacturing was much less labor intensive than a generation earlier and productivity had increased by a factor of five. Nevertheless, the mills had moved from an eight-hour day to a twelve-hour day—this in spite of evidence that the workers were exhausted and individually worked less efficiently when required to work twelve hours.[67] The workers had to be paid a subsistence wage whether they worked eight hours daily or twelve. Thus the extra cost to the employer of the twelve-hour day was near zero. Had the labor union been permitted by law to wield its institutional power to the same degree that the manufacturer wielded its power, worker efficiency would increase as well.

Commons's distinction between managerial and bargaining transactions exposed an important policy divide between traditional economists and Progressives, one that long outlived institutionalism itself. For traditionalists, wage bargains were simply a species of contract, and should be governed by the same contractual rules, including liberty to contract freely and an assumption of equality between the parties. By contrast, for the Progressives the labor bargain was something fundamentally different from contract law. Its hierarchical nature demanded greater State supervision. A century after the Progressive and neoclassical revolution, that view continues to influence our thinking about labor.

Commons's work continued the idea promoted by the historical school and institutionalism generally that markets are diverse, and that resources often move through society by mechanisms other than market transactions. This view survived in the writing of both economic historians and transaction cost economics long after institutionalism itself was cast aside by mainstream economists.[68] Institutionalism also remained robust in legal theory, particularly in the legacy of Legal Realism. Although the term "market" does describe the relationship between employers and employees, shareholders and management, husbands and wives, and voters and elected officials, it fails to capture important differences. This idea—that neoclassicism's abstraction and reductionism creates an illusion of simplicity and unjustified bias against State intervention—retained considerable vitality in the law.

5

Social Value, Taxation, and Public Finance

THE STATE COULD hardly function without making judgments about the welfare of its citizens. Governments devise tax schemes, which often take more from the well-off than the poor. They provide for defense and safety, public works, education, a monetary system and mail, environmental regulation, and even direct economic support. In a democratic society run by elected officials many of these judgments are made with little thought about the methodological problems of assessing or even defining "welfare."

The casualness of these everyday observations belies the ragged state of the science, however. Within economics, the measurement problem has broken into two distinct parts: market and nonmarket transfer. With some dissent from Progressives, both classical and neoclassical economics maintained a robust belief that voluntary market exchange increases welfare. That conclusion was based on assumptions of individual choice and freedom to trade. The bigger problem was *in*voluntary transfers such as taxes. When can a forced transfer from one person to another be shown to improve welfare? After initial debate, most mainstream economists began to conclude in the late 1930s that economic science lacked the observation and measurement tools to draw many useful conclusions about involuntary transfers.

In sharp contrast, social scientists saw human beings as having survival needs rather than preferences. Care for these needs emerged through the development of social institutions, including tribes, nations, communities, families, religions, and legal customs. Although the "preferences" of the economic actor were purely individual, the ways these institutions addressed survival needs had an undeniable social component. In addition, whereas neoclassical economics emphasized the extent to which preferences are individual, unique, and difficult to compare across persons, evolutionary theory emphasized the extent to which the requirements for survival and productivity are the same for those sharing a common environment.

Classical political economy had generally tied value to the cost of production, which did not depend on either individual or social group preferences. Indeed, the lack of a social component in classicism's value theory led some traditionalists to continue to defend classical theories of value against the marginalist onslaught.[1] By contrast, emergent marginalism in the early twentieth century toyed with a more "social" conception of economic value. Certain commodities or opportunities were thought to have a value to the group that was greater than the values that individuals asserted in the marketplace. Even relatively orthodox marginalists such as John Bates Clark believed that value contained this social element, but social value became a particularly powerful theme for the institutionalists.[2]

Thorstein Veblen reflected this idea in *The Theory of the Leisure Class* (1899).[3] Whether he was actually influenced by Clark is difficult to say. Veblen's book never mentioned Clark or, for that matter, any other British or American economists save Mill. As an evolutionist, Veblen preferred the term "habits" rather than "preferences" to describe human choice, and he rejected the neoclassical idea that human beings are economic actors with stable, generally autonomous preferences.[4] The economic conception of preference was deficient because the theory simply accepted them as given, with no inquiry into their sources or rationales. But "reasoning is largely controlled by other than logical, intellectual forces;...and the sentiment which animates men, singly or collectively, is as much, or more, an outcome of habit and native propensity as of calculated material interest."[5] Equilibrium was unimportant because human habits were the result of interaction of human variation and the environment, and were continuously changing.[6] The "evolution of social structure has been a process of natural selection of institutions," he wrote, reflecting "a natural selection of the fittest habits of thought."[7] Habits differed insofar as nature produced variation, but they were the same insofar as the natural selection process chooses certain habits for survival.[8]

In 1901 Edwin R.A. Seligman, a pioneer in marginalist analysis and Progressive tax policy, argued that "[v]alue in society depends upon the fact not only that each individual measures the relative urgency of his own different wants, but that he compares them, consciously or unconsciously with those of his neighbors." As a result, economic theory must consider social as well as individual components of value.[9] Michigan sociologist and economist Charles Horton Cooley faulted marginalist economics for taking individual subjective desire as its basic datum, for such desires are socially conditioned by existing institutions. As a result, Cooley argued, the economist unconsciously accepts existing institutions as given and loses his power to criticize them.[10]

Within the evolutionary view humans are more body than mind, so basic elements in the human list of wants are common to all of them, even though they might use surplus wealth differently. Veblen believed essential goods should be thought of as having a social value that was different than any sum of individual values.[11] Seligman justified the Progressive income tax by dividing goods into "necessities," "comforts," and "luxuries." A progressive tax scheme that reduced one person's luxuries in order to procure another's necessities increased social welfare.[12] Even Justice Holmes acknowledged in 1911 that certain "necessaries" such as "short rations in a shipwreck" might be made subject to greater State control than other commodities.[13]

If human choice is a product of evolution and explained by survival instincts, then sociology and psychology can contribute to economics by studying the source and nature of preference. For example, Wesley Clair Mitchell, an institutionalist student of Veblen and John Dewey, who led the National Bureau of Economic Research for twenty-five years, rejected the supremacy of individual rational choice as a working assumption, arguing that psychology and sociology suggested the contrary.[14] He denied that economic theory must rest upon the "simple facts of preference or choice, and [that] the psychological explanation of these preferences or choices is ... a matter of indifference to our science." Walton Hamilton, who was trained as an economist but spent much of his later career as a Yale law professor, argued in "The Institutional Approach to Economic Theory" that economics had to incorporate a "theory of motives ... in harmony with the conclusions of modern social psychology."[15]

Some economists, who might be regarded as institutionalism's "fellow travelers," tried to incorporate elements of both economic and Darwinian conceptions of welfare. For example, Clark's son John Maurice Clark argued that a complete economics must include both the "science" of observing preferences and developing mathematically the consequences of marginal utility theory, but also the "art" of examining the biological and social sources of preference. For Clark this entailed the use of welfare tests unrelated to state of mind, drawn from behavioral psychology or sociology. However, he would limit this social conception to "minimum standards relating to those necessities which are generally accepted as such."[16]

For some Progressives this conception of social value promised to unify economics with the other sciences. Simon Patten from the University of Pennsylvania's Wharton School believed that human consumption patterns are socially conditioned. As a result, sociology and economics should become a single science.[17] Edward A. Ross, who was both a sociologist and a marginalist economist, stressed that value is entirely a function of social conditioning. *Social Control* (1901), his most important contribution to sociology, was an extended argument that values are socially formed, that individual selfishness is in constant tension with social needs, and that sociology must study the relationship between individual instincts and social conditioning. Further, social values are a product of the evolutionary process, just as all physical and cultural characteristics of humanity. "[T]he valuations we are bred to are not native to us."[18]

Social Value in the Thought of Roscoe Pound

The American legal scholar whose thought most thoroughly incorporated evolutionary social conceptions of value was Roscoe Pound. Although he corresponded with Ely and was heavily influenced by Edward Ross, his work shows little sign that he read Veblen. Ross and Pound became friends at the University of Nebraska just after the turn of the century, and Ross inspired Pound's vision for melding law and social science that Pound came to call "sociological jurisprudence." Early on, Pound made his career arguing that individualistic legal doctrines such as liberty of contract were both "mechanical" and insufficiently reflective of modern social conceptions of value. He believed that although legal use of the term "liberty of contract" was relatively recent, its individualistic bias actually originated with the classical political economists.[19] Pound argued political economy had given the law an individualistic bias that ignored the social aspects of value inherent in the social sciences, particularly sociology.

Pound, as many Progressive Era intellectuals, drew much of his social value theory from the German Historical tradition, which was strongly nationalistic and institutionalist but minimized the importance of individual autonomy.[20] "Social interests," insofar as Pound articulated them, were things to be discovered by social scientists, and Pound had a rather technocratic view about social science methodology. He seemed to think that sociologists and psychologists could simply discover what was best for people. Even his theory of legislation has the ideal legislator largely ignoring the choices of his constituency. Rather, the legislator's job is to do the right thing, usually as dictated by social science inquiry. Pound paid little attention to economics, and was sometimes hostile toward it. Later in his life he equated "economics" in legal analysis with interest group politics.[21]

Pound's early jurisprudence was one of the most non-individualistic theories to be developed by a high profile thinker associated with an elite American legal institution, Harvard Law School. His thought was fundamentally inimical to neoclassical economic analysis, although it fits somewhat better with institutional economics. Later in his career, however, and embittered by the way some Legal Realists had treated his work, Pound moved to the right, objecting to what he saw as Legal Realism's advocacy of specialized agencies rather than courts to give effect to social science principles.[22]

Social Value under Fire: "Methodological Individualism"

The neoclassical view of welfare was based on far narrower assumptions than anything Veblen, Ross, or Pound accepted. If individuals do not have identical preferences, and if the differences are not precisely knowable, then the mathematics of marginalism can apply only to individuals. This observation, modest but revolutionary, appeared in one of Joseph Schumpeter's earliest English contributions to economic thought, written in Vienna in 1909, long before he immigrated to the United States. Schumpeter argued that if economics hopes to acquire anything approaching scientific precision it must adopt "methodological individualism" as a working procedure. "Almost every modern writer starts with wants and their satisfaction, and takes utility more or less exclusively as the basis of his analysis," Schumpeter wrote. "Without expressing any opinion about this *modus procedendi*, . . . it unavoidably implies considering individuals as independent units or agencies." In utility theory, "only individuals can feel wants." As a result, "marginal utilities do not depend on what society as such has, but on what individual members have." In sharp distinction to Veblen, Schumpeter concluded that no insights useful for economics could be gleaned by examining the sources of human preference and welfare. "For theory it is irrelevant *why* people demand certain goods: the only important point is that all things are demanded, produced, and paid for because individuals want them."[23]

Once economists accepted Schumpeter's suggestion that inquiries into the source of preference were not part of economics, then it did not matter whether human beings were the products of biological evolution or had been placed on earth with their preferences fully formed. Schumpeter believed, as most mainstream economists eventually would, that economics could maintain its scientific status only by limiting its conclusions to the preferences that people reveal by participating in markets.[24] The concept of "social value," as some kind of amalgam of individual values, could never be more than a vague "analogy."[25]

Schumpeter's critique served to divide economics from the social sciences. If the question was whether the evolutionary process yields individual needs sufficiently similar that one can generalize about them, then social scientists in other disciplines believed they had plenty to offer, particularly to legal policymakers who were seeking usable information for public policy. Increasingly, however, mainstream economists became skeptical, indifferent, and even hostile toward concepts of social value—or to any concept of value that could not be defined strictly in terms of individual preference. For most, the question was not whether individual utility functions have social origins. Most either conceded that they did or had nothing to say about the matter. Rather, the important issue was whether studying the social origins of preference added anything useful to economic science. Broadening the inquiry threatened to soften the scientific status of the discipline.

The last point is critical for what it says about the status of economics in the 1920s and 1930s. The principal place it claimed superiority over the other social sciences was in its use of mathematics. However, the hard mathematics of marginal utility economics applied to the *consequences* of a set of preferences assumed as given, stable, and rational. By contrast, study of the social sources of preference exposed economics to far mushier, less tractable questions that mainstream neoclassicists preferred be relegated to the other social sciences.

On the other side, sociologists and psychologists saw inquiries into the source of preference as the key to a unified scientific method. For example, Edward A. Ross had argued that what one person is willing to pay for a commodity is driven in large part by his perception of what others are willing to pay for it.[26] In lecture notes written in 1914, John Dewey protested that marginalist economics was driven by a strict individualism that severed the idea of human choice from more communal elements in valuation, particularly those that relate to education and productivity.[27] Throughout his career Dewey argued that social value was as important to economics as individual value, and that studies of the relationship between the two promised to unify psychology and economics.[28] Clarence Ayres, an institutional economist who became a prominent dissenter from neoclassicism in the 1930s and 1940s, believed that one could measure social value through productivity tests—for example, conducting experiments on the importance of milk for infants and then producing a "social value function" that would inform the State policymaker about how many resources should be committed to providing it.[29]

By the late 1930s elite legal theory was increasingly institutionalist, even though institutionalism was falling into disfavor in economic circles. By contrast, "welfare" economics as a discipline became increasingly neoclassical and antagonistic toward the redistributive policy agenda of the Legal Realists and the New Deal. As one historian of institutionalism has put it, these conflicting visions struggled mightily for the "soul" of economics.[30]

Welfare, Progressivity, and Tax Policy

The U.S. income tax had its roots in the financing of the very costly Civil War. In 1861, when tariffs and excise taxes proved insufficient, Congress passed an income tax and subsequently tinkered with rates and exemptions several times. The highest marginal tax rate was 10 percent on incomes above $5,000.[31] By 1872 the direct war debt was largely paid off and the tax was allowed to expire. However, ongoing obligations to pay Civil War pensions persisted for decades and continued the pressure for alternative revenue sources. The second federal income tax, instigated in part by the panic of 1893, was modest, with a 2 percent rate on incomes above $4,000. But the Supreme Court almost immediately declared the tax unconstitutional in its 5-4 *Pollock* decision of 1895.[32]

Morton J. Horwitz characterizes *Pollock* as the culmination of a half century movement toward identifying constitutional legitimacy with an anti-redistribution principle—a view heartily embraced by contemporary libertarian Constitutional law scholar Christopher Tiedeman. He saw the tax decision as an "object lesson in Constitutional construction."[33] What is striking, however, is the sources of mobilization in opposition to *Pollock*. The reaction represented an important turning point in legal thinking about progressivity. The contemporaneous revolution in economic thought created a new alignment between academics and the interest group politics of Progressivism. Politically, an important motivating factor was inequality of wealth, which reached its highest historical level during the Gilded Age and has subsequently been matched only by the early twenty-first century.[34]

By the early twentieth century a progressive income tax had bipartisan support, conservatives very possibly because they saw it as a way to stave off more radical measures.[35] The Sixteenth Amendment was ratified in 1913 and Congress soon passed a tax with increasing marginal rates that topped off at 6 percent.[36] During the Wilson administration the United States was once again confronted with a large war debt, and in 1916 raised the highest marginal rate to 15 percent. Thereafter the highest marginal rate increased dramatically, ultimately reaching 77 percent. From that point on tax policy became more divisive, with President Harding pushing through significant reductions.[37]

The Economic Argument for Progressivity

Taken to their extremes both the Reform Darwinist notions of welfare and those developed in marginalist economics prior to the 1930s would lead to significant redistribution of wealth. Left-leaning Darwinians such as Lester Ward viewed the controlled environment such as resulted from organized agriculture as much more productive than the natural environment of the jungle. Further, the farmer raising livestock does not typically heap all the resources on a small number of individuals. Rather, subject to minor variations, he gives them all equal "wealth." His goal is not "fairness" or equality of distribution for its own sake, but rather productivity. Nor does he measure value by considering states of mind, but rather such external indicia as freedom from disease, weight gain, milk or egg production, number of fruit per plant, and the like. That is, the indicia of success are external and based on productivity rather than choice.

Several things about the Progressive Era debate over differential tax rates are notable. *First*, the economists who supported the progressive tax drew on marginalist theory, but less explicitly than one might think. To a significant degree the arguments for progressivity were based on objective welfare judgments derived from the other social sciences. *Second*, marginalist analysis played a much more important role in tax administration, particularly in identifying the class of persons upon whom the ultimate burden of a tax would fall. *Third*, the amount of progressivity in the income tax during this period was relatively modest.

The Progressive Era economist with the greatest influence on judicial policy was Edwin R.A. Seligman.[38] He was the most prominent public finance economist of his day, and became a champion of the progressive income tax. He attended Columbia University and went to Germany for graduate studies. As a young faculty member at Columbia, where he spent his entire career, he enthusiastically aligned himself with the reformers in the 1880s debate over the future of economics. In 1902 he served as President of the American Economics Association.

Most of Seligman's work was devoted to two problems in tax theory that lay at the heart of Progressive legislative policy. The first was the rationale for progressive rather than constant or proportional income taxes. The second problem concerned the shifting and incidence of taxation—questions about when tax burdens are shifted from the person upon whom they appear to fall, and how to identify the classes upon whom the burden of a tax actually comes to rest.

At the turn of the century marginalist economists were trying to justify tax progressivity by engaging in interpersonal comparisons of utility. Seligman made the argument himself in his 1905 economics textbook.[39] The argument was that because people derived less utility from each dollar as their income rose, taxing higher incomes at higher levels would destroy less welfare per dollar of tax revenue received. Two neoclassical economists carried this position to the extreme—Thomas Nixon Carver in the United States and F.Y. Edgeworth in England. An optimal tax policy, argued Carver, should raise needed revenue through a "minimum of repression" of citizens. As the marginal utility of money declines as one has more, this suggested that the wealthy be taxed more heavily. Under a minimally repressive tax policy:

> The wealthiest man in the community would be taxed sufficiently to reduce his income and raise its final utility to a level with that of the next wealthiest man. Then these two would have to be taxed so as to raise the final utility of both their incomes to a level with that of the third, and so on till enough incomes were brought under the tax to raise enough revenue.[40]

Once sufficient revenue was raised, all other persons would be exempt from the tax.

In 1897 Edgeworth agreed in principle, although he differed in some details.[41] If every person's utility curve was identical, this implied that each person should be taxed until the remaining income of everyone was exactly the same. But Edgeworth blanched at the socialistic implications of this position and qualified it, suggesting that such leveling might reduce the incentive to produce and increase the birth rate among the lower economic classes.

Such economic defenses of progressivity were common through the 1920s. For example, Yale economist Irving Fisher tried to devise a statistical method for comparing utilities across families, thus justifying a progressive income tax.[42] In England, Cambridge University's Arthur Cecil Pigou defended progressivity in his 1928 book on public finance. He adhered to this position with only modest qualifications all the way through the third edition, which was not published until 1947 and revised shortly before his death in 1959.[43]

In contrast, by the late 1930s many mainstream economists had come to believe that interpersonal utility comparisons of this type were unscientific.

Lord Robbins, who most famously articulated this "ordinalist" argument, believed that the "conception of diminishing relative utility . . . does not justify the inference that transferences from the rich to the poor will increase total satisfaction. It does not tell us that a graduated income tax is less injurious to the social dividend than a non-graduated poll tax."[44] As Chapter 6 develops, mainstream American economists came to agree with Robbins, although most institutionalists and Legal Realists did not. "A belief in the comparability of diminishing marginal utility curves would be reasonable only if the nature and nurture of all men were identical," wrote Stanford University's Elmer Fagan in 1938. "A theory of progression whose logical validity and practical application depend upon so heroic an assumption as the identity of marginal utility curves will not be accepted."[45]

In 1908 Seligman acknowledged the power of marginal utility theory for justifying tax progressivity, but ultimately found the arguments unpersuasive, as had John Stuart Mill a half century earlier.[46] "Mathematics cannot help us here because the very first conditions fail us, the power to gauge with accuracy the mathematical relations of marginal utilities."[47]

Seligman ended up defending progressivity in taxation on objective rather than subjective welfare criteria. He called this the "faculty" theory and derived it from the notion that human provisions can be divided into three rough categories: necessities, comforts, and luxuries. Luxuries should be taxed at higher rates than comforts, and comforts at higher rates than necessities.[48]

Seligman's approach to progressivity retained its traction in tax policy precisely because it did not depend on a theory of interpersonal utility comparisons that mainstream economics eventually consigned to the trash heap. For example, in their influential writing on progressive taxation in the early 1950s, Walter J. Blum and Harry Kalven, Jr. found the case for progressivity in tax policy sustainable and even beyond "serious examination," even though nothing more than "sheer intuition" supported the use of interpersonal comparisons of utility.[49] By and large, the case for progressivity in the 1940s and after was based on objective welfare judgments rather than interpersonal comparisons of subjective utilities.

The Shifting and Incidence of Taxation

Any attempt to equalize welfare through the taxation system would be frustrated if those taxed can pass the burden to others. For example, a tax on monopoly profits would not equalize the monopolist's wealth with that of its customers if the monopolist could easily "shift" the tax by charging higher prices. Seligman became the Progressive Era's leading authority on the economics of passing on ("shifting") and identifying the group upon whom a tax burden ultimately falls ("incidence").[50]

Seligman was not the first person to consider these issues. Blackstone had concluded in the *Commentaries* that most taxes were shifted to consumers.[51] By contrast, Adam Smith believed that taxes were ultimately paid by landowners, provoking severe qualifications from Ricardo.[52] Others, including Jean-Baptiste Say, John Stuart Mill, and Alfred Marshall, also addressed the problem, as did several American political economists.[53] Cournot had anticipated marginalist analysis by examining the problem differently under competition and monopoly.[54] Because of its obvious practical implications the debate was hardly limited to economists. State revenue commissioners discussed the issue as early as the 1870s,[55] as did Thomas M. Cooley in his widely used *Treatise on Taxation*. Cooley followed the dominant thinking during the Gilded Age that most taxes would be shifted to final consumers. For example, a tax on land simply raised the price of agricultural products.[56]

What the pre-marginalist analysis of tax shifting generally lacked was a useable theory of fixed and variable costs. In general, taxes on variable costs are more readily shifted than taxes on fixed costs because variable costs determine pricing. Marginalist analysis also enabled its users to show how substitution rates, or "elasticities," affected shifting. Seligman's work produced an important debate with British economist F.Y. Edgeworth, leading to an outpouring of marginalist analysis of tax policy, much of it quite mathematical.[57] Between the beginning of the century and World War II the law and economics literature on the shifting and incidence of taxation was exceeded in volume only by the literature on the trust problem.[58]

Seligman worked out a scheme that favored taxation of a monopolist's earnings more heavily than the earnings of competitors, showing mathematically that a monopolist is likely to pass on only a relatively small portion of a tax. In a competitive market virtually the entire tax would be passed on. Most important, taxes imposed on sales tend to be passed on, whereas those imposed on fixed cost items such as land were less likely to be. Thus for example, a shirt-making factory would be unlikely to pass on a fixed annual property tax, but more likely to pass on a sales tax on its final product.

Seligman succeeded in what Progressive Era economists and social scientists accomplished only rarely: being cited by the courts. Under the practice of the day judges did not often cite works outside the law. The most frequent exception was Adam Smith's *Wealth of Nations*. Seligman was cited by the Supreme Court a half dozen times, however, and by lower courts as well.[59]

In its 1931 *Indian Motocycle* decision the Supreme Court held that a federal statute exempting local governments from federal taxation invalidated a tax placed on the initial sale of a motorcyle purchased by a police department. Even though the tax in question was not assessed directly against the municipality the majority found that it was effectively passed on to the ultimate buyer. In dissent, Justice Stone relied on Seligman for the proposition that one could not automatically infer that any upstream tax would come to rest on the ultimate purchaser.[60]

Under marginalist conceptions economists played an ever-increasing role in the formation of U.S. tax policy. However, the policy wound between the extreme view that any unequal or redistributive tax was an unjust and unconstitutional confiscation of property, and the alternative extreme that welfare would be maximized when wealth is equalized. The legal policy that the United States actually developed departed significantly from the first extreme and never came close to the second.

Constitutional Tax Policy and Public Finance

Two other issues of tax policy came under constitutional scrutiny in the late nineteenth and early twentieth centuries. One concerned the appropriate role of the State in defining and financing public goods. The other was the use of tax policy to control conduct with harmful effects on third parties.

A public good is something that, once created, benefits everyone. National defense is a commonly given example: everyone is protected whether or not he or she helps pay for it. Adam Smith devoted the final section of *The Wealth of Nations* to public finance, including a seventy-five page chapter on public works, which he defined as works "of such a nature, that the profit could never repay the expense to any individual" and thus must be produced by the government.[61] Under neoclassical analysis the theory of public goods became narrower and more technical, limited to goods that are both "nonexcludable," meaning that they benefit everyone, and also "nonrivalrous," meaning that one person's use does not limit what is left for others.[62] Many things that government provides, such as free streets or waterways, and certainly business subsidies, do not meet these requirements because exclusion is possible and overuse can burden others. As a result, these strict definitions invite the complaint that modern society provides "too many" public goods, in that tax revenues are being used to supply things that could be supplied privately, perhaps by charging a toll, or that encourage overuse because users do not pay the full cost of providing the good.

The constitutional theory of public goods originated in Gilded Age treatise arguments that governments could tax only for a "public purpose." The principal architects were Thomas M. Cooley, who wrote influential books on constitutional law and taxation, and John F. Dillon, who wrote an important book on the powers of municipalities.[63] The historical debate originated in complaints about states or municipalities that gave tax-financed subsidies to private business corporations.[64] These subsidies generally replaced alternative inducements that had been used earlier, including monopoly franchises or railroad land grants as an inducement to invest. Because the monopoly privilege could be granted at no out-of-pocket cost to the state and it already owned the land, neither type of inducement required the sovereign to raise significant revenue through taxation. The Jacksonian position on such inducements was hostile. Acting under Jackson appointee Chief Justice Roger B. Taney, the Supreme Court either struck them down or construed them very narrowly.[65] The Jacksonians were even more hostile to tax-generated direct subsidies, and the laissez-faire law writers such as Cooley and Dillon came out of this tradition.

The financial source of these subsidies was frequently tax-supported municipal bonds. During and after Reconstruction the bond issues were often challenged in court.[66] The leading case was *Savings & Loan Ass'n v. Topeka*, in which Justice Samuel F. Miller wrote the Court's opinion condemning the city's use of municipal bonds to subsidize a private corporation "for the purpose of building bridges, aiding railroads, water-power, or other works of internal improvement."[67]

Although this public purpose doctrine is sometimes associated with economic substantive due process, the Supreme Court was much more tolerant of tax-financed public projects than of protective labor regulation. In *Fallbrook Irrigation District* (1896) the Court held that California's public financing of irrigation in arid agricultural regions satisfied the public purpose requirement, even though the benefits flowed to only a small proportion of the taxpayers.[68] Twenty years later in *Green v. Frazier*, the Court upheld the use of tax monies to set up a flour mill, subsidize mortgages, and provide housing for tenant farmers. In this case the state legislature had declared that the purpose was public, and "we are not at liberty to interfere unless it is clear beyond reasonable controversy that rights secured by the federal Constitution have been violated."[69] After that, federal constitutional scrutiny of tax-financed subsidies declined considerably, although a few state courts continued to apply their own constitutions.[70]

The central concern of Gilded Age decisions such as *Topeka* was the use of tax revenues to subsidize business. Later cases ranged further, even to subsidies for provision of consumer goods. These uses went far beyond any mainstream economic conception of public goods, and often reflected nothing more than local politics. For example, in *Jones v. City of Portland* (1917), the Supreme Court upheld a statutory scheme for providing fuel to residents at cost.[71] Over a bitter dissent accusing the city of Lincoln, Nebraska, of "socialism and communism," that state's supreme court approved public funding to create a subsidized seller of oil and gasoline in competition with the plaintiff, rejecting his objection that there had never been local fuel shortages justifying such a public expenditure.[72] Other subsidy programs were clearly promotional and intended to attract industry into the municipalities that offered the subsidy.[73]

Within mainstream economics, the neoclassical theory of public goods became increasingly strident, arguing that private business competition would provide the proper amount of most goods, and that many subsidy programs were thinly disguised wealth transfer schemes. Many of the attacks on Keynesian public investment programs were of this nature. James Buchanan and Gordon Tullock later argued in their influential book *The Calculus of Consent* that public goods were inherently subject to excessive provision because individual voters anticipated that they would get more out than they put in. "Western governments have opened the way for more and more effective redistribution, which is accomplished indirectly through the tax financing of public goods and services."[74]

Another important tax issue confronting the courts concerned taxes that controlled undesirable or harmful behavior. Cambridge economist Arthur Cecil Pigou published his influential *Study in Public Finance* in 1928, which broadly supported such taxes. Pigou devoted an entire chapter to "Taxes and Bounties to Correct Maladjustments." Today we often call taxes used for this purpose "Pigouvian taxes," and they are used in such areas as environmental control of air pollution.[75]

"Pigouvian" taxes were actually well established before Pigou's time, however. Adam Smith spoke in *The Wealth of Nations* about a tax on carriages to offset the damage that they did to the roads, suggesting that the tax be proportional to weight because "each carriage is supposed to pay exactly for the wear and tear which that carriage occasions of the roads."[76] In the nineteenth century American states sometimes used taxes rather than outright prohibitions to control liquor consumption.[77] Other states did the same thing for lotteries and gambling.[78] Thomas M. Cooley devoted a chapter of his 1876 *Treatise* on taxation to "Taxes under the Power of Police," by which he meant the use of taxes as alternatives to prohibition or other types of regulation of harmful activities. Such a tax does not have "for its object the raising of revenue," but rather "the conservation of order..., the encouragement of industry, and the discouragement of pernicious employment."[79]

The Supreme Court upheld a federal Pigouvian tax on oleomargarine in 1904,[80] and another on narcotics in 1919.[81] The best known Pigouvian tax to reach the Supreme Court, however, was the child labor tax case of 1922.[82] In 1918 the Supreme Court had struck down a federal statute outlawing the use of child labor on goods destined for interstate shipment, finding that the statute exceeded both Congress's commerce power and the Tenth Amendment.[83] Congress responded by placing a 10 percent tax on the net income of employers using child labor. The tax was intended to level the playing field by making the exports of states that prohibited child labor more competitive with those that permitted it. The Supreme Court held that the provision was not a tax at all, but in fact a regulation of child labor, and struck it down for the same reasons that it had previously condemned the direct prohibition.

Just as is true of the tax subsidies, Pigouvian taxes were also challenged as products of legislative capture for the benefit of favored industries. One powerful example is the harsh reactions that states with strong dairy interests took against oleomargarine, a product invented and patented in Europe and introduced into the United States in the 1870s. Both dairy states and the federal government responded with an alarming range of restrictions, given that no harmful effects were ever established. Some states forbade margarine sales altogether. The Supreme Court struck down such a provision under the Commerce Clause.[84] Others prevented the margarine, an inherently white product, from being colored to resemble butter.[85] More than one state even required that it be colored pink, presumably to make it unpalatable. The Supreme Court struck down such a provision in 1898.[86] Finally, a number of states as well as the federal government taxed it, very likely in order to undermine its cost advantage over butter. In 1894 the Supreme Court upheld a Massachusetts statute that imposed both color limitations and labeling requirements on margarine, as well as a tax on its sale.[87] As noted above, it did the same thing for a federal tax in 1904.

The general course of tax history over the twentieth century was in the direction of less judicial supervision on constitutional grounds, with occasional exceptions for clearly discriminatory impositions or taxes levied without adequate notice. On the other side, mainstream economics became increasingly agnostic about the welfare effects of progressive income taxes, and increasingly strident against public goods' rationales for taxation schemes.

6

From Institutionalism to Legal Realism

THE AMERICAN INSTITUTIONALISTS were economists who dissented from neoclassical orthodoxy. They were a highly diverse group, but generally shared two beliefs. First was that marginalist economics' stripped down conception of the rational actor was inadequate to describe human behavior. Rather, economics should take both history and the biological sources of human motive much more seriously. Second, they shared significant doubts about the domain and legitimacy of markets. For the institutionalists, markets were only one of the mechanisms that move resources through society, and they resisted neoclassicism's attempt to reduce organizations to a market model. In addition, they believed that markets often work poorly and are responsible for many of society's economic evils, including maldistribution of wealth and loss of individual freedom.

Thorstein Veblen was the first American to define economics in terms of the institutions that create value and move resources through society. His *Theory of the Leisure Class* (1899) was subtitled *An Economic Study in the Evolution of Institutions.* Much of it was devoted to how the "evolution of social structure has been a process of natural selection of institutions."[1] Richard T. Ely's 1914 book on the common law and the distribution of wealth also spoke repeatedly about the economic effects of social and governmental institutions. Ely identified five "institutions in our economic order" that were mainly responsible for the distribution of wealth—namely, custom, competition, monopoly, governmental control, and benevolence.[2]

The self-referential term "institutional economics" was probably not coined until 1919, however, and then by a Legal Realist, Walton H. Hamilton. Around that time the movement became conscious of its own identity as a distinctive approach to economics.[3] Hamilton attended graduate school at the University of Michigan, studying economics under Henry Carter Adams and economics and sociology under Charles Horton Cooley, son of the Gilded Age constitutional law scholar Thomas M. Cooley. Both Adams and Cooley were dissenters from strict marginalism and strongly drawn to both the historical school as well as behavioral science.

Institutionalism was popular during the first three decades of the twentieth century. Its prominent writers included Veblen, Ely, Hamilton, John R. Commons, Robert Hale, and Edwin R.A. Seligman, as well as sympathizers such as John Dewey.[4] Others came a little later, including Wesley Mitchell, Gardiner C. Means, Clarence E. Ayres, William F. Ogburn, and Karl Polanyi, who taught in the United States after World War II. John Maurice Clark self-identified with the institutionalists and is often grouped among them, although much of his writing was more traditionally neoclassical. Institutionalism's influence was extraordinarily broad, touching the views of many who did not identify themselves with the movement. For example, during the early twentieth century the Harvard economics department, considered the country's best, was dominated by a "case study" method that focused on the historical development and unique features of individual industries or firms.[5] These studies were in sharp contrast to the relatively abstract nonhistorical analysis that had come to be associated with neoclassical economics. Studies by the United States Bureau of Corporations and its successor agency the Federal Trade Commission reflected a similar approach.[6] As Chapter 11 develops, after 1930 Harvard economists such as Edward S. Mason and Edward Chamberlin who generally did not identify themselves with institutionalism nevertheless incorporated strong assumptions about market diversity and fragility into their work on competition economics.

One striking difference between the neoclassical and institutionalist approaches to markets would become prominent during the New Deal. When markets work, they are all more or less alike and could be captured by the highly abstract mathematics of neoclassicism. When they fail, however, each one presents unique shortcomings and recipes for regulatory fixes. Justice Brandeis's formulation of the "rule of reason" for antitrust cases in 1918 reflects his institutionalism. In order to understand the competitive effects of a practice, he wrote, a court must "consider the facts peculiar to the business," as well as the "history of the restraint, the evil believed to exist," and "the reason for adopting the particular remedy."[7] That formulation turned the big antitrust case into some of the most costly and terrifying civil litigation ever known, generating thousands of pages of documents describing the history and unique features of an industry.

Within mainstream economics, institutionalism's claim to dominance was short-lived. It was already marginalized by 1930, and by 1940 institutionalists were virtual personae non grata within orthodox economic circles. That was true even of the American Economic Association, which had originated as a Progressive alternative to traditionalism but turned quickly to the right.[8] The debates in the AEA's became much more notable for attacks on institutionalism than for the institutionalist contributions themselves.[9] The mainstream was far more interested in developing technical apparatus—something that the rational actor assumptions of marginalism enabled but was inconsistent with the more historical, empirical, and descriptive accounts that institutionalists advocated.

Institutionalists believed that "institutions," broadly defined, were what moved resources through society. One institution is the market itself, but corporations, families, churches, political parties, legislatures, the judicial system, and clubs are all institutions. Many institutionalists were influenced by Edward Ross's conception of "social control," which saw a wide variety of social institutions as control devices regulating human behavior.[10] For John R. Commons, allocation decisions within institutions are a product of "working rules" and "transactions."[11] A working rule is one that the institution accepts for making decisions (e.g., "Father knows best," or "one person, one vote"). A transaction then refers to a particular decision.

Institutionalists believed that each of society's various institutions was unique, and that the working rules of each were proper subjects for economic study. This naturally demanded a great deal of empirical work. One might do empirical studies of how and why business corporations make decisions by observing their working rules and the transactions that resulted. Or one might do the same thing for families, the judicial system, or municipal government. But observations made about one institution would not necessarily apply to another.

For example, institutionalists emphasized that an important characteristic of the modern business corporation was the separation of ownership and control, or the fact that shareholders were absentee and managers represented only a small part of the ownership interest. Berle and Means's important New Deal era book on *The Modern Corporation* used institutionalist economics to uncover the corporation's flaws.[12] Adolf A. Berle, Jr. was an academic lawyer whose principal interest was corporate finance. Gardiner C. Means was a Harvard-trained economist who in addition to *The Modern Corporation* was recognized for his theory of "administered prices," explaining why markets with small numbers of firms did not seem to respond quickly to changes in demand.[13] While Berle was at Columbia he received a grant from the Rockefeller Foundation to do an interdisciplinary study of the American business corporation, and he hired Means as a research assistant to help with the economics. Means's statistical work became increasingly important, and by the time it was published they were coauthors.[14]

Institutionalists had a strong interest in the legal system, but they denigrated the common law almost as much as they disdained the market. Hope for the future lay in market-specific statutes and regulation. Whereas the institutionalists' accounts of the economy were descriptively rich, generalization and abstraction were the essence of neoclassicism and made its impressive mathematics possible. Indeed, institutionalism's inability to devise testable, general hypotheses explains why it failed to capture the minds of most young economists. Institutionalists were always doing elaborate historical or empirical studies about industries, firms, or legal institutions. All of the conclusions seemed quite descriptive and idiosyncratic, however, with no unifying theory to hold them together. Later empirical studies by the Legal Realists typically met the same fate.

This unsuccessful history notwithstanding, historians have always been drawn to institutionalism. Their movement occupies a position in history writing disproportionate to its presence within economics. Classic studies by such historians as Morton White, Henry Steele Commager, and Richard Hofstadter include lengthy appreciative appraisals of institutionalist economists such as Veblen, while ignoring economists who were much more influential within the mainstream, such as John Bates Clark, Irving Fisher, or Frank Knight.[15] The marginalist revolution working its way out in economics departments in the first three decades of the twentieth century was certainly as interesting and proved to be far more durable than anything institutionalism offered. It was also more technical, however, and often addressed to other professional economists rather than a broad range of policymakers.

Increasingly after the 1930s economists saw their discipline as concerned with individual market choices, but with little to say about the welfare consequences of State-imposed redistribution. The rational actor assumption became an essential component in the discipline's claim to scientific status. In the process neoclassical economics began to move back to the right, to a stronger commitment to the free market. Legal policymakers tended to find these arguments unpersuasive. Many of them simply abandoned mainstream economics as an important perspective on welfare.

The history of regulatory policy is analogous. After the 1940s mainstream economic thought increasingly believed that markets were more robust than previously believed. Neoclassical economists became critical of government intervention unless it corrected a "market failure," or the relatively uncommon situation where the market alone did not produce acceptable results. By contrast, most institutionalists found significant need for regulation. They believed that markets are feeble and highly imperfect instruments, often leading to monopoly or other inefficiencies.

This chapter considers some of the sources of American Legal Realism, but from a different viewpoint than most of the voluminous literature. The Legal Realists were, in essence, the lawyer branch of institutionalism. Although the Legal Realists often wrote about economics, the theory that they embraced was almost invariably institutionalist. That was true of Robert Hale, Walton Hamilton, Karl Llewellyn, Underhill Moore, and William O. Douglas.[16] After the ordinalist revolution in economics, institutionalism was gradually relegated to the fringe. Mainstream neoclassical economics began a "restoration" of the market to its earlier robust position and strongly limited the economic case for government intervention. By contrast, the Legal Realists continued a far more interventionist approach to economic law. Because Legal Realism was so dominant in New Deal and post–New Deal legal policy, the result was a sharp divide between economic theory and government policymaking.

Ordinalism and the Separation of Economics and Law

The ordinalist debate concerned the abstruse subject of interpersonal utility comparisons. Money has declining marginal utility for an individual, which means that the value someone places on her first dollar is likely to be greater than the value she places on her 100th. If so, why could not welfare be improved by transferring wealth from the rich to the poor, thus giving it to those who valued it more highly? Alfred Marshall found this argument persuasive and came to favor progressive income taxes and other forced wealth redistribution.[17] His successor at Cambridge, Arthur C. Pigou, agreed: A "transference of income from a relatively rich man to a relatively poor man of similar temperament, since it enables more intense wants to be satisfied at the expense of less intense wants, must increase the aggregate sum of satisfaction."[18] Prominent American economists, including Frank Taussig, John Bates Clark, Simon Patten, and Jacob Viner approved the use of interpersonal utility comparisons through the 1920s.[19]

Making utility comparisons across society requires two things. *First*, units of utility must be "cardinal," which means that the unit of measurement is constant. For example, two dollars have twice as much value as one dollar. By contrast, an "ordinal" measurement is a simple ranking with no weight assigned to it. *Second*, utility must be interpersonally comparable, which means that a unit of utility in the mind of one person is worth just as much as a unit in the mind of someone else. Reduced to fundamentals, the ordinalist critique was that "utility" refers to a purely mental state, making both cardinal measurement and interpersonal comparison impossible. Industrial economics, which assessed a business firm's wealth in constant dollars rather than utility, was not nearly as troubled by these problems.

The interpersonal utility debate invoked the "other minds" problem that underlay the Logical Positivist revolt against traditional conceptions of knowledge. The devastating effects of World War I on political liberalism and traditional religion had forced European intellectuals to redefine the proper boundaries of scientific inquiry. Logical Positivism emerged as an argument for eliminating metaphysics from scientific discourse. Under the Logical Positivism that grew out of the Vienna Circle, the meaning of a scientific statement was no more than the method by which it could be verified through empirical testing.[20] No concept of traditional social science suffered more under the Logical Positivist critique than "mental state," or one person's knowledge about the minds of others. In his classic 1936 book *Language, Truth and Logic*, A.J. Ayer argued that it was meaningless to talk about other people's minds except behaviorally, for one could observe only external actions.[21] Behaviorism in psychology tried to understand organisms entirely in terms of outward behavioral manifestations, rather than conjectures about state of mind.

In economics, the gateway to Logical Positivism was the relatively young London School of Economics (LSE), which was less tradition bound than Cambridge or Oxford. The two British economists most associated with the ordinalist revolution are Lionel Robbins and John Hicks.[22] Robbins was director of LSE in 1932, when he published his *Essay on the Nature and Significance of Economic Science*. As the Logical Positivists often did in their demonstrations against metaphysics, Robbins proposed a question thought to be scientific and then debated with himself about the method for answering it:

> Suppose that we differed about the satisfaction derived by A from an income of £1,000, and the satisfaction derived by B from an income of twice that magnitude. Asking them would provide no solution. Supposing they differed. A might urge that he had more satisfaction than B at the margin. While B might urge that, on the contrary, he had

> more satisfaction than A. We do not need to be slavish behaviourists to realise that here is no scientific evidence. There is no means of testing the magnitude of A's satisfaction as compared with B's. If we tested the state of their blood-streams, that would be a test of blood, not satisfaction. Introspection does not enable A to discover what is going on in B's mind, nor B to discover what is going on in A's. There is no way of comparing the satisfactions of different people.

Within the au courant language, this made the proposition that B receives more utility from a dollar than A does "meaningless." It "necessarily falls outside the scope of any positive science." Any attempt to quantify and compare one person's utility with that of another "is essentially normative. It has no place in pure science."[23]

Among neoclassicists Robbins's analysis swept the field.[24] The quoted passage about testing bloodstreams also made clear that objective welfare judgments had no place in economics because they did not measure mental state. Nevertheless, the novelty of Robbins's observations should not be exaggerated. He was hardly the first to observe that subjective feelings could not be compared across persons. Jeremy Bentham had lamented more than a century earlier that "one man's happiness will never be another man's happiness; a gain to one man is no gain to another; you might as well pretend to add 20 apples to 20 pears." Nonetheless, Bentham concluded that although the "addibility of the happiness of different subjects ... may appear fictitious," it was a proposition "without the allowance of which all political reasoning is at a stand."[25] By 1940 mainstream economists purported to abhor interpersonal comparisons of utility. To make them became one of economics' most conspicuous indiscretions. In the process theoretical economics either abandoned or severely limited efforts to link economic welfare to the distribution of wealth.

Robbins's critique also cut the knot between Darwinism and economics as mechanisms for assessing welfare. For Robbins, preferences were assumed to be absolutely subjective, completely autonomous to the individual, and unique. They reflected only the mental state of the person asserting them. Getting behind the preference to its source was impossible, because such inquiries depended on suppositions that could not be tested. Even though the other social sciences were just as influenced by the positivist revolution, they looked to external manifestations of welfare, such as observed health and productivity. That is, they responded to the "other minds" problem by creating welfare tests that did not depend on assumptions about mental state.

Ordinalism dominated economic thought to the extent that economists refused to make this jump.

By identifying welfare with individual preference, ordinalism also focused economics on consumption rather than production. In contrast, Cambridge economist Arthur Cecil Pigou strongly advocated for greater public investment in human productivity. By viewing human beings as engines of production rather than consumption, the interpersonal comparison problem became relatively unimportant. Pigou was the first economist to use the term "human capital," in the 1920s, a half century before the modern law and economics movement revived it. In his 1928 classic book on *Public Finance* Pigou observed that "there is such a thing as investment in human capital as well as investment in material capital." In that case "the distinction between economy in consumption and economy in investment becomes blurred."[26] Nicholas Kaldor, whose work laid much of the technical foundation for ordinalist welfare economics, observed in 1939 that policies that increase "physical productivity" are "quite unaffected by the comparability of individual satisfactions," for "in all such cases it is possible to make everybody better off than before."[27]

Reform Darwinists had already observed that scientific management of the environment, such as occurs for lower organisms in agriculture, need not identify success with subjective mental state. If the concern is productivity, then the criteria for promoting it tend to regard all individuals within a species as more or less the same.[28] Welfare economists after the ordinalist revolution often failed to appreciate how much of government intervention was intended to improve productivity rather than quality as measured by mental state. An important characteristic of State welfare policy during the New Deal and after was the development of external mechanisms for measuring welfare that did not involve assumptions about mental state. For example, from the 1940s through the 1960s Mollie Orshansky, an economist and statistician at the Social Security Administration, did the foundational work for what became the "poverty line," a measure that relates presumed welfare to external manifestations of well-being and productivity.[29]

By contrast, neoclassical economics became increasingly agnostic about the efficacy of public redistribution of wealth to improve the general welfare. In the process the discipline may have preserved scientific rigor, but the price was a significant loss of voice in policy matters. Increasingly during the New Deal and after the government did not bother itself with technical welfare economics. As far as professional economists were concerned, most of the government's expert decision-makers were institutionalists, statisticians, or else experts in industrial economics or antitrust, where the debate about interpersonal utility comparisons had little consequence. Only with the revival of anti-Keynesian, neoclassical economic policy in the 1970s and 1980s did neoclassical welfare economics and statecraft once again merge.[30]

The Legal Realists and Institutional Economics

Few legal intellectuals have captured our attention as much as the American Legal Realists.[31] They were not the first advocates of an interdisciplinary approach to law that included the social sciences. Roscoe Pound, John H. Wigmore, and others had done that a generation earlier. Nevertheless, students of American legal history, jurisprudence, law, and politics have never tired of Legal Realism. The Legal Realists successfully created the image that their thought was a true watershed in American law.

Our understanding of Legal Realism has unfortunately been distorted by Karl Llewellyn's widely publicized 1931 *Harvard Law Review* "list" of twenty Realists, which both exaggerated the movement's novelty and understated its breadth.[32] The list reflected Llewellyn's technocratic perception of law and social science, but also academic politics. He was attempting to distance himself from Pound and his Harvard colleagues. Llewellyn excluded both Felix Frankfurter and James Landis, although both names did appear on other lists of Realists that Llewellyn periodically created and privately sent to Pound. He discussed Adolf A. Berle and Thurman Arnold sympathetically, but declined to put them on the list. Also absent were nonlawyer academics who wrote about law, such as John Dewey, the prominent American philosopher; or institutionalist economists, including Robert Hale, a Harvard- and Columbia-trained lawyer-economist on the Columbia Law faculty, or Walton Hamilton. Hamilton's name did appear on two longer lists that Llewellyn privately sent to Roscoe Pound.[33]

While the Legal Realists often cited economics in addition to the social sciences as a source of law, the economics they drew from was almost invariably institutionalism. They largely ignored the ordinalist revolution in economics that was occurring even as they wrote. The Legal Realists were as diverse as the institutionalists. Nevertheless, several features stand out. *First,* together with the institutionalists they believed that resources often move through the economy by nonmarket means, that markets are deeply flawed social instruments, and that they differ greatly from one another. This fact also serves to explain the Legal Realists' preference for legislation over common law rules. For them, the analogies between economic markets and the common law were strong. Just as the metaphor of the "invisible hand" of the market, the neutral umpire of the common law was an unhelpful and potentially destructive image.

Second, just as the institutionalists, the Legal Realists were suspicious of analytic abstractions and unifying themes. They wanted to know how the world works, and the world was not a tidy place. Today we contrast the institutionalists with economic neoclassicism by looking at the endless descriptive examples. Neoclassical economics drew abstract figures that measured such things as "demand," or "marginal cost." By contrast, the institutionalists tended to speak, often historically, about specific firms, particular markets, or nonmarket alternatives, often in great detail. Their approach was more descriptive and historical rather than analytic.

The comparison of legal classicists and Legal Realists is just as stark. Consider Christopher Columbus Langdell's classical casebook on contracts, whose method transformed legal education in the late nineteenth century. Langdell divided the entire world of contracts into three analytic categories: "mutual consent, "consideration," and "conditional contracts." The cases were grouped by abstract doctrine, and completely indifferent to the markets in which they arose. Together with a little equity and a few statutory provisions such as the Statute of Frauds, the common law was considered to be the source of all contract doctrine. In the preface to his first edition Langdell lamented the "great and rapidly increasing number of reported cases." In contrast, however, "the number of fundamental legal doctrines is much less than is commonly supposed." The purpose of legal study was to have these doctrines "classified and arranged that each should be found in its proper place, and nowhere else."[34] Using Langdell as a model, law professors in the classical tradition attempted to organize the law around a relatively small number of highly abstract categories.

The torts casebook written by Leon Green, the most prominent Legal Realist in that field, was breathtakingly different. Green did not organize his casebook by analytic legal conception, but rather by the arenas in which disputes arose. Green's first chapter was entitled "Threats, Insults, Blows, Attacks, Wounds, and Fights." The second was "Surgical Operations; Treatment, Control, etc. of Sick, Disabled and Irresponsible Persons." Chapter 8 was entitled "Traffic and Transportation."[35] As one reviewer protested, Justice Cardozo's highly influential *Palsgraf* decision on proximate cause, which was rapidly becoming a staple in law school torts classes, was not contained in a chapter on "causation" or "proximate cause." There was no such chapter. Rather it was included in a subsection of chapter 8 entitled "passenger transportation."[36] For the first time, Green's casebook contained a section on "Conduct with Reference to Women," covering rape, seduction, alienation of affection, and slander of a woman's reputation. Although Green's 1900-page book made the law look chaotic, that observation would not have troubled Green or most of the other Legal Realists. The law was much more chaotic than its formalizers believed, and much more specific to the setting, or market, in which legal disputes occurred.

The course that the law eventually took was largely between the extremes proposed by Langdell and Green. On the one hand, legal analysis never abandoned its need to classify and organize conceptually. Although Green's casebook was published in several editions through the 1970s, it never occupied more than a small niche in American law schools. On the other hand, in every area from the Uniform Commercial Code to the market-specific regulatory agencies of the New Deal, the legal system rejected the universality of the common law in favor of more industry-specific or situational approaches.

Third, just as was true of the institutionalists in economics, the Legal Realists took an eclectic approach to law that ran against the grain of early twentieth-century scientism. The term "formalism," which Roscoe Pound used to attack the Langdellian classical tradition, had a powerful and generally nonpejorative meaning within science. For example, economists who used mathematics spoke of "formal" proofs, referring to proofs whose conclusions were strictly drawn from premises that were accepted within that discipline. The ordinalist revolution in neoclassical economics was very largely a process of *removing* economics from the less-formal disciplines of history and social science, with mathematics surviving as its only external and highly formal methodology. In sharp contrast, the Progressives such as Roscoe Pound, institutionalists, and Legal Realists used "formalism" as a dirty word, referring to the exclusion of insights that could be gleaned from other disciplines. Intellectual historians in the Progressive tradition largely adopted this nomenclature. For example, Morton G. White subtitled his influential 1949 book on Progressive social thought "The Revolt against Formalism."[37]

Fourth, both the institutionalists and the Legal Realists tended to be methodological empiricists rather than positivists. These terms are not always kept as distinct as they should be. An empirical methodology involves the collection of data by a "neutral" observer, who then forms a theory to account for it. By contrast, a positivist methodology begins with an hypothesis and then seeks to test it through a rigorous process of attempted falsification. In practice the two approaches are seldom pure. Empiricists either consciously or unconsciously bias their data gathering, thus coloring the results. For positivists, testing requirements are often satisfied by data that are merely consistent with the hypothesis, rather than with harsh efforts to prove it false.[38]

But in one important sense positivism came to be seen as methodologically superior. In a world that offers up far too much information, simply collecting data and then formulating conclusions that fit seems like a naïve process. The fate of institutionalism in economics and Legal Realism in law were very similar in this respect. Both produced numerous studies filled with statistics, charts, and tables. But the data often seemed pointless. Institutionalist writing (Veblen aside) was dominated by exhausting historical and empirical studies of particular industries or firms. The problem was not new. Writing about early nineteenth-century American science, when empiricism was coming into vogue, George H. Daniels observed the scientific concern with a "Deluge of Facts."[39] By the early twentieth century the problem was far worse. Today when we think of institutionalist/Legal Realist classics such as Berle and Means's *Modern Corporation*, we remember its powerful thesis about separation of ownership and control. We have largely forgotten the endless pages of charts and tables that often cast little light on their analysis. The Legal Realists who engaged in social science research were generally obsessed with facts, constantly overwhelmed by their variety and number,[40] and they found it difficult to do much with theory. The theory, when it came, was generally about legal process rather than legal substance.[41] In this regard, the Legal Realists were indebted to Pound, who also wrote more about legal institutions and legal process than about substantive law. Further, the love affair with the social sciences eventually wore off. In the late 1940s Jerome Frank lamented that the social sciences produced no laws or rules in the scientific sense, but only mountains of inconclusive data.[42]

Pound and the Realists

The Legal Realists were influential largely because they advocated statutory reform and distrusted traditional courts and the common law. Their ideas were actuated in complex statutes such as the Uniform Commercial Code, and also in the rise of agency regulation during the New Deal. Roscoe Pound deserves credit for his own efforts toward law reform, and more particularly for opening American legal scholarship to the social sciences. Pound did his most provocative writing in the first two decades of the twentieth century.[43] He paid scant attention to the institutionalist economists, completely ignoring Veblen and mentioning Commons only a few times in the context of labor law. In general, he associated economics with Karl Marx or interest group analysis and said little more.[44] Pound was completely taken with the early Reform Darwinist sociologists, however, particularly Lester Frank Ward and Edward A. Ross. He once described Ross's *Social Psychology* as "worth many volumes of the conventional analytical and historical jurisprudence."[45]

His many contributions notwithstanding, the Legal Realists treated Pound as the relic of a bygone era. By the time Legal Realism came to the fore in 1930 Pound was nationally prominent and in the second decade of his deanship at Harvard Law School. He had also become more conservative and critical of Progressive legislation, particularly of regulatory agencies, which he saw as having poorly defined quasi-judicial powers but without traditional protections for property rights.[46] He hardened in these views over his later career. His 1938 *Report* for the American Bar Association on regulatory agencies was severely critical of "administrative absolutism," and he repeated that accusation in his 1942 book on administrative law.[47] His rambling five-volume *Jurisprudence*, published in 1959 but incorporating many previously published articles and addresses, preached at length that "judicial justice" is superior to either "legislative justice" or "executive justice." The latter term was directed at regulatory agencies.[48] For all of his call for more social science in law, he expected it to be applied mainly by the courts.

Karl Llewellyn's famous 1930 call for a "realistic" jurisprudence was contemptuous of Pound's court-centric approach, as well as his excessive abstraction and "indeterminacy."[49] Pound's intemperate response then set off one of the most acrimonious debates in the history of academic law.[50] Despite Pound's earlier arguments for greater use of social science, in 1931 he objected to a "faith in masses of figures as having significance in and of themselves" or the belief that "the sole valid approach is by way of psychology."[51] Pound's stridency placed him in sharp controversy not only with Llewellyn, but also with Jerome Frank, for Pound strongly disliked Frank's book, *Law and the Modern Mind* (1930).[52]

Legal Realist Hessel Yntema later described the debate as the "baptism" of the Legal Realist movement, which largely defined itself at Pound's expense.[53] In retrospect, both Llewellyn and Pound behaved badly. Llewellyn was insufficiently respectful of Pound's early advocacy of a more open form of legal thought. For his part, Pound responded like a reactionary and clearly got the worst of the fight.[54]

Pound's work paved the way for Legal Realism, however, and today we rightfully regard both as important contributors to the progressive liberal tradition in American law. There were also profound differences. Pound's early writing on sociological jurisprudence reflected the heady optimism of social science during its founding years. It seemed to offer a cure for everything that afflicted society, including a legal system that was both "mechanical" and "formalistic"—two terms that Pound used often. Pound's 1911–1912 articles on the "Scope and Purpose" of sociological jurisprudence were themselves a formalistic variation on Auguste Comte's evolutionary law of the three stages,[55] an idea that other law and social science scholars picked up a few years later.[56] In Comte's thought human scientific knowledge had gone through a religious and a metaphysical stage, and was currently in a "positive," or scientific, stage. In Pound's model law and sociology went through four stages: mechanical, biological, psychological, and finally a stage of unification.[57] The mechanical stage was heavily driven by Newton and physics. The biological stage was to be found in Herbert Spencer and Darwin. The psychological stage depended on the sociological study of group action, mainly in Lester Frank Ward and several German thinkers.

Interestingly, Pound's psychological stage contained no mention of Freud, who was already well known among Americans. Freud had lectured in the United States in 1909 at the invitation of G. Stanley Hall, one of America's most prominent psychologists.[58] Pound's published writings over his entire career contain barely a half dozen mentions of Freud, most of them dismissive. In a 1938 article summarizing fifty years of jurisprudence, he briefly linked Freud to economic determinism and Marxism.[59] In contrast to Pound, the Legal Realists relied heavily on Freud.

Perhaps the biggest divide between Pound and the Legal Realists resulted from developments in the social sciences themselves, reflecting a new emphasis on technique and realization that making the world over was not in easy reach. For example, Robert Park's and Ernest Burgess's *Introduction to the Science of Sociology* (1921) largely set the discipline on a new track, emphasizing more technical empirical research, a preoccupation with methodology, and greater humility about results.[60] Albert Paul Weiss's *A Theoretical Basis of Human Behavior* (1925)[61] offered a far more naturalistic conception of human motivation, as did John B. Watson's *Behaviorism* (1925).[62] Although Pound lived and wrote into the 1960s, he ignored these authors and clung to a conception of social science that he had learned more than a half century earlier.

The Legal Realists largely shared Roscoe Pound's belief that legal study should focus on the institutions that make and administer the law. Indeed, on this score they were deeply indebted to Pound.[63] Whether they spoke of sociology and social control,[64] anthropology,[65] Freud and the fact-finding power of courts,[66] anti-conceptualism,[67] limitations on legal process,[68] the role of the contract in modern society,[69] deceptive advertising,[70] or the coercive power of the laissez-faire State,[71] the one thing the Legal Realists shared was an abhorrence of abstractions, and in particular the powerful abstractions such as the "market," which played such a dominant role in neoclassical economics.

Legal Realism, Institutionalism, and the New Deal

The New Deal, which brought many Legal Realists to political power, is known for its distrust of the market and enthusiasm for economic regulation. The collective weight of Legal Realist scholarship furthered the views that people are not simply the rational maximizers that dominate the landscape of neoclassical economics. Further, judges have broad discretion guided by a number of factors, of which formal legal analysis is only one. As Jerome Frank put it, "law may vary with the personality of the judge who happens to pass upon any given case."[72] As a result, facts are more important than law, and presentation counts for everything. Herman Oliphant argued that judges always "respond to the stimulus of the facts in the concrete cases before them rather than to the stimulus of over-general and outworn abstractions in opinions and treatises."[73] Llewellyn emphasized the great malleability of judicial precedent and the indeterminate nature of established legal canons of statutory construction.[74]

Although Legal Realism is notable for its numerous interdisciplinary outreaches in psychology, sociology, anthropology, and political science, it never reached the same accommodation with mainstream economics. Most Legal Realists found the other social sciences more useful for the analysis of legal rules. Further, the economics that they turned to was by 1930 decidedly out of favor among economists themselves. Just as Karl Llewellyn was underscoring the Legal Realist belief that legal conceptions should be cut up into smaller pieces for purposes of analysis,[75] neoclassical economists were rejecting differentiated institutional approaches and developing generalized models to explain all parts of the economy. Increasingly after the 1940s economists developed more positivistic scientific methodologies, whereas most Legal Realists never got beyond a kind of eclectic, unfocused empiricism.[76]

This strongly institutionalist motif showed up even in commercial areas that expressly invoked the market, and where the influence of traditional economics seemed obvious. Prominent examples are Underhill Moore's study of commercial banking and William O. Douglas's studies of business bankruptcy.[77] Institutionalist economics fit very well into the highly fact-laden, differentiated framework that the Legal Realists favored, whereas much more abstract and theoretical neoclassicism did not. This is true even of Legal

Realist fellow traveler Robert L. Hale, who wrote mainly about law and economics but is often grouped today with the Legal Realists. Hale, a trained economist who had a joint appointment in law and economics at Columbia, dedicated his career to illustrating imperfections in the market that might justify government regulation.[78]

In 1919 Legal Realist Walton Hamilton had tried to defend jurisprudential use of institutionalist economics. In an essay entitled "The Institutional Approach to Economic Theory," Hamilton objected to the excessive abstraction in neoclassical economic theory. Only an institutional approach was sufficiently comprehensive to account for the workings of markets and the full range of social phenomena that the legal system encounters. Further, the neoclassical urge to make economics more scientific by separating it from any political agenda was wrongheaded. After all, much of the writing of the classical political economists had been intended as political tracts rather than contributions to pure theory. Hamilton also argued that economics needed to be grounded in a more acceptable theory of human behavior, which considered the source of preference rather than just the preferences themselves.[79]

Hamilton was correct that the classicists had always written with policy concerns in mind. But neoclassical economics became increasingly obsessed with turning economics into a science. Marginalism promised to substitute mathematics for policy as the unifier of economic theory. Hamilton's paper was met with a volley of criticism from economists. Lewis H. Haney thought Hamilton's institutionalism was nothing more than a throwback to the historical economics of the late nineteenth century, in which factual description dominated over theory. "Professor Hamilton will not be able to develop any laws or build a science, but... his proposal will merely lead to an ever changing description of an ever changing environment."[80]

Six years later Karl Llewellyn offered economists a quite different defense of institutionalism in "The Effect of Legal Institutions on Economics."[81] Law itself is a costly, scarce resource, Llewellyn argued. As a result, economics should guide decisions about how the resources given to law are to be allocated. "As governmental energy is put to blocking robbery, it is drawn off of prohibition." One value of economic institutionalism is to inform policymakers about the costs and benefits of the legal system in different areas. Llewellyn suggested that areas deserving economic study were the use of form contracts to reduce the overall costs of high-volume transactions, administrative agencies and rule-making as less costly substitutes for legislation, and arbitration as an alternative to litigation. If Walton Hamilton's institutionalism was a throwback to the work of Veblen, Llewellyn's idea that economists should study the costs of the legal system was prescient, anticipating law and economics work done in the 1960s and after.

Why did institutionalism survive in legal theory so long after mainstream economists had rejected it? At the atmospheric level, the most likely answer lay in the relative weights given to equity and efficiency. During this period suffrage was continuously expanding to the disempowered—first to women and later to racial minorities. The Progressive coalition of the turn of the century, the New Deal coalition of the 1930s and 1940s, and even the Johnson coalition of the early 1960s succeeded politically because their principal political concerns were "economic" in the distributional sense.

The Progressive coalition, just as many others, became a victim of its own success. The economic failures of the Depression and the burdens of war gave way to the relative comfort and security of the 1950s. The Progressive concern began to shift away from wealth and toward other indicia of lack of privilege, such as race, extremist political or social views, indigent criminal defendants, alienage, and eventually abortion, affectional preference, and disabilities. Although *Brown v. Board of Education* and the civil rights movement were essential steps to fairness, they came at a price: the new Progressive concerns tended to divide rather than unite the coalition that had supported it. This was certainly true of the expansion of rights for racial minorities and accused criminals. Since the 1960s politically active welfare liberals have increasingly played the game of recognizing new groups as disadvantaged while losing or risking the allegiance of older ones. Meanwhile, as Gordon Tullock observed in the 1980s, government entitlement programs began to move up the social scale until their principal beneficiaries became, not the poor, but the employed and successful middle class.[82]

But the Progressive theory of welfare left a powerful legacy. The use of objective welfare judgments serves to remind us that technical methodologies in law and the social sciences are used for a purpose, that they often have alternatives, and that the search for methodological elegance should never trump the search for workable solutions. Neoclassical welfare economics under the ordinalists became so lashed to the mathematical constraints of its conception of welfare that it lost the ability to consider whether the conception was correct or—more relevantly—whether it was useful for the purpose at hand.

7

Recasting the Common Law: The Management of Risk and Relationship

THE COMMON LAW viewed private legal conflicts largely as discrete events in the past. The law's purpose was to make injured parties whole. Cambridge, Massachusetts, lawyer Francis Hilliard, author of the first American treatise on tort law in 1859, wrote that tort obligations rest on the "original moral duty, enjoined upon every person, so to conduct himself or exercise his own rights as not to injure another."[1] Damages were intended to compensate for injuries. The common law permitted additional, punitive damages for egregious conduct as early as the eighteenth century, although not frequently.[2] Nineteenth-century American courts became increasingly hostile toward punitive damages, mainly out of opposition to their redistributive and inherently criminal or "public" character.[3]

Nevertheless, the courts did develop some forward-looking legal rules addressing incentives and expectations. One example is the relationship between law and economic growth, reflected in early nineteenth-century disputes over whether monopoly grants furthered or discouraged entrepreneurial risk-taking.[4] The law often incorporated an implicit utilitarianism. By the twentieth century the common law was becoming an ideological battleground between those who saw the law in terms of redress for past wrongs and those who viewed it as a way of managing risk and ongoing business or personal relationships.

This chapter is concerned with these developments in the law of contract, real property, and torts, although similar changes occurred in other areas. One that has been extensively covered is family law, including its doctrines of married women's property rights, spousal abuse, interspousal immunities, and divorce. Historically the common law saw marriage as a black box that enclosed a man and a woman when their union was legally recognized. To say that conflicts that occurred inside the box were outside of the law's reach is an exaggeration. Nevertheless, the extent to which the legal system avoided peering inside is quite extraordinary.[5]

Historically, a man and a woman became a single legal person at the time of marriage. The woman lost virtually all legal control of her property, including the use of property that she had brought into the marriage. This situation was partially corrected over the course of the nineteenth century in a series of married women's property acts that gradually gave women a modicum of control.[6] Women were typically denied the power to make their own contracts, and under doctrines of interspousal immunity, husbands and wives could not sue each other or testify against one another. When a man abused his wife, including beating her, some courts looked aside, at least if the beating consisted of only "moderate correction." Right after the Civil War the North Carolina Supreme Court concluded that "family government is recognized by law as being as complete in itself as the State government is in itself.... [W]e will not interfere with or attempt to control it, in favor of either husband or wife, unless in cases where permanent or malicious injury is inflicted or threatened."[7] Historically, divorce was unlawful except by special legislative act. Statutes permitting judicial divorce upon proof of misconduct did not come into existence until the mid-nineteenth century.

Modern "no fault" statutes that largely permit divorce upon request are creatures of the 1960s and after.[8] Marriage increasingly became a relationship whose internal disputes could be regulated by the courts, reflecting that the black box had been opened. More generally, the common law's focus on discrete events in the past that produced "finality" for the future gave way to institutions and relationships that required ongoing supervision. In the process these institutions became more "public," with greater amounts of control based on externally imposed standards.

The balance of this chapter considers briefly how contract and property law changed so as to become overseers of ongoing risk and relationship. It then examines tort law at greater length.

Risk Sharing and the Relational Business Contract

Traditionally an enforceable contract was a completed event in historical time. The courts required a sufficiently definite "agreement," and this entailed that important terms such as prices and quantities be specified. Forward-looking provisions such as options or renewal clauses were enforced only if they were sufficiently explicit as to price, quantity, nature of the property, and the period during which the right could be exercised.[9]

In the late nineteenth century marginalist economists began to focus heavily on market exchange. The formal theory was developed within British economics about the time Holmes began arguing that the purpose of law is to regulate incentives, measured by an objective test.[10] In the influential writings of British economists F.Y. Edgeworth and Alfred Marshall, business firms were regarded as rational maximizers of firm value. Edgeworth developed an early version of the "contract curve," representing graphically the area in which mutually profitable trades would be made, and a "hedonical calculus" which assumed that an actor always tries to maximize its position. Building on Edgeworth, Marshall focused his work on business firm behavior and industrial organization, assuming once again that firms are profit maximizers.[11] Subjective will counted for little, and objectively defined rational expectations became a device for filling in "gaps," or unexplained elements, in business firm behavior.

The largely concurrent revolution in legal theory began with rejection of a "will" or subjective "meeting of the minds" theory of contract, and its replacement by an external standard, particularly in the writings of Holmes and Williston.[12] Just as in economics, this movement reflected an increasing divergence between commercial and noncommercial agreements that would have a powerful impact on the law. Although human beings have idiosyncratic preferences that are often difficult to classify or articulate, profit-maximization was assumed to be common to all firms and could be assessed by an outside observer. As a result the interpretation of commercial contracts came to depend less on uncovering the unique subjective wills of the parties, and more on standard trade practices, or judgments about rational business behavior in specific settings.

The neoclassical revolution in contract law was in sharp distinction to the formal common law, which had tried to develop unified theories that applied to all types of agreements. For example, Langdell's important casebook on contracts more-or-less indiscriminately mixed commercial and noncommercial contracts and even leases.[13] By the time of the Uniform Commercial Code in the mid-twentieth century, gap-filling in commercial contracts was common, but with rules that could be quite specific to different areas of enterprise.

Twentieth-century economics also became increasingly focused on market irregularities and imperfections. Objective standards in contract produced a growing sense that markets differ from one another and that "coercion," as the

Legal Realists used that term, could be present even in voluntary exchanges. Contract law gradually developed a greater sensitivity to situational diversity, inequality of bargaining position, and duress.[14]

In addition to economic theory, changing technologies of production and distribution also produced important modifications in contract law. The development of dedicated distribution networks permitted local firms to share entrepreneurial risks with suppliers, leading to agreements of longer duration and with more complex and open-ended terms.[15] For example, Gilded Age courts became increasingly willing to enforce contracts requiring dealers to perform to the manufacturer's "satisfaction," provided that dissatisfaction was not asserted "unreasonably."[16] By the 1920s dealership agreements increasingly contained termination clauses permitting the manufacturer to end the arrangement upon reasonable notice if the dealer's performance was deemed inadequate.[17] As Chapter 12 develops, much of the franchisee protection legislation implemented after World War II was directed at dealer termination provisions.

The most significant revisions undermined the traditional rule that a contract was not "complete" unless it contained a specified price, a specified quantity, and a specified good or service. Under a "requirements" contract a buyer agrees to purchase all its needs of a certain good over a defined period, but the quantity is not specified. An "output" contract does the same, except for sellers. Prior to the Civil War commercial requirements and output contracts were relatively rare.[18] Enforcement became more common in the latter part of the nineteenth century, provided that the court found a serious obligation on each side. For example, the courts permitted canners to enforce obligations to purchase all the corn that a farmer would grow in the coming year, or railroads to purchase all their needs for railroad ties.[19] If the contract permitted a firm not to purchase or sell anything at all, enforcement was typically denied. This was also true of many contracts setting up new dealerships but without a specific purchase commitment. A 1902 federal decision held that an agreement to sell "in such amounts or quantities as the acceptor might want" was void. The buyer "is not bound to want, desire, or take any of the articles mentioned."[20] For established businesses, the courts often observed that by committing to purchase all of its needs the buyer was providing its own historical use as evidence of the amount, thus enabling the court to fill the gap. The amount can be estimated based on "the future exercise of the business in good faith."[21]

Modern franchising contemplates that the supplier, or franchisor, will enter agreements with new and often inexperienced firms as franchisees.

Several courts refused enforcement of open-ended agreements when a new business had no track record.[22] Increasingly, however, decisions became more tolerant of requirements contracts even with new businesses. One decision observed that open-ended requirements contracts were valuable because they provided a "sure and steady" market, enabling new firms to enter.[23] Another concluded that a requirements contract between a can-making company and cannery reduced risk by providing assurance for the cannery's fluctuating can needs, which depended on the size of the harvest.[24] The 1916 *American Can* antitrust case recognized the value of long-term requirements contracting in the canning industry: "its advantages from the standpoint of the consumer were so great that it speedily went into almost universal use."[25] Increasingly such contracts were used to establish long-term distribution arrangements between suppliers and manufacturers, or between manufacturers and dealers.[26]

Justice Cardozo's well-known *Lady Duff-Gordon* decision (1917) on good faith actually reflected legal changes that had occurred over the preceding generation.[27] Lady Lucy Duff-Gordon, a prominent Manhattan fashion designer, had signed a contract with Otis W. Wood, giving him the exclusive right for one year to market garments with her endorsement. Lady Lucy then violated the agreement by endorsing clothing made for others and with no profits to Wood. The court found a contract even though Wood had not promised to do a specified amount of anything. Implicit in the agreement was Wood's obligation "to use reasonable efforts to bring profits and revenues into existence," and this was supported by the history and purpose of Wood's business.

Karl Llewellyn, who later became lead drafter of the Uniform Commercial Code, observed in 1931 that greater tolerance of open-ended contracts was called for "wherever long-range buyer-seller relations come to seem more important than exact definition of the risks to be shifted by the particular dicker in terms of quantity, quality, or price."[28] The Uniform Commercial Code treated long-term contracts without specific quantity terms as enforceable, provided that the quantities were such as "máy occur in good faith," and that the parties would not demand a quantity that was "unreasonably disproportionate" to historical experience.[29] Writing in 1939, Llewellyn observed that simple single-shot business exchanges do not exist anywhere except in "lunatic asylums" and when "haunting a first year [law school] class-room." What businesses actually do "is a thing materially more complex but vastly more sensible." They "offer, together with the promising and as its consequence, a continuing expectation and sense of security—an assurance in result as well as in expression—which has immediate and continuing value in itself."[30]

Courts increasingly incorporated a forward-looking theory of rational expectations into the law of business contracts, enforcing long-term franchise agreements that permitted the price, quantity, and even the goods to be subsequently specified and altered by the franchisor.[31] Dealers received much more generalized obligations to use their "best efforts." In upholding a 1925 franchise agreement a federal court observed that although simple agreements that failed to specify price or quantity might be unenforceable, "sales agency" agreements were different. "Where territory is to be exploited and orders to be solicited by salesmen, the number and amount of such orders cannot, of course, be foretold."[32] A 1927 franchise agreement in the home heating market provided that "The dealer agrees to pursue aggressively the merchandising of the burners and to employ only such methods as shall be consonant with the good repute and meet with the approval of the company."[33] A 1930 Ford franchise agreement required the dealer to provide an annual "estimate of the number of Ford automobiles . . . which dealer will purchase from company during each month." For its part, the company agreed "in its discretion" to "give careful consideration to such estimates but expressly reserving the right to follow or depart from" them.[34]

As Grant Gilmore observed in the mid-1950s, "the triumph of the good faith purchaser has been one of the most dramatic episodes in our legal history."[35] The commercial contractual relationship gradually developed as an alternative to the vertically integrated firm—"vertical integration by contract," as Friedrich Kessler described it in 1957.[36] This development served two quite distinctive purposes. First, it permitted firms to share the risk of expansion by shifting some development costs to local dealers and resellers. Second, it served the desirable social and political function of maintaining small locally owned businesses as an important part of the economic landscape. The increasing availability of contractual franchising made outright manufacturer ownership of retail stores unnecessary.

A prominent characteristic of business contracts is risk sharing. Even the simplest agreement tends to benefit buyers if the price subsequently goes up and sellers if it goes down. Long-term franchise contracts controlled risk even further by permitting the parties to readjust both price and quantity. Dealers were willing to make more specific investments in a seller's product if they had an assurance of ongoing supply. They could also capitalize on the value of the supplier's established goodwill, trademarks, or other intellectual property rights. In these ways the emerging franchise agreement resembled a marriage more than the mere sale of goods.

This switch from essentially backward-looking classical theories of value to forward-looking theories based on reasonable expectations provided greater realism about how people conduct their economic affairs. Nevertheless, franchise contracts were hierarchical, typically reflecting or giving more power to manufacturers than to dealers. Many critics from the Progressive Era to this day have called for greater legal supervision for the benefit of smaller dealers. As Chapter 12 develops, these concerns were to become a focus of both federal and state law, including statutory initiatives to limit the power of large producers to control independent local dealers.

Risk, Relationship, and Property

Property ownership was traditionally established by the law of conveyancing, which saw transfers as discrete events in time. Among the most problematic transfers was the lease, which established an ongoing relationship between landlord and tenant and had some features of both contract and property. During most of the nineteenth century contractual management was minimal, however, consisting mainly of the landlord's duty to guarantee undisturbed possession, and the tenant's duty to pay the rent and avoid committing "waste," or destruction of the longer-term value of the land.[37]

In the late 1800s courts began to limit the landlord's right of self-help eviction and required at least modest judicial procedures.[38] By the 1930s some courts were viewing leases more like contracts and less like conveyances.[39] Residential and even a few commercial leases were seen as giving the parties ongoing rights and obligations that had to be managed by the courts.[40] In the 1940s the federal government inaugurated residential rent controls under the Emergency Price Control Act, intended to combat the effects of wartime inflation. Later it largely ceded that role to the states.[41] Rent control by state and local governments entailed that in many residential leases the rent, the quality of the premises, and even the duration of the lease were regulated by statute.[42]

In a related development, the emergence of an implied warranty of habitability for residential leases in the 1960s and 1970s tracked the greater use of implied warranties in the second Restatement of Contracts, as well as the idea that building code violations made leases substantively unlawful and gave tenants a right of action.[43] The second Restatement of Property, published in 1977, recognized the implied warranty of habitability for residential leases.[44]

Equally important changes occurred in the law of land use, which in the nineteenth century was minimally regulated by the common law of trespass and nuisance, plus a few statutes limiting harmful uses. The guiding common law principle was that a person had significant freedom to use his own land but could not injure the rights of neighbors. Nuisance law was concerned with "nontresspasory" harms, such as pollution, noise, or immoral conduct. The statutory law typically reached only egregiously harmful uses such as the operation of slaughterhouses, brick kilns, or brothels within city limits. During the Gilded Age even these statutory provisions came under attack. Treatise writer John F. Dillon condemned the use of municipal statutes that authorized "condemnation and destruction of that as a nuisance which, in its nature, situation, or use, is not such."[45]

The law of nuisance exposed a contradiction in classical property rights theory. Often one person could not use his own property without harming a neighbor's rights. Building a house completely on one's own property could block a neighbor's sunlight, but American courts generally refused to recognize the right as actionable, occasionally citing concerns about restricting economic development.[46] One owner's use of water might deprive another owner of reasonable access. Or an owner's noisy machine might annoy a neighbor or interfere with her business. Classical nuisance law largely refused to "balance" competing rights except in the very general sense of dismissing claims when the injury was minimal, or applying "per se" rules where the activity violated a statute. The result was an unhelpful list of specific nuisances that resisted generalization. Francis Hilliard found nuisance law to cover "an undefined injury." He concluded that a general statement of the law was impossible and contented himself with a lengthy enumeration of activities that courts had addressed. His meandering discussion gave no thought to whether or how conflicting interests should be balanced.[47] In *The Common Law* (1881), Holmes ignored the subject. In "Privilege, Malice, and Intent," published thirteen years later, he characterized the common law mandate to use one's land without injuring another as "nothing but a benevolent yearning."[48]

The early twentieth century saw remarkable developments in this area. Most important was the rise of "regulatory" land use planning statutes, and the eventual development of utilitarian nuisance rules that incorporated a marginalist conception of cost and benefit. Municipalities began to use legislation in areas where the common law had refused to go, even including space and building height requirements. In 1885 the City of New York commenced statutory regulation of building heights.[49] In *Welch v. Swasey* (1909), the Supreme Court upheld Boston's downtown height restriction, even though the common law of nuisance had never declared tall buildings to be unlawful.[50] The author of the opinion was Justice Rufus Peckham, who only four years earlier had written the *Lochner* decision finding that a statutory limitation on working hours violated the liberty of contract protected by the Fourteenth Amendment.[51]

Land use became a vehicle for greatly expanding the role of regulatory boards in local government. In its 1926 *Euclid* decision the Supreme Court narrowly upheld an elaborate land use ordinance that specified building uses, heights, and densities. Justice Sutherland, who three years before had found minimum wage provisions for women to be beyond the state's police power, believed that urban land was persistently subject to market failure, making regulation acceptable.[52]

The need for specialized regulatory boards became apparent two years after *Euclid*, when the Supreme Court decided *Nectow v. Cambridge*.[53] Saul Nectow owned an undeveloped narrow lot in Cambridge, Massachusetts, that was zoned exclusively residential. However, it was wedged among a Ford Motor assembly plant, a soap factory, and the tracks of the Boston & Albany Railroad. The land was worthless for any residential structure. The Supreme Court held that if the effect of zoning was to destroy a property's entire value, the statute must provide either administrative relief or entitle the owner to compensation for a taking of property. With that the "zoning board of adjustment," called by various names, came into existence as one of the most important regulatory agencies in local government. Its job was to grant individual property owners relief in the form of "variances" or "exceptions," in the process saving municipalities from constitutional challenges. In practice, it has frequently been criticized for favoritism and special interest capture.[54]

The proliferation of zoning statutes after 1930 set the stage for a debate over the efficacy of private agreements as opposed to government regulation of land use. The modern law and economics movement largely originated as a dispute about using market- driven common law rules rather than regulation to control harmful land uses. The first Restatement of Torts (1939) expressly incorporated a utility balancing test into its doctrine of nuisance, declaring that nontrespassory conduct that harms another's land is unlawful "unless the utility of the actor's conduct outweighs the gravity of the harm."[55]

Increasingly the Supreme Court concerned itself with whether a land use provision was a lawful "regulation" or an unlawful "taking" of property without compensation. The Court tended to find a mere "regulation" when the provision did not require forced entry into someone's property or completely destroy its value, even though the property was worth much less as a result.[56] By contrast, "trespassory" provisions that actually imposed unwanted people or installations on private property or completely destroyed its value were routinely condemned.[57] The common law of nuisance no longer provided a meaningful constraint on regulatory power.

Finally was the creation of legal rules regulating residential housing discrimination. In 1948 the Supreme Court decided *Shelley v. Kraemer*, discussed in Chapter 3, which held that real estate covenants excluding African Americans or Asians were unenforceable, a conclusion that the Supreme Court had already reached on non-racial grounds for legislation in 1917.[58] In 1968 the federal Fair Housing Act both codified and broadened the right to nondiscrimination in the provision of housing, and in subsequent amendments expanded its protections to include gender, age, and family status.[59]

Tort Law: From Redress to Risk Management

The rise of modern technologies of production, transportation, and medicine produced many social benefits, but they also increased the danger of death or injury to person or property. The result was an unprecedented expansion of tort lawsuits in the decades around the turn of the twentieth century. In 1916 New York lawyer Arthur Ballantine complained that "more numerous than any other single class of cases in most city courts are suits against railroad and street railway corporations for damages on account of personal injuries." They often took up as much as half of the jury trial docket.[60] The development of modern tort law also provided the stage for important interest group clashes. Some interests, such as the railroads, were typically defendants who profited from reduced liability. For others, such as automobile drivers and passengers, or lawsuits between manufacturers, the effects were more random. Above all, these had an interest in reducing the number and cost of accidents as well as the costs of administering the tort and payment system.

Prior to the Civil War tort theory was very poorly developed. Holmes concluded in 1874 that torts is "not a proper subject for a law book." The field was little more than a collection of common law writs of trespass, trespass on the case for "indirect" wrongs, and actions of trover for the wrongful taking of property.[61] Negligence theory aspired to provide coherence. Thomas G. Shearman and Amasa A. Redfield's important treatise on negligence was published in 1869, and Holmes's unifying essays on tort theory came a little later.[62] As Chapter 2 develops, Holmes's theory of torts and crimes was pure marginalism: the law is not concerned with mental states but rather with regulation of conduct, and penalties should be adjusted to provide incentives to act appropriately.

Holmes's principal objection to strict liability was that in his mind it divorced liability from fault and thus failed to provide appropriate incentives. It could not be justified within a utilitarian framework that metered potentially dangerous conduct by applying differential penalties. The revival of strict liability in products cases several decades later came about as many came to believe that Holmes was incorrect.

The rise of negligence-based theories of tort liability were a tour de force in the development of the common law, but it came with a price. Proof of negligence and causation were fact intensive and costly, depending on a jury's ability to reconstruct the past and produce the objectively reasonable standard of care. That may not have been terribly difficult when the act was riding a speeding horse through a dark street. Evidence of negligence was often elusive in industrial accident cases, however. Machine production was complex, and many events leading to accidents were either out of view or impossible to reconstruct after the fact.

Beginning in the late nineteenth century and accelerating in the twentieth, tort law became recast as addressing problems of risk management rather than compensation for previous wrongs. This happened through a number of developments. *First* was the rise of negligence and the gradual development of a concept of objective foreseeability as a device for determining responsibility.[63] This set of concerns was formalized in the 1920s and woven into the definition of negligence in the first Restatement of Torts in the 1930s. *Second* was the gradual emergence of risk-based conceptions of causation. Closely related were developments in causation doctrine's much maligned stepsibling, "proximate cause," which had developed as a kind of sorting device for assigning legal liability to some causes but not others. *Third*, the adoption of negligence was followed by a realization that for many accidents related to industry and technology the administrative costs and uncertainties of a negligence rule were very high. The initial legal response was the rapid growth of the res ipsa doctrine, discussed below, followed by the rise of strict liability for dangerous and defective products in the 1940s and after.

The objective "reasonable person" standard for negligence originated prior to Holmes's influential writings in the 1870s and 1880s. In his 1859 treatise on torts Francis Hilliard wrote that "Negligence is said to consist in the omitting to do something that a reasonable man would do, or the doing something that a reasonable man would not do."[64] Sherman and Redfield echoed these words in their 1869 treatise.[65] An 1856 Illinois decision spoke of "reasonable" and "practicable vigilance."[66] Already in 1845 the Supreme Judicial Court of Massachusetts indicated that a passenger who jumped off a moving train car when its axle broke was not guilty of contributory negligence if jumping was an act of "reasonable precaution" under the circumstances.[67] Even earlier, the 1837 British decision in *Vaughn v. Menlove* established that negligence could not be measured by assessing an actor's state of mind.[68]

The Passing of Objective Causation

All types of private law require proof that the defendant "caused" the plaintiff's injury. The law of causation was divided into two parts: cause-in-fact, sometimes known as "but for" causation, and "proximate" cause, which is often called "legal" cause. In classical legal doctrine questions about conduct and the appropriate liability standard were sharply distinguished from questions about causation or proximate cause. As tort law became recast as a problem in risk management, however, the boundary between conduct and causation became obscured. The formal statement of the negligence test came to consider whether the defendant took reasonable—that is "cost justified"—precautions. Analysis of cost justification required considering both the amount of any expected harm and the probability that it would occur. At the same time, philosophical and actuarial conceptions of causation increasingly linked causation to probability. Legal Realist Leon Green noted the merger in 1923, when he argued that negligence and proximate cause were being decided by the same test.[69] Increasingly the standard for conduct became foreseeability of harm, which could be measured by the tools of probability, but causation also came to be measured by considering whether the defendant's conduct foreseeably increased the probability of an accident.

The demise of the "classical" theory of causation is one of the most important shifts in early twentieth-century tort law. Many of the cases involved railroads, whose lawyers struggled ingeniously to use the risk and uncertainty accompanying railroad technology to their advantage. Their academic champion was treatise writer Francis Wharton, an Episcopal priest, lawyer, and prolific author who defended a strict physical conception of causation, arguing that each harm results from a single "proximate" legal cause. This classical theory was countered by a progressive critique, which argued for a theory of "multiple" causation driven by policy concerns over management of risk, particularly where technology made the prediction of specific outcomes difficult.[70]

Within classical tort theory causation was regarded as presenting a question of physical science, considering whether the injury would have occurred "but for" the defendant's act or omission. A well-known late example is the

Second Circuit's 1920 decision in *New York Central R.R. v. Grimstad.* The plaintiff's husband, a barge captain, drowned after falling overboard in the presence of his wife. She alleged that the railroad which operated the barge was negligent because the barrage was not equipped with life buoys. Assuming negligence, the court nevertheless reversed the lower court's judgment for the plaintiff. "[T]here is nothing whatever to show that... if there had been a life buoy on board, the decedent's wife would have got it on time... or that, if she had, that she would have thrown it so that her husband could have seized it."[71] The rationale of *Grimstad* was the backward-looking logic that the plaintiff must be able to provide details showing that if the negligence had not occurred neither would the loss. Completely absent was any forward-looking concern that tort law should create incentives to take reasonable precautions.

"Proximate" cause became relevant only after causation had either been established or was assumed. The plaintiff had to show not only that the defendant caused the harm but that the conduct was sufficiently "proximate" so as to place it within the range of legal liability. As thus formulated, the doctrine was inconsistent with any theory that tort law should be used to manage risks. Rather it was about "remoteness" in the abstract. Juries typically received an instruction on proximate cause such as this one from an 1891 Colorado railroad case:

> In order for you to find for the plaintiff, you must find that the defendant's act was a "proximate cause" of the plaintiff's injuries. " 'Proximate cause" means the efficient cause, which in a natural and continuous sequence, unbroken by any new and independent cause, produced the event, and without which that event would not have occurred. A proximate cause must be that which immediately precedes and produces the effect, as distinguished from the remote, mediate or predisposing cause. It is thus the nearest, the immediate, the direct cause; the efficient cause; the cause that sets another or other causes in operation, or dominant cause.[72]

What is striking is not only that the instruction was so laden with essentially medieval classifications, but also the frequency with which courts took the issue away from the jury by deciding proximate cause as a matter of law. A good example is the 1898 decision of Massachusetts's highest court in *Stone v. Boston & Albany Railroad*.[73] On a September day in 1893 the railroad's loading terminal had been piled high with fuel oil stored in wooden barrels for winter heating demands. The railroad had been careless and several of the barrels had cracked, causing oil to drip under the wooden platform. A traveling salesman named Casserly was loading rubber boots into a boxcar when he tripped, spilling glowing ash from his pipe. The barrels were immediately engulfed in flames. As they exploded their staves shot into the air, and several landed in Stone's lumberyard across the tracks, completely destroying it. Stone lost his negligence case against the railroad, however, because, whether or not the dripping oil was the result of negligence, "The law will not look back from the injurious consequences beyond the last sufficient cause." The court found it too clear to be given to the jury that the last sufficient cause was Casserly's pipe, not the oil-soaked platform. Justice Holmes, who was on the bench at the time, agreed in silence.[74]

Looking backward, one can see that Casserly's act was more "proximate" in time to the accident than the negligently stored oil, which was already there. By contrast, looking forward from prior to the accident the dripping oil was an obvious and manageable hazard, but Casserly or any particular event that might have ignited it is nowhere in view. That is, the *Stone* analysis was bereft of any notion that the purpose of tort law is to control risks by penalizing avoidable conduct likely to cause harm.

Prior to the 1880s proximate cause had been a reasonably modest technical requirement that denied liability when an unlikely chain of events linked the defendant's conduct and the plaintiff's loss. For example, an 1863 New York decision used proximate cause language to deny liability when a railroad's train ran across fire hoses that were laid across the tracks, cutting them and preventing the fire department from saving the plaintiff's house.[75] But assertions of the doctrine grew dramatically in the last two decades of the century, mainly in railroad cases. The development can be traced through the consecutive editions of Shearman and Redfield's treatise on negligence. Both authors had been railroad lawyers, Redfield as general counsel for the Erie Railroad. When the *Treatise* was published in 1869 the treatment of proximate cause was less than one page long and cited four decisions.[76] The second and third editions were published in 1870 and 1880 and contained a single page on proximate cause. The 1888 fourth edition showed substantially greater treatment, and by the fifth edition in 1898 proximate cause had emerged as an entire lengthy chapter. In 1913 the editors of the sixth edition of Shearman and Redfield, by now both deceased, wrote that proximate cause had become "the most important and difficult part of the general definition of a right of action upon negligence." Thomas M. Cooley's contemporaneous treatise on torts shows the same development.[77]

By the 1910s two rather well-developed views about proximate cause divided the legal profession. Generally, railroad lawyers and other defense attorneys argued with considerable success that plaintiffs be required to show not only that the defendant "caused" the harm, but also—using Aristotelian language—that its action was an "efficient" cause and not merely a "condition" under which the harm had occurred.[78] This in turn required proof that the cause led to the harm "directly" and not "indirectly," that this path was through a "natural and continuous sequence" of events, and that no "intervening cause" or "superseding cause" had broken this sequence.

The most prominent theoretician of this position was Harvard Law professor Joseph H. Beale. His views became institutionalized in American conflict of laws doctrine when the first Restatement on Conflicts (1934) used proximate cause analysis to identify the state in which a legal right became "vested." Under that theory a single event determined which state could apply its law to a multistate dispute.[79] With great verbal ease, Beale could distinguish between "active" and "passive" causality, between "direct" and "indirect" consequences, and between "causes" and "conditions." His 1920 *Harvard Law Review* article on the subject resembles Alice's conversations in Wonderland:

> The whole problem may therefore be stated thus: when is one responsible for the operation (a) of an active force which he has created; (b) of an active force which acts upon a passive force which he created, or upon a passive force which he was legally bound to change? Each time one or more active causes operate on a condition to create a new condition, a new causal step is taken, ending with the given result. This result is the direct result of the active force or forces which last acted upon the immediately precedent condition, and is the indirect result of the earlier acting forces. The active force which brings about the result without the intervention—the subsequent coming into action—of any force is a direct cause of the result. All other forces are indirect. Every condition of what might be called the set stage on which the last active force acted is a precedent force; and of course no precedent force can operate to make a subsequent force remote.

Beale specifically rejected any suggestion that proximate cause be understood in relation to policy. There is no "pragmatic sanction for the law of proximate cause."[80]

The second theory of causation owed its modern origins largely to John Stuart Mill, whose *System of Logic* (1843) had become a popular American textbook. Mill attacked the Aristotelian distinction between "causes" and "conditions," which generally tried to identify a single relevant cause for an event.[81] Rather, cause refers to a set of antecedents, the whole of which are sufficient to bring about a particular result, and any one of which may have prevented it from occurring. The implication was that one could prevent an undesirable result by eliminating one of many alternative causes. Further causes could be ranked by the degree to which they increased the probability that a result would occur, or harm could be avoided by elimination or management of that cause. In sum, causation could be tied to a theory of probability and deterrence.

Mill's analysis provoked a sharp response from Francis Wharton. The theory of multiple causation, he wrote in 1874, would lead to "practical communism" in tort theory. " 'Here is a capitalist among these antecedents," some would think; "he shall be forced to pay."[82] In Wharton's mind the theory of multiple causation would turn the law into a political tool for the redistribution of wealth. "Reckless impecuniosity [would be] passed over when we are seeking for a responsible cause." Rather, plaintiffs would look back among alternative antecedents until they "hit…upon wealth without immediate friends."[83] Wharton decided that a "natural sequence" rule was far better than any manipulable foreseeability test. Only by looking for natural sequences of events could courts develop a scientific theory of proximate cause that would avoid unjustified legal manipulation of results.

Mill's more probabilistic approach resonated with some of the American pragmatist philosophers, however, and also with legal writers such as Nicholas St. John Green and Holmes. Both men were members of Boston's Metaphysical Club, a group of philosophers, social scientists, and legal academics that met to discuss scientific issues in the 1870s.[84] The group included Charles Sanders Peirce and William James, names most closely associated with philosophical Pragmatism, and James's brother Henry James, the novelist. The name "metaphysical" was intended to be ironic. Although the group's purpose was discussion of philosophical issues, the philosophy of the day was heavily concerned with eliminating metaphysics from scientific discourse. Pragmatism insisted that meaning be linked to measurable consequences.[85] This required a more scientifically rigorous conception of causation.

Peirce was the most influential philosopher of scientific method in the United States in the nineteenth century. He was also a marginalist, although his work was directed toward the process of scientific discovery rather than economics. Peirce corresponded with the British marginalist William Stanley Jevons, and visited him in England on at least one occasion.[86] In an 1875 essay he applied marginalist theory to scientific inquiry before marginalism had made its way into American economics.[87] Peirce observed that in the early period of any scientific discipline the cost of research tends to be low and the payoff high. As the discipline progresses, however, the incremental rate of progress diminishes and the investment in ever more specialized research becomes larger. He used calculus to try to determine the point at which further research was no longer cost justified. Peirce's own work on the theory of scientific inquiry later influenced the more marginalist of the institutionalist economists.[88]

Much of Peirce's work was addressed to questions of verification and language. Most of our misperceptions about the world result from our failure to use descriptive language carefully. Suppose we were debating whether a certain substance is "hard." What would we be disputing? We would have to mean that it responds in a certain way in certain situations. For example, something is hard when it cannot be scratched by many other substances. However, if that is our test for hardness, then our *entire* understanding of "hard" lies in the performance of that test. But suppose that this particular substance exists only in some remote place or only in Greek mythology. Then our debate is meaningless. "There is absolutely no difference between a hard thing and a soft thing so long as they are not brought to the test."[89]

The legal idea of "proximate" cause disturbed Peirce because it seemed completely untestable. "The idea of making the payment of considerable damages dependent upon a term of Aristotelian logic is most shocking," Peirce wrote at the turn of the century. "[T]here is nothing in the whole scholastic logic more justly an object of derision for any modern thinker than its weak confusion or thought in its doctrine of causes; nor in the whole doctrine is there any more manifest absurdity than the distinction between a proximate and a remote cause."[90] Speaking of a case in which a neighbor's cattle broke through the fence and destroyed the plaintiff's crop, Peirce noted that the judge found liability because the cattle owner's negligence was the "proximate cause" of the neighbor's injury. However, "the real reason why the judge awards damages... is that to allow a private person to undertake a business humanly sure in the long run to injure his neighbors... and then to allow him to pocket all the profits, and make his neighbors pay for incidental losses, would be to bring himself and his court into public contempt."[91]

The law must cut off liability somewhere. Peirce proposed foreseeability as a test. The breadth of legal liability would depend on human experience of how events occur.[92] Analyzed in Peirce's terms, however, proximate cause was not a theory about "cause" at all, but rather about the management of foreseeable harm.

American Pragmatism influenced an initially dissenting tradition of jurists to develop a view of causation based on management of foreseeable risks. Nicholas St. John Green was a Boston lawyer who lectured at the Harvard Law School and occasionally taught philosophy and political economy in Harvard College. He was also a friend of Peirce and Holmes and another founding member of the Metaphysical Club. Peirce later referred to him as "the Grandfather of Pragmatism."[93] Every assertion that "means anything," Green said in words echoing the Logical Positivism of a later generation, "indicates some sensible fact on the existence of which its truth depends."[94]

In 1870 Green started lecturing on torts at Harvard. After some conflict with Harvard's increasing formalism under Dean Langdell, he left in 1873 to become Dean at Boston University's law school. He remained there until his premature death in 1876. During his Harvard period Green wrote a formative essay entitled "Proximate and Remote Cause," where he critiqued the "natural sequence" test for proximate cause as a relic of medieval philosophy. Green relied on Mill's *Logic* and its theory of multiple causation. To every event there is "never a single antecedent, but always a set of antecedents taken together." We learn useful things about causation only when we investigate cause "for a practical purpose."

For example, when a man drowns many factors "cause" his death—"there must have been a man, and there must have been water." However, these causes have little policy significance. Rather,

> What one of the various circumstances necessary to the death we shall single out as the cause, to the neglect of the other circumstances, depends upon the question for what purpose we are investigating the death.... The man may have committed suicide; we say he himself was the cause of his death. He may have been pushed into the water by another; we say that other person was the cause. The drowned man may have been blind, and have fallen in while his attendant was wrongfully absent; we say the negligence of his attendant was the cause.... A medical man may say that the cause of his death was suffocation by water entering the lungs. A comparative anatomist may say that the cause of his death was the fact that he had lungs instead of gills like a fish. The illustration might be carried to an indefinite extent. From every point of view from which we look at the facts, a new cause appears.

One's purpose determines the relevant cause. If the purpose is to prevent further drownings in the same place we may decide that the drowning was "caused" by dangerous currents, and put up a "no swimming" sign. The problem of legal analysis of causation is that too often "philosophy and metaphysics are... brought into a discussion to which they do not belong." For Green,

> The phrase "chain of causation" which is a phrase in frequent use when this maxim is under discussion, embodies a dangerous metaphor. It raises in the mind an idea of one determinate cause, followed by another determinate cause, created by the first, and that followed by a third, created by the second, and so on, one succeeding another till the effect is reached.... There is nothing in nature which corresponds to this. Such an idea is a pure fabrication of the mind."[95]

Following after Nicholas Green, Holmes practically eliminated the idea of proximate cause from his own tort theory. For Holmes the purpose of tort law was to make some kinds of conduct costly, thus reducing people's incentive to engage in it. He argued that courts trace acts to their causes in such a way as to increase safety, while protecting the actor from liability for consequences that she could not control. To Holmes as to Green the only sensible empirical rule was foreseeability. "If the intervening events are of such a kind that no foresight could have been expected to look out for them, the defendant is not to blame for having failed to do so," he wrote in *The Common Law*. With that test Holmes largely dispensed with proximate cause.[96]

Holmes did not speak of foresight in terms of mathematical probabilities, and of course even tort law today generally does not. Computing probabilities is frequently impossible, particularly for the multi-causal accidents that have been the focus of proximate cause analysis. University of Pennsylvania law professor Francis Bohlen, who later became a Reporter for the Restatement of Torts, tried to create a more useful mechanism for defining the scope of liability for negligence. The notion of foreseeability is useful, he wrote in 1901, not because people can predict specific consequences, but because they can foresee who is in a "zone of danger." Bohlen recast the notion of foreseeability as a legal duty. A person has a duty to whomever might foreseeably be injured by his act. Although the railroad might not be able to predict the particular incident that would set fire to its dock, it could certainly foresee the danger that the dripping oil posed.[97]

Around the turn of the century a few courts began to recognize the theory of multiple causation by speaking about legal cause as a "substantial factor" or "material factor" in bringing about an undesirable result.[98] In 1912 Harvard Law professor Jeremiah Smith published a defense of this incipient test, which was incorporated into the Restatement of Torts in 1934. Completely avoiding the term "proximate cause," as all editions of the Restatement have, the provision declared that negligent conduct is a legal cause if the "conduct is a substantial factor in bringing about the harm."[99] This Restatement approach represented complete rejection of Wharton's position and adoption of Mill's theory of multiple causation.

Leon Green agreed that the language of proximate cause frequently hid or frustrated important social policies. Green was a plaintiff's tort lawyer who joined the University of Texas Law School faculty in 1915 and later became Dean of Northwestern Law School. The case that provoked Green's writing on proximate cause was *Seale v. Gulf, Colorado & Santa Fe Railroad* (1889). The railroad had neglected to remove dried brush from its right of way and then emitted sparks from one of its passing engines—both acts that were conceded to be negligent. The plaintiff's fifteen-year-old daughter was engulfed by the flames when she attempted to put the fire out to save her family's house. In dismissing the complaint the Texas Supreme Court wrote that "it is clear that but for the attempt of the deceased to put out the fire, her death would not have ensued. This act of hers was the new agency, which, supervening upon the original wrongful act of the appellee [the railroad], brought about the misfortune."[100] Green protested that the standard for negligence is guided by what the "ordinary prudent person" under the circumstances "should have foreseen as the probable consequence of his conduct." Many courts, including *Seale,* have found the defendant's acts to be "negligent" but then have gone on to find a lack of proximate cause because the consequences were not "foreseeable." They have applied the same test twice and have come to two different conclusions.[101]

The "phraseology of causation," Green wrote in 1930, lends itself " 'to learned dissertation about any situation which the judges do not understand." It is the last escape for judges who "have made up their minds" but "do not know how... to articulate their conclusions on a rational basis."[102] Green relied on an important book published in 1923 by British semanticists Charles K. Ogden and Ivor A. Richards, *The Meaning of Meaning*, which in turn had borrowed from Charles Sander Peirce. Ogden was a Logical Positivist, an editor of Bentham, and English translator of some of Ludwig Wittgenstein's early work. His book with Richards, which strongly influenced Legal Realist Jerome Frank,[103] combatted the idea that words correspond to things. The great strength of language lies in its abstraction—that one symbol can represent thousands of individual objects in the real world. However, therein lies language's greatest danger, for the single symbol suggests a uniformity that nature seldom reveals. Ogden and Richards took a generally positivistic position that was rapidly beginning to dominate the social sciences. "Every great advance in physics has been at the expense of some generally accepted piece of metaphysical explanation," they wrote. The implication for the law was clear. It must also abandon metaphysics and appropriate a more empirical language. "Word ritual under one guise or another has always been one of the primary methods of law administration," Leon Green concluded in 1928, citing *The Meaning of Meaning*, "but the first requisite of intellectual freedom, as much so in the study of the science of law as elsewhere, is a wholesome fear of words."[104]

The doctrine of proximate cause gradually became recast as relating to objective foreseeability and deterrence of harm, querying whether it was foreseeable that conduct would have produced harm of the type that actually occurred. Justice Cardozo's influential 1928 *Palsgraf* decison came to be identified with the new approach. Mrs. Palsgraf was standing on the far side of the platform of the Long Island Railroad Station. Several yards away a man carrying a paper sack was running to board a departing train. The conductor reached down to assist, an act that was probably negligent given the obvious risk. But the "obvious" risk is not what materialized. The man's sack did not contain his peanut butter sandwich, but rather fireworks, which exploded when he dropped it. The force of the explosion terrified people on the platform, who began stampeding and knocked over a set of scales next to Mrs. Palsgraf. Her injuries were mainly mental distress. Justice Cardozo's opinion denied liability, concluding that even if the railroad were negligent, its negligence was not "a wrong in its relation to the plaintiff," because "nothing in the situation gave notice that the falling package had in it the potency of peril to persons thus removed."[105]

As noted earlier, the three editions of the Restatement on Torts never use the term "proximate cause." The authors of the Third Restatement observed that although the term "has been in widespread use in judicial opinions," it "is an especially poor one to describe the idea to which it is connected." Rather, the Restatements employed the term "legal cause" to include both factual cause and scope of liability. However, as the authors acknowledged in 2011, the success of the Restatement's attempt to move judges from "proximate cause" and toward "legal cause" was in fact "quite limited."[106] A search of published negligence decisions in a single recent year, 2010, showed 410 that included discussions of "proximate cause."

Technology, Risk Management, and Accident Law

The typical mid-nineteenth century tort defendant was an individual, sometimes acting in the course of business although often not. The rise of the railroads and later the increase in factory production dramatically changed that.[107] By 1900 the American economy was far more industrialized and less agrarian. More production and transportation involved machinery. Further, distribution systems became more complex, with less purely internal production and more sharing through long-term contractual arrangements.

These changes had a profound influence on the tort system. *First*, along with the increase in machinery came more accidents, dramatically increasing the ratio of unintentional torts to intentional ones such as battery or assault. *Second*, accidents more commonly involved either shared fault or else ambiguity about which of many actors was to blame. *Third*, in a growing number of cases specific proof of a negligent act or causation became difficult to impossible. Classical tort law's distinct requirements of provable negligence and causation seemed unsatisfactory to address the twin tasks of making American society safer and compensating victims. The focus shifted to the identification of reasonable risks and their management. This entailed that losses from accidents be considered ex ante as opposed to ex post. As a result it was less important to identify precisely who was at fault or the nature of the negligent act, and more important to ensure that the similarly placed people received correct incentives in the future.

Tort law was also affected by two developments in the theory of risk management. The first was a greatly refined conception of risk that was inherent in marginal analysis. Classical political economists had a poor conception of risk because all of the important values were from the past. As soon as value is based on expected utility, however, risk enters the calculus. Further, risk shows up in numerous ways, including business investment, potentially dangerous activities, and even inactivity. Holmes, an important although mathematically nontechnical marginalist, understood this and made foresight, or anticipation of harm, an important element of his tort theory. In 1921 Frank H. Knight, an economist at the University of Chicago, published a path-breaking book entitled *Risk, Uncertainty, and Profit*, concerned with entrepreneurial risks.[108] Knight distinguished between "risk" and "uncertainty." A risk is a situation where a particular outcome is unknown but it can be calculated as a probability. For example, flipping a true coin produces a 50 percent chance of getting heads. Where probabilities can be estimated risk plays a major role in economic decision-making. By contrast, "uncertainty" deals with random future events whose probability cannot be estimated.[109]

One important problem for legal policy arises when the relevant risk includes harm to *others*. In such cases an actor who is not required to pay for those harms will take too much risk. For example, if a rancher is not held accountable when his cattle stray onto a neighbor's cornfield, the rancher will not have sufficient incentive to maintain sturdy fences.

The second development was the rise of actuarial science and insurance-based conceptions of risk. Determining policy coverage and rate making for casualty and liability insurance required risk to be monetized, which in turn required that it be assessed empirically and tied to specific behaviors. The seminal marginalist work on the subject was Allan H. Willett's *Economic Theory of Risk and Insurance* (1901), which was Willett's doctoral dissertation in political science at Columbia University.[110] Willett anticipated Knight's distinction between risk and uncertainty, and Knight relied on his work. But unlike Knight, Willett believed it both possible and actuarially necessary to place a probability on uncertainty as well.[111] That is, insurance had to assign a value even to unknowable risks, although the premium might be higher. The Casualty Actuarial Society was created in 1914 as the professional organization of insurance actuaries, devoted to problems of assessing the risk, size, and expected costs of accidents. In 1929, early in his academic career, Legal Realist and later Supreme Court justice William O. Douglas began writing about actuarial science and the shared liability of multiple actors.[112]

Estimating Forseeable Harm

Technologies such as railroads or mechanized manufacturing processes dramatically increased the number of accidents. The only way to eliminate railroad accidents altogether would be to eliminate railroads—a price that society was unwilling to pay. As Justice Holmes observed in 1929, "[m]any modern improvements must be expected to take their toll of life. When a railroad is built experience teaches that it is pretty certain to kill some people before it has lasted long."[113]

The question was how to reduce predicted harm. Because of its indifference to costs, Holmes's idea that a prudent person avoids foreseeable harms did not provide a precise calculus for determining the tolerable number of accidents. For example, limiting railroads to five mph would reduce the foreseeable number and severity of accidents. But a global five mph rule would make the railroads much less valuable. Foreseeability had to be "metered" in a way that would make it useful for determining the balance of risk and utility that society reasonably expects. In 1915 Yale professor Henry T. Terry attempted to put a finer point on Holmes's test by requiring judges to consider the "magnitude" of the risk—"A risk is more likely to be unreasonable the greater it is."[114] A decade later Harvard Law School professor Warren Seavey, later a Reporter for the first Restatement of Torts, defined foreseeability in terms of "the mathematical chance of injury,... the seriousness of the injury anticipated, the value of the interest subjected to injury, the value of the actor's interest being protected by his conduct, the chance of protecting his interests by other means, and all other relevant factors."[115] Seavey acknowledged that determining these values could be very difficult if they involved "moral" qualities. However, to the extent the query involved "standardized elements" of risk it would be possible to come up with a purely mathematical test for negligence.

Terry's and Seavey's attempts to add measurable content to foreseeability were incorporated into the Restatement of Torts (1934) by Francis Bohlen, its first reporter. The Restatement defined "negligence" as the taking of an unreasonable risk, and "unreasonableness" in terms of the "Magnitude of Risk and Utility of the Conduct," stating:

> (1) Where an act is one which a reasonable man would recognize as involving risk of harm to another, the risk is unreasonable and the act is negligent if the risk is of such magnitude as to outweigh what the law regards as the utility of the act or of the particular manner in which it is done.[116.]

This "risk-utility" balancing test—a nontechnical form of cost-benefit analysis—was pure marginalism in tort theory, defining liability in terms of the anticipated costs and benefits of a particular act. The test was first articulated in a 1935 court decision concerning an "attractive nuisance." A wrecking company had placed an inadequate fence around dangerous equipment, and a child who entered the property was injured. The court cited the Restatement definition in concluding that the "utility to the possessor [landowner] of maintaining the condition is slight as compared to the risk to young children involved therein."[117] Courts cited the Restatement's formulation a half dozen times in the 1940s, roughly thirty times in the 1950s, and roughly fifty times in the 1960s. In the 1960s the risk/utility test migrated from negligence doctrine to strict liability "without proof of fault" for dangerous and defective products. This occurred after it became clear that, notwithstanding the common law's attempt to maintain a sharp distinction between negligence and strict liability, when the results were recast in terms of risk management the standards were similar.

The next big step in marginalist analysis of foreseeable harm was Judge Learned Hand's decision in *Carroll Towing*, a World War II case that involved a collision in New York Harbor between a military boat and a barge. The barge pilot was away from his duties, and one disputed issue was whether his absence contributed to the plaintiff's losses.[118] Judge Hand's decision produced a famous algebraic formula for determining negligence that involved three variables: the probability of an accident, the expected harm, and the cost of precautions that would have prevented the accident. The formula, $B < PL$, states that an action is negligent if the Burden (B) of taking a precaution would be less than the Probability of a loss (P) times the anticipated size of the Loss (L). For example, if failure to take a precaution would lead to a 1 percent chance of an accident costing $1,000,000, then that failure is negligent if the cost of the precaution is less than $10,000. Thus the identification of negligence with failure to take "cost justified" precautions. As the Illinois Supreme Court put it in 1955, in another attractive nuisance case, "account must be taken of the cost and burden of taking precautionary measures."[119]

Like many great legal doctrines, the Hand formula was created in an idiosyncratic case where it could not possibly have been applied. Predicting the size of the accident and the relationship between a barge pilot's presence and the likelihood of harm seems farfetched.[120] Critical to effective administration of an accident system was good statistical data about losses and a large set of relatively similar situations. Here, actuarial science proved its worth for assessing accidents whose number and similarity enabled them to be grouped statistically. Writing in 1925, actuary Herbert P. Stellwagen concluded that fifty thousand automobiles would provide a "dependable volume" sufficient to develop reliable loss statistics.[121] By midcentury the expected accident cost side of the Hand formula had effectively been "monetized" for common and recurring accidents by converting statistical information about the expected risk and magnitude of accidents into a "casualty/liability" risk premium. In his 1970 best seller entitled *Settled Out of Court*, H. Laurance Ross noted that roughly 95 percent of accident claims were concluded by settlements negotiated privately among insurers, without the involvement of the judicial system.[122]

Managing Risk: Alternatives to Negligence

The complexity of machine production or organized distribution often made "fault" extremely difficult to observe. As machines and processes become more sophisticated, things increasingly happen out of human sight. Mass production goods often went by workers so quickly that they could never identify and later recall a particular problem, even if they made a good faith attempt. Further, the very accident about which the plaintiff complained often destroyed evidence of negligence. Finally, complex assembly and distribution systems meant that a good went through many hands before it reached the person who was injured.

The law has always been notorious for its fictions and shortcut-creating presumptions. Francis Hilliard discussed several in his 1859 American treatise on tort law.[123] For example, injuries to freight caused by common carriers were presumed to result from negligence.[124] Or surgical patients injured during the course of routine operations could have the negligence issue decided by the jury even if there was no evidence of a specific negligent act.[125] In the famous 1863 British decision of *Byrne v. Boadle* the plaintiff was walking down a city street when a barrel of flour came sailing out of an upper window and struck him.[126] The window opened into the defendant's bakery and warehouse. No witnesses could testify to any particular act of negligence. The defendant's lawyer argued that "Surmise is not to be substituted for strict proof" and there was "not a scintilla of evidence of negligence." But the court observed that "A barrel could not roll out of a warehouse without some negligence, and to say that a plaintiff who is injured by it must call witnesses from the warehouse to prove negligence seems to me preposterous." In certain cases "it may be said *res ipsa loquitur*"—"the act speaks for itself."

Sir Charles Pollock, Baron of the Court of Exchequer and author of *Byrne*, probably had no idea that the distinctively low tech facts of *Byrne v. Boadle* would be applied to hundreds of accidents arising out of the technologies of transportation or manufacturing that developed nearly a half century later. Things often went wrong for no apparent reason.

A good illustration is the long line of personal injury cases involving glass beverage bottles. In many the bottles had simply exploded. In others the bottles had jagged edges that cut the plaintiffs, or contained shards of broken glass, debris, insects or even mice, discovered only after the plaintiff had drunk some of the contents.[127] Most of the injuries resulted from the increasingly mechanized processes for making the bottles and filling them with carbonated beverages. Coca-Cola Co. was a frequent although by no means the only defendant. During the first four decades of the twentieth century hundreds of these cases reached the appellate courts.

Bottling technology had progressed rapidly in the early twentieth century, enabling the rise of the modern soft drink industry. Coca-Cola had been developed in the 1880s and Pepsi in the 1890s. The bottles themselves were made by a machine process. By the first decade of the twentieth century assembly lines processed thousands of bottles per hour. They were filled with water and syrup. The contents were then carbonated with CO_2 gas and fastened with a stopper or cap. Employees along the line watched the bottles go by and pulled out obviously broken or defective ones. But many things could happen that were hidden from view. The bottles could have cracks or imperfections that were hard to see, particularly on quick examination. The CO_2 injector could malfunction, perhaps giving an extra dose and increasing pressure on that bottle's contents. Or the cap could be improperly sealed. Once the bottles rolled off the assembly line and were placed into boxes for delivery they all looked alike.[128]

Between 1905 and 1944 Coca-Cola alone was the defendant in more than a hundred reported decisions considering whether to apply the res ipsa loquitur doctrine to an injury caused by an explosion or other failure in a soft drink bottle. Earlier cases generally rejected the doctrine. The first was a 1905 Georgia decision that insisted on specific proof of negligence when a Coke bottle exploded in the hand of a grocery store clerk who was placing the bottles on a shelf. "[A] plaintiff cannot avoid setting forth the particulars of the negligence relied on by averring that such matters are more peculiarly within the knowledge of the defendant."[129] Of course, the defendant might not be in a much better position than the plaintiff to know what had happened in the case of one particular bottle. Further, when a bottle exploded the evidence of what went wrong often evaporated. Beginning in the 1910s, however, the courts increasingly found res ipsa to apply to unexplained bottle injuries, provided that there was no evidence that the plaintiff's own mishandling had produced the injury.[130]

The bottling cases were hardly the only ones to apply res ipsa. What the cases tended to have in common was an injury indicating that something had gone wrong in the manufacturing process, but specific acts of negligence were impossible to prove. During the first four decades of the twentieth century judicial use of res ipsa in such cases increased some fortyfold. Effectively, res ipsa provided the back door through which strict liability entered the law.

Escola v. Coca-Cola Bottling Co. was a typical res ipsa case when it reached the California Supreme Court in 1944, after numerous decisions had already accepted the doctrine.[131] Gladys Escola was a waitress restocking Coke into a refrigerator when a bottle exploded in her hand. The cause was claimed to be either excessive gas in the bottle or else a hairline fracture that weakened the glass. The trial included testimony from an engineer for

Owens-Illinois Glass Company. He explained how the bottles were manufactured and tested by a sampling method that imposed extreme pressure and shock tests on one out of every six hundred bottles. The bottle in this case had been returned at least once, and the failure rate for used bottles was slightly higher than for new bottles. The plaintiff testified that she had handled the bottle carefully.

The California Supreme Court majority applied res ipsa, but today the decision is famous for Justice Roger Traynor's concurring opinion: "it should now be recognized that a manufacturer incurs an absolute liability when an article that he has placed on the market, knowing that it is to be used without inspection, proves to have a defect that causes injury to human beings." Justice Traynor offered three rationales for moving to a strict liability standard. First, it would give manufacturers a greater incentive to produce safer products by forcing them to bear the costs of losses. The manufacturer is in a much better position than the consuming public both to understand and to protect against the losses of dangerous and defective products. Second, the manufacturer is in a better position than the consumer to absorb and spread the losses. For the individual consumer such an injury is a lightning strike for which she is poorly prepared. For the manufacturer, however, the losses can be predicted and passed on as a cost of doing business. Finally, strict liability would dispense with the elaborate proof problems in an action for negligence when so much of the production process was unknown to the consumer. "An injured person . . . is not ordinarily in a position to . . . identify the cause of the defect, for he can hardly be familiar with the manufacturing process as the manufacturer himself is."[132]

An increasing volume of scholarship in the 1950s and 1960s debated the merits of strict liability. The leading proponents were Fleming James and William Prosser.[133] James's law school casebook on the law of torts, which had been published in 1942, already anticipated that the tort system should be designed so as to "distribut[e] losses in the socially desirable manner," just as insurance could do.[134]

California became the first state to adopt strict liability for injuries caused by dangerous and defective products, nearly two decades after *Escola*. Justice Traynor, now writing for a unanimous court, made clear that the theory being adopted was one of strict liability in tort, and not a doctrine of implied warranty in contract.[135] The Restatement (Second) of Torts adopted strict liability in tort for dangerous and defective products, extending liability all the way through the distribution chain from supplier to retailer.[136] Although California was the leader, nearly every American state followed suit.

The Cost of Accidents

Judge Hand's negligence opinion in *Carroll Towing* and Justice Traynor's opinion in *Escola* were written three years apart, and of course *Carroll Towing* did not involve a defective product. But the "risk/utility" test for negligence that emerged from *Carroll Towing* and the strict liability test advocated in *Escola* had one feature that powerfully united them: contrary to most people's sense that strict liability was more expansive than negligence, they in fact imposed similar levels of care, intended to minimize the cost of accidents. Judge Hand's algebraic formula found liability for negligence when the cost of taking a precaution was less than the expected cost of the accident that the precaution would have prevented. By requiring manufacturers to pay for all accidents caused by dangerous and defective products, however, the strict liability formulation produced the same result. A firm required to pay for every harm its products caused would take precautions up to the point that they became more costly than the expected cost of the accident itself.[137] The biggest differences were that under negligence a jury would determine after the fact where the line of cost justification was to be located. Under strict liability a firm made that decision for itself, paying either precaution costs or accident costs, whichever was cheaper. The "risk/utility" test for negligence eventually migrated into strict liability, considering whether the risk occasioned by a particular product design outweighed its utility.[138] In the process, tort law had become a thoroughly marginalist discipline, driven by a policy of reducing expected accident costs by considering rational expectations of risk and harm.

By the mid-1960s law writers and judges were in a full bore debate on the question of strict liability as opposed to negligence, as well as the role that marginal deterrence could play in formulating legal rules. For products, the entire manufacturing process was in the exclusive control of the producer, and much evidence of negligence was impossible to uncover. By contrast, in traffic accidents there often is evidence of specific acts of negligence (speeding, failure to yield, drunkenness). Further, accidents were frequently the result of a complex interaction of two parties, each of whom might have avoided it. The insurance industry was also present and in a position to spread losses.

In 1964 Walter J. Blum and Harry Kalven of the University of Chicago published an article that began an important debate on the issue of automobile accident liability.[139] Although neither was an economist, Blum was a renowned tax scholar and had taught himself economics in the process of developing theories about wealth distribution and taxation. Blum and Kalven's central concern was compensation plans, but they also addressed the problem of minimizing the overall number and cost of accidents by reducing both risk and magnitude. Blum and Kalven were skeptical that economics could contribute much. Speaking of deterrence, a problem that Kalven had developed in his own law school casebook on torts,[140] they concluded that the presence of multi-driver interaction made the economic deterrence problem virtually intractable. "A major difficulty here is that the thesis requires predictions about behavior of two populations and not just one."[141]

Blum and Kalven became the first lawyers to cite Ronald H. Coase's article on *The Problem of Social Cost,* which had been published four years earlier.[142] Coase, who is considered more fully in the Epilogue, had cast the accident problem as one of bargaining over a legal entitlement. A well-functioning market would produce the efficient result by giving the entitlement to the one who valued it most highly. Although Blum and Kalven appreciated Coase's observations, they viewed its bargaining model as innappropriate for automobile accidents. The illustrations in Coase's article were mainly of neighboring landowners, such as railroads and ranchers, with established relationships that made bargaining possible. However, "it is extremely awkward to imagine motorists and potential victims negotiating about their patterns of activity, and it would seem near fantasy to imagine what the terms of any bargain between them might be."[143]

In his 1970 book *The Cost of Accidents* Guido Calabresi argued that an efficient system of risk management must minimize the sum of three costs: accident costs, precaution costs, and administrative costs. In contrast to Blum and Kalven, Calabresi accepted a "Coasean" solution to the problem, not by requiring an actual bargain, but by estimating from external criteria who *would* have won the bargain had it been possible. Thus the "least cost avoider" entered the rhetoric of accident law, first in a federal appellate decision in 1980.[144] Imagine a train and a car speeding toward a grade crossing. The least efficient solution is obviously for them to collide, but that still leaves open the question of which must stop. Suppose we know that it costs $1 to stop a train and restart it, but only 10 cents to stop and restart a car. In that case the train would "buy" the right to proceed, and the car would willingly sell at a price between 10 cents and $1. By knowing this we do not have to make the bargain actually occur or pay anyone compensation. Coase had focused mainly on ways of stating tort problems as bargaining situations, whereas Calabresi focused on situations where the State had to predict bargaining outcomes. The result was that tort scholarship in the Calabresi mold is decidedly more interventionst than Coasean scholarship. Although their basic approaches were fundamentally the same,

Calabresi found market failures to be more common than Coase was willing to acknowledge.

For Calabresi, strict liability was the best solution to the products liability problem because manufacturers are in full control of the process. They are in "the best position to make the cost-benefit analysis between costs and accident avoidance and to act on that decision once it is made," he wrote in 1972.[145] By contrast, efficient deterrence rules for accident cases must deal with more complex situations that often relate two or more drivers and a sequence of decisions by each that could either produce or avoid the accident. The proper approach "would ask... Who is best suited to make the cost-benefit analysis between accident costs and accident avoidance costs?"[146] This called for a negligence inquiry for automobile accidents caused by driver error rather than defective products.

Multiple Actors and Risk Management

Risk-based theories of tort also produced more complex rules for allocating blame among multiple parties. Common law tort doctrine had generally adopted all-or-nothing rules that barred contributorily negligent plaintiffs from recovering anything. In the late nineteenth century this view manifested itself in widespread opposition to the idea that negligence could come in "degrees" calling for different levels of punishment.[147] In contrast, under "comparative" negligence courts could meter rewards and penalties by permitting negligent plaintiffs to recover, but with reduced damages to account for their own contribution to the bad result. This development required a conception of foreseeable magnitude and risk. A few states switched to comparative negligence in the early part of the twentieth century. By the 1970s nearly half of the states had adopted comparative negligence, and today virtually all have.[148]

The development of percentage allocation rules reflects the extent to which ideas about marginal deterrence affected common law theories of harm. When the concern is risk management, penalties must be metered so as to provide actors with the correct set of incentives. If multiple parties are to blame, penalties must be allocated among them as well. The traditional tort system, with its focus on compensation, never addressed this problem very successfully. Under traditional rules if a plaintiff sued three defendants in negligence and the three were found to be acting "in concert," then all three could be found liable together. Under common law rules of "joint and several liability," damages were ordinarily divided equally among the three, even if the guilt or contribution of each varied a great deal.[149] If the three defendants were not found to be acting "in concert," then negligence, causation, and damages had to be established against each one individually.[150] This made it possible for each of several defendants to blame the others, and plaintiffs who could not sort out liability or causation generally lost. For example, a 1907 Ohio decision held that when several businesses upstream independently discharged pollutants into a city's water supply, injury, causation, and damages had to be established separately against each one—a requirement that effectively precluded liability. "[T]he difficulty of separating the injury of each from the others would be no reason that one man should be held liable for the torts of others without concert."[151]

Railroading and factory manufacturing magnified these problems. Complex technologies frequently created situations in which negligence seemed clear, but "who's negligence?" was not. Alternatively, perhaps all defendants were negligent but only one of them "caused" the harm. Unraveling these issues could be both costly and speculative—as when one firm built the train engine, a second one maintained it, and a third one operated it.

During the early twentieth century the courts relaxed the common law's restrictions on allocation. *First*, they gradually switched away from contributory and toward comparative negligence rules. *Second*, courts became increasingly willing to permit recovery against a group of negligent defendants, even if only one was likely to have caused the harm. *Third*, the previously discussed doctrine of res ipsa was expanded so as to permit inferences of causation as well as negligence without explicit proof.

One again, a set of low tech cases provided the gateway. In *Oliver v. Miles* (1926) the two defendants were hunting partridges together when a covey of them flew over a nearby highway. Both defendants negligently shot across the highway, and one of their shots hit the plaintiff who was walking along the road. The plaintiff lost his eye, but he was unable to show which shooter had hit him.[152] Notwithstanding lack of evidence of causation the court sustained liability against both defendants on what can only be called a fiction that they were conspirators—"they were jointly engaged in the unlawful enterprise of shooting at birds flying over the highway" and as such "were in pursuit of a common purpose." The California Supreme Court's decision twenty years later in *Summers v. Tice*[153] expressly repudiated any conspiracy requirement. It was enough that each was negligent. The culmination of this thinking was "market share" liability approved by the California Supreme Court in its 1980 *Sindell* decision.[154] In that case the plaintiff had developed cancer, very likely as a result of her mother's use of DES (diethylstilbestrol) during pregnancy.

The drug was generic and any manufacturer's version could have caused the plaintiff's condition, but the plaintiff was unable to identify which particular manufacturer had supplied the drug. Following *Summers v. Tice*, the court held that because all manufacturers had produced the dangerous product, and its contents did not vary from one manufacturer to the other, damages should be shared by the manufacturers in proportion to their market share.

The marginalist revolution in tort law shifted judicial concern to risk management and deterrence of unreasonably harmful activity. The rules and remedies that provide proper levels of deterrence are not the same as the ones that compensate plaintiffs adequately, however. Damages are typically awarded in an amount needed to make the plaintiff "whole," which often bears little relationship to the amount needed to minimize the social cost of dangerous conduct. The solution for most courts is to use concerns about minimizing the cost of accidents to guide liability and granting of injunctions. By contrast, damages continue to provide compenation for past harm done.

PART THREE

The Neoclassical Firm and the Formation of Modern Business Policy

8

The Revolution in Corporate Finance

HISTORIANS WRITING FROM the Progressive Era through the 1970s often spoke in Darwinian terms about the rise of American business and the law governing it. They attributed the growth of the American business corporation to an evolutionary struggle for survival of the fittest,[1] and offered Social Darwinism to explain the law's tolerance of big business and hostility toward labor.[2] The evidence of Darwin was thin, however, consisting of little more than some speeches by nationally known business leaders such as Andrew Carnegie,[3] or Justice Holmes's famous statement in his *Lochner* dissent that the Fourteenth Amendment "does not enact Mr. Herbert Spencer's Social Statics."[4] When writing about Holmes's statement, the prominent midcentury historian Henry Steele Commager quipped that Holmes "was obviously wrong."[5]

Later historians accepted that the development of business policy during this period had almost nothing to do with any theory of evolution.[6] What was described as a Darwinian "survival of the fittest" was really nothing more than interest group conflict, technological change and obsolescence, or competition at work. To be sure, economic competition and Darwinian natural selection contained some superficial similarities. As the theory of competition was formalized in the twentieth century, however, it came to look less like Darwinian evolution and was increasingly driven by marginalist rational actor assumptions.

This chapter and the following four examine some of the most important of these debates. The first two look at corporate law, the third at patent policy and innovation, and the final two at competition policy and vertical control.

The "Watered" Stock Scandals

Since Andrew Jackson's time legal policy favored the business corporation as a device for managing the capital of multiple shareholders.[7] But the corporation could also be an instrument of deception when managers overstated corporate value in order to induce high share prices or favorable loan rates. Classical corporate finance theory assumed the unity of the corporation and its shareholders. Shareholders were regarded as in control, although they could be duped by management. The purpose of corporate finance law was twofold: to enable a corporation to finance its operations, but also to govern manager disclosure to actual or prospective lenders and shareholders.

The corporation was also a "person" in the eyes of the law, and after the 1880s even under the U.S. Constitution.[8] The business corporation owned its own assets and carried its own liabilities, posted its earnings and expenses to its own account, and made decisions about production and the distribution of profits. It conveyed property and appeared in court in its own name. Shareholders could come and go, but the corporate entity endured.

Prior to 1900 corporate finance was regulated mainly by the common law. The substantive rules were distinctly "classical." Value was thought to be a function of cost, which consisted mainly of the labor or investment that had gone into something. This theory of value was backward looking in time, asking what had been contributed in the past. Any attempt to take more out than the historical contribution would weaken the firm and perhaps send it to ruin. As Adam Smith once stated, "The real price of everything, what everything really costs to the man who wants to acquire it, is the toil and trouble of acquiring it."[9]

The paradigm example of classical value theory was the wage-fund doctrine, which held that the amount of wages that could be paid in the present was a function of the amount of "surplus" that remained from the previous period. The idea was highly intuitive. For example, the farmer working his field necessarily had to live off the previous year's produce. "If the corn is to be divided between the farmer and the labourer, the larger the proportion that is given to the latter, the less will remain for the former," wrote David Ricardo, an early nineteenth-century British political economist.[10] The moral that the classicists drew is that the rate of wages to be paid in the current period could not exceed the amount in a "fund" that represented accumulated surplus capital.

The classical theory of corporate finance followed the same principle. The value of a corporation was its paid-in capital, a backward-looking amount declared by the stated "par" value of shares.[11] For example, if a firm issued 10,000 shares at a par value of $5, these numbers represented the promoters' assurance that the firm's paid-in capital was $50,000. Disclosure of these numbers to creditors or prospective share purchasers assured them of a fund they could turn to in the event of a default. Stock was said to be "watered" when these numbers were exaggerated—for example, when controlling owners put real property or other assets into the corporation at greatly overstated values.[12] The term "watered" was derived from ranchers' practice of salting and overwatering cattle in order to increase their weight prior to sale.[13] Early Progressives made a career out of writing about the great "watered stock" controversies of the Gilded Age and early twentieth century.

A distinctive feature of the classical theory of corporate finance was that it could be understood by any commercially experienced judge. At the same time, however, the classical theory often had little to do with the current market value of a corporation, which is driven by expectations of profit rather than the amount previously paid in. Today the idea that value should be based on historical payments seems myopically backward looking. A firm with an enormous paid-up investment in an obsolete technology might be worthless. Another company with a small investment but a market-shifting innovation might be worth a fortune.

As the Pennsylvania Supreme Court stated the classical view in 1889, the stock certificate "stands in the hands of the subscriber for so much as, and no more than, the amount actually paid upon it."[14] William W. Cook, author of the most prominent corporate law treatise of the late nineteenth century, defended the traditional conception that a "share of stock is supposed, in theory, to represent its par value in money or money's worth, paid in or to be paid in to the corporation."

Cook, whose views echoed those of the New York corporate bar during its Gilded Age ascendancy,[15] largely reconstituted the publicly traded business corporation as a routine investment device for shareholders, rather than as a special prerogative of the State as in earlier corporate law writing. Cook's treatise was strongly focused on the rights of stockholders and their potential abuse at the hands of unscrupulous managers, whose interests he viewed as inconsistent with those of the corporation. Writing during a period of widespread stock scandal, he lamented that corporations "have been found to be efficient instruments of fraud, speculation, plunder, and illegal gain." Often the firms "become insolvent and stockholders lose their investments, while individuals become millionaires.... [E]normous fortunes are amassed by the few at the expense of the defrauded, but generally helpless, stockholders."[16]

Classical corporate finance theory was designed for common law rules of contract and fraud. The rules were regarded as self-executing, in the sense that any reasonable manager could comply with them. If the paid-in capital was in cash one could easily determine whether the stated par value of outstanding shares was adequately supported. Difficulties arose when contributions were noncash property such as real estate or other productive assets or intellectual property rights. Although these were prone to overvaluation, the common law of fraud addressed the problem. For example, the Illinois Supreme Court concluded that the rights to a penniless promoter's unwritten play and several unpatented inventions were not worth the $2,000,000 that the directors declared. Stock based on these assets "remained wholly unpaid."[17] Another found watering when a "nearly worthless" patent was valued by the promoters at more than $50,000. "If it had no ascertainable market value," then the directors could declare it only at "such price as could be realized by selling it to others for cash."[18] The courts tended to give promoters the benefit of the doubt if the evaluation had been made in good faith, even though subsequently proven wrong. The Supreme Court observed in 1886 that if the shareholders "honestly and in good faith put in property instead of money in payment of their subscriptions, third parties have no ground of complaint."[19] No state corporation law found stock to be watered merely because the capital originally paid in had subsequently become worthless. The decisive number was the value of the property at the time it had been paid in.[20]

This self-executing nature of classical corporate finance theory was essential if the financial relationships among a corporation's managers, shareholders, and creditors were to be governed by common law rules in the general courts. In the nineteenth century states were generally reluctant to create regulatory agencies. But during the Gilded Age corporate financial dealings grew far more complex than anything known earlier, except for some railroad corporations. Further, as the number of shareholders grew they also became more distant from the corporation's daily management.

Both the common law and the early incorporation acts approached the problem of watered stock by removing limited shareholder liability to one degree or another.[21] In 1824 Justice Story developed the "trust fund" doctrine while riding circuit. The Supreme Court followed in the 1870s.[22] The doctrine recognized a fictional trust against the assets of original shareholders who paid less into the corporation than the declared value indicated. Several states provided for some variation of the same thing by statute.[23] The influential New York General Incorporation Act of 1848 assessed double liability.[24] If the fund as originally paid in was smaller than stated, creditors could rely on the personal assets of shareholders to make up the difference.[25] However, the doctrine was subject to one important exception, which indicated a clear understanding that value and paid-in capital were not precisely the same: creditors were entitled to make independent judgments of corporate value and would be held to the consequences. For example, if a creditor knew that the capital had not been fully paid but loaned money anyway, he had implicitly valued the corporation by some other means than actual paid-in capital. He could not then go after the personal assets of shareholders in the event of insolvency.[26]

Early critics of corporate mismanagement largely accepted the classical theory without question. As Charles Francis Adams noted in an exposé of railroad watered stock scandals in the 1860s, value consists of all that which has been "extracted from the earth."[27] The story of the Erie Railroad stock scandal, which Adams exposed in a series of articles over a four-year period, became a model application of classical corporate finance theory to uncover great wrongdoing.[28] A giant corporation robbed both stock purchasers and creditors by issuing watered stock. Adams attacked the increasingly popular railroad practice of paying "stock dividends," which increased the number of shares without necessarily increasing the amount of capital that had been invested in the company. He also praised the recently enacted Illinois Constitution for its provision prohibiting railroads from issuing stock except for "money, labor or property actually received."[29]

Even in the early twentieth century most states still prohibited shares from being distributed unless the full stated par value had been paid into the corporation.[30] As William Cook noted, the problem of stock watering was made acute by the law of corporate limited liability, which he staunchly defended. Limited liability led to creation of the modern securities market. Without it, "the public would not dare to buy stocks, because they would be liable for corporate debts." As a result of limited liability "we find in some American corporations over 100,000 stockholders—total strangers to each other, and scattered all over the world." Indeed, as Cook later acknowledged, this very fact had permitted the "vast aggregations of capital which have revolutionized modern industry."[31]

One result of limited liability, however, was that creditors had to rely on the value of the corporation itself rather than its shareholders if default occurred. Cook strongly advocated for state "blue sky" laws, which prevented corporate promoters from selling stock that represented no value except the blue sky. The statues required a state agency or official to approve stock issues before they could be marketed, and thus became the first general use of nonjudicial regulatory intervention in the stock issuance process.[32]

The number of watered stock scandals increased dramatically during the Progressive Era, with a major wave during the period 1917–1920, and another one just at the onset of the Great Depression. Between 1911 and 1931, forty-seven out of forty-eight states passed blue sky laws. The statutes generally required registration of securities and sales personnel, the provision of detailed financial information to prospective purchasers, as well as a state official's prior approval of new stock offerings.[33]

One explanation for the growth of blue sky laws is that they were special interest legislation intended to protect mainly small banks who were losing savings deposits to securities investments. The banks themselves were regulated by state law excluding them from equity markets, and the blue sky laws may have been intended to make the securities less attractive as alternative investment vehicles.[34] There is little evidence, however, that blue sky law reporting requirements made securities less rather than more valuable to prospective shareholders with little close knowledge about a firm. As a result, others have argued that the statutes were long overdue reforms.[35] They were certainly responsive to the recent rise of the modern national securities markets, which placed a premium on investor confidence.[36] The markets also entailed that shareholders were even less involved in corporate affairs, however, and thus needed more and better quality disclosure.[37]

The Neoclassical Revolution in Corporate Finance Theory

Progressivism's "Muckrakers" wrote detailed exposés of financial scandals that occurred during the Gilded Age, an era named by Mark Twain for its superficial glitter that masked stunning inequalities and other social flaws.[38] The Muckrakers saw an indefensible maldistribution of wealth and power. Their principal target was the large American business corporation as well as the men who controlled them, including John D. Rockefeller, Andrew Carnegie, and railroad magnates Cornelius Vanderbilt, Leland Stanford, and Jay Gould.[39]

Nevertheless, a significant change was occurring in the theory of corporate valuation, emerging first in the economic literature and later migrating to the legal treatises, courts, and state legislatures. The marginalist revolution in economics recast the corporation as a forward-looking rational actor bent on maximizing profits, or shareholder value. The implications were profound and mainly of two kinds. First, "value" was based on expectations about the future rather than past investment. Second, as the model of profit maximization became formalized in the neoclassical literature the diverse preferences of not only shareholders but also of creditors and even managers became less important.

The term "watered" stock is quaint and largely obsolete today. Most shares are issued with no stated par value, or perhaps a very small nominal par value such as $1 per share. Although exaggerated valuations are still a problem, they do not typically involve what was paid in when a corporation was first formed. Rather, the exaggerations come from material misstatements about the firm's *prospects*, including assets and liabilities, as well as changes in products, markets, or legal obligations that could materially affect a firm's future earnings.

Beginning at the turn of the century, corporate finance writers began to argue that prospects of future profits rather than previous investment should drive corporate valuation. This led to a movement to drop the concept of "par" as an attribute of corporate share value.[40] Although this forward-looking theory provided a more realistic way to estimate corporate value, it also came with challenges. Prospects were much more amenable to manipulation. This change placed a greater premium on the good faith and reasonable expectations of managers, and also required much greater detail and accuracy in corporate reporting. The massive business bankruptcies that occurred during the Depression accelerated a demand for more aggressive regulation. It came at the federal level in the early 1930s.

Shareholders have undoubtedly always made investment decisions based on their expectations about future earnings, and prospective creditors have certainly made similar calculations, particularly for unsecured loans. The problem was that classical political economy and classical finance theory did not account for these forward-looking elements of human behavior.

In sharp contrast to classicism's focus on previously invested capital, neoclassicists viewed the value of a corporation as relating to the degree by which anticipated revenues would exceed anticipated expenses. As William Lough and Frederick Field observed in their Progressive Era treatise on corporate finance, "there is very seldom even a close correspondence between the original investment of capital and the value of a corporation's assets." As a result, "capitalization should be based upon the corporation's earning power, regardless of the capital investment." But this more realistic method of valuation was completely at odds with "the legal theory of capitalization." As a result, the law was "not much observed" by financiers, as opposed to litigators. Lough and Field concluded:

> The advantages of basing capitalization on earning power, rather than on capital investment, are two: First, the capitalization is thus brought into closer correspondence with the value of the capital assets; second,

the corporation's securities sell more readily, and for a higher total sum than under any other plan of capitalization.[41]

This marginalist revolution in corporate finance theory had several implications for corporate law. First, the entire concept of "par value," referring to previous investment, was worth little in measuring the value of a corporation. Lough and Field gave extended illustrations of situations in which "par" value differed widely from realistic value estimates.[42] George Kennan argued in 1916 that it was perfectly legitimate for the Chicago and Alton Railroad to reorganize in 1899 and greatly increase its capitalization, even though no additional capital had been paid in to the corporation. The new valuation simply represented the railroad's improved prospects.[43]

The principal counterargument acknowledged that anticipated ability to earn a profit was a theoretically superior measure of value than historically invested capital. Whereas invested capital was easily measurable, however, determining ability to earn a profit was a purely speculative exercise. Columbia University's James C. Bonbright observed that, on the one hand, removal of par value took away "false appearances." Rather, the investor will estimate value "on his knowledge of the real assets and the earning power, undeceived by a face value that means nothing." However, the purchaser must then depend "on the *valuation of the assets as stated by the company.*" As a result, he concluded, "the outstanding feature of corporations has now become, not *limited* liability, but no liability."[44]

Classical Corporate Finance in Decline

In 1909 the New York Bar Association supported legislation permitting shares to be issued "without the dollar mark"—that is, without a stated par value.[45] The statute, which was passed in 1912, permitted the company to state its capitalization in terms of current market value, reflecting the firm's reasonably anticipated prospects.[46] Other states followed, and by 1927 nearly forty had amended their corporation statutes to permit no-par shares. By 1947 every state except Nebraska and Kentucky had done so.[47] The new statutes permitted the shareholders or directors to declare the capital of the corporation, making changes periodically.

Many Progressives viewed no-par stock with considerable suspicion, seeing legislative capture by corporate entrepreneurs. "Probably the greatest single step in transferring control of property rights from stockholders to corporate managements was taken when the institution of no-par-stock was adopted into American corporation law," Adolf Berle wrote in his book on corporate finance in 1928.[48] Berle and Means repeated that claim five years later in *The Modern Corporation*, concluding that the movement toward no-par shares gave directors the power to "dilute at will" the value of outstanding shares. They had a point. One problem with the new methods of establishing value was that they were imprecise and susceptible of manipulation:

> What is a share of stock "worth." ... Curious as it may seem, the fact appears to be that liquid property, at least under the corporate system, obtains a set of values in exchange, represented by market prices, which are not immediately dependent upon ... the underlying values of the properties themselves. Two forms of property appear, one above the other, related but not the same. At the bottom is the physical property itself, still immobile.... Related to this is a set of tokens, passing from hand to hand..., which attain an actual value in exchange or market price only in part dependent upon the underlying property.... The tokens may, for instance, represent in their value an appraisal of the supposed ability of the particular management.[49]

Thus under no-par stock the value of a corporation—previously accessible to anyone who knew stated par and the number of shares—became a mystery. Most shareholders of widely held corporations were ignorant about the firm's value. Further, as Berle and Means suggested, corporate valuation could reflect the "supposed ability of the particular management"—an idea that seemed reprehensible to them but that later became a conventional component of corporate value.

These observations exacerbated the view held by many marginalist liberals, including John Maynard Keynes, that stock markets had become little more than "casinos" in which equity traders gambled, paying prices that had little to do with a corporation's true value. Only after considerable marginalist theorizing did this view give way to the modern belief discussed in the next chapter that capital markets are efficient and share prices generally reflect a company's worth.

In any event, the need for complete, *ongoing* disclosure to prospective shareholders loomed much larger under the marginalist theory of value. In the nineteenth century stock certificates had often been viewed as a form of "currency," in which the par value stated on the certificate was presumptive evidence of value. Even in 1924, after no-part stock had become well established, prominent corporate attorney Cornelius Wickersham observed that "gullible" purchasers continued to believe that the stated par value on a stock certificate represented the value of the shares.[50]

By the time of the blue sky laws and subsequently the federal securities acts, the perceived problem was not exaggeration of paid-in capital, but rather "balance sheet inflation." Section 11 of the federal statute created directors' liability for knowingly making false statements concerning any element of corporate value, and gave the right to bring a lawsuit to someone who purchased shares in reliance on such statements.[51]

The great corporate scandals of the Gilded Age produced an anti-business corporation rhetoric that remains with us today. Certainly there was a kernel of truth in the corporate scandal stories. Nonetheless, the Progressive muckraking account reflected a theory of corporate finance that was in the process of collapsing as corporate finance theory and the legal system shifted toward a more forward-looking method of valuation. Equally significant is the historical happenstance that the increase in corporate value during the late nineteenth century was unprecedented, making historical investment a particularly bad measure of corporate value.[52]

Nevertheless, the resiliency of the classical theory of corporate valuation was strong, lasting much longer than the classical wage fund doctrine. Even Progressive liberal economists who found the marginalist revolution quite useful in other areas were skeptical about no-par stock. For example, Progressive economist William Z. Ripley of Harvard's economics department was too much a marginalist to believe that "value" consists of historically invested capital. He nonetheless believed that the no-par share statutes were the breeding ground of "fraud and deception."[53] This theme would be repeated among Progressives, whether marginalist or not: whatever one might think of the process of removing par value as a basis for corporate valuation, doing so entailed considerably more managerial speculation, making some form of regulation essential.

Until pushed by changes in statutory law, the courts largely rejected the marginalist argument that the true value of a corporation was its earnings potential. As the Supreme Court concluded in 1892, in determining whether sufficient capital had been paid in, it would not look at intangibles reflecting on the earning power of the corporation, for these were "too unsubstantial and shadowy" to provide an estimate of value. The Court conceded "that the goodwill of a business may be the subject of barter and sale as between the parties to it." But in cases involving corporate default and a creditor allegation of watered stock, they provided no basis for determining value.[54] A 1905 New Jersey court—one of those most solicitous of corporate managers—rejected a declaration of corporate value that included "the capitalization of the annual profits expected to be realized from a favorable marketing of the product."[55] Most courts simply asked juries whether the value of money and property at the time it was paid in covered the stated par value of the shares, ignoring estimates based on anticipated profitability. The "only question for the jury is, was the property worth the amount of the stock."[56] Some public utilities also ran into trouble with watered stock rules when they attempted to follow a practice widely favored by economists of making rates by valuing assets at replacement costs rather than historical costs.[57]

By the late 1910s, however, a few courts began to hold that valuation could include reasonably anticipated profits. A 1919 federal decision permitted a mining company to base its value on ore that was anticipated but not yet actually discovered.[58] The "trust fund" doctrine gradually fell into disuse. Seymour Thompson, a longtime critic of the doctrine, concluded that it "in practicable application would be ruinous to the business management of corporations."[59]

In approving no-par statutes, railroad corporation lawyer and treatise author Victor Morawetz acknowledged that a business corporation must have a capital that cannot be impaired by the declaration of stock dividends. However, "it is not necessary that the amount of capital should be fixed by reference to the nominal or par amount of the shares." Then Morawetz noted the emergent view that in most cases the capital "is invested permanently in fixed plant or machinery which cannot again be converted into cash, and whose value, in great measure depends upon the profitableness of the company's business."[60]

In his influential treatise on corporate finance, Arthur Stone Dewing distinguished among economic, accounting, and legal conceptions of corporate capital. The legal and accounting conceptions relied heavily on the stated values of amounts that had previously been paid in. By contrast, businessmen and investors were interested mainly in the economic meaning of capital, which related to productive value. A corporation might have a patent for which it paid little or nothing, noted Dewing, but was nevertheless of great value. Rather than looking at a corporation's "capital" as that which had been paid in, it should be viewed as representing "anything of concrete and specific value, material or intangible, which affords definite help in enabling the corporation to conduct its business at a profit." In defending the rise of no-par shares, Dewing observed that "the right to participate in earnings is the fundamental characteristic of stock—not its right to participate in the property." As a result, no-par shares were designed to "record the proportional rights of their holders in the earnings of the corporation and ignore the amount of the contribution on which their rights were based."

Under the classical theory, par value was "the actual and substantial stake contributed by the owners of the business." However,

> as soon as the new corporation begins business operations, whatever correspondence between the value of its property and the nominal or money value of its capital stock that may have existed in the beginning, is lost immediately. Some of these operations result in a profit, in which case the corporate property is increased while the amount of outstanding capital stock remains the same; some operations result in a loss, and a discrepancy between the property and the par value of the capital stock arises in the opposite direction. The important thing to observe is that the equality between property and capital stock, however justified at the beginning, is upset by the very operations for which the corporation was organized."[61]

Dewing was more sanguine than other Progressives about the potential for abuse. With excessive optimism he predicted that no-par shares would serve to *increase* the participation of investors in corporate affairs. Having removed previously invested capital as a basis for estimating value, the prospective shareholder or lender would be "forced to investigate the earnings of the corporation, present and past, the history of the corporation and its managers, its standing in the industry, and the value of its shares with reference to current and future interest rates, as they are affected by the rise and fall of industrial activity." He predicted that no-par shares would "conserve the social capital by encouraging greater intelligence and acumen among investors."[62] Dewing's prophecy seriously underestimated the extent to which shareholders by the mid-twentieth century would become mere technical traders, with little subjective knowledge about the companies that they were purchasing.

How liability should be assessed when corporations with no-par stock were found to be undercapitalized initially confused the courts. Some decisions fulfilled the worst fears of the Progressive critics, holding that no-par shares effectively denied creditors a remedy provided that the corporation met legal minimum capitalization requirements. One federal court of appeals held in 1923 that the regime created by no-par statutes was essentially "let the creditor beware."[63] A decade later the Kansas Supreme Court held that subscribers who had not actually paid even the $1 nominal par value stated on the share certificates could be held liable only for that sum.[64]

Market-Based Evaluation

As Dodd and Baker pointed out in their widely used 1940 casebook on corporate law, the issuance of no-par shares did not absolve the corporation of an obligation to state its value to potential creditors. Rather, it shifted the focus away from historical paid-in capital to value based on reasonable expectations. Even the most sophisticated bookkeeping would seldom address the problem. "[A]s yet there is no known way of keeping books in other than monetary terms." As a result, "if Blackacre is acquired through the issue of no-par shares, it is necessary to apply to Blackacre some figure in dollars at which to enter it on the books.[65] Assessing value based on prospects required looking "beyond the ledger." One must know something about the markets in which the firm operated and their growth potential, things that accounting books seldom reveal.

In 1947 Carlos Israels noted that a corporation could avoid all stock watering liability by simply stating its capital conservatively—no greater than a price at which contributed property could readily be sold—and then add any additional evaluation as paid-in surplus. "The investing public has been 'educated' to the point where it is now quite willing to pay much more than par for a par value share.... Earnings or earnings possibilities appears to dominate investor thinking as to price."[66] In the second edition of their book on public control of corporations, Charles Tippets and Shaw Livermore noted that the problem of watered stock had been attended by "much loose thinking and writing." Although methods of estimating value existed, true value was virtually impossible to determine. Further, no methodology could remove risk from the act of investing. "[E]ven slight acquaintance with the conditions of competitive industry teaches that there is no typical relationship between value of physical assets and earning power. It may be very different for a chewing gum concern and a steel plant."[67] They identified stock as watered simply when its declared value "was larger than a reasonable capitalization rate applied to the earnings" would warrant.

The theory of the business corporation in the 1930s and after was marked by a sharp divergence between mainstream economists and corporate lawyers on one side, and institutionalists and Legal Realists on the other. After the collapse of institutionalism within economics, the anti-corporation mantle was carried largely by liberal lawyers who saw constant warfare between minority shareholders who were aligned with the public interest, and corporate managers who had many motives for abuse.

9

The Separation of Ownership and Control

THE "SEPARATION OF ownership and control" will forever be associated with Adolf A. Berle and Gardiner Means's *The Modern Corporation and Private Property* (1932), which *Time* magazine called the "economic bible of the New Deal."[1] They did not originate the idea. In *The Wealth of Nations* Adam Smith revealed his distrust of the business corporation as managers of "other people's money." As a result "it cannot well be expected, that they should watch over it with the same anxious vigilance" as when they invest their own. "Negligence and profusion, therefore, must always prevail, more or less, in the management of the affairs of such a company."[2] In 1914 Boston lawyer Louis Brandeis used "other people's money" as the title for a book about absentee management, focusing heavily on bankers and business corporations. He argued that the "trust problem" in the United States involved not only manufacturers' cartels, but also the "money trust."[3] In the 1920s Thorstein Veblen used the term "absentee ownership" to discuss the relationship between shareholders and corporate managers,[4] and in 1925 Robert Brookings, founder of the Progressive Brookings Institution, wrote of the "separation of ownership and management" in his scathing critique of business corporations.[5]

Today *The Modern Corporation* is regarded not only as one of the great policy documents of the New Deal, but also of Legal Realism. More than any other work of the period, Morton J. Horwitz observed, Berle and Means highlighted the relationship "between property and power."[6] Justice Brandeis cited it five times in his stinging dissent in *Liggett v. Lee* (1933), where the majority overturned a statute that taxed chain stores for the protection of single-firm retailers. Brandeis complained about "the economic and social results of thus removing all limitations upon the size and activities of business corporations and of vesting in their managers vast powers once exercised by stockholders." Relying on Berle and Means, he lamented that the small family firm:

> is being supplanted by huge concerns in which the lives of tens or hundreds of thousands of employees and the property of tens or hundreds of thousands of investors are subjected, through the corporate mechanism, to the control of a few men. Ownership has been separated from control; and this separation has removed many of the checks which formerly operated to curb the misuse of wealth and power.[7]

What is often unappreciated is the extent to which not only institutionalists and Legal Realists but also neoclassical economists took stock owners out of the decision-making calculus of the business firm. The main difference was normative, not descriptive. Berle and Means and other architects of New Deal policy saw the separation of ownership and control in the large firm as a source of corporate aggrandizement, inefficiency, monopoly, and social irresponsibility. By contrast, neoclassical economics saw separation of ownership and control as essential to efficient business firm behavior.

During the Progressive era several writers argued that managers' urge to control had made business corporations too large. Louis Brandeis wrote that large railroad combinations were formed simply to satisfy managers' lust for empire, even though these combinations were "obviously inefficient."[8] In 1911 he testified before a U.S. Senate committee that the "corporation may well be too large to be the most efficient instrument of production and of distribution." Further, "whether it has exceeded the point of greatest economic efficiency or not, it may be too large to be tolerated among the people who desire to be free."[9]

A central argument in Berle and Means's book was that business corporations become less efficient as their shareholders become more numerous and widely dispersed.[10] However, they also alluded several times to a monopoly problem—namely that larger firms tended to charge higher prices.[11] At about the same time Henry C. Simons, an economist at the University of Chicago, published *A Positive Program of Laissez Faire.* Simons argued that large corporations should be broken up because they lead to poor economic performance in the form of higher prices.[12] In 1937 Ferdinand Lundberg published *America's Sixty Families*, a bestseller arguing that a small handful of American families controlled nearly all of American wealth through management of its largest corporations and interlocking social relationships.[13]

The progressive critique of the business firm embraced two different and somewhat inconsistent arguments against large corporations. One, most closely identified with Brandeis, Berle, and Means, was that big companies were inefficient because their owners were not in charge and managers did not have the correct set of incentives. The other was that large business firms led to monopoly and higher prices. Corporate inefficiency would ordinarily injure stockholders whereas high monopoly profits would benefit them. These two critiques often stood side by side with their inconsistencies unexamined. In 1945 Judge Learned Hand complained that a monopoly might be bad not only because it charged high prices but because it "deadens initiative, discourages thrift, and depresses energy"—a conclusion that the Supreme Court enthusiastically endorsed a year later.[14] Justice William O. Douglas repeatedly cited *Other People's Money* in dissents from the 1940s through the 1960s, arguing that separation of ownership and control should be viewed as an antitrust problem.[15] In his concurring opinion in *Falstaff Brewing* in 1973, near the end of his career, he argued that one purpose of aggressive merger enforcement was to prohibit the growth of inefficiently large corporations "where men on the 54th floor with only balance sheets and profit and loss statements before them decide the fate of communities with which they have little or no relationship."[16]

In 1950, when Congress was about to expand the antitrust merger law, it listened to a great deal of testimony to the effect that American business firms had become too large to be efficient. Industrial economist George W. Stocking spoke of the United States Steel Corporation as

> a big sprawling inert giant, whose production operations were improperly coordinated; suffering from a lack of a long-run planning agency; relying on an antiquated system of cost accounting....; with inadequate knowledge of its domestic and no clear appreciation of its opportunities in foreign markets; with less efficient production facilities than its rivals...[17]

In the 1950s Carnegie Mellon economist Herbert Simon introduced the term "satisficing" to describe management behavior in large firms: managers would perform just well enough to avoid shareholder objections but would fail to maximize value.[18] In the popular literature on corporate management Peter Drucker repeatedly argued that American businesses had become too large, doing too many things internally that could more efficiently be purchased from other firms. "Do what you do best and outsource the rest" became his mantra in two dozen popular books, starting with the *Concept of the Corporation* in 1946.[19] The antihero in Sloan Wilson's best-selling 1955 novel *The Man in the Gray Flannel Suit* was the faceless bureaucrat, unappreciated, underpaid, and self-destructive—famously played on the screen a year later by Gregory Peck.[20]

The Firm as Relevant Actor

In sharp contrast to Berle and Means, neoclassical economists saw separation of ownership and control as essential for efficient business firm behavior and finance. Price theory and industrial organization, the disciplines addressing corporate behavior, treated the firm as a unified entity. To the extent shareholder preferences differed, they rarely showed up. Alfred Marshall, the great Cambridge industrial economist, assumed that the firm's goal was to maximize its profits. As for shareholders, he wrote in his *Principles* (1890), "as a rule they do not take much active part in engineering the business and controlling its general policy; and they take no part in superintending its details." As a result, "the great body of the shareholders of a joint-stock company are, save in a few exceptional instances, almost powerless."[21] The entire thrust of neoclassical corporate finance theory was to turn the shareholder into an investor concerned only with the maximization of firm value. The manager became a mere agent whose duty was to further that goal. Until the rise of agency cost models in the 1960s, neoclassical economics largely disregarded the ownership/control problem by assuming that both the firm and its shareholders had only profit maximization in mind.

Ronald Coase published *The Nature of the Firm* in 1937, when he was still an instructor at the London School of Economics.[22] This important article was initially overlooked but became very influential in business policy in the 1970s and after. Whether a firm makes something for itself or purchases it from others, he argued, depends entirely "on a comparison of the costs of carrying out these market transactions with the costs of carrying out these transactions within an organization, the firm."[23] The resulting decisions are not simply "operational"; they are also "structural." For example, if it was more profitable for an automobile manufacturer to make its own automobile bodies it would make them. If not, it would buy them. The former choice made the firm bigger, whereas the latter made it smaller.

Throughout his career Coase wrote with irritation about armchair economists whose theories are abstracted from reality.[24] Nevertheless, *The Nature of the Firm* was an exercise in pure marginalist theory about substitution between lower and higher value assets or processes. His introduction stated his purpose was to define the firm in a way that is "not only realistic" but is also "tractable by two of the most powerful instruments of economic analysis developed by Marshall, the idea of the margin and that of substitution." To be sure, Coase made some casual observations about manager behavior. He recalled overhearing a telephone conversation at a Union Carbide plant that gave him "a lively sense of the possibilities of substitution."[25] He also speculated in one place that the introduction of telephones might make firms bigger by reducing the costs of managing remote facilities, and elsewhere that it might make them smaller by reducing the costs of market negotiations with independent suppliers. But this hardly establishes that the highly analytic theory of marginal choice developed in *The Nature of the Firm* had significant empirical content.

Nevertheless, *The Nature of the Firm* did for the structural theory of the firm what the great theorems of corporate finance, discussed below, did for the firm's financial structure. They assumed a firm whose only goal was the pursuit of profits, which it achieved by relentlessly comparing the costs and benefits of doing things in different ways. The result was a moving target within which managers made continuous decisions about how and what to produce. The diverse opinions of shareholders, never mentioned in Coase's article, were not even relevant.

Manager Discretion: The Business Judgment Rule

One characteristic of neoclassical economics was greater sophistication about risk. Forward-looking theories of value formalized risk-taking by tying it to rational expectations. Perhaps coincidentally, late nineteenth- and early twentieth-century corporate law developed an expanded toleration of manager discretion under the "business judgment" rule. Entrepreneurial risk-taking would be discouraged if inactive shareholders distressed by a business decision gone bad could too easily hold managers liable. The business judgment rule was first articulated in its modern form during the Gilded Age. In its 1872 *Sperling's* decision the Pennsylvania Supreme Court stated that directors could be personally liable to shareholders for "fraud, embezzlement or willful misconduct or breach of trust for their own benefit." However, they are not liable "for mistakes of judgment, even though they may be so gross as to appear to us absurd and ridiculous."[26]

Few courts went that far. The *Sperling's* formulation competed with decisions preserving greater control for shareholders by holding directors liable for various degrees of negligence. In *Briggs v. Spaulding* (1891) the Supreme Court held that directors are obliged to use a level of care "which ordinary and diligent men would exercise."[27] Later, states began to formulate the rule so as to be more tolerant of director risk-taking, articulating the standard in terms such as "clear and gross negligence"[28] Beginning early in the twentieth century the Delaware courts were prone to defer to business judgments made in good faith. They later expanded their tolerance, eventually holding business judgments immune form shareholder challenge unless they were grossly negligent or intentionally made in bad faith.[29]

The Fading Shareholder: Fisher's Separation Theorem

Corporate finance theory at mid-twentieth century assumed well-functioning financial markets and minimal "agency costs," which are transaction or monitoring costs that are internal to the firm. In the 1970s agency cost theory became the dominant method of accounting for conflicts between shareholders and managers.[30] Economic historian Douglass C. North once argued that Berle and Means actually discovered agency costs within the firm, thus explaining the separation of owner and manager interests.[31] Stating the issue this way, however, forces it into a neoclassical framework that Berle and Means themselves would not have accepted.

In the first decade of the twentieth century, the brilliant Yale economist Irving Fisher developed his "separation theorem."[32] Fisher observed that shareholders, like all persons, set out to maximize their utility, which represents a list of desires, limited resources, and a set of values for prioritizing them. Firms, in contrast, set out to make profits. If individual shareholders' utility functions are both different and unknowable, they cannot be equated with firm profit-maximization, which is a relatively simple matter of deciding on the action that maximizes value. Fisher's separation theorem states that the firm's operations are governed solely by the profit-maximization objective and cannot be deduced from the preferences of individual shareholders.[33]

An economic and legal theory of the firm might adopt any one of these assumptions: (1) firm behavior is a composite of the aggregated wishes of its shareholders; (2) every shareholder wants profit-maximization, so any profit-maximizing decision has the shareholders' unanimous consent; or

(3) the firm should maximize value and stop caring about actual shareholder preferences.

Nineteenth-century corporate law adopted the first assumption, making the firm little more than the wishes of its collective shareholders.[34] In contrast, neoclassical economic and legal theories of the firm came to adopt either assumption (2) or (3). Those who rationalized the complete separation of ownership and control in widely held corporations often assumed that shareholders wanted to maximize their corporation's value. They noted that shares are held in large part by retirement funds, mutual funds, and other instruments for which value maximization is the articulated goal. Even here, however, there might be conflicting shareholder preferences for, say, high immediate dividends versus long-term reinvestment of profits. For the most part, however, the modern theory of corporate finance pays little attention to the actual preferences of shareholders insofar as they desire anything other than maximum firm value. In short, the theory assumed as a matter of technique that shareholders were unanimous. As a result the problem of ownership versus control could be disregarded.[35]

The Shareholder's Role: Exit or Voice

During the 1970s corporate finance theory was quite taken by a fictional assumption of shareholder unanimity. The literature did not sample actual shareholder preferences but instead assumed that all shareholders were profit-maximizers, although they could have different attitudes about risk. Indeed, *actual* polling of shareholder preferences as might occur in a shareholder meeting was thought to be a costly waste of time and resources. As Eugene Fama and Merton Miller, two architects of the efficient capital market hypothesis, summarized the literature in the early 1970s:

> Where there exist organized capital markets in which shares can be freely bought and sold and where these markets are perfect ... it is possible to develop an objective, operational decision criterion for management that (1) does not involve stockholder utility functions directly but (2) leads to precisely the same investment and operating decisions that each stockholder would make if he were running the firm himself.[36]

In the developing model managers used "voice," or control, to make their decisions, whereas shareholders used "exit," or trading of shares. The idea that shareholders maximize preferences by trading rather than controlling has been bedrock in corporate finance theory since the 1960s. The concept largely undermines the idea that a shareholder is an "owner" in any sense of the word that involves managerial power over the firm's behavior. Rather, the shareholder is indifferent to anything other than the risk adjusted rate of return or the trade-off between immediate income or longer-term growth. She sells on a moment's notice when a particular firm fails to meet her expectations.

Risk, Ownership, and Debt

One important difference between classical and neoclassical value theory lay in the treatment of risk and uncertainty. Because classicists measured value by looking at past averages, any quantitative concept of risk was difficult for them. Things such as the value of labor or the value of a business firm were measured by reference to previous investment. To be sure, people making investments consider risk. But the classical model of value did a poor job of theorizing such behavior. By contrast, marginalism's criteria of willingness-to-pay, or *expected* value, required consideration of probabilities. How to accommodate risk about future events became a central concern of neoclassical economics.

Historically, owners and creditors stood in two very different relationships to a firm. For example, Berle and Means did not lament the separation of *creditors* and control because creditors were not supposed to control anything. Ownership was a set of property rights in the form of stock, and owners were entrusted with operational decisions. By contrast, debt was contractual and gave creditors a right to collect periodic interest payments and eventually reclaim their principal. But debt gave them no say in the firm's operations unless insolvency was threatened.

Under the traditional theory of corporate finance a firm could reduce its cost of capital and thus increase its value by taking on debt. Typically, debt is cheaper because creditors have priority over shareholders when a firm must be dissolved, and debt is frequently secured by corporate property. However, if a firm borrows too much—that is, if it becomes excessively "leveraged"—then risk begins to rise because debt payments are obligatory whereas dividends are not. As a result, under traditional corporate finance theory, the cost of capital falls as the corporation takes on more debt, but rises again as the amount of debt becomes excessive. One important way of maximizing the firm's value is to find the optimal debt-to-equity ratio.[37]

The Modigliani-Miller theorem was named after its developers. Franco Modigliani was an Italian-born Jewish economist who fled Europe during the Italian Fascist purge. He eventually settled in the United States and made his career primarily at MIT. Merton Miller was an American economist who spent most of his senior career at the University of Chicago. The theorem, worked out in articles written in the late 1950s and early 1960s, states that in a perfectly functioning market for capital, the firm's value does not depend on the ratio of equity (ownership) to debt. Rather, a firm's value is determined entirely by its stream of earnings.[38]

Modigliani and Miller's reasoning was based on the difference between exit and voice. In a perfectly functioning capital market, all participants would optimize risk by making their *own* debt-to-equity substitutions. For example, an investor could purchase stock in a debt-free firm but borrow 40 percent of the money, leaving herself in a debt-equity position precisely equal to someone who used entirely her own money to purchase a firm with 40 percent indebtedness. The shareholder's power to exit and readjust his portfolio served to equalize risk-adjusted returns. Any time the market tended to value one firm higher than others based on its debt-to-equity ratio, rational investors would trade their shares back to equality. Stock ownership, or equity, becomes nothing more than one of two completely interchangeable ways of providing capital to the firm.

Given that debt is historically cheaper, the Modigliani-Miller analysis encouraged firms to take on more debt than had previously been thought optimal. As a result it has been blamed for excessive firm failures resulting from too much debt, particularly during periods of recession.[39]

The Efficient Capital Market Hypothesis

As the economic theory of competition developed through the first half of the twentieth century, the role of information became increasingly important. In *Risk, Uncertainty, and Profit* (1921), Frank Knight had argued that the smooth flow of information is essential to effective competition because it enables traders to evaluate risk.[40] At the same time, many early marginalists viewed stock markets with suspicion, regarding them as not conforming to the usual laws of supply and demand. Late nineteenth- and early twentieth-century stock gyrations seemed to confirm this, frustrating the application of basic economics to stock pricing. Even John Maynard Keynes, the most prominent economist of his generation, believed that stock markets were little more than "beauty contests" in which share prices rose and fell with no apparent relation to actual value.[41] In this regime so-called technical analysis of share prices flourished, with stock traders hoping to pick winners by searching for predictable patterns in pricing behavior.[42]

An emerging alternative theory was that, notwithstanding the frenzy with which stocks are often purchased and sold, overall pricing tends to reflect fundamental values. John Burr Williams, an influential economist who studied under Joseph Schumpeter, insisted that the price of shares reflected the intrinsic value that they represented—namely, reasonable expectations of future earnings and dividends.[43] Building on Williams's work, University of California economist Harry Markowitz developed the idea that an optimal portfolio consists of stocks of differing risk levels, with riskier investments offering higher rates of return but also more volatility.[44] That is to say, the shareholder should develop an investment portfolio that matches her own risk profile, and then "adjust" for changes in risk or return by making additional purchases or sales.

The efficient capital market hypothesis emerged from this theory. If capital markets work well stock prices will move quickly toward a level that equalizes risk-adjusted returns across stocks as well as alternative financial instruments. High risk and low risk stocks should produce the same return in the long run, because higher risk will be compensated through a stock price that yields a higher return. The all-important conclusion: one randomly selected mixture of stocks should perform just as well as another.

From that point the only missing ingredient was informational efficiency, or the idea that the market price of a security reflects what is known about it. If this information is accurate and quickly disseminated, the market price will tend to reflect rational expectations about value. Already in 1900 Louis Bachelier, a French mathematician, had argued in *The Theory of Speculation* that the *history* of commodity prices shows a random distribution, making it impossible to predict future prices from past price histories.[45] For example, repeated throws of a single true die will show a one-in-six chance of getting a five, but no sequence in historical throws provides useful information about the outcome of the next throw. As a result, an efficient investor can forget the historical research about price movements. Beginning in the 1930s, a number of "random walk" studies suggested the same thing for stock prices.[46]

In the 1960s Eugene Fama, who won the Nobel Prize in 2013, merged this theory about information flow with studies of pricing behavior, into what is now known as the efficient capital market hypothesis (ECMH).[47] The hypothesis generally states that in any market in which information flows freely, current market prices reflect investors' collective beliefs about value.

The hypothesis was popularized in a best-selling 1973 book by Princeton economist Burton Malkiel, entitled *A Random Walk Down Wall Street*.[48]

The ECMH comes in three versions. The weakest form states that current prices reflect all of the information contained from observations of previous trade prices. As a result, so-called technical analysis based on past price movements cannot predict future prices. A "semi-strong" form suggests that current prices reflect all public information, including not only technical information but also "fundamentals," which includes information about the performance and prospects of a firm. As a result, publicly known information has already been reflected in the market price, and trading on that information is of no use. If a business receives positive information, the stock price will immediately rise until its risk-adjusted value is the same as that of every other business. Finally, under the strong form even private information, including insider trading, is reflected in the stock price.[49] The two stronger versions have important policy implications for corporate disclosure and finance. They mitigate against hard regulation but in favor of disclosure.

The ECMH has been explicitly acknowledged in numerous court decisions involving claims of securities fraud. The "fraud on the market" theory was adopted by federal courts in the mid-1970s and approved by the Supreme Court in *Basic v. Levinson* (1988). The decision rested on the premise that stock prices are derived from publicly available information, so an important misstatement by corporate managers would distort investors' perception of the firm's value.[50] Further, because purchaser decisions are based on stock prices, the court could presume that share traders "relied" on the misinformation. This made it unnecessary to determine that each individual investor actually based a decision to buy or sell on false information, as the traditional common law of fraud required. The Supreme Court reiterated the theory in a 2013 decision: "The fraud-on-the-market premise is that the price of a security traded in an efficient market will reflect all publicly available information about a company; accordingly, a buyer of the security may be presumed to have relied on that information in purchasing the security."[51] At this writing the ECMH's relatively easy inference of causation has been called into question, however, and its use may be limited by the Supreme Court.[52]

The Separation of Ownership and Awareness

Every interesting factual assertion in Berle and Means's *Modern Corporation* has been disputed, including the fact of separation of ownership and control.[53]

In contemporary perception, however, Berle and Means were in the mainstream of 1930s' thought. Their views reflected widespread belief that stock ownership in large corporations was becoming more diffuse, and managers were not effectively controlled by owners. These beliefs even prompted congressional hearings in 1940.[54] The separation of ownership and control supplied a crucial rhetoric for the formation of corporate governance and finance theory, not only during the New Deal but for a long time after.

For Berle and Means and other Legal Realists, as well as institutionalist economists and later critics such as Ralph Nader,[55] separation of ownership and control led to business firm autocracy, irresponsibility, and waste. For the neoclassicists, by contrast, the assumption of separation was an essential prerequisite to efficient firm behavior and modern finance theory. By the 1970s marginalist price theory came to define every aspect of the business firm, including its behavior and structure. Insofar as corporate operations were concerned, stock ownership became no more than a detail. In an efficient capital market, investors maximize their returns by purchasing "index" funds, without knowing the products that a firm produces, the markets in which it operates, the makeup of its board of directors, or even the name of its CEO. Stock trading results from computer-generated algorithms that continuously rebalance portfolios. The personal investor who owns an index fund typically cannot even name the corporations that his fund owns.[56]

These developments represented a massive shift away from the nineteenth-century vision of the corporation as a device to facilitate investment by groups of active owner-operators. The result was not merely a separation of ownership and control, but a nearly complete separation of ownership and awareness. Undeniably, however, the shareholder who flipped stocks on a moment's notice served to decrease the corporation's social responsibility, at least to the extent that responsibility requires anything other than maximization of private firm value.

10

The Twisted Path to Innovation Policy

AMERICAN INTELLECTUAL PROPERTY (IP) law developed in relative isolation from any coherent economic policy concerning innovation. The history is mystifying because the Intellectual Property Clause is the only place the Constitution explicitly links its protections to a theory of incentives. Stating its purpose "to promote the progress of Science and useful Arts," the Constitution authorizes Congress to grant inventors and authors exclusive rights for "limited times."[1] The theory, borrowed from the 1624 British Statute of Monopolies, was that exclusive rights would motivate inventors and authors to create by permitting them temporarily to appropriate the value of their creations.[2] After those rights expired, the innovation would belong to the public. The "exclusive rights" and "limited times" formulation also indicates a concern for balancing inventor incentives against public access, something for which marginalist economics is well suited.

Historically, economists regarded patents with suspicion or else ignored them, as Adam Smith largely did in *The Wealth of Nations*. Patents were inimical to any theory of robust competition, which depended on rapid mobility of resources without government restraint—something the patent system undermined. Economists did not systematically confront the inner workings of the patent system until the mid-twentieth century. Most of the earlier American and English economic writing about patents concerned the use of patents that had already been created. The issues largely fell into the realm of competition policy rather than innovation policy as such. For example, price fixing, patent pooling, and patent ties were all discussed in an extensive literature.

But the patent system itself was a black box, largely accepted as given, except for frequent complaints that there were too many "worthless" patents. Already in 1894 Supreme Court justice David J. Brewer lamented that "so many worthless patents have been issued" that "perhaps the machinery now in use may not be the one adapted to work out the best results." Unless radical changes were made people would "rise in their wrath and abolish [the system] altogether."[3] The wrath never materialized however, and a half century later Alfred E. Kahn, one of America's most influential regulatory economists, complained again about the excess of "worthless patents." There were "too many vaguely drawn, excessively broad, uselessly narrow, wholly unworked patents."[4]

One reason the patent system was less important in early industrial economics than it became later is that the economic theory assumed that products were identical from one seller to another. For Alfred Marshall a market consisted of all goods that are completely alike, so customers care only about the price. His *Principles of Economics* (1890) contains only one sustained discussion of patents, concluding that patents are not worth a great deal because it is so easy to invent around them.[5] Marshall's massive *Industry and Trade* (1919), a 700-page book bearing the subtitle "A Study of Industrial Technique and Business Organization," described industry structure in painstaking detail. Marshall viewed patents mainly as increasing the cost of mechanized production. There was almost no discussion of the role of patents in promoting innovation. Marshall did note that many dominant firms "owed their first successes to the possession of important patents" suggesting that without patents there would be less dominance and more competition.[6] He observed, as an aside, that "If it were possible to adapt the duration of each patent grant to its peculiar conditions, the public interest would call for a specially long period for patents relating to processes to which the law of Increasing Return applied strongly, but in which its effects are slowly developed." He also suggested that trade secrets are worth more than patents when a product's novel features cannot readily be identified and copied. His comment was in reference to the dye industry, where processes for creating certain colors were kept secret and typically not patented.

Under Marshall's influence the model that dominated industrial economics through the 1930s assumed that consumer behavior and products remained constant.[7] Only in the 1930s did economists give serious attention to the ways product diversity and change fit into the theory. Because IP rights are all about change, only then did economists contemplate them more seriously. Marginalist analysis viewed patents as affecting incentives to innovate, but the encouragement was selective. Cambridge University's Arthur C. Pigou and Arnold Plant from the London School of Economics believed that people would invent without a patent system, but the availability of patenting biased inventing in the direction of things that could be patented.[8]

By contrast, economic institutionalists de-emphasized or rejected utilitarian impulses. They generally preferred a labor theory or one linked to Darwinian natural selection. Thorstein Veblen argued in *The Instinct of Workmanship* (1914) that the desire to create is not explained by utilitarianism but rather is a survival instinct developed through the evolutionary process.[9] This instinct was social, not individual, and was an important characteristic of the societies that survive the competitive struggle. For example, crop cultivation gave a survival advantage to those tribes that engaged in it. Veblen regarded individual appropriation as inimical rather than beneficial to technological progress because it severed innovation from group survival instincts. Harvard economics professor Frank Taussig, another institutionalist, argued in *Inventors and Money Makers* (1915) that the human "instinct of contrivance" had social and psychological origins unrelated to the search for profit.[10]

In addition to the institutionalists, several noneconomists rejected the idea that inducements to invent were individual and monetary. For example, Admiral Bradley A. Fiske was an important Progressive Era inventor of military technology such as telescopic sights for large guns. Fiske located the inventive spark in humanity's instinct to better itself, and as proving the superiority of white Europeans. The title of his book, "Invention, The Master-Key to Progress," was a thinly veiled illusion to the master race. These views were quite in keeping with Progressive Era theories of cultural evolution.[11]

Patent law has always been one of the most arcane of legal systems, with complex rules of interpretation developed by reference to previous law rather than any broader base of economic or empirical literature. Until the 1930s writing about patent law did not develop a "political economy" that encouraged policymakers to step back and consider the impact of the patent system on innovation and progress. Both legislative histories and the patent case law generally avoided economic examinations of such questions as whether patents facilitate or retard innovation, or produce social value in excess of costs. That judges did not address these questions is understandable, given that they simply interpret the statute. Over most of U.S. history Congress did not investigate them either, however, even though the Patent Act has been revised many times. In this sense patent law has resembled property law much more than anything that could be described as industrial or innovation policy. Real property lawyers and judges deciding boundary disputes rarely address fundamental questions about how much private property there should be, how widely it should be distributed, how property and wealth are related, or how broad is the power to exclude. Rather they apply a set of technical rules of long standing, sometimes aided with a little new technique, but rarely engaging broader social or economic issues.

Patent law has nothing resembling antitrust's rule of reason, where courts assess the competitive impact of a practice against the market in which it occurs. In this regard, the difference in economic content between the great antitrust debate leading to an expanded merger law in 1950 and the roughly contemporaneous debate over the 1952 Patent Act is striking. As the next chapter develops, antitrust policy was dominated by questions about the economic impact of various practices, including patent practices, on industry performance. Lawmakers did not always engage these economic issues competently, but they did engage them. In sharp contrast, the law governing patents shows little concern about the impact of the patent system on innovation or economic growth, the possibility of differential impact in different industries, or social benefits in relation to costs. In *Graham v. John Deere* the Supreme Court upheld and interpreted the 1952 Patent Act's requirement of "nonobvious" subject matter. But the Court did not suggest industry studies concerning whether too many patents were being granted, whether patents were furthering or stifling innovation, or anything approaching that.[12]

Patent law also presents a good case study of how interest groups influence legal policy. Questions about the proper duration or scope of patent rights or the balance between access and exclusion did not find consensus answers. One thesis of this book is that when a robust technical model fails to emerge, legislators are more likely to look to interest groups for solutions. In IP, rights holders are a more compact, homogenous group than consumers. Legislative IP law has been more prone to interest group control than nearly any other body of law, including antitrust. The result for most of our history has been continuous expansion of holder rights. Ironically, this expansion has occurred against a backdrop of commercial *product* life that has become steadily shorter. For example, today copyrights last far longer (typically, seventy years plus the life of the author) than the commercial life of most copyrighted works, entailing that the Constitution's requirement of "limited times" is largely meaningless. That is also true of patents in relatively fast-moving markets such as computers, telecommunications, and other information technologies.

"Property" or Flexible Tool of Economic Development? The Trivial Patent

Historically, the courts viewed patents as either "monopoly" or "property." If they were monopoly rights they were inherently powerful and their uses should be limited—a proposition that the Supreme Court once enthusiastically embraced. By contrast, if they were simply "property" then they were no more threatening to the economy than land titles. This binary view was largely supported by the classical political economists, who saw markets in terms of monopoly and competition, with no gradation from one to the other.

By contrast, marginalist economics saw markets in varying shades, believing that power, diversity, and change all exist on a continuum. These ideas gradually penetrated the analysis of innovation, but only decades after they were absorbed into competition policy. After World War II economists showed increasing interest in the operation of the patent system and its effects in different industries. One would never know this, however, from the congressional debates or case law on patents. For example, the "debate" discussed later between Joseph Schumpeter and Kenneth Arrow on the relation between market competition and innovation produced a cottage industry of economic studies—more than any other subject in the field of industrial organization.[13] It is cited a single time in the entire body of judicial patent cases.[14]

Notwithstanding the utilitarian language in the Constitution, the courts have generally imagined patents as "property" rights that cannot expand and shrink depending on changing ideas about economic development. Patents were treated as property in the rules for ownership and transfers, and also the Constitution's Takings (Eminent Domain) Clause.[15] For property rights generally, the Constitution limits the law's ability to "meter" the scope of ownership rights so as to track policies concerning innovation or economic development. To the contrary, property rights exist *in spite of* changing development concerns. This is in sharp contrast to antitrust, whose rights have always been defined in terms of changing economic circumstances and theory.

The law of property rights limited sovereign power to destroy the value of existing patents, but it said little about how many patents should be granted in the first place or what their scope should be. Under a strong natural rights conception fewer patents would be issued because only significant accomplishments deserved protection. By contrast, marginalist analysis might permit minor improvements to be patented under a kind of cost-benefit analysis. The historical record suggests as much. In the United States today about 225,000 utility patents are issued annually. For the first generation after the

Constitution was ratified, however, the number was fewer than a hundred per year. The first year that more than a thousand patents were issued was 1854, and the number did not consistently reach fifty thousand until the 1960s.[16]

Between 1790 and today the U.S. population grew by roughly seventy-five times (from four million under the 1790 census to three hundred million in 2010). During that same period the rate of patents issued annually increased more than ten thousand times. If we look only at the twentieth century, prior to 1950 patent growth roughly matched population growth, whereas during the second half it was nearly triple population growth. In the early 1950s economists George W. Stocking and Myron Watkins complained that the proliferation of patents was stifling competition, noting the alarming trend that the number of patents issued in the 1930s, around forty-five thousand annually, was double the rate of issuance in the 1890s.[17]

The relationship between issued patents and the rate of economic growth may be more relevant than the rate of population growth. However, it is also harder to assess.[18] The United States has experienced three technological revolutions that spurred economic growth over prolonged periods. The first was between 1750 and 1830, brought about mainly by interchangeable parts, the steam engine, and the cotton gin. The second was between 1870 and about 1900, brought about mainly by railroad expansion, electricity, the internal combustion engine, and machine production. The third was between 1960 and 2000, occasioned by the computer, modern telecommunications networks, and the Internet.[19] During the first of these periods patent issuance (beginning in 1790) was less than one hundred per year for the first part and roughly in the two- to three-hundred range during the remainder. During the second growth period annual patent issuance jumped considerably and roughly doubled over the period. During the third period the number of issued patents roughly tripled. However, the rate also increased fortyfold (from five hundred to twenty-four thousand) during the period from 1830 to 1870, which was of more modest innovation-induced growth, and it roughly doubled during the period 1900–1960, another slower period. The growth rate of patent issuance has been at least as large during periods of low growth as during high growth periods.

For all appearances, the American patent was becoming "marginalized." Too many patents contributed little to the stock of innovation. The Supreme Court had addressed the issue nearly a half century before Justice Brewer complained about the excess of worthless patents. Its first prolonged discussion of trivial patenting was *Hotchkiss v. Greenwood* in 1850. The Court rejected a patent for a doorknob with a porcelain handle. The prior technology had included a standard dovetail and groove arrangement for attaching a metal handle to the opening mechanism, and also handles made of porcelain that used a different mechanism. The patentee created a combination that used the established dovetail mechanism, only with a porcelain handle. Making this combination required only the ingenuity of "an ordinary mechanic acquainted with the business," and thus showed "an absence of that degree of skill and ingenuity which constitute essential elements of every invention."[20]

George Ticknor Curtis, author of the dominant patent law treatise at the time, described *Hotchkiss* as stating that simply using new materials in an old manufacture was insufficient for a patent unless the use of the new materials required significant ingenuity. Curtis himself stated rather strict criteria for inventiveness, suggesting that "the application of horse power, or water power, or steam power to a machine that has been moved by hand power, provided the change is within the ordinary knowledge and skill of any constructor, is not patentable."[21] He then distinguished new uses of old materials, new materials for old uses, cheaper ways of using an old material, and the application of established products in new areas—such as adapting the wire used for viola bows to women's hoop skirts.[22] Too low a standard of invention would permit "some follower in the track of genius, with just intellect enough to make a different mechanical device or contrivance" than already existed to commandeer the work of previous inventors.[23]

The Patent Act of 1836, in force at the time of *Hotchkiss*, permitted a patent on any "new and useful" device or process that is "not known or used by others."[24] This backward-looking inquiry created the very problem that *Hotchkiss* illustrates. Literally, the patentee's doorknob was not "known or used by others." Nonetheless, if any new but trivial juxtaposition of old devices or processes could qualify for a patent, they would be granted to many things that ordinary artisans could create on their own, diminishing public access while doing nothing to promote the progress of useful arts.

Ironically, immediately after *Hotchkiss* the rate of issued patents experienced one of its greatest increases ever—from 884 in 1850 to 4363 in 1860, fivefold growth in a single decade. The increase suggests a recurring question in patent history—namely, whether the Patent Office really changes its behavior in response to Supreme Court decisions tightening up patentability standards. The courts were less generous. They increasingly insisted on something more than "mere obvious manual changes following the beaten track of mechanical experience," as a New York court put it in 1867. It rejected a patent on an agricultural reaper that placed the operator's seat and a few controls in a more convenient location.[25] In its important *Rubber-Tip Pencil* decision

(1874) the Supreme Court rejected a patent for the modern eraser-tipped pencil, noting that both pencils and rubber erasers had been around for years. All the inventor had discovered was that compressing a small piece of rubber into a metal cylinder attached to the back of a pencil made the rubber stay in place. It did not matter that the resulting product was commercially successful.[26]

As Yale professor and patent treatise author William Callyhan Robinson attempted to explain in 1890, a particular device could have different "embodiments" that a trained observer could readily imagine, even though they were not identical with the existing device. One could not obtain a patent on a new embodiment of an old thing.[27] When the Supreme Court later began to articulate the requirement for patentability as works of "genius" rather than mere mechanical alterations, Congress intervened, restating the requirement as "nonobvious" subject matter in 1952.[28] "Nonobvious" can mean considerably less than "genius," as more than a half century of patent issuance under the new provision established.

The Origins of Patent Competition Policy: Prior to the Clayton Act

Since the first Patent Act was passed in 1790, its various versions have been concerned almost entirely with how patents are created, saying little about how they are subsequently used. Those questions were substantially left to the common law, to the judge-made "first sale" doctrine, and later to antitrust law. Not until 1952 did Congress control another judge-made doctrine, patent "misuse," which regulated abuses of issued patents. Questions about the use of issued patents were generally assessed under policies concerned with maintaining competition or furthering market transactions. Something resembling a "political economy" of innovation emerged first in these areas, beginning in the nineteenth century and expanding rapidly after the passage of the Clayton Act in 1914. Antitrust became important for dealing with these issues, in large part because the language of the antitrust laws was so spare, empowering judges to forbid practices that might "lessen competition" or "monopolize" markets, but providing few details. This was in sharp contrast to the increasingly detailed patent and other IP codes that gave judges much less room to maneuver. In sum, the economic study of patent use became far more sophisticated than the economic study of patent issuance.

The Sherman antitrust act (1890) never mentioned patents and did little to change judicial doctrine about them. During the quarter century between the

Sherman Act and the passage of the Clayton Act (1914) the Supreme Court confronted virtually every one of the issues that later became central to patent competition policy. These included pooling and price-fixing, unreasonable exclusion, compulsory licensing, and patent ties. The Court dismissed every complaint, either ignoring the Sherman Act or refusing to apply it. That would change abruptly after 1914, when a single mention of patents in the Clayton Act signaled a new course that severely limited patent rights while also integrating patent use more closely into competition policy.

Collusion, Exclusion, and Nonuse

Around the turn of the century the Supreme Court addressed major issues involving patented technologies that grew out of the Gilded Age revolution in machine production. The eclectic range of products included agricultural harrows, machine-made grocery bags, toilet paper, and office copy machines.

In 1900 harrows were horse-drawn implements that farmers used to break up ground. "Spring tooth" harrows had steel blades mounted so that they could spring up or to the side when they hit a rock, rather than breaking. Reed & Co. of Kalamazoo, Michigan, was apparently the first to obtain a patent, followed closely by several other small firms from Michigan and upstate New York. After several years of litigation, the firms "pooled," or shared, their patents by cross licensing them to one another. Under the pooling agreement the late-coming firms licensed from the earlier firms, but they also agreed on a minimum sale price for the harrows themselves. The pool then brought an action against a member for royalties and to enforce the price-fixing agreement.[29]

Justice Peckham, who authored the unanimous opinion for the Supreme Court, had also written the Court's opinion holding that price-fixing agreements among railroads were illegal per se under the Sherman Act.[30] Nevertheless, the Court concluded that the harrow price fix was "an appropriate and reasonable" requirement in a patent license because it tended to guarantee the value of the patents. Justice Peckham reasoned that the owner of a patent was entitled both to produce under the patent and to set the product's price. It followed that he could license these rights together or separately, just as a real property owner can sell some rights while retaining others. The Supreme Court unanimously adhered to this view a generation later in its *General Electric* decision.[31] The effect was to permit firms to fix a product price if the fix was contained in a patent licensing agreement.

The Supreme Court's 1908 *Paper Bag* decision was its first encounter with patent-based exclusion by a dominant firm. Several firms acting independently had developed and patented technology for making the modern stand-up grocery bag. The machines, which were a significant achievement, cut the paper, folded it, and glued the edges at high speed. Different patents took different approaches. William Liddell had invented a device that folded the paper at the appropriate places. He sold the patent to the Eastern Paper Bag Co., the dominant bag manufacturer, which was already using an alternative system that it regarded as equally good. Eastern then "shelved" the Liddell patent, electing to stay with its existing technology.[32]

When Continental Paper Bag Co. began producing with a technology somewhat similar to the Liddell patent, Eastern brought an infringement suit under the patent doctrine of equivalents. That doctrine, which had originated in an 1854 Supreme Court decision, enabled a patentee to bring an infringement action against technology that was not literally covered by a patent's claims, but was considered sufficiently "equivalent" so as to be deemed implicit in the patent's coverage.[33] Supporters of the doctrine generally observed that without it firms could "invent around" a patent by making trivial changes, thus undermining the patent's value. Critics argued that the doctrine had no natural limits and enabled patentees to shut down alternative technologies that were significant inventions in their own right. One well-known and far-reaching example is *Wright v. Curtiss*, where the court applied equivalents doctrine to shut down Curtiss's modern airplane that used metal wings and ailerons for steering and stability. The Wright brothers' technology had included fabric-covered flexible wings and cables that "warped" or twisted them. The decision enabled the Wrights to keep aircraft with rigid wings and ailerons from being manufactured, preventing the United States' use of metal-winged aircraft in World War I.[34]

The *Paper Bag* litigation exposed a battle that had been raging in patent law for some time. The more liberal view saw patents as utilitarian instruments for furthering innovation and making it available to the public. Under this view the technology described in unused patents should be available to others. It was expressed in the British Patent Act of 1902, which provided for compulsory licensing of unused patents.[35] The alternative view was that patents were property pure and simple, and could be used or not at the owner's will. For example, a farmer can remove a trespasser even if the farmer is not currently using the trespassed land.

Eastern, the dominant paper bag maker, pursued a business strategy of buying up patents and shutting them down so they would be unavailable to competitors. Eastern's counsel had been candid about this. "We do not make these machines because we do not need them," he said of the Liddell patent at oral argument. "We hold the patent to control." Federal judge James Aldrich objected to the suppression of competing technologies in this way. "[I]f a party may acquire and hold a single competing patent in deliberate and intentional nonuse for the purpose of overthrowing competitive conditions, and may have equitable injunction to that end, he may acquire and suppress all competing inventions." This would "reverse the whole constitutional and statutory project, in which the primary and leading purpose was to benefit the public and business."[36]

The Supreme Court rejected Adlrich's view that patent use must be subordinated to competition policy in this fashion. A patent was the "absolute property" of the inventor, and the two things that Eastern had done, acquisition and nonuse, were both fundamental attributes of property ownership. Any patent owner "may withhold the knowledge of it from the public, and he may insist upon all the advantages and benefits which the statute promises to him who discloses to the public his invention."[37] An unnamed writer in the *Yale Law Journal* supported the decision as properly rejecting the view that a patentee is a "quasi-trustee for the public," citing cases where dominant firms had kept patents secret until a rival started using the technology, and then sued for infringement. The "best jurisdictions have insisted on clinging to the elementary, constitutional idea of absolute right in a patentee."[38] By contrast, in the early 1920s economist John Maurice Clark criticized the purchase of patents "for the purpose of putting them to sleep." He observed that dominant firms might pay a great deal to acquire and suppress a patent that threatened increased competition. The result would be to restrain innovation.[39]

Distribution Policy: From the First Sale Doctrine to Antitrust

American legal policy toward product distribution was developed in patent law long before there were any antitrust laws. Although a few earlier decisions were more tolerant,[40] patent and antitrust case law became quite hostile toward manufacturer attempts to control how independent resellers resold their products. This hostility is enigmatic, given the importance of organized retail distribution systems to economic growth during this period and the common law's strong commitment to liberty of contract, particularly among business persons.

The mystery has two possible explanations, neither of which is completely satisfactory. First, the historical hostility reflects the common law's disdain for restraints on alienation: once a manufacturer sells a product the buyer/reseller should be able to do with it as she pleases. The common law policy dated back to the Middle Ages, and the Supreme Court expressed it repeatedly in the nineteenth century in patent cases and later in antitrust decisions through the 1960s. It survives even to this day in the first sale doctrine, which limits a patent or copyright owner's ability to restrict the use of a covered article once it has been sold.

A second answer is that when antitrust analysis of vertical practices began to incorporate economics, the prevailing theories of vertical integration were hostile. From the 1910s through the 1950s control of distribution was seen as a route to monopoly. The odd result was that courts routinely approved practices such as price-fixing by competitors through patent pools, even as they ferociously condemned distributional practices such as resale price maintenance and tying.

Tying occurs when a seller forbids a customer from buying a primary ("tying") product unless the customer also agrees to purchase a second, "tied" product. The initial cases were not antitrust cases, but patent disputes concerning "combination" patents. The issue went to the Supreme Court in the *Morgan Envelope* case in 1894.[41] The patentee owned three patents: on a dispenser, on special toilet paper, and on a combination on the use of the two together. Cheaper unpatented brands of toilet paper were available, however. When the defendant sold unpatented paper to owners of the patentee's dispenser, the patentee claimed contributory infringement of the combination patent. "Contributory" infringement occurs when someone knowingly sells something that enables the buyer to commit patent infringement. In the first half of the twentieth century contributory infringement claims became the principal vehicle by which patentees enforced patent ties.

The Supreme Court denied the patentee's action, however, relying on patent law's first sale, or "exhaustion," doctrine. The doctrine, which was not expressed in the Patent Act, dated to the early nineteenth century. Its most powerful statement was *Adams v. Burke*, a Civil War–era case that refused to enforce a restriction limiting the use of a patented coffin lid to burials within ten miles of Boston. When the patent owner attempted to enforce the restriction the Court held that the purchase of the patented lid "exhausted" the patentee's interest in that particular lid. "[W]hen the machine passes to the hands of the purchaser, it is no longer within the limits of the [patent] monopoly."[42]

Adams itself concerned a locational restriction, or "territorial restraint" in later antitrust parlance. The toilet paper case involved a tying arrangement. In 1908 the Supreme Court also applied the first sale doctrine in a copyright case to resale price maintenance. Bobbs-Merrill had published a pulp novel called *The Castaway*, by Hallie Ermine Rives, who wrote popular fiction and books on etiquette. Macy's Department Stores purchased the book and sold it for 89 cents, violating a printed restriction preventing resale of the book for less than $1.00. When Bobbs-Merrill sued for copyright infringement the Supreme Court held that the sale of the book exhausted the publisher's control over the purchased copies, making the price restriction unenforceable.[43]

By 1908 the Supreme Court had used IP law rather than antitrust law to deny enforcement to all of the major distribution restraints that would later become the subject of antitrust litigation. The one significant departure occurred in 1912, in *Henry v. A.B. Dick Co.*, and provoked an immediate congressional response. Dick manufactured a mimeograph machine, an early form of office copier in which the operator typed text on a carbonized stencil and wrapped it around an ink-filled drum. Dick sold the machine with a patent notice requiring purchasers to use its stencils, ink, and paper.[44] The Supreme Court enforced the tying restriction and Congress reacted with § 3 of the Clayton Act, passed in 1914 during Woodrow Wilson's first term. The provision condemned tying arrangements of all goods, "whether patented or unpatented," if the tie lessened competition.[45] For the first time, patent use had become an antitrust issue.

Why did Congress react so swiftly to the *Henry* tying arrangement case but not the agricultural harrow price-fixing case or the *Paper Bag* case permitting enforcement of unused patents? The government tried repeatedly without success to get the Supreme Court to overturn its rule permitting product price-fixing in patent license agreements. Several bills were presented to Congress, but they all failed.[46] Today the tying arrangement in *Henry* is widely regarded as competitively harmless, while horizontal price-fixing is equally widely regarded as anticompetitive. In any event, after the Clayton Act was passed patent use became a central concern of competition policy.

The Impact of the Clayton Act and the New Deal

In its first patent restraint case after the Clayton Act was passed the Supreme Court overruled *Henry*. The *Motion Picture Patents* case condemned an attempt by the owners of the market-dominating Edison motion picture projector to require purchasers of the projector to show only the company's films.[47] Edison's team had been one of the first inventors of the sprocketed projector reel and perforated film that engaged the sprocket.[48] This permitted the film to run faster and without the jerkiness of the earliest motion pictures. The tying restriction was a lingering vestige of an attempt to monopolize the entire U.S. motion-picture industry, at the time based in New York.[49] The attempt even included blacklisting of actors and actresses who worked on films produced by competitors.[50] Indeed, Hollywood soon became the center for film production because so many producers and artists fled New York to escape the legal reach of the film monopoly. Proximity to Mexico may have been one of Hollywood's attractions, because film producers were violating many of the Motion Picture company's patent restrictions.[51] By the time of trial the patents on the film had expired, although not those on the projector. The attempt to monopolize the industry had also largely fallen apart. Its principal effect was to hasten the film industry's relocation to southern California. Subsequent to the *Motion Picture* case the courts pursued tying arrangements relentlessly, initially under patent law and the judge-made doctrine of patent "misuse," and later under antitrust law.

The Clayton Act also brought the U.S. government much more actively into enforcement policy concerning patent use. All of the pre–Clayton Act decisions discussed previously were brought by private parties. Thereafter the government increasingly challenged perceived abuses of issued patents, mainly under the antitrust laws.[52] Both the antitrust case law and the economic and legal writing about the uses and abuses of patents and other IP rights increased exponentially.[53] The writing had little to offer, however, on topics such as the relationship between innovation and market structure, the optimal duration and scope of patents, or whether different industries should have different types of patent protection. With few exceptions, economists very largely accepted the patent system itself at face value, considering only whether issued patents were being used in competitively harmful ways.

Intellectual Property Monopolies: Institutionalism and the New Deal

As Chapter 6 relates, the Legal Realists who came to dominate federal economic policy during the New Deal were heavily influenced by the economic institutionalism of the Progressive Era. The institutionalists were deeply critical of IP rights, regarding them mainly as devices for perpetuating monopoly. Richard T. Ely's book *Monopolies and Trusts* (1900) acknowledged a relationship between patents and innovation, but largely spoke of them as monopolies. Ely suggested a number of reforms to the patent system. First, the government should be empowered "to purchase any patent at an appraised valuation" and place it in the public domain. Second, he advocated for global compulsory licensing: all patents should be granted "only on condition that the use of the patent shall be free to any one on payment to its owner of a reasonable royalty." A third reform was to place an annual tax on the use of patents, with a provision that the patent would lapse if the tax had not been paid.[54] Thorstein Veblen viewed IP rights as nothing more than a socially costly device for the preservation of monopoly. In the *Theory of Business Enterprise* (1919) he spoke of patents and trademarks as monopolies "resting on custom and prestige," and that they gave a "differential advantage" to their owners, but "no aggregate advantage to the community."[55]

After 1930 economic and legal writing focused increasingly on the role of IP rights in undermining competition. Edward Chamberlin's ground-shifting book on *Monopolistic Competition* (1933) pursued the relationship between IP rights and product differentiation. Existing theory, which assumed homogenous products, saw firms as competing in price so strenuously that they were unable to recover their fixed costs. As a result, collusion, monopolization, or ruin seemed inevitable. Under monopolistic competition firms did not compete by producing more and shaving prices. They avoided head-to-head competition by continuously differentiating their products so as to create little monopolies that were distinguishable in the eyes of consumers. Rather than overproduction, monopolistic competition theory saw chronic underproduction and unnecessarily high prices. Firms used trademarks and patents in order to protect their product space. Chamberlin argued that both patents and trademarks were exclusionary. Patents led to differentiation of products, whereas trademarks led to differentiation of brands. In the case of strong, well-recognized brands, he concluded, trademarks actually created more monopoly space between firms than patents did.[56]

Chamberlin created an industrial model in which patents and trademarks became an explicit part of business strategy. He concluded that IP rights were often "excessive" in the sense that there were too many in relation to any social value that they produced. Chamberlin's work was appealing to the Legal Realists, reinforcing their view that markets themselves are often instruments of coercion. In addition, the Legal Realists borrowed ideas developed in the 1910s and 1920s that property rights should be viewed less as a set of physical attributes and more as an abstract power to exclude vis-à-vis both others and the State. For example, Richard T. Ely had written that "the essence of property is in the relations among men arising out of their relations to a thing."[57] Wesley Hohfeld, whose work on legal concepts as balanced right/duty obligations made him a darling of the Legal Realists, also saw property rights as abstractions consisting of the power to exclude and the duty of others to respect that power.[58] Arthur L. Corbin argued that property "has ceased to describe any res, or object, of sense at all, and has become merely a bundle of legal relations."[59]

Legal Realist Jerome Frank concluded later that property and monopoly are "equivalent" because both create "the legally-protected power of an owner . . . to exclude others from its use except upon the owner's terms."[60] Frank developed this idea in several trademark decisions that came before the Second Circuit Court of Appeals. Although Frank was one of the more prolific Legal Realists, he was not an academic. He went from private practice to a series of positions in the New Deal administration. In 1941 Roosevelt appointed him to a federal judgeship on the Second Circuit, where he served until his death. Judge Frank's opinions on trademarks consistently characterized them as monopolies. "[T]he legal protection of trade-name does not engender competition," he wrote in a 1943 decision. "[O]n the contrary, it creates lawful monopolies, immunities from competition. And the legally forbidden invasions of those monopolies might often benefit consumers."[61] A concurring opinion in 1945, a year before the Lanham trademark act was passed, became Judge Frank's vehicle for a lengthy essay on monopoly and IP rights. Property ownership "is the essence of monopoly: the power to exclude others and thus economically to coerce them to pay what he demands for its use." Frank therefore objected to the tendency of the federal courts to call trademarks property rights, concluding that "the conventional assumption that trade-name protection importantly adds, in direct fashion, to consumers' economic welfare, has not yet been proved to be true in fact."[62]

The late 1940s saw significant law and scholarship on the monopolistic tendencies in trademark law.[63] In 1948 a federal court of appeals held that Sunkist could not invoke the recently passed Lanham trademark act against a food producer who used its name because of its "unconscionable efforts" to monopolize the word "Sunkist."[64] Arthur R. Burns saw product differentiation as one of the strongest signals that American markets were noncompetitive, and IP rights were the biggest culprit. Although patents are "held out as a bait to encourage the improvement of methods of production," in fact the "contribution of the patent law to the decline of price competition has passed far beyond the limits suggested by this principle."[65]

Other economists, including Berkeley's William Fellner and Harvard's John Kenneth Galbraith, argued that product differentiation induced by patents and trademarks effectively reduced the number of firms who actually competed with one another, thus making cartels more likely.[66] These views became more widespread in the 1950s and 1960s, with many writers arguing that brand advertising, product re-engineering, and even annual style changes in the automobile industry were anticompetitive.[67] They were fed by a popular literature that condemned product design and brand advertising as psychological manipulation of gullible consumers. Vance Packard's *The Hidden Persuaders* (1957) became a best seller. John Keats's *The Insolent Chariots* (1958) focused on automobile design changes and advertising.[68] Packard raised the specter that large manufacturers would use "psychological testing" in order to identify the repressed needs of consumers and then appeal to them through brand advertising. During 1957 Senate hearings on pricing in the automobile industry several economists cited annual style changes and excessive brand advertising as the principal reasons that the industry was not performing competitively.[69] A few years later Ralph Nader's bestseller *Unsafe at Any Speed* (1965) found automobiles to be infested with "designed-in dangers." Automobile makers had pushed brand appeal at the expense of quality and safety. Nader's book led young scholars such as Robert Reich and Robert Pitofsky to argue for increasing regulation of automobile advertising as well as safety.[70]

The Post–New Deal Attack on Patents

In the late 1930s perceived abuses of patents became a central focus of New Deal policy. Legal Realist Walton Hamilton wrote both a Temporary National Economic Committee (TNEC) monograph and many articles on the subject, stretching through the 1940s. He attacked firms that aggregated large numbers of patents or used restrictive licensing agreements to drown out competitors, and advocated broader use of compulsory licensing.[71] Working with Hamilton, Roosevelt's antitrust chief Thurman Arnold began an antitrust campaign against patent abuses. He championed the "leverage" theory that a firm could use its patents as a lever to acquire additional power in markets outside of the patent. In 1940 Arnold published a book about anticompetitive distribution practices entitled *The Bottlenecks of Business.* He described how the Ethyl Company used a patent on its ethyl antiknock compound, which was placed in gasoline in a.023 percent solution. Ethyl then required gasoline resellers using its compound to charge a specified price for the gasoline itself. As a result, Ethyl "required only one gallon of this patented fluid" to control the price of "forty-two hundred gallons of unpatented gasoline." The resulting *Ethyl* decision in the Supreme Court was one of the many times that the Court condemned patent abuses under a leverage theory.[72] Between 1938 and 1946 Arnold's Antitrust Division brought eighty-three antitrust patent abuse cases, a roughly tenfold increase from previous years.[73] Arnold also proposed legislation that would permit the Attorney General to intervene in patent infringement suits in order to have patents cancelled.[74] Like Walton Hamilton, he also recommended compulsory licensing.[75]

Prominent public intellectuals also criticized patents. Hungarian Michael Polanyi, who taught at Manchester but was widely read in the United States, argued in 1944 that the patent system was flawed in its basic conception. The system attempted to break up the stream of human knowledge with tiny "dams," each one becoming an obstacle to further progress.[76] Friedrich Hayek, then a professor at the London School of Economics shortly before he moved to the University of Chicago, voiced similar concerns.[77] Corwin Edwards joined the call for compulsory licensing of "unworked" patents.[78]

United States' law never adopted a general doctrine of compulsory licensing, even for unused patents. However, the emerging doctrine of patent "misuse" became an important vehicle for selective compulsory licensing and control of patent practices thought to be harmful. The doctrine was first hinted in the *Motion Picture Patents* case discussed previously. In 1931 the Supreme Court held that a patentee could not enforce a notice restriction requiring purchasers of its patented icebox to use its own dry ice. Borrowing from patent law's first sale doctrine, Justice Brandeis reasoned that a patentee was entitled to only a single royalty, but in this case was trying to leverage a second royalty on the unpatented ice.[79] The Supreme Court stated the mature version of the misuse doctrine in its 1942 *Morton Salt* decision, defining misuse as "the use of the patent to secure an exclusive right or limited monopoly not granted by the Patent Office and which it is contrary to public policy to grant."[80] Suppiger had been requiring purchasers of its patented salt injection machine used by canners to use its unpatented salt. Shortly afterward the government won an antitrust lawsuit condemning the International Salt Company of the very same practice.[81] The patent misuse doctrine thus migrated to antitrust law and for the next half century was used aggressively against all forms of tying, particularly when one of the products was protected by a patent or other IP right.

Whether or not patents were "monopolies," they did limit firm mobility by making it more difficult to enter markets with significant patent protection. For the classical political economists, mobility had been bedrock. Monopoly prices could not last as long as new firms were free to enter. In *The Theory of Monopolistic Competition* Chamberlin himself assumed easy entry into business. But Chamberlin's own pessimism about the industrial economy was exceeded by the "structuralist" theorists of industrial economists, notably Harvard's Edward Mason and his influential student Joe S. Bain. These views, discussed in the following chapter, worked their way into the law in writing by antitrust economists and lawyers.

The structuralists saw industries that were increasingly dominated by small numbers of firms and significant barriers to entry. They acknowledged that patents could encourage innovation, but found their overall impact to be negative. Mason's best-known legal policy article on the monopoly problem, published in 1937, never mentioned patents. Two years later, however, he argued for a "thorough going overhauling of existing patent legislation" so as to complement antitrust policy in dealing with both restrictive patent practices and the nonuse of patents in order to withhold technology from the market.[82]

Joe S. Bain, one of the most prominent antitrust economists of the 1950s and 1960s, largely regarded patents as socially costly impediments to competition. He associated them strongly with high barriers to entry.[83] In his influential 1959 textbook on industrial organization Bain recommended compulsory licensing of "each and every" patent. "While reasonably protecting the interest of the patent holder... by providing for reasonable royalties,... it would severely restrict or eliminate the use of patents as levers for collusive market control or as monopolistic barriers to entry."[84] In their formative book on *Antitrust Policy*, published that same year, Carl Kaysen and Donald F. Turner recommended compulsory patent licensing under the antitrust laws if a patent had not been used within five years of its issuance date and the "patentee was limiting its use in a way which was contrary to the public interest."[85] The influential 1955 *Report* of the Attorney General's Commission to Study the Antitrust Laws was generally more conservative, limiting compulsory licensing to cases of abuse. The Commission's members divided on the question of royalty-free licensing as an antitrust remedy. The majority thought it confiscatory and inappropriate, while a "substantial minority" disagreed.[86]

Prior to the 1952 Patent Act the Supreme Court invalidated patents routinely, for a variety of reasons.[87] In 1937 it unanimously rejected a patent on a vacuum tube as nothing more than an aggregation of older technologies and held that patentability required "inventive genius" rather than mere "mechanical skill."[88] Four years later the Court held that the Constitution required inventive genius.[89] In a concurring opinion to a 1950 decision Justice Douglas, joined by Justice Black, blamed the Patent Office for attempting "to get a broader, looser conception of patents than the Constitution contemplates." In the process it patented "a host of gadgets" that "obviously have had no place in the constitutional scheme of advancing scientific knowledge."[90] The Supreme Court's hostility toward patents led Justice Robert H. Jackson to remark in a dissent that "the only patent that is valid is one which this Court has not been able to get its hand on."[91]

Innovation and Economic Growth: The Schumpeter-Arrow "Debate"

Joseph Schumpeter's *Capitalism, Socialism and Democracy (*1942*)* was intended to defend free market capitalism against its Depression-influenced critics, particularly Keynes's view that the government should manage economic development so as to maintain stability. In the process, Schumpeter completely upended thinking about innovation, and implicitly about the role of the legal system in fostering it.[92] He viewed capitalism as an ongoing process of "creative destruction" by which innovation continuously displaced old industrial hierarchies with new ones. Looking back at the history of marginalist economic theory, he derided its emphasis on defects and failures in markets that created the impression we were living in an economic dark age. During this very period (the Depression aside) wealth had been created at an unprecedented rate. The reason, Schumpeter argued, was not price competition but rather innovation that continuously keeps markets in a frenzy. Schumpeter developed two controversial conclusions. One is that innovation contributes much more to economic growth than ordinary competitive processes. The second was that only monopolists or market- dominating firms were likely to be important innovators, for only they had the resources and relief from competitive pressure that costly innovation required.

Schumpeter's book almost single-handedly created a subdiscipline in economics concerning the relationship among innovation, economic growth, and monopoly.[93] His Harvard colleague Edward S. Mason concluded that Schumpeter's "drastic" argument completely undermined antitrust policy.[94] Schumpeter died in 1950, so one cannot characterize much of this literature as a "debate" with him, but two lines of thinking became central. First, Robert M. Solow, writing in the mid-1950s, performed empirical studies suggesting that Schumpeter was correct on his first point. Solow modeled an economy over the previous half century in which technology remained constant, comparing it with the actual economy. As much as 90 percent of economic growth was not accounted for. This "residual," he concluded, was the consequence of innovation.[95] By contrast, Kenneth Arrow took sharp issue with Schumpeter's other argument, namely that monopolists are the most likely innovators. In fact, Arrow argued, monopolists lack the competitive pressure to innovate, and they have much less to lose from failure to innovate.[96]

Although these economists were all writing about innovation, their work had an equally profound effect on antitrust law. Antitrust has always been preoccupied with the economics underlying its doctrines, as well as the role innovation plays in evaluating the consequences of business practices. By contrast, patent law has been much more myopic, generally preferring inward-looking doctrinal consistency over development of a political economy that relates innovation to market structure or economic performance. This difference became more pronounced in the 1970s, as antitrust increasingly viewed competition policy through consumers' eyes rather than those of producers. Consumers tend to benefit from low prices, high quality, and strong innovation, but they are almost never the best organized among the interest groups involved in the process. In sharp contrast, the IP laws have been dominated by the interests of producers, who gain from protection rather than access. One result has been widespread acceptance of Schumpeter's conclusion that innovation is a major contributor to economic growth, but also constant doubt whether patent law contributes much to innovation.[97]

The Failure of Patent Law as Innovation Policy

In the 1940s the practicing patent bar became increasingly alarmed about the Supreme Court's harsh treatment of the patent system. Giles Sutherland Rich, a leading patent lawyer, joined with Pasquale Federico to draft a new statute with the support of the New York Bar Association. The process exemplifies a tradition in which Congress virtually turned the drafting of complex IP legislation over to private producer interests. For example, drafting of the revised Copyright Act in 1976 was largely given to a committee dominated by copyright holders, who produced one of the greatest expansions of coverage for right holders at the expense of users.[98]

Rich was particularly vexed by the rapid expansion of patent "misuse" doctrine, as well as the high level of inventiveness that the Supreme Court required for patentability. The resulting 1952 Patent Act added a new section limiting patent misuse claims.[99] On inventiveness, the most significant addition was a requirement of "nonobvious" subject matter as a weaker alternative to the Supreme Court's requirement of "genius," which Rich regarded as seriously restrictive and too subjective.[100] As Judge Hand had observed in 1950, the patentability requirement was "as fugitive, impalpable, wayward, and vague a phantom as exists in the whole paraphernalia of legal concepts."[101]

What particularly provoked the supporters of the new Patent Act was the *A & P* decision invalidating a patent on an arm that could be placed on a grocer's counter and pushed forward to slide groceries toward the cashier.[102] The Rich Committee was upset by Justice Douglas's blunt concurrence stating that "the opinions of the Court have taken 'inventive genius' as the test," citing several decisions. The new test in the 1952 Act is that the invention must have been "nonobvious" at the time of its making to a person with "ordinary skill" in the area. Judge Hand concluded in 1955 that the provision was intended to restore the standard to its earlier position before the Supreme Court adopted the "inventive genius" test.[103] That standard guided the Patent Office and the courts toward patent grants for relatively minor inventions, occasionally resisted by the Supreme Court.[104]

By the late 1960s a growing consensus of producer groups had come to believe that generalist judges lacked the skills necessary to make good patent law. A 1975 *Report* of a Presidential Commission concluded that the federal courts were plagued by insufficient technical expertise and inconsistent decisions. Further, too many technical patent questions were given over to juries. The Commission recommended creation of a new appellate court to decide patent appeals.[105] The Federal Circuit was created in 1982 and given exclusive jurisdiction over appeals based on interpretations of the Patent Act. Giles Rich became one of its founding judges, serving until he was in his nineties.[106]

The Federal Circuit succeeded remarkably in strengthening the patent system after its deconstruction by the Supreme Court.[107] Not everyone was enamored of the change, however. Richard Posner observed the deep divisions among economists and antitrust lawyers over the role and effectiveness of the patent system. He doubted that eliminating the disciplinary effect of competing courts would solve it.[108] The court has also faced increasing criticism that its patent law too frequently serves to stifle rather than promote innovation.[109] What is most striking, however, is the extent to which both the drafters of the 1952 statute and the Federal Circuit have disregarded the economic literature affecting their field, far more than in any area of regulatory policy, including antitrust law. As a result, patent law has never escaped from producer capture and the kind of micro-micro analysis of boundaries that is more akin to property law than to the making of economic policy.

11

Structuralism in Competition Policy

NO AREA OF American law was more explicitly driven by economics than antitrust. Marginalist economics was heavily focused on business firm behavior and market performance—"industrial organization," as Alfred Marshall named this subdiscipline in *Principles of Economics* (1890), published the same year that the Sherman Act was passed.[1] Marshall also preferred the name "economics" to "political economy." The latter term was too closely associated with politics, which represented "the interests of only some part or parts of the nation" rather than society as a whole. In 1879 he and his coauthor/wife had argued that "economics" is a science rather than a political tool because it "brings together a great number of similar facts and finds that they are special cases of some great Uniformity which exists in nature."[2]

Nevertheless, marginalist analysis and even Marshall's own work threw the economic study of industry into division and disarray. First were the greatly increased technical demands. One advantage of classical political economy was its simplicity. The sharply increasing use of mathematics in neoclassical economics led to domination by professionals. Those without the technical skills tended to resist, and judges, legislators, and lawyers increasingly found its requirements beyond their grasp.

A second early effect of marginalism was to undermine the classical faith in competition. The emergent theory of fixed costs appeared to show that competitive outcomes were elusive and varied considerably from one market to another. Simply put, competition forces prices toward immediate costs, without leaving enough to cover capital costs. Yale economist Arthur Twining Hadley recognized the problem in the railroad industry in the 1890s.[3] In the early twentieth century this "ruinous competition" problem was generalized to all industries with significant fixed costs. The result served to justify the position of many economists that either monopoly or collusion in these industries was inevitable and the government could do little to correct it. Progressives for their part ignored the analysis, minimized its consequences, or argued that higher prices were a cost society should be willing to pay for industries populated by smaller firms. The stubbornness of these problems often led to policy conclusions that seem overly broad when considered in retrospect. Nevertheless, they would have severe, long-lasting implications for both antitrust and regulatory policy.

As Chapter 1 observes, economic marginalism developed simultaneously with the growth of the large business enterprise. When Adam Smith surveyed the economic landscape he saw farmers, blacksmiths, cobblers, and bakers—mainly small enterprises with low initial investment, easy entry, and little product differentiation other than a tradesman's reputation for quality. But economists writing during and after America's Gilded Age saw an economic world dominated by larger firms with significant investments in specialized plants and equipment.

Both classical political economy and the common law had always assumed easy entry and mobility of business. Except for utilities, common carriers, or a few other industries, government restrictions were regarded as harmful. An initial effect of the marginalist revolution was to undermine this presumption. The market itself became a hindrance to mobility, and the perceived role of the State changed from impediment to facilitator.

Classical political economy had the distinct advantage of not being technical. If they were writing today, the classical political economists would be regarded as public intellectuals writing about policy. "Competition" referred to rivalry that existed among two or more business persons.[4] For example, Adam Smith knew that competition required actors who knew about their market and had the freedom to act, which required that resources be mobile. But Smith and other classicists had only a vague idea about the relationship between competitive prices and cost. Further, the English classicists had little conception of "degrees" of competition. Augustin Cournot, writing in France in the 1830s, used mathematics to relate the number of firms in a market to the resulting price. Only with the rise of marginalism, however, did Cournot's work come into vogue in England and later in the United States.[5] Both Jevons and Léon Walras began to use some math in the 1870s, and Jevons and Marshall both acknowledged Cournot's influence.[6]

Cournot's mathematical model predicted that as the number of firms in the market became smaller, the price would rise, reaching the monopoly level at a single firm. His highly simplified theory of oligopoly influenced much of the marginalist theorizing about competition in the twentieth century.[7] Although acknowledging Cournot, Marshall nevertheless focused on the two simplest situations—competition and monopoly, with little thought for anything in between. By contrast, in her path-breaking study of price theory, *The Economics of Imperfect Competition*, Marshall's student Joan Robinson noted that although traditionally economists had treated competition as the norm and monopoly as a special case, "it is more proper to set out the analysis of monopoly, treating perfect competition as a special case."[8]

Soon after he immigrated to the United States Joseph Schumpeter reviewed Robinson's book. If competition is the exceptional case, he observed, then the geometry of marginalism, with its shifting curves, "cannot remain an academic curiosity." Our assumptions that markets are best left alone "cease to hold true" and "the list of cases in which collective political action can increase" welfare "becomes so extended as to make these cases the rule rather than more or less curious exceptions."[9] Schumpeter's statement about political action reflected an emergent 1930s' view that markets were frail institutions that varied a great deal from one another and often required government intervention to set them right.

The Perfect Market's Shrinking Domain

Marginalism provided industrial economics with a useable theory of costs and value, but the theory also created imposing problems. The classical political economists had only a general notion about the relation between costs and production. Marginalism changed that by developing mathematical concepts of fixed, variable, and marginal costs. Alfred Marshall noted that certain costs were highly responsive to demand in a short time period, whereas other costs such as those for land or durable plants or equipment were not. Whenever output lagged behind demand, the market price had little to do with cost. For example, "there is no connection between cost of reproduction and price in the cases of food in a beleaguered city."[10]

In 1900 many economists and antitrust writers saw the "ruinous competition" problem as so pervasive that either monopoly or collusion would be inevitable in many manufacturing markets.[11] Antitrust intervention would not solve the problem, for it did no more than condemn practices thought to be unavoidable. By the 1920s, however, a consensus began to emerge that truly ruinous competition existed in only a few industries. The literature began to develop important distinctions between long-run and short-run decision-making, largely in attempts to explain the great merger movement that occurred at the turn of the twentieth century.[12]

In 1923 American John Maurice Clark, professor at the University of Chicago and later Columbia, published a path-breaking book on pricing in manufacturing industries, *Studies in the Economics of Overhead Costs.* As Morris Copeland observed in a review, "[e]conomic theory has from the start proceeded as if all the costs incurred in any given period of time were directly traceable to the business transacted during that period."[13] In fact, planning occurred over the long run, which included decisions about the construction of plants as well as the quality and variety of products. Joan Robinson's *Economics of Imperfect Competition*, published a decade later, was the first systematic technical analysis of firms with significant fixed costs and diverse products.[14] In such markets, she reasoned, firms do not compete with each other nearly as sharply as under perfect competition. Prices tended to be higher and firms had an incentive to diversify their products in order to avoid head-to-head competition.

One important distinction between Marshall's *Principles* and Robinson's *Imperfect Competition* is in the two authors' conceptions of the "firm." For Marshall, the firm was in intense competition with other firms producing identical goods, or else a monopolist not facing any competitors at all. In sharp contrast, Robinson imagined a manufacturing world more like the one we actually have, in which products are more or less differentiated and yet compete. *Imperfect Competition*'s jolting conclusion was that real-world markets perform much less robustly than economists had imagined. Although the classicists were correct that true monopoly was the exception rather than the rule, they were far too sanguine about everything else. "Economists, misled by the logical priority of perfect competition in their scheme, were somehow trapped into thinking that it must be of equal importance in the real world." But in fact "the real world did not fulfill the assumptions of perfect competition."[15]

As Schumpeter observed, the previous practice of political economy had been to look "at the whole stretch of ground between the two limiting cases [monopoly and perfect competition] as rather unsafe and incapable of yielding determinate results." However, "[a]s the majority of practical cases lie on that stretch," the result was "highly unsatisfactory."[16] Robinson's ideological subtext was relatively clear. "We see on every side a drift towards monopolisation." Further, Robinson believed that capitalist entrepreneurs were systematically transferring wealth toward themselves and away from the one group that was unable to differentiate its output effectively—namely, labor.[17] Soon after *Imperfect Competition* was published, Robinson became a Keynesian and an active socialist in the British Labour Party.[18]

Harvard economist Edward Chamberlin developed further implications of product differentiation in his controversial and highly influential *Theory of Monopolistic Competition*, which was mathematically more sophisticated than Robinson's book.[19] Product differentiation undermined most of the arguments from prior to the 1930s that high fixed costs automatically led to ruinous competition. Firms making differentiated products did not simply manufacture more and more as long as price was above short-run cost. Rather, they invested in distinguishing their products in order to avoid head-to-head competition.

During the mid-twentieth century monopolistic competition became the ruling model of competition theory.[20] The theory suggested the worst of both worlds. Although prices were high, firms nevertheless did not earn monopoly profits because they spent their revenues distinguishing their products. The result was high prices, customer confusion, and excessive spending on advertising, promotion, and intellectual property rights. One result was an abrupt and dramatic change in the focus of competition policy. Antitrust became increasingly preoccupied with anticompetitive practices in product-differentiated markets. This change had two powerful implications. First was a dramatic expansion of antitrust law into issues involving vertical integration and distribution. Second was greater engagement with intellectual property law.

Antitrust Policy in the Second New Deal

The twenty-year period leading up to the New Deal has been described as an era of government-authorized cartels, or "cooperative competition."[21] The early New Deal carried this thinking to the extreme, substituting State planning and organized private ordering for competition.[22] The government's Antitrust Division was relegated to bringing a few "peanut" cases and staying out of the way.[23]

But in the late 1930s the Roosevelt administration undertook an abrupt and radical change in antitrust policy. The antitrust policies of the Second New Deal were highly suspicious of any form of agreement among rivals and increasingly hostile toward both dominant firms and vertical integration. The *Madison Oil* case (*Socony-Vacuum*) is an example of firms caught between the conflicting demands of two different government policies *within* successive Roosevelt administrations.[24] With encouragement from the National Recovery Administration, the petroleum industry had undertaken cartel-like self-regulation in order to limit output. Then, in an abrupt switch, the government issued a criminal indictment against the companies for the very same activities.[25]

One hesitates to ascribe too many policy implications to academic economists' ideas about industrial organization. Nevertheless, the facts are powerful, reflecting how quickly the growing number of new generation economists in the Roosevelt administration affected policy. Both the ruinous competition theories of the early century through the 1920s, and the monopolistic competition theories of the mid-1930s and after, saw severe problems in the traditional competitive model. But the implications for antitrust policy could not have been more different. The earlier views led naturally to the belief that less antitrust is better, that mergers were inevitable and should be broadly tolerated, and that competitor coordination through business associations was both necessary and publicly beneficial. By contrast, monopolistic competition theory saw a world of underperforming mini-monopolists who took anticompetitive advantage of intellectual property rights and vertical integration. These problems appeared to beg for aggressive antitrust solutions.

Structuralism in Competition Policy after the New Deal

Workable Competition

The work of Robinson and Chamberlin severely limited the classical idea that competition is robust and the natural tendency of markets. This fact explains at least part of the subsequent antitrust hostility toward such things as advertising and "excessive" product differentiation, which would reach its high point in the 1960s and 1970s.[26] At the same time, many members of the infant Chicago School rejected the theory of monopolistic competition for being too complex and overemphasizing industry structure rather than individual firm behavior.[27]

How one looks at monopolistic competition depends on the starting point. If perfect competition is the "norm," then monopolistic competition creates an image of sick industries, producing too little and spending too many resources on product differentiation, intellectual property rights, and advertising. By contrast, if one begins with unworkable competition and continuous collusion, then monopolistic competition may actually be an acceptable alternative. The all-important adjustments that competition policy had to make were, first, learning to live with imperfection. Second, policymakers had to distinguish those markets in which socially acceptable amounts of competition could be sustained through relatively passive antitrust enforcement, from those that would require more active regulation.

In 1940 John Maurice Clark thrust a consensus-forming paper into this mix. In *Workable Competition* he argued that although markets did contain many imperfections, their impact had been exaggerated. In reality, government policymakers could identify and enforce a degree of competition that was functionally adequate when compared with more regulatory alternatives. Further, "government need not assume the burden of doing something about every departure from the model of perfect competition."[28]

Workable Competition made the case for antitrust as the principal umpire of competition, while preserving a smaller domain for regulation by government agency. Important details had to be resolved, however, and a significant debate ensued between Harvard structuralists and behaviorists located mainly at the University of Chicago.[29] Nevertheless, widespread agreement emerged that Clark had salvaged the policy idea that while markets were imperfect, they were nevertheless sufficiently robust that only episodic government intervention would be necessary in most cases.[30]

The Rise of Structuralism

For the economic institutionalists, antitrust policy required different rules for different markets. As Legal Realist Walton Hamilton observed of the antitrust laws in 1932, "The simple uniformity of the older acts" must yield "to an accommodation of public oversight to the varying necessities of different trades."[31] After Chamberlin the idea that markets and even firms differed a great deal was picked up by more mainstream economists, particularly at Harvard. One byproduct that emerged in the 1950s was a series of single industry studies illustrating the competitive conditions in particular markets.[32] Contemporary regulatory policy, with its proliferation of different agencies in charge of different markets, was heavily driven by this conception of market diversity.

The relationship between economic institutionalism and emergent Harvard structuralism is undoubted, even though few Harvard economists considered themselves institutionlists. Structuralism clearly reflected the institutionalists' views that markets are frail, that they differ from one another, and that they require significant State intervention. Nevertheless, structuralism also thoroughly accommodated the neoclassical tools of marginalist analysis. The main difference is that traditional neoclassicists in the Alfred Marshall tradition relied on economic models that assumed uniform products and competition on price. By contrast, structuralists accepted the world after Robinson and Chamberlin, in which product differentiation had severe implications for market vitality. This enabled the structuralists to do a version of neoclassical economics that both was mathematical and had heightened views about monopoly, the anticompetitive consequences of entry barriers, intellectual property rights, and vertical control. Some of the most important antitrust decisions of the late 1940s and 1950s were written by people such as Justice William O. Douglas, who began his career as an institutionalist and never relented from his hostility toward these expressions of monopoly.

Harvard's economics department dominated economic thinking about competition policy from the 1940s through the 1960s and had a considerable influence on antitrust policy. Its principals were Chamberlin and Edward S. Mason, both on the Harvard economics faculty, and Joe S. Bain, who received his PhD under Mason but spent most of his career at the University of California at Berkeley. Donald F. Turner, another Harvard PhD, came to the law school in 1954 and Phillip Areeda in 1961. Carl Kaysen, also from Harvard, was at nearby MIT. Turner started out his career as a Bainian structuralist but changed his views in the 1970s. Areeda was never really a structuralist, although some of his writing about "no fault" monopoly was consistent with structuralist approaches.[33]

Already in 1937 Mason had observed that lawyers and economists used the term "monopoly" differently. Lawyers thought of monopoly as "restrictive or abusive practices," whereas economists identified it with market "control."[34] A dozen years later Mason concluded that lawyers had largely come around to the economists' view and increasingly were identifying monopoly as a structural rather than behavioral problem.[35]

Although Chamberlin's monopolistic competition dominated industrial economics, the policy emphasis gradually moved away from his particular model to oligopoly, which economists saw as far more threatening. In Chamberlin's story product differentiation and advertising were excessive, but easy entry and a large number of firms forced prices close to cost. This was unlikely in an oligopoly market with a small number of firms and high entry barriers. Joe Bain, who became the most prominent spokesperson for Harvard School structuralism, complained in 1950 that workable competition in oligopoly industries would be much more difficult to achieve.[36]

Bain found plenty of structural signs that competition was not workable in concentrated industries. Plants were too large and new entry was restrained, even though profits were much higher than Chamberlain had envisioned. Such markets should "be considered a case of unworkable competition." Further, such behavior was "determined by certain characteristics of the underlying market structure." In that case, "a demonstrated association between market structure and results would establish the more fundamental determinants of workability of competition."[37] Bain criticized those who found the relationship between structure and performance to be "indeterminate." Rather, a policymaker could "arrive at hypotheses concerning the systematic association of oligopolistic market structure and results." Bain then proposed a research agenda that related market structure to such things as the likelihood of collusion, profit margins, and innovation rates.[38]

The Structure-Conduct-Performance Paradigm

The Mason/Bain paradigm for industrial competition directly related an industry's structure to its performance, with "performance" referring to degree of competitiveness. Their evaluation tool became known as the "structure-conduct-performance," or S-C-P, paradigm, which tied together theories of oligopoly and product differentiation, and a great deal of empirical data.[39] Using it, industry structure was thought to determine behavior, and firms were largely powerless to deviate. For example, firms in concentrated industries (those with a small number of firms) could not avoid comparing their prices and determining whether to match their rivals. This conduct was in turn thought to dictate performance. If structure entails conduct and conduct entails performance, conduct itself drops out as a variable of interest. One could predict performance simply by knowing something about structure.

The S-C-P paradigm emerged in the 1950s as the dominant model of industry competition. Its reductionism contributed to its power. Conduct was thought to be too ambiguous to assess. A large firm's actions designed to increase its own sales were presumptively competitive, whereas actions designed to steal sales from rivals might be thought anticompetitive. But how does one tell the difference when the same act does both things? The S-C-P paradigm promised antitrust policymakers a way of addressing these problems without troubling themselves about the ambiguities inherent in analyzing conduct.

Bolstering Bain's commitment to the S-C-P paradigm was his belief that industrial concentration in America was too high. Firms were larger than necessary to be efficient, and many markets would function equally well with more firms. In the presence of high entry barriers, which Bain tended to find readily, this theory had strong implications for antitrust policy. It suggested that there was a concentration "ratchet" in the sense that even after a firm achieved efficient size, nothing kept it from growing larger still. Industrial concentration would tend to increase. [40] This would be exacerbated by a lax merger policy that permitted firms to grow larger by acquiring rivals.

The idea that firms were much larger than economically justified was the centerpiece of congressional hearings that led to a 1950 expansion of the anti-merger law.[41] Bain believed that overall, American industry exhibited a trend toward concentration—a theme that was reflected in subsequent merger decisions in the Supreme Court. Indeed, in 1960s'-era merger policy a "trend toward concentration" became a shorthand rationale for condemning mergers without detailed inquiry into specific effects.[42]

Further, Bain argued, vertical integration could increase the tendency toward concentration by locking vertically related firms together.[43] He cited vertical integration in automobile production and assembly. Suppose that automobile production required a 15 percent market share for efficiency, while assembly of parts required only 2 percent. By integrating manufacturing and assembly, and particularly by making the parts specific to one manufacturer's design, the automobile manufacturer effectively required its dedicated assembler to have a 15 percent share as well.

Bain also believed that product differentiation was an entry barrier. Established firms "may enjoy a product-differentiation advantage over potential entrants, because of the preference of buyers for established firms and products when compared with new ones."[44] Product-differentiated markets also tended to have more patent protection and more regimented distribution systems. Prices tended to be higher in more differentiated markets.

Bain criticized antitrust monopolization cases that analyzed monopoly "only indirectly through assault on the predatory or exclusionary actions of firms, and not directly as a structural phenomenon." The result was "lengthy and expensive" and largely indeterminate litigation, whose poor results were magnified because courts were usually "unwilling to remedy illegal monopolization by requiring structural changes through dissolution or dismemberment of offending firms." Following Bain, Vanderbilt economist George W. Stocking faulted the Supreme Court for excessive emphasis on "intent and conduct." which he believed had served to undermine several government cases against dominant firms.[45]

The principal case to shift the focus from conduct to market control was Judge Hand's 1945 *Alcoa* decision, which found that the Aluminum Company of America had engaged in unlawful monopolization. The government's challenge occasioned the longest trial in U.S. history, more than two years, with Thurman Arnold himself participating.[46] The Supreme Court could not manage the six-justice quorum to decide the closely watched case. President

Roosevelt had not yet filled the seat occupied by Justice Byrnes, eventually replaced by Wiley Rutledge. In addition Justices Jackson, Reed, Murphy, and Stone were all disqualified because they had participated in earlier government cases against *Alcoa*. Congress responded with a statute that designated the three most senior judges of the Second Circuit Court of Appeals as a substitute for the Supreme Court.[47]

Judge Learned Hand's *Alcoa* opinion proved to be a forceful statement of the S-C-P paradigm. First was the detailed attention he gave to defining a "relevant market" and assessing Alcoa's power. Second was his willingness to find unlawful monopolization on relatively minor misconduct. Third was his terse declaration that "we disregard any question of intent."[48]

Many antitrust experts, including Edward H. Levi of Chicago and Eugene Rostow of Yale, proclaimed the decision an important turning point, ending antitrust's preoccupation with immoral conduct and inaugurating a more refined approach based on the economics of market structure.[49] Beginning in the late 1940s, Supreme Court antitrust decisions frequently repeated these themes.[50] A few courts even entertained the view that antitrust law forbade monopoly "without fault" or "for its own sake."[51] The 1955 *Report* of the Attorney General's Commission on antitrust reflected the same impulse, emphasizing power a great deal but paying little more than lip service to conduct requirements.[52] In 1959 Donald F. Turner and Carl Kaysen proposed that the government be permitted to break up monopolies without any proof of anticompetitive conduct.[53] Although the courts never adopted that position, both the government and the courts accepted definitions of the monopolization offense that required much less harmful conduct than earlier cases had found.

The implications of the S-C-P paradigm on antitrust policy were far-reaching. Turner concluded that "[s]uch postwar decisions as *Alcoa* perceptibly decreased the law's requirement of bad conduct" and "perceptibly increased its attention to power." The *Alcoa* case "clearly consigned the abuse theory of monopolization to limbo."[54] In merger law the S-C-P paradigm entailed that mergers could be analyzed simply by determining the market shares of the firms involved, as the Court held in its 1963 *Philadelphia Bank* decision.[55] This view, somewhat modified, was incorporated into Merger Guidelines the Antitrust Division issued in 1968, when Turner was its head.[56]

The economists advocating the S-C-P paradigm and the courts worked in tandem. Which most influenced the other is difficult to say. The S-C-P paradigm matured in the economics literature in the 1950s, several years after the *Alcoa* decision. Industrial structure was first and foremost on the minds of Congress when it enacted the Cellar-Kefauver Amendments to the merger law in 1950.[57] Bain's concerns about a "trend" toward increased industrial concentration were anticipated in that statute's legislative history.[58] Indeed, a Federal Trade Commission (FTC) study in 1948 had warned that "if nothing is done to check the growth in concentration, either the giant corporations will ultimately take over the country, or the Government will be impelled to step in and impose some form of direct regulation in the public interest."[59]

Even these conclusions reflected institutionalist and Legal Realist views that stretched back to Adolf A. Berle and Gardiner C. Means's critique of rising concentration in *The Modern Corporation and Private Property*. They spoke of the "centripetal attraction which draws wealth together into aggregations of constantly increasing size," and warned that "the trend is apparent" and "no limit is as yet in sight."[60] The 1950 legislation followed a string of proposals in Congress to stop further concentration.[61] To be sure, these earlier proposals did not share the economists' concerns about reduced output and higher prices. The earlier concerns were heavily populist, addressed to aggregations of power as such. Derek Bok, an antitrust professor who later became President of Harvard University, observed that "the curious aspect of the debates is the paucity of remarks having to do with the effects of concentration on prices, innovation, distribution, and efficiency." Rather, "competition appeared to possess a strong socio-political connotation which centered on the virtues of the small entrepreneur to an extent seldom duplicated in economic literature."[62]

The S-C-P Paradigm in Decline

The dominant theme of the S-C-P paradigm was that antitrust should reduce the amount of monopoly in the economy.[63] By contrast, the guiding principle of the emergent Chicago School critique was that market power is not inherently a bad thing. Often monopoly and high concentration result from efficiency. The critique had originated at the University of Chicago in the thought of Frank Knight and Aaron Director, and then later George Stigler in price theory, Milton Friedman in macroeconomics, Gary Becker in law and economics, and Richard Posner in antitrust.[64]

The Chicago School launched a frontal attack on the S-C-P paradigm's identification of industrial concentration as an inherent evil. The most likely cause of concentration, Chicago economists argued, is economies that favor larger firms. Further, the rigid oligopoly theories of the S-C-P paradigm considerably understated the ingenuity of firms in finding ways to compete. The S-C-P paradigm tended to view oligopoly as a structural problem, which rather strictly related performance to the number of firms in a market and their size distribution. In contrast, the Chicago School tended to look at concentrated industries as presenting problems in competitive strategy, in which each market participant weighed the net effects of various actions and anticipated responses.[65] Two pillars of Chicago School revisionism were that larger firms tended to have lower costs than Bain had supposed, and that firms in concentrated markets behave much more competitively than Chamberlin, Mason, Bain, Kaysen, or Turner had supposed.[66]

Picking a date for any intellectual movement's demise is difficult. The Harvard School abandoned most parts of the S-C-P paradigm in the 1970s.[67] This was partly a reaction to the 1969 *Neal Report,* which had been secretly commissioned by President Lyndon Johnson in late 1967. He asked Phil C. Neal, Dean of the University of Chicago Law School, to lead a commission to propose antitrust reforms for American industry. Johnson requested the Commission's *Report* by June 30, 1968, intending its release to be part of the LBJ re-election strategy. However, Johnson's political standing was severely damaged by the unpopular war in Vietnam, and in March he announced that he would not seek re-election. The authors finished the *Report* nevertheless, and it was released early in 1969.[68] Its authors included six law professors, three economists, and three antitrust lawyers. The entire project took only seven months to complete, involved no new research, and contained virtually no citation. Yet it proposed expansive antitrust reforms, including a "Concentrated Industries Act," which would give the Attorney General a mandate to "search out" oligopolies and order breakups until no firm had a market share exceeding 12 percent.

Robert H. Bork, a professor member of the Commission, wrote a stinging dissent from the *Report's* recommendations and firmly aligned himself with the Chicago School critique.[69] William F. Baxter, another academic member, kept silent but would largely repudiate the *Report* later as he learned more about economics.[70] Bork went on to become a prominent D.C. Circuit judge and failed nominee for the Supreme Court. Baxter became head of the Antitrust Division during Ronald Reagan's first term in office in the early 1980s.

No Neal *Report* recommendation was ever enacted. The change in administration from Johnson to Nixon, who was elected in 1968, killed any political momentum for massive antitrust reform. President Nixon appointed George J. Stigler of the Chicago economics department to chair a competing

Commission, which included both Posner and Ronald Coase. The "Stigler Report" was never officially released, but it leaked out in May 1969, and was subsequently published.[71] The Stigler *Report* disagreed with the industrial concentration warnings in the Neal *Report*, largely rejected the correlation between market concentration and anticompetitive results, and made several technical recommendations for revision of the antitrust laws.

The tragedy of the Neal *Report* is that just as it was being written its perspective was on the verge of catastrophic collapse. Indeed, the *Report*'s release instigated a massive reaction among younger academics that eventually cast the S-C-P paradigm into the trash heap of defunct economic doctrines. In 1969, that same year, Nixon appointed conservative chief justice Warren E. Burger to succeed the much more liberal Earl Warren, signaling a rightward turn in Supreme Court antitrust law. In 1974 the Court gave the federal government its first defeat in a merger challenge in decades, concluding that the government could not simply rely on an increase in market shares but must show actual anticompetitive effects. The era of S-C-P had come to an end.[72]

12

Distribution and Vertical Control

MUCH OF THE history of legal and economic policy has emphasized the interest group clashes that produced it.[1] Regulatory history is often viewed as a political process in which well-organized interest groups obtain political advantage and protect their particular industry from competition, typically at the expense of consumers. But interest group politics cannot fully explain our regulatory past, especially not in areas where consensus is fairly strong. For example, in almost every state, electricity and natural gas have been delivered to retail customers by price-regulated monopolies. By contrast, groceries and shoes have been sold in competitive markets with little regulation except for brief periods of extremist flirtation. These results did not obtain simply because electric power interest groups were better organized than were grocers. Policymaking in these situations was driven by theory as well as politics. If the theory is controversial, however, or if many of its features were poorly understood, then interest group influence became more prominent and tended to dominate government policy. As a result, interest group pressures in a complex democracy cannot be ignored, particularly in a regime where fundamental changes in technology and corporate structure were causing many displacements of older small businesses. So it is with the law of vertical integration.

Vertical integration occurs when a firm does something internally that it might otherwise purchase on the market. Supporters generally referred to the practice as vertical "integration," emphasizing its efficiencies. For example, economist Lawrence Frank defined vertical integration in 1925 as "the functional coordination of one or more units in each of the several successive stages of production, so that they are all operated as a single, unified industrial process."[2] By contrast, critics including economic institutionalists and Legal Realists spoke of it as vertical "control" or vertical "restraints," terms that emphasized its perceived tendencies to limit small business freedom or create monopolies.

Few areas of economic law have experienced more fumbling, experimentation, and interest-group pressure than the law of vertical control. Nevertheless, vertical integration is not inherently monopolistic. For example, the nineteenth-century village cobbler who maintained his own shop, made three pair of shoes per week by hand, and sold them directly to consumers was vertically integrated "upstream" into shoemaking machinery and "downstream" into shoe retailing. With the rise of machine manufacture, the cobbler's individual functions gradually became vertically *dis*-integrated. For example, the formation of the United Shoe Machinery Company in 1899 created a firm that made only shoe-manufacturing equipment and leased it to shoe manufacturers, who in turn sold the shoes to distributors or perhaps directly to department stores for resale.[3] What had once been the work of a single firm now became that of at least three or four.

Vertical integration can occur when a firm simply begins doing something for itself, such as the cobbler who sells his own shoes directly to customers. This type of "de novo" vertical integration was regarded as the least damaging to competition, although U.S. legal policy in the 1930s and after became hostile. Second, a firm might acquire a different firm in a vertically related market, such as when Brown Shoe, a manufacturer, acquired Kinney Shoe's chain of retail stores in 1956.[4] The third type of vertical integration involved long-term, or "relational," contracts between two firms that maintained legally separate ownership. As detailed in Chapter 7, legal recognition of such agreements enabled modern franchising and the growth of independent dealer networks. Although contracts generally produced the loosest forms of vertical integration, they also invoked the angriest controversy and some of the most aggressive legislation.

Vertical integration never played much of a role in classical economic theory. The classicists assumed that the firm procured some of its needs on the market and did other things for itself depending on convenience. Adam Smith's *Wealth of Nations* included a chapter entitled "That the Division of Labour Is Limited by the Extent of the Market."[5] Smith argued that firms in larger markets tend to purchase more from others and do less for themselves, leading to vertical dis-integration. For example, in a small, isolated village, each farmer shoes his own horses, but a larger community may support a blacksmith who can perform the job better or at lower cost.

The early marginalist economists did not do much more than the classicists did. In 1919, late in life, the great Cambridge economist Alfred Marshall wrote a lengthy book entitled *Industry and Trade*, which was never as influential as his famous *Principles of Economics. Industry and Trade* contained detailed accounts of vertical integration, most of which Marshall attributed to cost savings or to firms' fussiness about quality. He anticipated the 1930s' view that product differentiation led to greater vertical integration. If components were unique to that firm's own product, such as Ford engines for Ford automobiles, then Ford would be more likely to make its own engines. *Industry and Trade* also contained an interesting discussion of the steel industry, suggesting that widespread collusion led to vertical integration as manufacturers tried to avoid cartel prices by refining their own steel.[6] Although Marshall's observations were realistic and ahead of their times, they were unfortunately not integrated into Marshall's general theory but instead were buried in a descriptive account of the details of industry drawn mainly from casual observation.

In the United States, both the institutionalists and later the Legal Realists were suspicious of vertical integration, seeing it as a step toward monopolistic control. For example, John R. Commons found it to be inherently monopolistic.[7] In *The Modern Corporation and Private Property,* Berle and Means saw the interests of managers as conflicting with those of owners, a phenomenon that they believed led to inefficiently large size and excessive vertical control.[8] In his 1940 book on *The Bottlenecks of Business* Thurman Arnold, head of the Justice Department's Antitrust Division, argued that vertical restrictions were at least partly to blame for the maldistribution of wealth because they drove so many small firms out of business.[9]

The most important dissenting voice was Ronald H. Coase, whose *The Nature of the Firm* was published in 1937, when Coase was still at the London School of Economics.[10] Coase saw vertical integration as a problem of comparing the costs of internal production against those of using the market. The theory was purely market-driven and completely non-monopolistic. But he was swimming upstream. Coase's essay was virtually ignored for more than a generation, even among economists. For example, Joe Bain's 1959 text on *Industrial Organization* contained lengthy discussions of vertical integration but never cited Coase.[11]

During the latter part of the New Deal U.S. antitrust policy embarked on a thirty-year war against vertical integration. Robert Bork complained in the 1950s that antitrust policy "consistently condemned" vertical integration without understanding it.[12] From today's perspective the law of vertical integration in the mid-twentieth century seems irrationally hostile, understating its economic value and exaggerating its potential for competitive harm. Aside from Coase, however, the legal theory was not far removed from the prevailing economics. For example, Bain saw vertical integration as much more pervasive than the search for economies justified. He found its rationales in the prospect of monopoly—mainly, higher entry barriers or market exclusion. Although Bain lacked good empirical data, he voiced "a considerable suspicion" that most vertical integration was "not justified on the basis of any cost savings." Bain cited the increase in vertical integration into distribution and sales as involving situations where "the rationale of the integration is... the increase of the market power of the firms involved rather than a reduction in cost."[13]

Bain was even more suspicious of vertical integration by contract, particularly if the contract involved the exclusion of rivals. For example, in single branding ("exclusive dealing") a supplier might insist that a dealer sell only its brand. "Most such practices or policies are dually effective in (a) restricting or weakening existing competition, and (b) preventing or discouraging the entry of new competitors." In sum, the mainstream economics of the day largely supported the hostility expressed in the case law.

In contrast, Alfred Chandler's panoramic Pulitzer-prize history of American business growth saw vertical integration largely as a consequence of technological developments and changes in markets. In a book that cited Ronald Coase's *The Nature of the Firm* only once and misnamed him "Richard,"[14] Chandler nevertheless argued that vertical integration occurred when it became more cost-effective for firms to use managers rather than markets to obtain materials or distribute their products. In Chandler's account an important engine of this revolution was the railroad. First, the railroads were the first firms large enough to accomplish things efficiently through managers rather than markets. Second, the railroads made it possible for other firms to combine spatially separated production and distribution functions under a single management.

Emergent Threats to Small Business

Progressive Era manufacturing firms often evolved from greater to lesser vertical integration. The Wright brothers—bicycle builders by trade—made many of their own aeroplane parts, as did many of the early automobile manufacturers. Henry Ford, whose impulse for vertical control approached paranoia, even grew his own soybeans for making plastic horn buttons.[15] As industries developed, however, their needs typically became more standardized and reliance on outside suppliers increased.[16] International Harvester, the largest early twentieth-century maker of agricultural implements, initially acquired and operated its own steel mills, mines, railroads, and parcels of land for growing lumber. It gave them up in the 1930s, partly because government antitrust authorities believed that vertical integration was leading to higher prices.[17]

The history of legal policy toward vertical integration in the United States reflects extraordinary antipathy and indecisiveness. Most of the historical problem was with corporations. The common law held very benign attitudes toward vertical expansion by internal growth. Simply integrating vertically into a new line of business was not an offense. At the same time, however, states were concerned about corporate power that they could not control. Nineteenth-century state corporate law often restricted vertical integration by corporate "business purpose" clauses. For example, a corporation chartered to operate a railroad might violate state corporate law by building a factory to manufacture its own tracks or cars. A benign legal environment later developed the "collateral transactions" rule, permitting corporations to integrate vertically into areas deemed essential to their operation. By the second decade of the twentieth century most large firms were incorporated under liberalized corporate law provisions that permitted them to engage in "any lawful business." After that corporate law did not significantly impede vertical integration.[18]

In the 1920s antitrust law began to condemn vertical integration by dominant firms if it displaced independent rivals. Vertical mergers also became increasingly suspect. As originally enacted the antitrust merger provision, § 7 of the Clayton Act, applied only to mergers between competitors and thus did not reach vertical mergers.[19] Congress corrected that oversight in 1950, and almost immediately the Justice Department launched an aggressive campaign against vertical mergers, supported by the Supreme Court.

Economists never developed a robust theory showing why a firm's participation in multiple stages of production or distribution is harmful. Vertical integration *did* cause obvious and painful economic dislocations, however, ruining thousands of small family businesses during the Great Depression. As a result it became a playground for special-interest groups seeking both state and federal protective legislation.[20] Many states began to levy "corrective" taxes against vertically integrated chain retailers. In *Liggett v. Lee* (1933) the Supreme Court overturned a Florida law taxing chains at a rate that increased as the chain operated in more counties. Justice Brandeis wrote a stinging dissent lamenting that the chains were running single store owners out of business.[21] Several states passed "divorcement" statutes that prohibited gasoline refiners from owning their own retail stations.[22] State regulation of franchising began mainly in the automobile industry and then passed into other markets. The principal perceived evils were manufacturers' increasing demands for larger investments by dealers, and also the tying of repair parts and financing to automobile sales.[23] At the federal level, the drafting of the Robinson–Patman Act in the mid-1930s was virtually taken over by the leading association of small wholesale grocers, largely after they had failed to combat the chain-store revolution with privately orchestrated boycotts.[24]

Economists and even lawyers knew that vertical integration could reduce the costs of distribution, but that fact did not always make them more sanguine. Some even regarded the cost savings themselves as harmful. Those concerns were manifest in the legislative history of 1950 amendments to the antitrust laws, and reflected in the Supreme Court's *Brown Shoe* decision in 1962.[25] At the government's request, the Court condemned a vertical merger into retailing precisely *because* it permitted the firm to undersell smaller, unintegrated rivals. The prevailing belief was that an economic landscape populated by small businesses was what the country really wanted—"for its own sake and in spite of possible costs," as Judge Hand described the goals of the antitrust laws in 1945.[26]

Contractual Vertical Integration: Liberty of Contract and Restraints on Alienation

Contractual vertical integration refers mainly to long-term franchise agreements between manufacturers and independent dealers. Late nineteenth- and early twentieth-century views of contractual integration invoked two common-law doctrines: liberty of contract and an equally strong policy against restraints on alienation. The common law was deeply committed to both principles, notwithstanding profound conflict between them. Liberty of contract entailed that contracting parties could agree to do anything not contrary to positive law or public policy. Further, vertical distribution agreements were contracts between experienced businesspersons who did not require any special solicitude from the law.

On the other side was the common law's deep hostility toward restraints on alienation, which generally took the form of restrictions on how a purchaser could use or sell the acquired property. Here, the law carved out a significant exception to liberty of contract even as the Supreme Court was elevating that doctrine to strong constitutional status. The *Dr. Miles* decision (1911), which condemned supplier agreements that set resale prices ("resale price maintenance," called "fair trade" by small retailers), came only six years after the *Lochner* decision struck down maximum-hours laws for laborers.[27]

The law's almost sacred regard for individual business autonomy expressed in the condemnation of alienation restraints was a significant legal obstacle to controlled distribution. Clearly an employer could tell its own employee operating a retail branch what price to charge, that he could sell only his employer's products, or that he must use only his employer's ink in the store's mimeograph machine. However, if the employee was an independently franchised small business and the relationship was contractual, the story was entirely different. All three of these practices were at one time regarded as unlawful per se under the antitrust laws—that is, they were presumed unlawful without proof of specific anticompetitive effects.

American legal policy toward business restraints on alienation developed in the mid-nineteenth century in patent and copyright law through the "first sale" doctrine, discussed in Chapter 10. The doctrine prohibited a firm from using the intellectual property laws to enforce a restriction on a protected good after it had been sold. However, the historical policy was hardly limited to intellectual property. The English common law's aversion to alienation restraints had its origins in the long English history of estates in land. Harvard Law professor John Chipman Gray's influential Gilded Age treatise, *Restraints on the Alienation of Property*, lauded both liberty of contract and the common-law rules prohibiting alienation restraints.[28]

In *Dr. Miles* the Supreme Court expressly incorporated the common-law policy against restraints on alienation into the Sherman Act, citing Gray's treatise as well as *Coke upon Littleton*, an early seventeenth-century edition of a fifteenth-century treatise on property law.[29] From *Dr. Miles* on, resale price maintenance was regarded as falling within the Sherman Act's prohibition of trade restraints. The Supreme Court's *Schwinn* decision more than a half century later still cited this "ancient rule against restraints on alienation" as a rationale for condemning territory restrictions imposed on bicycle dealers.[30]

In 1914 Congress passed Section 3 of the Clayton Act, migrating the concern with tying and single-branding from patent law into competition law. It also extended the concern from sales to leases and other nonsale transactions and made clear that the prohibition applied to unpatented goods. Patent law's first sale doctrine continued to apply to the sales of patented goods, but antitrust reached much more broadly. In its 1922 *United Shoe Machinery* decision and its 1936 *IBM* decision the Supreme Court condemned tying clauses in lease contracts of commercial machinery.[31]

Relational Franchise Contracts and the Fading Monopoly Requirement

As noted in Chapter 7, classical common law viewed contracts as governing discrete agreements in time: I will do this for you, and you pay me. Prior to the Gilded Age Judges were ambivalent toward open-ended agreements that had uncertain duration or that called for an indeterminate quantity or, even more, an uncertain price. But the essence of vertical integration by contract was the development of longer-term business relationships, contemplating future developments that could only be estimated when the relationship was formed. This type of contract required a forward-looking theory of rational expectations, and marginalist economics supplied the supporting theory.

A "relational" contract is open-ended in the sense that it contemplates ongoing adjustments among the parties, with periodic changes in price, quantity, or other terms. The earliest relational contracts were long-term patent licenses in which the licensee promised to pay a specified sum for each unit produced over a multi-year period, but the number of units could vary. In the mid-nineteenth century the McCormick Harvesting Co. used regional patent and trademark licenses to create ongoing relationships with local manufacturer-dealers who produced its machines locally and sold them to farmers, thus making national shipment of bulky equipment unnecessary.[32] The arrangement also permitted McCormick to share the risk and cost of developing a nationwide distribution system. Licensees agreed to be exclusive resale agents for McCormick's reapers in a certain territory, and that they would sell no reapers other than McCormick's. Singer reached similar agreements with sewing machine dealers.[33]

The developing franchise system typically involved the sale and resale of goods from manufacturers to independent dealers, and also licensing of trademarks and other intellectual property rights. The franchisees became part of the manufacturer's branded distribution network. Two of the largest early franchisors were retailers of consumer products—Western Auto and Ben Franklin Stores. Both originated in the 1920s and by 1960 had several thousand stores doing business under the franchisor's name.[34]

Automobile franchising began to develop before 1910. Henry Ford initially experimented with company-owned local offices and even with traveling salesmen showing his Model-T automobiles, but he soon turned to franchise relationships with locally owned dealerships. The franchise agreements required Ford to supply cars and permitted dealers to advertise themselves as part of the Ford enterprise. The agreements did not specify the quantity or wholesale price, and they required the dealers to make their best efforts to sell Ford vehicles. Eventually they came to require the dealers to stock and sell Ford repair parts and to perform service on Ford vehicles. In 1917 the National Automobile Dealers Association was formed as a way of empowering dealers against manufacturers, mainly by obtaining legislation.[35]

As a matter of state law, by the 1930s the courts had become increasingly comfortable with open-ended franchise agreements, provided they did not see a threat of monopoly.[36] They also tended to interpret the contracts literally and to enforce even harsh provisions against dealers who knowingly entered into them.[37] The common law was most likely to enforce long-term distribution contracts when they were fairly strict and tied the buyer's hands, thus tending to establish mutuality of obligation, but not when the buyer was free to deal with others. Under federal law, however, these considerations gradually flipped after the Clayton Act was passed. Both Congress and later the courts increasingly worried that such exclusivity provisions could create monopoly.[38] In 1922 the Supreme Court refused to enforce single-brand contracts covering the retailing of dress patterns. The agreement created a franchise relationship between a market- dominating pattern manufacturer and thousands of dry-goods stores across the country, giving the retailers steep discounts in exchange for their promise to sell the manufacturer's patterns exclusively. The very definiteness of the contract proved to be its undoing. The exclusivity provisions reached to many towns that had only a single dry-goods store. This made it impossible for customers to obtain competing patterns.[39]

Exclusive dealing also became widespread in the gasoline industry. The manufacturer's trademark could not be displayed on the gasoline itself, so buyers had to rely on signs posted at the retailer's station or pumps. In the early 1920s several courts rejected the Federal Trade Commission's claim that it was anticompetitive for refiners to provide branded pumps to locally owned stations on the condition that they sell only that manufacturer's gasoline. As one court put it:

> Every pumping station is an advertisement; each bears the name of the oil producer whose gasoline is supplied therefrom, if the retailer honestly observes his bargain. The system is a great convenience to the public; it has increased enormously the ease with which motor drivers may obtain "gas" even in remote and thinly settled districts.[40]

But by 1949 the Supreme Court had changed direction. In *Standard Stations* it condemned gasoline single-branding under aggressive antitrust rules that did not demand any showing of monopoly.[41]

The Supreme Court's increasing disapproval of contractual vertical integration, even when monopoly was not threatened, effectively forced firms to prefer ownership integration even when contract integration would have been preferable. That is, legal policy perversely destroyed the very small businesses it was intended to protect. Justice Douglas recognized this in an otherwise completely out-of-character dissent in a case involving Standard Oil of California. Douglas was both an aggressive enforcer of the antitrust laws and an outspoken supporter of independent small business. Nevertheless, he objected to the majority's decision condemning single-branding agreements. Rather than tolerating "split-pump" stations selling multiple brands, the refiners would simply open their own gasoline stations and terminate their arrangements with independents. As a result, Douglas complained, the majority's decision effectively "sets the stage for Standard and the other oil companies to build service-station empires of their own."[42] His prediction was largely correct.

Franchising and Intellectual Property Licensing

The common law identified the boundaries of firms in terms of purchase and sale. If a manufacturer sold to someone for resale, that buyer-reseller was a separate firm whose entrepreneurial freedom was worthy of protection. But if the manufacturer simply licensed a process or offered a good to someone under consignment, then the downstream actor was nothing more than an "agent" or broker of the manufacturer. The *economic* theory of distribution came to regard these contractual distinctions between firms and agents as unimportant, but they persisted much longer in the law. So manufacturers took advantage of the fact that patent and other intellectual property licenses had always contemplated open-ended relationships. In 1926 the Supreme Court held that General Electric could lawfully supply light bulbs to dealers on "consignment" and stipulate the price at which the dealers sold them.[43] However, fifteen years earlier in *Dr. Miles* the Supreme Court had warned that it, and not the parties, would decide whether a relationship with a dealer was a sale or a mere agency.[44] By the same token, a manufacturer could not create a patent licensing scheme that was a mere "sham" in order to avoid either the first-sale doctrine or the resale-price-maintenance rule. In *Victor Talking Machines*, the manufacturer "licensed" its patented phonographs to its seven thousand dealers, stipulating the resale price and imposing other dealer controls.[45] The Supreme Court found the arrangement to be nothing more than an attempt to evade the antitrust law of resale price maintenance.

A later experiment with intellectual property licensing that found greater legal success was the "business method" franchise, intended to avoid the first-sale doctrine as well as the harshest antitrust restrictions. Business method franchises typically did not involve the sale of goods at all, but rather included detailed contractual oversight of a franchisee's business. The franchisee received intellectual property rights from the franchisor, plus a standardized format that provided national or regional consumer recognition. Business-method franchises expanded significantly in the 1950s with the rise of such firms as McDonald's. Thomas Dicke observed that "by the late 1950s perceptive entrepreneurs realized that... there was more money to be made selling hamburger stands than in selling hamburgers."[46] McDonald's principal business was real estate. It typically purchased sites and leased them to franchisees at a price that depended on the dollar volume of the franchisee's sales. The franchisees purchased their own equipment and food products from other sources, following the franchisor's specifications. Neither the first-sale rule nor the resale price maintenance rule applied, because nothing was being resold. Except for a few brushes with the law of tying arrangements, which it generally won, McDonald's was able to develop a franchise system largely free of antitrust scrutiny.[47] Those franchises that were found guilty of unlawful tying were typically the ones that sold a physical product and insisted that the franchisee resell the franchisor's product exclusively.[48]

Small Business Campaigns: The Robinson-Patman Act, Fair Trade, and Dealer Protection

The interest group that complained most loudly about vertical integration was small business. But different types of vertical integration affected small business in different ways, and they responded accordingly. Small business tended to favor harsh rules against restraints on alienation when the practice was single-branding or tying, because these practices tended to injure them. But they strongly supported resale price maintenance, or "fair trade," which protected them from larger retailers. The rising chain store, which owned its own retail outlets, was a nearly unqualified disaster for small businesses, driving thousands into bankruptcy. Franchising was clearly harmful to truly independent small businesses, but it also gave them an opportunity to reorganize as franchisees, and many did so.

The Robinson-Patman Act

During the Great Depression small businesses felt assaulted by larger firms, particularly the emergent chain store. Thousands of small grocers went bankrupt and blamed the Great Atlantic and Pacific Tea Company ("A & P"), the fastest growing chain prior to World War II.[49] In contrast to smaller grocers, A & P either acquired its sources of supply or else entered into heavily managed contracts that required suppliers to package items in A & P–branded containers according to its specifications. Its practices benefitted customers in important ways, but also migrated buying habits away from fresh agricultural products toward processed ones. It brought nothing but devastation to small grocers.[50]

In 1934 the FTC published a stinging critique of chain stores, accusing them of undermining the traditional retail economy of family-owned stores, mainly by forcing suppliers to discriminate in price between larger and smaller buyers.[51] Congress followed two years later with the Robinson-Patman Act, enacted at the behest of small retail grocers, who were a powerful interest group. The statute made it unlawful for a seller to charge different prices to two different dealers who resold in competition with each other, if the effect was to injure the dealer forced to pay the higher price.

One notable thing about this controversial statute is the "flip" that occurred in its drafting, which essentially changed it from an anti–chain-store provision into an anti-franchise provision. Chains such as A & P owned their own stores. The Robinson-Patman Act applied only to "sales," however, so it did not cover transfers between A & P's warehouses and its individual stores. The statute was supposedly intended to cover A & P's *buying* practices—that is forcing suppliers such as Borden to charge A & P a lower price for dairy products than smaller grocers paid. But the buyer's liability section of the Act became a legislative afterthought that was never as effective as the main provision applying to discriminatory sales.[52] As a result, the dominant use of the Robinson–Patman Act was not against chain stores but rather against manufacturers who discriminated in price as between two independent *dealers*. For example, if a gasoline refiner rewarded a successful franchisee with lower wholesale prices, while a less ambitious franchisee paid more, this became grist for a Robinson-Patman claim.[53]

The impact of Robinson-Patman Act enforcement was perverse. By condemning differential sale prices to independent dealers, the statute encouraged large manufacturers and suppliers to integrate vertically into retailing even more than they already had.[54] For example, a refiner facing potential liability for charging two independent dealers different prices could solve the problem by acquiring at least one of them and operating it as a subsidiary. Frederick M. Rowe, one of the most discerning analysts of the statute, complained that enforcement of the Robinson-Patman Act was largely "unrelated" to the statute's intended purpose of disciplining large buyers. Rather, the most typical defendant was a small firm—often a supplier who favored one dealer over another through the provision of some allowance or award. Over a twenty-five-year enforcement period the FTC had filed a total of 11 out of 1040 complaints against large buyers—a record which Rowe described as an "enforcement fiasco." The typical defendant was "rarely a titan of the market, but more typically... the smaller concern trapped in the legal maze."[55]

"Fair Trade" and the Political Movement against *Dr. Miles*

Next to the Robinson-Patman Act, the most important federal legislation intended to protect small dealers was the 1937 Miller-Tydings Act, which permitted states to legalize resale price maintenance, or "fair trade" within their borders, and even impose prices on retailers who had not agreed to fair trade provisions.[56] Prior to 1911 trade associations of small retailers had had considerable success in pressuring manufacturers to set minimum retail prices for their goods, thus limiting the ability of large stores to undersell smaller ones. Several states permitted the practice.[57] However, in 1911 the Supreme Court's *Dr. Miles* decision applied federal antitrust law to condemn any agreement setting resale prices. Small store owners and their trade associations were devastated. Some states, such as California, refused to follow the federal rule unless the manufacturer was a monopolist engaged in interstate commerce.[58]

Attorney Louis Brandeis excoriated the *Dr. Miles* decision in a 1913 article in *Harper's Weekly*, complaining that small dealers would not be able to "secure fair prices." He argued that "when a trade-marked article is advertised to be sold at less than the standard price, it is generally done to attract persons to the particular store by the offer of an obviously extraordinary bargain. It is a bait—called by the dealers a 'leader.'" In fact, the low price "would more appropriately be termed a 'mis-leader'; because the very purpose of the cut-price is to create a false impression," luring people to purchase other, overpriced goods. Further, unreasonably close margins will force the manufacturer to "deteriorate the article in order to preserve his own profits."[59]

Brandeis, who would go on the Supreme Court in 1916, had been instrumental in the formation of the American Fair Trade League in

1912, designed to promulgate rules of "fair" competition and to combat aggressive price cutting in retailing.[60] The efforts included a campaign for voluntary compliance with "fair" retail markups. In 1920 Hills Brothers launched such a campaign, urging grocers to charge at least a 5 cent markup over the wholesale price. When Piggly Wiggly, a discounter, publicly advertised lower prices it immediately increased its sales. Other retailers capitulated.[61] The price war that erupted captured the Federal Trade Commission's attention, which condemned Hills Brothers of unlawful resale price maintenance.[62]

The 1920s and early 1930s saw massive political organizing by retailer associations, all seeking to have *Dr. Miles* either overruled or states permitted to obtain exceptions. Like many small business campaigns, it was pushed over the top by the Depression. The initial result was state "fair trade" statutes permitting resale price maintenance within the state's borders. By 1938 they had been enacted in all but five states. Almost none of the state court decisions found them unlawful for conflicting with *Dr. Miles*. Some condemned the statutes for improperly delegating price-setting power to private firms.[63] Other states upheld the statutes against a variety of challenges, generally finding that a manufacturer was entitled to protect its goodwill or trademarks by price maintenance.[64]

The Supreme Court legitimated fair trade in 1936. Its *Seagram Distillers* decision upheld an Illinois fair trade law against claims that it violated the Sherman Act, improperly delegated rate power to private firms, and interfered with interstate commerce. Justice Sutherland wrote that such laws were premised on the idea that for a retailer to undercut the manufacturer's posted price "is an assault upon the good will, and constitutes what the statute denominates 'unfair competition.'"[65] Congress soon followed with the Miller-Tydings Act, heavily supported by small retailer associations but vehemently resisted by large discounters such as R.H. Macy Co. The Act went further than *Seagrams*, permitting enforcement of announced resale prices even against cutters who had notice of the policy but had never signed a resale price maintenance agreement.

In the 1950s the political tide began to turn again. Large discounters had become a way of life. Consumers, whose rhetoric and feet moved in different directions, seemed to prefer low prices over a large population of small stores. The Miller-Tydings regime remained in place, although with declining state support, until 1975. Congress repealed it after being convinced that "fair trade" was mainly a way of protecting the higher margins of small sellers, leading to higher prices.[66]

Dealer Protection Laws

By World War II both federal and state legislators had come to believe that restricted distribution was a major cause of manufacturer abuse of dealers. Roughly half of the states passed automobile-dealer-franchise acts designed to protect dealers from harsh franchise terms.[67] A few provisions required a state agency to approve franchise agreements. Most forbade manufacturers from terminating dealers—except for proven cause—and from imposing unwanted goods on manufacturers. However, a move for federal legislation backfired when an inquiry by the Federal Trade Commission produced evidence that dealer collusion rather than manufacturer coercion created the impetus for most of the requested practices.[68]

The National Automobile Dealers Association turned to Congress. After a fifteen-year lobbying campaign interrupted by the war, Congress passed the Automobile Dealers' Day in Court Act in 1956.[69] The House Report justified the legislation by concluding that automobile manufacturer "concentration of economic power has increased to the degree that traditional contractual concepts are no longer adequate to protect the automobile dealers under their franchises."[70] The statute required manufacturers to act in good faith when canceling a franchise and gave the dealer a legal action to have good faith judicially determined. The preamble to the statute stated that it was intended "to balance the power now heavily weighted in favor of automobile manufacturers."

Contractual Integration and Antitrust Policy through the 1960s

Modern franchise distribution largely developed in a hostile legal environment. Interest-group pressures were obvious, but legal policymaking was disturbingly short of coherent economic theory to explain why contractual vertical integration was socially harmful. The situations can be divided into two classes. The first involved manufacturer control of the pricing, location, or internal operations of independent dealers. The second involved manufacturer limits on dealers' ability to sell competitors' goods. A single franchise agreement often did both things simultaneously. For example, an automobile manufacturer might specify a dealer's location or prices, which regulated distribution of its own cars, but also prohibit the dealer from selling the new cars of a different manufacturer. The auto manufacturer might also require dealers to use only the manufacturer's parts for repairs—a form of tying.

After the New Deal antitrust law developed a campaign against vertical integration by contract under a variety of legal and economic theories. Except where fair trade was authorized, the per se rule against resale price maintenance made that practice categorically illegal without regard to purpose or even the slightest possibility of monopoly.[71] The law of tying arrangements turned into a competitive travesty. Ties of ordinary commodities such as salt were condemned when no possibility of monopoly was in sight.[72] The Supreme Court continued to cite the traditional concern for dealer freedom from restraints on alienation.

Supreme Court doctrine showed undisguised hostility during the Warren Court era. In the *Schwinn* bicycle case (1967) the Supreme Court made it unlawful per se for a manufacturer to assign locations to its dealers or limit sales only to its own franchised retailers.[73] And in *Albrecht* (1968), it became unlawful per se for a newspaper to limit the maximum prices charged by its carriers.[74] *Albrecht* virtually guaranteed that many manufacturers would simply stop using independent dealer networks and switch to ownership vertical integration. High dealer prices could kill any manufacturer's distribution system, and dealers could be expected to charge high markups when they were relatively insulated from competition. That is precisely what happened in the newspaper industry. The independent carrier who purchased and resold newspapers became an artifact, replaced by employee carriers with subscription prices set by the newspaper itself.[75]

Writing in the late 1970s, then Yale law professor Robert Bork blamed an economically unsophisticated, overly paternalistic Supreme Court for these decisions.[76] But the Supreme Court was not the only or even the main culprit. With a few exceptions such as *Albrecht*, these antitrust cases were brought by the government itself. The *Schwinn* bicycle case was a government-enforcement action, and the Justice Department brief was signed by an odd trio. Thurgood Marshall, later to become one of the Supreme Court's great liberals, was the Solicitor General in charge of representing the government. The second signatory was Donald F. Turner, the Harvard Law professor then serving as head of the Antitrust Division. The third, and a principal drafter, was Richard A. Posner, serving as a staff attorney and assistant to the Solicitor General. The brief emphasized the legal policy against restraints on alienation but struggled to find any reason Schwinn's limitations on its dealers' locations were anticompetitive. It argued mainly that Schwinn was trying to preserve an image of high quality by avoiding discount stores. Limiting distribution to high-end dealers would facilitate advertising "stressing real or imagined differences" to persuade consumers that its brand was superior.[77]

Both Turner and Posner subsequently repudiated these positions.[78] The *Schwinn* era lasted only a decade. The *GTE Sylvania* decision in 1977 refused to condemn restricted distribution unless anticompetitive effects were proven.[79] A key ingredient in the switch was the replacement of Earl Warren by Chief Justice Warren Burger, who was more conservative and much more favorable toward vertical integration.

One notable feature of the law of vertical distribution restraints during this period was how unrelated it was to any coherent economic theory. As a result, the courts placed great significance on things that seem economically inconsequential. For example, in the law of resale price maintenance it did not matter whether collusion was occurring or whether the market was even prone to monopoly. But what *did* matter was whether there was a sale-plus-resale, as opposed to a mere consignment. The per se tying rule did not ask whether the markets were competitive or tied-up products were even capable of being monopolized. Exclusion was far more imagined than real. George and Rosemary Hale, among the more astute critics of vertical restraints law in the 1950s, observed that the courts articulated a "monopoly" theory of contractual restraints while never actually finding any monopoly.[80] Through all of it, the perceived protected interest was small business and independent dealers.

Antitrust and Ownership Integration: Leveraging Monopoly

Ownership vertical integration had been a target of populist opposition since the Civil War, particularly if it involved monopolies. The so-called Granger Cases were a response to railroad acquisitions or construction of grain elevators, which placed the railroads in the business of purchasing and storing grain as well as shipping it. This caused an outcry among farmers who believed that the railroad companies were using railroad/grain-elevator combinations to suppress the price of wheat, soybeans, and corn. The controversy culminated in state laws regulating elevator prices, which the Supreme Court approved in 1876.[81]

For most of the twentieth century, however, legal policy toward ownership vertical integration was less hostile than for vertical contracting. For one thing, sales through a wholly owned subsidiary did not involve restraints on alienation. Further, unilateral action never provoked as much disfavor as did exclusionary "combinations," or agreements. A few early cases condemned ownership integration found to be part of a scheme to monopolize. In the 1911 *American Tobacco* case the Supreme Court ordered the defendant to divest its retail stores as part of the breakup of a monopoly.[82] Kodak was condemned in 1915 for acquiring some wholesale camera distributors, apparently to exclude competing manufacturers from distribution channels.[83] A year later *Corn Products* condemned a corn-syrup manufacturer's acquisition of a candy factory and its entering into competition with its own customers, who were rival candy makers.[84] These early decisions attacked what the courts perceived to be strategic acquisitions used to deny rivals access to markets.

By contrast, the 1911 *Standard Oil* decision, which partly dissolved John D. Rockefeller's petroleum empire, took a largely benign attitude toward Standard's very significant vertical integration into transportation and marketing.[85] For two decades following *Standard Oil* the lower courts were favorably inclined toward vertical integration in the petroleum industry, even praising its efficiency.[86] In the 1920 *United States Steel* case the Supreme Court gave broad approval to ownership vertical integration, which it described as "a facility of industrial progress" that reduced costs and made production operate more smoothly.[87]

After the New Deal discomfort toward ownership vertical integration began to harden. Economists increasingly believed that the amount of vertical integration was excessive in relation to any cost savings it produced, and that it increased entry barriers and caused excessive product differentiation.[88] More generally, however, was the feeling that the Depression was a monopoly problem, and that widespread vertical integration was a sign of a sick industrial establishment. Cost savings were quickly reinterpreted as unfair advantages that threatened to destroy small business. University of Chicago economist Henry Simons argued that vertical integration should be permitted only "so far as clearly compatible with the maintenance of real competition."[89] A 1941 Temporary National Economic Committee monograph on the petroleum industry was extremely critical of vertical integration, claiming that it was inherently monopolistic.[90]

These feelings did not subside with the War. In 1948 Yale law professor and economist Eugene Rostow declared that the "essential instrument of economic power in the oil industry is integration," particularly into "transportation facilities." Vertical integration "is the basic means of achieving and maintaining monopolistic control over price."[91] Corwin Edwards believed that vertical integration was a significant bottleneck in the economy. He called for a statute that would determine the proper "proportioning" of vertical integration by any firm and order adjustments against those that were integrated excessively.[92] In one of its most hostile statements concerning vertical integration, the Supreme Court suggested that the vertically related divisions of a single firm could "conspire" with each other for purposes of the Sherman Act.[93] Thereupon followed a series of actions by the Justice Department against vertical integration, including most prominently the motion-picture industry. The claim was that independent film producers and exhibitors were being driven from the market. Justice Douglas wrote for the majority in the *Paramount Pictures* case (1948) that vertical integration violates the antitrust laws "if it was a calculated scheme to gain control over an appreciable segment of the market and to restrain or suppress competition, rather than an expansion to meet legitimate business needs."[94]

Many economists and antitrust policymakers from the 1940s through the 1960s saw a landscape marked by increasing product differentiation and vertical control, and declining competition. The courts became increasingly hostile, sometimes concluding that firms integrate vertically in order to force their own subsidiaries to purchase at monopoly prices;[95] or that vertically integrated firms received an unfair advantage because they could buy from their subsidiaries at cost, while others had to pay monopoly prices.[96] Writing in the mid-1950s, Robert Bork concluded that courts had developed a wholly irrational hostility toward vertical integration.[97]

The views of Joe Bain, the leading industrial economist of the Harvard School, were more moderate, but he also concluded that widespread vertical integration was excluding smaller firms unnecessarily.[98] Bain suggested that "undoing" vertical integration that was not justified by cost savings could "actually reduce barriers to entry without offsetting social loss and be conducive to more workable competition." His concerns were reflected a few years later in the Justice Department's 1968 Guidelines for challenging vertical mergers, drafted while Donald F. Turner was in charge of the Antitrust Division.[99]

The government's developing position was that it was anticompetitive for a firm to deal exclusively with its own subsidiaries or even to favor them, at least if the firm was relatively large. Because the main economic purpose of vertical integration is self-provision or self-distribution, the position was basically that vertical integration was legal only if it made no economic sense to do so in the first place. This argument carried the day in the *du Pont* merger case, when the Supreme Court condemned du Pont's acquisition of a large interest in General Motors stock on the theory that GM would discriminate in favor of du Pont in purchasing paints and fabrics that du Pont made.[100] On the theory that every senseless action deserves an equally senseless reaction,

General Motors and du Pont argued in return that GM "did not favor du Pont" at all.[101]

The extraordinary thing about vertical integration is its robust growth in American business practice in the face of a legal regime that was rarely accommodating and often hostile. But just as legal policymakers did not understand the economic rationales for vertical integration, they also did not appreciate the economic consequences of their own policies. Per se rules against contractual vertical integration shifted firms into ownership integration, often doing even greater harm to the small business interests that legislatures and courts had been trying to protect.

PART FOUR

Neoclassical Public Law

13

The Substantive Due Process Triumvirate: Health, Safety, and Morals

THE "SUBSTANTIVE DUE process" era describes a forty-year period in which the Supreme Court declared certain economic regulations unconstitutional. The Court did not use that term. Rather, it spoke of the "liberty" that the Constitution protects for making contracts or the security of property. A law interfering with contract or property rights might be upheld if it protected health, safety, or morals. However, that determination lay with the courts. As Justice Peckham observed in *Lochner*, which struck down a state statute limiting the labor of bakers to ten hours per day or sixty hours per week, a rule protecting people from their own labor contracts would place the State in the position of "a supervisor, or *pater familias*, over every act of the individual." Unless the proper effect can be shown, the case "gives rise to at least a suspicion that there was some other motive dominating the legislature than the purpose to subserve the public health or welfare."[1]

Vested Rights, Substantive Due Process, and the Constitutional Text

Prior to the Civil War, state regulation raised federal constitutional issues infrequently. All powers not granted to the federal government were reserved to the states. The most notable limitations were state debtor relief legislation that violated the Contract Clause or interfered with exclusive federal control over bankruptcy,[2] or limitations on state power that impeded interstate commerce.[3] Under the so-called vested rights doctrine, protection for contract or property was applied to rights that had been previously granted and were later taken away. For example, *Fletcher v. Peck* held that a land deed, once granted, could not be rescinded,[4] and the *Dartmouth College* case held that a granted corporate charter could not be modified so as to be less favorable to the grantee.[5] Chief Justice Taney's *Dred Scott* opinion also stated that a statute freeing a slave merely because his owner had brought him into free territory deprived the owner of property without due process.[6] Taney, a Democrat appointed by President Andrew Jackson, spoke similarly of patent term extensions applied retroactively to someone who had already purchased the patented good.[7] Later, this vested rights analysis was applied to property through specific enforcement of the Fifth Amendment's eminent domain clause.[8]

The origins of substantive due process doctrine lay in the state courts, particularly in the Midwest, where it grew out of a strong anti-regulation bias in Jacksonian democracy.[9] Michigan chief justice Thomas M. Cooley was a Jackson-inspired Democrat who became an abolitionist in the 1850s and switched to the Republican Party. His influential treatise on *Constitutional Limitations* was initially published in 1868, the same year the Fourteenth Amendment was ratified. Cooley focused mainly on state law, but later editions of his book and the works of other constitutional scholars argued that the Fourteenth Amendment's Due Process clause restricted economic legislation that did not take away a previously vested right.[10] For example, the hours-of-labor rule struck down in *Lochner v. New York* applied to contracts that were to be made in the future. The seventh edition of *Constitutional Limitations*, published in 1896 and the last one Cooley worked on prior to his death, illustrates what had become of the Fourteenth Amendment. The discussion of Due Process occupied sixty pages. Roughly two-thirds of a page addressed race and ethnic discrimination. The remainder dealt entirely with liberty of contract, economic relationships, and morals. A twenty-page discussion of equal protection included roughly two pages on race, mainly in footnotes. The balance discussed discriminatory economic regulation. These page counts actually understate the ratios, because Cooley also discussed the economic meaning of these clauses in other places, such as the power to tax.[11]

At the same time they were expanding limits on prospective regulation, Cooley and other constitutional law writers attacked the vested rights doctrine for favoring established interests at the expense of those not so favored.[12] Cooley railed at the *Dartmouth College* case for holding that contract or property rights, once created, could not be taken back. Cooley saw this principally as a monopoly problem. Under it some of the "most enormous and threatening powers in our country have been created." In his *Commentaries* law treatise writer Francis Wharton argued that the *Dartmouth College* vested rights doctrine should no longer be controlling, because it "fix[ed] social rights in a constant perpetual mould."[13] For Cooley and Wharton, embracing substantive due process and jettisoning much of vested rights doctrine were twin approaches to the problem of special interest capture of the legislative process. Their views are in some tension with classical liberal constitutionalism today, which would preserve *both* strong constitutional protection for vested rights and substantive limitations on the creation of future rights.[14] They also inferred, often without support, that prospective regulation and licensing conferred or threatened monopoly in the same way that vested exclusive privileges did.

The term legislative "capture" did not come into use until the mid-twentieth century. Nevertheless, Gilded Age state courts were increasingly concerned with legislation that favored one interest group at the expense of a broader set of interests or the general public. By that time, however, the anti-regulation ideology had veered from its original Jacksonian course. During the earlier period legislative capture was seen as protecting propertied interests (mainly Federalist and Whig) who used tight credit, monopoly grants, corporate control, and other vested rights to protect themselves from the competition of political and economic outsiders.[15] Increasingly after the Gilded Age the "capturing" entities were labor, small businesses, or economic reformers. Although these groups had differing motives, ranging from welfare improvement to elimination of competition or avoidance of free riding, they often found common ground on results.

Some court opinions reflected suspicion of capture. In *Jacobs* (1885) the New York Court of Appeals overturned a state statute prohibiting the manufacture of cigars in tenement houses. The law was directed at the practice of using mainly non-English-speaking immigrants to do piecework in their homes, rented to them by their employers, where child labor could not be controlled.[16] The legislation was sponsored by the Cigar-Makers' Union, whose concerns were undoubtedly to limit low cost competition from child labor and tenement house production.[17] Theodore Roosevelt was just beginning his Republican political career in the state legislature at the time and was being lobbied in both directions. Suspecting labor union instigation, he initially opposed the bill. His autobiography then recounts his visit to the tenements for himself, which changed his mind. Roosevelt's socialist reformer friend Jacob Riis later described the tenement cigar rollers' plight in a chapter of his 1890 bestseller *How the Other Half Lives*.[18] Nevertheless, the Court could not perceive "how the cigar maker is to be improved in his health or his morals by forcing him from his home and its hallowed associations and beneficent influences, to ply his trade elsewhere." As Chief Judge Robert Earl explained, if the legislature "passes an act ostensibly for the public health…, then it is for the courts to scrutinize the act and see whether it really relates to and is convenient and appropriate to promote the public health."

In fact, courts applying substantive due process seldom "scrutinized" for either capture or unwarranted monopoly. They simply assumed it and usually did not attempt to identify its source. *Lochner* itself stated the concern as "at least a suspicion that there was some other motive" but did not perform or even suggest an actual inquiry. Labor unions were promoters of the legislation in *Lochner, Jacobs*, as well as other labor protective cases. But by and large the parties did not argue that point and the courts did not cite it as even relevant. A year after *Jacobs* the Illinois Supreme Court struck down a statute requiring coal miners doing piecework to be paid by weight rather than by the "box," whose size could be manipulated by the employer.[19] The Pennsylvania Supreme Court overturned a statute that required iron workers paid by the ton to have the ton measured as 2000 pounds rather than the 2240 pounds that an employer specified, and that the payment be made in "lawful money" rather than goods.[20] In 1904 a New York court struck down a statute requiring training and an examination before a person could be certified to shoe horses,[21] and in 1910 the New York Court of Appeals invalidated a statute mandating that embalmers and undertakers be licensed and requiring an apprenticeship. The court concluded that the statute was not motivated by concerns for the "general health, morals and welfare of the state," but rather by the desire to create a monopoly.[22] That conclusion seems paranoid, given that the statute did not restrict the number of license holders but merely imposed a three-year educational requirement. Further, there was no evidence of monopoly, although there was considerable evidence of sanitation concerns from both the preparation of bodies and the embalming process itself. Regulation of undertakers was first passed in Virginia in 1894, and by 1900, twenty-three states had adopted them.[23] The court dwelt on the fact that the licensing requirement applied even to undertakers who did not embalm, but public health issues applied to both.

Licensing of professions much less threatening to the public health than the care of dead bodies had been widespread and generally unchallenged in United States throughout the nineteenth century vested rights era.[24] Increasing hostility during the Gilded Age seems to have resulted at least partly from confusion between licensing and "monopoly." Courts overturned regulations on the grounds that they created a monopoly, but without determining whether any actual monopoly was in prospect. By contrast, those that upheld the regulations often observed that mere licensing without exclusivity did not automatically create a monopoly.[25] While some Progressive Era licensing may have been intended to exclude those who could not afford to meet its requirements, particularly Afro-Americans, the evidence indicates that it did not have that effect.[26]

Whether substantive due process significantly limited the amount of regulation is debatable, but it did produce powerful rhetoric.[27] Estimates of the number of statutes that were overturned range widely, from roughly fifty to two hundred.[28] Of course, many federal decisions never made it to the Supreme Court, and most stayed entirely in state courts. In any event, more regulatory provisions survived than were struck down. For example, the government could forbid activities that were public nuisances at common law.[29] The courts were more suspicious of regulations that were novel, and particularly if they suggested class conflict or created a monopoly or other market advantage.

One of the biggest market changes during this period was in the status of the laborer. Increasing urbanization, the industrial revolution, and a large wave of immigrants had dramatically increased the ratio of employees to self-employed. The Bakeshop Act at issue in *Lochner* was the result of organizing efforts led by a coalition that included the New York Ladies' Health Protective Association and the International Bakers and Confectioners Union, aimed both at more sanitary shops and reducing hours of labor. Its opponents tended to be small bakeries run by mainly Italian and Jewish immigrants. The dispute reflected the economic realities that higher wages or improvements in working conditions were costly and the labor supply plentiful. A ten-hour rule that exempted some firms would give them anticompetitive cost advantages. But the legislation also reflected biases that were typical of trade and labor unions at the time, including racism and hostility toward immigrants.[30] The *Lochner* statute was neutral on these issues, however, and the Court cited no evidence that bakers of all ethnicities could not comply with its ten-hour provision.

The labor movement had to live with two harsh realities, one factual and one legal. The factual reality was that mechanization made factories more efficient, but employers controlled production. Both *Jacobs* and *Lochner* also revealed one source of production cost savings unrelated to mechanization -- namely, merging of production facilities into laborers' living quarters provided by the employers. Even here, producers very likely picked up the gains. There is no evidence, for example, that cigar rollers who worked in their tenement houses received greater compensation than those who worked in separate factories or paid less than market rates for rent. Strikes and attempts at organizing the laborers were common, although most failed because the labor supply was too abundant.[31]

In addition, technology and intellectual property rights increasingly served to differentiate manufactured products, thereby blunting head-to-head price competition. Unskilled and semiskilled labor had no such opportunity, however, and wages were competed to subsistence levels. Notwithstanding union efforts to restrict worker output, the labor market was considerably more competitive than many product markets.

Labor organizing and protective legislation very likely increased the operating costs of some firms, but there is no evidence that they reduced employment. Indeed, a bakery required to use employees sixty rather than eighty hours per week would likely hire more of them. These facts led to sharp debates among both economists and legal scholars, described in Chapter 14, about whether laborers were getting their fair share of the gains from economic progress.

The legal reality was that while firms had the capacity to organize into large single entities, laborers were individuals in the eyes of the law. Their organizations were generally treated as cartels and their efforts to limit output by restricting membership as boycotts.[32]

History writing about the substantive due process era has tended to focus on the Supreme Court's antipathy about economic regulation and its strong dislike of the labor movement.[33] The period was one of simultaneous technological and regulatory expansion. It saw new federal regulation of the railroads and railroad labor, monopolies, employer tort liability, food and drugs, and child labor. At the state and local level were wage and hours laws, child labor, product quality regulation, professional licensing, and land use. So judicial responses must be seen in perspective. For the most part judges were trained in the classical traditions of the later nineteenth century, whose common law system emphasized contract and property rights and backward-looking theories of value.

Ironically, they were also trained in the traditional tools of legal interpretation. Nevertheless, the most visible feature of substantive due process is that neither "liberty of contract" nor specific prohibitions of the statutes that the courts struck down were expressed in the Constitutional text. Nor were they supported by a fair reading of the constitutional history. The substantive due process era was the Supreme Court's first sustained experiment with constitutional "noninterpretivism," predicating judicial review on an economic theory accepted by a bare majority of the Supreme Court, but with no support in the constitution itself. The closest the U.S. Constitution or statutes ever came to defining a prospective liberty of contract was in the 1866 Civil Rights Act, which the Fourteenth Amendment was intended in part to justify. That provision gave all persons in the United States "the same right... as is enjoyed by white citizens" to make and enforce contracts. Tellingly, the statute said nothing about substantive limitations on the right to contract, other than that they could not discriminate as between white and nonwhite citizens.[34]

Further, the economic theory was in decline, swept under by the marginalist revolution. Justice Holmes's substantive due process dissents across two decades reflected both of these propositions. He objected in *Lochner* that the majority decided the case "upon an economic theory which a large part of the country does not entertain." But he also acknowledged that this did not drive his dissent. Rather, as he stated in *Lochner* and reiterated nearly two decades later in *Adkins*, the majority could not point to any "specific provisions of the Constitution" justifying their decisions.[35]

Exceptions to Liberty of Contract: Health, Safety, and Morals

In *Muller v. Oregon* the Supreme Court considered the constitutionality of a state statute that limited women laundry workers to ten hours of labor per day.[36] Attorney Louis Brandeis, who was defending the law, had the daunting task to convince the Court to approve a ten-hour statute for women laundry employees only three years after it had struck down a similar provision for bakers in *Lochner*. Brandeis and labor scholar and activist Josephine Goldmark submitted their now famous "Brandeis Brief" of evidence about the effects of long working hours on women, arguing that this evidence had been available to the legislature and served to justify their action.[37] The Brandeis Brief argued that a women's position as mother and principal caretaker justified increased State solicitude. The argument was more than faintly Darwinian. For example, it quoted an 1871 Report of the Massachusetts Bureau of Labor Statistics: "Like begets like," so "if the parents are feeble in constitution, the children must also inevitably be feeble."[38]

Although the Brandeis Brief is sometimes called a "social science" brief, much of the evidence it presented was hardly social science. The brief quoted a dozen reports of state bureaus of labor statistics, which had operated in twenty-nine states since Reconstruction to collect information about working conditions.[39] It also cited statements by the United States Industrial

Commission, the British Chief Inspector of Factories and Workshops, and a dozen physicians and physiologists about the effects of long hours on women and their children. One British physician stated that overworked girls often became sterile or produced sickly children. Some passages were written by obvious labor activists and even Progressive clergymen. One came from Thomas M. Cooley, whose strong ideas defending liberty of contract made exceptions for women. "The general rule undoubtedly is that any person is at liberty to pursue any lawful calling." But "some employments . . . may be admissible for males and improper for females."[40]

The *Muller* brief's table of contents maps Brandeis's and Goldmark's strategy. It opened with a section that "this is not class legislation," a category whose significance is discussed in the next chapter. It then recited a litany familiar to the Supreme Court: separate sections on the "Bad Effect of Long Hours on Health," on ". . . Safety," and on ". . . Morals."[41] Then followed another section, with the same three divisions, on the effects of *laundry* employment on health, safety, and morals.[42] For example, the Brief quoted a Massachusetts legislative report: "When the working day is so long that no time whatever is left for a minimum of leisure or home-life, relief from the strain of work is sought in alcoholic stimulants and other excesses."[43]

The genius of the Brandeis Brief was its simultaneous creativity and conservatism. Although the expansive quotation of agency reports and nonlegal sources was novel, the key to the brief's success was its organization around the "health, safety, or morals" triumvirate that the Court had often cited in locating the line between permissible and prohibited regulation.[44] Defenders had to convince the courts that theirs was not a mere interference in the market, but rather governed a value that the state was empowered to protect. The Court generally upheld a regulation on health or safety grounds if the health or safety in question was of someone *other* than the contracting parties. The parties themselves, if they were adults, were generally regarded as able to contract about their own safety and health, but they might not give due regard to the safety or health of customers or others whom their contract affected. Morals were treated differently, however. Here, the State was entitled to intervene even to protect the contracting parties from their own vices.

In *Lochner* the Supreme Court majority found that these conditions had not been met. Justice Peckham saw no evidence that long hours affected the "healthful quality of the bread" that bakers produced.[45] As bread consumers were not a party to the bakers' wage and hour bargain, regulation might be needed to protect their interests. Finding no such impact, Justice Peckham concluded that the full weight of long working hours fell upon the parties, who were adults with contractual capacity.[46]

The presence of external effects was thought to provide a constitutionally defensible rationale for regulation because, although contracting parties had a right to bargain for their own position, they did not have a right to impose harms on others. Four years after he authored *Lochner,* Justice Peckham wrote the Supreme Court's opinion in *Welch v. Swasey*, unanimously upholding a Boston statute limiting the height of downtown buildings. Peckham noted concerns that taller buildings imposed greater risks to nearby buildings, particularly of fire.[47] A generation later Justice Sutherland wrote the opinions in an analogous pair of decisions. He concluded in *Adkins* in 1923 that a minimum wage provision for women was unlawful because no reasonable relationship was shown between the wage provision and public health or morals.[48] But three years later he wrote the Court's opinion upholding comprehensive land use planning statutes—clear infringements of liberty of contract that caused significant harm to the plaintiff's downzoned property. Sutherland's rationale was that unregulated urban development had numerous harmful effects on others, including traffic congestion and fire hazards. As a result it could not be shown that the ordinance had "no substantial relation to the public health, safety, morals, or general welfare."[49]

Markets and Morals in Economic and Social Thought

The nineteenth century produced two sharply clashing visions of American society and the appropriate role of the State. The financial stakes were high and the debates were unambiguously political, but they were also influenced by theory. Classical political economists generally opposed most regulation. These included Americans John McVickar, Francis Wayland, Francis Bowen, Henry Carey, Amasa Walker, and Henry Vethake. These writers imported their arguments from the British political economists, even as they lamented Britain's turn toward greater government intervention. At the same time, however, they viewed economics and morals as complementary but sharply separated. Economics dealt with human incentives and self-interest. Morals dealt with obligations to the community and the Maker.

By contrast, emergent marginalism doubted the superiority of the market and seriously qualified the classical aversion to government interference. Many marginalists believed well into the 1930s that some wealth redistribution would improve overall welfare. Progressive intellectuals also found the gap between science and morals to be both exaggerated and bridgeable. Morality increasingly became identified with its social and economic consequences. As a political movement, Progressivism promoted active government involvement in both morals and the economy, often on grounds that were explicitly Christian.[50] Indeed, one of the reasons for the Progressives' enthusiasm about regulation is that they began to see wealth distribution as a moral issue. One visible manifestation was the Social Gospel, which attempted to refocus Christianity's concern on social welfare issues.[51] Progressive economist Richard T. Ely and economist-sociologist Edward A. Ross painted vivid pictures of wealthy businessmen as thieves who caused much greater social harm than traditional robbers. In 1907 Ross, then at the University of Wisconsin, published a book with the very religious title *Sin and Society: An Analysis of Latter-Day Iniquity*. President Roosevelt wrote the introduction. One chapter, entitled "Sinning by Syndicate," spoke of the evils of corporations, bankers, and trusts. Questions about the distribution of wealth "could scarcely arise" at a time when each family "lived wholly off the produce of its own farm," Ross observed. But the prevalence of modern wage labor changed that, requiring social decisions about how wealth should be divided between owners and workers.[52]

The problem with utilitarianism and marginalism was that they threatened to turn ethics, just as economics, into the study of what produces maximum satisfaction in *post*-fallen humanity. The classical political economists believed that the Fall had little impact for economic doctrine. A theory of religion, ethics, or even natural science might be clouded beyond repair by humanity's fall from grace. But economics was not concerned about the desires of some ideal or sinless humanity. It considered humanity as it was found. This perspective produced strong individualism in economic theory, but communitarianism in moral theory. Each person knew his own wants, and political economy was concerned with maximizing them. By contrast, the human being making moral decisions cannot trust his judgment, for his baser instincts constantly threaten to take over. He finds his moral compass in stable institutions, religion, and the community.

The best classical example of this distinction is Adam Smith himself. Smith's economic man in the *Wealth of Nations* always knows what he wants; it is only a matter of making the trades that will get him there.[53] In sharp contrast, the moral actor of Smith's *Theory of Moral Sentiments*, written seventeen years earlier, is always groping in the dark, distinguishing right from wrong by observing the actions of others. In this sense, Smith was a pure product of the conservative Scottish Enlightenment. The economic market was for him a work of pure beauty and orderliness just as the chemical tables were for Joseph Priestly, or the ordering of species for Thomas Jefferson.[54] The greatest manifestation of God's creative power was that the world did not *need* to be continuously corrected. In an often-quoted passage of *Sentiments* he compared the universe to the "wheels of the watch," which are "admirably adjusted to the end for which it was made.... If they were endowed with a desire and intention to produce it, they could not do it better." By contrast, the study of morals required one to look away from the watch itself and toward the watch's maker:

> The administration of the great system of the universe, however, the care of the universal happiness of all rational and sensible beings, is the business of God and not of man. To man is allotted a much humbler department, but one much more suitable to the weakness of his powers, and to the narrowness of his comprehension; the care of his own happiness, or that of his family.[55]

Political economy considered how fallen human beings maximized their actual desires in an imperfect world. By contrast, the science of morals required them to transcend their fallen state and objectify their sinful nature. In this task, humanity needed help from the Bible, from tradition and authority, and the Church. Although Smith's economics was strongly individualistic, his moral theory was based on continuous interpersonal comparison. He famously described the student of morals as an "impartial spectator:"

> We can never survey our own sentiments and motives, we can never form any judgment concerning them, unless we remove ourselves, as it were, from our own natural station, and endeavor to view them as at a certain distance from us. But we can do this in no other way than by endeavoring to view them with the eyes of other people, or as other people are likely to view them.

Someone growing up in absolute isolation would have no reference point for making moral judgments at all. But "bring him into society, and he is immediately provided with the mirror which he wanted before."[56]

Political economists in nineteenth-century America vehemently rejected consequentialist or utilitarian ethics, even as they robustly defended free markets.[57] Both political economy and ethics were concerned with human happiness, but they approached it differently. Political economy addressed how the individual maximized his own happiness through production and trading. Moral philosophy was concerned with how one determined the ethical course of action. John McVickar, professor of both political economy and moral philosophy at Columbia, instructed his students in the 1820s that "what religion condemns as contrary to duty and virtue, Political Economy proves to be equally opposed to peace, good order, and the permanent prosperity of the community."[58]

Individualism in economics and communitarianism in morals dominated orthodox American thought in the nineteenth century. American law was increasingly preoccupied with "liberty of contract" in economic matters, while readily approving serious interferences with contract when morals were at stake. These beliefs were widely held, transcending the diversity in religious doctrine that dominated Christian religion during this time. The moral science of a Unitarian such as Harvard's Francis Bowen closely resembled that of Baptist Francis Wayland, president of Brown University, notwithstanding their bitter antagonism in matters of theology.[59]

Wayland, an anti-Jacksonian, fancied himself a kind of American facsimile of Adam Smith. Just as Smith had published his *Moral Sentiments* and then his *Wealth of Nations*, so Wayland published his *Elements of Moral Science* in 1835 and his *Elements of Political Economy* in 1837. As Smith, Wayland regarded his two books as developing related parts of a single system of social philosophy. The principles of political economy "are so closely analogous to those of Moral Philosophy, that almost every question in one, may be argued on grounds belonging to the other." But while Wayland's *Political Economy* was an extended argument for laissez-faire, showing that self-interest and free trading yielded wealth and prosperity, his *Moral Science* was an extended argument against utilitarian ethics, or the idea that rightness or wrongness of any action should be based on consequences.[60]

Adam Smith's views about the differences between economic and moral science were equally well reflected by Henry Vethake, a Presbyterian just as Adam Smith, and also a Jacksonian. Vethake was professor and later provost of the University of Pennsylvania. His *Principles of Political Economy* (1844) abhorred State interference in private markets, attacked unionism, protective labor legislation, and State economic support for the poor, including unemployment compensation. Nevertheless, articles such as liquor may be treated differently because excessive consumption "has an injurious effect upon society." Conceding the power of the State to condemn such consumption on moral grounds, can the State derive any additional justifications from political economy? The answer must be no. "Politico-economically speaking, all these, being objects of men's desire, are to be regarded as useful objects." Rather, "the argument against the use of spirituous liquors, in so far as it applies with greater force to those liquors than to any other article of consumption, is altogether a moral one."[61]

Anti-Regulation Public Law and Government Control of Morals

From fundamentally Jacksonian roots, classical legal thought developed several principles of economic welfare that eventually came to be associated with substantive due process. Among these were that people should have equal access to market opportunities, and government should not interfere in the right to operate a lawful business. Monopoly grants, licensing restrictions, or other entry barriers were all suspect. In addition, taxation was appropriate only if it was for a "public" purpose, which did not include the provision of subsidies or similar incentives to private enterprise.[62]

The Jacksonian position on welfare and morality stands in sharp contrast. First, the prosperous families who benefitted most from the proactive economic policies of the early nineteenth century were typically from the more established and elite American churches. Their religion emphasized intellectual content over piety and social relations over antiworldliness. By contrast, the Jacksonians were a diverse coalition of outsiders, many of them quite fervent. Some, including Jackson appointee chief justice Roger B. Taney, were Catholics.[63] Others were pro-revival evangelicals reacting against the rationalism of the established churches.[64] Although these groups were very different from each other, as a collective they hardly believed that the State should extricate itself from moral affairs in the same way that it should remove itself from economic affairs. Catholics were strongly inclined to mingle the Church and the State as regulators of behavior. Many of the Jacksonian Protestant groups became crusaders for State-imposed morality.

The story of Jacksonian religion is complex. First, a political coalition between Protestant evangelicals and Catholics was no easy thing. Many of the evangelical groups defined their very existence by hatred of Catholicism. For their part, Catholics saw no salvation outside of the Catholic Church. For this reason many mainstream northern Baptists, including Francis Wayland, remained Whigs rather than joining the Jacksonians.[65] Second, disestablishment itself was instigated by Jacksonian anti-establishment thinking, particularly in Massachusetts and Connecticut.[66] Although Jackson was Presbyterian, he cultivated non-sectarianism and emphasized the multi-denominational nature of his support. The Jackson era created the notion that the United States has a kind of Christian national religion that tolerates but transcends denominational differences.

One might wonder why a movement emphasizing disestablishment would support regulation of morals with such fervor. But that is to read a twentieth-century conception of disestablishment into the nineteenth. Historically, disestablishment was largely a fiscal phenomenon. The primary issue was the use of tax monies to pay the clergy and support church operations. The controversies had relatively little to do with the State's power to regulate conduct, and did not venture into such questions as Bible reading or prayer in public schools or State regulation of marriage or public morals.[67]

An ironic impact of disestablishment was that it increased rather than decreased the role of the State as regulator of moral conduct. The government's growing moral hegemony resulted from revival movements that splintered the Protestant churches, populating the evangelical landscape with small denominations that were powerless to impose significant disciplinary authority. The State moved in to fill the vacuum.

Notwithstanding deep theological division, the population was relatively united on a broad range of morality questions. As a result, decisive coalitions sponsored statutes regulating conduct on principles associated with Christian morality generally. The great reform movements of the four decades before the Civil War were religiously motivated and tended to unite people with very different political and theological views.[68] Their goal was the enactment of civil legislation associated with Christian values in general. Here the regulatory state continued alive and well. Although liberty of contract forbade the State from regulating working conditions or licensing occupations, it did not prevent it from prohibiting marriage contracts between people of different races,[69] from shutting down lotteries, prohibiting the sale of alcoholic beverages, or forcing businesses to close their doors on Sunday.

Lotteries

Because it is contractual, the lottery is a striking example of the divergence between economic individualism and moral communitarianism in classical welfare policy. Just as economic antistatism was triumphing as an economic theory, the American position on lotteries was changing from toleration and use to hostility and strict regulation.

Lotteries had been common in colonial America among all except Quakers.[70] Alexander Hamilton supported their use to finance public projects, and the Continental Congress passed a resolution in 1775 "[t]hat a sum of money be raised by way of lottery for defraying the expense" of the anticipated military campaign.[71] In 1812 Congress authorized lotteries to raise money for street improvements in Washington, DC, and by 1820 it had authorized them about seventy times for various projects.[72] They were frequently used to finance public works projects, such as the construction of the Erie Canal system, which opened in 1825 just as the campaign against lotteries was beginning.[73] They were also used privately to support construction of educational facilities and churches. Indeed, churches were among the most common users of lotteries.[74] Lottery contracts were enforceable under the American common law.

Christian evangelicals launched a campaign against lotteries in the 1820s and 1830s, leading to restrictive state legislation. A principal instigator was Job Roberts Tyson, a Whig member of Congress from Pennsylvania. In 1833 Tyson published a *Brief Survey of the Great Extent and Evil Tendencies of the Lottery System*, arguing that lotteries produced sloth and immorality, particularly among the poor.[75] He produced evidence that lottery ticket purchases were common causes of insolvency, and that they frequently contributed to embezzlement and forgery. New York had already adopted an anti-lottery act in 1821 and expanded its prohibitions in 1833. Connecticut and Virginia followed in 1834.[76] The first Supreme Court decision upholding a statute forbidding lotteries came in a dispute challenging a prior state policy of encouraging them. In 1829 the Virginia legislature had authorized a corporation to use a lottery to finance a turnpike. In 1834, however, it passed another statute condemning lotteries and providing for expiration of the company's right in 1837. The company challenged the limitation, relying on the Supreme Court's *Dartmouth College* decision that reneging on a previously granted corporate charter violated the Constitution's Contract Clause.[77] The Court not only found no impairment, but also indicated how much opinion about lotteries had changed. "[T]he common forms of gambling are comparatively innocuous when placed in contrast with the widespread pestilence of lotteries. The former are confined to a few persons and places, but the latter infests the whole community."[78]

In 1880 the Supreme Court went much further. In 1867 the Mississippi legislature had chartered a corporation to issue lottery tickets, but a year later amended its constitution to declare that "the legislature shall never authorize any lottery, nor shall the sale of lottery tickets be allowed." The Court acknowledged that unilateral revocation of the corporate charter was ordinarily prohibited by the Contract Clause. Formerly, "when the sources of public revenue were fewer than now, they [lotteries] were used in some or all of the States." However, subsequent learning revealed that lotteries "are demoralizing in their effects, no matter how carefully regulated." As a result, "no legislature can bargain away the public health or the public morals." The Supreme Court then gave about as narrow an interpretation of the Contract Clause as had ever been applied to a state grant. "Any one... who accepts a lottery charter does so with the implied understanding that the people, in their sovereign capacity" may revoke it "any time when the public good shall require, whether it be paid for or not."[79]

The next major lottery campaign was against the Louisiana Lottery of the 1870s, which was widely promoted to ticket buyers scattered across the country. That "abuse" became the target of President Benjamin Harrison's reform agenda in the early 1890s, and eventually federal legislation forbidding the sale of lottery tickets in the mail.[80] The statute was upheld by a divided Court in *Champion v. Ames* (1903) as a legitimate exercise of the federal commerce power and not in violation of the Tenth Amendment. After quoting its earlier decisions about the immoralities of lotteries, the Supreme Court declared that "[w]e should hesitate long before adjudging that an evil of such appalling character, carried on through interstate commerce, cannot be met and crushed by the only power competent to that end."[81] Four dissenters protested that lottery tickets were not "articles of commerce," and thus not within federal power.

The Early Campaigns against Alcohol

Americans historically drank with moral stigma only for drunkenness. In the 1820s, however, Protestant churches began a century-long campaign against the evils of liquor that continued through the Progressive Era, culminating in the Eighteenth Amendment and Prohibition in 1919.[82] The campaign was originally manifested in sermons and tracts urging people to avoid alcohol. But New England's Whigs politicized it, targeting members of the Jacksonian coalition. Among these were poor European immigrants, who were believed to be heavy drinkers and, not coincidentally, heavily Catholic.[83] In the 1830s the American Temperance Society abandoned its previous policy of moral persuasion in favor of legislative prohibition.[84] By the end of the 1850s many states had passed statutes limiting or prohibiting the consumption of alcoholic beverages.[85]

Most mid- and late- nineteenth-century decisions rejected constitutional challenges to statutes that forbade trade in alcoholic beverages, closing down breweries and bars.[86] The Supreme Court typically upheld these statutes even though the businesses were legal when built and forced to close without compensation.[87] After the Eighteenth Amendment was ratified the courts upheld restrictions that went beyond what the Amendment required. In 1925 the Supreme Court held that a state could seize liquor legally purchased and stored in a private home when the consumption had subsequently become forbidden by statute. The older statute, in force when the liquor was purchased, "permitted the social serving of liquors and beverages in private residences and in ordinary social intercourse."[88] Further, the Eighteenth Amendment, which was in force at the time, applied only to" the manufacture, sale, or transportation of intoxicating liquors."

Sunday Laws

Sabbath breaking was already an offense in the Colonies, but evangelicals pursued it with renewed vigor during and after the Jackson era.[89] In part, this was a consequence of the "market revolution" that employed more people in the commercial marketplace rather than on the farm. Laws that prevented Sunday trade were defended with the observation that the citizenry was overwhelmingly Christian, no matter what the sect. Christians believed Sunday should be a day of rest. By midcentury many state courts were applying statutes or common law rules that prohibited the enforcement of contracts negotiated on Sunday, even as they were expanding liberty of contract as a general matter.[90] New York, the most commercial and cosmopolitan of nineteenth-century states, found a compromise. Its statute was interpreted to prohibit sales made in stores or public markets on Sundays, but to permit agreements negotiated in private.[91]

Moral Regulation in the Treatise Literature

By the 1880s moral philosophy was disappearing as an academic discipline in American universities. As intellectuals wrestled with Charles Darwin and marginalist economics, ethics became more anthropological, relativistic, and utilitarian. But the message of the moral philosophers survived in the great constitutional treatise writers. Their influential books largely preserved the classical position that, on individualist principles, the State must stay out of the economy, but on communitarian principles, it should retain a strong hand in the regulation of morals. Orthodox writer Francis Wharton expressed similar positions in his numerous treatises.[92]

No legal intellectual better symbolizes classical legal thought during this period than Michigan's Thomas M. Cooley. His treatises on *Constitutional Limitations* (1868) and *Taxation* (1876), and his edition of Blackstone's *Commentaries (*1871*)*, are three of the era's most influential legal texts.[93] Cooley's genius was to describe the State's "police power" as if it were broad, all the while interpreting it narrowly.

Although Cooley believed State regulation of the economy was suspect, regulation of morals was essential. For example, although the Constitution's Contract Clause prevented a state from impairing the obligation of a preexisting contract on economic grounds, it could do so on moral grounds. Cooley approved temperance statutes that closed down lawfully built distilleries. "Perhaps there is no instance in which the power of the legislature to make such regulations as may destroy the value of property, without compensation to the owner, appears in a more striking light than in the case of these statutes." Nevertheless, Cooley concluded that such statutes were valid, notwithstanding his more general position that State protection of private property was a "sacred right."[94]

Cooley's brief discussion approving Sunday closing laws offers another insight into his position on economic and moral regulation. Two arguments had been offered for such laws. The first was that Sunday closing benefits the individual in that "one day's rest in seven is needful to recuperate the exhausted energies of body and mind." A second was that such laws "require the proper deference and regard which those not accepting the common belief may justly be required to pay to the public conscience." Cooley found the second argument persuasive but not the first. People had liberty to contract for their own hours of labor, and each individual could protect himself from excessive job demands. But recognition of a public conscience could be achieved only by forcing religious deference. He made the same argument about blasphemy statutes. "The language which the Christian regards as blasphemous, no man in sound mind can feel under a sense of duty to make use of under any circumstances, and no person is therefore deprived of a right when he is prohibited, under penalties, from uttering it."[95]

Christopher G. Tiedeman, another prominent writer on state regulatory power, was more libertarian than Cooley. Even so, where morals were concerned self-determination quickly gave way to communitarian value. Tiedeman wrote in his 1886 Treatise on the *Limitations of Police Power* that "no man can be addicted to vices, even of the most trivial character, without doing damage to the material interests of society.[96] Although Tiedeman saw difficult philosophical problems in State regulation of vices that caused no injury to others, he did not believe they rose to constitutional status. The legislature must have discretion to decide when a vice was sufficiently harmful to warrant legal regulation.

The University of Chicago's Ernst Freund was more moderate than Cooley or Tiedeman. His 1904 treatise on the *Police Power* distinguished regulatory authority in three "spheres of activities." First was a "conceded sphere" involving public safety, order, and morals, where the police power is continually and properly growing. Second is a "debatable sphere" concerning the proper production and distribution of wealth; here, legislation is still in an "experimental stage." Third is an "exempt sphere" of economic, intellectual, and political movements where the Constitution gives individuals freedom from State control. The spheres "may overlap," leading to complex questions. For example, "religion and speech and press are primarily free, but that does not prevent them from being subjected to restraints in the interest of good order or morality."

Freund expressed concern about government restrictions that were paternalistically intended to protect individuals from self-abuse. Laws against gambling and excessive drinking were problematic because they restrain "the individual from temptation and acts, which, while hurtful to him, are not immediately offensive to others." Freund admitted he would have great difficulty with regulation of liquor consumption if drinking harmed only the drinker himself. But it was widely known that the damage of drunkenness quickly extends to the entire community. Regulation was thus appropriate. By the same rationale Sunday closing laws were perfectly justifiable "for the protection of the good order and comfort of the community established and recognized by common custom and convention."[97]

The progressive attack on substantive due process doctrine prior to the New Deal consisted of two prongs. The strategically more conservative prong, exhibited by Brandeis's brief in *Muller*, sought to stay within the traditional classical framework but move the Court toward broader views about the range of "health," "safety," or "morals" issues that justified government intervention. Although Brandeis himself believed in a much broader and purely economic basis for regulation, as became clear during his tenure on the Supreme Court, he knew how to win his cases. Over the three decades after *Muller* this approach met with some but limited success.

The more aggressive prong was a direct attack on markets themselves, arguing that they were deficient simply because they worked poorly or distributed wealth in unacceptable ways. An important consequence of the marginalist revolution was to provide more secular rationales for regulation based on purely economic, market failure considerations. Prior to the late 1930s the Supreme Court typically rejected such arguments except in the case of monopoly. When the Court finally switched to deferential analysis of economic regulation in the late 1930s, the triumvirate of "health, safety, and morals" became a relatively unimportant part of constitutional jurisprudence.

14

The Waning of Classical Labor Policy

MODERN LABOR POLICY developed during the Progressive Era and the New Deal. The period was as tumultuous in economics as in lawmaking. Anglo-American economic and legal thought in the nineteenth century were built on a robust faith in markets and free contract. Beginning around 1900 that faith was shaken to its roots, and then slowly restored following World War II. Yet the restoration never claimed the nearly universal assent that once existed among the classical political economists. Many economists writing during this period believed that markets were more fragile than previously believed. That was particularly true of economic institutionalists, who survived as New Deal policymakers long after they were marginalized within their own discipline. Further, distribution of wealth emerged as an issue that the market itself could not address.[1] Legislative policy toward wages, hours, the labor of women and children, and working conditions became the opening wedge for a much broader set of regulatory initiatives that developed prior to and during the New Deal. This chapter focuses mainly on labor policy, while the next chapter considers the new regulatory State more generally.

The constitutional debates over labor policy during this period reflected a divide that was partly generational, partly ideological, but generally economic. At the Supreme Court level the debate also encompassed two broad questions about governmental power. First was the power of *any* government to interfere with privately negotiated agreements, captured mainly in the doctrine of liberty of contract. The second had to do with the assignment of power as between Congress on one hand and states or federal agencies on the other. The Supreme Court considered this question of institutional competence mainly in decisions under the Commerce Clause, the Tenth Amendment, and the nondelegation doctrine limiting the power of regulatory agencies.

Keeping the two questions distinct is often difficult and frankly not always important. Many Supreme Court justices were ambivalent or even hostile toward *any* kind of regulation that could not be justified by health, safety, or morals concerns. To be sure, the pre–1940 case law on the constitutionality of economic regulation is doctrinally distinct in the legal sense. Law school curricula to this day consider the Commerce Clause, Tenth Amendment, and federal agency delegation cases to be so distinctive from state law substantive due process cases that they are often placed in different courses, one concerned with federal power and the other with individual rights.

As a matter of *economic* doctrine, however, the cases are much less distinctive. Judges who opposed labor regulation on economic principle searched for constitutional doctrine that provided support. Most political and social historians who are not overly preoccupied with legal doctrine have also seen a single state of mind expressed in diverse constitutional rules. Consider the Court-packing controversy of 1937. The popular story is a remarkably good one. President Roosevelt was fed up with Supreme Court decisions overturning New Deal legislation. In particular, *Schechter Poultry* invalidated portions of the National Industrial Recovery Act, which provided for both product and labor regulation.[2] FDR then proposed his ill-fated Judicial Procedures Reform Bill of 1937, which would have authorized the president to appoint up to six additional justices for each sitting justice who was more than seventy years and six months old. The bill faced enormous opposition and never passed, costing FDR considerable political capital. According to the story Associate Justice Owen Roberts "switched," thus giving the majority to the Supreme Court's moderate wing.

The issue on which Justice Roberts switched had little to do with federal legislation, however. During the period from *Lochner* (1905) through the early New Deal several Supreme Court decisions had limited state regulatory power, especially over labor. A second set of decisions was based on restrictive readings of congressional power. Only the second group implicated Roosevelt's New Deal agenda. In 1936 Justice Roberts had followed established precedent striking down a New York minimum wage law for women.[3] Shortly after the Court-packing plan was announced Roberts changed his vote in a virtually identical case, *West Coast Hotel v. Parrish*.[4] About two weeks later Justice Roberts "switched" on federal law as well, voting to sustain the National Labor Relations Act.[5]

In any event, the Roberts "switch in time" story is largely false. Justice Roberts had changed his mind well before the Court-packing announcement. Indeed, he would have switched in *Morehead*, the pre-packing decision, except that the challenger had waived an argument he believed to be critical—namely, whether the 1926 *Adkins* decision striking down a minimum wage statute for women should be overruled.[6] Justice Roberts voted to grant certiorari in *West Coast Hotel* in the Supreme Court's private conference prior to the Court-packing announcement. Further, he had privately declared his intention to switch sides right after the oral argument in December 1936, approximately two months prior to the Court-packing announcement. The weight we have historically given to Justice Robert's "switch" results from the fact that the Court was closely divided on New Deal legislation. Roberts was the rare justice who actually changed his mind rather than retiring or dying.

The "revolution" in Supreme Court jurisprudence was actually a gradual result of judicial appointments over four decades. The final switch resulted from the Supreme Court appointments that Roosevelt was able to make during the years following the Court-packing controversy. A divided Court that had produced many split decisions in wage and hours cases between *Lochner* (5-4) in 1905 and *Morehead* (5-4) in 1937 was transformed and thereafter gave overwhelming and often unanimous approval to economic regulation of nearly every type for the next half century.

Although the Roberts "switch in time" story is false, the change in constitutional doctrine was very real. It was driven in significant part by changes in economic thought, which worked their way into constitutional jurisprudence. The early century saw the rise of marginalist economics and institutionalism. Both favored government economic intervention that went far beyond traditional regulation of health, safety, and morals. Economics then entered the turbulent 1930s with John Maynard Keynes's *General Theory*, which might be called the *macro*economic "bible" of the Second New Deal, and also Edward Chamberlin's *Monopolistic Competition* and Berle and Means's *Modern Corporation*, two books that together became the New Deal's *micro*economic bibles.[7]

That constitutional theory would be slow to embrace this economic revolution is not surprising. Quite aside from the strength of important interest groups was the fact that nineteenth-century interpretation of the Constitution had been built on a distinctly classical theory of property rights. Ownership and stability based on previous investment were fiercely protected. By contrast, the Constitution says almost nothing about the defining concerns of marginalist theory—prospective value, risk management, or the distribution of wealth. The Constitution also says little about regulatory agencies with powers that might be characterized as executive, legislative, judicial, or some combination of all three. In sum, the movement from classical to neoclassical conceptions of property and value required considerable new thinking about the Constitution's meaning and flexibility toward changing economic ideas.

One thing that clearly paved the way, as the previous chapter notes, was that the substantive due process Court had thoroughly embraced the concept of constitutional lawmaking in disregard of the constitutional text. The Roosevelt coalition went no further, although the principal protected interests changed. Thus the announcement of the change required no more than a single footnote in the *Carolene Products* decision.[8]

Whether the New Deal was modern economic theory at work, blind and fumbling experimentation, or simple capitulation to interest groups has divided its historians ever since. Moderate and more left-leaning writers have viewed the New Deal as one of the great accomplishments of realist legal and economic policy.[9] Conservatives and libertarians have decried it as being damaging in fundamental ways to both the American economy and the American spirit.[10] The rhetorical advantage probably lay with the classicists. Classical theory made the case for market efficiency in the abstract, without regard to how resources are distributed. By contrast, those who found market failures to be ubiquitous had to acknowledge that the failures were diverse and not always well understood. Solutions often required the support of diverse interest groups, some of whom had more socially defensible positions than others. In the 1960s, public choice theory would push this point very far, often seeing only one set of interest group pressures while ignoring fundamentals that may have justified intervention. Indeed, an important shortcoming of public choice theory was that it established nonregulation as a "baseline," leading it to explain every instance of market intervention as a consequence of socially harmful capture.[11]

Appreciation of the new economics lurched rather than glided into Supreme Court jurisprudence, beginning with President Theodore Roosevelt's appointment of Justice Holmes in 1902. Until Franklin D. Roosevelt was able to flood the Court in the late 1930s, the relation between presidential political party and the position of Supreme Court appointees on regulation was remarkably haphazard. In addition to Holmes, Theodore Roosevelt appointed Justices Day and Moody. Day was the author of the decision striking down the federal child labor law.[12] Moody was more aligned with the Progressives, but he retired after less than four years. President Taft had six appointees in his four-year presidency. Chief Justice Edward Douglas White was a moderate, as were Horace Lurton and Charles Evans Hughes, who left the Supreme Court in 1916 and returned in 1930 as Chief Justice. By contrast, Taft appointees Joseph Lamar, Mahlon Pitney, and Willis Van Devanter voted fairly consistently against both state labor regulation and New Deal legislation. Van Devanter, together with Justices McReynolds, Sutherland, and Butler, were later dubbed the "Four Horsemen" of the Apocalypse, representing Conquest, War, Famine, and Death.[13] The name originated with popular Washington syndicated columnist Drew Pearson, whose "Washington Merry-Go-Round" columns on the Supreme Court were collected in 1936 as *The Nine Old Men.* He spoke repeatedly of the "Four Horsemen of Reaction." Later the term was picked up by Legal Realist Walton Hamilton in his severe attacks on the pre-1937 Court.[14]

President Wilson served eight years but had only three appointments. Of these Justice Louis Brandeis was a consistent liberal, whereas another, John H. Clarke, was a Progressive with a short career. Wilson's third appointment, James McReynolds, became another of the Four Horsemen and was also the Supreme Court's most notorious bigot. He was particularly hostile toward Jews such as Brandeis and disparaging of African American litigants, even turning his chair so that they saw only his back during oral argument.[15] President Harding made four appointments during his brief presidency of less than two-and-a-half years. Pierce Butler and George Sutherland were the remaining two Horsemen. By contrast, Edward T. Sanford, a justice for only seven years, was a moderate who dissented in *Adkins*, the first decision striking down a minimum wage statute for women employees. Another dissenter was Chief Justice Taft, whom Harding appointed in 1921, thus making Taft the only American to be both president and chief justice. President Coolidge, who succeeded Harding upon his death, appointed only one justice, Harlan Fiske Stone, who later became chief justice and was generally supportive of New Deal legislation. He wrote the Court's influential opinion in *Carolene Products* a year after the Court-packing controversy, giving broad support to economic regulation.[16] Finally, Herbert Hoover appointed Benjamin Cardozo and Roberts, and reappointed Hughes, this time as chief justice. Cardozo and Hughes were sympathetic to the progressive revolution, as was Roberts after his switch.

So prior to FDR the record of Supreme Court appointments shows little correlation between presidential political party and regulatory attitude of the justices. Beginning in late 1937, Roosevelt's appointments changed that, cementing the Court's new position and making its alignment more obviously political. These were Hugo Black (August 1937), Stanley Reed (January 1938), Felix Frankfurter (January 1939), and William O. Douglas (April 1939). FDR also appointed Frank Murphy (January 1940), James F. Byrnes (June 1941, succeeded fifteen months later by Wiley B. Rutledge), Robert

H. Jackson (July 1941), and Chief Justice Harlan Fisk Stone (July 1941). These appointments remade the Court, and for a time left only Justice Roberts as a non-FDR appointee.

"Class Legislation"

Of all constitutional debates in the first half of the twentieth century, few claimed more attention than those involving labor policy. As Horace Gray Wood's Gilded Age treatise on *Master and Servant* both reflected and facilitated, by *Lochner*'s time American law had developed a more "private" conception of the employment agreement, rejecting the more protectionist but highly diverse common law that had prevailed prior to the Civil War. Employment law increasingly became merged into the commercial law of contract. *Lochner* thus constitutionalized a relatively recent conception of the labor agreement.[17]

The late nineteenth century witnessed widespread labor disputes, often including strikes and violence. The Pullman rail car strike of 1894 was one of the most notorious, ending in Eugene V. Debs's criminal conviction under the antitrust laws. Business people in particular saw the threat of class warfare that America, unlike Europe, had until then managed to avoid.[18] In his Boston University commencement speech on "The Path of the Law" in 1897, then state justice Holmes observed that conservatives of his day were obsessed by the war between the classes and the threat of incipient socialism.[19]

Already in 1868 Thomas M. Cooley had written at length about the evils of "class legislation." His principal concerns were statutes that favored well-placed interest groups, particularly special favors granted in corporate charters. State courts occasionally used the term in that way.[20] Justice Harlan then introduced the term "class legislation" into the Supreme Court's lexicon in the *Civil Rights Cases* (1883), where he dissented from a decision striking down a federal statute condemning racial exclusion.[21] The Court later used the term in *Yick Wo* (1886), which condemned a San Francisco land use ordinance that discriminated against Chinese-run laundries, and again in its *Pollock* decision (1895), which struck down the progressive income tax.[22] By 1900 those supporting wage and hour laws increasingly felt obliged to show that the provision in question was not "class legislation," but rather could be justified on the traditional grounds permitting regulation of health, safety, or morals. For example, in *Petit* the Supreme Court held that a statute requiring barbershops to be closed on Sunday was an appropriate regulation of morals and not class legislation.[23] By contrast, the *Truax* decision struck down as class legislation an Arizona statute prohibiting employers from obtaining injunctions against striking laborers.[24] Gilded Age state courts also condemned some labor protective statutes as "class legislation."[25]

The history of working class poverty during this period is often muddled by its statistics. In 1879 public intellectual Henry George observed in *Progress and Poverty* that, notwithstanding significant economic growth, there was an "increased bitterness among the working classes."[26] Statistics collected later supported both parts of George's observation. On the one hand, real wages in the United States grew during the Gilded Age and Progressive Era, except for a four-year reversal in nonunion wages following the 1893 depression.[27] But the real story lies in wage disparities and wealth distribution. The rising upper and middle classes obtained an increasing share of wealth at the expense of untrained and semiskilled labors. Indeed, some attempts to reconstruct a "poverty line' for the 1890s conclude that about 40 percent of American families lived below it.[28] Americans were literally becoming wealthier on the backs of the poor. The labor union grew to prominence amidst a growing feeling that, while aggregate American wealth was increasing, labor was falling behind.

For their part, American industrialists largely defended the growing wealth disparity by arguing that most of the new wealth came from entrepreneurial risk-taking and advances in technology, not from improvements in labor efficiency.[29] Of course, that avoided the question of exactly how labor was to become more efficient, as the needs for labor were entirely derivative of the technology. It also ignored that industrialists were in a position to differentiate their products and thereby blunt price competition. By contrast, unskilled and semiskilled labor competed only on price. As a result, most labor markets were more competitive than were production markets.

Nonetheless, in *Adkins* Justice Sutherland wrote for the Court that a state minimum wage statute improperly interfered with the "just equivalence" between "the amount to be paid and the service to be rendered." Justice Butler repeated that phrase in *Morehead*, which struck down another minimum wage provision, and Justice Sutherland repeated it yet again in his dissent in *West Coast Hotel*.[30] The term reflects a distinctly moral view of markets that differentiated classical political economy from the more nominalist views of the marginalists. For the latter, a wage increase meant only that the equilibrium would land in a different place. The employer would hire up to the point that the value of the next employee just equaled the extra cost. If demand did not change, an employer required to pay more would hire fewer workers or shift more production to labor-reducing technology. As both institutionalist John R. Commons and Keynes pointed out, however, demand *did* change. Increased wages also put money into laborers' pockets, and whether a higher minimum wage increased or diminished output depended on the circumstances. Keynes was strongly influenced by Commons on this point.[31]

Legally, the decks were stacked against the labor movement in important ways. As Commons complained in 1924, an incorporated employer was treated by the law as a single entity, no matter how large. By contrast, laborers were legal individuals. If two of them agreed with each other about wages, the law saw a cartel.[32] Whereas an employer could refuse to hire anyone he pleased, an agreement among laborers not to work was a boycott. Both cartels and boycotts were treated much more harshly than unilateral acts. It is no surprise that during its early decades the Sherman Antitrust Act became a potent union-busting device.[33]

Another problem was an ironic result of the "free labor" ideology that permeated the labor movement following Reconstruction. Labor advocates identified the right to obtain or leave one's job with the abolition of slavery and the Thirteenth Amendment.[34] But the right of worker mobility also served to create investment risks for employers. Why would an employer pay to train a worker who might quit his job and take his costly training elsewhere? Employers universally treated day or hourly labor as a variable cost. Workers could be hired when demand increased and quickly let go when it declined. There were no provisions for wage substitutes or medical care during layoffs. These practices had become the default rule in employment agreements during the Gilded Age when they were institutionalized in Wood's influential treatise on the law of *Master and Servant*. Up to that time American courts had generally followed the English rule which provided, in Blackstone's words, that once menial (unskilled) servants were hired, they must be maintained "as well when there is work to be done, as when there is not."[35]

The meaning of "free labor" changed over time, and in ways that were largely unfavorable to organized labor. During the New Deal "free labor" was considered by many to be a right to organize, while others thought of it as a right to be free of a closed shop. The latter view became a part of labor policy in 1947, when the Taft-Hartley Act permitted states to enact "right to work" laws that typically give employees the wage benefits of a union contract while not requiring them to join a union or pay its dues. In one of the most powerful examples of free riding, the impact of "right to work" became wages that were significantly lower in right-to-work states.[36]

The situation led to the deep irony that the American employer was more loyal to his machinery than to his workers. Employer-owned equipment had to be maintained even when it was not working because of slack demand, but the employer could lay off most laborers on short notice and without owing them anything. This state of affairs led so moderate an economist as John Maurice Clark to propose in the early 1920s that labor be treated as a fixed cost for purposes of dealing with layoffs.[37] That is, employers should be required to enter long-term commitments with employees and support them even when they were not working, as they did their factories and machinery. Although his proposal received acclaim at a meeting of the American Economic Association, it never went beyond that until support for laid-off workers became reflected in collective bargaining agreements or unemployment compensation provisions that became part of the Social Security Act of 1935.[38]

Labor Protective Legislation: Racism, Equalizing Costs, or Worker Welfare?

Labor union strategy in the Gilded Age was fundamentally the same as producer strategy. Just as the technological revolution created surplus production capacity, so too technology plus the immigration waves of the 1880s and 1890s produced an unprecedented labor surplus. In order to improve wages and working conditions labor needed to limit its output, just as producers needed to limit theirs in order to keep profits up. The unions turned to closed shop agreements, exclusion of certain groups, or public intervention in the form of minimum wage or maximum hours laws. Unions were responsible for their share of the racial and ethnic exclusion that pervaded Gilded Age and Progressive Era thought. Around 1910 virtually every northern trade union excluded African Americans from membership.[39] Union members widely believed that African Americans were strikebreakers because they were willing to work for lower wages and under more adverse conditions.[40] In its 1906 *Hodges* decision the Supreme Court held that the civil rights statutes did not apply when a group of white workers violently attacked a sawmill in order to drive away its African American employees. Although the act was certainly criminal, it was outside of federal power to regulate, and the Tenth Amendment reserved this power to the states.[41]

Race and ethnic prejudice also played a role in protective legislation, as did the desire to encourage immigrant assimilation. For example, the ten-hour law struck down in *Lochner* may have had its greatest effect on immigrant bakery owners, particularly Italians and Jews, whose employees often spoke no English.[42] Nevertheless, the statute applied to every "biscuit, bread or cake bakery or confectionery establishment" in the entire state. The labor movement recognized that if hours limitations were not imposed across an entire industry the exempted employers would obtain competitive advantages, particularly where wages were driven to subsistence levels no matter how much the laborer worked. The *Lochner* statute followed after legislation elsewhere in the urban east that since the mid-nineteenth century had limited the hours of many types of workers. By the time of *Lochner* North Carolina had enacted an eleven-hour law for all manufacturing, South Carolina and Georgia had similar legislation for textile workers, four states regulated the maximum hours of bakers, and several others regulated the maximum hours of women or minors. State court challenges to these statutes produced mixed results.[43] These provisions followed after a series of Factory Acts passed in Great Britain across the nineteenth century. The Acts initially limited the hours of women and children but by the mid-1850s began extending their provisions to male laborers.[44]

Although *Lochner*'s ten-hour provision may have hindered ethnic baker employers, it was quite sympathetic with the concerns of the employees. Many Italian and eastern European laborers had been brought into the United States under the Padrone system, a form of indentured servitude, or peonage. An 1885 federal statute had made it unlawful to prepay the passage of immigrants in order to place them under peonage contracts. However, the Padrones continued to control labor within their ethnic groups well into the twentieth century.[45] Employees, including bakers, were brokered out by the Padrones. At the time of *Lochner* Italian workers were themselves in the process of organizing against the Padrone system.[46] An 1896 *New York Times* article entitled "War on Filthy Bakeries," published a few months before the *Lochner* statute was passed, described how women's groups had been campaigning against the bakeries, whose walls were described as "covered with vermin." According to the article, bakers worked between 12 and 20 hours daily and slept on bread troughs or mattresses thrown over flour barrels. Many were permitted to leave the shops only once per week, and some reported that they would be fired for telling outsiders about working conditions.[47] Three years later Congress conducted hearings on the effects of the law that confirmed the *New York Times* account. Prior to the legislation bakers often "worked twenty-four hours without cessation; sixteen and eighteen hours were quite common; twelve and thirteen hours was the rule." Further, they were often "forced under contract with their employers to make the bake shops their home, sleep in in them… The law struck at the eradication of all those things."[48] The state's brief was candid about the legislation's paternalism: the "habits" of some immigrants "must be changed so that in due course of time there may be that assimilation which has made so successful our previous immigrations."[49]

The *Lochner* statute contained both the hard ten-hour rule and also a set of sanitary regulations readily subject to the manipulation of any inspector bent on ethnic discrimination. *Lochner* struck down only the ten-hour provision. In his largely ignored dissent, Justice Harlan (joined by Justices White and Day) described how both bakery hours and working conditions were the most difficult and unhealthy "imaginable," relying on an *Annual Report* of the New York Bureau of Labor Statistics.[50]

Prior to 1930 most Supreme Court constitutional law involving wages, hours, or working conditions concerned the states. By contrast, most federal government involvement before the New Deal was with tort liability for work-related accidents and some child labor and railroad labor regulation. In 1911 the Court upheld a federal provision limiting the hours of railroad workers in interstate commerce to ten per day. Applying the same "health, safety, and morals" criteria that governed state regulation, the Court found that Congress was justified in declaring a link between the safety of railroad passengers and the alertness of railroad workers.[51] Federal regulation of employer tort liability was initially struck down in 1908, but in 1912 the Court upheld a redrafted statute that applied only to workers engaged in interstate commerce.[52] The Court also overturned an attempt to give federal protection to union organizing of railroad laborers.[53] A general child labor statute, cast as a prohibition on the interstate shipment of goods manufactured with child labor, was struck down in 1918 under the Commerce Clause and the Tenth Amendment.[54]

The Sherman Antitrust Act was frequently applied to labor union activities prior to 1914.[55] In that year Congress passed the Clayton Act at the behest of the Wilson administration, which sought to create an antitrust immunity for labor organizing. The statute was not very effective, however, and a broad antitrust immunity had to await the Norris-Laguardia anti-injunction Act[56] and Wagner Act[57] during the New Deal, and the Taft-Hartley Act of 1947.[58]

The Passing of the Wage-Fund Doctrine and the "Residual Claimant"

The wage-fund doctrine, which dominated classical economic and legal theory in the nineteenth century, held that the total fund available for the payment of wages was the capital that the firm had retained from previous production. The theory was distinctly pre-marginalist, determining value by looking back at what had already been paid in. Under the theory a firm reserved surplus earnings in each period as a "fund" available to pay wages in the following period. If the firm was to thrive, its gross wages during the second period could not exceed the amount of capital that had been saved. Otherwise the fund would be depleted, and producers would suffer declines in output and perhaps be driven into bankruptcy. The result for laborers would be unemployment and starvation. Thus the wage-fund theory argued for a "natural" rate of wages and against labor unions or legislative interference. Judicial opinions such as *Adkins v. Children's Hospital* (1923) followed its logic in striking down legislative attempts to increase wages.[59]

The wage-fund theory was generally drawn from simple agrarian analogies, in contexts where there was no labor contract at all but only self-employment. For example, the farmer laboring in his field had to live on last year's corn, not the immature corn that was currently growing in the field. Yale political economist William Graham Sumner, one of the staunchest American defenders of the doctrine, ridiculed its critics for thinking "that a man who was tilling the ground in June could eat the crop he expected to have in September, or that a tailor could be wearing the coat which he was making."[60]

Marginalist economics completely upended the classical wage-fund doctrine, substituting a forward-looking theory of value based on reasonable expectations. When a business person hired a laborer, what counted was not previous investment in capital, a backward-looking number, but rather the worker's *expected* contribution to the production process. If a worker added 15 cents per hour in value, the employer would be willing to pay any amount up to 15 cents less the costs of maintaining the worker. Marginalism provided a unifying model for all of the elements that go into production, including wages, John Bates Clark argued in "Wages and Interest as Determined by Marginal Productivity."[61] An entrepreneur would invest in his own skills, in land, factories, equipment, and labor up to the point that the additional investment was just enough to pay for itself. For example, if changing to a new machine required an incremental investment of $100 per year but the entrepreneur predicted $110 in increased profits, he would buy the new machine. If the machine promised increased profits of only $90 per year, he would not. So too with labor.

This technical change in the theory of value transformed economic thinking about labor during the early twentieth century. In particular, it led to the widespread belief that labor was not getting its fair share. Undifferentiated and excessive worker competition persistently drove wages much lower than the average worker's contribution to his employer. The result was seen by many Progressives as a kind of legally sanctioned theft, in which noncompetitive employers were able to suppress wages by exploiting labor abundance and disorganization. The two solutions to the problem were the essentially private one of union organizing, and the public one of statutory wage and hours provisions.

The rhetoric of this debate often referred to the "residual claimant" of the wage agreement. The underlying doctrine originated with William Stanley Jevons, the first serious English marginalist, who had rejected the wage-fund theory.[62] Francis Walker, MIT president and a severe American critic of the wage-fund doctrine, argued in his *Political Economy* that the four factors of production were land, capital, entrepreneurship, and labor. Wages represented the value left over when land, capital, and entrepreneurship were paid for. "The whole remaining body of wealth daily or annually created, is the property of the laboring class, their wages, or the remuneration of their services."[63] John Bates Clark had already argued in the late 1880s that under perfect competition each element of production should receive its "marginal product." Thus labor should receive the value that it adds to the firm.[64] The residual claimant became a forceful part of Keynes's argument in the *General Theory* (1935) that in a competitive market labor would tend to earn its "marginal net product," or the increase that it contributed to the firm's value.[65] Clark's and Keynes' limitation to competitive markets was where the rub occurred. If the labor market was highly competitive, while the more diversified manufacturing market was not, then employers would be in a position to suppress wages and keep for themselves much of labor's contribution.[66] The firm belief that markets were becoming less competitive on the production side than the worker side fueled this view.

Much of the history writing about the Progressive Era labor movement has emphasized the moral and political character of the arguments for regulated wages.[67] But Progressive economists believed they were engaged in economic science. They were fond of noting that only the *marginal* laborer, or the last laborer to be hired, received precisely his contribution to the production process. Laborers who were hired earlier by definition contributed more than their wages, assuming that all laborers were paid the same amount. This meant that laborers, generally among the lowest of America's economic classes, were contributing more to the production process than they took out, adding to the wealth of capitalists while living under subsistence conditions themselves. Under the welfare economics of the day, total welfare would increase if any surplus created by the production process was given to those who were worse off. For many Progressives this theory justified State intervention on behalf of labor, such as minimum wage laws—a view that was reflected among economically sophisticated writers in the law reviews. For example, Harvard professor and Legal Realist Thomas Reed Powell observed that the Constitution was utterly silent on the question of minimum wage laws. As a result the rulings did not reflect interpretation of the Constitution at all, but only the "outlook and temper" of the justices.[68]

Writing in his early career, institutionalist John R. Commons initially agreed with John Bates Clark that if the laborer were indeed "free" he could obtain the marginal value of his contribution by changing jobs, or else capitalize it by becoming an entrepreneur.[69] By 1924, however, Commons had changed his position, and argued vehemently that unionization was the mechanism by which labor could recover its total contribution, just as incorporation and trade associations were the means by which business entrepreneurs could recover theirs. Writing at a time when businesses were frenetically organizing into trade associations in order to limit production, as the next chapter develops, Commons saw laborers' resentment of the worker who accepted low wages or long hours as no different than producer resentment of price cutters:

> When business men call upon laborers to "produce," and criticize them for restricting production, they are calling upon them to do that which they themselves do not. For they, like the laborers, produce, not indiscriminately, but they produce in limited quantities, in order to maintain the price in their market.[70]

For the Progressives the developing economics of marginal utility revealed nothing but oppression for the working class.[71]

Objective Judgments of Laborer Welfare

The debate over legislated minimum wages turned Progressive Era economists' attention to the welfare effects of State-mandated rather than individually negotiated wages. This in turn invited the question whether welfare could be measured objectively and socially, or only subjectively and individually through contracting processes. Both progressive and more centrist economists tended to believe that one could show scientifically that a certain minimum level of income was necessary for the American worker to sustain self and family.[72]

During the first two decades of the century a mountain of literature dealt with the scientific measurement of the "living wage"—or the minimum income that would enable a family to have an acceptable standard of living.[73] In the 1910s and 1920s the United States Bureau of Labor Statistics, which had been established in 1894, greatly expanded its statistical studies of wages and purchasing power.[74] Glendower Evans, a Progressive and close friend of William James, defended the use of objective criteria for a "minimum standard of living" for the woman wage earner.[75] She noted how a state wage board attempted to construct the minimum family budget—by such devices as calling "a representative connected with a department store" in order to obtain "an estimate for clothing." The resulting minimum weekly budget of $8.71 included 10 cents for "church." In an article on "Wage Theories and Wage Policies," addressing the problem of objective welfare criteria and wage policy, John R. Commons argued that economics since Adam Smith had properly been divided into a theory of value, which was devoted to the measurement of individual market choices; and a theory of prosperity, which was devoted to social welfare.[76] Public wage policy belonged to the latter. Likewise William F. Ogburn, who later became prominent for his theory of cultural lag, noted several methodological difficulties in determining a minimum standard of living but advocated the approach nonetheless.[77]

During the 1910s and 1920s, when most state minimum wage legislation was passed, the momentum in American economic theory was with marginalists, who advocated some sort of regulatory intervention in the marketplace. Until 1937 the biggest hurdle was the Supreme Court. Afterward, constitutional law rarely interfered with the statutory development of wage and hour regulation.

15

The Regulatory State and Federalism

HISTORY WRITING ABOUT the New Deal has focused heavily on economic policy. Those who believe that the market shortcomings that New Dealers identified were real and required correction also tend to think that the constitutional revolution was justified. The Constitution had to be "opened up" to reflect a more complex and forward-looking understanding of markets and society. By contrast, critics tend to be confident about markets and doubtful that the New Deal regulatory agenda represented anything more than special interest capture. They have even more serious doubts that regulatory agencies have the capacity to increase wealth or make the economy better. In these debates economic theory is the dog, and constitutional theory but the tail.

While the new economics transformed thinking about industrial production and the American worker, it reached most other areas of the economy as well. The powerful rhetoric of the Progressives created a straw man—namely a nineteenth-century laissez-faire economy in which each person was left to himself and big business prospered at the expense of weaker members of society. That claim was very far from the truth. The United States had a strong tradition of regulation at every governmental level that stretched back to the commonwealth ideal of Revolutionary times and maintained a growing presence throughout the nineteenth century.[1]

Historically, most regulation was enacted without any formal economic theory to support it. That is very likely true even today. Legislators or aldermen listen to people petition that they need this or that regulation, and the legislative body decides whether to comply. Beginning in the late nineteenth century Progressive lawyers, economists, and political leaders began to call for more elaborate and centralized government control of many aspects of the economy in addition to the health, safety, and morals that had traditionally justified regulation.

Market Failure and the Threat to Property Rights

As Chapter 13 observed, American courts around 1900 tended to approve market interventions tied to the triumvirate of "health, safety, or morals." Regulation was constitutionally permissible if the problem that the legislature identified pertained to the health or safety of someone *other* than the contracting parties. Market participants were presumably able to take care of themselves, with some exceptions for women and children. By contrast, regulation of morals was permissible even if the morals were those of the contracting party. Even within classical political statecraft, people needed protection from their own moral shortcomings.

Health and safety regulation became the opening wedge for a more secular doctrine of "externalities"—the idea that certain market interventions are socially beneficial if the contracting parties are not likely to consider harms that their agreements impose on other members of society. For example, the Supreme Court could justify comprehensive land use regulation while rejecting wage and hours legislation. Urban development often imposed significant burdens on people who were not a party to the development agreement, whereas the burden of labor agreements fell mainly on the contracting employer and employee.

Classical political economists had a strong conception of property rights. The legal term "vested rights" captured this conception and accounts for the close link between property theory and contract theory. Certain values, once created, could not be taken away. The main body of the Constitution did this in the Contract Clause, which applied to the states.[2] The Fifth Amendment's Takings Clause and the Fourteenth Amendment's Equal Protection and Due Process Clauses later did this as well. In cases involving railroads the Supreme Court recognized takings-like protection for corporations in 1886 under the Equal Protection Clause[3] and in 1897 under the Due Process Clause.[4]

The quick infiltration of marginalist economics into the economic curriculum around the turn of the twentieth century was nothing less than revolutionary. Although neoclassical theory did not completely undermine traditional notions of property rights, it weakened classical doctrine in several respects. Markets began to look much more vulnerable to imperfections. Further, distribution of wealth became an important ingredient in measuring the welfare produced by an economy. Finally, neoclassicism saw value as willingness to pay for the next unit—that is, its theory of value was forward rather than backward looking. State Justice Holmes, perhaps the first marginalist lawyer, had observed already in an 1895 eminent domain damages case, that "all values are anticipations of the future."[5] While forward-looking assessments provided a more satisfying behavioral account of how markets work, they necessarily involved more prediction based on technical formulations and information that could be quite specific to the market in question.

The fights over marginalism between the "old" and "new" generation of economists are legendary. For the most part, however, it was not economists' personal wealth that was at stake. For young economists in particular there was more to be gained from acquiring new territory than from repairing old fences.[6] One's position on the backward-looking wage-fund doctrine or the forward-looking marginal value theory of labor could make or ruin academic reputations. But to the extent the marginal value theory argued for significantly higher wages and unionization or greater public investment in infrastructure, vast amounts of wealth were at stake as well. One can say the same thing about progressive taxation, government price regulation, or regulatory agencies. The new generation of economists that flooded American universities in the late nineteenth and early twentieth centuries took on these issues in ways that clearly threatened established property rights if the legal system were to take them seriously.[7]

A "market failure" is a situation where the market is unlikely to change on its own, but prices are higher than they should be, quantity or quality are too low, or certain people are affected in unnecessarily harmful ways.[8] More practically, relevant market failure occurs when government intervention can make things better. Although the classicists did not use the term "market failure," they understood the concept. Beginning with Adam Smith they considered whether the "self interest" that leads to individual trading is sufficient to produce adequate value.[9] The general answer was yes, but even the classicists recognized some exceptions. One was John Stuart Mill's discussion of natural monopoly. Speaking of the British Post Office, a government-created monopoly, Mill wondered whether "instead of being centralized in a single concern" the London postal business "were divided among five or six competing companies." Each would have to maintain "almost as large an establishment as is now sufficient for the whole," and each would have "to send letter-carriers into every street." As a result, the total costs of operating a single postal system for the entire city was much lower than the cost of a competitive system.[10]

Under marginalism the concept of market failure became more secular and also more technical. As the theory of perfect competition was formalized, economists began to realize that the conditions for achieving it are quite strict. Early in the twentieth century they began incorporating competitive breakdowns into the theory of industrial organization.[11] Cambridge economist Arthur C. Pigou made the study of market failure central to his *Economics of Welfare*, which was highly influential in the United States after the 1920s and remains so, notwithstanding withering criticism by Ronald Coase.[12] A significant portion of the "rehabilitation" of the market that occurred in the 1960s and after took the form of an attack on Pigou.

A distinctive feature of the emergent conception of market failure is diversity. When markets succeed they tend to be alike and a uniform policy of nonintervention works for all. When markets fail, however, they do so in specific ways that require different corrections, including "Pigouvian" taxes such as those discussed in Chapter 5, or more direct forms of regulatory intervention. Progressives through the New Deal, and institutionalists in particular, were obsessed with the diverse nature of market failure. Two principles were bedrock. The first was that market failure was ubiquitous. The second was that each market or institution required study in order to determine its own unique rules of operation. The Legal Realists picked up this mantle, both making the case that economic law must be freed from abstraction, and later implementing market-specific regulations. The resulting New Deal regulatory regime had not only more regulation, it also led to different regulatory agencies for each industry, with differing views about the regulatory problems in each market and differing agendas for solving them.

The development of complex theories of market failure led to a tension in economics that emerged full-blown in the 1930s and after. Marginalist economics itself had highly analytic roots, based on reductionist assumptions about rational behavior. But these analytic conceptions produced results that varied considerably with market conditions. For example, as a higher proportion of a firm's costs are fixed, competition becomes more difficult to sustain. Healthy competition also requires that participants have good information, that product flows freely among them, and that new firms can enter easily. But the presence of these factors varied considerably from one market to the next. Markets with fewer firms appeared to perform less competitively. The rise of theories about product differentiation in the 1930s suggested that product diversity could have a powerful impact on competition, and that intellectual property rights affected these outcomes. As Berle and Means argued, the separation of ownership and control could make business firms perform in undesirable ways.[13] However, the problem manifested itself differently depending on firm size or organizational structure. As the weight of these differences became more pronounced, economic policy study became more specific to the industry and much more empirical. Public law followed a similar course.

These views were to have a significant impact on both the amount and the diversity of regulatory law.

The discussions of market failure in this period also included concerns regarded today as "distributive"—that is, having to do with how resources are divided among more and less wealthy individuals. Important architects of market failure theory such as Pigou wrote prior to the ordinalist revolution discussed in Chapter 6. They tended to believe that social welfare increased as wealth was more equal. Uneven distribution of wealth was itself a "market failure" concern to the extent that market forces could not be relied on to correct it.

But the concern with satisfaction of wants does not tell the whole story. Because people are producers as well as consumers, redistribution was also thought essential to facilitate increased worker productivity and consumer demand. For example, John Maurice Clark, who relied heavily on Pigou's work, argued the economic case for greater investment in worker productivity through education and higher wages.[14] This focus is critical to understanding welfare policy of the New Deal Era, which was intended to increase worker training and productivity as well as consumer confidence.

During the New Deal American regulatory policy set out on a two-pronged venture, both to correct market failure and to promote "fairness," or "equal access." For example, the historical preoccupation with "universal service" in public utility law reflected both efficiency and distributive values. Efficiency required monopoly, but monopoly in turn gave the regulated firm a duty to serve all customers in a reasonably nondiscriminatory manner. These concerns originated in the common law of public service companies and quickly migrated into regulatory policy. They are strongly reflected in the law review writing prior to the New Deal.[15]

Overproduction, Associationalism, and the First New Deal

Franklin D. Roosevelt's New Deal was a mélange of fiscal and regulatory experiments. It was also two quite different experiments, reflecting inconsistent economic policies. To oversimplify, the policy initiatives of the First New Deal (1933) were largely industry-driven efforts to restrict production in order to get prices up, plus some government cajoling for better wages and working conditions. The principal policy initiatives of the Second New Deal (1934 and after) were stimulation of demand, more aggressive labor legislation and antitrust policy, and social and labor security. Both policies were built on a premise of pervasive market failure, but the perceived failures and fixes in the first New Deal were quite different from those in the second.

By the late 1920s the concern with overproduction had become conventional in the economics literature. As developed in Chapter 11, neoclassical economics initially struggled to incorporate fixed costs into its theories about pricing and output. High fixed costs forced competitive firms to increase output, driving prices too low to cover long- term investment. Fixed costs also gave large firms cost advantages over smaller firms. The predicted result was cycles of overproduction and business losses, attempts at collusion in order to keep output down, and mergers. "Ruinous competition" became not only an economic but also a legal term of art that appeared frequently in the case law. These ideas were repeatedly confirmed during the Gilded Age and Progressive Era, as firms turned increasingly to machine production and were able to increase output many times over.[16] They counseled against strong antitrust enforcement.

One political response prior to the New Deal was various forms of "associationalism," or the development of voluntary trade associations that operated on a vaguely defined boundary between coordination and outright collusion.[17] Associationalism often led to industry-initiated codes of "fair dealing," exchanges of information among producers, including quantity reporting and warnings to avoid overproduction. On the eve of the Depression the United States had more than two thousand national and local trade associations of this kind.[18] At the same time, it is hard to overlook the simultaneous efforts by business to keep product output down and its unrestrained and often cruel resistance toward any attempts to reduce output in labor markets in order to get wages up.

In the case of product output restraints the government largely stood aside, but occasionally challenged extreme practices under the antitrust laws. In the late 1910s it challenged a trade association in the lumber industry whose stated purpose was "to disseminate among members accurate knowledge of production and market conditions so that each member may gauge the market intelligently instead of guessing at it." The result would be to substitute " 'co-operative competition' for cutthroat competition, or keeping prices at reasonably stable and normal levels."[19] The Supreme Court condemned the association. The government also obtained an antitrust decree against the linseed oil trade association for using an elaborate reporting mechanism designed to detect price cutting.[20]

The Hoover administration's approach to the overproduction problem was to permit business firms to form their own associations. The First New

Deal approach was more aggressive, including both antitrust immunity and government-mandated limitations on output in order to get prices up and, optimistically, to increase wages. The National Recovery Administration, which was organized in 1933, and collateral agencies such as the Petroleum Administrative Board, cooperated with businesses in the drafting of mandatory "codes" intended to achieve these goals.[21]

As for worker wages and hours, the differences between the First and Second New Deals have been unnecessarily exaggerated. The NRA Codes almost universally provided for worker welfare. Some Codes assessed requirements about working conditions and permitted laborers to organize into unions. From the onset Roosevelt's first Secretary of Labor, Frances Perkins, made the minimum wage, the forty-hour week, workers compensation, and unemployment compensation central to her labor policy.[22] In retrospect the Codes reflected naiveté about business willingness to abide by the labor portion of the typically underenforced provisions, but the requirements were clearly there.

On the other hand, one unmistakable difference between the First and Second New Deals was the attitude toward *product* output restrictions. The earlier period viewed overproduction as the problem, and the Codes together with lax antitrust policy tended to limit production. In sharp contrast, the antitrust aggressiveness of the Second New Deal was intended to get output up. Some of the very practices that had been encouraged during the early years of the New Deal were challenged as antitrust violations a few years later.

The thinking behind the NRA Codes of the First New Deal was that reduced output would yield high product prices, which would produce the surplus necessary to increase wages. NRA official Arthur Heath Onthank described the process in "How Codes Are Made," a defense of administration policy. Firms made proposals for their industry. Then the government encouraged them to "organize" their production in ways that today would be regarded as collusion.[23] Reflecting in 1934 on the brief history of the administration, Clair Wilcox acknowledged that firms involved in implementing the Codes were much more enthusiastic about fixing product prices than raising wages. "In actuality it has been possible for some employers to violate the hour and wage provisions of the codes; to reduce hours and increase production without substantially increasing employment." At the same time, the Codes had clearly "boosted prices," in part by limiting the use of efficient machinery, and by "prolonging the life of relatively inefficient producers." As a result, "production and prices have outrun consumer incomes and the expected expansion of buying power has failed to materialize."[24] It is little wonder, as Ellis Hawley observed, that the industry-driven NRA codes were already unpopular and near political collapse before the Supreme Court's *Schechter* decision invalidated them.[25]

Because the perceived failures in each industry were unique, the codes varied a great deal from one industry to another. For example, the "hot oil" provision that the Supreme Court struck down in *Panama Refining* prohibited the interstate shipment of petroleum produced in excess of production quotas. "In most cases the Code provisions for curtailment of production will be of great assistance in preserving interstate commerce," wrote a commentator in the *Yale Law Journal*. They would "tend to eliminate waste and loss of oil, both underground and on the surface."[26] When competing companies owned rigs over the same underground pool they were forced to pump as quickly as possible or risk drainage by their rivals. Once abandoned, however, the costs of restarting a well were very large. "It is often more expensive to recondition abandoned wells than to drill new ones."[27]

Chief Justice Hughes wrote the Court's decision condemning the hot oil provision. The statute did "not seek to lay down rules for the guidance" of officials concerning how excess production was to be defined or identified.[28] As a result, Congress had inappropriately delegated a legislative power to the executive branch and had not "sufficiently defined" a framework to guide rule-making. As Justice Cardozo complained in his lone dissent, "ascertainment" of the specific facts of the hot oil problem "was a task too intricate and special to be performed by Congress itself through a general enactment in advance of the event."[29]

The *Schechter Poultry* decision, which dismantled what remained of the NRA, involved a very different industry. The "Live Poultry Code" regulations concerning unhealthy ("sick") chickens were intended to limit output as well as control product quality, but the Code also limited work to forty hours per week, required wages of at least 50 cents per hour, and prohibited child labor. It also permitted the workers to form unions. This time the Court's decision was unanimous, striking the Code down under both the Commerce Clause and as an improper delegation of legislative power to the executive branch. Justice Cardozo wrote a concurring opinion indicating that in this case the Code had gone too far. "Here in effect is a roving commission to inquire into evils and upon discovery correct them."[30] It is one thing for a Code to condemn conduct clearly recognized as improper or unfair, he explained. But in this case the Code's coverage "becomes as wide as the field of industrial regulation.... This is delegation running riot."[31]

The regulatory agenda of the New Deal strongly reflected the view of its policymakers that market failure is market specific. This required detailed study of the conditions in individual markets thought to be in distress. That process began early in Roosevelt's administration through the Code promulgation process and culminated in the forty-three monographs and thirty volumes of hearing reports produced by the Temporary National Economic Committee (TNEC) between 1938 and 1941 on every facet of American industry.[32]

It is easy to criticize the New Deal for undue experimentation or perhaps even excessive attentiveness to interested industry participants. But the nature of market failure is to invite market-specific fixes. The Constitution's framers had already recognized this for markets where they had foreseen problems, such as intellectual property, national mail delivery, and bankruptcy. In the past the Supreme Court had recognized that market-specific regulation was beyond Congress's ability to achieve, and had more than once assented to acts of delegation. It is important not to exaggerate the novelty of both the delegation of administrative duties and, necessarily, of administrative law.[33]

The constitutional debate over New Deal regulation exists at two levels. First is the question whether market failure is in fact as ubiquitous and diverse as the New Dealers imagined. Second is whether the Constitution is flexible enough to accommodate the expansive delegation of legislative power that becomes practically essential if the answer to the first question is yes. Once Roosevelt was able to flood the Supreme Court with his own appointees both of these issues were politically resolved in favor of broad regulatory power. The Administrative Procedure Act, which was passed in 1946, was later interpreted to permit agency rule-making with little more specific direction than Congress had provided in the NRA.[34] The *Final Report* of the Attorney General's Committee on Administrative Procedure, which recommended the Act, identified fifty-one federal regulatory agencies, including some thirty-five created during the New Deal.[35]

The Second New Deal

The Second New Deal shifted the federal government's focus more sharply toward labor and unemployment, as well as stimulation of demand. The National Labor Relations Act ("Wagner Act," 1935) limited the ability of employers to exclude labor unions and largely introduced modern collective bargaining.[36] The Works Progress Administration (WPA, 1935) used federal funds to employ people in public works projects and also acted as a welfare agency to distribute food, clothing, and some housing.[37] The Social Security

Act (1935) created the Social Security Administration and led to the modern system of federally paid retirement and disability benefits.[38] The federal government made a dramatic about-face on competition policy, largely dropping the concern about limiting production and inaugurating aggressive antitrust enforcement under the leadership of Thurman Arnold.

Historians have generally seen the Second New Deal as an abrupt change from the First, and have often explained it as Roosevelt's continuous experimentation to find answers to economic problems that seemed to defy solution. However, the Second New Deal also shows the influence of deep changes in economic theory that had come to the forefront of academic economics. One of these was Keynesian macroeconomic policy. The other was the monopolistic competition revolution.

Stimulation of Demand

Roosevelt met John Maynard Keynes in 1934. Keynes had written an "Open Letter to the President" in the *New York Times* advocating "reasoned experiment" with the economy.[39] He argued that the Depression resulted principally from slack demand. As a result, stimulation rather than austerity was the only rational fix. In addition, Keynes urged that recovery be given priority over more durable structural reforms. Further, the way to recovery is through the "increase of national purchasing power resulting from governmental expenditure, which is financed by loans and is not merely a transfer through taxation from existing incomes."

Although Roosevelt found Keynes very abstract, his ideas for stimulation by government spending were easy to grasp. As his predecessor Herbert Hoover, FDR had been committed to balancing the budget. He had been unable to do so, however, and Keynes provided a way out. He stated somewhat defensively in a 1936 campaign speech, "To balance our budget... would have been a crime against the American people. To do so we should either have had to make a capital levy that would have been confiscatory, or we should have set our face against human suffering with callous indifference."[40] In 1937 the administration renewed its effort to balance the budget, but recession re-emerged, threatening several years of improvement.[41] Then, for fiscal year 1938, FDR proposed his first budget with an intentional deficit, in this case of $3 billion. Jerome Frank, who was about to become Chair of the Securities Exchange Commission, protested that it was far too little. His views largely reflected the consensus among Legal Realists and the Left, which was thoroughly enamored of Keynes.[42]

The federal government took an unprecedented role in managing the greater economy through deficit spending, creation of jobs through non-market mechanisms, support for distressed workers so as to enable them to re-enter the market, and control of inflation and access to money. Roosevelt took more-or-less seriously Keynes's theory that economic depression required government stimulation of consumption, including provision of jobs for the building of infrastructure. Keynes himself was relentlessly experimental, just as Roosevelt, and he emphasized the extent to which different situations required different fixes. Keynes contemplated loosely specified public-private partnerships to address problems of underemployment and consumer distress.[43] "For all the fumbling and hesitancy with which [the Keynesian measures] have been applied," Yale law professor Eugene V. Rostow conceded in 1941, "it may be said positively that these techniques have worked."[44]

The End of Associationalism: Branded Distribution and Monopolistic Competition

The economic theory of overproduction that drove associationalism had been based on a model of machine production of standardized commodities. Overproduction and ruinous competition were serious threats because of the combination of high fixed costs and head-to-head price competition. That economic model was reflected in antitrust policy during the 1910s and 1920s. Most of the big antitrust cases occurred in industries for standardized products—railroad transportation, oil and linseed, tobacco, metal cans, wire nails, wood products, and the like. But the industrial landscape was changing rapidly. More products became branded and differentiated from one another. Particularly affected were automobiles, office equipment, appliances, medicines, motion pictures, and a little later, commercially prepared foods and data processing.

Along with differentiation came a massive increase in product advertising, particularly in the 1920s with the growth of New York advertising agencies such as J. Walter Thompson and BBDO.[45] The use of trademarks increased dramatically, particularly on goods produced for interstate shipment. The Lanham Trademark Act was eventually passed in 1946, providing uniform and expansive federal protection for trademarks used in interstate commerce.[46] The Act reflected a shift in product distribution practices that was well underway, de-emphasizing the common law's historical concern with "origin," expressed in the offense of "passing off" one's goods as if they were made by someone else.[47] The new focus turned to "brands."[48] For example, beginning in the 1920s trademark infringement could be found even if the infringer put the brand owner's mark on a noncompeting product that the owner did not make.[49]

Branding and product differentiation served to blunt price competition between manufacturers of otherwise competing products. Advertising agencies had recognized this and promoted the idea before economists discovered it. In the early 1920s the J. Walter Thompson agency sent out a flyer to potential customers, urging them to take advantage of trademarks in order to differentiate their products. "In the majority of cases" where the manufacturer does not use a trademark "his name never reaches the consumer. His trade is necessarily precarious, and he is constantly in danger of the kind of cut-throat competition that shaves the lowest margin of profit to nothing."[50] In 1917 Arthur Acheson's book on trademarking argued that firms could satisfy their zest to be monopolists by promoting trademarks. "Monopolies created in this manner are safe from the interference of the law," he somewhat prematurely urged.[51]

Dramatic increases in brand advertising were quite inconsistent with the theory of overproduction in mainstream economics. Brand advertising is a wasted expense if everyone's product is identical. As a result, the impact of Edward H. Chamberlin's *Theory of Monopolistic Competition*, published in 1933, is difficult to exaggerate.[52] For markets where products could reasonably be differentiated, Chamberlin's model brought the concern with fixed costs and overproduction to an abrupt end. Notwithstanding its technical complexity, the Chamberlin model was beguilingly realistic. Firms did not need to race to produce more. Instead they could invest in distinguishing their products from rivals.

The theory of monopolistic competition changed the landscape of industrial economics dramatically.[53] Like most big ideas it produced both critics and variations, but there is little doubt about its profound impact on U.S. antitrust policy from the Second New Deal through the 1960s. Under Chamberlin's model each firm became a little "monopolist" of its own unique output. Profits are no higher than the competitive level, however, because new firms continuously enter the market while existing ones invest in shifting their products so as to claim every niche in product space. Instead of overproduction, the monopolistic competition model produces long-term *under*production and costly unused capacity. This in turn meant that prices would be higher than under perfect competition, although not as high as under monopoly.

Monopolistic competition had a large number of policy implications. The chronic underproduction that it predicted seemed to cry out for antitrust or regulatory cures. Another was that product differentiation was "excessive," in that its principal effect was not to benefit consumers but rather to enable firms to avoid head-to-head competition. This concern with excessive differentiation also led to severely critical attitudes about intellectual property rights and even product advertising. Both played a significant part in antitrust policy in the late 1940s and after.

Antitrust policy's tacit support for collusive associations came to an abrupt end.[54] In March 1938, Roosevelt appointed Thurman Arnold to head the Antitrust Division, and he quickly expanded its staff from a few dozen to more than three hundred lawyers. Arnold launched an aggressive antitrust campaign that quickly moved into new enforcement areas involving intellectual property, restrictive distribution contracts, and vertical integration in product-differentiated industries such as automobiles, motion pictures, fabricated aluminum, and the American Medical Association.[55] These cases moved American antitrust policy far beyond its traditional concern with cartels and dominant firms, and placed antitrust on an expansion road that did not noticeably diminish for forty years. The merits of that expansion have been debated extensively, with critics accusing antitrust of losing its focus on production efficiency, developing a virtual loathing of intellectual property rights, and fretting too much about socially harmless product differentiation or distribution practices that courts did not fully understand.[56]

Nevertheless, the first signs of economic recovery coincided with the Second New Deal and preceded the economic expansion that resulted from the war efforts. Substantial expansion of American Gross Domestic Product began in the mid-1930s, with the brief, previously noted recession in 1938. GDP expanded quickly after 1940. Unemployment began to fall in 1934, but was above 15 percent in every year prior to the war except for 1936. Then it fell sharply.[57] A case can be made that the government-enforced cartelization policies of the First New Deal actually prolonged the Depression by limiting output expansion. The switch toward government stimulation of demand and output expansion that began in 1935 pointed the country on a truer course to recovery.

National Markets and the Passing of Dual Federalism

While the Constitution mandates "federalism" as a governmental structure for the United States, that term has morphed and re-morphed many times. Disputes about the proper division of regulatory power between the federal government and the states have been heavily market driven. In one sense the New Deal did little more than recognize that achievements in production, transportation, and communication had made markets much bigger than before. As a result regulation by individual states tended to be less complete, more self-serving and opportunistic, and less calculated to achieving uniformities that are essential if large markets are to function properly.

The nineteenth and early twentieth centuries are often said to be dominated by "dual federalism," in which the states and the federal government occupied separate but ill-defined regulatory spheres.[58] The post–New Deal era is described as a period of "national supremacy," which does not use the word "federalism" because supposedly there was none. Looking back from 1950, constitutional historian Edward Corwin described the period as the "passing" of dual federalism.[59] Later came "cooperative federalism," which in fact is a kind of national supremacy in which the federal government conditions funding on state cooperation in certain regulatory ventures. Finally the "New federalism" refers to distinctly postwar policies or Supreme Court decisions that shifted the balance back toward the states, particularly for "traditional" functions of state or local government.

Federalism in the text of the Constitution bears little resemblance to the theoretical and highly ideological doctrine that subsequently developed. The drafters of the Constitution were practical people. They were fully aware of the importance of local control over local matters, but also of the failure of decentralized government under the Articles of Confederation. Already in the late eighteenth century they understood that certain markets, such as the postal service, intellectual property, and bankruptcy, required either national uniformity or limitations on state self-dealing. In other areas the development occurred later. For example, the call for increased federal oversight of business corporations was a direct result of changes in state law that permitted corporations to operate in many states and do their business nationally.

The U.S. Constitution recognizes only the federal government and the individual states as "sovereign." Then it divides the power to make laws among them. In some areas, such as those covered by the Commerce Clause, the federal government shares regulatory power with the states in ways that are not specified in much detail. In others, Congress has exclusive "enumerated" powers that the Constitution specifically grants, while the states have all "residual" powers—a point reiterated by the Tenth Amendment. Historically states have had sovereignty over criminal law within state borders, marriage and divorce, property located within the state including probate, internal operations of state and local government, the structural law of business corporations, most tort law, and much of contract law. Even these can be subject to a significant federal overlay when multistate interests are prominent or federally recognized rights are involved.

During the age of dual federalism these lines were thought to be hard even if not particularly clear. Congress could not assert power within the state's domain in areas where it did not have constitutional authority to regulate on its own. Neither could it impose obligations on the states that infringed their own sovereign authority.[60] Although the Civil War Constitutional Amendments shifted important powers away from the states to the federal government, the Court read them narrowly when traditional state regulation of intrastate private conduct was concerned. Most notably, in the *Civil Rights Cases* the Court concluded that Congress lacked the power to regulate private racial exclusion practices that had historically been the prerogative of state law.[61] A generation later in *Hodges* the Court refused to permit the federal government to criminalize violent behavior by private white citizens against African American workers, observing that under the Tenth Amendment intrastate crimes of violence were a matter for the states.[62]

The Impact of *Erie v. Tompkins*

The U.S. Constitution permits the federal courts to decide cases between citizens of different states. In certain circumstances an out-of-state plaintiff, such as a creditor, can sue a local debtor in federal court rather than state court. Alternatively, an out-of-state defendant sued in state court can "remove" the case to the federal court. The drafters' intentions were mainly to free out-of-state litigants from local prejudice. Both the Diversity Clause and the Federal Judiciary Act that implemented it were drafted long before there was any significant federal economic regulation except where the Constitution assigned exclusive control to the federal government. The Diversity Clause thus addressed situations in which a state court would have applied the common law or else a state statute.

In *Swift v. Tyson* (1842) the Supreme Court held that in a diversity case involving an interstate commercial dispute the federal Court was not bound by the law of the state where the claim arose. Rather, it could follow the courts' own view of the common law.[63] In its 1855 *Watson* decision the Court extended *Swift* to a state insolvency statute that limited an out-of-state creditor's right to recover.[64] The key was that the statute was determined to be "general," pertaining to the commercial law, rather than "local." In *Erie v. Tompkins*, decided a year after the Court-packing controversy, the Supreme Court overruled *Swift* and held that in diversity cases the federal courts must follow state law. Justice Brandeis, generally an advocate of expanded federal power, wrote the majority opinion. Justices Butler and MacReynolds, the two remaining Four Horsemen who had more or less consistently opposed federal power, dissented.[65]

Quoting the late Justice Holmes out of context, Justice Frankfurter later referred to the *Swift* conception of the common law as a "brooding omnipresence."[66] That was also a completely unfair characterization of the views of Justice Story, who wrote *Swift*. Nevertheless, it expressed a mindset in Legal Realist theory of national law, which is that it exists only when the Constitution or the federal government acting through Congress says it does. In 1938, when *Erie* was decided, national regulatory authority was expanding at a breathtaking rate. If Congress could validly control a particular facet of interstate commerce, as it was frequently doing, then those regulations were supreme over inconsistent state laws. But if Congress chose not to regulate a certain area, then there was no abstract "general law" left.

Justice Brandeis had emphasized this point a generation earlier, in the *International News* case. The Supreme Court majority held that the defendant's newswire service had committed the common law tort of unfair competition when it copied stories from rival Associated Press for its own customers. In the 1909 Copyright Act Congress had rejected copyright protection for freshly written, or "hot," news stories prior to copyright registration.[67] Given that the Constitution gave Congress exclusive control over copyright, in Brandeis's view there was no common law "tort" remaining. The Supreme Court was simply using judge-made tort law to expand the scope of copyright protection, an area that the Constitution assigned exclusively to Congress.

Justice Story, the greatest commercial law scholar of his generation,[68] faced a much different situation in the 1840s when the Court decided *Swift*. Although the Constitution gave Congress the power to "establish... uniform laws on the subject of Bankruptcies,"[69] it did not create federal authority to establish a uniform commercial law. The combination of federal bankruptcy law and idiosyncratic state commercial law led to numerous difficulties in determining when a federal bankruptcy court must honor the contract, property, and corporation law of the individual states.[70] Prior to *Erie* the Supreme Court had acknowledged that, owing to variations in state law, uniform federal bankruptcy law could yield "different results in different states."[71] Within commercial law itself, state legal control over an increasingly interstate commercial market led to inconsistency and self-dealing. Conflicts over commercial practices were numerous, particularly between large commercial states such as New York, which tended to have many creditors, and smaller noncommercial states in the South and West, which tended to have debtors. Further, Story believed that Congress lacked the power to impose a uniform law of commercial contracts under the Commerce Clause, a view that the Supreme Court would confirm in *Paul v. Virginia*, holding that contracts are not "articles of commerce."[72]

By contrast, Congress had the power to regulate the personal injury liability of interstate railroads in the late 1930s, when *Erie* was decided. In this case, however, it had not done so. As a result, the issue remained with state tort law. This is the meaning of Justice Brandeis's statement that the "course pursued" in *Swift's* deprecation of state law in diversity decisions was unconstitutional. To the extent that Congress had chosen not to federalize the law, the Tenth Amendment guaranteed that the right was retained by the states.

Erie was a tort case, traditionally part of the common law where state uniformity was not essential. *Swift* had created several "mismatches" in areas of local interest, something that the courts interpreting it frequently recognized.[73] But the flip side was that *Erie* created mismatches in areas where national uniformity was important but Congress had not acted so as to impose it. As for commercial law itself, it is no coincidence that drafting of the Uniform Commercial Code began only a few years after *Erie* forced the federal courts to apply state law to interstate commercial disputes. The Code's principal drafter, Karl Llewellyn, would have preferred a federal statute, something that the Commerce Clause prior to *Wickard v. Filburn* (1942) would have permitted only for interstate transactions. A few months prior to *Wickard* Llewellyn had written William Draper Lewis, the Director of the American Law Institute, that "The way to get rid of the troubles of the Erie R.R. v. Tompkins case, and to offer to international commercial transactions a single, clear and modernized law, is by Congressional action."[74] *Erie* portended chaos in commercial law to the extent that interstate commercial transactions would be treated differently depending on the state whose law was being applied.

A similar situation arose in trademark law, an area not within Congress's exclusive power under the Constitution. In 1879 the Supreme Court had held that trademarks did not fall within the Intellectual Property Clause's express limitation to "writings and discoveries."[75] As a result, states had the authority to regulate trademarks and Congress could regulate them only under its commerce power. *Erie* threatened chaos to the extent that weak federal protection entailed that the scope of trademarks held by multistate firms varied from state to state. In 1940 Harvard Law professor and free speech scholar Zechariah Chafee complained that the uniform body of interstate trademark law established by the federal courts under *Swift* "is now likely to be torn into pieces because of the *Tompkins* case."[76] Two years later the Supreme Court's *Pecheur Lozenge* decision fulfilled Chafee's prediction, applying idiosyncratic state common law to a company that marketed its brand nationally.[77] One of Congress's purposes in enacting the Lanham Act in 1946, which greatly expanded federal protection of trademarks and unfair competition, was to provide the uniformity that *Erie* took away from the federal judiciary.[78]

Constitutional Recognition of the Neoclassical Market and Partial Retreat

The emergence of interstate markets was both a technological and a conceptual phenomenon. Technologically, it was driven heavily by the transportation revolution, mainly the railroads, and also by the rise of large-scale production that required firms to seek out larger markets. Even classicists such as Adam Smith understood the relationship between the technologies of transportation and the size of markets. Writing before the age of railroads, he observed that "by means of water-carriage a more extensive market is opened to every sort of industry than what land-carriage alone can afford." As a result, cities located along the coast tended to conduct trade over a much greater geographic range than inland cities.[79]

Neoclassical economics developed much more abstract and forward-looking ideas about markets, which the legal system gradually accommodated. Alfred Marshall no longer spoke of the market as a place where traders meet to exchange goods and haggle over prices, an image that was local as well as physical. Rather, the market was the geographic area over which prices tend to move toward an equilibrium.[80] The "market" became an abstraction identified by geometric figures showing the relationship between cost and demand. The new conception was to have a profound effect, first on the economic idea and later on the legal idea of the market. A producer of beet sugar in New York might be packing it for railroad shipment to Boston or Chicago. Even the farmer's decision about how much to grow depended critically on the geographic range over which sales could be made. Neoclassical economics collapsed questions about how much to grow, how much to manufacture, and how much to ship into a single one defined by the anticipated size of the market.

From the Gilded Age the Supreme Court had perpetuated a classical, backward- looking distinction between "manufacturing" and "commerce," holding in 1895 that the federal antitrust laws did not reach an in-state sugar manufacturing trust even though the product was destined for shipment across state lines.[81] In 1918 *Hammer v. Daghenhart* struck down a federal statute prohibiting the employment of children to produce goods that were shipped interstate within thirty days of their manufacture. The thirty-day limitation indicates that interstate shipment was not an afterthought. The goods in question were being manufactured in fulfillment of orders from out of state. Nevertheless, the Supreme Court held that the regulation of child labor is manufacturing, not commerce, and is thus a "purely state authority," relying on the Tenth Amendment as well as the Commerce Clause. Many states had already limited child labor under their power to regulate health, safety, and morals, and nationally child labor was in decline.[82] The Supreme Court had unanimously held in 1913 that an Illinois child labor statute did not violate the Equal Protection Clause.[83] North Carolina, where *Hammer* arose, prohibited employing children under twelve. The federal statute set the minimum age at fourteen.[84] Nevertheless, critics such as Thomas Reed Powell and Edward Corwin argued that *Hammer* would perpetuate a race to the bottom. States competing in national markets would try to reduce labor costs by relaxing child labor rules.[85] Supporting their argument was that most state child labor provisions prohibited the employment of children within the state, but permitted importation of goods produced by children elsewhere.

Justice Holmes's dissent in *Hammer* made the more neoclassical point that the statute in question referred exclusively to the kinds of goods that could be transported across state lines. It was a regulation of "commerce," not of child labor. As a result, the "Act does not meddle with anything belonging to the States." Indeed, if "there were no Constitution and no Congress their power to cross the line would depend upon their neighbors."[86]

The Supreme Court persisted in the manufacturing/commerce distinction through the mid-1930s, although by dwindling majorities. In *Carter* (1936) a 5-4 majority used it to overturn the Bituminous Coal Conservation Act, which created a commission establishing wages, hours, and production standards in the hard coal industry.[87] After Court-packing, the unanimous decisions in *Darby* (1941) and *Wickard* (1942) indicated nearly complete federal supremacy regarding the commerce power. *Darby* explicitly acknowledged that *Hammer* was no longer the law, and upheld the Fair Labor Standards Act's prohibition of interstate shipment of goods unlawfully manufactured under it. Darby had been charged both with paying less than the minimum wage of 25 cents per hour, and requiring employees to work more than the statutorily permitted forty-four hours per week. The Court also held, in conflict with *Hammer*, that the Tenth Amendment does no more than state "a truism that all is retained which has not been surrendered."[88] The following year *Wickard* adopted a thoroughly neoclassical conception of markets. The Court unanimously held that the federal commerce power extended not merely to the interstate shipment of goods, but to their production if the impact "affected" interstate commerce.[89] In antitrust, the federal courts began to think of federal power in terms of market scope rather than local act. In 1945 Judge Learned Hand held that Sherman Act jurisdiction should be measured by an "effects" test that asked not where an anticompetitive practice had occurred, but where it caused higher prices or other types of competitive harm.[90] The Supreme Court observed in a 1949 antitrust case, "If it is interstate commerce that feels the pinch, it does not matter how local the operation which applies the squeeze."[91]

The ink on *Wickard* was barely dry, however, when two new issues restored at least some state autonomy. In *Parker v. Brown* (1943)[92] the Court unanimously held that a state could regulate its own agricultural production even if inconsistent with federal antitrust policy. *Parker* involved a state-administered program limiting California raisin production. The scheme itself was a leftover of the first New Deal policy of using output limitations to stimulate prices.[93] The production allocations were controlled by producers themselves, and the program amounted to little more than a cartel benefitting California growers. Further, California produced 95 percent of the raisins consumed in the United States and roughly half of the world supply. Most of the raisins were destined for interstate shipment. The lower court had condemned the output restriction as an impermissible burden on interstate commerce. The Supreme Court not only rejected that conclusion but also held that the output limitation was not inconsistent with the Sherman Act.

Parker recognized what came to be an important protection for state regulation of local economic issues—namely, the antitrust "state action" immunity. The doctrine did not rest on any federal assessment of the merits of a state or local regulation, but only on the federal court's conclusion that the state had adequately articulated its regulatory goals. The doctrine has operated ever since to permit substantial state and local control of commercial activities, even if they have a significant extraterritorial impact or represent relatively clear instances of local special interest capture. It remains one of the biggest concessions to federalism in Commerce Clause jurisprudence.[94] Its domain is restricted, however, to the relatively "passive" regulation imposed by antitrust law.

Insurance regulation was a different story. In *South-Eastern Underwriters* (1944), the Supreme Court applied the federal antitrust laws to the largely state-regulated insurance industry.[95] Insurance had traditionally been regulated entirely by state law, largely on the rationale that insurance contracts "are not articles of commerce" and are thus within the control of state common law.[96] The *South-East Underwriters* decision held that an agreement among insurance companies to fix rates was fully reachable under the Sherman Act, notwithstanding that the industry was regulated by state law nearly everywhere.[97] Congress almost immediately responded with the McCarran-Ferguson Act, which created an antitrust exemption for the industry to the extent that it was regulated by state law.[98] The result preserved state regulation for an industry whose sellers were increasingly multistate firms doing national business. Economist Irwin Stelzer complained in the mid-1950s that the provision led to balkanization of a national market, permitting states to favor home-grown companies and exclude outsiders.[99] State insurance regulation retained its antitrust immunity even if the regulation in question was self-serving, parochial, or anticompetitive, provided that the state actually imposed at least minimal oversight. The McCarran-Ferguson Act remains to this day as one of the great—and socially costly—compromises between federal and state regulatory power.

Epilogue

THE NEW DEAL AT BAY

LEGAL REALISM LEFT American legal theory holding an empty bag. It was a "destructive movement," Grant Gilmore lamented in 1951. "We stand amid the wreck and ruin of a jurisprudence which cannot be rebuilt."[1] To say that law was "positive" or "legislative" was consistent with the period's waning modernism, but neither term provided useful content to legal policy. At the same time, Legal Realism's cynicism should not be exaggerated. Although it appeared in popular books such as Jerome Frank's *Law and the Modern Mind*,[2] many Realists ended up working in government. For all appearances they were enthusiastic supporters of a new age of legislation, redistribution, nonjudicial regulation, and expertise. They went from rebellion to establishment in a brief time.

The Great Depression, the War, and the massive changes brought about by government wrought considerable anxiety about law. If law was to be the product of policy science, then where was the science? A central question for legal theory became whether social science and economics were consistent with democratic policymaking, and promised legal institutions that could facilitate growth and defensible concepts of liberty, democratic participation, and fairness. The initial attempt at a positive answer, driven strongly by Legal Realist values, was a search for nonmarket mechanisms of impartial policymaking. When that quest failed, economists, legal scholars and later policymakers increasingly returned to more market-driven approaches.

While the period following World War II desperately sought consensus, the writing of American intellectuals only showed how elusive consensus could be. Influential works of American social history, including Oscar Handlin's *The Uprooted* and Will Herberg's *Protestant, Catholic, Jew*, both undermined the myth that the United States was a single great "melting pot," blending all cultural identities into one slightly off-white batter. Herberg settled for the idea of a "triple" melting pot, which included Protestants, Catholics, and Jews but slighted Muslims, Hindus, Buddhists, or the variety of other religions practiced by millions of Native, Chinese, and other immigrant Americans.[3] *Brown v. Board of Education* and later Bull Connor's televised fire hosing of nonviolent demonstrators dramatically exposed the nation to the reality of racial conflict.[4] Senator Joseph McCarthy's campaign to root out Communists became a symbol of 1950s' suppression of dissent.[5]

Reconstructing and Delimiting the Common Law

The search for rational consensus in law was driven as much by practical considerations as ideological ones. One heroic effort was the Restatement projects of the American Law Institute (ALI), which were never intended to be either radically revisionist or particularly jurisprudential. They were substantially motivated by professional developments. From its founding in 1878, the American Bar Association had made rationalization and uniformity of the law one of its objectives.[6] A year later West Publishing Company inaugurated the Regional Reporter System, which large numbers of lawyers began using in the 1880s and 1890s.[7] The books were relatively inexpensive and collected the important case law of all of the states, organized by region. The relative insignificance of the West was clear in how the states were grouped. Kansas, in the center of the country, was in the *Pacific Reporter*. Lawyers now had an inexpensive way of comparing their own law with that of nearby states and were shocked to discover the degree of diversity.[8]

The ALI was a relative latecomer to unification. It was founded in 1923 and directed by William Draper Lewis, a Republican Progressive, friend of Theodore Roosevelt, and former Dean of the University of Pennsylvania Law School. The ALI's stated purpose was "to promote the clarification and simplification of the law and its better adaptation to social needs."[9] The first Restatements included Contracts (1932), Agency (1933), Conflict of Laws (1934), Property (1936), Restitution (1937), and Torts (1938–1939). Controversy continues about whether the Restatement project was "reformist."[10] Some of its reporters, such as Harvard's Joseph Beale who was in charge of Conflict of Laws, were ardent anti-reformers.[11] In addition, the first Restatement grew out of a pre-*Erie v. Tompkins* mentality that was inclined to look for a single best legal rule.[12]

Legal Realists were almost uniformly critical. Leon Green thought that the torts Restatement was an exercise in pure formalism.[13] Yale Law School Dean

Charles Clark, also an advisor on the Property Restatement, first heaped praise on the Restatement of Contracts for its assembly of the great legal minds of the day. Then he dismantled the entire document, criticizing its excessive formalism and its substitution of citation for rigorous analysis. The Institute's "formula" served "to press the fruitful activities of its scholars into the dry pulp of the pontifical and vague black letter generalities."[14] In an unpublished paper the University of Iowa's Percy Bordwell criticized the Property Restatement's treatment of future interests as "a combination of ancient or rather early medieval history, analytic jurisprudence and reportorial legislation but not a statement of the positive law." In a subsequent review of the entire Restatement of Property he predicted its failure. "Legislation is legislation and scholarship is scholarship, but the Institute is not a legislature and its ways are not those of scholarship."[15] Myres McDougal said much the same.[16]

Tulane Legal Realist Mitchell Franklin believed that the Restatements were "transitional" documents paving the way for codification.[17] "At the very least, the historic function of the American Law Institute is its role of affording a transition from the classic American law of the nineteenth and early twentieth centuries to a new American law." Samuel Williston, Reporter for the Restatement on Contracts, observed that "in every other civilized country," judge-made law eventually "became unwieldy" and "a code has followed.... [M]y own belief is that we shall repeat the history of other countries.... This Restatement... will serve as a better foundation for a code."[18]

In important ways the Restatement's drafters looked backward, attempting to rationalize a diverse and inconsistent body of legal rules. Grant Gilmore's argument that the ALI's Restatement agenda was to hold off Legal Realism was certainly overstated.[19] When the Restatements were conceived in the late 1920s, the impact of Legal Realism was not yet ominous. The biggest impulse toward change came from Holmes's less radical but nevertheless transformative ideas about the purpose and effects of the common law. The Restatement project was reformist in this more limited sense.

For example, the Williston-directed Restatement of Contracts was strongly influenced by Holme's highly commercial orientation, with its emphasis on shared expression rather than internal state of mind, its concern about creating proper incentives, its emphasis on remedies, and its generally amoral attitude about performance. The provision on nuisance law in the Restatement of Torts, drafted just as legislative land use regulation was becoming prominent, was an exercise in pure marginalism. "Nontrespassory" harms to the land of others, including noise, smoke, excessive water, immoral conduct, and other activities, were unlawful, "unless the utility of the actor's conduct outweighs the gravity of the harm."[20] This "harm/utility" formulation had never appeared in the case law, but it applied a kind of marginalist cost-benefit analysis to private land use disputes. The Restatement test was borrowed from the work of another Holmesian, Judge Learned Hand's opinion in *Smith v. Staso Milling Co.*, which had held that nuisance injunctions should be subjected to a utility balancing test.[21] In 1942 a Connecticut court became the first to apply this section, concluding that the operation of a castor oil plant would not be enjoined simply because a small number of workers at neighboring businesses were allergic to castor bean dust. This approach required 'balancing" of competing interests, and in this case the castor oil facility had taken every step to limit its emissions. The only alternative was to close the plant, but it was under contract to the army and "its product is indispensable to the prosecution of the war." Under the Restatement approach, "Regard must be had not only for the interests of the person harmed but also for the interests of the actor, for the interests of the community, and, under the present circumstances, for the nation."[22]

Unlike the reforms later promoted by the Legal Realists, the Restatements continued to operate within a framework that acknowledged the centrality of the common law and (implicitly) the market, as well as the essential role of the courts. Whether or not law was legislative in character, within the Restatement conception it was still largely made by judges. In addition, the Restatements perpetuated the view that the same body of common law rules could be applied across the full range of human activity, without specialized rules for different situations.

By contrast, the Legal Realists were increasingly obsessed with market diversity, leading them away from both the Restatement vision and the common law itself. They were more supportive of the uniform law approach that was already underway when the first Restatements were drafted. The National Conference of Commissioners on Uniform State Laws, which had been organized in the early 1890s, strove to unify state law by promoting uniform legislation. Its principal projects were a series of "model acts" that state legislators could adopt.[23] Its early achievements were uniform acts in commercial law, including negotiable instruments (1896), warehouse receipts (1906), the highly influential Uniform Sales Act (1906), and bills of lading (1908). These statutes attempted to harmonize the law made in state courts with the "general" commercial law *Swift v. Tyson* (1842) imposed on federal judges in diversity cases. As Justice Story had stated in *Swift*, "The law respecting negotiable instruments may be truly declared... to be in a great measure, not the law of a single country only, but of the commercial world."[24] Story did not foresee the extent to which *Swift* produced divisions between the federal and numerous state courts. By 1908 the Uniform Negotiable Instruments Act had been enacted in thirty-five states, and the Uniform Sales Act was to have even greater success.[25] Most of the uniform acts were later merged into the Uniform Commercial Code, with its nine distinct articles for different areas of commercial activity.[26]

Drafting on the Uniform Commercial Code began in 1940 and turned into a joint effort in 1942. Chastened by its harsh treatment from the Legal Realists, the ALI joined in. Karl Llewellyn was the principal drafter, but as the code developed it contained little of the radical critique that the Legal Realists had envisioned. The UCC was first and foremost a consensus document, deducing the law from observed behavior in commercial markets. Llewellyn famously queried bankers "If I were a cheque and I arrived in your bank where would I go?"[27] The UCC's revisionism was largely limited to deviations from common law rules that business persons regarded as unrealistic or as reflecting judicial ignorance of how the business world works. For the most part, the market remained alive and well.

The Restatement Second project was initiated in 1952, after Legal Realism had been woven into the legal fabric and state diversity imposed by *Erie v. Tompkins* was well established. The Reporters of the second Restatements were largely centrists. They included E. Allan Farnsworth on Contracts, with Arthur Linton Corbin as advisor; A. James Casner on Property, and William Prosser and John W. Wade on Torts. The greatest changes in mindset lay in the second Restatements' decreasing trust of markets and greater regard for consumers and other vulnerable or unsophisticated participants. This resulted in a softening of the merchant-oriented rules of contract law, as expressed in the Restatement (Second) of Contracts (1979). In addition was the formal embrace of strict liability for defective products in the Restatement (Second) of Torts § 402A (1977). Grant Gilmore saw in these developments a subtle "coming together" between contract law and tort law. Both threatened an "explosion of liability." The gradual death of nineteenth century tort doctrine that tied liability to fault "matches the decline and fall of nineteenth century consideration and contract theory."[28]

The Promises and Limitations of Public Governance

Elite legal thought through the 1960s was dominated by two conflicting trends. *First* was an attempt to justify and define the more legislative approaches that Legal Realism and the New Deal promoted. *Second* was the increasing view that legislation is inherently unstable, inefficient, and prone to capture by special interests. In the 1960s and after the second of these largely disemboweled the first.

The Transformation of Substantive Due Process: Liberty Rights and Special Interest Capture

The Supreme Court recognized the end of the *Lochner* era in its 1938 *Carolene Products* decision.[29] The aftermath produced two quite different lingering effects. *First*, although the Court largely stopped second-guessing economic legislation, substantive due process analysis of *non*market liberties continued unabated and even expanded. *Second*, the Supreme Court lost its most important tool for combating special interest capture. In this sense, *Carolene Product's* strong presumption of constitutionality represents the high point of a confidence in the legislative process whose defense had yet to be articulated. A generation later that view would become the target of public choice and rent-seeking theory, which once again picked up the anti-legislation/anti-regulation mantle.

On the first effect, *Lochner* became shorthand for a set of essentially contract rights against the State. But as *Carolene Products* itself acknowledged in its famous fourth footnote, the theory of preferences that drove Anglo-American economic and political theory included other human choices that were not strictly economic at all. A significant number of Supreme Court decisions during and after the *Lochner* era recognized liberties outside the realm of ordinary economic bargaining. Already in 1890 Brandeis and coauthor Samuel D. Warren argued in the *Harvard Law Review* for a legally protected right to privacy, even though Brandeis later became one of *Lochner's* strongest critics.[30] The Supreme Court's *Buchanan v. Warley* decision (1917) discussed in Chapter 3 hinted at protection for noneconomic liberty in its condemnation of residential racial segregation by zoning.[31] *Meyer v. Nebraska* (1923) found that people had a liberty right to learn a foreign language. The Court struck down a World War I–era statute that made it unlawful for any school to teach a foreign language to children who had not yet reached the eighth grade. The opinion, written by Horseman Justice James McReynolds, provided an interesting list of constitutionally protected liberty rights:

> ... not merely freedom from bodily restraint but also the right of the individual to contract, to engage in any of the common occupations of

> life, to acquire useful knowledge, to marry, establish a home and bring up children, to worship God according to the dictates of his own conscience, and generally to enjoy those privileges long recognized at common law as essential to the orderly pursuit of happiness by free men.[32]

The Court relied on *Lochner, Adkins*, and several other substantive due process decisions. Two years later, *Peirce v. Society of Sisters* overturned a state statute that closed parochial schools, including Catholic schools. Justice McReynolds wrote the opinion.[33] In *Skinner v. Oklahoma* (1942) the Court recognized a right of procreation, striking down a statute that provided for more-or-less automatic sterilization of certain convicted criminals.[34] This liberty right took wing in the 1960s, providing greatly expanded constitutional protection for an assortment of "fundamental" rights that the text of the Constitution did not explicitly embrace. What most of the cases had in common is that significant interest groups opposed the conduct, often on moral or religious grounds, but the conduct itself was typically consensual and caused little or no injury to third parties. *Loving v. Virginia* recognized a constitutional right to marry, striking down statutory bans on interracial marriage ("miscegenation").[35] *Griswold v. Connecticut* struck down a statute forbidding the distribution and use of contraceptives, in the process recognizing a fundamental right to privacy.[36] *Roe v. Wade* (1973) recognized and defined a woman's right to have an abortion.[37] Finally, *Lawrence v. Texas* held that the State may not prohibit consensual sexual activity between adults of the same sex.[38]

The second effect of *Carolene Products* was that its deference toward economic regulation largely undermined the Supreme Court's ability to limit "capture" by special interest groups. In retrospect, neither *Lochner*-style economic due process nor *Carolene Products'* extreme deference was a good vehicle for ferreting out the harmful effects of special interest control of legislation. The *Lochner* approach either condemned legislation without regard to capture or assumed capture without proof. *Carolene Products* went to the opposite extreme, largely removing the Court's ability to limit special interest economic legislation unless it ran afoul of an explicit constitutional provision. The development of public choice theory, discussed below, was an attempt to recover this lost element of substantive due process.

Carolene Products itself illustrates the problem. The statute in question grew out of the same dairy industry campaign that led to the suppression of oleomargarine, discussed in Chapter 5.[39] The "filled milk" provision that the Court upheld prohibited sellers from inserting non-milk oils into their milk products. Carolene's product, then called "Milnut," contained evaporated milk with a small amount of coconut oil. The mixture whipped very easily, thus making it a substitute for pure cream. The product is sold to this day under the name "Milnot," owned by J.M. Smucker's, Inc. It contains considerably less fat than whipping cream and no saturated fat. From the beginning, the principal purpose of the legislation was not to protect consumers from a harmful product, but rather to protect the dairy industry from competition.

Legal Interpretation and Judicial Review

One important legacy of Legal Realism was the belief that all of law, including common law, is essentially public in character. As a result the traditional distinction between private and public law is either porous or untenable. In *Shelley v. Kraemer* (1948) the Supreme Court held that mere judicial enforcement of a private racially restrictive covenant implicates "state action" under the Fourteenth Amendment, suggesting that even common law contracts could be "public."[40] The courts declined to jump the precipice, however, and held *Shelley* closely to its facts. In 1956 the Supreme Court refused to apply it in *Black v. Cutter Laboratories*, which upheld judicial enforcement of a private arbitration board's dismissal of a worker for membership in the Communist Party.[41] The Court rejected Mabel Black's protest that judicial enforcement of the decision violated her First Amendment rights, finding no state action but only a private labor agreement. In 1959 the Legal Realist Leon Green wrote that even tort law was "Public Law in Disguise."[42] A year later, however, Ronald Coase would declare in "The Problem of Social Cost" how utterly private the law could be.[43] Green's article has largely been forgotten, while Coase's is the most cited of all time.

A second legacy of Legal Realism was the belief that law is fundamentally democratic and legislative, but also complex and best interpreted by experts. One influential attempt to reconstruct a practical and lawyerly defense of legal interpretation was Henry Hart and Albert M. Sacks' book of teaching materials entitled *The Legal Process*.[44] The book came out in 1958 in a mimeographed "tentative edition," which Harvard Law School distributed free upon request to interested law teachers. Thus it remained, widely used but with minimal revision, for nearly forty years until Foundation Press published it even though it had become conceptually obsolete.[45] *The Legal Process* had been intended for a course in legislation, but evolved to include administrative decision-making and even some common law approaches. Its central message was that law could be improved through increased institutional competence, greater transparency, and "reasoned elaboration" designed to discover the law's underlying purpose. Legal policy for Hart and Sacks is inherently democratic and legislative, but statutes are never sufficiently complex to describe the entire reality to which they apply. They are the products of political compromise, ambiguous and open-ended. The job of the expert decision-maker is to use interpretative tools in order to locate a statute's "meaning" and then apply it to the case at hand.

Meanwhile, Henry Hart's other coauthor Herbert Wechsler wrote "Neutral Principles of Constitutional Law," intended both to defend and limit the Supreme Court's counter-democratic decision in *Brown v. Board of Education*.[46] Wechsler believed that *Brown* adequately elaborated its conclusion that separate public schools were "inherently unequal," but he faulted the Court's subsequent and unelaborated decisions desegregating municipally owned bathhouses and publicly sponsored operas.[47] Unlike schools, these facilities were voluntary rather than mandatory and thus did not fit within *Brown's* rationale without further explanation. Looking back to the era of substantive due process, Wechsler saw that the Court's willingness to permit state restrictions on labor unions but unwillingness to permit labor-protective legislation as another instance of superficially non-neutral decision-making. For Wechsler as for Hart and Sacks, the key to principled lawmaking was for the courts to identify some neutral rationale that justified differential treatment and then provide a reasoned explanation. Unstated but lurking in the background, of course, was that "neutral" principles existed, could be discovered, and even yield determinate results, if only enough process and elaboration were applied. One harsh critique was that Wechsler's "neutral" principles did not even reach to mandatory desegregation of public facilities, a burden that Wechsler carried to his grave.[48]

Yale professor Alexander Bickel concluded from his own exhaustive study of the Fourteenth Amendment that the *Brown* desegregation decision was neither explicitly contemplated nor foreclosed by the Amendment's drafters and proponents. As a result the decision was permissible and attained further legitimacy because it was unanimous.[49] Given that the Court had discretion to go either way and that its result was socially just, Bickel wholeheartedly supported it. In *The Least Dangerous Branch*, a constitutional law classic that cemented Bickel's position as one of his field's greatest scholars, Bickel wove a powerful, prolegislative argument that judicial review is disruptive to democratic process and must be used sparingly.[50] He brought the terms "counter-majoritarian difficulty" and "passive virtues" into constitutional discourse, emphasizing that judicial review can readily be overused and in the process can threaten democratic institutions and undermine public confidence in government. The Court must search relentlessly for non-constitutional alternatives and always write decisions striking down statutes as narrowly as possible.

The Critique of Political Markets

Hart, Sacks, Wechsler, and Bickel all understood that legislation is imperfect and incomplete. They were nonetheless committed to the view that both legislation and administrative law were worth preserving. Increasingly after the 1950s, however, critics from law, economics, and political science all began to see legislative and administrative processes as so deeply flawed that they rarely reveal the social will. Regulation in particular seemed very costly in relation to results, a point that James M. Landis brought home in his 1960 *Report on Regulatory Agencies* to president-elect Kennedy. Landis's report was influential because during the heyday of Legal Realism he had been the author of an important and far more optimistic book, *The Administrative Process*.[51]

Landis had been the first Chairman of the Securities Exchange Commission, as well as Dean of the Harvard Law School. His 1938 book on *The Administrative Process* was intended to defend the infant administrative state from some of its harshest critics, including the American Bar Association and older Progressives such as Roscoe Pound, who believed the agencies threatened absolutism and arbitrary decision-making.[52] Roosevelt's own Brownlow Committee *Report* (1937) had concluded that administrative agencies were a "headless" fourth branch of government that lacked democratic accountability, and required greater supervision from the executive branch.[53] Although Landis's lectures were given just after the Court-packing controversy, most of Roosevelt's new Court appointments had not yet been made and the current Supreme Court was hostile. The year before an opinion by Justice Sutherland had likened the truncated procedures of the Securities and Exchange Commission, Landis's own agency, to the "intolerable abuses of the Star Chamber."[54]

Landis's defense of the administrative state must be read against this background. He was in essence writing a brief. He defended agencies as more flexible than courts, and more able to command expertise, and acknowledged that they needed to be accountable to the designated branches of government. He also argued that agency rule-making could make them more proactive, seeing problems in advance rather than waiting for litigation, as courts must do.

Landis's *Report* to president-elect Kennedy twenty-two years later revealed how much the gleam had left the rose. Landis lamented that agencies were much costlier than anticipated, and that they lacked coordination among one another and often issued inconsistent orders. Effective rule-making was often undermined by industry interference: "the regulatees have become the regulators."[55] What is strikingly absent from Landis's *Report*, however, is any suggestion that a greater range of business firm activities be removed from agency control. There may have been problems, but he did not see deregulation as a solution.

Landis was hardly the first to note the problem of special interest capture of government process. As noted previously, *Lochner*-era decisions often assumed it. In fact, American political thinkers had been aware of it since James Madison expressed concern that interest groups ("factions') would hijack the government for their own ends. Madison wrote in *The Federalist* No. 10 that guarding against factions required both cohesiveness among citizens and checks and balances incorporated into the structure of government.[56]

A hallmark of Progressivism was its faith in grass roots political markets and a belief that the solution to special interest problems was broader and more direct involvement by voters. The muckraking journalists of the early twentieth century largely saw corruption and lack of popular involvement as going hand in hand. That was the principle theme of Progressive muckraker Lincoln Steffans's 1906 book *The Struggle for Self-Government.* His better-known book, *The Shame of The Cities*, emphasized ballot corruption as the cause of municipal government failure.[57]

Progressive Era social scientists firmly believed that government reform was an essential goal of their disciplines. In his departing address as President of the American Political Science Association, Woodrow Wilson defined political science as "the accurate and detailed observation of these processes by which the lessons of experience are brought into the field of consciousness, transmuted into active purposes, put under the scrutiny of discussion, sifted, and at least given determinate form in law."[58] Soon after he left Princeton to become governor of New Jersey and then U.S. president.

"Law" was the operative word in Wilson's statement, but law coming from where? Wilson believed that voters were too unsophisticated to make difficult policy decisions directly. Nevertheless, he was committed to broad voter participation in the election of wise and honest officials.[59] During his presidency the Constitution was augmented by the Seventeenth Amendment, which provided for direct election of U.S. Senators, and the Nineteenth Amendment, which extended the vote to women. Wilson himself was initially opposed to women's suffrage, but ostensibly changed his mind after observing the role of women in the war effort.[60] By contrast to the Progressives, the political philosophy of the New Deal was much more inclined toward governance by administrative agencies, with much of the decision-making delegated to experts, and with less direct forms of political accountability.

These visions of the relationship between democracy and good government all had their critics. The interest group theory that developed in the young discipline of political science was preoccupied with legal institutions at every level. Reacting to the overly abstract and optimistic visions of democracy that characterized the nineteenth-century study of government, the new generation called for more realism and harsher critiques. Arthur Bentley's highly influential *Process of Government* (1908) examined how interest groups affected government decision-making within Congress, the presidency, courts, state legislatures, and even political parties. He subtitled his book "A Study of Social Pressures."[61] The influential leftist historian Charles Beard argued in 1913 that the U.S. Constitution represented the triumph of commercial interests and those owning mainly personal property, as over against more agrarian interests whose wealth was largely in land. Beard attempted to show first that the membership of the Constitutional Convention was disproportionately composed of owners of securities, traders and shippers, and other forms of commercial wealth; and second that the Constitution protected these interests by devices such as restrictions on state debtor relief laws.[62]

Interest group theory also played an important role in the writing of the economic institutionalists and Legal Realists. Their work also reflected an urge to use economics and law as tools of reform. In mainstream economics resources flow without friction to the place where they will do the most good. In the real world, the institutionalists argued, organizations and special interests always get in the way. The most influential institutionalist attack on collective decision processes was Berle and Means's *The Modern Corporation*, which was fundamentally about the power of management to wrest control from shareholders, who were much more diffuse and had smaller individual stakes.[63] Significantly, however, Berle and Means saw legislation as a cure, as if it could somehow be immune from special interest influence.

An important characteristic of institutionalism was its identification of the specific institutions that make public decisions, rather than the more abstract approaches that characterized neoclassical economics. Corporations are different from courts, which are different from agencies, which are different from legislatures. Institutionalist economist John R. Commons wrote a posthumously published book entitled *The Economics of Collective Action*, concerned with how organized group action could leverage power in nongovernmental institutional settings, such as bargaining between employers and employees.[64]

The heavily empirical approach championed by Berle, Means, and Commons explained the value of institutionalism and Legal Realism, but also suggests why they ultimately failed. Their strength lay in their study of specific institutions in the real world, but they too often became bogged down in detail. Critics complained about the lack of methodological rigor in work that variously called upon exhaustive example, political theory, history, and even Darwin and Freud to explain group political behavior.[65]

The study of public decision-making became more formalized in post-institutionalist writing by political scientists and sociologists. Of particular importance were C. Wright Mills, *The Power Elite* (1956); Anthony Downs, *An Economic Theory of Democracy* (1957); and Robert A. Dahl's *Who Governs?* (1961).[66] These books emphasized the role of government as umpire among competing interest groups. Writing on a backdrop of utilitarian political philosophy, their authors examined the ways that interest groups could influence outcomes and in some cases distort true community choices in existing institutions.

The explosion of economics literature on social choice in the 1960s defies description in a few paragraphs.[67] In contrast to the political scientists, economists developed abstract but analytically more rigorous accounts of collective decision- making under strictly marginalist principles. The term "public choice" entered the legal literature in reference to works by Kenneth Arrow, Mancur Olson, James Buchanan, and Gordon Tullock, all of whom were trained economists. As a matter of pure theory, Arrow's *Social Choice and Individual Values* may be the most important to economists and political theorists. The books with the greatest policy influence, however, were James Buchanan and Gordon Tullock's *The Calculus of Consent* (1962) and Mancur Olson's *The Logic of Collective Action* (1965). Olson's formalization of interest group theory most influenced the set of legal critiques that today are associated with the terms "regulatory capture" and "deregulation."[68]

Public choice theory was as cynical about legislation and regulation as Legal Realism was about the common law. The economic critique was beguilingly simple. Voluntary exchanges are efficient because everyone gains, provided that nonparties are not injured. But democracies in which each person gets a vote make very few decisions unanimously. When is a decision for the social good if some people oppose it? Prior to the rise of ordinalism in the 1930s neoclassical economists thought they had a partial answer: society is better off when resources are transferred from the wealthy to the poor, even if some wealthy object. That answer was never complete, however, because not all disputes divide the poor and the wealthy. In any event, by the 1950s most economists were rejecting any view that justified involuntary wealth transfers by engaging in interpersonal comparisons of utility.

The formal theory of political markets began with the Marquis de Condorcet's discovery in the late eighteenth century that voting processes are prone to failure of equilibrium, or "cycling." When votes are not unanimous we cannot be assured of a stable outcome. To illustrate, suppose the symbol *p* means "prefer" as between two alternatives—for example "A*p*B" means that a voter prefers choice A over choice B. Then imagine a simple society with three voters and three choices, A, B, and C. The voters have these preferences:

Voter 1: A*p*B*p*C
Voter 2: B*pCpA*
Voter 3: C*p*A*p*B

In a majority vote between alternative A and B, A wins because both Voters 1 and 3 prefer A over B. Then, in a vote between A, the winner, and C, C wins. Voters 2 and 3 prefer C over A. Thus the "social" decision at this point indicates that C wins, because a majority prefers C over A, and A over B. A minimum condition of rational behavior in the neoclassical framework is "transitivity," which means that if an individual prefers X over Y and Y over Z, she must prefer X over Z. However, in the above illustration if a vote is taken on C versus B, B wins because Voters 1 and 2 prefer B over C. At that point we could start over again and have a vote between B and A, but that would place us in an infinite cycle. In sum, the "social" choice of as few as three individuals on as few as three issues can be "irrational," in the sense that it results in endless cycling with no final outcome. The conclusion: it may be impossible to identify the correct "social choice" from one person/one vote systems. Kenneth Arrow formalized this observation and derived a mathematical proof, usually called the "General Impossibility Theorem," or "Arrow's Impossibility Theorem," that the aggregation of votes cannot yield a stable social choice unless the vote is unanimous.

Whether Arrow's analysis applies to government policy depends on whether the policy incorporates shared rules that serve to force consensus. The vote-cycling story assumes that preferences are "naked," in the sense that each person chooses what she wants without constraint. However, if we had three scientists or even three appellate judges applying a given body of rules, their choices would be much more constrained and cycling would occur far less often.[69] The Progressive and New Deal reliance on experts assumed that decision-makers were applying theory to policy, and not simply asserting naked preferences. Further, the degree of determinacy need not be all that great. For example, the Supreme Court is an ideologically diverse body that decides controversial cases in which the law is usually "soft." If their votes were simply random they would be unanimous in 1 out of 256 cases. In fact, above 30 percent of the Supreme Court's decisions are unanimous.

The Calculus of Consent is less technical than Arrow's work. It also rejected interpersonal comparisons of utility and acknowledged that unanimous choices are true social choices. Realizing that unanimity is impossible to achieve, Buchanan and Tullock explored whether the unanimity rule can be relaxed. Rules that require less than unanimous decision-making impose costs on naysayers, but sometimes an outcome resembling unanimity is possible if "side payments" compensate the losers.[70] In that case everyone would be at least as well off—a condition that Richard Epstein developed in an important 1985 book as a theory of eminent domain.[71] *The Calculus of Consent* included a complex analysis of "logrolling," or vote trading in legislative bodies, to illustrate its harmful and beneficial uses.

The Logic of Collective Action appealed to a broad audience from the day it was published. Although Mancur Olson located interest group theory squarely inside of neoclassical economics, he did it in a nontechnical way that was more accessible than Arrow and less strident than Buchanan and Tullock. Olson relied heavily on the economic theory of cartels.[72] A cartel attempts to achieve the monopoly rate of price and output. However, an individual firm can make more by increasing output and shaving price. If everyone does that, however, the cartel will fall apart. Cartels work much better when they are small and well disciplined, with a set of common interests. Difficulties of detection and discipline in larger groups enable an individual member to "free ride" on the efforts of others or even defect. One problem with very large groups, Olson observed, is that the additional return produced by the efforts of each individual member is very small. By contrast, in the very small group the defection of a single member can throw the entire group into disarray.

Olson's book reached two very powerful conclusions. The first one, less emphasized in the later literature, is that excessive free riding leads to underinvestment in public goods, or infrastructure. Each individual would rather not contribute anything at all, trusting that others will take care of the problem.[73] Olson's second theory, for which his book became famous, was that small and well-organized interest groups are much more effective in getting their message across than large groups. Much of the subsequent public choice attack on regulation was based on this premise—namely that regulation tends to benefit regulated firms, who are few in number and well organized, rather than their customers, who are likely to be numerous, diverse, and disorganized.

The most powerful rhetoric of the deregulation movement in the late 1970s and after was that regulation too often succumbed to "capture" by the regulated at the expense of the more general public. For example, Olson's theory provided a powerful explanation for why so many regulatory agencies hear the voices of regulated firms more clearly than those of consumers—why, for example, intellectual property law has always been so protective of producers. It also explains why individuals vote for state right-to-work laws in order to avoid the individual costs of joining a union, even though their act undermines collective bargaining and results in significantly lower wages in right-to-work states.[74]

Public choice theory has made the Supreme Court more sensitive to the role of interest groups in obtaining legislation. Justice Scalia has frequently spoken of statutes as the results of compromise among competing interest groups.[75] Nevertheless, such recognition sometimes turns the Court in surprising directions. For example, the important *Chevron* decision in 1984 recognized that statutes often reflect ambiguity resulting from deals between competing interest groups. The Court then ruled that the regulatory agency should be free to adopt any reasonable interpretation of an ambiguous statute.[76] The result, which occurred during the early years of the deregulation movement, has been to give agencies enormous discretion to make rules in areas where Congress has not spoken precisely on the issue.

The Rehabilitation of Private Markets

Public choice theory was not the only onslaught against the New Deal regulatory State. Beginning in the 1950s and accelerating in the 1960s neoclassical economics gradually rehabilitated private markets, eventually concluding that most of them worked tolerably well, if not perfectly. The Chicago School moved from being a "lunatic fringe," as Richard A. Posner once paraphrased what its detractors called it,[77] to mainstream legitimacy. The Coasean revolution directed many writers in economics and law to the study of very tiny markets. In the process Coase's writing served to undermine the privileged position that Legal Realism had given regulation over the common law.

The New Learning in Industrial Economics

The high point of antitrust interventionism in the United States was in the 1950s and 1960s, reflecting an almost paranoid concern with industrial "concentration"—or small number of firms in a market. In 1950 Congress expanded the coverage of the anti-merger law, § 7 of the Clayton Act. Over a fifteen-year period policymakers offered a series of proposals for "deconcentrating" American industry by breaking up large firms. A final serious proposal offered by Michigan senator Philip A. Hart was presented to the Senate in 1972 as the Industrial Reorganization Act. The proposal was supported by Ralph Nader, whose study group report, *The Closed Enterprise System,* argued that the economy was dominated by noncompetitive market structures that made it impossible for smaller firms to compete.[78]

None of these bills passed. Increasingly the dominant writing in industrial economics, together with legal scholarship by such writers as Robert H. Bork and Richard A. Posner, began a general rehabilitation of the market.[79] Questioning almost every premise of the structuralist school, the new learning largely restored the classical faith that high prices would encourage new firms to come into a market, making durable monopoly rare.[80]

In 1974 a group of influential economists and lawyers met at Airlie House in Warrenton, Virginia, in a conference that signaled a turning point in antitrust and industrial policy. The proceedings were published as *Industrial Concentration: The New Learning.* That book, widely used in antitrust and industrial policy classes for two decades, indicated just how much dominant thinking about the "monopoly problem" had shifted. Essays by Chicago School scholars John S. McGee, Yale Brozen, Harold Demsetz, and Posner argued that concentration did not threaten competition nearly as much as the structuralists had assumed. Large firm size was driven mainly by economic efficiency, and competition could be robust with many fewer firms than the now ageing Harvard School had supposed. The Airlie House conference also heard protests from defenders of structuralism, but increasingly these voices were drowned out.[81]

Micromarkets and the Common Law: Coase

Few twentieth-century scholars have had more influence on legal thought than Ronald H. Coase (1910–2013). He was born in a London suburb where his parents worked as telegraph operators for the British post office. His formative economic education and what legal education he had were at the

London School of Economics in the 1920s and early 1930s, during its heyday under the leadership of Lionel Robbins.[82] His 1937 essay on *The Nature of the Firm* lay ignored for a generation, but later it had a pervasive influence on thinking about the structure of the business firm and the rationales for vertical integration.[83] Coase moved to the United States in the 1950s and taught at SUNY Buffalo, and then at the Universities of Virginia and Chicago. His most famous article, *The Problem of Social Cost*, was published in 1961 while he was at Virginia, whose economics department was second only to Chicago's in attempting to forge free market solutions to problems commonly thought to be the province of government.[84]

Coase's foil was Arthur C. Pigou, Alfred Marshall's successor as professor of economics at Cambridge University. In *The Economics of Welfare*, Pigou addressed the problem of "externalities," or harmful effects that a person's activities have on others. The idea did not originate with Pigou, or for that matter, not even with economists. By the 1910s the Supreme Court's liberty of contract jurisprudence had a well-developed theory of externalities as a justification for regulation. For example, regulation of working conditions might be justified if unrestricted contracting affected other people—the "healthful quality of the bread," as Justice Peckham put it in *Lochner* (1905).[85] As Coase presented Pigou's position, the government needed to intervene in such cases in order to protect bystander victims. Pigou and later Coase used the example of a railroad whose trains emit sparks that might start fires injuring neighboring farmers.[86] Coase famously argued that government intervention may not be necessary because private bargaining could address such problems.

What became the most famous actual case in *The Problem of Social Cost* was a nuisance law dispute involving Dr. Octavius Sturges, a London physician who specialized in pneumonia and other diseases of the lungs. Sturges shared a duplex with Frederick Horatio Bridgman, confectioner to the Queen. Bridgman used a large mechanical mortar and pestle to break down chocolate and other substances. Dr. Sturges complained that the pounding machine interfered with his ability to diagnose patients with his stethoscope.[87] Against the argument that this dispute required State intervention, Coase argued that Sturges and Bridgeman could simply have bargained with each other over Bridgman's continued use of the mortar and pestle. For example, if Sturges valued the right to be free of the pounding by £100, while Bridgeman valued the right to use his machine by only £80, then use of the machine would end. If these values were reversed, however, then the use would continue. Coase concluded that in a well-functioning market the two parties would bargain their way to an "efficient" result and that this the outcome would depend strictly on relative values and not on who might win the lawsuit.

The Problem of Social Cost is the most cited law review article of all time. Every nook and cranny of Coase's argument has been explored. Coase made a powerful argument that legal entitlements can be traded in markets just as much as ordinary products and services. For example, the right to pollute or to be free of pollution is tradeable. As in any market, unrestrained trading ordinarily produces efficient results, something that cannot always be said of government intervention. Many areas of law that were thought to be "public" or "quasi-public," such as environmental or eminent domain law, could be reconceived as "private" to the extent that they reflected bargaining disputes among affected persons.

Coase's concern was with very small markets. *Sturges v. Bridgman* involved bargaining between a single physician and confectioner over the use of a single two-unit house. To the extent that Coase turned the problem of legal disputes into one of bargaining, it was at a microscopic level, not the large areas that are typically covered by legislation such as zoning laws. Later economists in this tradition, such as Oliver E. Williamson, wrote about economic decision-making within a single firm, including decisions about whether to make or buy inputs and of specialized contract practices with suppliers or distributors.[88] The "Coase Theorem," as Chicago economist George J. Stigler later named it, is subject to many qualifications and variations. Efficient outcomes might be more elusive if bargainers have high bargaining ("transaction") costs. Some disputes might involve many more than two bargainers, making efficient outcomes more difficult to reach. For example, if the spark-emitting railroad is not guilty of a nuisance but the aggregated farmers along the railroad's path have the greater value, then the farmers must pay off the railroad. Organizing them and getting them to agree on each farmer's contribution could be heroic, particularly if they differ in size, amount of injury, and so on. Each one individually might not want to pay anything at all, assuming that others would bear the burden. Mancur Olson would make this very argument just a few years later in *The Logic of Collective Action*, but it also applies to the Coasean situation if many bargainers are involved.

The Coasean literature includes both supporters and detractors, and within the fields of both economics and law.[89] James Buchanan, coauthor of *The Calculus of Consent*, and Harold Demsetz debated the relative costs and benefits of private bargaining compared to government intervention.[90] Another debate concerned "alienability," or the transferability of legal entitlements. Coase's argument depended on people's ability to negotiate to the efficient solution by waiving their legal claims, something that the common law permits but statutes such as the zoning laws typically do not.[91]

The Problem of Social Cost had a significant impact on 1960s' and 1970s' thinking about environmental law, natural resources, and land use planning, all of which were subject to extensive regulation. In law school casebooks on property, "private" land use restrictions moved from the back burner to the front. Economically inclined law teachers drew blackboard pictures of polluting smokestacks and downwind homes, asking students about the relative merits of regulation or private bargaining to address environmental policy. Property scholars compared the rights created by zoning statutes with negotiable common law nuisance rules or private covenants.[92]

In 1964 Allen Kneese wrote his now classic book *The Economics of Regional Water Quality Management*, relying on Coase in a chapter dedicated to the use of private markets to make water allocation decisions.[93] Environmental policy turned increasingly to "market based" pollution control systems that permitted firms to bid for pollution rights or even trade them.[94] Under these systems the Environmental Protection Agency set "gross" standards for particular pollutants. Companies could bid for the rights to discharge them, presumably assigning them to the producer whose output was the most valuable or who had the highest pollution reduction costs.

Similar developments occurred in accident law, as Chapter 7 recounts. Drawing on Coase, Guido Calabresi suggested that liability for automobile accidents should be assigned to the person who *would* have obtained the obligation if bargaining had been possible—the "cheapest cost avoider," in the terminology of law and economics. Calabresi's and Richard A. Posner's work also called for rethinking of the appropriate roles of negligence and strict liability in torts and gave support to the drafters of the Second Restatement of Torts, which embraced strict liability for harms caused by dangerous and defective products.[95]

Neither Coase, Posner, nor Calabresi single-handedly invented law and economics. Economic analysis of law was well developed in the earlier history of legal thought, as portions of this book discuss. The *Journal of Law and Economics* was established at the University of Chicago about six years before Coase moved there and three years before *The Problem of Social Cost* was published. Posner's ground-shifting book entitled *Economic Analysis of Law* was published in 1973.[96] He was a law student at Harvard when *Social Cost* was published and accepted his first academic position at Stanford Law School in 1968, focusing on antitrust law. He moved to the University of Chicago in

1969 and became an appellate judge when Ronald Reagan appointed him in 1981.

Posner's *Economic Analysis of Law* expanded the domain of law and economics to nearly every legal area. Posner included lengthy sections on the common law, family law, regulation, corporate and securities law, tax and wealth distribution, constitutional law, and federalism. His early work became associated with the position that economic efficiency is the most defensible goal for legal rules. Redistribution may be appropriate too, but it should be explicit and direct rather than disguised in costly regulations or subsidies.

Coase and Posner have become symbols of everything that people both love and hate about law and economics. Some legal scholars were put off by the extent to which Posner marshaled arguments based on expected utility for every conceivable legal problem, including such things as marriage and prostitution, as well as his willingness to assume that competition did or could exist in many areas where it seemed impossible to achieve.[97] But Posner has proven to be a nimble scholar. An important key to the success of his work, and to the law and economics movement generally, has been an ability to marshal its insights into a positive and evolving program for legal reconstruction, something that other twentieth-century critiques including Legal Realism and Critical Legal Studies were never able to accomplish. Perhaps the legal achievement that comes closest is John Rawls's *Theory of Justice* (1971), whose powerful anti-utilitarian argument for increasing expected welfare by improving the lot of the worst off was particularly influential in the 1980s and 1990s. Although Rawls's book has been cited more frequently than Coase's *Social Cost*, Rawls did not make nearly as dramatic a jump from classes in legal theory to applied law.

The (Partial) Dismantling of the Regulatory State

By the 1970s a consensus was emerging that much regulation was excessive, poorly designed, or both. First, industrial economists increasingly came to believe that markets were more robust than previously thought and required government intervention less frequently. Second, public choice theory appeared to make a strong case that regulation too often led to capture, benefitting regulated firms rather than the consumers it was declared to protect.[98] Regulation seemed much more costly than anticipated and produced less appealing results. In 1982 appellate judge Stephen G. Breyer, who had been a professor of administrative law at Harvard Law School and would later become Associate Justice of the Supreme Court, wrote a highly influential book, *Regulation and Its Reform.*[99] The book was all the more influential because Breyer was not a member of the Chicago School or even a fellow traveler. He was a Democrat, appointed to the bench by Jimmy Carter and elevated to the Supreme Court by Bill Clinton. Breyer illustrated how certain markets, such as trucking and air travel, had been "mismatches" from the start because these industries were either structured competitively or capable of being made so. Indeed, a principal effect of trucking regulation had been to make it nearly impossible for new firms to enter a market in which entry should be quite easy.

Mancur Olson's thesis about interest group capture, the Coasean literature on bargaining alternatives to regulation, and the social choice/voting literature all coalesced in the 1960s and 1970s to make a powerful intellectual case for dismantling New Deal regulation. But very likely the most important factor was a poor track record, including the high public costs of administration and the even higher private costs of compliance. Small businesses and new entrants complained that the regulatory process favored large firms. Consumer benefits were often illusory. In addition, as Landis's 1960 *Report* had already pointed out, there were way too many "jurisdictional" squabbles, inconsistent mandates, or other costly trade-offs, often caused by self-serving intervention by Congress.

Bruce Ackerman and William T. Hassler confirmed many of these problems in *Clean Coal/Dirty Air* (1981), a now classic discussion of how political processes can corrupt good intentions. As one reviewer put it, the book revealed "power-conscious congressmen, scheming staff persons, intrepid industry lobbyists, overzealous environmentalists, and insecure bureaucrats who connive, cajole, and caress one another into supporting a law and a set of regulations that may actually produce an increase in the nation's air pollution at an enormous cost to businesses and taxpayers."[100]

Deregulation of railroads, trucking, and airlines produced lower consumer prices and greatly increased the entry of new firms. In other areas it had less success. Most occurred in stages, and pinpointing a single year in which an industry was "deregulated" is impossible.[101] Trucking and railroad regulation were low-hanging fruit because the industries were competitively structured. Deregulation began in the late 1970s and early 1980s, just at the end of the Carter administration.[102] The Interstate Commerce Commission, created in 1887 and America's oldest major federal regulatory agency, was dismantled in 1995.

Passenger air travel regulation under the Civil Aeronautics Board (CAB) was a true maze of price regulation, restrictions on service, and subsidies for struggling carriers. The CAB's explicit concern was "unfair" competition, but that came to mean any competition at all. For example, the CAB made it illegal for Aloha Airlines to include rental cars in traveler vacation packages, because this would give Aloha an "unfair advantage" over its competitor Hawaiian Airlines.[103] One wonders how a practice can be anticompetitive when customers like it and any firm can do it. During the high point of CAB regulation in the late 1970s, airlines were forbidden from offering movies, and even the size of the sandwich in passenger meals was regulated. In 1977 the dispute over sandwich size prompted Alfred Kahn, who had just been appointed director of the CAB, to wonder "is this what my mother raised me to do?" Kahn, an economist from Cornell University, went on to become one of the great economist proponents of deregulation.[104]

The airline industry was deregulated in several steps, beginning with the Airline Deregulation Act of 1978, which authorized the CAB to approve deviations from regulated fares.[105] The United States also negotiated several "open skies" agreements with foreign countries, allowing greater access by foreign carriers into U.S. markets. The CAB itself was abolished in 1984.[106] Today, pricing is left to the discretion of each carrier, enforced only by the antitrust laws, and then only rarely. No one regulates the size of sandwiches, which have largely disappeared in any event.

The story of telecommunications deregulation is more complex. The national telephone system took the first steps in the late 1970s, when the courts began to doubt AT&T's long-held position, supported by the Federal Communications Commission, that its network should not be forced to interconnect with anyone. Previously, in the 1956 *Hush-A-Phone* decision the FCC had gone so far as to forbid a firm from selling an entirely non-electronic plastic cup that fit over a phone mouthpiece so that a caller could whisper into it and keep his words confidential. The appellate court reversed, thus cracking the long-held rule prohibiting all "foreign attachments" to the monopoly telephone network.[107]

During the 1960s several firms that provided two-way radio services tried to interconnect electronically with the AT&T system. Carterfone, a technology developed by Thomas Carter, enabled truckers to use Citizens' Band radio to access the phone system to talk to their families or others while on the road. AT&T objected to the interconnection, but in 1968 the FCC changed its position and permitted Carter to proceed.[108] The case damaged AT&T's reputation because it publicized the extent to which AT&T's regulatory actions could actually inhibit innovations that consumers wanted.

In the early 1980s AT&T was to a very significant extent deregulated by the antitrust laws rather than legislation. An appellate court held that antitrust law required the AT&T network to interconnect with rivals.[109] MCI, then a very young company, was permitted to provide long distance services in competition with AT&T. At about the same time AT&T agreed to be broken up in order to resolve an antitrust action brought by the government. The decree severed local operating companies from long distance.[110] The principal protagonist was William F. Baxter, a Stanford law professor who was head of the Antitrust Division during Ronald Reagan's first term. AT&T also severed its Western Electric division, thus ending an era in which purchasers of telephone service were required to lease their phones from AT&T. The result was a flood of new entrants into the markets for devices such as telephones, fax machines, and the like, and also into long distance communications.

The deregulation movement has not been confined to great New Deal edifices. It also included purely local regulation. As initially approved by the Supreme Court's 1926 *Euclid* decision, zoning involved fairly rigid government specifications of land use, with a checkerboard of parallel streets and a strong preference for single-family homes.[111] These earliest zoning statutes were "cumulative," meaning that higher uses excluded lower ones, but not vice versa, with single-family homes ranking highest and heavy industry lowest. Beginning in the 1950s and 1960s, however, more communities turned to "exclusionary" zoning, which excluded in both directions. One significant downside was the increased use of zoning to exclude on the basis of wealth or race, mainly by requiring very large lots or eliminating multifamily housing. Some state courts overturned these provisions, holding that communities could not use zoning to exclude their "fair share" of a regional cross section of the population.[112] Federal law never went that far.

Zoning regulation historically tied particular parcels of land to specific uses. Not only was this process inflexible, it also required planners to be expert predictors of future economic development. A great deal of land in rapidly growing communities was zoned when it was still being used primarily for agriculture. Although deviations were possible, a landowner had to show some kind of need or hardship. Beginning in the 1950s, however, some communities began to permit areas within the zoned community to "float," and have their uses determined later. Early decisions were skeptical, sometimes exhibiting overt hostility to market-driven outcomes. One 1960 decision, widely reprinted in law school property casebooks, reflected this antimarket bias: under a floating zone provision "the development itself would become the plan, which is manifestly the antithesis of zoning."[113]

Two subsequent initiatives changed the course of urban land use planning in the United States. Once was statutes that provided for significantly greater flexibility, permitting the market rather than public planners to determine housing needs. The other was the dramatic revitalization of "private" zoning-like restrictions. The best-known example of the first is the "planned unit development," or PUD, which abandoned the 1920s' notion that single-family homes should be on equal lots located on parallel streets. The PUD form gave private developers the ability to negotiate the layout of planned subdivisions. Already in 1949, Prince George's County, Maryland, authorized two builder-planned communities, with varying building styles, irregular streets, common land areas, and community facilities.[114] The thinking was that economically interested developers had every incentive to make their developments as attractive as possible to customers, and thus could be expected to respond better than government planners to anticipated housing needs.[115] The PUD approach incidentally favored larger home builders, reflecting a reality in which ever more homes were built by firms who constructured more than a hundred homes per year.[116]

The other development was the dramatic rise of private restrictive covenants, or "servitudes," as zoning substitutes. The result was the kind of tiny markets that Coase had imagined in the *Problem of Social Cost*. Under a servitude system the relevant land use decision could be made by an owners' association that controlled a few units rather than the thousands that might be under a city's zoning board. The popularity of restrictive covenants increased after the Supreme Court's decision in *Buchanan v. Warley*, discussed in Chapter 3, which struck down racially exclusive zoning.[117] Home developers then turned to private racially restrictive covenants, which the Supreme Court initially upheld in 1926.[118] It changed its mind in 1948 in *Shelley v. Kraemer*.[119] Developers also began to use private covenants to control other aspects of subdivisions, such as housing size, density, placement on lots—many of the same things that zoning controlled. In its important 1938 *Neponsit* decision the New York Court of Appeals approved a subdivision covenant scheme that created a private homeowner's association to manage the subdivision and required individual property owners to pay an ownership fee.[120] *Neponsit* helped create the legal framework for private contractual alternatives to zoning. Initially the growth of such subdivisions was slow. In 1964 fewer than five hundred subdivisions in the United States were managed by private homeowners' associations. By 2000 the number had grown to roughly 225,000.[121]

The impact of these "private residential governments" is manifold. First, often there is more "regulation" as such than even zoning ordinances provide.

For example, private subdivisions often control building materials, landscaping, pet ownership, and permissible uses much more elaborately than zoning typically does. At the same time, however, the regulations are both private and contractual, in the sense that everyone agrees to them as a condition of buying a home in a particular development. In a very real sense residential land use law had moved from the public back into the private legal sphere.

Conclusion

The legal world in the United States today is more "private" than it was from the New Deal through the 1960s. Some of that development was clearly a socially beneficial response to regulatory excesses. But democracy's movements often lack moderation. On the way to whatever short-lived equilibrium it may attain, it gyrates between extremes.

Deregulation has had a significant effect on American infrastructure, privatizing parts of it and diminishing what is left over. A common complaint about expansive regulation is overinvestment in infrastructure. In the early 1960s Harvey Averch and Leland Johnson famously argued that because regulated firms are guaranteed a profitable rate of return on their investment they are tempted to enlarge the base on which this return is computed. They "gold plate," or overinvest in infrastructure such as pipelines, electric lines, telecommunications, and transportation facilities.[122] Deregulation has largely removed that incentive. In sharp contrast, the actors in the markets envisioned by Ronald Coase do not invest if they cannot appropriate the results. Although the great public works projects of the New Deal era may have given us too many train stations, courthouses, universities, schools, highways, or other public facilities, privatization has provided too little. And the distributional impact should not be forgotten: infrastructure is often of greater benefit to the poor than the wealthy.

The deregulation of residential communities has had a similar effect. Private residential governments have reduced the value of the traditional community as a public good. Once the private subdivision has its own private park, recreational facilities, and security force, its owners are less likely to vote tax increases to support public parks or increase the government's police force. Robert Reich termed this phenomenon "the secession of the successful."[123] A few courts have relied on esoteric historical rules such as the "public trust" doctrine to force subdivisions to open truly scarce facilities to a larger population. For example, in 1984 the New Jersey Supreme Court required a private homeowners' association to open its privately owned beach to the public.[124]

Nonetheless, the deregulation movement has not taken us back to some idealized notion of the nineteenth century, although some proponents may long for that. Thanks to urbanization and technological development, the world is critically more dependent on infrastructure today than it was a century ago. And of course the environment is the ultimate infrastructure, because everyone participates but each person individually benefits more by corrupting than by improving it. For these reasons the deregulation movement may largely have run its course, even though some ideological support remains. Infrastructure provides the platform on which social and legal systems develop, and societies with better platforms have the advantage. The trick is to develop shared resources in ways that facilitate economic and social growth for all members of society rather than favoring particular interest groups. This is one of the biggest challenges facing democratic legal systems in the neoclassical era.

Notes

INTRODUCTION

1. Charles Darwin, THE DESCENT OF MAN AND SELECTION IN RELATION TO SEX (New York: D. Appleton, 1871).
2. *See* Henri F. Ellenberger, THE DISCOVERY OF THE UNCONSCIOUS: HISTORY AND EVOLUTION OF DYNAMIC PSYCHIATRY (New York: Basic Books, rev. ed. 1994); Daniel C. Dennett, DARWIN'S DANGEROUS IDEA: EVOLUTION AND THE MEANINGS OF LIFE (New York: Simon & Schuster, 1995).
3. *See, e.g.*, Duncan Kennedy, THE RISE AND FALL OF CLASSICAL LEGAL THOUGHT (Washington, DC: Beard Books, 2006); William M. Wiecek, THE LOST WORLD OF CLASSICAL LEGAL THOUGHT: LAW AND IDEOLOGY IN AMERICA, 1886–1937 (New York: Oxford, 1998); Morton J. Horwitz, THE TRANSFORMATION OF AMERICAN LAW: THE CRISIS OF LEGAL ORTHODOXY, 1870–1960, at 9–63 (New York: Oxford, 1992); Herbert Hovenkamp, ENTERPRISE AND AMERICAN LAW, 1836–1937 (Cambridge, MA: Harvard Univ. Press, 1991).
4. Adam Smith, AN INQUIRY INTO THE NATURE AND CAUSES OF THE WEALTH OF NATIONS London: W. Strahan & T. Cadell, 1776); William Blackstone, COMMENTARIES ON THE LAWS OF ENGLAND (Oxford: Clarendon Press, 1765–1769).
5. On institutionalism, *see* Chapters 4–6; on Keynes, *see* Chapter 15; *and* Teodoro Dario Togati, KEYNES AND THE NEOCLASSICAL SYNTHESIS: EINSTEINIAN VERSUS NEWTONIAN MACROECONOMICS (New York: Routledge, 1998).
6. Grant Gilmore, THE DEATH OF CONTRACT (Columbus: Ohio State Univ. Press, 1974). *See* Arthur Linton Corbin, CORBIN ON CONTRACTS: A COMPREHENSIVE TREATISE ON THE WORKING RULES OF CONTRACT LAW (St. Paul, MN: West, 1950); RESTATEMENT OF THE LAW (FIRST) CONTRACTS (1931); RESTATEMENT OF THE LAW (SECOND) CONTRACTS (1975–1981); Uniform Commercial Code (1942–1952).
7. *See* Chapter 2.
8. Henry Sumner Maine, ANCIENT LAW: ITS CONNECTION WITH THE EARLY HISTORY OF SOCIETY AND ITS RELATION TO MODERN IDEAS (London: John Murray, 1861). *See* Roscoe Pound, THE SPIRIT OF THE COMMON LAW 155

(Boston: Marshall Jones Co., 1921) (discussing Maine's antistatism). On Maine, *see* David M. Rabban, LAW'S HISTORY: AMERICAN LEGAL THOUGHT AND THE TRANSATLANTIC TURN TO HISTORY 115–49 (New York: Cambridge, 2013).

9. KENNEDY, CLASSICAL LEGAL THOUGHT, *supra* note 3; HORWITZ, TRANSFORMATION OF AMERICAN LAW, *supra* note 3.
10. *E.g.*, Richard A. Epstein, THE CLASSICAL LIBERAL CONSTITUTION: THE UNCERTAIN QUEST FOR LIMITED GOVERNMENT (Cambridge, MA: Harvard Univ. Press, 2014).
11. William Graham Sumner, WHAT SOCIAL CLASSES OWE EACH OTHER (New York: Harper, 1883); William Graham Sumner, FOLKWAYS: A STUDY OF THE SOCIOLOGICAL IMPORTANCE OF USAGES, MANNERS, CUSTOMS, MORES, AND MORALS (Boston: Ginn, 1906); James Coolidge Carter, LAW: ITS ORIGIN, GROWTH AND FUNCTION (New York: Putnam, 1907). *See* Chapter 1.
12. *See* Chapter 8.
13. *See* the Epilogue.
14. *See* Chapter 10.
15. *See* HOVENKAMP, ENTERPRISE AND AMERICAN LAW, *supra* note 3.
16. Thomas S. Kuhn, THE STRUCTURE OF SCIENTIFIC REVOLUTIONS (Chicago: Univ. of Chicago Press, 1962); Arthur O. Lovejoy, THE GREAT CHAIN OF BEING: A STUDY OF THE HISTORY OF AN IDEA (Cambridge, MA: Harvard Univ. Press, 1936); Joseph A. Schumpeter, HISTORY OF ECONOMIC ANALYSIS (New York: Oxford, 1954); Merle Curti, THE GROWTH OF AMERICAN THOUGHT (New York: Harper & Row, rev. ed. 1951); Richard Hofstadter, SOCIAL DARWINISM IN AMERICAN THOUGHT, 1860–1915 (Philadelphia: Penn. Press, 1944).
17. Morton J. Horwitz, THE TRANSFORMATION OF AMERICAN LAW, 1780–1860, AT 253–54 (Cambridge, MA: Harvard Univ. Press, 1977), quoting Oliver Wendell Holmes, Jr., *Privilege, Malice, and Intent*, 8 HARV. L. REV. 1, 7 (1894); *and* Karl N. Llewellyn, THE COMMON LAW TRADITION: DECIDING APPEALS 38 (Boston: Little, Brown, 1960).
18. *E.g.*, Paul A. Lombardo, THREE GENERATIONS, NO IMBECILES: EUGENICS, THE SUPREME COURT, AND *BUCK V. BELL* (Baltimore: Johns Hopkins Univ. Press, 2008); Charles A. Lofgren, THE PLESSY CASE: A LEGAL-HISTORICAL INTERPRETATION (New York: Oxford, 1987).
19. Tony Freyer, ANTITRUST AND GLOBAL CAPITALISM, 1930–2004 (New York: Cambridge Univ. Press, 2009); Rudolph J.R. Peritz, COMPETITION POLICY IN AMERICA: HISTORY, RHETORIC, LAW (New York: Oxford, 1996); HOVENKAMP, ENTERPRISE, *supra* note 3; William J. Novak, THE PEOPLE'S WELFARE: LAW AND REGULATION IN NINETEENTH-CENTURY AMERICA (Chapel Hill: Univ. of North Carolina Press, 1996).
20. Charles E. Rosenberg, THE TRIAL OF THE ASSASSIN GUITEAU: PSYCHIATRY AND THE LAW IN THE GILDED AGE (Chicago: Univ. of Chicago Press, 1995);

James Mohr, DOCTORS AND THE LAW: MEDICAL JURISPRUDENCE IN NINETEENTH-CENTURY AMERICA (New York: Oxford, 1993); Lawrence M. Friedman & Robert Percival, THE ROOTS OF JUSTICE: CRIME AND PUNISHMENT IN ALAMEDA COUNTY, CALIFORNIA, 1870–1910 (Chapel Hill: Univ. of North Carolina Press, 1981).

21. RABBAN, LAW'S HISTORY, *supra* note 8.
22. HENRY HART, JR. & ALBERT SACKS, THE LEGAL PROCESS (tent. ed., 1958). *See* the Epilogue.

CHAPTER 1

1. John Dewey, THE INFLUENCE OF DARWIN ON PHILOSOPHY 3 (New York: Henry Holt, 1910).
2. Erasmus Darwin, ZOONOMIA; OR, THE LAWS OF ORGANIC LIFE ([1794] American edition, Philadelphia: Edward Earle, 1818). Erasmus Darwin was Charles Darwin's grandfather. *See also* Jean-Baptiste Lamarck, ZOOLOGICAL PHILOSOPHY: AN EXPOSITION WITH REGARD TO THE NATURAL HISTORY OF ANIMALS ([1809]; Eng. trans. by Hugh Elliot, London: Macmillan, 1984).
3. Henry Adams, THE EDUCATION OF HENRY ADAMS 224, 231 (Boston: Houghton Mifflin, 1918).
4. Most prominently in Sir Edward Burnett Tylor, PRIMITIVE CULTURE: RESEARCHES INTO THE DEVELOPMENT OF MYTHOLOGY, PHILOSOPHY, RELIGION, ART, AND CUSTOM (London: John Murray, 1871); Lewis Henry Morgan, ANCIENT SOCIETY (New York: Henry Holt, 1877). *See* George W. Stocking, JR., RACE, CULTURE, AND EVOLUTION: ESSAYS IN THE HISTORY OF ANTHROPOLOGY (New York: Free Press, 1968).
5. *E.g.*, John B. Watson, BEHAVIORISM 144 (New York: People's Institute, 1925). *See also* John B. Watson, PSYCHOLOGY FROM THE STANDPOINT OF A BEHAVIORIST (Philadelphia: Lippincott, 1919); Stephen Sheldon Colvin & William Chandler Bagley, HUMAN BEHAVIOR (New York: Macmillan, 1913); William McDougall, AN INTRODUCTION TO SOCIAL PSYCHOLOGY (London: Methuen, 1908); Ivan Petrovich Pavlov, CONDITIONED REFLEXES: AN INVESTIGATION OF THE PHYSIOLOGICAL ACTIVITY OF THE CEREBRAL CORTEX (London: Oxford, 1927); Albert Paul Weiss, A THEORETICAL BASIS OF HUMAN BEHAVIOR (Columbus: R. G. Adams, 1925). For a good historical survey, *see* Robert A. Boakes, FROM DARWINISM TO BEHAVIOURISM: PSYCHOLOGY AND THE MINDS OF ANIMALS (New York: Cambridge Univ. Press, 1984).
6. Holmes to Laski (Nov. 23, 1928), *in* HOLMES-LASKI LETTERS: THE CORRESPONDENCE OF MR. JUSTICE HOLMES AND HAROLD J. LASKI, 1916–1935, at 1113 (Mark DeWolfe Howe ed., Cambridge, MA: Harvard Univ. Press, 1953).

7. *E.g.*, Franklin Henry Giddings, THE THEORY OF SOCIOLOGY (Philadelphia: Am. Acad. Pol. & Soc. Sci., 1894); Lester Frank Ward, NEO-DARWINISM AND NEO-LAMARCKISM (Washington: Gedney & Roberts, 1891); Lester Frank Ward, THE PSYCHIC FACTORS OF CIVILIZATION (Boston: Ginn, 1893); Lester Frank Ward, GLIMPSES OF THE COSMOS: A MENTAL AUTOBIOGRAPHY (New York: Putnam, 6 vols. 1913–1918).
8. Frederick Jackson Turner, THE SIGNIFICANCE OF THE FRONTIER IN AMERICAN HISTORY (Madison: State Historical Society of Wisconsin, 1894).
9. *See* Thomas R. Malthus, AN ESSAY ON THE PRINCIPLE OF POPULATION (London: J. Johnson, 1798); Thomas R. Malthus, PRINCIPLES OF POLITICAL ECONOMY (London: John Murray, 1820). On Malthus's influence on Darwin, *see* Janet Browne, CHARLES DARWIN: VOYAGING, A BIOGRAPHY 385–90 (New York: Knopf, 1995). *See* Lionel Robbins, AN ESSAY ON THE NATURE & SIGNIFICANCE OF ECONOMIC SCIENCE 55 (London: Macmillan, 1st ed. 1932; 2d ed. 1935).
10. Charles Darwin, THE DESCENT OF MAN AND SELECTION IN RELATION TO SEX (New York: Appleton, 1871). *See, e.g.*, Vol. I, ch. 5 (intellectual and moral faculties, including religion); TYLOR, PRIMITIVE CULTURE, *supra* note 4; MORGAN, ANCIENT SOCIETY, *supra* note 4; Oliver Wendell Holmes, JR., THE COMMON LAW 11, 19, 34 (Boston: Little, Brown, 1881).
11. *See* Richard Hofstadter, SOCIAL DARWINISM IN AMERICAN THOUGHT, 1860–1915 (Philadelphia: Penn Press, 1944); Henry Steele Commager, JR., THE AMERICAN MIND: AN INTERPRETATION OF AMERICAN THOUGHT AND CHARACTER SINCE THE 1880's (New Haven, CT: Yale, 1950); Morton G. White, SOCIAL THOUGHT IN AMERICA: THE REVOLT AGAINST FORMALISM (New York: Viking, 1949).
12. Herbert Spencer, SOCIAL STATICS 67 (1850; New York: D. Appleton & Co., rev. 1875). *See* HERBERT SPENCER: CRITICAL ASSESSMENTS OF LEADING SOCIOLOGISTS (John Offer, ed., London: Routledge, 2 vols. 2000), in particular, Kenneth E. Bock, "Darwin and Social Theory," vol. 2 *id.* at 120.
13. *See* Ryan Alan, JOHN DEWEY AND THE HIGH TIDE OF AMERICAN LIBERALISM 22–23 (New York: Norton, 1995).
14. SPENCER, SOCIAL STATICS, *supra* note 12, 185–87, 288–89, 373, 405; 2 Herbert Spencer, PRINCIPLES OF SOCIOLOGY: POLITICAL INSTITUTIONS 542 (1872; American edition. New York: Appleton, 1882).
15. William Graham Sumner, "Rights," "Some Natural Rights," and "Equality," written between 1887 and 1906. Quotations are from ESSAYS OF WILLIAM GRAHAM SUMNER (Albert Galloway Keller & Maurice R. Davie, eds., New Haven, CT: Yale, 1934), I, 358–62, 363–68, 421–23, 448–53.
16. William Graham Sumner, WHAT SOCIAL CLASSES OWE TO EACH OTHER 141–42 (New York: Harper, 1883).

17. Charles Darwin, THE VARIATION OF ANIMALS AND PLANTS UNDER DOMESTICATION (London: John Murray, 1868).
18. HOFSTADTER, SOCIAL DARWINISM IN AMERICAN THOUGHT, *supra* note 11, at 67; Lester Frank Ward, DYNAMIC SOCIOLOGY (New York: D. Appleton, 1883).
19. WARD, GLIMPSES OF THE COSMOS III, *supra* note 7, at 32–35; IV, 352–55; II, 169.
20. Albion W. Small, THE MEANING OF SOCIAL SCIENCE 83 (Chicago: Univ. of Chicago Press, 1910).
21. *See generally*, Robert E.L. Faris, CHICAGO SOCIOLOGY, 1920–1932 (San Francisco: Chandler, 1967); L.L. Bernard & Jessie Bernard, ORIGINS OF AMERICAN SOCIOLOGY: THE SOCIAL SCIENCE MOVEMENT IN THE UNITED STATES (New York: Crowell, 1943); John C. Burnham, LESTER FRANK WARD IN AMERICAN THOUGHT (Washington, DC: Public Affairs Press, 1956).
22. For Pound's reliance on Ward, *see* Roscoe Pound, The Scope and Purpose of Sociological Jurisprudence, 24 HARV. L. REV. 591 (1911), and 25 HARV. L. REV. 140, 142, 489 (1911); and Roscoe Pound, JURISPRUDENCE, 5 vols. (St. Paul, MN: West, 1959), I, *passim*.
23. *See* Patrick S. Atiyah, THE RISE AND FALL OF FREEDOM OF CONTRACT 36–60 (New York: Oxford, 1979).
24. Henry Maine, ANCIENT LAW: ITS CONNECTION WITH THE EARLY HISTORY OF SOCIETY AND ITS RELATION TO MODERN IDEAS 296 (London: John Murray, 1861).
25. *See* Chapters 13–15. On the Jacksonian period, *see* Charles Sellers, THE MARKET REVOLUTION: JACKSONIAN AMERICA, 1815–1846 (New York: Oxford, 1991); Herbert Hovenkamp, ENTERPRISE AND AMERICAN LAW, 1836–1937 (Cambridge, MA: Harvard Univ. Press, 1991).
26. In addition to HOFSTADTER'S SOCIAL DARWINISM, *see* COMMAGER, THE AMERICAN MIND, *supra* note 11, at 359–73; WHITE, SOCIAL THOUGHT IN AMERICA, *supra* note 11; Robert McCloskey, AMERICAN CONSERVATISM IN THE AGE OF ENTERPRISE, 1865–1910, at 26–30 (Cambridge, MA: Harvard Univ. Press, 1951). *See also* Owen M. Fiss, TROUBLED BEGINNINGS OF THE MODERN STATE, 1888–1910, at 47–49 (OLIVER WENDELL HOLMES DEVISE HISTORY OF THE SUPREME COURT OF THE UNITED STATES (vol. 8, Stanley N. Katz ed., New York: Macmillan, 1993).
27. For example, the "Monkey Trial" of 1925: Scopes v. State, 289 S.W. 363 (Tenn. 1927). *See* Edward J. Larson, SUMMER FOR THE GODS: THE SCOPES TRIAL AND AMERICA'S CONTINUING DEBATE OVER SCIENCE AND RELIGION (New York: Basic, 2006).
28. Herbert Hovenkamp, The Political Economy of Substantive Due Process, 40 STAN. L. REV. 379–447 (1988).
29. For example, Roscoe Pound, Liberty of Contract, 18 YALE L. J. 454 (1909). *See* Herbert Hovenkamp, The Cultural Crises of the Fuller Court, 104 YALE L.J. 2309 (1995).

30. *See* Arnold M. Paul, CONSERVATIVE CRISIS AND THE RULE OF LAW: ATTITUDES OF BAR AND BENCH, 1887–1895, at 22 & n. 10 (Ithaca, NY: Cornell, 1960).
31. Holmes to Lady Pollock, July 2, 1895, *in* 1 THE CORRESPONDENCE OF MR. JUSTICE HOLMES AND SIR FREDERICK POLLOCK, 1874–1932, at 57–58 (Cambridge, MA: Harvard Univ. Press, 2d ed. 1961). *See also* Holmes to Harold Laski, Sept. 15, 1916; Aug. 24, 1924), 1 HOLMES-LASKI CORRESPONDENCE 19–20 (Cambridge, MA: Harvard Univ. Press, 1950); Holmes to Morris Cohen, Feb. 5, 1919, PORTRAIT OF A PHILOSOPHER: MORRIS R. COHEN IN LIFE AND LETTERS 321 (Lenora Rosenfield ed., New York: Harcourt, 1962).
32. On evolution and Holmes, *see* Oliver Wendell Holmes, Jr., Law in Science and Science in Law, 12 HARV. L. REV. 443, 449 (1899); Oliver Wendell Holmes, Jr., Primitive Notions in Modern Law, 10 AM. L. REV. 422, 429–30 (1876). *And see* Albert W. Alschuler, LAW WITHOUT VALUES: THE LIFE, WORK, AND LEGACY OF JUSTICE HOLMES (Chicago: Univ. of Chicago Press, 2000).
33. Lester Frank Ward, Social and Biological Struggles, 13 AM. J. SOC. 289, 292 (1907).
34. *See* David Wigdor, ROSCOE POUND: PHILOSOPHER OF LAW 55–62 (Westport, CT: Greenwood Press, 1974); Herbert Hovenkamp, Evolutionary Models in Jurisprudence, 64 TEX. L. REV. 645 (1985).
35. *See, e.g.*, Richard A. Epstein, THE CLASSICAL LIBERAL CONSTITUTION: THE UNCERTAIN QUEST FOR LIMITED GOVERNMENT 338–39, 370–72, 581–91 (Cambridge, MA: Harvard Univ. Press, 2014); David N. Mayer, LIBERTY OF CONTRACT: REDISCOVERING A LOST CONSTITUTIONAL RIGHT (Washington, DC, Cato: 2011); David E. Bernstein, REHABILITATING LOCHNER: DEFENDING INDIVIDUAL RIGHTS AGAINST PROGRESSIVE REFORM (Chicago: Univ. of Chicago Press, 2011); Michael J. Phillips, THE LOCHNER COURT, MYTH AND REALITY: SUBSTANTIVE DUE PROCESS FROM THE 1890S TO THE 1930S (New York: Praeger, 2000); Howard Gillman, THE CONSTITUTION BESIEGED: THE RISE AND DEMISE OF LOCHNER ERA POLICE POWERS JURISPRUDENCE (Durham, NC: Duke, 1993); Paul Kens, JUDICIAL POWER AND REFORM POLITICS: THE ANATOMY OF LOCHNER V. NEW YORK (Lawrence: Univ. Press of Kansas, 1990).
36. *See* HOVENKAMP, ENTERPRISE, *supra* note 25, chs. 7–9, 14–17; GILLMAN, CONSTITUTION BESIEGED, *supra* note 35, at 19–60; SELLERS, MARKET REVOLUTION, *supra* note 25.
37. Edward S. Corwin, CONSTITUTIONAL REVOLUTION, LTD. 82–90 (Claremont, CA: Claremont Colleges, 1941). Corwin relied in part on the PhD dissertation of one of his students. *See* Benjamin Twiss, LAWYERS AND THE CONSTITUTION: HOW LAISSEZ FAIRE CAME TO THE SUPREME COURT (New York: Oxford, 1941).
38. Lochner v. New York, 198 U.S. 45, 75 (1905).
39. *See* WILLARD L. KING, MELVILLE WESTON FULLER (1950); Richard Skolnik, Rufus Peckham, *in* 3 THE JUSTICES OF THE UNITED STATES SUPREME COURT

1789–1969, at 1685 (Leon Friedman & Fred L. Israel eds., New York: Chelsea House, 1969); James F. Watts, Jr., *Edward Douglass White, in* 3 THE JUSTICES OF THE SUPREME COURT, *supra*, at 1633.

40. *E.g.*, Adkins v. Children's Hosp., 261 U.S. 525, 568 (1923).
41. *See* Joel Francis Paschal, MR. JUSTICE SUTHERLAND: A MAN AGAINST THE STATE 8–15 (Princeton, NJ: Princeton Univ. Press, 1951). *Contrast* Hadley Arkes, THE RETURN OF GEORGE SUTHERLAND: RESTORING A JURISPRUDENCE OF NATURAL RIGHTS 42–43 (Princeton, NJ: Princeton Univ. Press, 1994) (questioning Sutherland's Social Darwinism); Samuel R. Olken, Justice George Sutherland and Economic Liberty: Constitutional Conservatism and the Problem of Factions, 6 WILLIAM & MARY BILL OF RIGHTS J. 1 (1997) (similar).
42. 2 Herbert Spencer, THE PRINCIPLES OF ETHICS 111–13, 202–03 (New York: Appleton, 1891); MAINE, ANCIENT LAW, *supra* note 24, in particular ch. 9.
43. *See, e.g.*, SPENCER, SOCIAL STATICS, *supra* note 12, 22–27 (1850; rev. ed. 1872).
44. Herbert Spencer, THE MAN VERSUS THE STATE 159 (London: Williams & Norgate, 1884).
45. MAINE, ANCIENT LAW, *supra* note 24, at 110, 299–301, 333 (1861; rep. edition 1963).
46. William G. Sumner, The Mores of the Present and the Future, 13 YALE REV. 233 (1909), *reprinted in* 1 ESSAYS OF WILLIAM GRAHAM SUMNER 86 (Albert Galloway Keller & Maurice R. Davie eds., New Haven, CT: Yale, 1934).
47. MAINE, ANCIENT LAW, *supra* note 24. *See* David M. Rabban, LAW'S HISTORY: AMERICAN LEGAL THOUGHT AND THE TRANSATLANTIC TURN TO HISTORY, ch. 3 (New York: Cambridge Univ. Press, 2013); Kunal M. Parker, Context in History and Law: A Study of the Late Nineteenth-Century American Jurisprudence of Custom, 24 L. & HIST. REV. 473 (2006).
48. *See* Dorothy Ross, THE ORIGINS OF AMERICAN SOCIAL SCIENCE 98–140 (New York: Cambridge Univ. Press, 1991); Mary O. Furner, ADVOCACY AND OBJECTIVITY: A CRISIS IN THE PROFESSIONALIZATION OF AMERICAN SOCIAL SCIENCE, 1865–1905, at 45–50 (Lexington: Univ. of Kentucky Press, 1975). On German influences on the American legal academy, *see* Mathias Reimann, "A Career in Itself—the German Professoriate as a Model for American Legal Academia," *in* THE RECEPTION OF CONTINENTAL IDEAS IN THE COMMON LAW WORLD, 1820–1920, at 165 (Mathias Reimann ed., Berlin: Duncker & Humblot, 1993).
49. On the cultural evolutionists' embrace of Darwin, *see* John W. Burrow, EVOLUTION AND SOCIETY: A STUDY IN VICTORIAN SOCIAL THEORY 118–19, 134–53 (London: Cambridge Univ. Press, 1966); John Higham, HISTORY 94–95 (Englewood Cliffs, NJ: Prentice-Hall, 1965); Peter Stein, LEGAL EVOLUTION: THE STORY OF AN IDEA 88, 100 (New York: Cambridge Univ. Press, 1980); Hovenkamp, *Evolutionary Models, supra* note 34, at 645. The most elaborate

Progressive era study of the relation between law and evolution is EVOLUTION OF LAW: SELECT READINGS ON THE ORIGIN AND DEVELOPMENT OF LEGAL INSTITUTIONS (Albert Kocourek & John H. Wigmore eds., Boston: Little, Brown, 3 vols. 1915–1918).

50. William Graham Sumner, FOLKWAYS: A STUDY OF THE SOCIOLOGICAL IMPORTANCE OF USAGES, MANNERS, CUSTOMS, MORES, AND MORALS (Boston: Ginn, 1906).

51. James Coolidge Carter, THE PROPOSED CODIFICATION OF OUR COMMON LAW (New York: Evening Post, 1884); James Coolidge Carter, THE PROVINCES OF THE WRITTEN AND THE UNWRITTEN LAW (New York: Banks & Brothers, 1889); James Coolidge Carter, LAW, ITS ORIGIN, GROWTH AND FUNCTION 268 (New York: Putnam, 1907). *See also* Pound's very negative review: Roscoe Pound, James C. Carter's Law: Its Origin, Growth and Function, 24 POL. SCI. Q. 317 (1909) (book review); *and* Mathias Reimann, The Historical School against Codification: Savigny, Carter, and the Defeat of the New York Civil Code, 37 AM. J. COMP. L. 95 (1989).

52. Thomas M. Cooley, Sources of Inspiration in Legal Pursuits, 9 W. JURIST 515, 517 (1875). *Accord* John F. Dillon, COMMENTARIES ON THE LAW OF MUNICIPAL CORPORATIONS 23 (Boston: Little, Brown, 1890).

53. Thomas M. Cooley, A TREATISE ON THE CONSTITUTIONAL LIMITATIONS WHICH REST UPON THE LEGISLATIVE POWER OF THE STATES OF THE AMERICAN UNION 21 (Boston: Little, Brown, 1868).

54. *Brown*, 347 U.S. 483 (1954). *See* C. Vann Woodward, THE STRANGE CAREER OF JIM CROW 103 (New York: Oxford, 4th ed. 2002) (discussing Sumner's *Folkways*).

55. Plessy v. Ferguson, 163 U.S. 537, 551 (1897).

56. Hofstadter emphasized this point in SOCIAL DARWINISM, *supra* note 11, at 37–51.

57. *See* Michael J. Klarman, FROM JIM CROW TO CIVIL RIGHTS: THE SUPREME COURT AND THE STRUGGLE FOR RACIAL EQUALITY 321–43 (New York: Oxford, 2004).

58. Jeremy Bentham, THE PHILOSOPHY OF ECONOMIC SCIENCE (c. 1793), *reprinted in* 1 WERNER STARK, JEREMY BENTHAM'S ECONOMIC WRITINGS: CRITICAL EDITION BASED ON HIS PRINTED WORKS AND UNPRINTED MANUSCRIPTS 113 (London: Allen & Unwin, 1952). *See also* JEREMY BENTHAM, PRINCIPLES OF THE CIVIL CODE, part 1, ch. 6 (first published 1802), 1 The Works of Jeremy Bentham (John Bowring ed., Edinburg: William Tait, 1838). On the influence of Bentham on thinking about marginal deterrence, *see* Bernard E. Harcourt, THE ILLUSION OF FREE MARKETS: PUNISHMENT AND THE MYTH OF NATURAL ORDER (Cambridge, MA: Harvard Univ. Press, 2011).

59. *See* Joseph Schumpeter, HISTORY OF ECONOMIC ANALYSIS 529–30, 569–70 (New York: Oxford, 1954); N. B. de Marchi, Mill and Cairnes and the Emergence of Marginalism in England, 4 HIST. POL. ECON. 344 (1972).

60. Jeremy Bentham, AN INTRODUCTION TO THE PRINCIPLES OF MORALS AND LEGISLATION [1789] (J.H. Burns & H.L.A. Hart eds., London: Athlone, 1970); Jeremy Bentham, THE THEORY OF LEGISLATION (POSTHUMOUS) (London: Trulbner, 1864).
61. *See* Mark Blaug, ECONOMIC THEORY IN RETROSPECT 277–310 (New York: CambridgeUniv. Press, 5th ed. 1997). Schumpeter's biased but brilliant account traces its origins mainly to Cournot and lesser authors who wrote in the first half of the nineteenth century. *See* SCHUMPETER, HISTORY OF ECONOMIC ANALYSIS, *supra* note 59, at 463; William Jaffe, *Leon Walras's Role in the "Marginal Revolution" of the 1870s*, 4 HIS. POL. ECON. 379 (1972).
62. Alfred Marshall & Mary Paley Marshall, THE ECONOMICS OF INDUSTRY (London: Macmillan, 1879). *See* Lionel Robbins, Richard T. Ely lecture, Economics and Political Economy, 71 AM. ECON. REV. 1 (May 1981).
63. William Stanley Jevons, THE THEORY OF POLITICAL ECONOMY 1, 59–60 (London: Macmillan, 1871). Alfred Marshall also deserves some credit. *See* 1 THE EARLY ECONOMIC WRITINGS OF ALFRED MARSHALL 2 (J.K. Whitaker ed., London: Macmillan, 1975).
64. Carl Menger, PRINCIPLES OF ECONOMICS ([1871], Eng. trans. by James Dingwell & Bert F. Hoselitz, New York: NYU Press, 1981). *See* Herbert Hovenkamp, *The First Great Law & Economics Movement*, 42 STAN. L. REV. 993, 996–97 (1990).
65. Clark probably came to his marginalism independently. *See* John B. Clark, THE PHILOSOPHY OF WEALTH: ECONOMIC PRINCIPLES NEWLY FORMULATED, chs. 4–5 (Boston: Ginn, 1886); SCHUMPETER, HISTORY OF ECONOMIC ANALYSIS, *supra* note 59, at 870.
66. Alfred Marshall, PRINCIPLES OF ECONOMICS 158 (London: Macmillan, 1890). *See also id.* at 15–16 (8th ed. 1920).
67. Joseph A. Schumpeter, Robinson's Economics of Imperfect Competition, 42 J. POL. ECON. 249, 256 (1934).
68. *See* David McCullough, THE GREAT BRIDGE: THE EPIC STORY OF THE BUILDING OF THE BROOKLYN BRIDGE (New York: Simon & Schuster, 1983); Jill Jones, CONQUERING GOTHAM: A GILDED AGE EPIC: THE CONSTRUCTION OF PENN STATION AND ITS TUNNELS (New York: Penguin, 2008); David McCullough, THE PATH BETWEEN THE SEAS: THE CREATION OF THE PANAMA CANAL, 1870–1914 (New York: Simon & Schuster, 1978); David Carden, THE ANDERTON BOAT LIFT (Witney, England: Black Dwarf, 2000). On the Corliss Centennial Engine, including a frontpiece photograph, *see* Howard Mumford Jones, THE AGE OF ENERGY: VARIETIES OF AMERICAN EXPERIENCE, 1865–1915 (New York: Viking, 1971).
69. MARSHALL, PRINCIPLES OF ECONOMICS, *supra* note 66, Book V, chs. 1–3, Book VI, ch. 11 (1890).
70. Irving Fisher, Mathematical Investigations in the Theory of Value and Prices, 9 TRANSACTIONS OF THE CONNECTICUT ACADEMY 28, 38 (July 1892). The

machine is illustrated on page 38. *See* William C. Brainard & Herbert E. Scarf, *How to Compute Equilibrium Prices in 1891*, 64 AM. J. ECON. & SOC. 57 (2005).

71. Dr. Miles Medical Co. v. John D. Park & Sons Co., 220 U.S. 373, 412 (1911).
72. Holmes to Frank Taussig, July 19, 1911, OWH Papers, *quoted in* THE LEGACY OF OLIVER WENDELL HOLMES, JR. 281 (Robert W. Gordon ed., Palo Alto, CA: Stanford, 1992).
73. International Harvester Co. of Am. v. Kentucky, 234 U.S. 216, 221 (1914).
74. *See* Chapter 14.
75. *See* Yuval P. Yonay, THE STRUGGLE OVER THE SOUL OF ECONOMICS: INSTITUTIONALIST AND NEOCLASSICAL ECONOMISTS IN AMERICA BETWEEN THE WARS 29–48 (Princeton, NJ: Princeton Univ. Press, 1998).
76. MARSHALL, PRINCIPLES OF ECONOMICS, *supra* note 66, at 10–13 (1890).
77. *E.g.*, Louis Menand, THE METAPHYSICAL CLUB: A STORY OF IDEAS IN AMERICA (New York: Farrar, Straus, and Giroux, 2001).
78. Thorstein Veblen, *Why Is Economics Not an Evolutionary Science?*, 12 Q.J. ECON. 373, 384 (1898).
79. BENTHAM, THEORY OF LEGISLATION, *supra* note 60, at 105.
80. *Id.* at 107–08, 325–26.
81. *Cf.* Gary S. Becker, *Crime and Punishment: An Economic Approach*, 76 J. POL. ECON. 169 (1968).

CHAPTER 2

1. *See* Chapter 3; Loving v. Virginia, 388 U.S. 1 (1967) (striking down Virginia statute banning interracial marriage).
2. *See, e.g.*, Hamilton Cravens, THE TRIUMPH OF EVOLUTION: AMERICAN SCIENTISTS AND THE HEREDITY-ENVIRONMENT CONTROVERSY, 1900–1941, at 157–90 (Philadelphia: Univ. of Pennsylvania Press, 1978); John P. Jackson, JR. & Nadine M. Weidman, RACE, RACISM, AND SCIENCE: SOCIAL IMPACT AND INTERACTION (Santa Barbara, CA: ABC-CLIO, 2004). On the survival of genetics, *see* Richard J. Herrnstein & Charles Murray, THE BELL CURVE: INTELLIGENCE AND CLASS STRUCTURE IN AMERICAN LIFE (New York: Free Press, 1994).
3. *See* Edward Lurie, LOUIS AGASSIZ: A LIFE IN SCIENCE (Chicago: Univ. of Chicago Press, 1960); Jon H. Roberts, *Louis Agassiz on Scientific Method, Polygenism, and Transmutation: A Reassessment*, 2 ALMAGEST 76 (2011). *See also* Herbert Hovenkamp, SCIENCE AND RELIGION IN AMERICA, 1800–1860, at 165–86 (Philadelphia: Univ. of Pennsylvania Press, 1978); CRAVENS, *supra* note 2, at 157–90.
4. *E.g.*, Edward A. Ross (Progressive sociologist), *The Causes of Race Superiority*, 18 ANNALS AM. ACAD. POL. & SOC. SCI. 67, 67–89 (1901); G. Stanley Hall (Progressive psychologist), *The Negro in Africa and America*, 12 PEDAGOGICAL SEMINARY 350 (1905); John R. Commons (Progressive economist), RACES AND

IMMIGRANTS IN AMERICA (New York: Macmillan, 1907); Franklin Henry Giddings (Progressive psychologist), THE PRINCIPLES OF SOCIOLOGY 328 (New York: Macmillan, 1896).

5. EDWARD A. ROSS, SOCIAL CONTROL (New York: Macmillan, 1901); *and see* DOROTHY ROSS, THE ORIGINS OF AMERICAN SOCIAL SCIENCE 176–80 (New York: Cambridge Univ. Press, 1991).
6. ROSS, SOCIAL CONTROL, *supra* note 5, at 60–61.
7. *See* Peter Bowler, THE ECLIPSE OF DARWINISM: ANTI-DARWINIAN EVOLUTION THEORIES IN THE DECADES AROUND 1900, at 60–66 (Baltimore: Johns Hopkins, 1983); Edward Larson, EVOLUTION: THE REMARKABLE HISTORY OF A SCIENTIFIC THEORY (New York: Modern Library, 2004).
8. Charles Horton Cooley, SOCIAL ORGANIZATION: A STUDY OF THE LARGER MIND 296 (New York: Scribner, 1909). Cooley was a sociologist at the University of Michigan, and the son of Thomas M. Cooley, Michigan Supreme Court justice and influential treatise author.
9. Simon N. Patten, *The Failure of Biologic Sociology*, 4 ANNALS AM. ACAD. POL. & SOC. SCI. 63 (1894); Simon N. Patten, *The Relation of Economics to Sociology*, 5 ANNALS AM. ACAD. POL. & SOC. SCI. 117 (1895); Franklin H. Giddings, *Utility, Economics and Sociology*, 5 ANNALS AM. ACAD. POL. & SOC. SCI. 82 (1894).
10. ROSS, SOCIAL CONTROL, *supra* note 5, at 106, 110, 112, 345.
11. *See* Louis Menand, THE METAPHYSICAL CLUB 49–69 (New York: Farrar, Straus & Giroux, 2001); Thomas C. Grey, *Holmes and Legal Pragmatism*, 41 STAN. L. REV. 787 (1989); Max H. Fisch, *Justice Holmes, the Prediction Theory of Law, and Pragmatism*, *in* PEIRCE, SEMEIOTIC, AND PRAGMATISM: ESSAYS BY MAX FISCH 6 (Kenneth L. Ketner & Christian J.W. Kloesel eds., Bloomington: Indiana Univ. Press, 1986); Robert Samuel Summers, INSTRUMENTALISM AND AMERICAN LEGAL THEORY 20–34 (Ithaca, NY: Cornell Univ. Press, 1982).
12. Oliver Wendell Holmes, JR., THE COMMON LAW 11, 19, 34 (Boston: Little, Brown, 1881), citing Edward Tylor, PRIMITIVE CULTURE: RESEARCHES INTO THE DEVELOPMENT OF MYTHOLOGY, PHILOSOPHY, RELIGION, ART, AND CUSTOM (London: J. Murray, 1871).
13. *E.g.*, David M. Rabban, LAW'S HISTORY: AMERICAN LEGAL THOUGHT AND THE TRANSATLANTIC TURN TO HISTORY, 215–67 (New York: Cambridge Univ. Press, 2013); G. Edward White, OLIVER WENDELL HOLMES, JR. (New York: Oxford Univ. Press, 2006); G. Edward White, JUSTICE OLIVER WENDELL HOLMES: LAW AND THE INNER SELF (New York: Oxford Univ. Press, 1995); Mark DeWolfe Howe, OLIVER WENDELL HOLMES: THE SHAPING YEARS (Cambridge, MA: Harvard Univ. Press, 1957).
14. RABBAN LAW'S HISTORY, *supra* note 13, at 513–14.
15. HOLMES, COMMON LAW, *supra* note 12, at 108. *See* Harry L. Pohlman, JUSTICE OLIVER WENDELL HOLMES & UTILITARIAN JURISPRUDENCE (Cambridge, MA: Harvard Univ. Press, 1984).
16. HOLMES, COMMON LAW, *supra* note 12, at 117, 149, 300–05.

17. *See also* Oliver Wendell Holmes, Jr., *The Theory of Torts*, 7 AM. L. REV. 652 (1873); Holmes, *Primitive Notions in Modern Law*, Part I, 10 AM. L. REV. 422 (1876); Part II, 11 AM. L. REV. 641 (1877).
18. *See* Samuel L. Williston, THE LAW OF CONTRACTS (New York: Baker, Voorhis & Co., 1920); Arthur L. Corbin, *Quasi-contractual Obligations*, 21 YALE L.J. 533 (1912); Arthur L. Corbin, *Discharge of Contracts*, 22 YALE L.J. 513 (1913).
19. Mainly, in Holmes, *The Theory of Torts, supra* note 17; and HOLMES, COMMON LAW, *supra* note 12, chs. 3 & 4.
20. HOLMES, COMMON LAW, *supra* note 12, at 49–51.
21. *Id.* at 63, 108, 303.
22. Warren A. Seavey, *Negligence—Subjective or Objective*, 41 HARV. L. REV. 1, 10, 27 (1927).
23. United States v. Carroll Towing Co., 159 F.2d 169 (2d Cir. 1947). *See* Chapter 7.
24. Oliver Wendell Holmes, Jr., *The Path of the Law*, 10 HARV. L. REV. 457, 458, 461, 471, 473–74 (1897).
25. HOLMES, COMMON LAW, *supra* note 12, at 92. *See* Nicholas St. John Green, *Proximate and Remote Cause*, 4 AM. L. REV. 201 (1870). *See* Chapter 7.
26. Charles Sanders Peirce, COLLECTED PAPERS OF CHARLES SANDERS PEIRCE (Charles Hartshorne & Paul Weiss eds., six vols, Cambridge, MA: Harvard Univ. Press, 1931–1935), VI at 275, 28–66; William James, ESSAYS IN RADICAL EMPIRICISM 155 *et seq.* (New York: Longmans, Green, 1912).
27. HOLMES, COMMON LAW, *supra* note 12, at 49–51.
28. *E.g.*, William James, PRAGMATISM: A NEW NAME FOR SOME OLD WAYS OF THINKING, ch. 1 (New York: Longmans, Green, 1907).
29. HOLMES, COMMON LAW, *supra* note 12, at 146–47.
30. On this point, *see* 2 Mark DeWolfe Howe, JUSTICE OLIVER WENDELL HOLMES: THE PROVING YEARS, 1870–1882, at 44–49 (Cambridge, MA: Harvard Univ. Press, 1963); E. Donald Elliott, *Holmes and Evolution: Legal Process as Artificial Intelligence*, 13 J. LEGAL STUD. 113, 126–40 (1984); Jan Vetter, *The Evolution of Holmes, Holmes and Evolution*, 72 CALIF. L. REV. 343, 363 (1984).
31. *E.g.*, Catherine Drinker Bowen, YANKEE FROM OLYMPUS: JUSTICE HOLMES AND HIS FAMILY (Boston: Little, Brown, 1944).
32. Oliver W. Holmes, Jr., *Law in Science and Science in Law*, 12 HARV. L. REV. 443 (1899). *See* Herbert Hovenkamp, *Evolutionary Models in Jurisprudence*, 64 TEX. L. REV. 645, 659–62 (1985).
33. Oliver Wendell Holmes, Jr., "Introduction," RATIONAL BASIS OF LEGAL INSTITUTIONS xxxi (John H. Wigmore & Albert Kocourek eds., New York: Macmillan, 1923).
34. Underhill Moore, *Rational Basis of Legal Institutions*, 23 COLUM. L. REV. 609, 612, 617 (1923).
35. *E.g.*, Philip P. Wiener, EVOLUTION AND THE FOUNDERS OF PRAGMATISM 172–89 (Cambridge, MA: Harvard Univ. Press, 1949).

36. 1 Cesare Lombroso, L'HOMME CRIMINEL 155–58 (Paris: Felix Alcan, 1887). On Lombroso's work, *see* Stephen Jay Gould, THE MISMEASURE OF MAN 123–43 (New York: Norton, 1981); David G. Horn, THE CRIMINAL BODY: LOMBROSO AND THE ANATOMY OF DEVIANCE (New York: Routledge, 2003).
37. Cesare Lombroso & Guglielmo Ferrero, CRIMINAL WOMAN, THE PROSTITUTE, AND THE NORMAL WOMAN (1893; English trans. by Nicole Rafter & Mary Gibson, Durham, NC: Duke Univ. Press, 2004).
38. August Drahms, THE CRIMINAL, HIS PERSONNEL AND ENVIRONMENT: A SCIENTIFIC STUDY 144, 133, 373 (New York: Macmillan, 1900). For a survey of other contemporaneous studies, *see* Leonard Doncaster, HEREDITY IN THE LIGHT OF RECENT RESEARCH 165–66 (Cambridge: Cambridge Univ. Press, 1910).
39. *See* Harry C. Sharp, "Vasectomy as a Means of Preventing Procreation in Defectives," 53 J. AM. MED. ASSN. 1897 (1899). *See* S. Severin Buschmann, *Vasectomy*, 2 IND. L. J. 259 (1926).
40. *E.g.*, C.N. Ellinwood, *Vasectomy: An Argument for Its Therapeutic Use in Certain Mental Diseases and as a Means of Diminishing Crime and the Number of Criminals*, 2 CAL. STATE J. MED. 60 (1904).
41. *Laws of Indiana*, 1907, at 377–78 (Indianapolis: Burford Contractor for State Printing, 1907). *See* Robert L. Osgood, *The Menace of the Feebleminded: George Bliss, Amos Butler, and the Indiana Committee on Mental Defectives*, 97 IND. MAG. HIST. 253 (2001); Alexandra Minna Stern, *"We Cannot Make a Silk Purse Out of a Sow's Ear": Eugenics in the Hoosier Heartland*, 103 IND. MAG. HIST. 3 (2007).
42. Williams v. Smith, 190 Ind. 526 (1921).
43. Buschmann, *Vasectomy, supra* note 39, at 260. *See* State v. Feilen, 70 Wash. 65, 126 P. 75 (1912) (tracing the history of vasectomy as a crime control device; vasectomy of defendant convicted of raping a child was not cruel and unusual punishment). *See also* Edwin Black, WAR AGAINST THE WEAK: EUGENICS AND AMERICA'S CAMPAIGN TO CREATE A MASTER RACE (New York: Four Walls Eight Windows, 2003); Mark A. Largent, BREEDING CONTEMPT: THE HISTORY OF COERCED STERILIZATION IN THE UNITED STATES (New Brunswick: Rutgers Univ. Press, 2008); Marouf Arif Hasian, JR., THE RHETORIC OF EUGENICS IN ANGLO-AMERICAN THOUGHT (Athens: Univ. of Georgia Press, 1996); Gregory M. Dorr, *Defective or Disabled?: Race, Medicine, and Eugenics in Progressive Era Virginia and Alabama*, 5 J. GILDED AGE & PROGRESSIVE ERA 359 (2006).
44. Buck v. Bell, 274 U.S. 200, 206–08 (1927) (construing Va. Code § 1095h (1924)). *See* Gregory Michael Dorr, SEGREGATION'S SCIENCE: EUGENICS AND SOCIETY IN VIRGINIA (Charlottesville: Univ. of Virginia Press, 2008); Paul A. Lombardo, THREE GENERATIONS, NO IMBECILES: EUGENICS, THE SUPREME COURT, AND *BUCK V. BELL* (Baltimore: Johns Hopkins Press, 2008); Thomas C. Leonard, *Eugenics and Economics in the Progressive Era*, 19 J. ECON. PERSP. 207 (2005). On

the Catholic position, *see* Edward J. Larson, SEX, RACE, AND SCIENCE: EUGENICS IN THE DEEP SOUTH 107–15 (Baltimore: Johns Hopkins Univ. Press, 1995).

45. *See, e.g.*, Joel D. Hunter, *Sterilization of Criminals*, 5 J. CRIM. L. CRIMINOLOGY & POLICE SCI. 514 (1915). For a critique written after the movement had subsided, *see* Stanley P. Davies & Frankwood E. Williams, SOCIAL CONTROL OF THE MENTALLY DEFICIENT 94–120 (New York: Thomas Y. Crowell, 1930). *See also* CRAVENS, TRIUMPH OF EVOLUTION, *supra* note 2; Mark H. Haller, EUGENICS: HEREDITARIAN ATTITUDES IN AMERICAN THOUGHT (New Brunswick, NJ: Rutgers, 1963).

46. Mickle v. Henrichs, 262 F. 687 (D. Nev. 1918).

47. F. Emory Lyon, *Race Betterment and the Crime Doctors*, 5 J. CRIM. L. & CRIMINOLOGY 887 (1915).

48. *Buck*, 274 U.S. at 207. *See* Mary L. Dudziak, *Oliver Wendell Holmes as a Eugenic Reformer: Rhetoric in the Writing of Constitutional Law*, 71 IOWA L. REV. 833 (1986).

49. Albert E. Wiggam, *The Rising Tide of Degeneracy: What Everybody Ought to Know about Eugenics*, 53 WORLD'S WORK 25 (1927).

50. Albert E. Wiggam, THE FRUIT OF THE FAMILY TREE (Indianapolis, IN: Bobbs-Merrill, 1924).

51. Steven Selden, *Transforming Better Babies into Fitter Families: Archival Resources and the History of the American Eugenics Movement, 1908–1930*, 149 PROC. AM. PHIL. SOC'Y 199 (2005) (containing amazing photos).

52. *See* Charles Buckman Goring, THE ENGLISH CONVICT: A STATISTICAL STUDY (London: H.M. Stationery, 1913); William A. White, *Method and Motive from the Psychiatric Viewpoint*, 5 J. AM. INST. CRIM. L. & CRIMINOLOGY 348 (1914). Tracing the development is Max Schlapp & Edward Smith, THE NEW CRIMINOLOGY: A CONSIDERATION OF THE CHEMICAL CAUSATION OF ABNORMAL BEHAVIOR (New York: Boni & Liveright, 1928).

53. Arthur Cleveland Hall, CRIME IN ITS RELATIONS TO SOCIAL PROGRESS 380–86 (New York: Columbia, 1902).

54. *E.g.*, Sigmund Freud, THE PSYCHOPATHOLOGY OF EVERYDAY LIFE (1901; Eng. trans. by A.A. Brill, London: Unwin, 1914). *See* Lucille Ritvo, DARWIN'S INFLUENCE ON FREUD: A TALE OF TWO SCIENCES (New Haven, CT: Yale, 1990); Frank Sulloway, FREUD, BIOLOGIST OF THE MIND: BEYOND THE PSYCHOANALYTIC LEGEND 238 (New York: Basic, 1979).

55. New York: Macmillan, 1923, 18–19, 204.

56. *See* William Graham Sumner, FOLKWAYS: A STUDY OF THE SOCIOLOGICAL IMPORTANCE OF USAGES, MANNERS, CUSTOMS, MORES, AND MORALS (Boston: Ginn, 1906).

57. William Alanson White, INSANITY AND THE CRIMINAL LAW 13 (London: Macmillan, 1923). White borrowed several ideas from James George Frazer, a British anthropologist whose book *The Golden Bough* was a highly popular and influential theory about the evolution of human cultural norms. *See*

James G. Frazer, THE GOLDEN BOUGH: A STUDY IN COMPARATIVE RELIGION (London: Macmillan, 1890).

58. WHITE, INSANITY, *supra* note 57, at 229.
59. *See* William A. White, *Sterilization of Criminals*, 8 J. AM. INST. CRIM. L. & CRIMINOLOGY 499, 500 (1917). On the Institute, *see* Jennifer Devroye, *The Rise and Fall of the American Institute of Criminal Law and Criminology*, 100 J. CRIM. L. & CRIMINOLOGY 7 (2010).
60. The proposed statute is discussed in Edwin R. Keedy, *Insanity and Criminal Responsibility*, 30 HARV. L. REV. 535, 724 (Parts I and II, 1917).
61. John Charles Bucknill, UNSOUNDNESS OF MIND IN RELATION TO CRIMINAL ACTS 117 (London: S. Highley, 1854).
62. Sage v. State, 91 Ind. 141, 145 (1883); United States v. Lee, 15 D.C. (4 Mackey) 489 (1886). *See also* Commonwealth v. Wireback, 190 Pa. 138, 42 A. 542 (1899); Commonwealth v. Cooper, 219 Mass. 1, 106 N.E. 545 (1914); Kirby v. State, 68 Tex. Crim. 63, 150 S.W. 455 (1912).
63. People v. Willard, 150 Cal. 543, 89 P. 124 (1907).
64. GILBERT'S CRIMINAL CODE § 1220 (Albany, NY: Matthew Bender, 1923).
65. Clarence Darrow, CRIME: ITS CAUSE AND TREATMENT 40 (New York: Crowell, 1922).
66. The text of Darrow's appeal can be found at http://law2.umkc.edu/faculty/projects/ftrials/leoploeb/darrowclosing.html.
67. Hal Higdon, THE CRIME OF THE CENTURY: THE LEOPOLD AND LOEB CASE (New York: Putnam, 1975); Paula Fass, *Making and Remaking an Event: The Leopold and Loeb Case in American Culture*, 80 J. AM. HIS. 919 (1993). A contemporary account focusing on the medical questions is Maurice Urstein, LEOPOLD AND LOEB: A PSYCHIATRIC-PSYCHOLOGICAL STUDY (New York: Lecouver Press, 1924).
68. Quoted in HIGDON, *supra* note 67, at 22.
69. *A Symposium of Comments from the Legal Profession, in the Loeb-Leopold Murder of Franks in Chicago, May 21, 1924*, 15 J. CRIM. L. & CRIMINOLOGY 395, 404 (1925); John H. Wigmore, *The Judge's Sentence in the Loeb-Leopold Murder*, 19 ILL. L.REV. 167 (1924).
70. 1 Francis Wharton & William Draper Lewis, A TREATISE ON CRIMINAL LAW 49 & n.1 (Philadelphia: Kay, 1st ed. 1846; 10th ed. 1896).
71. Sheldon S. Glueck, *Ethics, Psychology and the Criminal Responsibility of the Insane*, 14 J. CRIM. L. & CRIMINOLOGY 208 (1923).
72. Roscoe Pound, *Introduction*, FRANCIS B. SAYRE, A SELECTION OF CASES ON CRIMINAL LAW xxxvii (Rochester, NY: Lawyers' Cooperative 1927).
73. Sheldon S. Glueck, MENTAL DISORDER AND THE CRIMINAL LAW 89, 93–95 (Boston: Little, Brown, 1925).
74. John Barker Waite, *Irresistible Impulse and Criminal Liability*, 23 MICH. L. REV. 443, 450–51 (1925).
75. Thomas V. Moore, DYNAMIC PSYCHOLOGY 9 (Philadelphia: Lippincott, 1924).

CHAPTER 3

1. *See* Reginald Horsman, RACE AND MANIFEST DESTINY: THE ORIGINS OF AMERICAN RACIAL ANGLO-SAXONISM 117–57 (Cambridge, MA: Harvard Univ. Press, 1981); Michael J. Klarman, FROM JIM CROW TO CIVIL RIGHTS: THE SUPREME COURT AND THE STRUGGLE FOR RACIAL EQUALITY 360–67 (New York: Oxford Univ. Press, 2004). On the Progressive Era in particular, *see* David W. Southern, THE PROGRESSIVE ERA AND RACE: REACTION AND REFORM, 1900–1917 (Wheeling, IL: Harlan Davidson, 2005).
2. Brief for Defendant in Error, Muller v. Oregon, 208 U.S. 412 (1908). *See* Chapter 13.
3. Berea College v. Kentucky, 211 U.S. 45 (1908). On Berea College, *see* Shannon H. Wilson, BEREA COLLEGE: AN ILLUSTRATED HISTORY (Lexington: Univ. Press of Kentucky, 2006); Elisabeth Sinclair Peck, BEREA'S FIRST CENTURY, 1855–1955 (Lexington: Univ. Press of Kentucky, 1955).
4. Kentucky, Maryland, Delaware, and Missouri.
5. *See* Stephen J. Gould, THE MISMEASURE OF MAN 20–145 (New York: Norton, 1981); Hamilton Cravens, THE TRIUMPH OF EVOLUTION: AMERICAN SCIENTISTS AND THE HEREDITY-ENVIRONMENT CONTROVERSY, 1900–1941, at 15–55, 157–265 (Philadelphia: Univ. of Pennsylvania Press, 1978).
6. Plessy v. Ferguson, 163 U.S. 537, 544 (1896).
7. *Berea College*, 123 Ky. at 221, 225–26, 94 S.W. at 626–28. *See* 211 U.S. 45, 53–58 (1908); Note, *Constitutionality of a Statute Compelling the Color Line in Private Schools*, 22 HARV. L. REV. 217, 218 (1909); *The Berea College Case*, 14 VA. L. REG. 643, 643–44 (1908).
8. *Brief for Defendant in Error* 40–41 (discussing Sanford B. Hunt, *The Negro as Soldier*, 7 ANTHROPOLIGICAL REV. 40 (1869)). On Hunt, *see* John S. Haller, JR., OUTCASTS FROM EVOLUTION: SCIENTIFIC ATTITUDES OF RACIAL INFERIORITY, 1859–1900, at 30–34 (Urbana: Univ. of Illinois Press, 1971).
9. *See* Samuel George Morton, CRANIA AMERICANA: OR, A COMPARATIVE VIEW OF THE SKULLS OF VARIOUS ABORIGINAL NATIONS OF NORTH AND SOUTH AMERICA 290 (Philadelphia: Dobson, 1839). Morton's work was later continued by Josiah C. Nott & George R. Gliddon, TYPES OF MANKIND (Philadelphia: Lippincott, 1854). *See* John P. Jackson, JR. & Nadine M. Weidman, RACE, RACISM, AND SCIENCE: SOCIAL IMPACT AND INTERACTION 39–59 (Santa Barbara, CA: ABC-CLIO, 2005); William R. Stanton, THE LEOPARD'S SPOTS: SCIENTIFIC ATTITUDES TOWARD RACE IN AMERICA, 1815–1859, at 24–44 (Chicago: Univ. of Chicago Press, 1960).
10. Samuel George Morton, *Observations on the Size of the Brain in Various Races and Families of Man*, 4 PROC. ACAD. NAT. SCI. PHILADELPHIA, 209, 221–24 (1849); *and see* Samuel G. Morton, CRANIA AEGYPTIACA: OR, OBSERVATIONS ON EGYPTIAN ETHNOGRAPHY, DERIVED FROM ANATOMY, HISTORY AND THE MONUMENTS (Philadelphia: J. Penington, 1844).

11. *Brief for Defendant in Error* 42, Berea College.
12. *Id.* at 41, quoting William B. Smith, THE COLOR LINE: A BRIEF IN BEHALF OF THE UNBORN 81 (New York: McClure, Phillips, 1905).
13. *E.g.*, Alexander Bickel & Benno Schmidt, THE JUDICIARY AND RESPONSIBLE GOVERNMENT, 1910–1921, at 731 n.10, IX OLIVER WENDELL HOLMES DEVISE HISTORY OF THE SUPREME COURT OF THE UNITED STATES (New York: Macmillan, 1984).
14. *See* Paul A. Carter, THE SPIRITUAL CRISIS OF THE GILDED AGE (DeKalb, IL: Northern Illinois Univ. Press, 1971) (post-Darwin); Herbert Hovenkamp, SCIENCE AND RELIGION IN AMERICA, 1800–1860, at 165–210 (Philadelphia: Univ. of Pennsylvania Press, 1978) (pre-Darwin).
15. Perhaps the earliest statement of this view is Samuel S. Haldeman, *Enumeration of Recent Fresh-Water Mollusca*, 4 B.J. NAT. HIST. 468, 481–84 (1844). Darwin agreed. *See* Darwin to Charles Lyell, June 21, 1859, in Darwin Correspondence Database, http://www.darwinproject.ac.uk/entry2470 (last visited Nov. 30, 2013).
16. *See* C. Vann Woodward, THE STRANGE CAREER OF JIM CROW (New York: Oxford Univ. Press, 1955). The controversy over Woodward's original "Jim Crow" thesis is summarized in Howard N. Rabinowitz, *More than the Woodward Thesis: Assessing the Strange Career of Jim Crow*, 75 J. AM. HIST. 842 (1988). *See also* Don E. Fehrenbacher, THE DRED SCOTT CASE 580–82 ((New York: Oxford, 1978). *Cf.* Pamela Brandwein, RETHINKING THE JUDICIAL SETTLEMENT OF RECONSTRUCTION (New York: Cambridge Univ. Press, 2011), who sees the judicial system as more protective of black civil rights than has been the consensus.
17. Howard N. Rabinowitz, RACE RELATIONS IN THE URBAN SOUTH: 1865–1890, at 259–81 (New York: Oxford Univ. Press, 1978). On exclusion's extensions into the north, *see* Margaret Garb, *Drawing the "Color Line": Race and Real Estate in Early Twentieth-Century Chicago*, 32 J. URB. HIST. 773 (2006); WHEN DID SOUTHERN SEGREGATION BEGIN? (John David Smith ed., New York: Palgrave, 2002).
18. *See* Howard N. Rabinowitz, *From Exclusion to Segregation: Southern Race Relations, 1865–1890*, 63 J. AM. HIST. 325, 325–27 (1976).
19. *See* FEHRENBACHER, DRED SCOTT, *supra* note 16, at 35.
20. RABINOWITZ, RACE RELATIONS, *supra* note 17, at 162–64.
21. *See* An Act to Establish a System of Public Instruction, Pub. L. No. 53, 1870 Ga. Laws 49, 57; An Act to Establish and Maintain a System of Free Common Schools for the State of Arkansas, No. LII, § 107, 1868 Ark. Acts 163, 196; An Act to Establish a System of Public Free Schools for the State of Texas, ch. LXVIII, § 3(7), 1870 Tex. Gen. Laws 113, 114. The 1876 Texas Constitution, written immediately after Reconstruction, made segregated public education mandatory. Tex. Const. 1876, art. VII, § 7; *see also* Act of Aug. 11, 1868, 1868 Ala. Acts 148 (segregation in public schools mandatory unless all parents consented to integration); Act of

Apr. 12, 1869, ch. 184, § 50, 1868–1869 N.C. Pub. Laws 458, 471 (separate schools for children of each race). On Tennessee, *see* Act of Mar. 5, 1867, ch. XXVII, § 17, 1866–1867 Tenn. Pub. Acts 33, 39–40; Joseph H. Cartwright, The Triumph of Jim Crow: Tennessee Race Relations in the 1880's, at 7–13 (Knoxville: Univ. of Tenn. Press, 1976).

22. *See* Brief for Appellees on Reargument at 31, app. B at 22–23, app. C at 8–18, Briggs v. Elliott, *consolidated with* Brown v. Bd. of Educ., 347 U.S. 483 (1954).
23. *See* RABINOWITZ, RACE RELATIONS, *supra* note 17, at 182–91.
24. *Id.* at 327; Roger A. Fischer, *A Pioneer Protest: The New Orleans Street-Car Controversy of 1867*, 53 J. Negro Hist. 219 (1968).
25. DeCuir v. Benson, 27 La. Ann. 1 (1875); Hall v. DeCuir, 95 U.S. 485 (1877).
26. *See* Pearson v. Duane, 71 U.S. (4 Wall.) 605, 615 (1866); Brown v. Memphis & C.R. Co., 5 F. 499, 502 (C.C.W.D. Tenn. 1880).
27. Act of Feb. 23, 1869, No. 38, § 1, 1869 La. Acts 37.
28. *Benson*, 27 La. Ann. at 9; *Record* 9, *Hall*, 95 U.S. 485.
29. Act of Oct. 18, 1870, Pub. L. No. 258, 1870 Ga. Laws 398.
30. *See* Stanley J. Folmsbee, *The Origin of the First "Jim Crow" Law*, 15 J.S. HIST. 235 (1949).
31. WILLIAM GILLETTE, RETREAT FROM RECONSTRUCTION, 1869–1879, at 186–235 (Baton Rouge: Louisian State Univ. Press, 1979).
32. The Civil Rights Cases, 109 U.S. 3, 25 (1883).
33. 163 U.S. 537, 551 (1896).
34. Civil Rights Act of 1875, ch. 114, § 1, 18 Stat. 335, 335–36 (emphasis added).
35. United States v. Newcomer, 11 Phila. 519, 27 F. Cas. 127, 128 (D.C. Pa. 1876).
36. Charge to Grand Jury—The Civil Rights Act, 30 F. Cas. 999, 1000–01 (C.C.W.D.N.C. 1875) (No. 18,258).
37. United States v. Dodge, 25 F. Cas. 882, 883 (W.D. Tex. 1877) (No. 14,976). In his generally excellent book on the subject, Charles Mangum misconstrued *Dodge,* observing that it "upheld" the 1875 Civil Rights statute but not mentioning that it also held that separate but equal accommodations complied with it. See Charles Staples Mangum, THE LEGAL STATUS OF THE NEGRO 29 (Chapel Hill: Univ. of N.C. Press, 1940).
38. *Record,* Civil Rights Cases, 109 U.S. at 3. *See also* Gray v. Cincinnati S. Ry., 11 F. 683 (C.C. Ohio, 1882) (Ohio railroad had duty to provide cars that were equal, although not necessarily integrated, and thus could not relegate Afro-American woman with sick child to the smoking car). *Cf.* Smoot v. Kentucky Cent. Ry. Co., 13 F. 337 (C.C.D. Ky. 1882) (declaring Civil Rights Act unconstitutional and holding that train could exclude Afro-American woman with first class ticket from ladies' car).
39. *Brief of the United States* 1–2, The Civil Rights Cases, 109 U.S. 3 (1883).
40. Act of July 23, 1866, ch. 217, 14 Stat. 216. *See Brief for Respondents* 12–13, Bolling v. Sharpe, 347 U.S. 497 (1954).

41. State v. McCann, 21 Ohio St. 198 (1871).
42. GEORGE A. RUTHERGLEN, CIVIL RIGHTS IN THE SHADOW OF SLAVERY: THE CONSTITUTION, COMMON LAW, AND THE CIVIL RIGHTS ACT OF 1866, at 88–90 (New York: Oxford Univ. Press, 2012).
43. United States v. Buntin, 3 Ky. L. Rptr. 630, 10 F. 730, 735 (C.C. Ohio 1882).
44. Act of Mar. 2, 1888, ch. 27, § 1, 1888 Miss. Laws 48.
45. Act of July 10, 1890, No. 111, § 1, 1890 La. Acts 152, 153.
46. Louisville, N.O. & T. Ry. v. Mississippi, 133 U.S. 587, 594 (1890) (Harlan, J., dissenting). Harlan was the lone dissenter in the *Civil Rights Cases*. Justice Bradley was one of the dissenters in the *Slaughter-House Cases*, which had declined to apply the Fourteenth Amendment to a state monopoly provision. Slaughter-House Cases, 83 U.S. 36, 112–14 (1872). *See* Herbert Hovenkamp, ENTERPRISE AND AMERICAN LAW, 1836–1937, at 105–24 (Cambridge, MA: Harvard Univ. Press, 1991).
47. *Plessy v. Ferguson*, 163 U.S. 537, 555–64 (1896).
48. Brief of the State of Mississippi at 4, Louisville, N.O. & T. Ry. v. Mississippi, 133 U.S. 587 (1890).
49. On the facts and the racial classification system, see *Brief on Behalf of Defendant in Error, Plessy v. Ferguson*; and see Mark E. Elliott, COLOR-BLIND JUSTICE: ALBION TOURGEE AND THE QUEST FOR RACIAL EQUALITY FROM THE CIVIL WAR TO *PLESSY V. FERGUSON* 262–96 (New York: Oxford Univ. Press, 2006).
50. *Plessy*, 163 U.S. at 551–52.
51. *See, e.g.*, Henry Wiencek, MASTER OF THE MOUNTAIN: THOMAS JEFFERSON AND HIS SLAVES (New York: Farrar, Straus and Giroux, 2012); Lucia C. Stanton, "THOSE WHO LABOR FOR MY HAPPINESS": SLAVERY AT THOMAS JEFFERSON'S MONTICELLO (Charlottesville: Univ. of Virginia Press, 2012).
52. Charge to Grand Jury—The Civil Rights Act, 30 F. Cas. 999, 1000 (C.C.W.D.N.C. 1875) (No. 18,258).
53. *See* 7 Charles Fairman, THE HISTORY OF THE SUPREME COURT OF THE UNITED STATES: RECONSTRUCTION AND REUNION, 1864–1888, pt. 2, at 564 (Holmes Devise History of the Supreme Court, New York: Macmillan 1987). On Bradley's position on civil rights, *see* G. Edward White, *The Origin of Civil Rights in America*, 64 CASE WEST. RES. L. REV. (2014).
54. *See* Marvin Harris, THE RISE OF ANTHROPOLOGICAL THEORY: A HISTORY OF THEORIES OF CULTURE 80–179 (New York: Crowell, 1968).
55. GOULD, MISMEASURE, *supra* note 5, at 30–112. Dispute continues over Gould's claim that Morton intentionally mismeasured skulls in order to exaggerate racial bias. See Michael Weisberg, *Remeasuring Man*, 2014 EVOLUTION AND DEVELOPMENT (forthcoming) (concluding that Gould was generally correct)..
56. Hunt, *The Negro as a Soldier, supra* note 8, at 48–54.
57. Joseph Barnard Davis, *On the Weight of the Brain in the Negro*, 7 ANTHROPOLOGICAL REV. 190, 190–192 (1869). For the conclusions about brain

weight and level of civilization, *see* JOSEPH BARNARD DAVIS, AN ATTEMPT TO ASCERTAIN THE AVERAGE WEIGHT OF THE BRAIN IN THE DIFFERENT RACES OF MANKIND (Philadelphia: Academy of Natural Sciences of Philadelphia, 1866).

58. LEWIS HENRY MORGAN, ANCIENT SOCIETY 3–18, 29–45, 550–554 (New York: Henry Holt, 1877).
59. Frederick L. Hoffman, *The Race Traits and Tendencies of the American Negro*, 11 PUB. AM. ECON. ASS'N 1, 310–329 (1896). On Hoffman, *see* Francis J. Sypher, *The Rediscovered Prophet: Frederick L. Hoffman (1865-1946)*, COSMOS CLUB (2011), http://www.cosmos-club.org/web/journals/2000/sypher.html (last visited Oct. 13, 2013).
60. Hunt, *The Negro as a Soldier, supra* note 8, at 52.
61. Nathaniel S. Shaler, *Our Negro Types*, 29 CURRENT LIT. 44–47 (1900). *See also* Nathaniel S. Shaler, THE NEIGHBOR: THE NATURAL HISTORY OF HUMAN CONTACTS 59–64 (Boston: Houghton, Mifflin, 1904). On Gilded Age perceptions, *see* Peggy Pascoe, WHAT COMES NATURALLY: MISCEGENATION LAW AND THE MAKING OF RACE IN AMERICA (New York: Oxford Univ. Press, 2009).
62. On Lamarckian thought in the United States, *see* HOVENKAMP, SCIENCE AND RELIGION, *supra* note 14, at 189–210; Donald K. Pickens, EUGENICS AND THE PROGRESSIVES (Nashville, TN: Vanderbilt Univ. Press, 1968).
63. *See, e.g.*, Eugene S. Talbot, DEGENERACY: ITS CAUSES, SIGNS, AND RESULTS 99–103 (London: W. Scott, 1898; 1904); W.A. Dixon, *The Morbid Proclivities and Retrogressive Tendencies in the Offspring of Mulattoes*, 20 JAMA 1, 1–2 (1893).
64. *See* William F. Brundage, LYNCHING IN THE NEW SOUTH: GEORGIA AND VIRGINIA, 1880–1930, at 58–60 (Urbana: Univ. of Illinois Press, 1993). On the extent to which the FDR administration obtained southern allegiance by refusing to clamp down on lynching, see Ira Katznelson, FEAR ITSELF: THE NEW DEAL AND THE ORIGINS OF OUR TIME 84–96, 141–70 (New York: W.W. Norton, 2014).
65. Pace v. Alabama, 106 U.S. 583, 585 (1882).
66. 379 U.S. 184 (1964).
67. James Hugo Johnston, RACE RELATIONS IN VIRGINIA & MISCEGENATION IN THE SOUTH (Amherst: Univ. of Massachusetts Press, 1970); Ira Berlin, Many Thousands Gone: The First Two Centuries of Slavery in North America (Cambridge, MA: Harvard, 1998).
68. *See* State v. Ross, 76 N.C. 242 (1877).
69. 42 U.S.C § 1981 (1866). *E.g.*, Green v. State, 58 Ala. 190 (1877) (not the purpose of federal Civil War Amendments to interfere with a traditional state power); State v. Gibson, 36 Ind. 389 (1871).
70. Perez v. Lippold, 32 Cal. 2d 711, 198 P.2d 17 (1948).
71. Loving v. Virginia, 388 U.S. 1, 2 (1967).
72. State v. Gurry, 121 Md. 534, 548–51, 88 A. 546, 552–53 (1913) (improperly destroyed vested property rights); Carey v. City of Atlanta, 143 Ga. 192, 202, 84 S.E. 456,

460 (1915) (taking property without due process of law); State v. Darnell, 166 N.C. 300, 305, 81 S.E. 338, 340 (1914) (unlawful restraint on transferability of property). California cities had previously passed exclusion statutes directed at the Chinese. They were invalidated under the Equal Protection Clause. *In re* Lee Sing, 43 F. 359, 360–62 (C.C.N.D. Cal. 1890).

73. 245 U.S. 60, 70–71 (1917).
74. On Warley, *see* Russell Wigginton, *"But He Did What He Could": William Warley Leads Louisville's Fight for Justice, 1902–1946*, 76 FILSON HIST. Q. 427 (2002).
75. Quoted in Benno C. Schmidt, Jr., *Principle and Prejudice: The Supreme Court and Race in the Progressive Era: Part 1: The Heyday of Jim Crow*, 82 COLUM. L. REV. 444, 512 (1982).
76. Alpheus T. Mason, BRANDEIS: A FREE MAN'S LIFE 477–81 (New York: Viking, 1946). On Storey, *see* William B. Hixson, JR., MOORFIELD STOREY AND THE ABOLITIONIST TRADITION (New York: Oxford Univ. Press, 1972); Susan D. Carle, *From Buchanan to Button: Legal Ethics and the NAACP* (Part II), 8 UNIV. CHI. L. SCH. ROUNDTABLE 281, 285–89 (2001).
77. *Supplemental and Reply Brief for Defendant in Error on Rehearing* at 123, 142–254, 173–74 Buchanan v. Warley, 245 U.S. 60 (1917); John Vertrees, *The Fifteenth Amendment and Blacks and Whites in the United States*, 6 LAW. & BANKER 129, 129–42 (1913).
78. *See* Benjamin A. Gould, INVESTIGATIONS IN THE MILITARY AND ANTHROPOLOGICAL STATISTICS OF AMERICAN SOLDIERS 471 (New York: U.S. Sanitary Commission, 1869).
79. James Bryce, *Thoughts on the Negro Problem*, 153 N. AM. REV. 641, 643–44, 647–51 (1891). On Bryce, *see* John T. Seaman, JR., A CITIZEN OF THE WORLD: THE LIFE OF JAMES BRYCE (New York: Tauris, 2006).
80. ALEXANDER HARVEY SHANNON, RACIAL INTEGRITY AND OTHER FEATURES OF THE NEGRO PROBLEM 22 (Nashville, TN: M.E. Church, 1907).
81. Noted in HARRIS, RISE OF ANTHROPOLOGICAL THEORY, *supra* note 54, at 127.
82. *See* SHANNON, RACIAL INTEGRITY, *supra* note 80, at 16–95.
83. *See* Supplemental and Reply Brief at 182–98, Buchanan v. Warley (quoting Frank U. Quillin, THE COLOR LINE IN OHIO: A HISTORY OF RACE PREJUDICE IN A TYPICAL NORTHERN STATE 1–11, 125–65 (Ann Arbor, MI: G. Wahr, 1913)). *See* Paul Finkelman, *The Strange Career of Race Discrimination in Antebellum Ohio*, 55 CASE W. RES. L. REV. 373 (2004).
84. Buchanan v. Warley, 245 U.S. 60, 81–82 (1917).
85. *See* David E. Bernstein, REHABILITATING LOCHNER: DEFENDING INDIVIDUAL RIGHTS AGAINST PROGRESSIVE REFORM 85–87 (Chicago: Univ. of Chicago Press, 2011).
86. Plessy v. Ferguson, 163 U.S. 537 (1896); Brown v. Bd. of Educ., 347 U.S. 483 (1954).
87. Corrigan v. Buckley, 271 U.S. 323, 330 (1926). Clement E. Vose, CAUCASIANS ONLY: THE SUPREME COURT, THE NAACP, AND THE RESTRICTIVE COVENANT

CASES 17–41 (Berkeley: California Press, 1959), which relies heavily on Moorfield Storey's correspondence concerning *Corrigan*. State court decisions upholding racially restrictive covenants after *Corrigan* include Hemsley v. Sage, 194 Okla. 669, 154 P.2d 577 (1944); Burkhardt v. Lofton, 63 Cal. App. 2d 230, 146 P.2d 720 (1944). Cases finding improper restraints on alienation include Williams v. Commercial Land Co., 1931 WL 2034 (Ohio App. 1931); White v. White, 108 W.Va. 128, 150 S.E. 531 (1929).

88. Shelley v. Kraemer, 334 U.S. 1, 8–9, 13 (1948).
89. Erwin Chemerinsky, CONSTITUTIONAL LAW: PRINCIPLES AND POLICIES 663–704 (New York: Aspen, 3d ed. 2006).
90. 347 U.S. 483, 494 n.11 (1954). Sociologist Kenneth B. Clark probably had more to do with Warren's use of social science data than any other social scientist. *See, e.g., Brown*, 347 U.S. at 494 n.11 (citing Kenneth B. Clark, THE EFFECT OF PREJUDICE AND DISCRIMINATION ON PERSONALITY DEVELOPMENT (Washington, DC: Federal Security Agency, 1950)). *See* Risa L. Goluboff, THE LOST PROMISE OF CIVIL RIGHTS 243 (Cambridge, MA: Harvard Univ. Press, 2007) (criticizing the Court for relying on psychological damage as its theory of harm).
91. *See* Paul Popenoe & Roswell H. Johnson, APPLIED EUGENICS 280–303 (New York: Macmillan, 1918); Edward M. East & Donald F. Jones, INBREEDING AND OUTBREEDING: THEIR GENETIC AND SOCIOLOGICAL SIGNIFICANCE 245–65 (Philadelphia: Lippincott, 1919).
92. *See Psychological Examining in the United States Army*, 15 MEMOIRS NAT'L ACAD. SCI. 705–42 (Robert Yerkes ed., Washington, DC: U.S. GPO, 1921); Robert M. Yerkes, *Testing the Human Mind*, 131 ATLANTIC MONTHLY 358, 358–70 (1923).
93. *See* GOULD, MISMEASURE, *supra* note 5, at 192–225.
94. *See* Richard Lynn, RACE DIFFERENCES IN INTELLIGENCE: AN EVOLUTIONARY ANALYSIS (Augusta, GA: Washington Summit, 2006); Richard J. Hernstein & Charles Murray, THE BELL CURVE: INTELLIGENCE AND CLASS STRUCTURE IN AMERICAN LIFE (New York: Free Press, 1994).
95. VA. CODE § 20–50 (1924).
96. Rhinelander v. Rhinelander, 219 N.Y.S. 548 (N.Y. App. Div. 1927), *aff'd* 245 N.Y. 510 (1927). See the perceptive treatment in Angela Onwuachi-Willig, ACCORDING TO OUR HEARTS: *RHINELANDER V. RHINELANDER* AND THE LAW OF THE MULTIRACIAL FAMILY (New Haven, CT: Yale Univ. Press, 2014).
97. *See* Franz Boas, *Human Faculty as Determined by Race*, 43 PROC. AM. ASS'N FOR ADVANCEMENT SCI. 301 (1894); Franz Boas, *Some Recent Criticisms of Physical Anthropology*, 1 AM. ANTHROPOLOGIST 98, 106 (1899). *See* Franz Boas, RACE, LANGUAGE AND CULTURE (New York: Macmillan, 1940). For a summary and analysis of Boas's work, *see* HARRIS, RISE OF ANTHROPOLOGICAL THEORY, *supra* note 54, at 250–89; Vernon J. Williams, JR., RETHINKING RACE: FRANZ BOAS AND HIS CONTEMPORARIES (Lexington: Univ. Press of Kentucky, 1996).

98. Edward B. Reuter, THE MULATTO IN THE UNITED STATES: INCLUDING A STUDY OF THE ROLE OF MIXED-BLOOD RACES THROUGHOUT THE WORLD 320, 325–26, 375–76 (Boston: R.G. Badger, 1918).
99. Melville J. Herskovits, THE AMERICAN NEGRO: A STUDY IN RACIAL CROSSING, 41–48, 51–66 (New York: Knopf, 1928); Melville J. Herskovits, THE ANTHROPOMETRY OF THE AMERICAN NEGRO 234–80 (New York: Columbia Univ. Press, 1930).
100. Gunnar Myrdal, AN AMERICAN DILEMMA: THE NEGRO PROBLEM AND MODERN DEMOCRACY 3–25, 83–153 (New York: Harper, 1944). *See* WILLIAM J. BARBER, GUNNAR MYRDAL: AN INTELLECTUAL BIOGRAPHY (Basingstoke, England: Palgrave Macmillan, 2007).
101. Shelley v. Kraemer, 334 U.S. 1, 20 (1948).
102. Application for Leave to File Brief Amicus and Brief Amicus Curiae on Behalf of Congress of Industrial Organizations and Certain Affiliated Organizations at 20–22 & nn.2-5, Shelley v. Kraemer, 334 U.S. 1 (1948) (quoting anthropologist RALPH LINTON, THE STUDY OF MAN 39 (New York: D. Appleton-Century Co., 1936)). On the CIO and race discrimination at this time, *see* Michael Goldfield, *Race and the CIO: The Possibilities for Racial Egalitarianism during the 1930s and 1940s*, 1993 INT'L LABOR AND WORKING-CLASS HIS. 1 (Fall 1993); on the New Deal administration's lack of enthusiasm to do anything about segregation prior to World War II, see IRA KATZNELSON, FEAR ITSELF, *supra*, note 64, at 132-225..
103. Brief of the United States as Amicus Curiae at 25–39 nn.8–11, Shelley v. Kraemer, 334 U.S. 1 (1948).
104. On *Brown, see, e.g.*, Petition for Rehearing at 26–31, Barrows v. Jackson, 346 U.S. 249 (1953), *reh'g denied*, 346 U.S. 841 (1953); *and see* Idus A. Newby, CHALLENGE TO THE COURT: SOCIAL SCIENTISTS AND THE DEFENSE OF SEGREGATION, 1954–1966 (New Orleans: LSU Press, 1967). On *Loving, see* Brief and Appendix on Behalf of Appellee, State of Virginia, Loving v. Virginia, 388 U.S. 1 (1967) (lengthy discussion of scientific race theories).

CHAPTER 4

1. *E.g.*, John Bates Clark, THE CONTROL OF TRUSTS (New York: Macmillan, 1901); Richard T. Ely, MONOPOLIES AND TRUSTS (New York: Macmillan, 1900). *See* Hans Thorelli, THE FEDERAL ANTITRUST POLICY: ORIGINATION OF AN AMERICAN TRADITION (Baltimore: Johns Hopkins Press, 1955); Herbert Hovenkamp, ENTERPRISE AND AMERICAN LAW, 1836–1937, at 241–348 (Cambridge, MA: Harvard Univ. Press, 1991).
2. The professional economic journals in the United States developed at roughly the same time as the law school law reviews. The *Quarterly Journal of Economics*, the first specialized economics journal in either Britain or America, began publication at Harvard in 1886. The *Journal of Political Economy* started publication at

Chicago in 1892. The *American Economic Review* began publication under that banner in 1911 under the auspices of the American Economic Association, but predecessors were published under the titles "Publications" or "Proceedings" of the AEA, or the AEA "Quarterly." *See* HOVENKAMP, ENTERPRISE, *supra* note 1, at 171–206; Mary O. Furner, ADVOCACY AND OBJECTIVITY: A CRISIS IN THE PROFESSIONALIZATION OF AMERICAN SOCIAL SCIENCE, 1865–1905, at 35–58 (Lexington: Univ. Press of Kentucky, 1975).

3. Charles Francis Adams, *The State and the Railroads*, ATLANTIC MONTHLY 360 (Mar. 1876), 691 (June 1876). On ADAMS, *see* Thomas K. McCraw, PROPHETS OF REGULATION 1–79 (Cambridge, MA: Harvard Univ. Press, 1984). On the railroad problem, *see* Herbert Hovenkamp, *Regulatory Conflict in the Gilded Age: Federalism and the Railroad Problem*, 97 YALE. L.J. 1017–72 (1988).
4. Henry Carter Adams, *Economics and Jurisprudence*, 8 SCI. 15 (July 2, 1886). On the German Historical School and the study of particular industries, *see* HOVENKAMP, ENTERPRISE, *supra* note 1, at 298–307.
5. Henry C. Adams, *The Relation of the State to Industrial Action*, 1 PUB. AM. ECON. ASSN. 7, 13, 55 (1887).
6. Id. at 60, 64, 68–75.
7. John S. Mill, PRINCIPLES OF POLITICAL ECONOMY, WITH SOME OF THEIR APPLICATIONS TO SOCIAL PHILOSOPHY, Bk. 2, ch. 14, § 13 (London: Parker, 1848). Adam Smith had a limited conception of natural monopoly. *See* Adam Smith, AN INQUIRY INTO THE NATURE AND CAUSES OF THE WEALTH OF NATIONS, Book V, ch. 1.121 (London: Strahan & Cadell, 1776) (suggesting that insurance, banking, municipal water supplies, and canals fell into this category).
8. David Ricardo, ON THE PRINCIPLES OF POLITICAL ECONOMY AND TAXATION (London: J. Murray, 1817). On the land issue and the treatment of Ricardo by American economists, *see* HOVENKAMP, ENTERPRISE, *supra* note 1, at 70–71, 187–91.
9. Arthur C. Pigou, WEALTH AND WELFARE (London: Macmillan, 1912); Arthur C. Pigou, THE ECONOMICS OF WELFARE (London: Macmillan, 1920; 4th ed. 1932).
10. Joan Robinson, THE ECONOMICS OF IMPERFECT COMPETITION, ch. 27 (London: Macmillan, 1933).
11. Edward Chamberlin, THE THEORY OF MONOPOLISTIC COMPETITION (Cambridge, MA: Harvard Univ. Press, 1933).
12. John Maurice Clark, SOCIAL CONTROL OF BUSINESS (Chicago: Univ. of Chicago Press, 1926).
13. *See, e.g.*, John Bates Clark, THE DISTRIBUTION OF WEALTH: A THEORY OF WAGES, INTEREST AND PROFITS (New York: Macmillan, 1899); Thomas Nixon Carver, THE DISTRIBUTION OF WEALTH (New York: Macmillan, 1904); John R. Commons, THE DISTRIBUTION OF WEALTH (New York: Macmillan, 1893); Richard T. Ely, PROPERTY AND CONTRACT IN THEIR RELATIONS TO THE

DISTRIBUTION OF WEALTH (2 volumes, New York: Macmillan, 1914); Rufus Cope, THE DISTRIBUTION OF WEALTH (Philadelphia: Lippincott, 1890); Charles W. MacFarlane, VALUE AND DISTRIBUTION (Philadelphia: Lippincott, 1899); John K. Ryan, DISTRIBUTIVE JUSTICE (New York: Macmillan, 1916); Charles B. Spahr, AN ESSAY ON THE PRESENT DISTRIBUTION OF WEALTH IN THE UNITED STATES (New York: Crowell, 1896); David A. Wells, RECENT ECONOMIC CHANGES, AND THEIR EFFECT ON THE PRODUCTION AND DISTRIBUTION OF WEALTH AND THE WELL-BEING OF SOCIETY (New York: D. Appleton, 1889).

14. Alfred Marshall, PRINCIPLES OF ECONOMICS 130 (New York: Macmillan, 8th ed. 1920); COMMONS, THE DISTRIBUTION OF WEALTH, *supra* note 13, at 10. *See* Chapter 6.
15. *E.g.*, Carol Aronovici, *Housing and the Housing Problem*, 51 ANNALS AM. ACAD. POL. & SOC. SCI. 1 (1914); Carol Aronovici, *Cost Factors in Housing Reform*, 51 ANNALS AM. ACAD. POL. & SOC. SCI. 25 (1914); John J. Murphy, *Some Effects of Housing Regulation*, 51 ANNALS AM. ACAD. POL. & SOC. SCI. 99 (1914); Alvah Hunt Doty, *The Federal Government and the Public Health*, 166 N. AM. REV. 543 (1898).
16. ELY, PROPERTY AND CONTRACT, *supra* note 13; Robert L. Hale, *Coercion and Distribution in a Supposedly Non-coercive State*, 38 POL. SCI. Q. 470, 477 (1923). On Hale, *see* Barbara H. Fried, THE PROGRESSIVE ASSAULT ON LAISSEZ FAIRE: ROBERT HALE AND THE FIRST LAW AND ECONOMICS MOVEMENT (Cambridge, MA: Harvard Univ. Press, 1998).
17. 1 William James, PRINCIPLES OF PSYCHOLOGY 185 (New York: Holt, 1890). On behaviorism, *see* John B. Watson, BEHAVIORISM (New York: People's Institute, 1924); John B. Watson, PSYCHOLOGY FROM THE STANDPOINT OF A BEHAVIORIST (Philadelphia: Lippincott, 1919); Ivan Pavlov, CONDITIONED REFLEXES: AN INVESTIGATION OF THE PSYCHOLOGICAL ACTIVITY OF THE CEREBRAL CORTEX (Eng. trans. by G.V. Anrep, London: Oxford, 1927); Albert Paul Weiss, A THEORETICAL BASIS OF HUMAN BEHAVIOR (Columbus, OH: Adams, 1925); John Dewey, HOW WE THINK (Boston: D.C. Heath, 1910); Robert M. Yerkes, *Behaviorism and Genetic Psychology*, 14 J. PHIL., PSYCH. & SCI. METHOD 154 (1917); Edgar A. Singer, Jr., *Mind as an Observable Object*, 8 J. PHIL., PSYCH. & SCI. METHOD 180 (1911); Ralph Barton Perry, *The Mind Within and the Mind Without*, 6 J. PHIL. PSYCHOL. 169 (1909). On Watson, *see* David Cohen, J. B. Watson, THE FOUNDER OF BEHAVIOURISM (London & Boston: Routledge, 1979); Edward A. Purcell, JR., THE CRISIS OF DEMOCRATIC THEORY: SCIENTIFIC NATURALISM AND THE PROBLEM OF VALUE 34–38 (Lexington: Univ. Press of Kentucky, 1973).
18. Oliver Wendell Holmes, JR., THE COMMON LAW (Boston: Little, Brown, 1881).
19. WATSON, BEHAVIORISM, *supra* note 17, at 6.
20. Gilbert Ryle, THE CONCEPT OF MIND (London: Hutchinson's, 1949).

21. John Maurice Clark, *Recent Developments in Economics, in* RECENT DEVELOPMENTS IN THE SOCIAL SCIENCES 259 (E.C. Hayes ed., Philadelphia: Lippincott, 1927). *See also* Morris Copeland's call for treating value theory as a behavioral science. Morris A. Copeland, *Economic Theory and the Natural Science Point of View*, 21 AM. ECON. REV. 67 (1931); Bernard F. Haley, *The Psychological Basis of the Marginal Utility Theory of Value*, Proceedings, Pacific Collegiate Economic and Commercial Conference 1 (1928); Frank A. Fetter, *Value and the Larger Economics*, 31 J. POL. ECON. 587 (1923); Rexford G. Tugwell, *Human Nature in Economic Theory*, 30 J. POL. ECON. 317 (1922).
22. Frank A. Fetter, *Price Economics versus Welfare Economics*, 10 AM. ECON. REV. 467, 719–21 (1920).
23. Wesley Mitchell, *The Prospects of Economics, in* THE TREND OF ECONOMICS 31 (Rexford G. Tugwell, ed., New York: Knopf, 1924).
24. Irving Fisher, *A Statistical Method for Measuring "Marginal Utility" and Testing the Justice of a Progressive Income Tax, in* ECONOMIC ESSAYS CONTRIBUTED IN HONOR OF JOHN BATES CLARK 157–93 (J.H. Hollander ed., New York: Macmillan, 1927).
25. *Report of the Sixty-Third Meeting*, BRITISH ASSN. FOR ADVANCEMENT OF SCIENCE 843 *et seq.* (1894).
26. *See* Gerald Frank Shove, *The Place of Marshall's Principles in the Development of Economic Theory*, 52 ECON. J. 294, 316–17 (1942). *See also* Robert Cooter & Peter Rappoport, *Were the Ordinalists Wrong about Welfare Economics?*, 22 J. ECON. LIT. 507 (1984).
27. *E.g.*, Malcolm Rutherford, THE INSTITUTIONALIST MOVEMENT IN AMERICAN ECONOMICS, 1918–1947 (Cambridge: Cambridge Univ. Press, 2011).
28. *E.g.*, Geoffrey M. Hodgson, THE EVOLUTION OF INSTITUTIONAL ECONOMICS: AGENCY, STRUCTURE, AND DARWINISM IN AMERICAN INSTITUTIONALISM (London: Routledge, 2004); Yuval P. Yonay, THE STRUGGLE OVER THE SOUL OF ECONOMICS: INSTITUTIONALIST AND NEOCLASSICAL ECONOMISTS IN AMERICA BETWEEN THE WARS (Princeton, NJ: Princeton Univ. Press, 1998); Mark Blaug, ECONOMIC THEORY IN RETROSPECT 712–14 (3d ed. London: Cambridge, 1999).
29. John Maurice Clark, *Book Review*, 27 J. POL. ECON. 218, 219 (1919) (reviewing Charles Horton Cooley, SOCIAL PROCESS (New York: Scribners, 1918)).
30. *See* Frank Knight, *Marginal Utility Economics, in* 5 ENCYCLOPAEDIA OF THE SOCIAL SCIENCES 357 (Edwin R.A. Seligman ed., New York: Macmillan, 1931); Spurgeon Bell, *Fixed Costs and Market Price*, 32 Q.J. ECON. 507 (1918) (discussing inadequacy of classical cost theory).
31. John Bates Clark, ESSENTIALS OF ECONOMIC THEORY AS APPLIED TO MODERN PROBLEMS OF INDUSTRY AND PUBLIC POLICY 132 (New York: Macmillan, 1907).
32. Principally, in COMMONS, THE DISTRIBUTION OF WEALTH, *supra* note 13.

33. *See* Morris Copeland, *Commons's Institutionalism in Relation to Problems of Social Evolution and Economic Planning*, 50 Q.J. ECON. 333, 335 (1936). *See also* John R. Commons, INSTITUTIONAL ECONOMICS (New York: Macmillan, 1934).
34. *See* David M. Rabban, LAW'S HISTORY: AMERICAN LEGAL THOUGHT AND THE TRANSATLANTIC TURN TO HISTORY 115–70, 218–28 (New York: Cambridge Univ. Press, 2013).
35. *See* Chapter 1, discussing Englishman Edward Tylor, PRIMITIVE CULTURE (London: J. Murray, 1871); and American Lewis Henry Morgan, ANCIENT SOCIETY (New York: Henry Holt, 1877).
36. *E.g.*, Edward A. Ross, SOCIAL CONTROL (New York: Macmillan, 1901 (sociology); August Drahms, THE CRIMINAL (New York: Macmillan, 1900) (criminology, physiology, sociology psychology); Lester F. Ward, DYNAMIC SOCIOLOGY (New York: Appleton, 1883) (economics, sociology). On the influence of Darwin on American thought outside the biological sciences, *see* Louis Menand, THE METAPHYSICAL CLUB: A STORY OF IDEAS IN AMERICA (New York: Farrar, Straus, and Giroux, 2001); PURCELL, CRISIS OF DEMOCRATIC THEORY, *supra* note 17; Paul Crook, DARWIN'S COAT-TAILS: ESSAYS ON SOCIAL DARWINISM (New York: Peter Lang, 2007); Carl N. Degler, IN SEARCH OF HUMAN NATURE: THE DECLINE AND REVIVAL OF DARWINISM IN AMERICAN SOCIAL THOUGHT (New York: Oxford, 1991); Mike Hawkins, SOCIAL DARWINISM IN EUROPEAN AND AMERICAN THOUGHT, 1860–1945 (New York: Cambridge Univ. Press, 1997).
37. *See, e.g.*, Thorstein Veblen, THE THEORY OF THE LEISURE CLASS: AN ECONOMIC STUDY IN THE EVOLUTION OF INSTITUTIONS 194 (New York: Macmillan, 1899). *See also* Thorstein Veblen, THE PLACE OF SCIENCE IN MODERN CIVILISATION AND OTHER ESSAYS 444 (New York: Huebsch, 1919).
38. *See* Chapter 1; *and* EVOLUTION OF LAW: SELECT READINGS ON THE ORIGIN AND DEVELOPMENT OF LEGAL INSTITUTIONS (Albert Kocourek & John H. Wigmore eds., Boston: Little, Brown, 1915–1918); ROSS, SOCIAL CONTROL, *supra* note 36; Edward A. Ross, SIN AND SOCIETY: AN ANALYSIS OF LATTER-DAY INIQUITY (Boston: Houghton, Mifflin, 1907); Albert G. Keller, *Law in Evolution*, 28 YALE L.J. 769 (1919); W. Jethro Brown, *Law and Evolution*, 29 YALE L.J. 394 (1920); Arthur L. Corbin, *The Law and the Judges*, 3 YALE REV. 234 (1914). *See* Herbert Hovenkamp, *Evolutionary Models in Jurisprudence*, 64 TEX. L. REV. 645 (1985).
39. John R. Commons, *Law and Economics*, 34 YALE L.J. 371, 372 (1925).
40. Biographical and economic studies of Veblen include John Patrick Diggins, THORSTEIN VEBLEN: THEORIST OF THE LEISURE CLASS (Princeton, NJ: Princeton Univ. Press, 1999); John Hobson, VEBLEN (Fairfield, NJ: Kelley, 1991); cited earlier: YONAY, STRUGGLE OVER THE SOUL OF ECONOMICS, *supra* note 28; Douglas F. Dowd, THORSTEIN VEBLEN (New Brunswick, NJ: Transaction, 2000); David Riesman, THORSTEIN VEBLEN: A CRITICAL

INTERPRETATION (New York: Scribner, 1953). *See also* Joseph Dorfman, THORSTEIN VEBLEN AND HIS AMERICA (New York: Viking, 1934); William M. Dugger, *Veblen's Radical Theory of Social Evolution*, 40 J. ECON. ISSUES 651 (2006); George Liagouras, *Socio-Economic Evolution and Darwinism in Thorstein Veblen: A Critical Appraisal*, 33 CAMBRIDGE J. ECON. 1047 (2009).

41. *E.g.*, Alex Beam, *The Naughty Professor*, STANFORD MAG., 1997, *available at* http:www.stanfordalumni.orgnewsmagazine1997sepoctarticlesveblen.html. Contrast Russell H. Bartley, *Unexamined Moments in the Life of Thorstein Veblen*, ELEGANT TECHNOLOGY (1997), *available at* http:www.elegant-technology.com-TVbarRI.html. The accusations originated in DORFMAN, THORSTEIN VEBLEN AND HIS AMERICA, *supra* note 40.

42. Thorstein Veblen, *Why Is Economics Not an Evolutionary Science?*, 12 Q.J. ECON. 373 (1898).

43. Thorstein Veblen, THE THEORY OF BUSINESS ENTERPRISE 269–71 (New York: Scribners, 1904).

44. Thorstein Veblen, ABSENTEE OWNERSHIP AND BUSINESS ENTERPRISE IN RECENT TIMES: THE CASE OF AMERICA (New York: Huebsch, 1923).

45. Liggett v. Lee, 288 U.S. 517, 565 (1933) (striking down statute taxing chain stores at higher rates than single store firms) (Brandeis, J., dissenting).

46. *See* Robert M. Crunden, MINISTERS OF REFORM: THE PROGRESSIVES' ACHIEVEMENT IN AMERICAN CIVILIZATION, 1889–1920, at 12–14 (New York: Basic Books, 1982). On Ely's life, *see* Richard T. Ely, GROUND UNDER OUR FEET: AN AUTOBIOGRAPHY (New York: Macmillan, 1938); Benjamin G. Rader, THE ACADEMIC MIND AND REFORM: THE INFLUENCE OF RICHARD T. ELY IN AMERICAN LIFE (Lexington: Univ. Press of Kentucky, 1966).

47. On Ely's problems with universities, *see* FURNER, ADVOCACY AND OBJECTIVITY, *supra* note 2, at 87–92, 100–01, 115–24, 247–55.

48. 2 JOHNS HOPKINS UNIV. STUDIES IN HISTORY AND POLITICAL SCIENCE 143–202 (Mar. 1884).

49. Simon Newcomb, *The Two Schools of Political Economy*, 14 (N.S.) PRINCETON REV. 291 (1884).

50. *See* Richard T. Ely, *Recent American Socialism*, 3 JOHNS HOPKINS UNIV. STUDIES IN HISTORICAL AND POLITICAL SCIENCE 233–304 (1885); William Graham Sumner, COLLECTED ESSAYS IN POLITICAL AND SOCIAL SCIENCE (New York: Henry Holt, 1885). The debate continued in *Science* magazine and was later anthologized as SCIENCE ECONOMIC DISCUSSION (New York: The Science Company, 1886). *See* Albert E. Moyer, A SCIENTIST'S VOICE IN AMERICAN CULTURE: SIMON NEWCOMB AND THE RHETORIC OF SCIENTIFIC METHOD 108–26 (Berkeley: Univ. of California Press, 1992).

51. *See* Richard T. Ely, *The Founding and Early History of the American Economic Association*, 26 PAPERS & PROCEEDINGS, SUPPLEMENT, AM. ECON. ASSN. 144 (1936); *and see* Alfred W. Coats, *The First Two Decades of the American Economic*

Association, 50 AM. ECON. REV. 556 (1960); Alfred W. Coats, *The Political Economy Club: A Neglected Episode in American Economic Thought*, 51 AM. ECON. REV. 624 (1961).

52. Richard T. Ely, SOCIALISM AND SOCIAL REFORM 309 (New York: Crowell, 1894).

53. ELY, PROPERTY AND CONTRACT, VOL. 1, *supra* note 13, at 579–80; 2 *id.* at 579, 586–618 (italics in original).

54. *E.g.*, Williams v. Walker-Thomas Furniture Co., 350 F.2d 445 (D.C. Cir. 1965). *See* Grant Gilmore, THE DEATH OF CONTRACT 99–101 (Columbus: Ohio State Univ. Press, 1974).

55. *See* Herbert Hovenkamp, *The Political Economy of Substantive Due Process*, 40 STAN. L. REV. 379, 412–20 (1988).

56. COMMONS, THE DISTRIBUTION OF WEALTH, *supra* note 13; John R. Commons, LEGAL FOUNDATIONS OF CAPITALISM (New York: Macmillan, 1924). On Commons, *see* Katherine V.W. Stone, *John R. Commons and the Origins of Legal Realism; or, the Other Tragedy of the Commons, in* 2 TRANSFORMATIONS IN AMERICAN LEGAL HISTORY (Daniel W. Hamilton & Alfred L. Brophy eds., Cambridge, MA: Harvard Univ. Press, 2009); John R. Commons, MYSELF (New York: Macmillan, 1934).

57. *See* COMMONS, INSTITUTIONAL ECONOMICS, *supra* note 33, at 651; COMMONS, LEGAL FOUNDATIONS, *supra* note 56, at 67–68.

58. *E.g.*, Wesley C. Mitchell, *Commons on the Legal Foundations of Capitalism*, 14 AM. ECON. REV. 240 (1924); Wesley C. Mitchell, *Commons on Institutional Economics*, 25 AM. ECON. REV. 635 (1935); Walton H. Hamilton, *Law and Economics*, 19 AM. ECON. REV. SUPPLEMENT, PAPERS AND PROCEEDINGS 56 (1929); Walton H. Hamilton, *The Institutional Approach to Economic Theory*, 9 AM. ECON. REV. 309 (1919); Karl N. Llewellyn, *What Price Contract?—An Essay in Perspective*, 40 YALE L.J. 704 (1931); Karl N. Llewellyn, *The Effect of Legal Institutions upon Economics*, 15 AM. ECON. REV. 665 (1925).

59. *E.g.*, Oliver E. Williamson, THE ECONOMIC INSTITUTIONS OF CAPITALISM 3–6, 10 (New York: Free Press, 1985). *See* Herbert Hovenkamp, *Coase, Institutionalism, and the Origins of Law and Economics*, 86 IND. L.J. 499 (2011).

60. Ronald H. Coase, *The Nature of the Firm*, 4 ECONOMICA (n.s.) 386, 392 (1937). *See* Chapter 12.

61. COMMONS, LEGAL FOUNDATIONS, *supra* note 56, at 147.

62. *See* John R. Commons, *The Problem of Correlating Law, Economics and Ethics*, 8 WIS. L. REV. 3, 10 (1932).

63. COMMONS, LEGAL FOUNDATIONS, *supra* note 56, at 323, 386–87.

64. John R. Commons, ECONOMICS OF COLLECTIVE ACTION, esp. at 25–35 (New York: Macmillan, 1951).

65. COMMONS, LEGAL FOUNDATIONS, *supra* note 56, at 296. On the problem of "conspiracy" and incorporation of labor unions during the Progressive Era, *see*

Herbert Hovenkamp, *Labor Conspiracies in American Law, 1880–1930*, 66 TEX. L. REV. 919, 958–62 (1988).

66. COMMONS, LEGAL FOUNDATIONS, *supra* note 56, at 297, quoting Hitchman Coal & Coke Co. v. Mitchell, 245 U.S. 229, 271 (1917) (Brandeis, J., dissenting).

67. COMMONS, LEGAL FOUNDATIONS, *supra* note 56, at 322.

68. *See, e.g.*, Douglass C. North, STRUCTURE AND CHANGE IN ECONOMIC HISTORY (New York: Norton, 1981); Karl Polanyi, THE GREAT TRANSFORMATION (New York: Farrar & Rinehart, 1944); Oliver E. Williamson, MARKETS AND HIERARCHIES: ANALYSIS AND ANTITRUST IMPLICATIONS (New York: Free Press, 1975).

CHAPTER 5

1. *E.g.*, Silas M. Macvane, *Marginal Utility and Value*, 7 Q.J. ECON. 255, 269 (1893); Silas M. Macvane, *Analysis of Cost of Production*, 1 Q.J. ECON. 481, 483 (1887).

2. John Bates Clark, THE PHILOSOPHY OF WEALTH 10–20, 35–37, 61–63 (Boston: Ginn, 1886).

3. Thorstein Veblen, THE THEORY OF THE LEISURE CLASS: AN ECONOMIC STUDY OF INSTITUTIONS (New York: Macmillan, 1899).

4. *See also* Thorstein Veblen, *Why Is Economics Not an Evolutionary Science?*, 12 Q.J. ECON. 373 (1898); Veblen, *The Preconceptions of Economic Science*, part 3, 14 Q.J. ECON 240 (1900). Veblen did reflect on Clark's work a decade later in Veblen, *Professor Clark's Economics*, 22 Q.J. ECON. 147 (1908). *See* Geoffrey M. Hodgson, *Thorstein Veblen and Post-Darwinian Economics*, 16 CAMBRIDGE J. ECON. 285, 292 (1992).

5. Thorstein Veblen, *The Socialist Economics of Karl Marx and His Followers, Part II: The Later Marxism*, 21 Q.J. ECON. 299 (1907).

6. Thorstein Veblen, *The Evolution of the Scientific Point of View* 37, 10 UNIV. OF CALIFORNIA CHRONICLE, *reprinted in* Thorstein Veblen, THE PLACE OF SCIENCE IN MODERN CIVILISATION AND OTHER ESSAYS 37 (New York: Huebsch, 1919).

7. VEBLEN, THE THEORY OF THE LEISURE CLASS, *supra* note 3, at 188. *See also* Malcolm Rutherford, *Thorstein Veblen and the Processes of Institutional Change*, 16 HIST. POL. ECON. 331 (no. 3, 1984).

8. Thorstein Veblen, *The Limitations of Marginal Utility*, 17 J. POL. ECON. 620, 626 (1909).

9. Edwin R.A. Seligman, *Social Elements in the Theory of Value*, 15 Q.J. ECON. 321, 323–24 (1901). *See also* IRVING FISHER, MATHEMATICAL INVESTIGATIONS IN THE THEORY OF VALUE AND PRICES 89 (Transactions of the Connecticut Academy, Vol. 9, July 1892); Simon Patten, *The Scope of Political Economy*, *in* Simon N. Patten, ESSAYS IN ECONOMIC THEORY 192 (Rexford G. Tugwell ed., New York: Knopf, 1924); John H. Gray, *Economics and the Law*, 5 AM. ECON. REV. SUPP. 3 (1915) (policy economics should be concerned with group needs

rather than individual preferences). For a recap of the debate, *see* Jacob Viner, *The Utility Concept in Value Theory and Its Critics*, 33 J. POL. ECON. 369, 638 (1925).

10. Charles H. Cooley, *The Institutional Character of Pecuniary Valuation*, 18 AM. J. SOC. 543, 546–50 (1913).
11. *See* Thorstein Veblen, *Industrial and Pecuniary Employments, in* VEBLEN, THE PLACE OF SCIENCE IN MODERN CIVILISATION AND OTHER ESSAYS 298, 307–11, *supra* note 6.
12. Edwin R.A. Seligman, *Progressive Taxation in Theory and Practice*, 9 PUB. AM. ECON. ASS'N 1, 132–33 (no. 1/2 1894); Edwin R.A. Seligman, *The Theory of Progressive Taxation*, 8 PUB. AM. ECON. ASS'N 52 (1893).
13. Dr. Miles Medical Co. v. John D. Park & Sons Co., 220 U.S. 373, 412 (1911).
14. Wesley C. Mitchell, *The Rationality of Economic Activity*, 18 J. POL. ECON. 97, 197 (1910); Wesley C. Mitchell, *Human Behavior and Economics: A Survey of Recent Literature*, 29 Q.J. ECON. 1, 2 (1914). On Mitchell's influence on institutional economics and Legal Realism, *see* Malcolm Rutherford, THE INSTITUTIONALIST MOVEMENT IN AMERICAN ECONOMICS, 1918–1947: SCIENCE AND SOCIAL CONTROL 10–53, 112–60 (New York: Cambridge Univ. Press, 2011); Yuval P. Yonay, THE STRUGGLE OVER THE SOUL OF ECONOMICS: INSTITUTIONALIST AND NEOCLASSICAL ECONOMISTS IN AMERICA BETWEEN THE WARS 51–72 (Princeton, NJ: Princeton Univ. Press, 1998).
15. 9 AM. ECON. REV. SUPP. 309, 316 (1919). On Hamilton and institutionalism, *see* RUTHERFORD, THE INSTITUTIONALIST MOVEMENT, *supra* note 14, at 57–95.
16. John Maurice Clark, *Economic Theory in an Era of Social Readjustment*, 9 AM. ECON. REV. SUPP. 280 (1919); John Maurice Clark, *Economics and Modern Psychology*, 26 J. POL. ECON. 1, 7, 10–12 (1918); John Maurice Clark, *The Concept of Value—A Rejoinder*, 29 Q.J. ECON. 709, 712 (1915).
17. *See* Simon N. Patten, *The Failure of Biologic Sociology*, 4 ANNALS AM. ACAD. POL. & SOC. SCI. 63 (1894); Simon N. Patten, *The Relation of Economics to Sociology*, 5 ANNALS AM. ACAD. POL. & SOC. SCI. 117 (1895); Simon N. Patten, *The Effect of the Consumption of Wealth on the Economic Welfare of Society, in* SCIENCE ECONOMIC DISCUSSION 123 (Henry C. Adams ed., New York: Science Co., 1886). *See* Daniel M. Fox, THE DISCOVERY OF ABUNDANCE: SIMON N. PATTEN AND THE TRANSFORMATION OF SOCIAL THEORY (Ithaca, NY: Cornell, 1967).
18. Edward A. Ross, SOCIAL CONTROL 329–32, 338–49 (New York: Macmillan, 1901).
19. Roscoe Pound, *Liberty of Contract*, 18 YALE L.J. 454, 455–56, 460 (1909). Pound relied for his critique of the classicists on Henry Rogers Seager, INTRODUCTION TO ECONOMICS (New York: Henry Holt, 1904), replaced in later years by his more influential PRINCIPLES OF ECONOMICS (New York: Henry Holt, 1913). Seager was trained in the German Historical School but was a fairly orthodox marginalist and among the more conservative of the Progressive economists. *See also* Roscoe Pound, *Mechanical Jurisprudence*, 8 COLUM. L. REV. 605 (1908).

20. On Pound's use of history, *see* David M. Rabban, LAW'S HISTORY: AMERICAN LEGAL THOUGHT AND THE TRANSATLANTIC TURN TO HISTORY 423–70 (New York: Cambridge Univ. Press, 2013). Pound relied mainly on RUDOLF VON JHERING, LAW AS A MEANS TO AN END 332–33 (Eng. trans. by Isaac Husik, Boston: Boston Book Co., 1913). *See* Roscoe Pound, *Making Law and Finding Law*, 82 CENTRAL L.J. 351, 358 (1916); Pound, *The Scope and Purpose of Sociological Jurisprudence*, pt. 1, 24 HARV. L. REV. 591 (1911); pt. 2: 25 HARV. L. REV. 140 (1912); pt. 3: 25 HARV. L. REV. 489, 490 (1912); Pound, *Social Problems and the Courts*, 18 AM. J. SOC. 331, 341 (1912); Pound, *Legislation as a Social Function*, 18 AM. J. SOC. 755, 762 (1913).
21. *E.g.*, Roscoe Pound, *The Economic Interpretation and the Law of Torts*, 53 HARV. L. REV. 365, 383 (1940).
22. *See, e.g.*, Roscoe Pound, *Public Law and Private Law*, 24 CORNELL L.Q. 469 (1939).
23. Joseph A. Schumpeter, *On the Concept of Social Value*, 23 Q.J. ECON. 213–16 (1909). On methodological individualism, *see* Mark Blaug, THE METHODOLOGY OF ECONOMICS 129–56 (New York: Cambridge Univ. Press, 1980). On Schumpeter, *see* THOMAS K. MCCRAW, PROPHET OF INNOVATION: JOSEPH SCHUMPETER AND CREATIVE DESTRUCTION (Cambridge, MA: Harvard Univ. Press, 2007).
24. *See, e.g.*, Frank H. Knight, *The Nature of Economic Science in Some Recent Discussion*, 24 AM. ECON. REV. 225 (1934).
25. Schumpeter, *Concept of Social Value, supra* note 23, at 220, 222.
26. Edward A. Ross, *The Sociological Frontier of Economics*, 13 Q.J. ECON. 386, 394 (1899).
27. Rick Tilman, Thorstein Veblen, John Dewey, C. Wright Mills AND THE GENERIC ENDS OF LIFE 168–74 (Lanham, MD: Rowman & Littlefield, 2004).
28. John Dewey, INDIVIDUALISM OLD AND NEW 9, 135, 168–71 (New York: Minton, Balch, 1930); Dewey, *Theory of Valuation*, 2 INTERNATIONAL ENCYCLOPEDIA OF UNIFIED SCIENCE 19–50 (Chicago: Univ. of Chicago Press, 1930); *and see* John Dewey, THEORY OF VALUATION (Chicago: Univ. of Chicago Press, 1939).
29. Clarence E. Ayres, THE INDUSTRIAL ECONOMY 305 (Boston: Houghton Mifflin, 1952).
30. YONAY, STRUGGLE OVER THE SOUL, *supra* note 14. *See also* Geoffrey M. Hodgson, THE EVOLUTION OF INSTITUTIONAL ECONOMICS: AGENCY, STRUCTURE, AND DARWINISM IN AMERICAN INSTITUTIONALISM (London: Routledge, 2004).
31. *See* Sheldon D. Pollack, WAR, REVENUE, AND STATE BUILDING: FINANCING THE DEVELOPMENT OF THE AMERICAN STATE (Ithaca, NY: Cornell Univ. Press, 2009); Robert Stanley, DIMENSIONS OF LAW IN THE SERVICE OF ORDER: ORIGINS OF THE FEDERAL INCOME TAX, 1861–1913, at 16–20 (New York: Oxford Univ. Press, 1993).

32. Pollock v. Farmers' Loan & Trust Co., 158 U.S. 601 (1895). The contemporary debate over the *Pollock* decision includes Edwin R.A. Seligman, *Is the Income Tax Constitutional and Just?*, FORUM 56 (Mar. 1895); A.C. Miller, *National Finance and the Income Tax*, 3 J. POL. ECON. 255 (1894); Charles Bullock, *Direct Taxes and the Federal Constitution*, 9 YALE REV. 429 (1901); 10 YALE REV. 6, 144 (1902); Charles J. Bullock, *The Origin, Purpose and Effect of the Direct-Tax Clause of the Constitution*, 15 POL. SCI. Q. 217, 452 (1900); Max West, *The Income Tax and the National Revenues*, 8 J. POL. ECON. 433 (1900).
33. Morton J. Horwitz, THE TRANSFORMATION OF AMERICAN LAW, 1870–1960: THE CRISIS OF LEGAL ORTHODOXY 19–20 (New York: Oxford Univ. Press, 1992); Christopher Tiedeman, *The Income Tax Decisions as an Object Lesson in Constitutional Construction*, 6 ANNALS AM. ACAD. POL. & SOC. SCI. 268 (1895).
34. For statistics on wealth inequality in the late nineteenth century, *see* Peter H. Lindert & Jeffrey G. Williamson, *Growth, Equality, and History*, 22 EXPLORATIONS ECON. HIS. 341 (1985).
35. *See* Doris Kearns Goodwin, THE BULLY PULPIT: THEODORE ROOSEVELT, WILLIAM HOWARD TAFT, AND THE GOLDEN AGE OF JOURNALISM 517, 548–50, 594–98 (New York: Simon & Schuster, 2014);Ajay K. Mehrotra, MAKING THE MODERN AMERICAN FISCAL STATE: LAW, POLITICS, AND THE RISE OF PROGRESSIVE TAXATION, 1877–1929 (New York: Cambridge Univ. Press, 2014);Martin J. Sklar, THE CORPORATE RECONSTRUCTION OF AMERICAN CAPITALISM, 1890–1916 (New York: Cambridge Univ. Press, 1988).
36. On ratification, *see* MEHROTRA, SHARING THE BURDEN, *supra* note 35; John D. Buenker, THE INCOME TAX AND THE PROGRESSIVE ERA (New York: Garland, 1985). The tax was upheld in Brushaber v. Union Pac. R.R. Co., 240 U.S. 1 (1916); Stanton v. Baltic Mining Co., 240 U.S. 103 (1916). *See* John F. Witte, THE POLITICS AND DEVELOPMENT OF THE FEDERAL INCOME TAX (Madison: Univ. of Wisconsin Press, 1985).
37. For a good brief history, *see* Dennis J. Ventry, Jr., *Equity versus Efficiency and the U.S. Tax System in Historical Perspective*, *in* TAX JUSTICE: THE ONGOING DEBATE 25–70 (Joseph J. Thorndike & Dennis J. Ventry, Jr. eds., Washington, DC: Urban Institute Press, 2002).
38. On Seligman's career, *see* 4 Joseph Dorfman, THE ECONOMIC MIND IN AMERICAN CIVILIZATION, 1918–1933, at 257–66 (New York: Viking, 1959); MEHROTRA, SHARING THE BURDEN, *supra* note 35. Mary O. Furner, ADVOCACY AND OBJECTIVITY: A CRISIS IN THE PROFESSIONALIZATION OF AMERICAN SOCIAL SCIENCE, 1865–1905, at 67–110, 207–22 (Lexington: Univ. Press of Kentucky, 1975).
39. EDWIN R.A. SELIGMAN, PRINCIPLES OF ECONOMICS, ch. 12 (New York: Longmans, 1905).
40. Thomas Nixon Carver, *The Ethical Basis of Distribution and Its Application to Taxation*, 6 ANNALS AM. ACAD. POL. & SOC. SCI. 79 (1895). *See also* Thomas

Nixon Carver, *The Minimum Sacrifice Theory of Taxation*, 19 POL. SCI. Q. 66, 72 (1904); Francis Amasa Walker, *The Bases of Taxation*, 3 POL. SCI. Q. 1, 14 (1888).

41. Francis Y. Edgeworth, *The Pure Theory of Taxation*, 7 ECON. J. 46, 55 (1897).
42. Irving Fisher, *A Statistical Method for Measuring "Marginal Utility" and Testing the Justice of a Progressive Income Tax*, *in* ECONOMIC ESSAYS, CONTRIBUTED IN HONOR OF JOHN BATES CLARK 157–93 (J.H. Hollander ed., New York: Macmillan, 1927).
43. Arthur C. Pigou, A STUDY IN PUBLIC FINANCE (London: Macmillan, 1928; 3d ed. 1947, revised 1960). *See* the third revised edition, chs. 4–7.
44. Lionel Robbins, AN ESSAY ON THE NATURE AND SIGNIFICANCE OF ECONOMIC SCIENCE 136, 141 (London: Macmillan, 1932; 2d ed. 1935).
45. Elmer D. Fagan, *Recent and Contemporary Theories of Progressive Taxation*, 46 J. POL. ECON. 457, 465 (1938).
46. EDWIN R.A. SELIGMAN, PROGRESSIVE TAXATION IN THEORY AND PRACTICE (Baltimore: AEA, 1894; 2d ed. 1908).
47. *Id.* at 223, 283–85, 705–11; EDWIN R.A. SELIGMAN, THE INCOME TAX 31–32 (New York: Macmillan, 1911; 2d ed. 1914). As Mill had observed in 1848, "Whether the person with £10,000 a year cares less for £1,000 than the person with only £1,000 a year cares for £100, and if so, how much less, does not appear to me capable of being decided with the degree of certainty on which a legislator or a financier ought to act." 2 John Stuart Mill, PRINCIPLES OF POLITICAL ECONOMY, Book V, ch. ii, § 2 at 398 (London: J.W. Parker, 1849).
48. SELIGMAN, THE INCOME TAX, *supra* note 47, at 32–33. Seligman drew upon Francis A. Walker, *The Bases of Taxation, supra* note 40, at 14.
49. Walter J. Blum & Harry Kalven, Jr., *The Uneasy Case for Progressive Taxation*, 19 U. CHI. L. REV. 417 (1952). *See also* Walter J. Blum & Harry Kalven, JR., THE UNEASY CASE FOR PROGRESSIVE TAXATION (Chicago: Univ. of Chicago Press, 1953).
50. *See, e.g.*, EDWIN R.A. SELIGMAN, THE SHIFTING AND INCIDENCE OF TAXATION (New York: Macmillan, 1896; rev. ed. 1899); Seligman, *On the Shifting and Incidence of Taxation*, 7 PUB. AM. ECON. ASSN. 7, 119 (1892); Seligman, *The General Property Tax*, 5 POL. SCI. Q. 24 (1890); Seligman, *The Taxation of Corporations*, 5 POL. SCI. Q. 269, 438 (1890). For modern applications, *see* Sarah B. Lawsky, *On the Edge: Declining Marginal Utility and Tax Policy*, 95 MINN. L. REV. 904 (2011).
51. COMMENTARIES ON THE LAWS OF ENGLAND, bk I, ch. viii (1766).
52. Adam Smith, AN INQUIRY INTO THE NATURE AND CAUSES OF THE WEALTH OF NATIONS, Book V, ch. ii (London: Strahan & Cadell, 1776); David Ricardo, ON THE PRINCIPLES OF POLITICAL ECONOMY AND TAXATION, chs. 9–16 (London: J. Murray, 1817).
53. Jean-Baptiste Say, A TREATISE ON POLITICAL ECONOMY, Book III, ch. x (1803; Eng. trans. of 4th ed. by C.R. Prinsep, Boston: Wells & Lilly, 1821); MILL, PRINCIPLES OF POLITICAL ECONOMY, *supra* note 47, Book V, chs. ii–iii; Alfred

Marshall, PRINCIPLES OF ECONOMICS 442 (London: Macmillan, 1890); Francis A. Walker, POLITICAL ECONOMY 606–10 (New York: Henry Holt, 3d ed. 1888).

54. Augustin Cournot, RESEARCHES INTO THE MATHEMATICAL PRINCIPLES OF THE THEORY OF WEALTH, chs. 6–8 ([1838]; Eng. trans. by Nathaniel T. Bacon; Irving Fisher ed., New York: Macmillan, 1897).

55. *See* David Wells, REPORT OF THE NEW YORK TAX COMMISSION (New York: Martin B. Brown, 1872); Albert Bolles, *Report of the Revenue Commission*, Pennsylvania Legislature, May 25, 1889, at 142 (1890).

56. Thomas McIntyre Cooley, A TREATISE ON THE LAW OF TAXATION: INCLUDING THE LAW OF LOCAL ASSESSMENTS 38–39 (Chicago: Callaghan, 1st ed. 1876, 2d ed. 1886).

57. *See* Laurence S. Moss, *The Seligman-Edgeworth Debate about the Analysis of Tax Incidence: The Advent of Mathematical Economics, 1892–1910*, 69 AM. J. ECON. & SOC. 524 (2010).

58. In addition to Seligman, *see* Edward A. Ross, *Seligman's "Shifting and Incidence of Taxation,"* 3 ANNALS AM. ACAD. OF POL. & SOC. SCI. 444 (1893); Adolph C. Miller, *On Incidence of Taxation*, 1 J. POL. ECON. 444, 450 (1893); Thomas Nixon Carver, *The Shifting of Taxes*, 5 YALE REV. 258 (1897); T.S. Adams, *Effect of Income and Inheritance Taxes on the Distribution of Wealth*, 5 AM. ECON. REV. SUPP. 234 (1915); Harry Gunnison Brown, *Some Frequently Neglected Factors in the Incidence of Taxation*, 28 J. POL. ECON. 499 (1920).

59. Helvering v. Griffiths, 318 U.S. 371, 373 n.4 (1943); Graves v. New York, 306 U.S. 466, 484 n.4 (1939); United States v. Jacobs, 306 U.S. 363, 367 n.6 (1939); Norfolk & W. Ry. v. North Carolina, 297 U.S. 682, 684 n.1 (1936); Concordia Fire Ins. Co. v. Illinois, 292 U.S. 535, 552 (1934); DuPont v. Commissioner of Internal Revenue, 118 F.2d 544, 545 n.2 (3d Cir. 1941); *In re* Newland, 115 F.2d 165, 166 n.4 (3d Cir. 1940); New Consumers Bread Co. v. Commissioner of Internal Revenue, 115 F.2d 162, 163 n.6 (3d Cir. 1940).

60. Indian Motocycle Co. v. United States, 283 U.S. 570, 581 n.5 (1931).

61. SMITH, WEALTH OF NATIONS, *supra* note 52, Book V, ch. 1, pt. iii.

62. Paul A. Samuelson, *The Pure Theory of Public Expenditure*, 36 REV. ECON. & STAT. 387 (1954).

63. Thomas M. Cooley, A TREATISE ON THE CONSTITUTIONAL LIMITATIONS WHICH REST UPON THE LEGISLATIVE POWER OF THE STATES OF THE AMERICAN UNION 487 (Boston: Little, Brown, 1868); COOLEY, A TREATISE ON THE LAW OF TAXATION, *supra* note 56; John F. Dillon, TREATISE ON THE LAW OF MUNICIPAL CORPORATIONS (Chicago: Cockroft, 1872).

64. *See* Herbert Hovenkamp, ENTERPRISE AND AMERICAN LAW, 1836–1937, ch. 3 (Cambridge, MA: Harvard Univ. Press, 1991).

65. *E.g.*, Proprietors of the Charles River Bridge v. Proprietors of the Warren Bridge, 36 U.S. 420 (1837). The debate is recounted in HOVENKAMP, ENTERPRISE, *supra* note 64, at 110–14.

66. Exhaustively described in Charles Fairman, THE OLIVER WENDELL HOLMES DEVISE HISTORY OF THE SUPREME COURT OF THE UNITED STATES: RECONSTRUCTION AND REUNION: 1864–1888, at 918–1116 (New York: Macmillan, 1971).
67. Citizens' Saving & Loan Ass'n v. City of Topeka, 87 U.S. 655 (1874).
68. Fallbrook Irrigation Dist. v. Bradley, 164 U.S. 112 (1896).
69. Green v. Frazier, 253 U.S. 233, 240–41 (1920).
70. *E.g.*, Carothers v. Town of Booneville, 169 Miss. 511, 153 So. 670 (1934).
71. Jones v. City of Portland, 245 U.S. 217 (1917).
72. Standard Oil Co. v. City of Lincoln, 114 Neb. 243, 208 N.W. 962 (1926).
73. Note, *Municipal Subsidies and the Industrialization of the South*, 47 YALE L.J. 1412 (1938).
74. James M. Buchanan & Gordon Tullock, THE CALCULUS OF CONSENT: LOGICAL FOUNDATIONS OF CONSTITUTIONAL DEMOCRACY 198 (Ann Arbor: Univ. of Michigan, 1962).
75. *See, e.g.*, Louis Kaplow & Steven Shavell, *On the Superiority of Corrective Taxes to Quantity Regulation*, 4 AM. L. & ECON. REV. 1 (2002).
76. SMITH, WEALTH OF NATIONS, *supra* note 42, Book V, ch. 1, pt. iii, art. 1.
77. *E.g.*, Youngblood v. Sexton, 32 Mich. 406 (1875); J.F. Baker & Co. v. Panola County, 30 Tex. 86 (1867); City of Hannibal v. Guyott, 18 Mo. 515 (1853).
78. Washington v. State, 13 Ark. 752 (1853) (tax on billiard parlors); Wendover v. City of Lexington, 15 B.Mon. 258 (Ky. App. 1854) (lottery tax).
79. COOLEY, TAXATION, *supra* note 56, ch. 19, 586–606.
80. McCray v. United States, 195 U.S. 27 (1904).
81. United States v. Doremus, 249 U.S. 86 (1919).
82. Bailey v. Drexel Furniture Co., 259 U.S. 20 (1922).
83. Hammer v. Dagenhart, 247 U.S. 251 (1918); *see* Chapter 14.
84. Schollenberger v. Pennsylvania, 171 U.S. 1 (1898).
85. State v. Rippeth, 71 Ohio St. 85 (1904). *See* Ruth Dupré, *"If It's Yellow, It Must Be Butter": Margarine Regulation in North America since 1886*, 59 J. ECON. HIST. 353 (1999); Geoffrey P. Miller, *Public Choice at the Dawn of the Special Interest State: The Story of Butter and Margarine*, 77 CAL. L. REV. 83 (1989).
86. Collins v. New Hampshire, 171 U.S. 30 (1898). *See also* State v. Bruce, 55 W.Va. 384 (1904).
87. Plumley v. Massachusetts, 155 U.S. 461 (1894).

CHAPTER 6

1. Thorstein Veblen, THE THEORY OF THE LEISURE CLASS: AN ECONOMIC STUDY IN THE EVOLUTION OF INSTITUTIONS 188 (New York: Macmillan, 1899).
2. 1 Richard T. Ely, PROPERTY AND CONTRACT IN THEIR RELATIONS TO THE DISTRIBUTION OF WEALTH 55 (New York: Macmillan, 1914).

3. Walton Hamilton, *The Institutional Approach to Economic Theory*, 9 AM. ECON. REV. 316 (May 1919). *See* MALCOLM RUTHERFORD, THE INSTITUTIONALIST MOVEMENT IN AMERICAN ECONOMICS, 1918–1947, at 3–11 (Cambridge: Cambridge Univ. Press, 2011).
4. *See also* Charles H. Cooley, *The Institutional Character of Pecuniary Valuation*, 18 AM. J. SOC. 543, 546–50 (1913); Morris Copeland, *Economic Theory and the Natural Science Point of View*, 21 AM. ECON. REV. 67, 68 (1931). Good writing on institutionalism includes RUTHERFORD, THE INSTITUTIONALIST MOVEMENT, *supra* note 3; Geoffrey M. Hodgson, THE EVOLUTION OF INSTITUTIONAL ECONOMICS: AGENCY, STRUCTURE, AND DARWINISM IN AMERICAN INSTITUTIONALISM (London: Routledge, 2004).
5. *See, e.g.*, Melvin T. Copeland, THE COTTON MANUFACTURING INDUSTRY OF THE UNITED STATES (Cambridge, MA: Harvard Univ. Press, 1912); Arthur S. Dewing, CORPORATE PROMOTIONS AND REORGANIZATIONS (profiling numerous industries) (Cambridge, MA: Harvard Univ. Press, 1914). On this historical approach to industrial economics, *see* Herbert Hovenkamp, *The Antitrust Movement and the Rise of Industrial Organization*, 68 TEX. L. REV. 105, 111–15 (1989).
6. U.S. Bureau of Corporations studies include: THE STEEL INDUSTRY (in three parts: 1911, 1912, 1913); THE BEEF INDUSTRY (1905); TRANSPORTATION AND FREIGHT RATES IN CONNECTION WITH THE OIL INDUSTRY (1906); THE PETROLEUM INDUSTRY: POSITION OF THE STANDARD OIL COMPANY IN THE PETROLEUM INDUSTRY (1907); THE INTERNATIONAL HARVESTER CO. (1913). FTC studies include: REPORT ON THE BOOK-PAPER INDUSTRY (1917); REPORT ON FLOUR MILLING AND JOBBING (1918); REPORT ON CANNED FOODS (1918); REPORT ON THE MEAT-PACKING INDUSTRY (1919); REPORT ON LEATHER AND SHOE INDUSTRIES (1919); REPORT ON THE GRAIN TRADE (1920).
7. Bd. of Trade v. United States, 246 U.S. 231, 238 (1918).
8. *See* Richard T. Ely, *The Founding and Early History of the American Economic Association*, 26 AM. ECON. REV. 144 (1936); A.W. Coats, *The First Two Decades of the American Economic Association*, 50 AM. ECON. REV. 555 (1960).
9. *See, e.g.*, Paul T. Homan, *An Appraisal of Institutional Economics*, 22 AM. ECON. REV. 10 (1932); *Panel Discussion, Institutional Economics*, 22 AM. ECON. REV. SUPP. 105–16 (1932).
10. Edward A. Ross, SOCIAL CONTROL: A SURVEY OF THE FOUNDATIONS OF ORDER (New York: Macmillan, 1901).
11. John R. Commons, LEGAL FOUNDATIONS OF CAPITALISM 67–68, 121 (New York: Macmillan, 1924).
12. Adolf A. Berle, JR. & Gardiner C. Means, THE MODERN CORPORATION AND PRIVATE PROPERTY (New York: Harcourt, Brace & World, 1932).
13. *See* Frederic S. Lee, POST-KEYNESIAN PRICE THEORY 44–66 (New York: Cambridge Univ. Press, 1999).

14. *See* Adolf A. Berle, JR., NAVIGATING THE RAPIDS, 1918–1971 (New York: Harcourt Brace, 1973); Jordan A. Schwarz, LIBERAL: ADOLF A. BERLE AND THE VISION OF AN AMERICAN ERA (New York: Free Press, 1987).
15. *E.g.*, Morton White, SOCIAL THOUGHT IN AMERICA: THE REVOLT AGAINST FORMALISM (New York: Viking, 1949) (numerous references to Veblen; none to Clark, Fisher, or Knight); Henry Steele Commager, THE AMERICAN MIND (New Haven, CT: Yale, 1950) (lengthy discussion of Veblen; no mention of Knight; single mention of John Bates Clark, incorrectly lumped with the "classical economists" (236)); Richard Hofstadter, THE AGE OF REFORM (New York: Knopf, 1955) (several mentions of Veblen, Ely, and Commons; none of Clark, Fisher, or Knight).
16. *See* Robert L. Hale, *Coercion and Distribution in a Supposedly Non-coercive State*, 38 POL. SCI. Q. 470 (1923); Robert L. Hale, *Bargaining, Duress and Economic Liberty*, 43 COLUM. L. REV. 603 (1943); Hamilton, *Institutional Approach to Economic Theory, supra* note 3; Walton Hamilton, *Law and Economics*, 19 AM. ECON. REV. 56 (1929); William O. Douglas, *A Functional Approach to the Law of Business Associations*, 23 U. ILL. L. REV. 673 (1929); Underhill Moore & Theodore S. Hope, Jr., *An Institutional Approach to the Law of Commercial Banking*, 38 YALE L.J. 703 (1929).
17. Alfred Marshall, PRINCIPLES OF ECONOMICS 108 (London: Macmillan,1890).
18. *See* Arthur C. Pigou, THE ECONOMICS OF WELFARE 89 (London: Macmillan, 1924; 4th ed. 1932).
19. *See* 1 Frank William Taussig, PRINCIPLES OF ECONOMICS 132 (New York: Macmillan, 3d ed. 1921) ("inequality of incomes brings a less sum of human happiness than equality of incomes"); John Bates Clark, *The Ultimate Standard of Value*, 1 YALE REV. 258 (1893); Simon N. Patten, *The Scope of Political Economy*, 2 YALE REV. 264 (1894) (similar); Jacob Viner, *The Utility Concept in Value Theory and Its Critics (pts. 1 & 2)*, 33 J. POL. ECON. 369, 638 at 644 (1925) ("Changes in the relative distribution of income as between different classes will bring about changes in the amount of welfare, even though the aggregate real income of the community remains the same").
20. *See* THE CAMBRIDGE COMPANION TO LOGICAL EMPIRICISM (Alan Richardson & Thomas Uebel eds. Cambridge: Cambridge Univ. Press, 2007). For a good historical background, *see* Allan Janik & Stephen Toulmin, WITTGENSTEIN'S VIENNA (New York: Simon and Schuster, 1973).
21. Alfred J. Ayer, LANGUAGE, TRUTH, AND LOGIC 20 (New York: Dover, 1936).
22. *See* William H. Beveridge, THE LONDON SCHOOL OF ECONOMICS AND ITS PROBLEMS, 1919–1937, at 46–58 (London: Allen & Unwin, 1960).
23. Lionel Robbins, AN ESSAY ON THE NATURE & SIGNIFICANCE OF ECONOMIC SCIENCE 139–40 (London: Macmillan, 2d ed. 1935). *See also* Lionel Robbins, *Interpersonal Comparisons of Utility: A Comment*, 48 ECON. J. 635 (1938).

24. *See, e.g.*, I.M.D. Little, CRITIQUE OF WELFARE ECONOMICS 55–58 (Oxford: Clarendon Press, 1950); Roy F. Harrod, *Scope and Method of Economics*, 48 ECON. J. 383 (1938); John R. Hicks, *The Foundations of Welfare Economics*, 49 ECON. J. 696 (1939); Nicholas Kaldor, *Welfare Propositions of Economics and Inter-personal Comparisons of Utility*, 49 ECON. J. 549 (1939).
25. Quoted in Wesley C. Mitchell, *Bentham's Felicific Calculus*, 33 POL. SCI. Q. 161, 172 (1918).
26. Arthur C. Pigou, A STUDY IN PUBLIC FINANCE 29 (London: Macmillan, 1928). *Cf.* Gary S. Becker, HUMAN CAPITAL (Chicago: Univ. of Chicago Press, 3d ed. 1993).
27. Kaldor, *Welfare Propositions, supra* note 24.
28. *See* Chapter 1.
29. *E.g.*, Mollie Orshansky, *Counting the Poor: Another Look at the Poverty Profile*, 28 SOC. SEC. BULL. 3 (1965); Mollie Orshansky, *Measuring Poverty*, *in* THE SOCIAL WELFARE FORUM 211 (New York: Columbia, 1965).
30. An approachable introduction is Steven M. Sheffrin, RATIONAL EXPECTATIONS (New York: Cambridge Univ. Press, 2d ed., 1996).
31. A sampling of the scholarship on Legal Realism includes the following books, although there are many excellent articles as well. Hanoch Dagan, RECONSTRUCTING AMERICAN LEGAL REALISM & RETHINKING PRIVATE LAW THEORY (New York: Oxford Univ. Press, 2013); Neil Duxbury, PATTERNS OF AMERICAN JURISPRUDENCE (New York: Oxford Univ. Press, 1995); Morton J. Horwitz, THE TRANSFORMATION OF AMERICAN LAW: THE CRISIS OF LEGAL ORTHODOXY: 1870–1960, at 169–92 (New York: Oxford Univ. Press, 1992); N.E.H. Hull, ROSCOE POUND AND KARL LLEWELLYN: SEARCHING FOR AN AMERICAN JURISPRUDENCE (Chicago: Univ. of Chicago Press, 1997): Laura Kalman, LEGAL REALISM AT YALE, 1927–1960 (Chapel Hill: Univ. of North Carolina Press, 1986); Brian Leiter, NATURALIZING JURISPRUDENCE: ESSAYS ON AMERICAN LEGAL REALISM AND NATURALISM IN LEGAL PHILOSOPHY (New York: Oxford Univ. Press, 2007); Edward A. Purcell, JR., THE CRISIS OF DEMOCRATIC THEORY: SCIENTIFIC NATURALISM AND THE PROBLEM OF VALUE (Lexington: Univ. Press of Kentucky, 1973); Wilfred E. Rumble, JR., AMERICAN LEGAL REALISM: SKEPTICISM, REFORM AND THE JUDICIAL PROCESS (Ithaca, NY: Cornell Univ. Press, 1968); John Henry Schlegel, AMERICAN LEGAL REALISM AND EMPIRICAL SOCIAL SCIENCE (Chapel Hill: Univ. of North Carolina Press, 1995); William Twining, KARL LLEWELLYN AND THE REALIST MOVEMENT (London: Weidenfeld and Nicolson, 1973); G. Edward White, THE CONSTITUTION AND THE NEW DEAL (Cambridge, MA: Harvard Univ. Press, 2000).
32. Karl N. Llewellyn, *Some Realism about Realism—Responding to Dean Pound*, 44 HARV. L. REV. 1222, 1226–27 & n.18 (1931).

33. On Llewellyn's various list of Realists and the rationales for some of his choices, *see* HULL, ROSCOE POUND AND KARL LLEWELLYN, *supra* note 31, at 103–18.
34. Christopher Columbus Langdell, A SELECTION OF CASES ON THE LAW OF CONTRACTS, preface, viii, xi (Boston: Little, Brown, 1871).
35. Leon Green, THE JUDICIAL PROCESS IN TORTS CASES (St. Paul, MN: West, 1932).
36. Harry Shulman, *The Judicial Process in Tort Cases* (REVIEWING GREEN, *SUPRA*, NOTE 35), 45 HARV. L. REV. 1445 (1932), discussing Palsgraf v. Long Island R.R., 248 N.Y. 339, 162 N.E. 99 (1928). Shulman was a professor at Yale Law School and was its Dean from 1954 to 1965.
37. WHITE, SOCIAL THOUGHT IN AMERICA, *supra* note 15.
38. *E.g.*, Dierdre N. McCloskey, *The Loss Function Has Been Mislaid: The Rhetoric of Significance Tests*, 75 AM. ECON. REV. 201 (1985). For a good discussion of the issue in economics, *see* Bruce Caldwell, BEYOND POSITIVISM: ECONOMIC METHODOLOGY IN THE TWENTIETH CENTURY (London: Routledge, rev. ed. 1994).
39. George H. Daniels, AMERICAN SCIENCE IN THE AGE OF JACKSON 102–18 (New York: Columbia, 1968).
40. *E.g.*, Jerome Frank, LAW AND THE MODERN MIND (New York: Brentano's, 1930).
41. *E.g.*, Roscoe Pound, *Courts and Legislation,* 7 AM. POL. SCI. REV. 361 (1915); Roscoe Pound, *Justice According to Law (pts. 1–3)*, 13 COLUM. L. REV. 696 (1913), 14 COLUM. L. REV. 1, 103 (1914). On the Legal Realists' increasing concern with procedure, *see* SCHLEGEL, AMERICAN LEGAL REALISM, *supra* note 31, at 495–519.
42. Jerome Frank, COURTS ON TRIAL: MYTH AND REALITY IN AMERICAN JUSTICE 209–10 & n.62 (Princeton, NJ: Princeton Univ. Press, 1949).
43. *See, e.g.*, Roscoe Pound, *The Causes of Popular Dissatisfaction with the Administration of Justice*, 29 A.B.A. REP. 395 (1906); Roscoe Pound, *Liberty of Contract,* 18 YALE L.J. 454 (1909); Roscoe Pound, *Mechanical Jurisprudence*, 8 COL. L. REV. 605 (1908); Roscoe Pound, *The Scope and Purpose of Sociological Jurisprudence*, 24 HARV. L. REV. 591 (1911); 25 HARV. L. REV. 140, 489 (1912) (three parts).
44. His most extensive discussion is in *Scope and Purpose, supra* note 43, at 162–68.
45. *Id.* at 509 (referring to Edward A. Ross, SOCIAL PSYCHOLOGY (New York: Macmillan, 1908)). *See also* Roscoe Pound, *Social Problems and the Courts*, 18 AM. J. SOC. 331, 341 (1912); Roscoe Pound, *Legislation as a Social Function*, 18 AM. J. SOC. 755, 762 (1913); Roscoe Pound, *Making Law and Finding Law*, 82 CENTRAL L.J. 351, 358 (1916).
46. *See* Roscoe Pound, *The Limits of Effective Legal Action*, 3 A.B.A. J. 55 (1917).
47. Roscoe Pound, *Report of the Special Committee on Administrative Law*, 63 ANN. REP. A.B.A. 331, 342–43 (1938); ROSCOE POUND, ADMINISTRATIVE LAW: ITS GROWTH, PROCEDURE, AND SIGNIFICANCE 35 (Pittsburgh: Univ. of Pittsburgh Press, 1942).
48. 1 ROSCOE POUND, JURISPRUDENCE 447–55 (St. Paul, MN: West, 1959).

49. Karl N. Llewellyn, *A Realistic Jurisprudence—The Next Step*, 30 COL. L. REV. 431, 431–35 & n.3 (1930).
50. Roscoe Pound, *The Call for a Realist Jurisprudence*, 44 HARV. L. REV. 697 (1931). Llewellyn's response is Karl Llewellyn, *Some Realism about Realism, supra* note 32.
51. Roscoe Pound, *Call for Realist Jurisprudence*, 44 HARV. L. REV. 697, 702–08.
52. FRANK, LAW AND THE MODERN MIND, *supra* note 40.
53. Hessel Yntema, *American Legal Realism in Retrospect*, 14 VAND. L. REV. 317 (1960).
54. For an excellent account of the debate, including unpublished correspondence, *see* N.E.H. Hull, *Some Realism about the Llewellyn-Pound Exchange over Realism: The Newly Uncovered Private Correspondence, 1927–1931*, 1987 WIS. L. REV. 921.
55. AUGUSTE COMTE, COURS DE PHILOSOPHIE POSITIVE (Paris: Bachelier, 6 vols. 1830–1842). *See* Harriet Martineau's English translation and condensation: HARRIET MARTINEAU, THE POSITIVE PHILOSOPHY OF AUGUSTE COMTE (2 vols. London: J. Chapman, 1st ed. 1853).
56. *E.g.*, Albert G. Keller, *Law in Evolution*, 28 YALE L.J. 769, 769–70 (1919); EVOLUTION OF LAW: SELECT READINGS ON THE ORIGIN AND DEVELOPMENT OF LEGAL INSTITUTIONS (Albert Kocourek & John H. Wigmore eds., Boston: Little, Brown, 1915–1918) (3 vols.).
57. Pound, *Scope and Purpose, supra* note 43, at 491.
58. *See* NATHAN HALE, FREUD AND THE AMERICANS: THE BEGINNINGS OF PSYCHOANALYSIS IN THE UNITED STATES, 1876–1917 (New York: Oxford Univ. Press, 1971). For contemporary commentary, *see* James Putnam, *Personal Impressions of Sigmund Freud and His Work, with Special Reference to His Recent Lectures at Clark University*, 4 J. ABNORMAL PSYCH 293 (1909–1910).
59. Roscoe Pound, *Fifty Years of Jurisprudence*, 51 HARV. L. REV. 777, 784, 786 (1938).
60. ROBERT PARK & ERNEST BURGESS, INTRODUCTION TO THE SCIENCE OF SOCIOLOGY (Chicago: Univ. of Chicago Press, 1921).
61. ALBERT PAUL WEISS, A THEORETICAL BASIS OF HUMAN BEHAVIOR (Columbus, OH: R.G. Adams, 1925).
62. John B. Watson, BEHAVIORISM (New York: People's Institute, 1925). The internal conflicts in social science during this period are recounted in PURCELL, THE CRISIS OF DEMOCRATIC THEORY, *supra* note 31, at 15–46.
63. *See* N.E.H. Hull, *Reconstructing the Origins of Realistic Jurisprudence: A Prequel to the Llewellyn-Pound Exchange over Legal Realism*, 1989 DUKE L.J. 1302; HORWITZ, TRANSFORMATION II, *supra* note 31, at 169–82.
64. *E.g.*, Moore & Hope, *An Institutional Approach to the Law of Commercial Banking, supra* note 16; Underhill Moore & Charles Callahan, *Law and Learning Theory: A Study in Legal Control*, 53 YALE L.J. 1 (1943); Thurman Arnold, *Law Enforcement—An Attempt at Social Dissection*, 42 YALE L.J. 1 (1932).
65. KARL LLEWELLYN & E. ADAMSON HOEBEL, THE CHEYENNE WAY (Norman: Univ. of Oklahoma Press, 1941); Huntington Cairns, *Law and Anthropology*, 31 COL. L. REV. 32 (1931).
66. *E.g.*, FRANK, LAW AND THE MODERN MIND, *supra* note 40.

67. *E.g.*, Llewellyn, *A Realistic Jurisprudence*, *supra* note 49.
68. *E.g.*, FRANK, LAW AND THE MODERN MIND, *supra* note 40; Charles E. Clark, *Fact Research in Law Administration*, 2 CONN. BAR J. 211 (1928); William O. Douglas & J. Howard Marshall, *A Factual Study of Bankruptcy Administration and Some Suggestions*, 32 COL. L. REV. 25 (1932).
69. *E.g.*, Karl N. Llewellyn, *What Price Contract?—An Essay in Perspective*, 40 YALE L.J. 704 (1931).
70. Milton Handler, *False and Misleading Advertising*, 39 YALE L.J. 22 (1929).
71. *E.g.*, Hale, *Coercion and Distribution*, *supra* note 16; Standard Brands v. Smidler, 151 F.2d 34, 38–39 (2d Cir. 1945) (Frank, J., concurring).
72. FRANK, LAW AND THE MODERN MIND, *supra* note 40, at 111. *See also* Jerome Frank, *Are Judges Human?*, 80 U. PA. L. REV. 17, 22–23 (1931).
73. Herman Oliphant, *A Return to Stare Decisis*, 14 A.B.A. J. 71, 75 (1928).
74. Karl Llewellyn, THE BRAMBLE BUSH: ON OUR LAW AND ITS STUDY 72–75 (New York: Oceana, 1930); Karl Llewellyn, *Remarks on the Theory of Appellate Decision and the Rules or Canons about How Statutes Are to Be Construed*, 3 VAND. L. REV. 395, 399–406 (1950).
75. *See* Llewellyn, *Some Realism about Realism*, *supra* note 32, at 1237.
76. *See* Robert W. Gordon, *Professors and Policymakers: Yale Law School Faculty in the New Deal and After*, *in* HISTORY OF THE YALE LAW SCHOOL: THE TERCENTENNIAL LECTURES 75–137 (Anthony T. Kronman ed., New Haven, CT: Yale Univ. Press, 2004); KALMAN, LEGAL REALISM AT YALE, *supra* note 31; John Henry Schlegel, *American Legal Realism and Empirical Social Science: From the Yale Experience*, 28 BUFF. L. REV. 459 (1979).
77. *E.g.*, Moore & Hope, *An Institutional Approach to the Law of Commercial Banking*, *supra* note 16; Underhill Moore & Gilbert Sussman, *Legal and Institutional Methods Applied to the Debiting of Direct Discounts—III, the Connecticut Studies*, 40 YALE L.J. 752 (1931); others of this series of pieces can be found at 40 YALE L.J. 381; 40 YALE L.J. 555; 40 YALE L.J. 752; 40 YALE L.J. 928; 40 YALE L.J. 1055; and 40 YALE L.J. 1219. On Moore's research methodology, *see* John Henry Schlegel, *American Legal Realism and Empirical Social Science: The Singular Case of Underhill Moore*, 29 BUFF. L. REV. 195, 244–49 (1980). *See also* William O. Douglas & Dorothy S. Thomas, *The Business Failures Project—A Problem in Methodology*, 39 YALE L.J. 1013 (*1930*); Douglas & Marshall, *supra* note 68; Douglas, *A Functional Approach*, *supra* note 16.
78. *See* Hale, *Bargaining, Duress and Economic Liberty*, *supra* note 16; Hale, *Value to the Taker in Condemnation Proceedings*, 31 COL. L. REV. 1 (1931); Hale, *Coercion and Distribution*, *supra* note 16.
79. Hamilton, *The Institutional Approach*, *supra* note 3, at 312–16.
80. Lewis H. Haney, *Comments*, 9 AM. ECON. REV. SUPP. 321 (1919).
81. 15 AM. ECON. REV. 665, 668–75 (1925). *See also* RUTHERFORD, THE INSTITUTIONALIST MOVEMENT, *supra* note 3, at 242–47, 330–31.

82. *See* Gordon Tullock, ECONOMICS OF INCOME REDISTRIBUTION, esp. at 111–50 (Boston: Kluwer-Nijhoff, 1983); Gordon Tullock, THE ECONOMICS OF SPECIAL PRIVILEGE AND RENT SEEKING (Boston: Kluwer, 1989).

CHAPTER 7

1. 1 Francis Hilliard, THE LAW OF TORTS OR PRIVATE WRONGS 82 (Boston: Little, Brown, 1859).
2. *E.g.*, Wilkes v. Wood, Lofft 1, 98 Eng. Rep. 489 (C.P. 1763). In the United States, *see* Coryell v. Colbaugh, 1 N.J.L. 90 (1791); Hanna v. Sweeney, 78 Conn. 492, 62 A. 785 (1906). Hilliard treated punitive damages briefly in his treatise on tort remedies. *See* Francis Hilliard, THE LAW OF REMEDIES FOR TORTS, OR PRIVATE WRONGS 442–43, 456 (Boston: Little, Brown, 1867).
3. *See* Morton J. Horwitz, THE TRANSFORMATION OF AMERICAN LAW, 1870–1960: THE CRISIS OF LEGAL ORTHODOXY 115 (New York: Oxford Univ. Press, 1992).
4. The seminal work is James Willard Hurst, LAW AND ECONOMIC GROWTH: THE LEGAL HISTORY OF THE LUMBER INDUSTRY IN WISCONSIN, 1836–1915 (Cambridge, MA: Harvard Univ. Press, 1964). *See also* Morton J. Horwitz, THE TRANSFORMATION OF AMERICAN LAW, 1780–1860 (Cambridge, MA: Harvard Univ. Press, 1977). In the context of enterprise liability, *see* Herbert Hovenkamp, ENTERPRISE AND AMERICAN LAW, 1836–1937, at 1–67, 105–70 (Cambridge, MA: Harvard Univ. Press, 1991).
5. *See* Lawrence M. Friedman, A HISTORY OF AMERICAN LAW 146–47 (New York: Simon & Schuster, 3d ed. 2005); Michael Grossberg, GOVERNING THE HEARTH: LAW AND THE FAMILY IN NINETEENTH-CENTURY AMERICA (Chapel Hill: Univ. of North Carolina Press, 1985).
6. *See* Peggy A. Rabkin, FATHERS TO DAUGHTERS: THE LEGAL FOUNDATIONS OF FEMALE EMANCIPATION (Westport, CT: Greenwood, 1980); Norma Basch, IN THE EYES OF THE LAW: WOMEN, MARRIAGE, AND PROPERTY IN NINETEENTH-CENTURY NEW YORK (Ithaca, NY: Cornell Univ. Press, 1982); Richard H. Chused, *Married Women's Property Law: 1800–1850*, 71 GEO. L.J. 1359 (1983).
7. State v. Rhodes, 61 N.C. 453 (1868).
8. J. Herbie DiFonzo, BENEATH THE FAULT LINE: THE POPULAR AND LEGAL CULTURE OF DIVORCE IN TWENTIETH-CENTURY AMERICA (Charlottesville: Univ. of Virginia Press, 1997).
9. *E.g.*, Jennings-Heywood Oil Syn. v. Houssiere-Latreille Oil Co., 119 La. 793, 44 So. 481 (1907); Merchant v. O'Rourke, 111 Iowa 351, 82 N.W. 759 (1900). On lease covenants, *see* Mecklenburg Real Estate Co. v. Kyoleum Co., 142 Tenn. 295, 219 S.W. 821 (1920), following Chancellor Kent's decision in Rutgers v. Hunter, 6 Johns, Ch. 215 (N.Y. 1810).

10. *See* Chapter 2.
11. Francis Ysidro Edgeworth, MATHEMATICAL PSYCHICS: AN ESSAY ON THE APPLICATION OF MATHEMATICS TO THE MORAL SCIENCES 94–104 (London: Kegan Paul, 1881); Edgeworth, *The Hedonical Calculus*, 4 MIND 394 (1879); Alfred Marshall, PRINCIPLES OF ECONOMICS 196–97, 371, 421–46, 555, 794 (London: Macmillan, 1890). On Marshall and profit maximization, *see* Maria Cristina Marcuzzo & Eleonora Sanfilippo, *Profit Maximization in the Cambridge Tradition of Economics*, FIGHTING MARKET FAILURE: COLLECTED ESSAYS IN THE CAMBRIDGE TRADITION OF ECONOMICS 70–86 (Maria Cristina Marcuzzo ed., London: Routledge, 2011).
12. Samuel Williston, THE LAW OF CONTRACTS (New York: Baker, Voorhis, 1920).
13. Christopher C. Langdell, A SELECTION OF CASES ON THE LAW OF CONTRACTS (Boston: Little, Brown, 1871).
14. *E.g.*, Arthur L. Corbin, CORBIN ON CONTRACTS (St. Paul, MN: West, 1950); *see* Lawrence M. Friedman, CONTRACT LAW IN AMERICA: A SOCIAL AND ECONOMIC CASE STUDY 97–107 (Madison: Univ. of Wisconsin Press, 1965); Grant Gilmore, THE DEATH OF CONTRACT (Columbus: Ohio State Univ. Press, 1974).
15. *See* Alfred D. Chandler, JR., THE VISIBLE HAND: THE MANAGERIAL REVOLUTION IN AMERICAN BUSINESS (Cambridge, MA: Harvard Univ. Press, 1977), which covers the Colonial period through the mid-twentieth century. Glenn Porter & Harold C. Livesay, MERCHANTS AND MANUFACTURERS: STUDIES IN THE CHANGING STRUCTURE OF NINETEENTH-CENTURY MARKETING (Baltimore: Johns Hopkins Press, 1971); Ian R. Macneil, *Contracts: Adjustment of Long-Term Economic Relations under Classical, Neoclassical, and Relational Contract Law*, 72 NW. U. L. REV. 854 (1978); Charles J. Goetz & Robert E. Scott, *Principles of Relational Contracts*, 67 VA. L. REV. 1089 (1981).
16. *E.g.*, Grinnell v. Kiralfy, 55 Hun 422 (N.Y. S. Ct. 1890).
17. *E.g.*, Mills-Morris Co. v. Champion Spark Plug Co., 7 F.2d 38 (6th Cir. 1925).
18. A few exceptions are: Mason v. Cowan's Administrator, 40 Ky. 7 (1840) (farmer agreed to provide purchaser with all hogs raised in a year); *cf.* Cherry v. Smith, 22 Tenn. 19 (1842) (enforcing contract to ship "up to" 150 barrels of salt).
19. *E.g.*, Jones v. Binford, 74 Me. 439 (1883); Fontaine v. Baxley, 90 Ga. 416 (1892).
20. Cold Blast Transp. Co. v. Kansas City Bolt & Nut Co., 114 F. 77 (8th Cir. 1902); *see also* A. Santaella & Co. v. Otto F. Lange Co., 155 F. 719 (9th Cir. 1907); Crane v. C. Crane & Co., 105 F. 869, 871 (7th Cir. 1901).
21. Marx v. Am. Malting Co., 169 F. 582 (6th Cir. 1909); Ellis v. Dodge Bros., 246 F. 764 (5th Cir. 1917); Rosenthal v. Empire Brick & Supply Co., 108 N.Y. Sup. 347 (1st Dept 1908); Scott v. Stevenson Co., 130 Minn. 151, 153 N.W. 316 (1915); Lima Locomotive & Machine Co. v. Nat'l Steel Castings Co., 155 F. 77 (6th Cir. 1907); Manhattan Oil Co. v. Richardson Lubricating Co., 113 F. 923 (2d Cir. 1902).

22. Oakland Motor Car Co. v. Indiana Auto. Co., 201 F. 499 (7th Cir. 1922) (prospective car dealership); Nebraska Aircraft Corp. v. Varney, 282 F. 608 (8th Cir. 1922) (prospective aircraft dealership).
23. Garden City Sand Co. v. S. Fire Brick & Clay Co., 124 Ill. App. 599, 606, *aff'd*, 223 Ill. 616 (1906); *see also* Rozier v. St. Louis & S.F.R.R., 147 Mo. App. 599 (1910) (buyer's agreement to purchase quarry's output served as inducement for quarrier to enter the business).
24. Bloomington Canning Co. v. Union Can Co., 94 Ill. App. 62 (1901).
25. United States v. Am. Can Co., 230 F. 859 (D.C. Md. 1916).
26. *E.g.*, Connersville Wagon Co. v. McFarlan Carriage Co., 166 Ind. 123 (1904) (wheel manufacturer's supply contract to wagon manufacturer); Weil v. Chicago Pneumatic Tool Co., 138 Ark. 534 (1919) (truck manufacturer and dealer in trucks and parts); Phares v. Stover, 136 Ga. 843 (1911) (dealership agreement to sell various unnamed articles); Olson v. Whiffen, 175 Ill. App. 182 (1912) (bottling supplies to bottlers).
27. Wood v. Lucy, Lady Duff-Gordon, 222 N.Y. 88, 118 N.E. 214 (1917); *and see* Steven J. Burton, *Breach of Contract and the Common Law Duty to Perform in Good Faith*, 94 HARV. L. REV. 369 (1980).
28. Karl Llewellyn, *What Price Contract?—An Essay in Perspective*, 40 YALE L.J. 704, 705, 727 (1931).
29. UCC § 2–306.
30. Karl N. Llewellyn, *Our Case-Law of Contract: Offer and Acceptance, II*, 48 YALE L.J. 779, 789–90 (1939).
31. *See* Thomas S. Dicke, FRANCHISING IN AMERICA: THE DEVELOPMENT OF A BUSINESS METHOD, 1840–1980, at 155 (Chapel Hill: Univ. of North Carolina Press, 1992); Lawrence Howard Seltzer, A FINANCIAL HISTORY OF THE AMERICAN AUTOMOBILE INDUSTRY (Boston: Houghton Mifflin, 1928); Clare Elmer Griffin, *Wholesale Organization in the Automobile Industry*, 3 HARV. BUS. REV. 424 (1925); Richard Langlois & Paul Robertson, *Explaining Vertical Integration: Lessons from the American Automobile Industry*, 49 J. ECON. HIST. 361 (1989).
32. Marrinan Med. Supply v. Ft. Dodge Serum Co., 47 F.2d 458, 462 (8th Cir. 1931).
33. Silent Automatic Burner Co. v. Silent Automatic Corp., 214 Wis. 342, 252 N.W. 274 (1934).
34. Ford Motor Co. v. Kirkmyer Motor Co., 65 F.2d 1001, 1002–03 (4th Cir. 1933).
35. Grant Gilmore, *The Commercial Doctrine of Good Faith Purchase*, 63 YALE L.J. 1057, 1057 (1954).
36. Friedrich Kessler, *Automobile Dealer Franchises: Vertical Integration by Contract*, 66 YALE L.J. 1135 (1957).
37. On the nineteenth-century American law of waste, *see* HORWITZ, THE TRANSFORMATION OF AMERICAN LAW, 1780–1860, *supra* note 4, 54–58.

38. *See* Tom G. Geurts, *The Historical Development of the Lease in Residential Real Estate*, 32 REAL EST. L.J. 356 (2004).
39. *E.g.*, Dale E. Bennett, *The Modern Lease—An Estate in Land or a Contract (Damages for Anticipatory Breach and Interdependency of Covenants)*, 16 TEX. L. REV. 47 (1937).
40. *See* Mary Ann Glendon, *The Transformation of American Landlord-Tenant Law*, 23 B.C. L. Rev. 503 (1982).
41. Pub. L. No. 421, 77th Cong. 2d Sess. (Jan. 30, 1942). *See* Federal Housing and Rent Act of 1947, 61 Stat. 193 (1947). *See* John W. Willis, *The Federal Housing and Rent Act of 1947*, 47 COLUM. L. REV. 1118 (1947). New York City had regulated rents earlier. *See* Robert M. Fogelson, THE GREAT RENT WARS: NEW YORK, 1917–1929 (New Haven, CT: Yale Univ. Press, 2013)
42. *See* John W. Willis, *A Short History of Rent Control Laws*, 36 CORNELL L.Q. 54, 87–88 (1950); *see also* Bowles v. Willingham, 321 U.S. 503, 516–21 (1944) (upholding rent control as wartime emergency measure).
43. *E.g.*, Javins v. First Nat. Realty Corp., 428 F.2d 1071 (D.C. Cir. 1970); Amanuensis, Ltd. v. Brown, 65 Misc.2d 15, 318 N.Y.S.2d 11 (Civ. Ct. 1971); Reste Realty Corp. v. Cooper, 53 N.J. 444, 251 A.2d 268 (1969); Mease v. Fox, 200 N.W.2d 791 (Iowa 1972).
44. RESTATEMENT (SECOND) OF PROPERTY, LANDLORD AND TENANT §§ 5.4, 5.5 (1977).
45. 1 John Forrest Dillon, TREATISE ON THE LAW OF MUNICIPAL CORPORATIONS 409, 410 (Chicago: Cockroft, 1872); *see also* Thomas M. Cooley, A TREATISE ON THE CONSTITUTIONAL LIMITATIONS WHICH REST UPON THE LEGISLATIVE POWER OF THE STATES OF THE AMERICAN UNION (Boston: Little, Brown, 1868).
46. Parker & Edgarton v. Foote, 19 Wend 309 (N.Y. 1838); 2 Emory Washburn, A TREATISE ON THE AMERICAN LAW OF REAL PROPERTY 62 (Boston: Little, Brown, 1860–1862). *See also* Stuart Banner, AMERICAN PROPERTY: A HISTORY OF HOW, WHY, AND WHAT WE OWN 16–18 (Cambridge, MA: Harvard Univ. Press, 2011).
47. 2 HILLIARD, LAW OF TORTS, *supra* note 1, at 66.
48. Oliver W. Holmes, Jr., *Privilege, Malice, and Intent,* 8 HARV. L.REV. 1, 3 (1894).
49. *See* Michael R. Montgomery, *Keeping the Tenants Down: Height Restrictions and Manhattan's Tenement House System, 1885–1930*, 22 CATO J. 495, 503–04 (2003).
50. Welch v. Swasey, 214 U.S. 91 (1909).
51. *See* Lochner v. New York, 198 U.S. 45 (1905).
52. *See* Village of Euclid v. Ambler Realty Co., 272 U.S. 365 (1926); Adkins v. Children's Hosp., 261 U.S. 525, 545 (1923).
53. 277 U.S. 183 (1928).
54. *See* Jesse Dukeminier, Jr. & Clyde Stapleton, *The Zoning Board of Adjustment: A Case Study in Misrule*, 50 KY. L.J. 273 (1962).

55. RESTATEMENT (FIRST) TORTS § 826 (1939).
56. *E.g.*, Penn Cent. Transp. Co. v. New York City, 438 U.S. 104 (1978); Goldblatt v. Town of Hempstead, N.Y., 369 U.S. 590 (1962); Hadacheck v. Sebastian, 239 U.S. 394 (1915) (excluding brick kilns in city limits; petitioner's land 87.5 percent less valuable as a result).
57. Pennsylvania Coal Co. v. Mahon, 260 U.S. 393 (1922); United States v. Causby, 328 U.S. 256 (1946) (harmful flyovers by military aircraft). Commentary from the 1960s includes Frank I. Michelman, *Property, Utility, and Fairness: Comments on the Ethical Foundations of "Just Compensation" Law*, 80 HARV. L. REV. 1165 (1967); Joseph L. Sax, *Takings and the Police Power*, 74 YALE L.J. 36 (1964).
58. Shelley v. Kraemer, 334 U.S. 1 (1948); Buchanan v. Warley, 245 U.S. 60 (1917).
59. 42 U.S.C. § 3601 *et seq* (1968).
60. Arthur A. Ballantine, *A Compensation Plan for Railway Accident Claims*, 29 HARV. L. REV. 705 (1916). Ballantine became a prominent tax attorney and served as undersecretary of the treasury to President Hoover. He was a founding partner of Dewey, Ballantine, once a prominent New York law firm.
61. Oliver Wendell Holmes, Jr., Book Review 5 AM. L. REV. 340 (1871) (review of C.G. ADDISON, THE LAW OF TORTS (New York: Cockcroft, 1870)). *See* John Wigmore, *Justice Holmes and the Law of Torts*, 29 HARV. L. REV. 601 (1916).
62. Thomas G. Shearman & Amasa A. Redfield, A TREATISE ON THE LAW OF NEGLIGENCE (New York: Baker, Voorhis, 1869); Oliver W. Holmes, Jr., *The Theory of Torts*, 7 AM. L. REV. 652 (1873); Oliver Wendell Holmes, Jr., *Privilege, Malice, and Intent*, 8 HARV. L. REV. 1 (1894); Oliver Wendell Holmes, JR., THE COMMON LAW (Boston: Little, Brown, 1881).
63. In the United States, Brown v. Kendall, 60 Mass. (6 Cush.) 292 (1850) (Shaw, C.J., adopting a negligence interpretation of writ of trespass on the case). *See* G. Edward White, TORT LAW IN AMERICA: AN INTELLECTUAL HISTORY 12–19, 112–84 (New York: Oxford Univ. Press, 2003); Peter Karsten, HEART VERSUS HEAD: JUDGE-MADE LAW IN NINETEENTH-CENTURY AMERICA 97–128 (Chapel Hill: Univ. of North Carolina Press 1997); HORWITZ, THE TRANSFORMATION OF AMERICAN LAW, 1780–1860, *supra* note 4, at 85–99.
64. 1 HILLIARD, LAW OF TORTS, *supra* note 1, at 124.
65. SHEARMAN & REDFIELD, NEGLIGENCE, *supra* note 62, at 322.
66. Frink v. Potter, 17 Ill. 406 (1856).
67. Ingalls v. Bills, 9 Metcalf 1, 50 Mass. 1 (1845).
68. Vaughan v. Menlove, 132 Eng. Rep. 490 (C.P. 1837).
69. Leon Green, *Are Negligence and "Proximate" Cause Determinable by the Same Test?—Texas Decisions Analyzed*, 1 TEX. L. REV. 243, 423 (1923).
70. *See* Herbert Hovenkamp, *Pragmatic Realism and Proximate Cause in America*, 3 J. LEGAL HIST. 3, 6–7, 14–18 (1982) (discussing Wharton's disparagement of multiple causation). For an alternative account, *see* KARSTEN, HEART VERSUS HEAD, *supra* note 63, at 101–05.

71. New York Cent. R.R. v. Grimstad, 264 F. 334 (2d Cir. 1920).
72. Blythe v. Denver & Rio Grande Railway Co., 25 P. 702 (Colo. 1891); *see also* Melville Peck, THE DOCTRINE OF PROXIMATE CAUSE AND LAST CLEAR CHANCE (Richmond, VA: Peck, 1914).
73. 51 N.E. 1 (Mass. 1898). *See* Leon Green, RATIONALE OF PROXIMATE CAUSE 203 *et seq*. (Kansas City, MO: Vernon, 1927).
74. Holmes served on the Supreme Judicial Court of Massachusetts from 1882 to 1902, when he was appointed by President Theodore Roosevelt to the U.S. Supreme Court.
75. Mott v. Hudson River R. Co., 1 Rob 585 (N.Y. 1863).
76. SHEARMAN & REDFIELD, NEGLIGENCE, *supra* note 62, at 6. *Cf.* KARSTEN, HEART VERSUS HEAD, *supra* note 63, at 102–03, who finds others.
77. SHEARMAN & REDFIELD, NEGLIGENCE, *supra* note 62, at 46 (6th ed. 1913); Thomas M. Cooley, A TREATISE ON THE LAW OF TORTS (Chicago: Callaghan, 1880; 2d ed. 1888; 3d ed. 1907).
78. On Aristotle's nomenclature of causation, *see* David Ross, ARISTOTLE 74–79 (London: Methuen, 1923).
79. RESTATEMENT (FIRST) CONFLICT OF LAWS §§ 312, 377–378 (1934). Beale defended this approach in 3 Joseph H. Beale, A TREATISE ON THE CONFLICT OF LAWS 1969 (New York: Baker, Voorhis, 1935).
80. Joseph H. Beale, *The Proximate Consequences of an Act*, 33 HARV. L. REV. 633, 641 (1920); *see also* James Angell McLaughlin, *Proximate Cause*, 39 HARV. L. REV. 149 (1925); Albert Levitt, *Cause, Legal Cause and Proximate Cause*, 21 MICH. L. REV. 34, 160 (1922).
81. *See* John Stuart Mill, A SYSTEM OF LOGIC, RATIOCINATIVE AND INDUCTIVE 241, 378 (London: John W. Parker, 1843) (New York: Harper, 8th ed. 1874); *see* H.L.A. Hart & Tony Honore, CAUSATION IN THE LAW 19 (Oxford: Clarendon Press, 2d ed. 1985).
82. Francis Wharton, A SUGGESTION AS TO CAUSATION (Cambridge, MA: Riverside Press, 1874). Wharton's *Suggestion* was originally an appendix to the first edition of his TREATISE ON THE LAW OF NEGLIGENCE (Philadelphia: Kay & Brother, 1874). *See* Hovenkamp, *Pragmatic Realism, supra* note 70, at 3, 6–7, 14–18.
83. Francis Wharton, THE LIABILITY OF RAILWAY COMPANIES FOR REMOTE FIRES: PROXIMATE AND REMOTE CAUSE 5, 17, 18 (St. Louis, MO: Jones, 1878). Wharton borrowed most of his ideas from Rhode Island reformer and businessman Rowland Gibson Hazard's Two Letters on Causation and Freedom in Willing Addressed to John Stuart Mill (London: Longmans, 1869).
84. *See* Louis Menand, THE METAPHYSICAL CLUB: A STORY OF IDEAS IN AMERICA (New York: Farrar, Straus & Giroux, 2001).
85. On American Pragmatism, *see* Horace S. Thayer, MEANING AND ACTION: A CRITICAL HISTORY OF PRAGMATISM (Indianapolis, IN: Bobbs-Merrill, 1968); Bruce Kuklick, THE RISE OF AMERICAN PHILOSOPHY:

CAMBRIDGE, MASSACHUSETTS, 1860–1930, at 104ff (New Haven, CT: Yale Univ. Press, 1977). On Peirce and causation theory, *see* Ian Hacking, THE TAMING OF CHANCE 200–03 (New York: Cambridge Univ. Press, 1990).

86. *See* Vincent Batts, Thomas Cook & John Lincourt, *Hypothetical Fallibilism in Peirce and Jevons*, 15 TRANSACTIONS CHARLES S. PEIRCE SOC'Y 132 (1979).
87. Charles S. Peirce, *Note on the Theory of the Economy of Research*, 1875 COAST SURVEY REPORT 197–201, *reprinted in* THE WRITINGS OF CHARLES S. PEIRCE: 1879–1884, at 73 (Christian J.W. Kloesel ed., Bloomington: Indiana Univ. Press, 1989); *see also* Charles Sanders Peirce, *The Doctrine of Necessity Examined*, THE MONIST 321–37 (1892).
88. *See* E.E. Liebhafsky, *The Influence of Charles Sanders Peirce on Institutional Economics*, 27 J. ECON. ISSUES 741 (1993).
89. Charles S. Peirce, *How to Make Our Ideas Clear*, 12 POPULAR SCI. MONTHLY 286, 299 (1878). Other quotations are from Charles Sanders Peirce, COLLECTED PAPERS OF CHARLES SANDERS PEIRCE 358ff, 388ff, 464ff, 470ff, 491ff (Charles Hartshorne & Paul Weiss eds., Cambridge, MA: Harvard Univ. Press, 1931–1935). These essays were written in the 1860s and 1870s.
90. Charles Sanders Peirce, *Review of Sidney Edward Mezes's Ethics: Descriptive and Explanatory*, 73 THE NATION 325, 326 (1901), *reprinted in* 8 COLLECTED PAPERS OF CHARLES SANDERS PEIRCE 122, 123 (Cambridge, MA: Harvard, 1958).
91. PEIRCE, REVIEW OF SIDNEY EDWARD MEZES'S ETHICS, *supra* note 90 at 326.
92. PEIRCE, 6 COLLECTED PAPERS, *supra* note 89, at 28–66, 275 (Cambridge, MA: Harvard Univ. Press, 1965); *compare* William James, ESSAYS IN RADICAL EMPIRICISM 155 *et seq.* (London: Longmans, Green, 1912).
93. PEIRCE, 5 COLLECTED PAPERS, *supra* note 89, at 12–13. For more on Nicholas St. John Green, *see* Philip P. Wiener, EVOLUTION AND THE FOUNDERS OF PRAGMATISM 152–71 (Cambridge, MA: Harvard Univ. Press, 1949); KUKLICK, THE RISE OF AMERICAN PHILOSOPHY, *supra* note 85, at 47ff. On the relationship between Green and Holmes, see MENAND, METAPHYSICAL CLUB, *supra* note 84, at 222–27.
94. The statement is quoted in his obituary in 12 DAEDULUS: PROC. AM. ACAD. ARTS & SCI. 289, 290 (1876).
95. Nicholas St. Green, *Proximate and Remote Cause*, 4 AM. L. REV. 201, 211–12 (1870).
96. HOLMES, THE COMMON LAW, *supra* note 62, 92.
97. Francis H. Bohlen, *The Probable or the Natural Consequences as the Test of Liability in Negligence*, 40 (n.s.) AM. L. REG. 79, 148 (1901). On Bohlen's career and the Restatement (First) of Torts, *see* WHITE, TORT LAW IN AMERICA, *supra* note 63, 310–16.
98. Pletcher v. Scranton Traction Co., 185 Pa. 147, 39 A. 837 (Pa. 1898); *see also* Bergen County Traction Co. v. Heitman's Adm'r, 61 N.J.L. 682, 40 A. 651 (N.J. Err. & App. 1898).

99. Jeremiah Smith, *Legal Cause in Actions of Tort*, 25 HARV. L. REV. 303 (1912); RESTATEMENT OF TORTS § 421 (1934). *See* Henry W. Edgerton, *Legal Cause*, 72 U. PA. L. REV. 211, 343 (1924).
100. Seale v. G.C. & S.F. Rwy. Co., 65 Tex. 274 (1889).
101. Green, *Are Negligence and "Proximate Cause" Determinable by the Same Test?*, *supra* note 69, at 243, 248, 251; GREEN, RATIONALE OF PROXIMATE CAUSE, *supra* note 73, at 71, 122.
102. Leon Green, JUDGE AND JURY 223 (Kansas City, MO: Vernon, 1930).
103. *See* Jerome Frank, LAW AND THE MODERN MIND (New York: Brentano's, 1930), *passim.*
104. Leon Green, *The Duty Problem in Negligence Cases*, 28 COLUM. L. REV. 1014, 1016–17 (1928); *see* Charles K. Ogden & Ivor A. Richards, THE MEANING OF MEANING 18, 44 (London: Kegan Paul, 1923). On Ogden's and Richards's indebtedness to Peirce, *see* THAYER, MEANING AND ACTION, *supra* note 85, at 305–06.
105. *E.g.*, Palsgraf v. Long Island R.R., 248 N.Y. 339, 341, 162 N.E. 99 (N.Y. 1928); *see* Arthur L. Goodhart, *The Unforeseeable Consequences of a Negligent Act*, 39 YALE L.J. 449 (1930).
106. RESTATEMENT (THIRD) OF TORTS, PHYSICAL AND EMOTIONAL HARM § 6, Special Note (2010–2011); *see also* RESTATEMENT (THIRD) OF TORTS, PHYSICAL AND EMOTIONAL HARM § 26, Comment A.
107. *See* James W. Ely, JR., RAILROADS AND AMERICAN LAW (Lawrence: Univ. Press of Kansas, 2002).
108. Frank H. Knight, RISK, UNCERTAINTY AND PROFIT (Boston: Houghton Mifflin, 1921).
109. *See* Milton Friedman & L.J. Savage, *The Utility Analysis of Choices Involving Risk*, 56 J. POL. ECON. 279 (1948); *and see* John Von Neumann & Oskar Morgenstern, THEORY OF GAMES AND ECONOMIC BEHAVIOR (Princeton, NJ: Princeton Univ. Press, 1944), which quantified many of Knight's observations about risk, in particular the idea that economic actors maximize their expected utility.
110. Allan H. Willett, ECONOMIC THEORY OF RISK AND INSURANCE (New York: Columbia Univ. Press, 1901).
111. On this point, *see* KNIGHT, RISK, UNCERTAINTY, *supra* note 108, at 59–60.
112. William O. Douglas, *Vicarious Liability and Administration of Risk, I & II*, 38 YALE LJ. 584, 720 (1929).
113. Nashville Ry. v. White, 278 U.S. 456, 459 (1929).
114. Henry T. Terry, *Negligence*, 29 HARV. L. REV. 40 (1915).
115. Warren A. Seavey, *Negligence—Subjective or Objective?*, 41 HARV. L. REV. 1, 7–8 (1927). On Seavey, *see* Warren A. Seavey & Donald B. King, A HARVARD LAW PROFESSOR: WARREN A. SEAVEY'S LIFE AND THE WORLD OF LEGAL EDUCATION 65 (Buffalo, NY: W.S. Hein, 2005).
116. RESTATEMENT (FIRST) OF TORTS §§ 284, 291. *See* Patrick J. Kelley, *The First Restatement of Torts: Reform by Descriptive Theory*, 32 S. ILL. U. L.J. 93 (2007).

117. Gimmestad v. Rose Bros. Co., 194 Minn. 531, 537, 261 N.W. 194 (1935) (citing Restatement, Torts (Tentative Draft No. 4) § 209).
118. United States v. Carroll Towing Co., 159 F.2d 169 (2d Cir. 1947).
119. Kahn v. James Burton Co., 5 Ill. 2d 614, 623 (1955). *See also* Knight v. Kaiser Co., 305 P.2d 248, 254 (Cal. App. 1957) (using same language). The Hand formula is explained and a version of it defended in Richard A. Posner, *A Theory of Negligence*, 1 J. LEGAL STUD. 29 (1972).
120. On the complex facts, *see* Stephen Gilles, United States v. Carroll Towing Co.: *The Hand Formula's Home Port, in* TORTS STORIES 11, 12–14 (Robert Rabin & Stephen Sugarman eds., New York: Foundation Press, 2003).
121. Herbert P. Stellwagen, *Automobile Rate Making*, 11 PROC. CASUALTY ACTUARIAL SOC'Y 276, 285 (1925).
122. *See* H. Laurence Ross, SETTLED OUT OF COURT: THE SOCIAL PROCESS OF INSURANCE CLAIMS ADJUSTMENT 141 (Chicago: Aldine, 1970).
123. 1 HILLIARD, LAW OF TORTS, *supra* note 1.
124. *E.g.*, Johnson v. Hudson Rwy. 20 N.Y. 65 (N.Y. 1859).
125. HILLIARD, LAW OF TORTS, *supra* note 1, at 129, *discussing* Leighton v. Sargent, 7 Fost. 460 (N.H. 1853).
126. Byrne v. Boadle, 159 Eng. Rep. 299 (Ex. 1863).
127. *E.g.*, Wilkes v. Memphis Grocery Co., 23 Tenn. App. 550 (1939) (dead flies in bottle; refusing to apply res ipsa); Perry v. Kelford Coca-Cola Bottling Co., 196 N.C. 175 (1928); Rozumailski v. Philadelphia Coca-Cola Bottling Co., 296 Pa. 114 (1929); Atlanta Coca-Cola Bottling Co. v. Holbrook, 40 Ga. App. 269 (1929) (tin wrappers found in bottle, poisoning contents); Reece v. Durham Coca-Cola Bottling Co., 197 N.C. 661 (1929) (insect); Yates v. Coca-Cola Bottling Works, 14 Tenn. App. 7 (1931) (decomposed fly or bug; res ipsa rejected); Coca- Cola Bottling Co. v. Rowland, 16 Tenn. App. 184 (1932) (decomposed mouse; refusing to apply res ipsa).
128. *See* J. C. Louis & Harvey Z. Yazijian, THE COLA WARS (New York: Everest House, 1980); John J. Riley, A HISTORY OF THE AMERICAN SOFT DRINK INDUSTRY: BOTTLED CARBONATED BEVERAGES, 1807–1957 (Washington, DC: American Bottlers of Carbonated Beverages, 1958).
129. Hudgins v. Coca-Cola Bottling Co., 122 Ga. 695, 50 S.E. 974 (1905).
130. *E.g.*, Payne v. Rome Coca-Cola Bottling Co., 10 Ga. App. 762 (1912) (applying res ipsa); Atlanta Coca-Cola Bottling Co. v. Danneman, 25 Ga. App. 43 (1920); Coca-Cola Bottling Works v. Shelton, 214 Ky. 118 (1926); Birn v. Coca Cola Bottling Corp., 31 Ohio N.P. 441, 1933 WL 1644 (Ohio Com. Pl. 1933) (refusing to apply res ipsa because plaintiff had set bottle in sun on a hot day).
131. Escola v. Coca-Cola Bottling Co., 150 P.2d 436, 437, 440, 460, 463 (Cal. 1944). On *Escola, see* MARK GEISTFELD, Escola v. Coca-Cola Bottling Co.: *Strict Products Liability Unbound, in* TORTS STORIES, *supra* note 120, at 229.
132. *Escola, supra*, 150 P.2d at 463.

133. *See* Fleming James, Jr., *General Products—Should Manufacturers Be Liable without Negligence?*, 24 TENN. L. REV. 923 (1957); Fleming James, Jr., *Products Liability, II*, 34 TEX. L. REV. 192, 228 (1955); William L. Prosser, *The Assault upon the Citadel (Strict Liability to the Consumer)*, 69 YALE L.J. 1099 (1960); William L. Prosser, *The Fall of the Citadel (Strict Liability to the Consumer)*, 50 MINN. L. REV. 791 (1966).
134. Harry Schulman & Fleming James, JR., CASES AND MATERIALS ON THE LAW OF TORTS, at vii (Chicago: Foundation, 1942).
135. Greenman v. Yuba Power Prods., Inc., 377 P.2d 897 (Cal. 1963); *see also* Vandermark v. Ford Motor Co., 391 P.2d 168 (Cal. 1964) (extending strict liability to retailers). On the debate over whether strict liability doctrine should develop out of contract and warranty doctrine rather than tort doctrine, *see* Peter W. Huber, LIABILITY: THE LEGAL REVOLUTION AND ITS CONSEQUENCES (New York: Basic, 1988); George L. Priest, *The Invention of Enterprise Liability: A Critical History of the Intellectual Foundations of Modern Tort Law*, 14 J. LEGAL STUD. 461, 505–11 (1985).
136. RESTATEMENT (SECOND) OF CONTRACTS § 402A (1981).
137. *See* John Prather Brown, *Toward an Economic Theory of Liability*, 2 J. LEGAL STUD. 323 (1973); Richard A. Posner, *Strict Liability: A Comment*, 2 J. LEGAL STUD. 205 (1973).
138. Principally by John Wade, Dean of Vanderbilt Law School. *See* John W. Wade, *On the Nature of Strict Tort Liability for Products*, 44 MISS. L.J. 825 (1973); *see, e.g.*, Byrns v. Riddell, Inc., 113 Ariz. 264 (1976) (football helmet); Cepeda v. Cumberland Eng'g Co., Inc., 76 N.J. 152 (1978) (pellet-crushing machine).
139. Walter J. Blum & Harry Kalven, Jr., *Public Law Perspectives on a Private Law Problem—Auto Compensation Plans*, 31 U. CHI. L. REV. 641 (1964).
140. Charles O. Gregory & Harry Kalven, JR., CASES AND MATERIALS ON TORTS 690–702 (Boston: Little, Brown, 1959).
141. Blum & Kalven, *Public Law Perspectives*, *supra* note 139, at 701.
142. Ronald H. Coase, *The Problem of Social Cost*, 3 J.L. & ECON. 1 (1960). On Blum and Kalven's treatment of Coase, *see* Steven G. Medema, *Legal Scholarship and the Coase Theorem in the 1960s* (2014) (BePress Working Paper, available at http://works.bepress.com/steven_medema/1/).
143. Blum & Kalven, *Public Law Perspectives*, *supra* note 139, at 700.
144. Ins. Co. of North Am. v. Forty-Eight Insulations, Inc., 633 F.2d 1212, 1231 (6th Cir. 1980).
145. Guido Calabresi & Jon T. Hirschoff, *Toward a Test for Strict Liability in Torts*, 81 YALE L.J. 1055, 1060 (1972).
146. Guido Calabresi, *Optimal Deterrence and Accidents*, 84 YALE L.J. 656, 666 (1975). *See also* Richard A. Posner, *Guido Calabresi's The Cost of Accidents: A Reassessment*, 64 MD. L. REV. 12 (2005). For a good historical background, *see* Laura Kalman, *Some Thoughts on Yale and Guido*, 76 LAW & CONTEMP. PROBS. (2014).

147. *E.g.*, Francis Wharton, A TREATISE ON THE LAW OF NEGLIGENCE 21–58 (Philadelphia: Key and Brother, 1st ed. 1874, 2d ed. 1878); Nicholas St. John Green, *The Three Degrees of Negligence*, 8 AM. L. REV. 649 (1874); *see* HORWITZ, TRANSFORMATION OF AMERICAN LAW, 1870–1960, *supra* note 3, at 112–18.
148. *See* Victor E. Schwartz & Eveyn F. Rowe, COMPARATIVE NEGLIGENCE, § 1.01 (Indianapolis, IN: A. Smith Co., 5th ed. 2010). On the history, *see* WHITE, TORT LAW IN AMERICA, *supra* note 63, at 164–68.
149. *E.g.*, Union Stock Yards Co. v. Chicago, Burlington, & Quincy R.R., 196 U.S. 217 (1905).
150. *E.g.*, Matthews v. Delaware, L. & W. R. Co., 56 N.J.L. 34, 27 A. 919 (N.J. Sup. 1893).
151. City of Mansfield v. Brister, 76 Ohio St. 270 (1907).
152. Oliver v. Miles, 144 Miss. 852, 110 So. 666, 668 (Miss. 1926).
153. Summers v. Tice, 33 Cal. 2d 80, 199 P.2d 1 (1948); *see also* Reyher v. Mayne, 90 Colo. 586, 10 P.2d 1109 (Colo. 1932).
154. Sindell v. Abbott Labs., 607 P.2d 924 (Cal. 1980).

CHAPTER 8

1. *E.g.*, Merle E. Curti, THE GROWTH OF AMERICAN THOUGHT 634 (New Brunswick: Transaction Pub., 3d ed. 1964); Arthur S. Miller, THE SUPREME COURT AND AMERICAN CAPITALISM 51 (New York: Free Press, 1968); D.K. Adams, AMERICA IN THE 20TH CENTURY: A STUDY OF THE UNITED STATES SINCE 1917, at 27 (New York: Cambridge Univ. Press, 1967); Howard Ross Smith, GOVERNMENT AND BUSINESS: A STUDY IN ECONOMIC EVOLUTION 251 (New York: Ronald Press, 1958); Samuel P. Hays, THE RESPONSE TO INDUSTRIALISM, 1885–1914, at 108 (Chicago: Univ. of Chicago Press, 1957).
2. *E.g.*, Benjamin Twiss, LAWYERS AND THE CONSTITUTION: HOW LAISSEZ FAIRE CAME TO THE SUPREME COURT (Princeton, NJ: Princeton Univ. Press, 1942); Richard Hofstadter, SOCIAL DARWINISM IN AMERICAN THOUGHT, 1860–1915, at 5-6 (Philadelphia: Univ. of Pennsylvania Press, 1944); Clyde E. Jacobs, LAW WRITERS AND THE COURTS: THE INFLUENCE OF THOMAS E. COOLEY, CHRISTOPHER G. TIEDEMAN, AND JOHN F. DILLON UPON AMERICAN CONSTITUTIONAL LAW (Berkeley: Univ. of California Press, 1954); Arnold M. Paul, CONSERVATIVE CRISIS AND THE RULE OF LAW: ATTITUDES OF BAR AND BENCH, 1887–1895 (Ithaca, NY: Cornell Univ. Press, 1960); Alfred H. Kelly AND Winfred A. Harbison, THE AMERICAN CONSTITUTION: ITS ORIGINS AND DEVELOPMENT (New York: W.W. Norton, 1963).
3. *E.g.*, Andrew Carnegie, *The Gospel of Wealth*, 148 N. AM. REV. 653 (1889), reprinted with other speeches and essays in ANDREW CARNEGIE, THE GOSPEL OF WEALTH AND OTHER WRITINGS (David Nasaw ed., New York: Penguin, 2006).
4. Lochner v. New York, 198 U.S. 45, 65 (1905).

5. Henry Steel Commager, THE AMERICAN MIND: AN INTERPRETATION OF AMERICAN THOUGHT AND CHARACTER SINCE THE 1880S, at 82–90, 372–73 (New Haven, CT: Yale, 1950).
6. *E.g.*, Robert C. Bannister, SOCIAL DARWINISM: SCIENCE AND MYTH IN ANGLO-AMERICAN SOCIAL THOUGHT (Philadelphia: Temple Univ. Press, 1979). *See also* Mike Hawkins, SOCIAL DARWINISM IN EUROPEAN AND AMERICAN THOUGHT, 1860–1945: NATURE AS MODEL AND NATURE AS THREAT (Cambridge: Cambridge Univ. Press, 1997), which is more qualified than Bannister.
7. *See* Herbert Hovenkamp, ENTERPRISE AND AMERICAN LAW, 1836–1937, at 11–66 (Cambridge, MA: Harvard Univ. Press, 1991).
8. Santa Clara Co. v. S. Pacific R.R., 118 U.S. 394, 396 (1886); HOVENKAMP, ENTERPRISE, *supra* note 7, ch. 4; Morton J. Horwitz, Santa Clara *Revisited: the Development of Corporate Theory*, 88 W. VA. L. REV. 173, 174 (1985).
9. Adam Smith, AN INQUIRY INTO THE NATURE AND CAUSES OF THE WEALTH OF NATIONS 13 (Chicago: Univ. of Chicago Press, 1952 [1776]).
10. David Ricardo, PRINCIPLES OF POLITICAL ECONOMY AND TAXATION II, 35 (London: J. Murray, 3d ed. 1821). On the Wage Fund theory and the *Lochner*-era Supreme Court, *see* Chapter 14.
11. On the early history, focusing on Massachusetts, *see* Oscar Handlin & Mary Handlin, COMMONWEALTH: A STUDY OF THE ROLE OF GOVERNMENT IN THE AMERICAN ECONOMY: MASSACHUSETTS, 1774–1861, at 144–50 (Cambridge, MA: Harvard Univ. Press, 1941, rev. ed. 1969).
12. *See, e.g.*, William W. Cook, A TREATISE ON STOCK AND STOCKHOLDERS AND GENERAL CORPORATION LAW, §§ 21, 22, 28, 29 (Chicago: Callaghan, 2d ed. 1889); 4 Seymour D. Thompson, COMMENTARIES ON THE LAW OF CORPORATIONS § 3903 (Indianapolis, IN: Bobbs-Merrill, 2d ed. 1910).
13. Lawrence E. Mitchell, THE SPECULATION ECONOMY: HOW FINANCE TRIUMPHED OVER INDUSTRY 95–98 (San Francisco: Berrett-Koehler, 2007).
14. Appeal of Lehigh Ave. Rwy. Co., 499, 129 Pa. 405 (1889).
15. *See* Robert Gordon, *Legal Thought and legal Practice in the Age of American Enterprise, 1870-1920*, *in* PROFESSIONS AND PROFESSIONAL IDEOLOGIES IN AMERICA, 1730–1940 (Gerald L. Geison ed., Chapel Hill: Univ. of North Carolina Press, 1983); Morton J. Horwitz, THE TRANSFORMATION OF AMERICAN LAW, 1870–1960: THE CRISIS OF LEGAL ORTHODOXY 78–97 (New York: Oxford Univ. Press, 1992).
16. COOK, STOCK AND STOCKHOLDERS, *supra* note 12, at 667.
17. Gillett v Chicago Title & Trust Co., 230 Ill. 373, 82 N.E. 891, 904–05 (1907).
18. Garden City Sand Co. v. Crematory Co., 205 Ill. 42, 68 N.E. 724 (1903).
19. Coit v. North Carolina Gold Co., 119 U.S. 343, 344–45 (1886). *See also* Carr v. Le Fevre, 27 Pa. 413 (1856) (contribution of coal mining property at appraised value was proper if no reason existed for thinking that the appraisal had been fraudulently obtained).

20. *E.g., Coit*, 119 U.S. at 346–47. *See also* 2 John C. Bonbright, THE VALUATION OF PROPERTY 799 (New York: McGraw-Hill, 1937).
21. On the progression of legal doctrine, *see* HOVENKAMP, ENTERPRISE, *supra* note 7, 49–64.
22. Wood v. Dummer, 3 Mason 308, 30 Fed. Cas. 435 (C.C. Me. 1824); Sawyer v. Hoag, 84 U.S. (17 Wall.) 610 (1873).
23. These included New York, Pennsylvania, Indiana, and Michigan, as well as others. *See* Herbert Hovenkamp, *The Classical Corporation in American Legal Thought*, 76 GEO. L.J. 1593, 1655 (1988).
24. 1848 N.Y. Laws, ch. 40. *See* HOVENKAMP, ENTERPRISE, *supra* note 7, ch. 5.
25. *E.g.*, Camden v. Stuart, 144 U.S. 104, 114 (1892); Handley v. Stutz, 139 U.S. 417 (1891) (construing Kentucky provision that made incorporating stockholders personally liable for the value of unpaid installments).
26. Coit v. North Carolina Gold Co., 119 U.S. 343, 347 (1886).
27. Charles Francis Adams, *Railroad Inflation*, 108 N. AM. REV. 130, 130–31 (1869).
28. *See* Charles Francis Adams, *The Railroad System*, 104 N. AM. REV. 476 (1867); Adams, *Legislative Control over Railway Charters*, 1 AM. L. REV. 451 (1867); Adams, *The Erie Railroad Row*, 3 AM. L. REV. 41 (1868); Adams, *A Chapter of Erie*, 109 N. AM. REV. 30–106 (1870); Adams, *Railway Problems in 1869*, 110 N. AM. REV. 116 (1870); Adams, *Railway Commissions*, 2 J. SOC. SCI. 233–36 (1870); Adams, *The Government and the Railroad Corporations*, 112 N. AM. REV. 31 (1871). On Adams's career in railroad regulation, *see* Thomas K. McCraw, PROPHETS OF REGULATION, ch. 1 (Cambridge, MA: Harvard Univ. Press, 1984).
29. Ill. Const., Art. XI, § 13 (1869). *See* Charles Francis Adams, *The Government and the Railroad Corporations*, 112 N. AM. REV. 31, 52 (1871).
30. *See* THOMPSON, COMMENTARIES ON THE LAW OF CORPORATIONS, *supra* note 12, §§ 3903, 3918.
31. William W. Cook, *"Watered Stock"—Commissions—"Blue Sky Laws"—Stock without Par Value*, 19 MICH. L. REV. 583, 584 (1921). On the development of limited liability in American corporate law, *see* HOVENKAMP, ENTERPRISE, *supra* note 7, ch. 5.
32. Cook, "*Watered Stock*," *supra* note 31, at 584, 591.
33. *See* Louis Loss & Edward M. Cowett, BLUE SKY LAWS (Boston: Little, Brown, 1958); Paul G. Mahoney, *The Origins of the Blue-Sky Laws: A Test of Competing Hypotheses*, 46 J. L. ECON. 229, 230–32 (2003) (table organized by adoption date and provisions).
34. *See* Jonathan R. Macey & Geoffrey P. Miller, *Origin of the Blue Sky Laws*, 70 TEX. L. REV. 347, 365 (1991). Mahoney, *supra* note 33, sees a more complex set of causes, mainly political, in which the relative power of small bank lobbying seemed to affect the type of statute that was passed.
35. Joel Seligman, *The Historical Need for a Mandatory Corporate Disclosure System*, 9 J. CORP. L. 1 (1983). *See also* Joel Seligman, THE TRANSFORMATION OF WALL

STREET: A HISTORY OF THE SECURITIES AND EXCHANGE COMMISSION AND MODERN CORPORATE FINANCE 19, 20, 38 (Boston: Houghton Mifflin, 1982).

36. Thomas R. Navin & Marian V. Sears, *The Rise of a Market for Industrial Securities, 1887–1902*, 29 BUS. HIS. REV. 105 (1955). *See also* Naomi R. Lamoreaux & Jean-Laurent Rosenthal, *Corporate Governance and the Plight of Minority Shareholders in the United States before the Great Depression*, *in* CORRUPTION AND REFORM: LESSONS FROM AMERICA'S ECONOMIC HISTORY 125 (Edward Glaeser & Claudia Goldin eds., Chicago: Univ. of Chicago Press, 2006).

37. *See* John Coffee, *The Rise of Dispersed Ownership: The Roles of Law and State in the Separation of Ownership and Control*, 111 YALE L.J. 1 (2001); Mark J. Roe, *Political Preconditions to Separating Ownership from Corporate Control*, 53 STAN. L. REV. 539, 585–87 (2000); William G. Roy, SOCIALIZING CAPITAL: THE RISE OF THE LARGE INDUSTRIAL CORPORATION IN AMERICA 16–18 (Princeton, NJ: Princeton Univ. Press, 1997); Alfred D. Chandler, SCALE AND SCOPE: THE DYNAMICS OF INDUSTRIAL CAPITALISM 144–45 (Cambridge, MA: Harvard Univ. Press, 1990). *See also* Mark J. Roe, STRONG MANAGERS, WEAK OWNERS: THE POLITICAL ROOTS OF AMERICAN CORPORATE FINANCE (Princeton, NJ: Princeton Univ. Press, 1994).

38. Mark Twain & Charles Dudley Warner, THE GILDED AGE: A TALE OF TODAY (Oxford: Oxford Univ. Press, 1873).

39. For a detailed account, including muckrakers' interactions with presidents Roosevelt and Taft, *see* Doris Kearns Goodwin, THE BULLY PULPIT: THEODORE ROOSEVELT, WILLIAM HOWARD TAFT, AND THE GOLDEN AGE OF JOURNALISM 254, 324–26, 467–540 (New York: Simon & Schuster, 2014). *See also* Walter M. Brasch, FORERUNNERS OF REVOLUTION: MUCKRAKERS AND THE AMERICAN SOCIAL CONSCIENCE (Lanham, MD.: Univ. Press of Am, 1990); Louis Filler, THE MUCKRAKERS: CRUSADERS FOR AMERICAN LIBERALISM (Washington, DC: Regnery, 1968).

40. *E.g.*, Cook, *"Watered Stock," supra* note 31.

41. William Henry Lough & Frederick William Field, CORPORATION FINANCE: AN EXPOSITION OF THE PRINCIPLES AND METHODS GOVERNING THE PROMOTION, ORGANIZATION AND MANAGEMENT OF MODERN CORPORATIONS 125, 127, 128, 130–31 (New York: Alexander Hamilton Inst., 1909; 7th ed. 1916).

42. *Id.* at 390–95.

43. George Kennan, THE CHICAGO & ALTON CASE: A MISUNDERSTOOD TRANSACTION 28–34 (Garden City, NJ: Country Life Press, 1916).

44. James Bonbright, *No-Par Stock: Its Economics and Legal Aspect*, 38 Q. J. ECON. 440, 447–48 (1924) (italics in original); James Bonbright, *Earning Power as a Basis of Corporate Capitalization*, 35 Q.J. ECON. 482 (1921). Bonbright was a political scientist and economist who later became prominent for his work on public utility regulation. For similar criticism, *see* William Z. Ripley, RAILROADS: FINANCE

AND ORGANIZATION 90–91 (New York: Longmans, 1915); Edward H. Warren, *Safeguarding the Creditors of Corporations*, 36 HARV. L. REV. 509 (1923).

45. William Z. Ripley, *MAIN STREET AND WALL STREET* 46 (Boston: Little, Brown, 1927).
46. Act of April 15, 1912, §§ 19–23 of the Stock Corporation Law. *See also* John S. Parker, CORPORATION MANUAL § 8 (New York: Corp. Manual Co., 1908).
47. *See* 5 THOMPSON, *supra* note 12, § 3627; Carlos Israels, *Problems of Par and No-Par Shares: A Reappraisal*, 47 COL. L. REV. 1279 (1947).
48. Adolf A. Berle, JR., STUDIES IN THE LAW OF CORPORATION FINANCE 64 (Chicago: Callaghan, 1928).
49. Adolf A. Berle, JR. & Gardiner C. Means, THE MODERN CORPORATION AND PRIVATE PROPERTY 159, 285–86 (New York: Harcourt, 1932).
50. Cornelius Wickersham, *The Progress of the Law on No Par Value Stock*, 37 HARV. L. REV. 464, 464 (1924). *See also* Cornelius W. Wickersham, A TREATISE ON STOCK WITHOUT PAR VALUE OF ORDINARY BUSINESS CORPORATIONS (Albany, NY: Bender, 1927).
51. *See In re* Haddam Distillers Corp., 1 S.E.C. 37 (1934); *In re* Thomas Bond, Inc., 5 S.E.C. 60 (1939).
52. *See* Sean Dennis Cashman, AMERICA IN THE GILDED AGE 1–40 (New York: NYU Press, 3d ed. 1993); Alfred D. Chandler, THE VISIBLE HAND: THE MANAGERIAL REVOLUTION IN AMERICAN BUSINESS (Cambridge, MA: Harvard Univ. Press, 1977).
53. RIPLEY, MAIN STREET, *supra* note 45, at 49.
54. Camden v. Stuart, 144 U.S. 104, 115 (1892).
55. See v. Heppenheimer, 69 N.J. Eq. 36, 53 61 A. 843, 848, 850 (1905).
56. Van Cleve v. Berkey, 143 Mo. 109 (1898).
57. Ohio & Col. Smelting & Refining Co. v. Pub. Utils Comm'n, 68 Colo. 137 (1920). *See also* Missouri v. Sw. Bell, 262 U.S. 276, 298–99 (1923) (Brandeis, J., concurring, joined by J. Holmes).
58. Clinton Mining & Mineral Co. v. Jamison, 256 F. 577, 579, 582 (3d Cir. 1919).
59. 5 THOMPSON, *supra* note 12, § 3425 at 260.
60. Victor Morawetz, *Shares without Nominal or Par Value*, 26 HARV. L. REV. 729 (1913).
61. 1 Arthur S. Dewing, THE FINANCIAL POLICY OF CORPORATIONS 55–56, 68, 71–73 (New York: Ronald, 1919).
62. *Id.* at 75. *Cf.* Richard H. Hollen & Richard S. Tuthill, *Uses of Stock Having No Par Value*, 7 A.B.A. J. 579 (1921) (no-par stock forces the investor to look at the corporation's current value before making an investment decision, rather than focusing on that which was historically paid in.).
63. Johnson v. Louisville Trust, 293 F. 857 (C.C.A. 6th 1923).
64. Norton v. Lamb, 144 Kan. 665, 62 P.2d 1311 (1936).

65. E. Merrick Dodd & Ralph J. Baker, CASES AND MATERIALS ON BUSINESS ASSOCIATIONS 1004 (Brooklyn, NY: Foundation Press, 1940).
66. Israels, *supra* note 47, at 1292–93.
67. Charles S. Tippetts & Shaw Livermore, BUSINESS ORGANIZATIONS AND PUBLIC CONTROL 378 (New York: Van Nostrand, 2d ed. 1941).

CHAPTER 9

1. Adolf A. Berle, JR. & Gardiner C. Means, THE MODERN CORPORATION AND PRIVATE PROPERTY (New York: Macmillan, 1932). *See* TIME, Apr. 24, 1933. On the writing of *The Modern Corporation, see* Thomas K. McCraw, *In Retrospect: Berle and Means*, 18 REV. AM. HIST. 578 (1990).
2. *See* Adam Smith, AN INQUIRY INTO THE NATURE AND CAUSES OF THE WEALTH OF NATIONS, Book 5, ch. 1, § 3.1.2 (Dublin: Whitestone, 1776). On other literature prior to Berle and Means, *see* Herbert Hovenkamp, ENTERPRISE AND AMERICAN LAW, 1836–1937, at 357–62 (Cambridge, MA: Harvard Univ. Press, 1991).
3. Louis Dembitz Brandeis, OTHER PEOPLE'S MONEY: AND HOW THE BANKERS USE IT (New York: Stokes, 1914).
4. Thorstein Veblen, ABSENTEE OWNERSHIP: BUSINESS ENTERPRISE IN RECENT TIMES (New York: Huebsch, 1923).
5. Robert S. Brookings, INDUSTRIAL OWNERSHIP: ITS ECONOMIC AND SOCIAL SIGNIFICANCE, ch. 1 (New York: Macmillan, 1925).
6. Morton J. Horwitz, THE TRANSFORMATION OF AMERICAN LAW: THE CRISIS OF LEGAL ORTHODOXY: 1870–1960, at 166 (New York: Oxford Univ. Press, 1992). *See also* James Willard Hurst, THE LEGITIMACY OF THE BUSINESS CORPORATION IN THE LAW OF THE UNITED STATES, 1780–1970, at 70–72 (Charlottesville: Univ. Press of Virginia, 1970).
7. Louis K. Liggett Co. v. Lee, 288 U.S. 517, 564–65 (1933). On *Liggett, see* Edward A. Purcell, JR., BRANDEIS AND THE PROGRESSIVE CONSTITUTION 142–43 (New Haven, CT: Yale Univ. Press, 2000).
8. BRANDEIS, OTHER PEOPLE'S MONEY, *supra* note 3, at 183. For similar views, *see* William Z. Ripley, MAIN STREET AND WALL STREET 3–15, 38–43, 76–77 (Boston: Little, Brown, 1927).
9. Statement of Louis D. Brandeis, *Hearings Before the Senate Committee on Interstate Commerce Pursuant to S. Res. 98*, 62d Cong., 2d Sess., vol. I, at 1174 (1911).
10. BERLE & MEANS, MODERN CORPORATION, *supra* note 1, at 9.
11. *Id.* at 308, 345–46; Berle reiterated the monopoly point in Adolf A. Berle, JR., POWER WITHOUT PROPERTY: A NEW DEVELOPMENT IN AMERICAN POLITICAL ECONOMY (New York: Harcourt, Brace, 1959).
12. Henry C. Simons, "A Positive Program of Laissez Faire: Some Proposals for a Liberal Economic Policy" (1934), *reprinted in* Henry C. Simons, ECONOMIC POLICY FOR A FREE SOCIETY (Chicago: Univ. Chicago Press, 1948).

13. Ferdinand Lundberg, AMERICA'S SIXTY FAMILIES (New York: Vanguard, 1937).
14. United States v. Aluminum Co. of Am., 148 F.2d 416, 427 (2d Cir. 1945); Am. Tobacco Co. v. United States, 328 U.S. 781, 813 (1946).
15. Baltimore & O.R. Co. v. United States, 386 U.S. 372, 452 (1967); Standard Oil Co. v. United States, 337 U.S. 293, 318 (1949); United States v. Columbia Steel Co., 334 U.S. 495, 535–36 (1948).
16. United States v. Falstaff Brewing Corp., 410 U.S. 526, 539–43 (1973).
17. *Study of Monopoly Power: Hearings Before the Subcomm. on the Study of Monopoly Power of the House Comm. on the Judiciary*, 81st Cong., 2d Sess. 967 (1950).
18. Herbert A. Simon, *A Behavioral Model of Rational Choice*, 69 Q.J. ECON. 99 (1955). *See also* James G. March & Herbert A. Simon, ORGANIZATIONS 168 (New York: Wiley, 1958).
19. Peter F. Drucker, CONCEPT OF THE CORPORATION (New York: John Day, 1946); DRUCKER, THE PRACTICE OF MANAGEMENT (New York: Harper, 1954); DRUCKER, TECHNOLOGY, MANAGEMENT AND SOCIETY (New York: Harper, 1970).
20. Sloan Wilson, THE MAN IN THE GRAY FLANNEL SUIT (New York: Simon & Schuster, 1955).
21. Alfred Marshall, PRINCIPLES OF ECONOMICS, Book IV. ch. xii, §§ 29, 30 (London: Macmillan, 1890). *See* Mark J. Roe, STRONG MANAGERS, WEAK OWNERS: THE POLITICAL ROOTS OF AMERICAN CORPORATE FINANCE (Princeton, NJ: Princeton Univ. Press, 1994); Eugene F. Fama & Michael C. Jensen, *Separation of Ownership and Control*, 26 J.L. & ECON. 301 (1983).
22. Ronald H. Coase, *The Nature of the Firm*, 4 ECONOMICA (N.S.) 386 (1937); *see* Herbert Hovenkamp, *Coase, Institutionalism, and the Origins of Law and Economics*, 86 IND. L.J. 499 (2011).
23. Ronald H. Coase, *The Nature of the Firm: Origin*, 4 J.L. ECON. & ORG. 3, 17 (1988).
24. *E.g.*, Ronald H. Coase, *The Lighthouse in Economics*, 17 J.L. & ECON. 357, 357–60, 372–76 (1974). His 1991 Nobel Prize lecture restated that theme. Ronald H. Coase, The Institutional Structure of Production, *in* ECONOMIC SCIENCES 1991–1995, at 12–13 (Torsten Persson ed., Singapore: World Scientific, 1997).
25. *See* Coase, *Nature of the Firm: Origin, supra* note 23, at 8–10, 13.
26. Sperling's Appeal, 71 Pa. 11, 20–21 (1872); *see* Lawrence M. Friedman, A HISTORY OF AMERICAN LAW 390–95 (New York: Simon & Schuster, 3d ed. 2005).
27. Briggs v. Spaulding, 141 U.S. 132, 152 (1891).
28. Spiegel v. Beacon Participations, Inc., 8 N.E.2d 895, 904 (Mass. 1937).
29. Whitmer v. William Whitmer & Sons, Inc., 99 A. 428, 431 (Del. Ch. 1916); Robinson v. Pittsburgh Oil Ref. Corp., 126 A. 46 (Del. Ch. 1924); Blish v. Thompson Automatic Arms Corp., 30 Del. Ch. 538, 64 A.2d 581 (Del. 1948); Dann v. Chrysler Corp., 40 Del.Ch. 103, 174 A.2d 696 (Del. Ch. 1961).

30. *See, e.g.*, Michael C. Jensen & William H. Meckling, *Theory of the Firm: Managerial Behavior, Agency Costs and Ownership Structure*, 3 J. FIN. ECON. 305, 308–09 (1976).
31. Douglass C. North, *Comment on Stigler and Friedland: "The Literature of Economics: The Case of Berle and Means,"* 26 J.L. & ECON. 269, 270 (1983).
32. Fisher developed the fundamental theory in Irving Fisher, THE NATURE OF CAPITAL AND INCOME (New York: Macmillan, 1906); Irving Fisher, THE RATE OF INTEREST: ITS NATURE, DETERMINATION AND RELATION TO ECONOMIC PHENOMENA (New York: Macmillan, 1907). He presented the mature theorem in Irving Fisher, THE THEORY OF INTEREST AS DETERMINED BY IMPATIENCE TO SPEND INCOME AND OPPORTUNITY TO INVEST IT (New York: Macmillan, 1930).
33. *See Irving Fisher's Theory of Investment, available at* http://cepa.newschool.edu/het/essays/capital/fisherinvest.htm. *See also* Richard A. Brealey ET AL., PRINCIPLES OF CORPORATE FINANCE 22 (Boston: McGraw-Hill Irwin, 9th ed. 2007).
34. *See* HOVENKAMP, ENTERPRISE, *supra* note 2, at 42–48.
35. *See* George J. Stigler & Claire Friedland, *The Literature of Economics: The Case of Berle and Means*, 26 J.L. & ECON. 237, 240 (1983).
36. Eugene F. Fama & Merton H. Miller, THE THEORY OF FINANCE 69 (New York: Holt, Rinehart & Winston, 1972). *See also* Steinar Ekern & Robert Wilson, *On the Theory of the Firm in an Economy with Incomplete Markets*, 5 BELL J. ECON. & MGMT. SCI. 171 (1974); Sanford J. Grossman & Joseph E. Stiglitz, *Stockholder Unanimity in Making Production and Financial Decisions*, 94 Q.J. ECON. 543 (1980); Oliver Hart, *On Shareholder Unanimity in Large Stock Market Economies*, 47 ECONOMETRICA 1057 (1979); Hayne Leland, *Information, Managerial Choice and Stockholder Unanimity*, 45 REV. ECON. STUD. 527 (1977); Louis Makowski, *Competition and Unanimity Revisited*, 73 AM. ECON. REV. 329 (1983).
37. For the traditional view, *see* Benjamin Graham, DAVID DODD & SIDNEY COTTLE, SECURITY ANALYSIS: PRINCIPLES AND TECHNIQUE 539–49 (New York: McGraw-Hill, 4th ed. 1962).
38. Franco Modigliani, 3 THE COLLECTED PAPERS OF FRANCO MODIGLIANI, at xiii (Andrew Abel ed., Cambridge, MA: MIT Press 1980). *See* Franco Modigliani & Merton H. Miller, *The Cost of Capital, Corporation Finance and the Theory of Investment*, 48 AM. ECON. REV. 261, 264, 295–96 (1958); Franco Modigliani & Merton H. Miller, *Dividend Policy, Growth, and the Valuation of Shares*, 34 J. BUS. 411 (1961).
39. Nevins D. Baxter, *Leverage, Risk of Ruin and the Cost of Capital*, 22 J. FIN. 395 (1967); Joseph E. Stiglitz, *A Re-examination of the Modigliani-Miller Theorem*, 59 AM. ECON. REV. 784 (1969). *See* Anat R. Admati, Peter Conti-Brown & Paul Pfleiderer, *Liability Holding Companies*, 59 UCLA L. REV. 852 (2012).

40. Frank H. Knight, RISK, UNCERTAINTY, AND PROFIT 78–87 (Boston: Houghton-Mifflin, 1921).
41. John Maynard Keynes, GENERAL THEORY OF EMPLOYMENT, INTEREST AND MONEY 156 (New York: Harcourt, Brace, 1936). *See also* John Hicks, VALUE AND CAPITAL: AN INQUIRY INTO SOME FUNDAMENTAL PRINCIPLES OF ECONOMIC THEORY (Oxford: Clarendon Press, 1939); Robert Rhea, THE DOW THEORY: AN EXPLANATION OF ITS DEVELOPMENT AND AN ATTEMPT TO DEFINE ITS USEFULNESS AS AN AID IN SPECULATION (New York: Barron's, 1932).
42. *See* Lawrence E. Mitchell, THE SPECULATION ECONOMY: HOW FINANCE TRIUMPHED OVER INDUSTRY 274–75 (San Francisco: Berrett-Koehler, 2007).
43. John Burr Williams, THE THEORY OF INVESTMENT VALUE 54–58 (Cambridge, MA: Harvard Univ. Press, 1938). *See also* Benjamin Graham & David Dodd, SECURITY ANALYSIS: PRINCIPLES AND TECHNIQUE 15–18, 404–11 (New York: McGraw-Hill, 1951) (emphasizing a strategy of "value investing" by studying fundamentals when searching for undervalued stocks).
44. *See* Harry Markowitz, *Portfolio Selection*, 7 J. FIN. 77 (1952).
45. Louis Bachelier, THE THEORY OF SPECULATION: THE ORIGINS OF MODERN FINANCE ([1900]; Eng. trans. by Mark Davis & Alison Etheridge, Princeton, NJ: Princeton Univ. Press, 2006).
46. *See* Holbrook Working, *A Random-Difference Series for Use in the Analysis of Time Series*, 29 J. AM. STAT. ASS'N 11, 11–12 (1934); Alfred Cowles III, *Can Stock Market Forecasters Forecast?*, 1 ECONOMETRICA 309, 323–24 (1933) (professional stock pickers did not do better than random selection).
47. Eugene F. Fama, *The Behavior of Stock-Market Prices*, 38 J. BUS. 34, 39 (1965). On the history, *see* Michael C. Jensen & Clifford W. Smith, JR., THE MODERN THEORY OF CORPORATE FINANCE 2–20 (New York: McGraw-Hill, 1984). *See also* Eugene F. Fama, *Efficient Capital Markets: A Review of Theory and Empirical Work*, 25 J. FIN. 383, 388 (1970).
48. Burton G. Malkiel, A RANDOM WALK DOWN WALL STREET (New York: Norton, 1973).
49. *See* Stephen A. Ross ET AL., CORPORATE FINANCE 352–57 (New York: McGraw-Hill/Irwin 10th ed. 2013).
50. *E.g.*, Blackie v. Barrack, 524 F.2d 891 (9th Cir. 1975); Basic, Inc. v. Levinson, 485 U.S. 224 (1988). On the fraud-on-the-market hypothesis in litigation prior to *Basic, see* Barbara Black, *The Strange Case of Fraud on the Market: A Label in Search of a Theory*, 52 ALB. L. REV. 923 (1988).
51. Amgen, Inc. v. Connecticut Retirement Plans, 133 S. Ct. 1184, 1190 (2013).
52. Erica P. John Fund, Inc. v. Halliburton Co., 718 F.3d 423 (5th Cir. 2013), cert. granted, 134 S.Ct. 636 (2013).
53. Stigler & Friedland, *The Literature of Economics, supra* note 35, at 244.
54. The empirical work leading up to *The Modern Corporation* was developed in Gardiner C. Means, *The Separation of Ownership and Control in American*

Industry, 46 Q.J. ECON. 68 (1931). *See also* Robert Gordon, *Stockholdings of Officers and Directors in American Industrial Corporations*, 50 Q.J. ECON. 622 (1936); Robert Gordon, *Ownership by Management and Control Groups in the Large Corporation*, 52 Q.J. ECON. 367 (1938); *Investigation of Concentration of Economic Power: Hearing Before the Temp. Nat'l Econ. Comm. Cong. of the U.S.*, 76th Cong., Monograph No. 29 (1940) (statement of Raymond Goldsmith, et al. in "The Distribution of Ownership in the 200 Largest Non-financial Corporations").

55. *See* Ralph Nader, *The Concord Principles: An Agenda for a New Initiatory Democracy* (Feb. 1, 1992), *available at* http://www.co-intelligence.org/CIPol_ConcordPrinciples.html.
56. *See* Donald R. Stabile, FORERUNNERS OF MODERN FINANCIAL ECONOMICS: A RANDOM WALK IN THE HISTORY OF ECONOMIC THOUGHT 90–95 (Northampton, MA: Edward Elgar, 2005).

CHAPTER 10

1. U.S. CONST. art. 1, § 8, cl. 8.
2. 21 Jac. I, ch. 3, § 6 (Eng. 1624) (authorizing letters patent for a "Term of fourteen Years or under" for the "sole Working or Making of new Manufactures within this Realm, to the true and first Inventor...."). *See* Adam Mossoff, *Rethinking the Development of Patents: An Intellectual History, 1550–1800*, 52 HASTINGS L.J. 1255 (2001); Tyler T. Ochoa & Mark Rose, *The Anti-monopoly Origins of the Patent and Copyright Clause*, 84 J. PAT. & TRADEMARK OFF. SOC'Y 909 (2002).
3. David J. Brewer, *The Patent System*, 3 YALE L.J. 149, 151, 157 (1894).
4. Alfred E. Kahn, *Fundamental Deficiencies of the American Patent Law*, 30 AM. ECON. REV. 475, 483–84 (1940).
5. Alfred Marshall, PRINCIPLES OF ECONOMICS, Book IV, ch. Xi, § 5, n.133 (London: Macmillan, 1890).
6. Alfred Marshall, INDUSTRY AND TRADE: A STUDY OF INDUSTRIAL TECHNIQUE AND BUSINESS ORGANIZATION; AND OF THEIR INFLUENCES ON THE CONDITIONS OF VARIOUS CLASSES AND NATIONS 344, 264, 327 (London: Macmillan, 1919).
7. *See* Neil Hart, EQUILIBRIUM AND EVOLUTION: ALFRED MARSHALL AND THE MARSHALLIANS (New York: Palgrave Macmillan, 2012).
8. *See* Arthur C. Pigou, THE ECONOMICS OF WELFARE 185 (London: Macmillan, 4th ed. 1932); Arnold Plant, THE ECONOMIC THEORY CONCERNING PATENTS FOR INVENTIONS, 1 ECONOMICA 30, 31–32 (1934).
9. Thorstein Veblen, THE INSTINCT OF WORKMANSHIP AND THE STATE OF THE INDUSTRIAL ARTS 102–08, 185–95 (New York: Macmillan, 1914).
10. Frank W. Taussig, INVENTORS AND MONEY-MAKERS: RELATIONS BETWEEN ECONOMICS AND PSYCHOLOGY (New York: Macmillan, 1915). *See also* Floyd

L. Vaughan, ECONOMICS OF OUR PATENT SYSTEM (New York: Macmillan, 1925).

11. Bradley A. Fiske, INVENTION, THE MASTER-KEY TO PROGRESS xxi, 8–80 (New York: Dutton, 1921).
12. Graham v. John Deere Co., 383 U.S. 1, 17–18 (1966).
13. Christina Bohannan & Herbert Hovenkamp, CREATION WITHOUT RESTRAINT: PROMOTING LIBERTY AND RIVALRY IN INNOVATION, ch. 1 (New York: Oxford Univ. Press, 2012).
14. Festo Corp. v. Shoketsu Kinzoku Kogyo Kabushiki Co., 234 F.3d 558, 639 (Fed. Cir. 2000), rev'd, 535 U.S. 722 (2002) (Newman, J., dissenting).
15. *See* Adam Mossoff, *Patents as Constitutional Private Property: The Historical Protection of Patents under the Takings Clause*, 87 B.U. L. REV. 689 (2007).
16. The data are gathered at http://www.uspto.gov/web/offices/ac/ido/oeip/taf/h_counts.pdf.
17. GEORGE W. STOCKING & MYRON W. WATKINS, MONOPOLY AND FREE ENTERPRISE 455–59 (New York: Twentieth Century Fund, 1951).
18. For one approach, finding an indeterminate relationship between patent grant rates and state economic growth, *see* Glynn S. Lunney, Jr., *Patents and Growth: Empirical Evidence from the States*, 87 N.C. L. REV. 1467 (2009).
19. *See* Robert J. Gordon, "Is U.S. Economic Growth Over? Faltering Innovation Confronts the Six Headwinds" (working paper, National Bureau of Economic Research, Aug. 2012), *available at* http://www.nber.org/papers/w18315.
20. Hotchkiss v. Greenwood, 52 U.S. 248, 267 (1850).
21. George Ticknor Curtis, A TREATISE ON THE LAW OF PATENTS FOR USEFUL INVENTIONS 68–69, 76 (Boston: Little, Brown, 4th ed. 1873).
22. *Id.* at 70, referring to Young v. Lippman, 9 Blatchf. 277, 30 Fed. Cas. 846 (C.C.N.Y. 1872).
23. CURTIS, *supra* note 21, at 114.
24. Patent Act of 1836, ch. 357, § 6, 5 Stat. 117 (July 4, 1836).
25. Kirby v. Beardsley, 5 Blatchf. 438, 14 F. Cas. 654 (C.C.N.Y. 1867).
26. Rubber-Tip Pencil Co. v. Howard, 87 U.S. 498 (1874).
27. WILLIAM CALLYHAN ROBINSON, THE LAW OF PATENTS FOR USEFUL INVENTIONS 312–15, 333–34 (Boston: Little, Brown, 1890).
28. 35 U.S.C. § 103 (1952). *See* John F. Duffy, *Inventing Invention: A Case Study of Legal Innovation*, 86 TEX. L. REV. 1 (2007).
29. E. Bement & Sons. v. Nat'l Harrow Co., 186 U.S. 70 (1902).
30. United States v. Trans-Missouri Freight Ass'n, 166 U.S. 290 (1897).
31. United States v. Gen. Electric Co., 272 U.S. 476 (1926).
32. Cont'l Paper Bag Co. v. E. Paper Bag Co., 210 U.S. 405 (1908).
33. Winans v. Denmead, 15 How. 330 (1853).
34. Wright Co. v. Herring-Curtiss Co., 204 F. 597 (W.D.N.Y. 1913). The history is recounted in Mfrs. Aircraft Ass'n, Inc. v. United States, 77 Ct. Cl. 481, 485 (1933).

35. 2 Edw. 7, c. 34, § 3 (1902). *See* Thomas Terrell, THE LAW AND PRACTICE RELATING TO LETTERS PATENT FOR INVENTIONS 248 (London: Sweet & Maxwell, 4th ed. 1906).
36. Cont'l Paper Bag Co. v. E. Paper Bag Co., 150 F. 741, 747, 749–50 (1st Cir. 1906).
37. *Cont'l Paper Bag*, 210 U.S. at 424. Only Justice Harlan dissented. The lengthy litigation is discussed in BOHANNAN & HOVENKAMP, CREATION WITHOUT RESTRAINT, *supra* note 13, at 295–99.
38. Comment, *The Effect of Nonuse on a Patentee's Remedy against Infringement*, 18 YALE L.J. 52, 54 (1908).
39. John Maurice Clark, STUDIES IN THE ECONOMICS OF OVERHEAD COSTS 146 (Chicago: Univ. of Chicago Press, 1923).
40. *E.g.*, Victor Talking Mach. Co. v. The Fair, 123 F. 424 (7th Cir. 1903) (enforcing resale price maintenance restriction on patented article).
41. Morgan Envelope Co. v. Albany Perforated Wrapping Paper Co., 152 U.S. 425 (1894).
42. Adams v. Burke, 84 U.S. (17 Wall) 453 (1873).
43. Bobbs-Merrill Co. v. Straus, 210 U.S. 339, 349–51 (1908); HALLIE ERMINIE RIVES, THE CASTAWAY (Indianapolis, IN: Bobbs-Merrill, 1904).
44. Henry v. A.B. Dick Co., 224 U.S. 1, 31–32 (1912).
45. 15 U.S.C. § 14 (1914).
46. On congressional efforts, *see Preliminary Report, TNEC, Sen. Doc. No. 95, 76th Cong., 1st Sess. 16, 17* (1939). Later efforts directed to Congress are recounted in United States v. Line Material Co., 333 U.S. 287, 362–63 & n.30 (1948).
47. Motion Picture Patents Co. v. Universal Film Mfg. Co., 243 U.S. 502, 517–18 (1917).
48. Ownership of the technology itself was disputed. *See* Charles Musser, THE EMERGENCE OF CINEMA: THE AMERICAN SCREEN TO 1907, at 130–80 (Berkeley: Univ. of California Press, 1994).
49. *See* Merle R. Thompson, TRUST DISSOLUTION 252–58 (Boston: Badger, 1919).
50. On the history, *see* Michael Conant, ANTITRUST IN THE MOTION PICTURE INDUSTRY: ECONOMIC AND LEGAL ANALYSIS 16–21, 77–80 (Berkeley: Univ. of California Press, 1960); Benjamin B. Hampton, HISTORY OF THE AMERICAN FILM INDUSTRY FROM ITS BEGINNINGS TO 1931, at 8–11, 17–24, 34, 64–76, 79–81 (New York: Dover, 1970).
51. Arthur Knight, THE LIVELIEST ART: A PANORAMIC HISTORY OF THE MOVIES 39 (New York: Macmillan, rev. ed. 1978).
52. *E.g.*, Patterson v. United States, 222 F. 599 (6th Cir. 1915); United States v. United Shoe Mach. Co., 247 U.S. 32 (1918); United Shoe Mach. Corp. v. United States, 258 U.S. 451 (1922); United States v. Gen. Electric Co., 272 U.S. 476 (1926); Standard Oil Co. v. United States, 283 U.S. 163 (1931).
53. A few of the more important examples are Bauer & Cie. v. O'Donnell, 229 U.S. 1 (1913); Ideal Wrapping Mach. Co. v. George Close Co., 23 F.2d 848 (D. Mass. 1928);

Victor Talking Mach. Co. v. Kemeny, 271 F. 810 (3d Cir. 1921); Straus v. Victor Talking Mach. Co., 297 F. 791 (2d Cir.1924). Contemporary discussion includes Floyd L. Vaughan, *The Relation of Patents to Industrial Monopolies*, 147 ANNALS AM. ACAD. POL. & SOC. SCI. 40 (Jan. 1930); Horace R. Lamb, *The Relation of the Patent Laws to the Federal Anti-trust Laws*, 12 CORN. L.Q. 261 (1927); David L. Podell & Benjamin S. Kirsch, *Patent Pools and the Anti-trust Laws*, 13 A.B.A. J. 430 (1927); Harry Toulmin, *The Patent Law and the Sherman Law*, 1 VA. L. REV. 445 (1914). *See also* F. Granville Munson, *Control of Patented and Copyrighted Articles after Sale*, 26 YALE L.J. 270 (1917); Rome G. Brown, *The Right to Refuse to Sell*, 25 YALE L.J. 194 (1916).

54. Richard T. Ely, *Monopolies and Trusts* 44–49, 246–47, 267 (New York: Macmillan, 1900).
55. Thorstein Veblen, THE THEORY OF BUSINESS ENTERPRISE 55, 139–40 (New York: Scribners, 1919).
56. Edward H. Chamberlin, THE THEORY OF MONOPOLISTIC COMPETITION: A RE-ORIENTATION OF THE THEORY OF VALUE 57–64 (Cambridge, MA: Harvard Univ. Press, 1933).
57. 1 Richard T. Ely, PROPERTY AND CONTRACT IN THEIR RELATIONS TO THE DISTRIBUTION OF WEALTH 96 (New York: Macmillan, 1914).
58. Wesley N. Hohfeld, FUNDAMENTAL LEGAL CONCEPTIONS AS APPLIED IN JUDICIAL REASONING, 26 YALE L.J. 710 (1917).
59. Arthur L. Corbin, TAXATION OF SEATS ON THE STOCK EXCHANGE, 31 YALE L.J. 429 (1922).
60. Standard Brands v. Smidler, 151 F.2d 34, 38–39 (2d Cir. 1945) (Frank, J., concurring).
61. E. Wine Corp. v. Winslow-Warren, Ltd., 137 F.2d 955 (2d Cir. 1943).
62. *Standard Brands*, 151 F.2d at 38–39 n.7, 41.
63. *E.g.*, Sigmund Timberg, *Trade-Marks, Monopoly, and the Restraint of Competition*, 14 L. & CONTEMP. PROBS. 323 (1949); Ralph S. Brown, Jr., *Advertising and the Public Interest: Legal Protection of Trade Symbols*, 57 YALE L.J. 1165 (1948).
64. California Fruit Growers Exch. v. Sunkist Baking Co., 166 F.2d 971, 974 (7th Cir. 1948).
65. Arthur R. Burns, THE DECLINE OF COMPETITION 11 (New York: McGraw-Hill, 1936).
66. *See, e.g.*, William J. Fellner, COMPETITION AMONG THE FEW: OLIGOPOLY AND SIMILAR MARKET STRUCTURES 292–93 (New York: Knopf, 1949); John Kenneth Galbraith, *Monopoly and the Concentration of Economic Power*, *in* A SURVEY OF CONTEMPORARY ECONOMICS 99–102 (Howard S. Ellis ed., New York: AEA, 1949).
67. *E.g.*, LEONARD WEISS, ECONOMICS AND AMERICAN INDUSTRY 331–32, 336–39 (New York: Wiley, 1961); Robert Lanzillotti, *The Automobile Industry*, *in* THE STRUCTURE OF AMERICAN INDUSTRY: SOME CASE STUDIES 321–34 (Walter Adams ed., New York: Macmillan, 3d ed. 1961).

68. Vance Packard, THE HIDDEN PERSUADERS (New York: D. McKay, 1957); John Keats, THE INSOLENT CHARIOTS (Philadelphia: Lippincott, 1958).
69. Senate Subcomm. On Antitrust and Monopoly of the Comm. On the Judiciary, *Study of Administered Prices in the Automobile Industry, 85th Cong., 2d Sess* (1958). *See* ADMINISTERED PRICES: AUTOMOBILES (U.S. Gov't Print. Off., 1958).
70. Ralph Nader, UNSAFE AT ANY SPEED: THE DESIGNED-IN DANGERS OF THE AMERICAN AUTOMOBILE (New York: Grossman, 1965); Robert Pitofsky, *Beyond Nader: Consumer Protection and the Regulation of Advertising*, 90 HARV. L. REV. 661 (1977); Robert B. Reich, *Toward a New Consumer Protection*, 128 U. PA. L. REV. 1 (1979).
71. Walton H. Hamilton, PATENTS AND FREE ENTERPRISE (Washington, DC: U.S. Gov't Print. Off., 1941). *See also* Walton H. Hamilton & Irene Till, *Antitrust—The Reach after New Weapons*, 26 WASH. U. L.Q. 1 (1940); Walton H. Hamilton, *A New Patent Policy*, 17 CURRENT HIST. 338 (1949); Walton H. Hamilton, *Whitewashing the Patent System*, 109 NEW REPUBLIC 278 (1943); Walton H. Hamilton, *Property Rights in the Market*, 2 J. LEGAL & POL. SOC. 10 (1943). *See also* Walton H. Hamilton, THE POLITICS OF INDUSTRY (New York: Knopf, 1957).
72. Thurman W. Arnold, THE BOTTLENECKS OF BUSINESS 26 (New York: Reynal & Hitchcock, 1940). *See* Ethyl Gasoline Corp. v. United States, 309 U.S. 436 (1940).
73. *See* Staff Report to H.R. Committee on Small Business, *United States versus Economic Concentration and Monopoly* 215–34 (1947).
74. Mortimer Feuer, *Patent Abuse versus National Interest*, 2 LAWYERS GUILD REV. 1 (1942).
75. Thurman Arnold, *The Abuse of Patents*, ATLANTIC, July 1942, *reprinted in* 24 J. PAT. OFF. SOC'Y 531 (1942). *And see* Corwin D. Edwards, *Thurman Arnold and the Antitrust Laws*, 58 POL. SCI. Q. 338 (1943); *Investigation of the Misuse of Patent Privileges* (Dep't of Justice Dec. 11, 1939). *See also* Spencer Weber Waller, *The Antitrust Legacy of Thurman Arnold*, 78 ST. JOHN'S L. REV. 569 (2004); Steven Wilf, *The Making of the Post-war Paradigm in American Intellectual Property Law*, 31 COLUM. J.L. & ARTS 139 (2008).
76. Michael Polanyi, *Patent Reform*, 11 REV. ECON. STUD. 61 (1944).
77. Friedrich A. Hayek, INDIVIDUALISM AND THE ECONOMIC ORDER 114 (Chicago: Univ. of Chicago Press, 1948).
78. Corwin D. Edwards, MAINTAINING COMPETITION: REQUISITES OF A GOVERNMENTAL POLICY 216–43 (NewYork: McGraw-Hill, 1949). *See also* Fritz Machlup, THE POLITICAL ECONOMY OF MONOPOLY: BUSINESS, LABOR, AND GOVERNMENT POLICIES (Baltimore: Johns Hopkins Press, 1952).
79. Carbice Corp. v. Am. Patents Dev. Corp., 283 U.S. 27, 30–33 (1931).
80. Morton Salt Co. v. G.S. Suppiger Co., 314 U.S. 488, 492 (1942).
81. Int'l Salt Co. v. United States, 332 U.S. 392 (1947).
82. Edward S. Mason, *Monopoly in Law and Economics*, 47 YALE L.J. 34 (1937); Edward S. Mason, *Methods of Developing a Proper Control of Big Business*, 18 PROCEEDINGS AM. ACAD. POL. SCI. 40, 45–46 (1939).

83. Joe S. Bain, BARRIERS TO NEW COMPETITION: THEIR CHARACTER AND CONSEQUENCES IN MANUFACTURING INDUSTRIES 148–50 (Cambridge, MA: Harvard Univ. Press, 1956).
84. Joe S. Bain, INDUSTRIAL ORGANIZATION 623 (New York: Wiley, 1959).
85. Carl Kaysen & Donald F. Turner, ANTITRUST POLICY: AN ECONOMIC AND LEGAL ANALYSIS 176–77 (Cambridge, MA: Harvard Univ. Press, 1959).
86. *Report*, ATTORNEY GENERAL'S NATIONAL COMMITTEE TO STUDY THE ANTITRUST LAWS 255 (U.S. Gov't Print. Off., 1955).
87. In addition to the cases discussed in the text, *see* Universal Oil Prods. Co. v. Globe Oil Ref. Co., 322 U.S. 471 (1944) (insufficient disclosure); Marconi Wireless Tel. Co. v. United States, 320 U.S. 1 (1943) (lack of inventiveness); U.S. Indus. Chems., Inc. v. Carbide & Carbon Chems. Corp., 315 U.S. 668 (1942) (unreasonable broadening of reissued patent); Detrola Radio & Television Corp. v. Hazeltine Corp., 313 U.S. 259 (1941) (anticipation); Toledo Pressed Steel Co. v. Standard Parts, Inc., 307 U.S. 350 (1939) (lack of inventiveness).
88. Mantle Lamp Co. v. Aluminum Prods. Co., 301 U.S. 544, 546 (1937).
89. Cuno Eng'g Corp. v. Automatic Devices Corp., 314 U.S. 84, 91 (1941).
90. Great Atl. & Pac. Tea Co. v. Supermarket Equip. Corp., 340 U.S. 147, 154 (1950).
91. Jungerson v. Ostby & Barton Co., 335 U.S. 560, 572 (1949) (Jackson, J., dissenting).
92. JOSEPH A. SCHUMPETER, CAPITALISM, SOCIALISM AND DEMOCRACY 101–06 (New York: Harper, 1942). *See* THOMAS K. MCCRAW, PROPHET OF INNOVATION: JOSEPH SCHUMPETER AND CREATIVE DESTRUCTION (Cambridge, MA: Harvard Univ. Press, 2007).
93. *See, e.g.*, Simon Kuznets, *Toward a Theory of Economic Growth*, *in* NATIONAL POLICY FOR ECONOMIC WELFARE AT HOME AND ABROAD (Robert Lekachman ed., Garden City, NY: Doubleday, 1955); Moses Abramovitz, *Economics of Growth*, *in* 2 A SURVEY OF CONTEMPORARY ECONOMICS 132, 139 (Bernard Haley ed., Homewood, IL: R.D. Irwin AEA, 1952); John Maurice Clark, *Competition: Static Models and Dynamic Aspects*, 45 AM. ECON. REV. 450 (1955).
94. Edward S. Mason, *Schumpeter on Monopoly and the Large Firm*, 33 REV. ECON. & STAT. 139 (1951).
95. *See* Robert M. Solow, *A Contribution to the Theory of Economic Growth*, 70 Q.J. ECON. 65 (1956).
96. Kenneth J. Arrow, *Economic Welfare and the Allocation of Resources for Innovation*, in ESSAYS IN THE THEORY OF RISK BEARING (Amsterdam: North-Holland, 1971). Galbraith sided with Schumpeter on this issue. *See* John K. Galbraith, AMERICAN CAPITALISM: THE CONCEPT OF COUNTERVAILING POWER 89–99 (Boston: Houghton Mifflin, 1952).
97. *See* BOHANNAN & HOVENKAMP, CREATION WITHOUT RESTRAINT, *supra* note 13, chs. 1, 4–5.
98. *Id.* at 133–38.
99. 35 U.S.C. § 271(d) (1952; amended: 1988). For Rich's position, *see* Giles S. Rich, *Contributory Infringement*, 31 J. PAT. OFF. SOC'Y 449, 464–66 (1949).

100. *See* Giles S. Rich, *Laying the Ghost of the "Invention" Requirement*, 14 FED. CIR. B.J. 163, 171 (2004).
101. Harries v. Air King Prods. Co., 183 F.2d 158, 162 (2d Cir. 1950).
102. Great Atl. & Pac. Tea Co. v. Supermarket Equip. Corp., 340 U.S. 147, 154 & n.1 (1950).
103. Lyon v. Bausch & Lomb Optical Co., 224 F.2d 530 (2d Cir. 1955).
104. Graham v. John Deere, 383 U.S. 1 (1966); Anderson's-Black Rock, Inc. v. Pavement Salvage Co., 396 U.S. 57 (1969).
105. *Commission on Revision of the Federal Court Appellate System Structure and Internal Procedures: Recommendations for Change*, 67 F.R.D. 195 (1975).
106. For a good historical perspective on the Federal Circuit, *see* Rochelle Dreyfuss, *The Federal Circuit: A Case Study in Specialized Courts*, 64 N.Y.U. L. REV. 1 (1989); Rochelle Dreyfuss, *In Search of Institutional Identity: The Federal Circuit Comes of Age*, 23 BERKELEY TECH. L.J. 787 (2008).
107. *See* Robert P. Merges, *One Hundred Years of Solicitude: Intellectual Property Law, 1900–2000*, 88 CAL.L.REV. 2187, 2224–32 (2000).
108. Richard Posner, THE FEDERAL COURTS: CRISIS AND REFORM 147–60 (Cambridge, MA: Harvard Univ. Press, 1985).
109. *E.g.*, James Bessen & Michael J. Meurer, PATENT FAILURE: HOW JUDGES, BUREAUCRATS, AND LAWYERS PUT INNOVATORS AT RISK (Princeton, NJ: Princeton Univ. Press, 2008); Dan L. Burk & Mark A. Lemley, THE PATENT CRISIS AND HOW THE COURTS CAN SOLVE IT (Chicago: Univ. of Chicago Press, 2009); BOHANNAN & HOVENKAMP, CREATION WITHOUT RESTRAINT, *supra* note 13, chs. 4–5.

CHAPTER 11

1. Alfred Marshall, PRINCIPLES OF ECONOMICS xx, 300 (London: Macmillan, 1890).
2. Alfred Marshall & Mary Paley Marshall, THE ECONOMICS OF INDUSTRY *2* (London: Macmillan, 1879).
3. Arthur Twining Hadley, ECONOMICS: AN ACCOUNT OF THE RELATIONS BETWEEN PRIVATE PROPERTY AND PUBLIC WELFARE 158, 295 (New York: Putnam, 1896); *see* Herbert Hovenkamp, *Regulatory Conflict in the Gilded Age: Federalism and the Railroad Problem*, 97 YALE L.J. 1017, 1017–72 (1988).
4. *See* George J. Stigler, *Perfect Competition, Historically Contemplated*, *65* J. POL. ECON. 1, 1–3 (1957); Adam Smith, AN INQUIRY INTO THE NATURE AND CAUSES OF THE WEALTH OF NATIONS 56–57 (London: W. Strahan, 1776).
5. *See* Irving Fisher, *Introduction* to ANTOINE AUGUSTIN COURNOT, RESEARCHES INTO THE MATHEMATICAL PRINCIPLES OF THE THEORY OF WEALTH ix, ix–xii ([1838]; Eng. trans. by Nathaniel T. Bacon, New York: A.M. Kelley, 1960); Martik

Shubik, *Cournot, Antoine Augustin, in* 1 THE NEW PALGRAVE: A DICTIONARY OF ECONOMICS 708, 708–12 (John Eatwell et al. eds., London: Macmillan, 1987).

6. William. Stanley Jevons, THE THEORY OF POLITICAL ECONOMY 3, 85 n.1 (London: Macmillan, 1871); Léon Walras, ELEMENTS OF PURE ECONOMICS 83–91 ([1874]; Eng. trans. by William Jaffé, London: Allen & Unwin, 1954); MARSHALL, PRINCIPLES OF ECONOMICS, *supra* note 1, at X–XI, 67, 149, 384.
7. *See* Mark Blaug, ECONOMIC THEORY IN RETROSPECT chs. 8–11, 15 (New York: Cambridge Univ. Press, 4th ed. 1985).
8. Joan Robinson, THE ECONOMICS OF IMPERFECT COMPETITION 92–94, 307 (London: Macmillan, 1933).
9. Joseph A. Schumpeter & A.J. Nichol, *Robinson's Economics of Imperfect Competition*, *42* J. POL. ECON. 249, 250–51, 256 (1934).
10. MARSHALL, PRINCIPLES OF ECONOMICS, *supra* note 1, at 445, 529.
11. Herbert Hovenkamp, ENTERPRISE AND AMERICAN LAW, 1836–1937, at 302–22 (Cambridge, MA.: Harvard Univ. Press, 1991); THE MAKING OF COMPETITION POLICY: LEGAL AND ECONOMIC SOURCES 92–103 (Daniel A. Crane & Herbert Hovenkamp eds., New York: Oxford Univ. Press, 2013).
12. *See, e.g.*, Eliot Jones, THE TRUST PROBLEM IN THE UNITED STATES 197–200 (New York: Macmillan, 1921); Myron W. Watkins, INDUSTRIAL COMBINATIONS AND PUBLIC POLICY: A STUDY OF COMBINATION, COMPETITION AND THE COMMON WELFARE ch. 3 (Allyn Young ed., Boston: Houghton Mifflin, 1927); Eliot Jones, *Is Competition in Industry Ruinous*, *34* Q.J. ECON. 473, 491–97 (1920); *see also* 2 F.W. Taussig, PRINCIPLES OF ECONOMICS 53–54 (New York: Macmillan, 1st ed. 1911, 3d ed. 1921); Spurgeon Bell, *Fixed Costs and Market Price*, *32* Q.J. ECON. 507, 509–22 (1918); Frank H. Knight, *Cost of Production and Price over Long and Short Periods*, *29* J. POL. ECON. 304, 306–10 (1921). On the merger movement, *see* Naomi R. Lamoreaux, THE GREAT MERGER MOVEMENT IN AMERICAN BUSINESS, 1895–1904 (New York: Cambridge Univ. Press, 1985).
13. John Maurice Clark, STUDIES IN THE ECONOMICS OF OVERHEAD COSTS (Chicago: Univ. of Chicago Press, 1923); Morris A. Copeland, *Book Review*, *40* POL. SCI. Q. 296, 296 (1925) (reviewing Clark's *Overhead Costs*).
14. ROBINSON, IMPERFECT COMPETITION, *supra* note 8, at 4–5, 51, 179–80, 316–17.
15. Id. at 4–5.
16. Schumpeter & Nichol, *Robinson's Economics of Imperfect Competition, supra* note 9, 250, 256.
17. ROBINSON, IMPERFECT COMPETITION, *supra* note 8, at 281–304, 307.
18. *See* Prue Kerr, *Joan Robinson and Socialist Planning in the Years of High Theory*, *31* CAMBRIDGE J. ECON. 489, 491–503 (2007).
19. Edward Chamberlin, THE THEORY OF MONOPOLISTIC COMPETITION: A RE-ORIENTATION OF THE THEORY OF VALUE (Cambridge, MA: Harvard Univ. Press, 1933).

20. *See* Joseph A. Schumpeter, HISTORY OF ECONOMIC ANALYSIS 1150–51 (New York: Oxford Univ. Press, 1954).
21. *See* Rudolph J.R. Peritz, COMPETITION POLICY IN AMERICA, 1888–1992: HISTORY, RHETORIC, LAW 76–89 (New York: Oxford Univ. Press, 1996); Jason E. Taylor & Peter G. Klein, *An Anatomy of a Cartel: The National Industrial Recovery Act of 1933 and the Compliance Crisis of 1934*, *26* RES. ECON. HIST. 235, 242–48 (2008).
22. *See* Chapter 15; Michael E. Parrish, ANXIOUS DECADES: AMERICA IN PROSPERITY AND DEPRESSION, 1920–1941, at 296–99 (New York: Norton, 1992).
23. Ellis W. Hawley, THE NEW DEAL AND THE PROBLEM OF MONOPOLY: A STUDY IN ECONOMIC AMBIVALENCE 373 (Princeton, NJ: Princeton Univ. Press, 1966); Ira Katznelson, FEAR ITSELF: THE NEW DEAL AND THE ORIGINS OF OUR TIME 229–41 (New York: W.W. Norton, 2014).
24. United States v. Socony-Vacuum Oil Co., 310 U.S. 150, 201–10 (1940).
25. *See* HAWLEY, *supra* note 23, at 374. Daniel Crane notes that the *Madison Oil* indictment stretched back to cover a time period when the defendants were acting under the orders of Harold Ickes, FDR's Secretary of the Interior, under the authority of section three of the National Industrial Recovery Act. Daniel A. Crane, *The Story of* United States v. Socony-Vacuum: *Hot Oil and Antitrust in the Two New Deals*, *in* ANTITRUST STORIES 91–119 (Eleanor M. Fox & Daniel A. Crane eds., New York: Foundation Press, 2007).
26. *E.g.,* William S. Comanor & Thomas A. Wilson, ADVERTISING AND MARKET POWER 245 (Cambridge, MA: Harvard Univ. Press, 1974).
27. *E.g.*, George J. Stigler, *Monopolistic Competition in Retrospect*, *in* FIVE LECTURES ON ECONOMIC PROBLEMS 22–24 (London: LSE, 1949).
28. John Maurice Clark, *Toward a Concept of Workable Competition*, *30* AM. ECON. REV. 241, 241–46, 256 (1940).
29. On the Harvard and Chicago Schools, *see* Herbert Hovenkamp, THE ANTITRUST ENTERPRISE: PRINCIPLE AND EXECUTION 31–38 (Cambridge, MA: Harvard Univ. Press, 2005).
30. *See, e.g.*, STAFF OF TEMP. NAT'L ECON. COMM., 76th Cong., INVESTIGATION OF CONCENTRATION OF ECONOMIC POWER: COMPETITION AND MONOPOLY IN AMERICAN INDUSTRY, Monograph No. 21, at 8–9 (Washington, DC: U.S. G.P.O., 1940) (written by Clair Wilcox); Corwin D. Edwards, MAINTAINING COMPETITION: REQUISITES OF GOVERNMENTAL POLICY 9–10 (New York: McGraw-Hill, 1949); George J. Stigler, *The Extent and Bases of Monopoly*, *32* AM. ECON. REV. SUPP. 1, 2–3 (1942).
31. Walton H. Hamilton, *The Problem of Anti-trust Reform*, *32* COL. L. REV. 173, 176–77 (1932).
32. *See, e.g.*, Carl Kaysen, *UNITED STATES V. UNITED SHOE MACHINERY CORPORATION*: AN ECONOMIC ANALYSIS OF AN ANTI-TRUST CASE (Cambridge, MA: Harvard

Univ. Press, 1956); Samuel M. Loescher, IMPERFECT COLLUSION IN THE CEMENT INDUSTRY (Cambridge, MA: Harvard Univ. Press, 1959); Jesse W. Markham, COMPETITION IN THE RAYON INDUSTRY (Cambridge, MA: Harvard Univ. Press, 1952); James W. McKie, TIN CANS AND TIN PLATE: A STUDY OF COMPETITION IN TWO RELATED MARKETS (Cambridge, MA: Harvard Univ. Press, 1959); Merton J. Peck, COMPETITION IN THE ALUMINUM INDUSTRY, 1945–1958 (Cambridge, MA: Harvard Univ. Press, 1961).

33. HOVENKAMP, ANTITRUST ENTERPRISE, *supra* note 29, at 35–38.
34. Edward S. Mason, *Monopoly in Law and Economics*, 47 YALE L.J. 34, 43 (1937).
35. *See* Edward S. Mason, *The Current Status of the Monopoly Problem in the United States*, 62 HARV. L. REV. 1265, 1271–76 (1949).
36. *See* Joe S. Bain, *Workable Competition in Oligopoly: Theoretical Considerations and Some Empirical Evidence*, 40 AM. ECON. REV. 35, 37–38 (1950). *See also* George W. Stocking & Myron W. Watkins, MONOPOLY AND FREE ENTERPRISE 87–93 (New York: Twentieth Century Fund, 1951).
37. Bain, *Workable Competition in Oligopoly*, *supra* note 36, at 38.
38. *See* Joe S. Bain, BARRIERS TO NEW COMPETITION: THEIR CHARACTER AND CONSEQUENCES IN MANUFACTURING INDUSTRIES 21–24 (Cambridge, MA: Harvard Univ. Press, 1956); Joe S. Bain, INDUSTRIAL ORGANIZATION 174 (New York: Wiley, 1959). *See also* Joe S. Bain, *Conditions of Entry and the Emergence of Monopoly*, *in* MONOPOLY AND COMPETITION AND THEIR REGULATION 215, 219–26 (Edward H. Chamberlin ed., London: Macmillan, 1954).
39. *See* Herbert Hovenkamp, *Introduction to The Neal Report and the Crisis in Antitrust*, 5 COMPETITION POL'Y INT'L 217, 219–22 (2009); HOVENKAMP, ANTITRUST ENTERPRISE, *supra* note 29, at 36–37.
40. *See* BAIN, INDUSTRIAL ORGANIZATION, *supra* note 38, at 152–55, 160, 358.
41. *See* S. REP. No. 81-1775, at 3 (2d Sess. 1950).
42. *E.g.*, United States v. Phila. Nat'l Bank, 374 U.S. 321, 363 (1963); Brown Shoe Co. v. United States, 370 U.S. 294, 322–23, 346 (1962); *cf.* BAIN, INDUSTRIAL ORGANIZATION, *supra* note 38, at 189.
43. *See* BAIN, INDUSTRIAL ORGANIZATION, *supra* note 38, at 158–59, 358.
44. *Id.* at 236–40.
45. George W. Stocking, *The Rule of Reason, Workable Competition, and Monopoly*, 64 YALE L.J. 1107, 1124 (1955). Stocking was best known for his coauthored book STOCKING & WATKINS, MONOPOLY AND FREE ENTERPRISE, *supra* note 36.
46. United States v. Alum. Co. of Am. ("*Alcoa*"), 148 F.2d 416 (2d Cir. 1945). *See* Spencer Weber Waller, *The Story of* Alcoa, *in* ANTITRUST STORIES, *supra* note 25, at 121, 127.
47. 58 Stat. 272.
48. *Alcoa*, 148 F.2d at 431. *See also* Donald F. Turner, *Antitrust Policy and the* CELLOPHANE *Case*, 70 HARV. L. REV. 281, 281–82 (1956) (critiquing the "purpose and intent" approach).

49. *See* Edward H. Levi, *The Antitrust Laws and Monopoly*, *14* U. CHI. L. REV. 153, 175 (1947); Eugene V. Rostow, *Monopoly under the Sherman Act: Power or Purpose?*, *43* ILL. L. REV. 745, 746–62 (1949).
50. Am. Tobacco Co. v. United States, 328 U.S. 781, 810–11 (1946). *See also* United States v. Paramount Pictures, Inc., 334 U.S. 131, 173 (1948); United States v. Griffith, 334 U.S. 100, 106–08 (1948).
51. United States v. United Shoe Mach. Corp., 110 F. Supp. 295, 343–45 (D. Mass. 1953), *aff'd per curiam*, 347 U.S. 521 (1954).
52. *Report*, The Attorney General's National Committee to Study the Antitrust Laws 43–60 (1955). *See* Ward S. Bowman, Jr., *The Report of the Attorney General's National Committee to Study the Antitrust Laws*, *4* J. INDUS. ECON. 81 (1956).
53. Carl Kaysen & Donald F. Turner, ANTITRUST POLICY: AN ECONOMIC AND LEGAL ANALYSIS 46, 111–19 (Cambridge, MA: Harvard Univ. Press, 1959). The proposal was renewed in 3 Phillip E. Areeda & Donald F. Turner, ANTITRUST LAW: AN ANALYSIS OF ANTITRUST PRINCIPLES AND THEIR APPLICATION ¶¶ 614–23 (New York: Little, Brown, 1978). The present author has preserved it, largely for its historical value, in 3 Phillip E. Areeda & Herbert Hovenkamp, ANTITRUST LAW: AN ANALYSIS OF ANTITRUST PRINCIPLES AND THEIR APPLICATION ¶¶ 630–38 (New York: Aspen, 4th ed. 2015).
54. Turner, *Antitrust Policy and the* Cellophane *Case*, *supra* note 48, at 281–92.
55. United States v. Phila. Nat'l Bank, 374 U.S. 321, 364 (1963).
56. The 1968 Guidelines are still available on the Antitrust Division's website. *See* 1968 Merger Guidelines, http://www.justice.gov/atr/hmerger/11247.pdf. *See* Oliver E. Williamson, The Merger Guidelines of the U.S. Department of Justice—In Perspective, http://www.usdoj.gov/atr/hmerger/11257.pdf (last visited April 28, 2014).
57. *See* Edward S. Mason, ECONOMIC CONCENTRATION AND THE MONOPOLY PROBLEM 371–81 (Cambridge, MA: Harvard Univ. Press, 1957); Derek C. Bok, *Section 7 of the Clayton Act and the Merging of Law and Economics*, *74* HARV. L. REV. 226, 234–36 (1960).
58. *See Amending Sections 7 and 11 of the Clayton Act: Hearings on H.R. 515 Before Subcomm. No. 2 of the Comm. on the Judiciary H. of Reps.*, 80th Cong. 7 (1947) (statement of Kefauver that "[the] increased concentration of economic power is dooming free enterprise.").
59. Federal Trade Commission, REPORT ON THE MERGER MOVEMENT: A SUMMARY REPORT *68* (U.S. G.P.O., 1948).
60. Adolf A. Berle, JR. & Gardiner C. Means, THE MODERN CORPORATION AND PRIVATE PROPERTY 18 (New York: Macmillan, 1932). *See* Chapter 9.
61. *See* Note, *Corporate Consolidation and the Concentration of Economic Power: Proposals for Revitalization of Section 7 of the Clayton Act*, *57* YALE L.J. 613, 620–26 (1948).

62. Bok, *Section 7, supra* note 57, at 236–37. *See also* Herbert Hovenkamp, *Derek Bok and the Merger of Law and Economics*, *21* U. MICH. J.L. REFORM 515, 516 (1988).
63. *See, e.g.*, KAYSEN & TURNER, ANTITRUST POLICY, *supra* note 53, at 82.
64. *See, e.g.*, Frank H. Knight, RISK, UNCERTAINTY AND PROFIT (Boston: Houghton, 1921); George J. Stigler, THE ORGANIZATION OF INDUSTRY (Homewood, IL: R.D. Irwin, 1968) (collecting earlier articles); Milton Friedman, ESSAYS IN POSITIVE ECONOMICS (Chicago: Univ. of Chicago Press, 1953); Gary S. Becker, THE ECONOMICS OF DISCRIMINATION (Chicago: Univ. of Chicago Press, 1957). *See* Richard A. Posner, *The Chicago School of Antitrust Analysis*, *127* U. PA. L. REV. 925 (1979).
65. *See* Posner, *Chicago School, supra* note 64, at 931–32; George J. Stigler, *A Theory of Oligopoly*, *72* J. POL. ECON. 44 (1964).
66. *See, e.g.*, Harold Demsetz, *Industry Structure, Market Rivalry, and Public Policy*, *16* J.L. & ECON. 1, 1 (1973).
67. 3 AREEDA & TURNER, ANTITRUST LAW, *supra* note 53, ¶ 347.
68. *Report of the White House Task Force on Antitrust Policy* (May 27, 1969), originally published at 115 CONG. REC. 11, 13890 (1969). *See* Stephen Calkins, *Antitrust Modernization: Looking Backwards*, *31* J. CORP. L. 421 (2006).
69. See Separate Statement of Robert H. Bork, 2 ANTITRUST L. & ECON. REV. 53 (Winter 1968).
70. *See* Richard Schmalensee, *Bill Baxter in the Antitrust Arena: An Economist's Appreciation*, *51* STAN. L. REV. 1317, 1319 (1999).
71. 115 CONG. REC. 12, 15933–15942 (June 16, 1969); *reprinted in* 2 ANTITRUST L. & ECON. REV. 13 (No. 3, Spring, 1969).
72. United States v. Gen. Dynamics Corp., 415 U.S. 486, 497 (1974).

CHAPTER 12

1. *See, e.g.*, THE REGULATED ECONOMY: A HISTORICAL APPROACH TO POLITICAL ECONOMY (Claudia Goldin & Gary D. Libecap eds., Chicago: Univ. of Chicago Press, 1994); Gabriel Kolko, RAILROADS AND REGULATION: 1877–1916, at 3 (Princeton, NJ: Princeton Univ. Press, 1965).
2. Lawrence K. Frank, *The Significance of Industrial Integration*, 33 J. POL. ECON. 179, 179 (1925).
3. *See* United States v. Winslow, 227 U.S. 202, 217 (1913); Carl Kaysen, *UNITED STATES V. UNITED SHOE MACHINERY CORPORATION:* AN ECONOMIC ANALYSIS OF AN ANTI-TRUST CASE 2–3 (Cambridge, MA: Harvard Univ. Press, 1956).
4. United States v. Brown Shoe Co., 370 U.S. 294 (1962).
5. Adam Smith, AN INQUIRY INTO THE NATURE AND CAUSES OF THE WEALTH OF NATIONS BK. I, ch. 3 (London: W. Strahan & T. Cadell, 1776). *See* George J. Stigler, *The Division of Labor Is Limited by the Extent of the Market*, 59 J. POL. ECON. 185, 185 (1951).

6. Alfred Marshall, INDUSTRY AND TRADE: A STUDY OF INDUSTRIAL TECHNIQUE AND BUSINESS ORGANIZATION; AND OF THEIR INFLUENCES ON THE CONDITION OF VARIOUS CLASSES AND NATIONS 147–48, 156, 373–81, 559–61 (London: Macmillan, 1919).
7. John R. Commons, LEGAL FOUNDATIONS OF CAPITALISM 270 (New York: Macmillan, 1924).
8. Adolf A. Berle & Gardiner C. Means, THE MODERN CORPORATION AND PRIVATE PROPERTY (New York: Harcourt, 1932).
9. Thurman Arnold, THE BOTTLENECKS OF BUSINESS 1–15 (New York: Reynal & Hitchcock, 1940).
10. Ronald H. Coase, *The Nature of the Firm*, 4 ECONOMICA (n.s.) 386, 404–05 (1937).
11. Joe S. Bain, INDUSTRIAL ORGANIZATION 138–41, 168–69, 261–71 (New York: Wiley, 1959).
12. Robert Bork, *Vertical Integration and the Sherman Act: The Legal History of an Economic Misconception*, 22 U. CHI. L. REV. 157, 159 (1954).
13. BAIN, INDUSTRIAL ORGANIZATION, *supra* note 11, at 168–69, 330, 331, 357–58.
14. Alfred D. Chandler, JR., THE VISIBLE HAND: THE MANAGERIAL REVOLUTION IN AMERICAN BUSINESS 515 n.3 (Cambridge, MA: Harvard Univ. Press, 1977).
15. George Hale, *Vertical Integration: Impact of the Antitrust Laws upon Combinations of Successive Stages of Production and Distribution*, 49 COL. L. REV. 921, 922 (1949).
16. *See* Richard N. Langlois & Paul L. Robertson, *Explaining Vertical Integration: Lessons from the American Automobile Industry*, 49 J. ECON. HIST. 361, 365 (1989).
17. *See* FTC, CAUSES OF THE HIGH PRICES OF FARM IMPLEMENTS 672–75 (1920); *International Harvester*, FORTUNE 21 (Aug. 1933).
18. *See* Herbert Hovenkamp, ENTERPRISE AND AMERICAN LAW, 1836–1937, at 335–60 (Cambridge, MA: Harvard Univ. Press, 1991); for the contemporary view, *see* Victor Morawetz, A TREATISE ON THE LAW OF PRIVATE CORPORATIONS §§ 362–365, 393 (Boston: Little, Brown, 2d ed. 1886).
19. Clayton Act, ch. 323, § 7, 38 Stat. 730 (1914).
20. On the political environment at midcentury, *see* Joseph C. Palamountain, JR., THE POLITICS OF DISTRIBUTION (Cambridge, MA: Harvard Univ. Press, 1955).
21. Liggett v. Lee, 288 U.S. 517 (1933). *See* PALAMOUNTAIN, POLITICS OF DISTRIBUTION, *supra* note 20, at 159–87; Godfrey M. Lebhar, CHAIN STORES IN AMERICA, 1859–1962, at 125–55 (New York: Chain Store Pub. Corp., 3d ed. 1963).
22. *See* Asher Blass & Dennis Carlton, *The Choice of Organizational Form in Gasoline Retailing and the Cost of Laws That Limit That Choice*, 44 J.L. & ECON. 511, 511–12 (2001).
23. *See* Thomas S. Dicke, FRANCHISING IN AMERICA: THE DEVELOPMENT OF A BUSINESS METHOD, 1840–1980, at 45–84 (Chapel Hill: Univ. of North Carolina Press, 1992) (Ford Motor Company franchising practices 1903–1956).

24. *See* Frederick M. Rowe, PRICE DISCRIMINATION UNDER THE ROBINSON-PATMAN ACT 3–25 (Boston: Little, Brown, 1962); Wholesale Grocers' Ass'n v. FTC, 18 F.2d 866 (8th Cir. 1927) (condemning grocers' association boycott of chain store suppliers). *See* Richard C. Schragger, *The Anti-Chain Store Movement, Localist Ideology, and the Remnants of the Progressive Constitution, 1920–1940*, 90 IOWA L. REV. 1011 (2005).
25. *See* Derek C. Bok, *Section 7 of the Clayton Act and the Merging of Law and Economics*, 74 HARV. L. REV. 226, 234–36 (1960); Herbert Hovenkamp, *Derek Bok and the Merger of Law and Economics*, 21 U. MICH. J.L. REFORM 515, 524–28 (1988); Brown Shoe Co. v. United States, 370 U.S. 294 (1962).
26. United States v. Aluminum Co. of Am., 148 F.2d 416, 429 (2d Cir. 1945).
27. Dr. Miles Med. Co. v. John D. Park & Sons Co., 220 U.S. 373, 397 (1911); Lochner v. New York, 198 U.S. 45, 59 (1905). Justice Holmes dissented in both cases.
28. John Chipman Gray, RESTRAINTS ON THE ALIENATION OF PROPERTY, at iii–viii (Boston Book Co., 1883; 2d ed. 1895).
29. *Dr. Miles*, 220 U.S. at 404–05, 409. *See* Lord Chief Justice Edward Coke's *Commentary upon Littleton* (1628), which was Volume 1 of Coke's *Institutes of the Lawes of England*, a largely verbatim copy of Sir Thomas Littleton's *Tenures*, first printed in 1481 or 1482. 1 COKE ON LITTLETON bk. 3, ch. 5, § 360, at 223 (n.p. 1628).
30. United States v. Arnold, Schwinn & Co., 388 U.S. 365, 380 (1967).
31. United Shoe Machinery Corp. v United States, 258 U.S. 451 (1922); International Business Machines Corp. v. United States, 298 U.S. 131 (1936).
32. *See* Seymour v. McCormick, 57 U.S. 480, 490 (1853); McCormick v. Gray, 54 U.S. 26 (1851). McCormick later changed to a more centralized distribution system with wholly owned outlets. *See* CHANDLER, VISIBLE HAND, *supra* note 14, at 305–07, 402–08.
33. Ruth Brandon, SINGER AND THE SEWING MACHINE: A CAPITALIST ROMANCE 117 (Philadelphia: Lippincott, 1977).
34. *See* Martin Mendelsohn, INTERNATIONAL FRANCHISING: AN OVERVIEW 4–5 (Amsterdam: Elsevier, 1984).
35. *See* DICKE, *supra* note 23, at 59–74; Sally H. Clarke, TRUST AND POWER: CONSUMERS, THE MODERN CORPORATION, AND THE MAKING OF THE UNITED STATES AUTOMOBILE MARKET (New York: Cambridge Univ. Press, 2007).
36. *E.g.*, Buggs v. Ford Motor Co., 113 F.2d 618 (7th Cir. 1940).
37. Ford Motor Co. v. Kirkmyer Motor Co., 65 F.2d 1001, 1006 (4th Cir. 1933); Bushwick-Decatur Motors, Inc. v. Ford Motor Co., 116 F.2d 675, 677 (2d Cir. 1940).
38. On the congressional concern, *see* H.R. REP. No. 63-1168, at 11–12 (1914).
39. Standard Fashion Co. v. Magrane-Houston Co., 258 U.S. 346, 351–57 (1922).
40. Standard Oil Co. v. FTC, 273 F. 478, 480 (2d Cir. 1921). The Supreme Court agreed with the Second Circuit in FTC v. Sinclair Co., 261 U.S. 463 (1923).

41. Standard Oil Co. v. United States, 337 U.S. 293, 302 (1949).
42. *Id.* at 316, 318–20.
43. United States v. Gen. Elec. Co., 272 U.S. 476, 481–83 (1926).
44. Dr. Miles Med. Co. v. John D. Park & Sons Co., 220 U.S. 373, 394–98 (1911).
45. Straus v. Victor Talking Mach. Co., 243 U.S. 490, 494–96, 500–01 (1917).
46. DICKE, FRANCHISING IN AMERICA, *supra* note 23, at 3.
47. *See, e.g.*, Principe v. McDonald's Corp., 631 F.2d 303 (4th Cir. 1980).
48. *E.g.*, Siegel v. Chicken Delight, Inc., 448 F.2d 43, 47–48 (9th Cir. 1971).
49. *See* ROWE, PRICE DISCRIMINATION, *supra* note 24, at 3–35; PALAMOUNTAIN, POLITICS OF DISTRIBUTION, *supra* note 20, at 169–222.
50. *See* Marc Levinson, THE GREAT A&P AND THE STRUGGLE FOR SMALL BUSINESS IN AMERICA (New York: Hill and Wang, 2011); James M. Mayo, THE AMERICAN GROCERY STORE 78–82 (Westport, CT: Greenwood, 1993).
51. FTC, FINAL REPORT ON THE CHAIN STORE INVESTIGATION 57–58, 85–97 (1934); *see* Ellis W. Hawley, THE NEW DEAL AND THE PROBLEM OF MONOPOLY 248–50 (Princeton, NJ: Princeton Univ. Press, 1966).
52. *See* 14 HERBERT HOVENKAMP, ANTITRUST LAW ¶ 2361 (3d ed. 2012).
53. *E.g.*, Standard Oil Co. v. FTC, 340 U.S. 231, 249–50 (1951).
54. *See* Richard A. Posner, THE ROBINSON-PATMAN ACT 26–27 (Washington, DC: Am. Enterprise Inst., 1976); Philip Elman, *The Robinson-Patman Act and Antitrust Policy: A Time for Reappraisal*, 42 WASH. L. REV. 1, 11–13 (1966).
55. ROWE, PRICE DISCRIMINATION, *supra* note 24, at 536–42.
56. Pub. L. No. 314, 75th Congress, 1st Sess. (1937). On the history of the numerous attempts to limit *Dr. Miles, see* E.R.A. Seligman & Robert Love, PRICE CUTTING AND PRICE MAINTENANCE: A STUDY IN ECONOMICS (New York: Harper, 1932); Harry Kantor & Anne Goulden, RESALE PRICE MAINTENANCE LEGISLATION IN THE UNITED STATES (Washington, DC: N.R.A., 1935).
57. *E.g.*, Grogan v. Chaffee, 156 Cal. 611 (1909).
58. D. Ghirardelli Co. v. Hunsicker, 164 Cal. 355 (1912).
59. Louis Brandeis, *Competition That Kills*, HARPER'S WEEKLY, Nov. 15, 1913. *See* Gerald Berk, LOUIS D. BRANDEIS AND THE MAKING OF REGULATED COMPETITION, 1900–1932 (New York: Cambridge Univ. Press, 2009).
60. *See* Laura D. Phillips, AMERICAN FAIR TRADE: PROPRIETARY CAPITALISM, NETWORKS, AND THE NEW COMPETITION, 1890–1940 (New York: Cambridge Univ. Press, 2014).
61. *See* Mark Pendergrast, UNCOMMON GROUNDS: THE HISTORY OF COFFEE AND HOW IT TRANSFORMED OUR WORLD 150–64 (New York: Basic, 2d ed. 2010).
62. Hills Bros. v. FTC, 9 F.2d 481 (9th Cir. 1926).
63. Lentheric v. Grant, 13 N.Y.S.2d 169 (N.Y. 1939); Coty, Inc. v. Hearn Dept. Stores, 284 N.Y.S. 909 (N.Y. Sup. 1935). *See* Note, *Fair Trade Legislation: The Constitutionality of a State Experiment in Resale Price Maintenance*, 49 HARV. L. REV. 811 (1936).

64. *E.g.*, Johnson & Johnson v. Weissbard, 191 A. 873 (N.J. App. 1937).
65. Old Dearborn Distr. Co. v. Seagram-Distillers Corp., 299 U.S. 183, 193 (1936).
66. Consumer Goods Pricing Act, 89 Stat. 801 (1975). *See* S. Rep. No. 466, 94th Cong., 1st Sess. 2 (1975).
67. *See* Friedrich Kessler, *Automobile Dealer Franchises: Vertical Integration by Contract*, 66 YALE L.J. 1135, 1169 & n.224 (1957).
68. FTC, ANNUAL REPORT 24–25 (1939).
69. Automobile Dealers' Day in Court Act, Pub. L. No. 1026, 70 Stat. 1125 (1956) (codified at 15 U.S.C. §§ 1221–1225 (2006)); *see* Donald P. McHugh, *The Automobile Dealer Franchise Act of 1956*, 2 ANTITRUST BULL. 353, 354 (1957).
70. H.R. REP. No. 2850, at 3 (1956).
71. On the development of the case law, *see* 8 PHILLIP E. AREEDA & HERBERT HOVENKAMP, ANTITRUST LAW ¶¶ 1620–1627 (3d ed. 2011).
72. *E.g.*, Int'l Salt Co. v. United States, 332 U.S. 392, 395–96 (1947).
73. United States v. Arnold, Schwinn & Co., 388 U.S. 365, 382 (1967).
74. Albrecht v. Herald Co., 390 U.S. 145, 153 (1968).
75. *See, e.g.*, Paschall v. Kan. City Star Co., 727 F.2d 692, 704 (8th Cir. 1984) (en banc).
76. Robert H. Bork, THE ANTITRUST PARADOX: A POLICY AT WAR AGAINST ITSELF 210–16 (New York: Basic, 1978).
77. Brief of the United States at 46–51, United States v. Arnold, Schwinn & Co., 388 U.S. 365 (1967) (No. 25).
78. 3 PHILLIP E. AREEDA & DONALD F. TURNER, ANTITRUST LAW ¶ 734c, at 262 (1978); Richard A. Posner, *The Next Step in the Antitrust Treatment of Restricted Distribution: Per Se Legality*, 48 U CHI. L. REV. 6, 7–8 (1981).
79. Cont'l T.V., Inc. v. GTE Sylvania, Inc., 433 U.S. 36, 36–37 (1977).
80. George Ellery Hale & Rosemary D. Hale, MARKET POWER: SIZE AND SHAPE UNDER THE SHERMAN ACT 49 (Boston: Little, Brown, 1958).
81. Munn v. Illinois, 94 U.S. 113, 135–36 (1876); *see* HOVENKAMP, ENTERPRISE AND AMERICAN LAW, *supra* note 18, ch. 12.
82. United States v. Am. Tobacco Co., 221 U.S. 106, 187–88 (1911).
83. United States v. Eastman Kodak Co., 226 F. 62, 79–80 (W.D.N.Y. 1915).
84. United States v. Corn Prods. Refining Co., 234 F. 964, 984–90, 1013 (S.D.N.Y. 1916).
85. Standard Oil Co. v. United States, 221 U.S. 1, 76–77 (1911).
86. *See, e.g.*, United States v. Standard Oil Co., 47 F.2d 288, 309–11 (E.D. Mo. 1931).
87. United States v. U.S. Steel Corp., 251 U.S. 417, 442 (1920).
88. *See, e.g.*, Arthur R. Burns, THE DECLINE OF COMPETITION: A STUDY OF THE EVOLUTION OF AMERICAN INDUSTRY 445 (New York: McGraw-Hill, 1936). See *also* Arthur R. Burns, *The Organization of Industry and the Theory of Prices*, 45 J. POL. ECON. 662, 671 (1937) (vertical integration inefficient because it "blurs" costs by disguising transfer prices).

89. Henry Simons, *A Positive Program for Laissez-Faire* 20–21 (1934), *reprinted in* SIMONS, ECONOMIC POLICY FOR A FREE SOCIETY (Chicago: Univ. of Chicago Press, 1948).
90. *See* Roy C. Cook, *Control of the Petroleum Industry by Major Oil Companies* 51–52 (TNEC Monograph No. 39, 1941).
91. Eugene V. Rostow, A NATIONAL POLICY FOR THE OIL INDUSTRY 71–76, 117 (New Haven, CT: Yale, 1948).
92. Corwin Edwards, MAINTAINING COMPETITION 130 (New York: McGraw-Hill, 1949).
93. United States v. Yellow Cab Co., 332 U.S. 218, 227 (1947).
94. United States v. Paramount Pictures, Inc., 334 U.S. 131, 174 (1948). The problem had already been noted during the New Deal. *See* Daniel Bertrand et al., *The Motion Picture Industry—A Pattern of Control* (TNEC Monograph No. 43, 1941).
95. *Yellow Cab Co.*, 332 U.S. at 226–27.
96. United States v. N.Y. Great Atl. & Pac. Tea Co., 173 F.2d 79, 85 (7th Cir. 1949).
97. Robert Bork, *Vertical Integration and the Sherman Act: The Legal History of an Economic Misconception*, 22 U. CHI. L. REV. 157, 181 (1954).
98. Joe S. Bain, *BARRIERS TO NEW COMPETITION: THEIR CHARACTER AND CONSEQUENCES IN MANUFACTURING INDUSTRIES* 142–166, 212 (Cambridge, MA: Harvard Univ. Press, 1956).
99. U.S. DEP'T OF JUSTICE, 1968 MERGER GUIDELINES 9–10 (1968).
100. United States v. E. I. du Pont de Nemours & Co., 353 U.S. 586, 588–89 (1957). *See* Brief for the United States at 113, *du Pont*, 353 U.S. 586 (No. 3).
101. Brief for Appellee Gen. Motors Corp. at 171, *du Pont*, 353 U.S. 586 (No. 3).

CHAPTER 13

1. Lochner v. New York, 198 U.S. 45, 62–63 (1905). A better historical case can be made that the 14th Amendment's Privileges and Immunities Clause was intended to include a few of the rights later recognized as part of Due Process, but this reading was rejected by the Supreme Court majority in the Slaughter-House Cases, 83 U.S. 36 (1872). See Kurt T. Lash, THE FOURTEENTH AMENDMENT AND THE PRIVILEGES AND IMMUNITIES OF AMERICAN CITIZENSHIP ix-x, 228-254 (New York: Cambridge Univ. Press 2014). The federal liberty of contract cases almost never mentioned the Privileges and Immunities clause, although a few state courts did. *See, e.g.*, People v. Ringe, 197 N.Y. 143, 151 (1910); People v. Beattie, 89 N.Y.S. 193 (N.Y.A.D. 1904)
2. *E.g.*, Ogden v. Saunders, 25 U.S. 213 (1827); Sturges v. Crowinshield, 17 U.S. 122 (1819). *See* 1 G. Edward White, LAW IN AMERICAN HISTORY 227, 241 (New York: Oxford Univ. Press, 2012).
3. *E.g.*, Gibbons v. Ogden, 22 U.S. (9 Wheat.) 1 (1824); Wilson v. Blackbird Creek Marsh Co., 27 U.S. (2 Pet.) 245 (1829).

4. 10 U.S. 87 (1810).
5. Dartmouth Coll. v. Woodward, 17 U.S. 518 (1819).
6. Dred Scott v. Sanford, 60 U.S. 393, 450 (1856).
7. Bloomer v. McQuewan 55 U.S. 539, 553 (1852).
8. *E.g*, Pennsylvania Coal Co. v. Mahon, 260 U.S. 393 (1922).
9. Herbert Hovenkamp, *The Cultural Crises of the Fuller Court*, 104 YALE L.J. 2309, 2319–2320 (1995); Herbert Hovenkamp, ENTERPRISE AND AMERICAN LAW, 1836–1937, at 171–92 (Cambridge, MA: Harvard Univ. Press, 1991); Charles Sellers, THE MARKET REVOLUTION: JACKSONIAN AMERICA, 1815–1846, at 50–54 (New York: Oxford Univ. Press, 1991). *See* Ryan Williams, *The One and Only Substantive Due Process Clause*, 120 YALE L.J. 408 (2010); Edward Corwin, *The Doctrine of Due Process of Law before the Civil War*, 24 HARV. L. REV. 366, 460 (1911); Learned Hand, *Due Process of Law and the Eight-Hour Day*, 21 HARV. L. REV. 495 (1908) (criticizing the doctrine as without historical foundation).
10. Thomas M. Cooley, A TREATISE ON THE CONSTITUTIONAL LIMITATIONS (Boston: Little, Brown, 1868). *See also* Christopher Tiedeman, A TREATISE ON THE LIMITATIONS OF POLICE POWER IN THE UNITED STATES (St. Louis, MO: F.H. Thomas, 1886); John Dillon, TREATISE ON THE LAW OF MUNICIPAL CORPORATIONS (New York: Cockcroft, 1872).
11. COOLEY, CONSTITUTIONAL LIMITATIONS, *supra* note 10, at 829–90 (due process; racial rights at 869); 554–574 (equal protection; race discrimination discussed mainly in footnotes) (7th ed. Boston: Little, Brown 1896).
12. *See* Herbert Hovenkamp, *The Classical Corporation in American Legal Thought*, 76 GEO. L.J. 1593, 1622–24 (1988).
13. COOLEY, CONSTITUTIONAL LIMITATIONS, *supra* note 10, at 335 (2d ed. 1871); Francis Wharton, COMMENTARIES ON AMERICAN LAW 556 (Philadelphia: Kay and Brother, 1884).
14. *E.g.*, Richard A. Epstein, THE CLASSICAL LIBERAL CONSTITUTION: THE UNCERTAIN QUEST FOR LIMITED GOVERNMENT 15–19 (Cambridge, MA: Harvard Univ. Press, 2014).
15. SELLERS, MARKET REVOLUTION, *supra* note 9; HOVENKAMP, ENTERPRISE, *supra* note 9, at 17–41, 93–104, 183–92.
16. *In re* Jacobs, 98 N.Y. 98, 110 (1885). *See* Chaim M. Rosenberg, CHILD LABOR IN AMERICA: A HISTORY, ch. 6 (Jefferson, NC: McFarland, 2013). On the industry at the time and the facts of *Jacobs, see* Eileen Boris, *"A Man's Dwelling House Is His Castle": Tenement House Cigarmaking and the Judicial Imperative, in* WORK ENGENDERED: TOWARDS A NEW HISTORY OF AMERICAN LABOR LAW 114 (Ava Baron ed., Ithaca, NY: Cornell Univ. Press, 1994).
17. *See* William E. Forbath, *The Ambiguities of Free Labor: Labor and the Law in the Gilded Age*, 1985 WISC. L. REV. 767, 795. On the union's organizing activities, see T.Wesley Glocker, *The Structure of the Cigar Makers' Union* 43-80, in STUDIES IN

AMERICAN TRADE UNIONISM (Jacob H. Hollander & George E. Barnett, eds., New York: Henry Holt, 1912).

18. Theodore Roosevelt, AN AUTOBIOGRAPHY 79–81 (New York: Scribners, 1913); Jacob A. Riis, HOW THE OTHER HALF LIVES: STUDIES AMONG THE TENEMENTS OF NEW YORK, CH. 12 (New York: Scribners, 1890). For a fuller account of Roosevelt's involvement, *see* Doris Kearns Goodwin, THE BULLY PULPIT: THEODORE ROOSEVELT, WILLIAM HOWARD TAFT, AND THE GOLDEN AGE OF JOURNALISM 37, 64, 77-85, 213-217, (New York: Simon & Schuster, 2014).
19. Millett v. People, 117 Ill. 294, 7 N.E. 631 (1886).
20. Godcharles v. Wigeman, 113 Pa. 431 (1886).
21. People v. Beattie, 96 A.D. 383, 89 N.Y.S. 193 (N.Y.A.D. 1904).
22. People v. Ringe, 197 N.Y. 143, 151 (1910). *See also* Wyeth v. Thomas, 200 Mass. 474 (1909) (striking down similar statute; no mention of monopoly).
23. *See* David Foos, *State Ready-to-Embalm Laws and the Modern Funeral Market*, 2012 MICH. ST. L. REV. 1375.
24. See William J. Novak, The People's Welfare: Law & Regulation in Nineteenth Century America 90–95 (Chapel Hill: Univ. N.C. Press, 1996); Lawrence M. Friedman, *Freedom of Contract and Occupational Licensing, 1890–1910: A Legal and Social Study*, 53 CAL. L. REV. 487 (1965).
25. Springer & Kimmell v. Town of Westernport, 140 Md. 506 (1922); Rapp v. Venable, 15 N.M. 509 (1910); State v. Call, 121 N.C. 643 (1897) (licensing of physicians did not create a monopoly). *See also* Noe v. Town of Morristown, 128 Tenn. 350 (1913) (condemning slaughter-house license provision that permitted only a single firm in the city to slaughter animals); Eagle Cliff Fishing Co. v. McGowan, 70 Or. 1 (1914) (condemning particular interpretation of commercial salmon fishing license that operated to create a monopoly); Burlington & Henderson County Ferry Co. v. Davis, 48 Iowa 133 (1878) (licensing a single firm to operate a ferry unlawful). In the Supreme Court, *see* Dent v. West Virginia, 129 U.S. 114 (1888) (unanimously upholding state licensing requirement for physicians).
26. Marc T. Law et al., *Effects of Occupational Licensing Laws on Minorities: Evidence from the Progressive Era*, 52 J.L. & ECON. 351 (2009).
27. *See, e.g.*, Matthew Lindsay, *In Search of "Laissez-Faire Constitutionalism,"* 123 HARV. L. REV. FORUM 55 (2010); Jed Shugerman, *Economic Crisis and the Rise of Judicial Elections and Judicial Review*, 123 HARV. L. REV. 1061 (2010).
28. At the lower end, *see* Charles Warren, *A Bulwark to the State Police Power—The United States Supreme Court*, 13 COL. L. REV. 667 (1913); Charles Warren, *The Progressiveness of the United States Supreme Court*, 13 COL. L. REV. 294 (1913). For the two hundred estimate, *see* Robert McCloskey, THE AMERICAN SUPREME COURT 101 (Chicago: Univ. Chicago Press, 1994); Felix Frankfurter, MR. JUSTICE HOLMES AND THE SUPREME COURT (Cambridge, MA: Harvard Univ. Press, 1938). *But see* Michael Phillips, THE LOCHNER COURT, MYTH AND

REALITY: SUBSTANTIVE DUE PROCESS FROM THE 1890S TO THE 1930S, ch. 2 (Westport, CT: Praeger, 2001) (disputing the two hundred figure as exaggerated).

29. *E.g.*, Mugler v. Kansas, 123 U.S. 623 (1887) (manufacturing of alcoholic beverages akin to nuisance); Waters pierce Oil Co. v. Town of New Iberia, 47 La. Ann. 863 (1895) (ordinance prohibiting storage of dynamite inside city limits merely proscribed a common law nuisance). *See also* State v. Heidenhain, 42 La. Ann. 483 (1890) (state had discretion to determine that smoking in streetcars was a nuisance).
30. *See* Robert Zieger, FOR JOBS AND FREEDOM: RACE AND LABOR IN AMERICA SINCE 1865 (Lexington: Univ. Press of Kentucky, 2010).
31. RIIS, HOW THE OTHER HALF LIVES, *supra* note 18, at 137–44.
32. *See* Herbert Hovenkamp, *Labor Conspiracies in American Law*, 66 TEX. L. REV. 919–65 (1988).
33. For divergent views, *see* Barry Cushman, RETHINKING THE NEW DEAL COURT: THE STRUCTURE OF A CONSTITUTIONAL REVOLUTION (New York: Oxford Univ. Press, 1998); David Bernstein, REHABILITATING *LOCHNER*: DEFENDING INDIVIDUAL RIGHTS AGAINST PROGRESSIVE REFORM (Chicago: Univ. Chicago Press, 2011).
34. 14 Stat. 27–30 (April 9, 1866), codified at 42 U.S.C. § 1981 (1866).
35. Lochner v. New York, 198 U.S. 45, 75 (1905); Adkins v. Children's Hosp., 261 U.S. 525, 567–68 (1923). *See* Herbert Hovenkamp, *The Political Economy of Substantive Due Process*, 40 STAN. L. REV. 379 (1988).
36. Muller v. Oregon, 208 U.S. 412 (1908).
37. Louis D. Brandeis, Brief for Defendant in Error, Muller v. Oregon, 208 U.S. 412 (1908) [hereinafter BRANDEIS BRIEF]. Goldmark was also Brandeis's sister-in-law.
38. *Id.* at 50–51.
39. On state bureaus of labor statistics, *see* Susan Carter, Roger Ransom & Richard Sutch, *The Historical Labor Statistics Project at the University of California*, 24 HIST. METHODS 52 (1991).
40. COOLEY, CONSTITUTIONAL LIMITATIONS, *supra* note 10, at 889 (7th ed., 1903).
41. BRANDEIS BRIEF, *supra* note 37, at 28–42, 42–44, 44–46.
42. *Id.* at 106–09 (health), 109 (safety), and 109–11 (morals).
43. *Id.* at 44.
44. *E.g.*, Bacon v. Walker, 204 U.S. 311, 317 (1907) (citing health, safety, and morals; upholding statute that forbade grazing sheep within two miles of residential area); Cal. Reduction Co. v. Sanitary Reduction Works, 199 U.S. 306, 324 (1905) (upholding ordinance limiting places for disposal of garbage); Jacobson v. Massachusetts, 187 U.S. 11 (1905) (upholding compulsory vaccination statute, citing medical opinion about health and safety); Austin v. Tennessee, 179 U.S. 343 (1900) (upholding limitations on the sale of cigarettes to minors, citing health, safety, and morals). Following *Muller*: Near v. Minnesota, 283 U.S. 697, 707 (1931) (Butler, J., dissenting, police power should be limited to statutes that

appropriately regulate health, safety, or morals); Nectow v. Cambridge, 277 U.S. 183, 187 (1928) (requiring that regulation have a "substantial relation to the public health, the public morals, the public safety or the public welfare"); Bunting v. Oregon, 243 U.S. 426 (1917) (upholding ten-hour law for mill workers, citing legislative statement that it was to protect public health); Adams v. Tanner, 244 U.S. 590, 593 (1917) (striking down provision that prohibits charging employees fees for job-related goods or services; "nothing... that in any way threatens or endangers the public health, safety, or morals."); Coppage v. Kansas, 236 U.S. 1, 16 (1915) (striking down statute forbidding employers from requiring employees to sign promises not to join unions; no relationship with "public health, safety, morals, or general welfare."); Lochner v. New York, 198 U.S. 45 (1905) (bakers' hours' statute not "a valid exercise of the police power to protect the public health, safety, morals, or general welfare.").

45. *Lochner*, 198 U.S. at 62.
46. Prior to *Lochner* the Court had acknowledged some exceptions. *See* Holden v. Hardy, 169 U.S. 366 (1898) (coal miners); Atkin v. Kansas, 191 U.S. 207 (1903) (municipal employer).
47. Welch v. Swasey, 214 U.S. 91, 107 (1909).
48. Adkins v. Children's Hosp., 261 U.S. 525, 555–56 (1923).
49. Village of Euclid v. Ambler Realty Co., 272 U.S. 365, 391–95 (1926).
50. *See, e.g.*, Robert Crunden, MINISTERS OF REFORM: THE PROGRESSIVES' ACHIEVEMENT IN AMERICAN CIVILIZATION, *1889–1920* (Champaign: Univ. of Illinois Press, 1985).
51. *See, e.g.*, Gary Dorrien, SOCIAL ETHICS IN THE MAKING: INTERPRETING AN AMERICAN TRADITION (New York: Wiley-Blackwell, 2010); Robert Handy, THE SOCIAL GOSPEL IN AMERICA, 1870–1920 (New York: Oxford Univ. Press, 1966). On Richard T. Ely and the Social Gospel, *see* Benjamin Rader, *Richard T. Ely. Lay Spokesman for the Social Gospel*, 53 J. AM. HIS. 61 (1966).
52. Edward Alsworth Ross, SIN AND SOCIETY: AN ANALYSIS OF LATTER-DAY INIQUITY, ix–xi, 21–42, 103–32 (Boston, Houghton, Mifflin, 1907).
53. *See* Adam Smith, AN INQUIRY INTO THE NATURE AND CAUSES OF THE WEALTH OF NATIONS, Bk. I, chs. 1–2 (Dublin: Whitestone, 1776).
54. *See, e.g.*, Daniel Joseph Boorstin, THE LOST WORLD OF THOMAS JEFFERSON (New York: Holt, 1948).
55. ADAM SMITH, THE THEORY OF THE MORAL SENTIMENTS 168–69, 386 ([1759] Liberty Edition reprint, 1976).
56. *Id.* at 203–04.
57. On the strong aversion of elite American Protestants to utilitarianism, *see* Daniel Howe, THE UNITARIAN CONSCIENCE: HARVARD MORAL PHILOSOPHY, 1805–1861, at 65–66 (Middletown, CT: Wesleyan, 1988); on evangelicals, *see* Donald Meyer, THE INSTRUCTED CONSCIENCE: THE SHAPING OF THE AMERICAN NATIONAL ETHIC (Philadelphia: Penn. Press, 1972).

58. John McVickar, *Concluding Remarks*, *in* John R. McCulloch, OUTLINES OF POLITICAL ECONOMY 136–37 (New York: Wilder & Campbell, 1825).
59. *See* Francis Bowen, LOWELL LECTURES, ON THE APPLICATION OF METAPHYSICAL AND ETHICAL SCIENCE TO THE EVIDENCES OF RELIGION (Boston: Little, Brown, 1849).
60. Francis Wayland, THE ELEMENTS OF MORAL SCIENCE 36, 100–02, 131 (New York: Cooke, 1835).
61. HENRY VETHAKE, THE PRINCIPLES OF POLITICAL ECONOMY 14, 306–07, 322–31 (unionism); 332–35 (hours legislation); 343–56 (welfare law and unemployment compensation) (Philadelphia: Nicklin, 1844). On Vethake, *see* Joseph Dorfman & Rexford Guy Tugwell, EARLY AMERICAN POLICY: SIX COLUMBIA CONTRIBUTORS 155–204 (North Stratford, NH: Ayer, 1960).
62. *See* Chapter 5; HOVENKAMP, ENTERPRISE, *supra* note 9, at 36–41.
63. *See* GLYNDON VAN DUESEN, THE JACKSONIAN ERA, 1828–1848, at 92–96 (New York, Harper, 1959).
64. *See, e.g.*, SELLERS, MARKET REVOLUTION, *supra* note 9, at 202–36.
65. *See* William G. McLoughlin, NEW ENGLAND DISSENT, 1630–1833: THE BAPTISTS AND THE SEPARATION OF CHURCH AND STATE (Cambridge, MA: Harvard Univ. Press, 1971).
66. *See* 2 *id.* at 915–1063, 1189–262.
67. *See* Arthur R. Schlesinger, THE AGE OF JACKSON 350–60 (Boston: Little Brown, rev. ed. 1945).
68. *See* Robert H. Abzug, COSMOS CRUMBLING: AMERICAN REFORM AND THE RELIGIOUS IMAGINATION (New York: Oxford Univ. Press, 1994); George H. Thomas, REVIVALISM AND CULTURAL CHANGE: CHRISTIANITY, NATION BUILDING, AND THE MARKET IN THE NINETEENTH-CENTURY UNITED STATES (Chicago: Univ. of Chicago Press,1989).
69. *E.g.*, Green v. State, 58 Ala. 190 (1877). *See* Chapter 3; *and* 1 Joel Prentiss Bishop, NEW COMMENTARIES ON MARRIAGE, DIVORCE, AND SEPARATION §§ 680–695 (Chicago: Flood, 1891) (anti-miscegenation statutes constitutional under Civil War amendments).
70. *See* Lester G. Lindley, CONTRACT, ECONOMIC CHANGE, AND THE SEARCH FOR ORDER IN INDUSTRIALIZING AMERICA 29 (New York: Garland, 1993).
71. 1. J. Cont. Cong. 535 (1775); 1 Joseph Stancliffe Davis, ESSAYS IN THE EARLIER HISTORY OF AMERICAN CORPORATIONS, 349, 380–81, 385, 520–21; *Appendix B*, 520–22 (Cambridge, MA: Harvard Univ. Press, 1917).
72. *See* 1 WHITE, LAW IN AMERICAN HISTORY, *supra* note 2, at 253–54.
73. *See* John Lilburn Thomas, THE LAW OF LOTTERIES, FRAUDS AND OBSCENITY IN THE MAILS 4 (Littleton, CO: Rothman, 1900). *See also* Joel Prentiss Bishop, COMMENTARIES ON THE LAW OF STATUTORY CRIMES 582–87 (Boston, Little, Brown, 1873); Carol Sheriff, THE ARTIFICIAL RIVER: THE ERIE CANAL AND THE PARADOX OF PROGRESS, 1817–1862, at 21 (New York: Hill and Wang, 1996).

74. *See* John Ezell, FORTUNE'S MERRY WHEEL: THE LOTTERY IN AMERICA 20–25 (Cambridge, MA: Harvard Univ. Press, 1960); Ainsworth Spofford, *Lotteries in American History* 177, 1892 *Annual Report*, American Historical Association (1893).
75. Philadelphia: William Brown, 1833.
76. 2 Anson P. Stokes, CHURCH AND STATE IN THE UNITED STATES 26 (New York: Harper, 1950).
77. Dartmouth College, 17 U.S. (4 Wheat.) 518 (1819). On the Contract Clause in the early nineteenth century, see HOVENKAMP, ENTERPRISE, *supra* note 9, at 17–35.
78. Phalen v. Virginia, 49 U.S. (8 Howard) 163, 168 (1850).
79. Stone v. Mississippi, 101 U.S. 815, 818–19, 821 (1880). *See also* Douglas v. Kentucky, 168 U.S. 488 (1897), permitting Kentucky to amend its constitution so as to require municipalities to renege on preexisting lottery contracts.
80. *See* EZELL, FORTUNE'S MERRY WHEEL, *supra* note 74, at 263–69.
81. Champion v. Ames, 188 U.S. 321, 356–58 (1903).
82. *See* Richard Hamm, SHAPING THE EIGHTEENTH AMENDMENT: TEMPERANCE REFORM, LEGAL CULTURE AND THE POLITY, 1880–1920 (Chapel Hill: Univ. North Carolina Press, 1995).
83. *See* ABZUG, COSMOS CRUMBLING, *supra* note 68, at 102; SELLERS, MARKET REVOLUTION, *supra* note 9, at 261–63.
84. Ian R. Tyrrell, SOBERING UP: FROM TEMPERANCE TO PROHIBITION IN ANTEBELLUM AMERICA, 1800–1860, at 159–224 (Westport, CT: Greenwood, 1979).
85. *See* Ernst Freund, THE POLICE POWER: PUBLIC POLICY AND CONSTITUTIONAL RIGHTS 192–219 (Chicago: Callaghan, 1904).
86. *E.g.,* State v. Murphy, 71 Vt. 127 (1898) (upholding statute that closed down bars without compensation); Craig v. Werthmueller, 78 Iowa 598 (1889) (upholding statute limiting liquor sales to businesses with permits); Carleton v. Rugg, 149 Mass. 550 (1889) (similar).
87. Mugler v. Kansas, 123 U.S. 623 (1887) (claims for compensation for closing down a distillery would not be "seriously entertained").
88. Samuels v. McCurdy, 267 U.S. 188 (1925).
89. *See* Bertram Wyatt-Brown, *Prelude to Abolitionism: Sabbatarian Politics and the Rise of the Second Party System*, 58 J. AM. HIS. 316 (1971); Paul E. Johnson, A SHOPKEEPER'S MILLENNIUM: SOCIETY AND REVIVALS IN ROCHESTER, NEW YORK, 1815–1837 (New York: Hill and Wang, 1978).
90. *See, e.g.,* Hulett v. Stratton, 5 Cush. (Mass.) 539 (1850) (contract made on Sunday to sell a horse unenforceable); Murphy v. Simpson, 14 B. Mon. (Ky.) 419 (1854) (same, interpreting a statute); Lyon v. Strong, 6 Vt. 219 (1834) ("No court will lend its aid to a man who founds his cause of action upon an illegal or immoral act. . . ."); Sayre v. Wheeler, 31 Iowa 112 (1870) (refusing to enforce promissory note executed

on Sunday). *See* Elisha Greenhood, THE DOCTRINE OF PUBLIC POLICY IN THE LAW OF CONTRACTS, REDUCED TO RULES 549–51 (Chicago: Callaghan, 1886).

91. Batsford v. Every, 44 Barb. 618 (N.Y. Supp. 1865); Boynton v. Page, 13 Wend. 425 (N.Y. 1835).

92. *E.g.*, Francis Wharton, A TREATISE ON THE CRIMINAL LAW OF THE UNITED STATES (Philadelphia: Kay and Brother, 7th ed. 1874) at § 2384 (Sunday laws, blasphemy and other religious offenses), § 2429 (lotteries), § 2403 (gambling), § 2433 (liquor).

93. COOLEY, CONSTITUTIONAL LIMITATIONS, *supra* note 10; Thomas McIntyre Cooley, A TREATISE ON THE LAW OF TAXATION, INCLUDING THE LAW OF LOCAL ASSESSMENTS (Chicago: Callaghan, 1876; 2d ed. 1883); William Blackstone, COMMENTARIES ON THE LAWS OF ENGLAND (T.M. Cooley ed., Chicago: Callaghan, 1871).

94. COOLEY, CONSTITUTIONAL LIMITATIONS, *supra* note 10, at 436, 584, 704, 708, 719–20 (6th ed.1890).

95. COOLEY, CONSTITUTIONAL LIMITATIONS, *supra* note 10, at 671–74 (7th ed. 1903).

96. TIEDEMAN, LIMITATIONS OF POLICE POWER, *supra* note 10, at 149, 150, 153; Christopher Tiedeman, THE UNWRITTEN CONSTITUTION OF THE UNITED STATES: A PHILOSOPHICAL INQUIRY INTO THE FUNDAMENTALS OF AMERICAN CONSTITUTIONAL LAW (New York: Putnam, 1890). *See* David Mayer, *The Jurisprudence of Christopher G. Tiedeman*, 55 MIS. L. REV. 95 (1990).

97. FREUND, POLICE POWER, *supra* note 85, quotes from § 500 at 537, and 7–11, 173, 192–93.

CHAPTER 14

1. On the aversion of the American classical political economists to wealth redistribution, *see, e.g.*, Francis Wayland, THE LIMITATIONS OF HUMAN RESPONSIBILITY (Boston: Gould, 1838); and 2 Joseph Dorfman, THE ECONOMIC MIND IN AMERICAN CIVILIZATION, 1606–1865, at 520, 557, 571–72, 592–93, 717, 734–35, 764, 793 (New York: Viking, 1946).
2. Schechter Poultry Co. v. United States, 295 U.S. 495 (1935).
3. Morehead v. New York *ex rel.* Tipaldo, 298 U.S. 587 (1936).
4. 300 U.S. 379 (Mar. 29, 1937).
5. NLRB v. Jones & Laughlin Steel Corp., 301 U.S. 1 (Apr. 12, 1937) (5-4).
6. Adkins v. Children's Hosp., 261 U.S. 525 (1923). *See Morehead*, 298 U.S. at 604–05. For detailed accounts, *see* Jeff Shesol, SUPREME POWER: FRANKLIN ROOSEVELT VS. THE SUPREME COURT (New York: Norton, 2010); Burt Solomon, FDR V. THE CONSTITUTION: THE COURT-PACKING FIGHT AND THE TRIUMPH OF DEMOCRACY (New York: Walker, 2009); Barry Cushman, RETHINKING THE

NEW DEAL COURT: THE STRUCTURE OF A CONSTITUTIONAL REVOLUTION 92–104 (New York: Oxford Univ. Press, 1998).

7. John Maynard Keynes, THE GENERAL THEORY OF EMPLOYMENT, INTEREST AND MONEY (London: Macmillan, 1936); Edward Chamberlin, THE THEORY OF MONOPOLISTIC COMPETITION (Cambridge, MA: Harvard Univ. Press, 1933); Adolf A. Berle & Gardiner C. Means, THE MODERN CORPORATION AND PRIVATE PROPERTY (New York: Macmillan, 1933).
8. United States v. Carolene Prod. Co., 304 U.S. 144, 153 n.4 (1938).
9. *E.g.*, Ellis W. Hawley, THE NEW DEAL AND THE PROBLEM OF MONOPOLY: A STUDY IN ECONOMIC AMBIVALENCE (Princeton, NJ: Princeton Univ. Press, 1966); Morton J. Horwitz, THE TRANSFORMATION OF AMERICAN LAW, 1870–1960: THE CRISIS OF LEGAL ORTHODOXY 193–247 (New York: Oxford Univ. Press, 1992).
10. *E.g.*, Richard A. Epstein, THE CLASSICAL LIBERAL CONSTITUTION: THE UNCERTAIN QUEST FOR LIMITED GOVERNMENT 6–14, 34–39, 117–20, 164–200, 271–75 (Cambridge, MA: Harvard Univ. Press, 2014); Burton Folsom, JR., NEW DEAL OR RAW DEAL? HOW FDR'S ECONOMIC LEGACY HAS DAMAGED AMERICA (New York: Threshold, 2008).
11. See the Epilogue.
12. Hammer v. Dagenhart, 247 U.S. 251 (1918).
13. *See The Book of Revelation* 6:1–8. However, their votes against government intervention were not as consistent as is sometimes imagined. *See* Barry Cushman, *The Secret Lives of the Four Horseman*, *83* VA. L. REV. 559 (1997).
14. Drew Pearson & Robert Allen, THE NINE OLD MEN 13, 18, 55 (New York: Doubleday, 1936); Walton Hamilton & George Braden, *The Special Competence of the Supreme Court*, *50* YALE L.J. 1319 (1941); Walton Hamilton, *Lions under the Throne*, *56* YALE L.J. 1458, 1459 (1947) (book review).
15. *See* A. Leon Higginbotham, Jr., *An Open Letter to Justice Clarence Thomas from a Federal Judicial Colleague*, *140* U. PA. L. REV. 1005 (1992) (describing incident where Justice McReynolds turned his back to Charles Hamilton Houston, a prominent African American lawyer).
16. United States v. Carolene Prod. Co., 304 U.S. 144 (1938).
17. Horace Gray Wood, MASTER AND SERVANT (Albany, NY: John D. Parsons, 1877; 2d ed. 1886). On the more paternalistic nature of nineteenth-century common law and its deviations from commercial contract law, *see* Karen Orren, BELATED FEUDALISM: LABOR, THE LAW, AND LIBERAL DEVELOPMENT IN THE UNITED STATES 55–62, 80–99, 175–78 (Cambridge: Cambridge Univ. Press, 1991); PHILIP SELZNICK et al., LAW, SOCIETY AND INDUSTRIAL JUSTICE 123–28 (New York: Russell Sage, 1969). Antebellum American employment law was in fact extremely diverse. *See* Christopher Tomlins, FREEDOM BOUND: LAW, LABOR AND CIVIC IDENTIFY IN COLONIZING ENGLISH AMERICA, 1580–1865 at 230–35 (New York: Cambridge Univ. Press, 2010). This history serves to

undermine any argument that the Constitution required a particular version of it.

18. *See* David R. Papke, THE PULLMAN CASE: THE CLASH OF LABOR AND CAPITAL IN INDUSTRIAL AMERICA (Lawrence: Univ. Press of Kansas, 1999); United States v. Debs, 64 F. 724 (C.C.N.D. Ill. 1894); and *In re* Debs, 158 U.S. 564 (1895) (denying habeas corpus petition); David Montgomery, THE FALL OF THE HOUSE OF LABOR: THE WORKPLACE, THE STATE, AND AMERICAN LABOR ACTIVISM, 1865–1925 (New York: Cambridge Univ. Press, 1987). On the legal response, *see* Howard Gillman, THE CONSTITUTION BESIEGED: THE RISE AND DEMISE OF LOCHNER ERA POLICE POWERS JURISPRUDENCE 61–100 (Durham, NC: Duke Univ. Press, 1993). On the formative influence of the railroad labor disputes and the rise of the New Deal, *see* Jon R. Huibregtse, AMERICAN RAILROAD LABOR AND THE GENESIS OF THE NEW DEAL, 1919–1935 (Gainesville: Univ. Press of Florida, 2010).
19. Oliver Wendell Holmes, Jr., *The Path of the Law*, 10 HARV. L. REV. 457, 467–68 (1897).
20. Thomas M. Cooley, A TREATISE ON CONSTITUTIONAL LIMITATIONS 391–96 (Boston: Little, Brown, 1868). Cooley collected all these statutes in his index under the title "class legislation." *Id.* at 642. *See also* Caruthers v. Andrews, 42 Tenn. 378 (1865); Carlisle Borough v. Marshall, 36 Pa. 397 (1860).
21. Civil Rights Cases, 109 U.S. 3, 48 (1883). *See* Chapter 3.
22. Yick Wo v. Hopkins, 118 U.S. 356, 368 (1886); Pollock v. Farmers' Loan & Trust Co., 157 U.S. 429, 596 (1895).
23. Petit v. Minnesota, 177 U.S. 164 (1900).
24. Truax v. Corrigan, 257 U.S. 312 (1921).
25. State v. Fire Creek Coal & Coke Co., 33 W.Va. 188 (1889) (striking down as class legislation statute that forbad company from charging a higher markup in company stores selling to employees then it did in its stores open to the general public); State v. Goodwill, 33 W.Va. 179 (1889) (striking down statute requiring miners' wages to be paid in lawful money rather than scrip); in re Mary Maguire, 7 P.C.L.J. 357 (Cal. 1881) (striking down statute that prevented women from working as waitresses in bars).
26. Henry George, PROGRESS AND POVERTY 487 (New York: Appleton, 1879).
27. Albert Rees, REAL WAGES IN MANUFACTURING, 1890–1914, at 38 (Princeton, NJ: Princeton Univ. Press, 1961). *See also* Charles Hoffmann, THE DEPRESSION OF THE NINETIES: AN ECONOMIC HISTORY (Westport, CT: Greenwood, 1970).
28. *See* Alan Trachtenberg, THE INCORPORATION OF AMERICA: CULTURE AND SOCIETY IN THE GILDED AGE *90* (New York: Hill and Wang, 2007).
29. *See* Daniel E. Saros, LABOR, INDUSTRY, AND REGULATION DURING THE PROGRESSIVE ERA 133 (New York: Routledge, 2009).
30. Adkins v. Children's Hosp., 261 U.S. 525, 558 (1923); Morehead v. New York *ex rel.* Tipaldo, 298 U.S. 587, 612 (1936); West Coast Hotel v. Parrish, 300 U.S. 379, 410.

31. *See* 2 Robert Skidelsky, JOHN MAYNARD KEYNES: THE ECONOMIST AS SAVIOUR, 1920–1937, at 229 (London: Macmillan, 1992); Charles Whalen, *John R. Commons and John Maynard Keynes on Economic History and Policy: The 1920s and Today*, 42 J. ECON. ISSUES 225 (2008).
32. JOHN R. COMMONS, LEGAL FOUNDATIONS OF CAPITALISM 296–98 (New York: Macmillan, 1924).
33. *See* Herbert Hovenkamp, ENTERPRISE AND AMERICAN LAW, 1836–1937, chs. 18–19 (Cambridge, MA: Harvard Univ. Press, 1991); Daniel R. Ernst, LAWYERS AGAINST LABOR: FROM INDIVIDUAL RIGHTS TO CORPORATE LIBERALISM (Urbana: Univ. of Illinois Press, 1995).
34. *See* Eric Foner, FREE SOIL, FREE LABOR, FREE MEN: THE IDEOLOGY OF THE REPUBLICAN PARTY BEFORE THE CIVIL WAR 75–76 (New York: Oxford Univ. Press, 1970). *See also* Robert J. Steinfeld, COERCION, CONTRACT, AND FREE LABOR IN THE NINETEENTH CENTURY (New York: Cambridge Univ. Press, 2001); William E. Forbath, *The Ambiguities of Free Labor: Labor and the Law in the Gilded Age*, 1985 WIS. L. REV. 767, 773.
35. WOOD, MASTER AND SERVANT, note 17; *see* William Blackstone, COMMENTARIES ON THE LAW OF ENGLAND, Bk. I, Ch. 14, 425 (St. George Tucker, ed. Philadelphia: William Young Birch, 1803).
36. National Labor Relations Act § 14(b), 29 U.S.C. § 164(a) (1947); See Heidi Shierholz & Elise Gould, *The Compensation Penalty of "Right to Work" Law* (Economic Policy Institute, Feb. 17, 2011), *available at* http://www.epi.org/publication/bp299/. On the passage of Taft-Hartley, *see* Ira Katznelson, FEAR ITSELF: THE NEW DEAL AND THE ORIGINS OF OUR TIME 394 (New York: W.W. Norton, 2014).
37. John Maurice Clark, STUDIES IN THE ECONOMICS OF OVERHEAD COSTS 46–69 (Chicago: Univ. of Chicago Press, 1923). *See* Laurence Shute, JOHN MAURICE CLARK: A SOCIAL ECONOMICS FOR THE TWENTY-FIRST CENTURY 57 (New York: St. Martin's, 1997).
38. 49 Stat. 620 (1935). *See* Edwin Witte, *Development of Unemployment Compensation*, 55 YALE L.J. 21 (1945).
39. Herbert Hovenkamp, *Social Science and Segregation before* Brown, 1985 DUKE L.J. 624. *See also* Bruce Nelson, DIVIDED WE STAND: AMERICAN WORKERS AND THE STRUGGLE FOR BLACK EQUALITY (Princeton, NJ: Princeton Univ. Press, 2001); THE BLACK WORKER: RACE, LABOR, AND CIVIL RIGHTS SINCE EMANCIPATION (Eric Arnesen ed., Urbana: Univ. of Illinois Press, 2007). For a survey of the literature, *see* Paul Moreno, *Unions and Discrimination*, 30 CATO J. 67 (2010).
40. Eric Arnesen, *Specter of the Black Strikebreaker: Race, Employment, and Labor Activism in the Industrial Era*, 44 LAB. HIST. 319, 322 (2003).
41. Hodges v. United States, 203 U.S. 1 (1906).
42. David E. Bernstein, REHABILITATING LOCHNER: DEFENDING INDIVIDUAL RIGHTS AGAINST PROGRESSIVE REFORM (Chicago: Univ. of Chicago Press, 2011).

43. Joseph G. Rayback, HISTORY OF AMERICAN LABOR 95–100, 265 (rev. ed. New York: Macmillan 2008). *See* Commonwealth v. Beatty, 15 Pa. Super. 5 (Pa. Sup. Ct. 1900) (upholding statute limiting hours of women and minors); Ritchie v. People, 155 Ill. 98 (1895) (striking down womens' forty hour statute).
44. *See* Alexander Redgrave, THE FACTORY ACTS (London: Shaw, 1878; 9th ed. 1902).
45. 23 Stat. 332 (Feb. 26, 1885). Litigated examples of the Padrone system after 1900 include Tenth Nat. Bank of Philadelphia v. Smith Const. Co., 242 Pa. 269 (1913); Commonwealth v. Diori, 53 Pa.Super. 353 (1912). *See also*Gunther Peck, REINVENTING FREE LABOR: PADRONES AND IMMIGRANT WORKS IN THE NORTH AMERICAN WEST, 1880–1930 (New York: Cambridge Univ. Press, 2000);Hasia R. Diner, HUNGERING FOR AMERICA: ITALIAN, IRISH & JEWISH FOODWAYS IN THE AGE OF MIGRATION 69–70 (Cambridge, MA: Harvard Univ. Press, 2001);Don Lescoheir & Elizabeth Brandeis, *Working Conditions and Labor Legislation*, *in* 3 HISTORY OF LABOR IN THE UNITED STATES, 1896–1932, at ix, 85–90 (John R. Commons et al. eds., New York: Macmillan, 1935);John R. Commons & John B. Andrews, PRINCIPLES OF LABOR LEGISLATION 42–47 (New York: Harper 1916); REPORT ON IMMIGRATION AND ON EDUCATION 431–35 (U.S. Indus. Comm'n. 1902). On peonage and indentured servitude prior to the Civil War, *see* TOMLINS, FREEDOM BOUND, *supra* note 17, 7–65.
46. *See* Richard Gambino, BLOOD OF MY BLOOD: THE DILEMMA OF THE ITALIAN-AMERICANS 116–19 (New York: Guernica, 2000); Calvin Winslow, *Italian Workers on the Waterfront: The New York Harbor Strikes of 1907 and 1919*, *in* THE LOST WORLD OF ITALIAN AMERICAN RADICALISM 99 (Gerald Meyer ed., Westport, CT.: Praeger, 2003). On labor organizing among Italian bakers in San Francisco at this time, *see* Paola A. Sensi-Isolami, *Italian Radicals and Union Activists in San Francisco, 1900–1920*, p. 189 in the same volume.
47. NEW YORK TIMES, April 8, 1896 (archives, *available at* http://query.nytimes.com/mem/archive-free/pdf?res=9505E3D9123EE333A2575BC0A9629C94679ED7CF (last visited April 30, 2014).
48. Testimony of Mr. Daniel O-Leary, Chief Factory Inspector of the State of New York 26, 38–39 (March 8, 1899), in 7 U.S. HOUSE, REPORT OF THE INDUSTRIAL COMMISSION ON THE RELATIONS AND CONDITIONS OF CAPITAL AND LABOR (56th Cong.2d session, Washington, U.S. Gov't Printing Office, 1901).
49. Brief for Defendant 14, Lochner v. New York, 198 U.S. 45 (1905).
50. *Lochner* 198 U.S. at 46 n.1, 70–71. *See also* Simone Cinotto, THE ITALIAN AMERICAN TABLE: FOOD, FAMILY, AND COMMUNITY IN NEW YORK CITY 108–10 (Champaign: Univ. of Illinois Press, 2013).
51. Balt. & Ohio R.R. Co. v. ICC, 221 U.S. 612, 618–19 (1911).
52. Howard v. Illinois Central R.R., 207 U.S. 463 (1908); Mondou v. N.Y., New Haven & Hartford R.R. Co., 223 U.S. 1 (1912) (Justice Van Devanter, one of the Four Horsemen, upholding statute).

53. Adair v. United States, 208 U.S. 161 (1908).
54. Hammer v. Dagenhart, 247 U.S. 251 (1918).
55. HOVENKAMP, ENTERPRISE, *supra* note 33, chs. 18–19; ERNST, LAWYERS AGAINST LABOR, *supra* note 33.
56. 47 Stat. 70, 29 U.S.C. §§ 101 *et seq.* (1932).
57. 29 U.S.C. §§ 151 *et seq.* (1935), properly known as the National Labor Relations Act.
58. 61 Stat. 136 (1947).
59. Adkins v. Children's Hosp., 261 U.S. 525, 557 (1923); *see* HOVENKAMP, ENTERPRISE, *supra* note 33, ch.16.
60. William G. Sumner, *Wages, in* COLLECTED ESSAYS IN POLITICAL AND SOCIAL SCIENCE 36, 50 (New York: H. Holt, 1885).
61. 10 J. POL. ECON. 105 (1901).
62. *See* William Stanley Jevons, THE THEORY OF POLITICAL ECONOMY, *Preface to the First Edition* vi–xlix (New York: Macmillan, 2d ed. 1879).
63. Francis A. Walker, POLITICAL ECONOMY 223 (New York: Henry Holt, 1883).
64. John Bates Clark, *Possibility of a Scientific Law of Wages,* 4(1) PUBLICATIONS AM. ECON. ASS'N 37 (1889); John Bates Clark, CAPITAL AND ITS EARNINGS (Baltimore: AEA, 1888); John Bates Clark, THE DISTRIBUTION OF WEALTH: A THEORY OF WAGES, INTEREST AND PROFITS (New York: Macmillan, 1899). Other American critics include Stuart Wood, *A New View of the Theory of Wages,* 3 Q.J. ECON. 462 (1889); Richard T. Ely, PROPERTY AND CONTRACT IN THEIR RELATIONS TO THE DISTRIBUTION OF WEALTH 2–4 (New York: Macmillan, 1914); Charles A. Tuttle, *The Workman's Position in the Light of Economic Progress,* 3(1) PUBLICATIONS AM. ECON. ASS'N 199, 209 (1902).
65. KEYNES, GENERAL THEORY, *supra* note 7, ch. 2 (1936) (1973 reprint edition: Macmillan-Cambridge for Royal Economic Society).
66. *See* Rosanne Currarino, THE LABOR QUESTION IN AMERICA: ECONOMIC DEMOCRACY IN THE GILDED AGE 69–79 (Urbana: Univ. of Illinois Press, 2011).
67. *E.g.,* Sidney Fine, LAISSEZ FAIRE AND THE GENERAL-WELFARE STATE: A STUDY OF CONFLICT IN AMERICAN THOUGHT, 1865–1901 (Ann Arbor: Univ. of Michigan Press, 1956); Richard Hofstadter, THE AGE OF REFORM: FROM BRYAN TO F.D.R. (New York: Knopf, 1955).
68. Thomas Reed Powell, *The Judiciality of Minimum-Wage Legislation,* 37 HARV. L. REV. 545, 546 (1924). *Accord* George Gorham Groat, *Economic Wage and Legal Wage,* 33 YALE L.J. 489 (1924); Leo Wolman, *Economic Justification of the Legal Minimum Wage,* 14 AM. LAB. LEGIS. REV. 226 (1924).
69. John R. Commons, THE DISTRIBUTION OF WEALTH 42–43 (New York: Macmillan, 1893).
70. COMMONS, LEGAL FOUNDATIONS, *supra* note 32, at 305–06.
71. *See, e.g.,* Jacob H. Hollander, *Political Economy and the Labor Question,* 176 N. AM. REV. 563 (1903). Hollander was an economist at Johns Hopkins.

72. *E.g.*, Arthur N. Holcombe, *The Legal Minimum Wage in the United States*, *2* AM. ECON. REV. 21 (1912); 2 Frank W. Taussig, PRINCIPLES OF ECONOMICS, chs. 56–57 (New York: Macmillan, 1911).
73. A few examples are Margaret Stecker, *Family Budgets and Wages*, *11* AM. ECON. REV. 447 (1921) (discussing numerous others); NATIONAL WAR LABOR BOARD, MEMORANDUM ON THE MINIMUM WAGE AND INCREASED COST OF LIVING (U.S. G.P.O., 1918); Frank Streightoff, THE STANDARD OF LIVING AMONG THE INDUSTRIAL PEOPLE OF AMERICA (Boston: Houghton Mifflin, 1911); Louise More, WAGE-EARNERS' BUDGETS: A STUDY OF STANDARDS AND COST OF LIVING IN NEW YORK CITY (New York: Holt, 1907); Robert Chapin, THE STANDARD OF LIVING AMONG WORKINGMEN'S FAMILIES IN NEW YORK CITY (New York: Charities Pub., 1909). For critiques, *see* Valeska Bari, *From Minimum Wage to Mass Production*, *16* (n.s.) YALE REV. 57, 65 (1926), arguing that although legal minimum wages were theoretically determined by scientific analysis of cost-of-living data, in practice politics almost always intervened; Arthur Lucas, *A Recommendatory Minimum Wage Law: The First Decade of the Massachusetts Experiment*, *14* AM. ECON. REV. 39 (1924) (citing administrative difficulties in minimum wage determination). For historical background, *see* Donald Stabile, THE LIVING WAGE: LESSONS FROM THE HISTORY OF ECONOMIC THOUGHT (Cheltenham, U.K.: Edward Elgar, 2008).
74. *See* Joseph Goldberg & William Moye, THE FIRST HUNDRED YEARS OF THE BUREAU OF LABOR STATISTICS 65–75 (U.S. G.P.O., 1985).
75. Glendower Evans, *The Social Aspects of the Public Regulation of Wages*, *5* AM. ECON. REV. SUPP. 270 (1915); *see also* Dorothy Douglas, *American Minimum Wage Laws at Work*, *9* AM. ECON. REV. 701, 713, 734 (1919).
76. John R. Commons, *Wage Theories and Wage Policies*, *13* AM. ECON. REV. SUPP. 110 (1923).
77. William Ogburn, *The Standard-of-Living Factor in Wages*, *13* AM. ECON. REV. SUPP. 118 (1923). *See* OGBURN, SOCIAL CHANGE WITH RESPECT TO CULTURE AND ORIGINAL NATURE (New York: Huebsch, 1922).

CHAPTER 15

1. Frank Bourgin, THE GREAT CHALLENGE: THE MYTH OF LAISSEZ-FAIRE IN THE EARLY REPUBLIC (New York: Harper, 1990); Oscar Handlin & Mary Flug Handlin, COMMONWEALTH: A STUDY OF THE ROLE OF GOVERNMENT IN THE AMERICAN ECONOMY: MASSACHUSETTS, 1774–1861 (Cambridge, MA: Harvard Univ. Press, 1969); James Willard Hurst, LAW AND THE CONDITIONS OF FREEDOM IN THE NINETEENTH-CENTURY UNITED STATES (Madison: Univ. of Wisconsin Press, 1956); Herbert Hovenkamp, ENTERPRISE AND AMERICAN LAW, 1836–1937, at 171–192 (Cambridge, MA: Harvard Univ. Press, 1991); William J. Novak, THE PEOPLE'S WELFARE: LAW AND REGULATION

IN NINETEENTH-CENTURY AMERICA (Chapel Hill: Univ. North Carolina Press, 1996).

2. U.S. CONST. art. I, § 10, cl. 1.
3. Santa Clara County. v. S. Pac. R.R., 118 U.S. 394 (1886).
4. Chicago, Burlington & Quincy R.R. Co. v. City of Chicago, 166 U.S. 226 (1897) (dicta).
5. Lincoln v. Commonwealth, 164 Mass. 368, 41 N.E. 489,491 (1895).
6. *See* Dorothy Ross, THE ORIGINS OF AMERICAN SOCIAL SCIENCE 98–121, 172–218 (New York: Cambridge Univ. Press, 1991); Paul Bernard, THE MAKING OF THE MARGINAL MIND: ACADEMIC ECONOMIC THOUGHT IN THE UNITED STATES, 1860–1910 (Ph.D. diss., Univ. of Mich., 1990).
7. *See* Burton Bledstein, THE CULTURE OF PROFESSIONALISM: THE MIDDLE CLASS AND THE DEVELOPMENT OF HIGHER EDUCATION IN AMERICA (New York: Norton, 1976); Mary O. Furner, ADVOCACY AND OBJECTIVITY: A CRISIS IN THE PROFESSIONALIZATION OF AMERICAN SOCIAL SCIENCE, 1865–1905 (Lexington: Univ. Press of Kentucky, 1975).
8. The classic definition is from Francis M. Bator, *The Anatomy of Market Failure*, 72 Q.J. ECON. 351, 351 (1958).
9. Adam Smith, AN INQUIRY INTO THE NATURE AND CAUSES OF THE WEALTH OF NATIONS IV.ix (Dublin: Whitestone, 1776). On the development of market failure theory among the classical political economists, *see* Bernard E. Harcourt, THE ILLUSION OF FREE MARKETS: PUNISHMENT AND THE MYTH OF NATURAL ORDER (Cambridge, MA: Harvard Univ. Press, 2011); Steven G. Medema, THE HESITANT HAND: TAMING SELF-INTEREST IN THE HISTORY OF ECONOMIC IDEAS 5–52 (Princeton, NJ: Princeton Univ. Press, 2009).
10. John S. Mill, PRINCIPLES OF POLITICAL ECONOMY: WITH SOME OF THEIR APPLICATIONS TO SOCIAL PHILOSOPHY I.9.6 (London: Parker, 1848).
11. *See* Chapter 11. On Marshall's contributions, *see* MEMORIALS OF ALFRED MARSHALL 44 (Arthur C. Pigou ed., London: Macmillan, 1925).
12. Pigou's book came out initially in 1912 under the title WEALTH AND WELFARE (London: Macmillan, 1912). It was then expanded through four editions during his lifetime as THE ECONOMICS OF WELFARE (London: Macmillan, 1920; 4th ed. 1932). On Coase's critiques, *see* Herbert Hovenkamp, *The Coase Theorem and Arthur Cecil Pigou*, 51 ARIZ. L. REV. 633 (2009).
13. *See* Chapter 9.
14. John Maurice Clark, STUDIES IN THE ECONOMICS OF OVERHEAD COSTS 357–85 (Chicago: Univ. of Chicago Press, 1923); *and see* Donald R. Stabile, *Pigou's Influence on Clark: Work and Welfare*, 29 J. ECON. ISSUES 1133 (1995).
15. *See, e.g.*, Gustavus H. Robinson, *The Public Utility Concept in American Law*, 41 HARV. L. REV. 277 (1928); Charles K. Burdick, *The Origin of the Peculiar Duties of Public Service Companies*, 11 COLUM. L. REV. 514 (1911); Bruce Wyman, *The Law of the Public Callings as a Solution of the Trust Problem*, 17 HARV. L. REV. 156 (1904).

See also George L. Priest, *The Origins of Utility Regulation and the "Theories of Regulation" Debate*, 36 J.L. & ECON. 289 (1993); Herbert Hovenkamp, *Regulatory Conflict in the Gilded Age: Federalism and the Railroad Problem*, 97 YALE L.J. 1017 (1988).

16. *See* HOVENKAMP, ENTERPRISE, *supra* note 1, ch. 23; In particular, *see* Arthur Twining Hadley, ECONOMICS: AN ACCOUNT OF THE RELATIONS BETWEEN PRIVATE PROPERTY AND PUBLIC WELFARE 158, 295 (New York: Putnam, 1896); John Bates Clark, *The Limits of Competition*, 2 POL. SCI. Q. 45, 55 (1887).
17. *See* Ellis Hawley, *Three Facets of Hooverian Associationalism: Lumber, Aviation, and Movies, 1921–1930*, *in* BUSINESS-GOVERNMENT COOPERATION 1917–1932: THE RISE OF CORPORATIST POLICIES 213 (Robert F. Himmelberg ed., New York: Garland, 1994); Ellis W. Hawley, *Herbert Hoover and the Sherman Act, 1921–1933: An Early Phase of a Continuing Issue*, 74 IOWA L. REV. 1067, 1085–101 (1989); Guy Alchon, THE INVISIBLE HAND OF PLANNING: CAPITALISM, SOCIAL SCIENCE, AND THE STATE IN THE 1920S, at 43–47, 63–67 (Princeton, NJ: Princeton Univ. Press, 1985). *See also* Isaiah L. Sharfman, *The Trade Association Movement*, 16 AM. ECON. REV. 203 (1926).
18. *See* Ellis W. Hawley, *Herbert Hoover, the Commerce Secretariat, and the Vision of an "Associative State," 1921–1928*, 61 J. AM. HIST. 116 (1974). For harsh criticism from the perspective of the Second New Deal, *see* CLAIR WILCOX, COMPETITION AND MONOPOLY IN AMERICAN INDUSTRY 220–25 (TNEC Monograph 21, U.S. Gov't Print. Off., 1940). *See also* William J. Barber, FROM NEW ERA TO NEW DEAL: HERBERT HOOVER, THE ECONOMISTS, AND AMERICAN ECONOMIC POLICY, 1921–1933 (New York: Cambridge Univ. Press, 1985).
19. Am. Column & Lumber Co. v. United States, 257 U.S. 377, 392, 394 (1921).
20. United States v. Am. Linseed Oil Co., 262 U.S. 371 (1923).
21. The NRA was established by the National Industrial Recovery Act, 48 Stat. 195 (1933). The Petroleum Administrative Board was organized a year later. Ellis W. Hawley, THE NEW DEAL AND THE PROBLEM OF MONOPOLY 214–15 (Princeton, NJ: Princeton Univ. Press, 1966).
22. Kirstin Downey, THE WOMAN BEHIND THE NEW DEAL: THE LIFE AND LEGACY OF FRANCES PERKINS (New York: Random House, 2009).
23. Arthur Heath Onthank, *How Codes Are Made*, *in* AMERICA'S RECOVERY PROGRAM 69 (Adolf A. Berle, Jr. et al. eds., New York: Oxford Univ. Press, 1934).
24. Clair Wilcox et al., *Introduction*, AMERICA'S RECOVERY PROGRAM, *id.*
25. Ellis W. Hawley, THE NEW DEAL AND THE PROBLEM OF MONOPOLY: A STUDY OF ECONOMIC AMBIVALENCE 124–27 (Princeton, NJ: Princeton Univ. Press, 1966). Hawley's book includes a detailed discussion of the code provisions. *Id.* at 53–71.
26. Comment, *Constitutionality of Government Control of Oil Production*, 43 YALE L.J. 610, 614 (1934).

27. *Statement of Joint Stripper Well Conference of Kansas, Texas, and Olkahoma*, Sen. Hearing on S. 1712, H.R. 5755, 73d Cong., 1st Sess. at 177–78 (1933).
28. Panama Ref. Co. v. Ryan, 293 U.S. 388, 415 (1935).
29. *Id.* at 437.
30. A.L.A. Schechter Poultry Corp. v. United States, 295 U.S. 495, 523–24, 551–52 (1935). *See* Barry Cushman, RETHINKING THE NEW DEAL COURT: THE STRUCTURE OF A CONSTITUTIONAL REVOLUTION 37–40, 92–93, 156–71 (New York: Oxford Univ. Press, 1998). *See also* Richard A. Epstein, THE CLASSICAL LIBERAL CONSTITUTION: THE UNCERTAIN QUEST FOR LIMITED GOVERNMENT 270–78 (Cambridge, MA: Harvard Univ. Press, 2014) (defending *Panama* and *Schechter*).
31. *Schechter*, 295 U.S. at 552–53.
32. *See Publications of the Temporary National Economic Committee*, 31 AM. ECON. REV. 347 (1941). The TNEC publications have been digitized and made available online by the Boston Public Library. *See* www.bpl.org/online/govdocs/temporary_national_economic_committee.htm#Monographs.
33. *E.g.*, J.W. Hampton, Jr. & Co. v. United States, 276 U.S. 394 (1928) (approving executive agency to regulate customs duties); Interstate Commerce Comm'n v. Goodrich Transit Co., 224 U.S. 194 (1912) (upholding ICC reporting requirements). On the earlier history, *see* Jerry L. Mashaw, CREATING THE ADMINISTRATIVE CONSTITUTION: THE LOST ONE HUNDRED YEARS OF AMERICAN ADMINISTRATIVE LAW (New Haven: Yale Univ. Press, 2012).
34. 60 Stat. 237 (1946); William E. Nelson, THE ROOTS OF AMERICAN BUREAUCRACY, 1830–1900 (Cambridge, MA: Harvard Univ. Press, 1982). *See* George B. Shepherd, *Fierce Compromise: The Administrative Procedure Act Emerges from New Deal Politics*, 90 NW. U. L. REV. 1557 (1996).
35. United States Attorney General's Committee on Administrative Procedure, *Final Report*, S. Doc. No. 8, 77th Cong., 1st Sess. app. A at 251–52 (1941).
36. *See* David M. Kennedy, FREEDOM FROM FEAR: THE AMERICAN PEOPLE IN DEPRESSION AND WAR, 1929–1945, at 290–324 (New York: Oxford Univ. Press, 1999).
37. Nancy E. Rose, PUT TO WORK: THE WPA AND PUBLIC EMPLOYMENT IN THE GREAT DEPRESSION (New York: Monthly Review Press, 2009).
38. KENNEDY, FREEDOM FROM FEAR, *supra* note 36, at 257–72.
39. N.Y. TIMES, Dec. 31, 1933. *See* KENNEDY, FREEDOM FROM FEAR, *supra* note 36, at 354–380. On Keynes's influence on New Deal policy, *see* William J. Barber, DESIGNS WITHIN DISORDER: FRANKLIN D. ROOSEVELT, THE ECONOMISTS AND THE SHAPING OF AMERICAN ECONOMIC POLICY, 1933–1945 (New York: Cambridge Univ. Press, 1996); Theodore Rosenof, ECONOMICS IN THE LONG RUN: NEW DEAL THEORISTS AND THEIR LEGACIES, 1933–1993 (Chapel Hill: Univ. North Carolina Press, 2009); Robert Skidelsky, JOHN MAYNARD KEYNES: 1883–1946: ECONOMIST, PHILOSOPHER, STATESMAN (New York: Penguin, 2005).

40. FDR, *Address* at Forbes Field, Pittsburgh, Oct. 1, 1936, in *The American Presidency Project* (Gerhard Peters & John T. Woolley eds.), *available at* http://www.presidency.ucsb.edu/ws/index.php?pid=15149#axzz1uNdFvw6X (last visited May 13, 2013).
41. Michael Lind, LAND OF PROMISE: AN ECONOMIC HISTORY OF THE UNITED STATES 287–88 (New York: Harper-Collins 2012); John Maynard KEYNES: CRITICAL ASSESSMENTS 77–85 (John C. Wood ed., London, Routledge, 1994).
42. KENNEDY, FREEDOM FROM FEAR, *supra* note 36, at 358–60.
43. John Maynard Keynes, THE GENERAL THEORY OF EMPLOYMENT, INTEREST, AND MONEY 378 (New York: Harcourt, Brace, 1936). *See* Robert Skidelsky, *The Relevance of Keynes*, 35 CAMBRIDGE J. ECON. 1 (2011). The business community reacted cautiously but was generally supportive. *See* Robert M. Collins, THE BUSINESS RESPONSE TO KEYNES, 1929–1964 (New York: Columbia Univ. Press, 1981).
44. Eugene V. Rostow, *Bituminous Coal and the Public Interest*, 50 YALE L.J. 543, 591–92 (1941). While editor-in-chief of the Yale Law Journal Rostow had written a somewhat lukewarm review of the General Theory. See Review, 47 YALE L.J. 498 (1938).
45. *See* Mark Tungate, ADLAND: A GLOBAL HISTORY OF ADVERTISING 28–29 (Philadelphia: Kogan Page, 2007); Stephen R. Fox, THE MIRROR MAKERS: A HISTORY OF AMERICAN ADVERTISING AND ITS CREATORS 5–7 (New York: Morrow, 1984). On the Gilded Age and Progressive Era, *see* James D. Norris, ADVERTISING AND THE TRANSFORMATION OF AMERICAN SOCIETY, 1865–1920 (New York: Greenwood, 1990).
46. 60 Stat. 427 (1946).
47. *E.g.*, Mosler Safe Co. v. Ely-Norris Safe Co., 273 U.S. 132 (1927) (Holmes, J.).
48. On this historical concern, *see* Frank I. Schechter, *The Rational Basis of Trademark Protection*, 40 HARV. L. REV. 813 (1927).
49. *See, e.g.*, Four Roses Prods. Co. v. Small Grain Distilling & Drug Co., 29 F.2d 959 (D.C. Cir. 1928) (maker of home brew syrup could infringe trademark owned by whiskey distiller); Yale Electric Corp. v. Robertson, 26 F.2d 972 (2d Cir. 1928) (Judge Hand, maker of flashlight infringed trademark owned by lock maker). *See* Mark Bartholomew, *Advertising and the Transformation of Trademark Law*, 38 N.M. L. REV. 1 (2008).
50. *See* Ross D. Petty, *The Codevelopment of Trademark Law and the Concept of Brand Marketing in the United States before 1946*, 31 J. MACROMARKETING 85, 91 (2011). *See also* J. Walter Thompson, THINGS TO KNOW ABOUT TRADE-MARKS: A MANUAL OF TRADEMARK INFORMATION (New York: Thompson, 1911). *And see* Shelby D. Hunt, *The Theory of Monopolistic Competition, Marketing's Intellectual History, and the Product Differentiation versus Market Segmentation Controversy*, 31 J. MACROMARKETING 73 (2011).

51. Arthur Acheson, TRADE-MARK ADVERTISING AS AN INVESTMENT 45 (New York: Evening Post Pub., 1917).
52. Edward H. Chamberlin, THE THEORY OF MONOPOLISTIC COMPETITION (Cambridge, MA: Harvard Univ. Press, 1933). On Chamberlin's influence on antitrust policy, *see* Chapter 11.
53. On Chamberlin's model as a solution to the overproduction problem, *see* Jan Keppler, MONOPOLISTIC COMPETITION THEORY: ORIGINS, RESULTS, AND IMPLICATIONS 46–121 (Baltimore: Johns Hopkins Univ. Press, 1994); Steven Brakman & Ben J. Heijdra, *Introduction*, THE MONOPOLISTIC COMPETITION REVOLUTION IN RETROSPECT 1, 4–7 (Steven Brakman & Ben J. Heijdra eds., Cambridge: Cambridge Univ. Press, 2004).
54. *See* Spencer Weber Waller, THURMAN ARNOLD: A BIOGRAPHY (New York: NYU Press, 2005); Wilson D. Miscamble, *Thurman Arnold Goes to Washington: A Look at Antitrust Policy in the Later New Deal*, 56 BUS. HIST. REV. 1 (1982). For Arnold's own statement of his views, *see* Thurman W. Arnold, *Prosecution Policy under the Sherman Act*, 24 A.B.A. J. 417 (1938).
55. For a good brief account, *see* Spencer Weber Waller, *The Antitrust Legacy of Thurman Arnold*, 78 ST. JOHN'S L. REV. 569 (2004).
56. *E.g.*, Robert H. Bork, THE ANTITRUST PARADOX: A POLICY AT WAR WITH ITSELF (New York: Basic Books, 1978).
57. Economic statistics on the New Deal are available at http://www.shmoop.com/great-depression/statistics.html (last visited May 2014).
58. On the origins of dual federalism in nineteenth century commercial law, *see* HOVENKAMP, ENTERPRISE, *supra* note 1, at 79–82.
59. *See* Edward S. Corwin, *The Passing of Dual Federalism*, 36 VA. L. REV. 1 (1950).
60. *E.g.*, Prigg v. Pennsylvania, 41 U.S. (16 Pet.) 539, 622 (1842) (declining to enforce federal statute that required state officials to cooperate actively in returning runaway slaves).
61. Civil Rights Cases, 109 U.S. 3 (1883); *see* Chapter 3.
62. Hodges v. United States, 203 U.S. 1 (1906).
63. Swift v. Tyson, 41 U.S. 1 (1842).
64. Watson v. Tarpley, 59 U.S. 517 (1855). *See* HOVENKAMP, ENTERPRISE, *supra* note 1, at 89–91.
65. Erie R. Co. v. Tompkins, 304 U.S. 64 (1938). The other two Horsemen had retired—Van DeVanter in 1937 and Sutherland in January 1938, three months before *Erie* was decided.
66. Guar. Trust Co. v. York, 326 U.S. 99, 102, 109 (1945), quoting Justice Holmes's dissent in S. Pac. Co. v. Jensen, 244 U.S. 205, 222 (1917).
67. Int'l News Serv. v. Associated Press, 248 U.S. 215, 264–65 & n.16 (1918).
68. *See* Joseph Story, COMMENTARIES ON THE LAW OF BILLS OF EXCHANGE, FOREIGN AND INLAND, AS ADMINISTERED IN ENGLAND AND AMERICA (Boston: Little, Brown, 1843).

69. U.S. CONST. art. 1, § 8, cl. 4.
70. In particular, *see* the divided decision in Ogden v. Saunders, 25 U.S. 213 (1827), in which Chief Justice Marshall wrote his only published dissent.
71. Stellwagen v. Clum, 245 U.S. 605, 613 (1918); *Ex parte* Christy, 44 U.S. 292 (1845); *and see* Alfred Hill, *The Erie Doctrine in Bankruptcy*, 66 HARV. L. REV. 1013 (1953).
72. Paul v. Virginia, 75 U.S. 168 (1868).
73. *See* HOVENKAMP, ENTERPRISE, *supra* note 1, at 89–96.
74. Karl Llewellyn to William Draper Lewis (Feb. 27, 1942) (American Law Institute Archives), *quoted in* Allen R. Kamp, *Downtown Code: A History of the Uniform Commercial Code, 1949–1954*, 49 BUFF. L. REV. 359, 375 n.50 (2001). On Llewellyn's preference for federal legislation, *see* William L. Twining, KARL LLEWELLYN AND THE REALIST MOVEMENT 277–79 (London: Weidenfeld & Nicolson, 1973); *and see* Karl N. Llewellyn, *The Needed Federal Sales Act*, 26 VA. L. REV. 558 (1940).
75. Trade-Mark Cases, 100 U.S. 82 (1879).
76. Zechariah Chafee, Jr., Unfair Competition, 53 HARV. L. REV. 1289, 1299 (1940).
77. Pecheur Lozenge Co. v. Nat'l Candy Co., 315 U.S. 666 (1942).
78. Lanham Act. 60 Stat. 427 (1946).
79. SMITH, WEALTH OF NATIONS, *supra* note 9, Bk. I, ch. 3.
80. *See* Lawrence A. Boland, *Difficulties with the Element of Time and the Principles of Economics*, *in* ALFRED MARSHALL: CRITICAL ASSESSMENTS 60 (John Wood ed., London: Routledge, 1996).
81. United States v. E.C. Knight Co., 156 U.S. 1 (1895). *See* Owen M. Fiss, TROUBLED BEGINNINGS OF THE MODERN STATE, 1888–1910, at 257–92 (Holmes Devise History of the Supreme Court. (New York: Macmillan, 1993)); Charles W. McCurdy, *American Law and the Marketing Structure of the Large Corporation, 1875–1890*, 38 J. ECON. HIST. 631 (1978).
82. Courts upholding or applying state child labor provisions include Platt v. S. Photo Material Co., 4 Ga. App. 159, 60 S.E. 1068 (Ga. Ct. App. 1908) (1906 Georgia statute); Am. Car & Foundry Co. v. Armentraut, 214 Ill. 509, 73 N.E. 766 (Ill. 1905) (1897 statute); Queen v. Dayton Coal & Iron Co., 95 Tenn. 458, 32 S.W. 460 (Tenn. 1895) (1881 statute).
83. Sturges & Burn Mfg. Co. v. Beauchamp, 231 U.S. 320 (1913).
84. Hammer v. Dagenhart, 247 U.S. 251, 268 n.1, 275–76 (1918).
85. Thomas Reed Powell, *Child Labor, Congress and the Constitution*, 1 N.C. L. REV. 61, 63–64 (1922); Edward S. Corwin, *Congress' Power to Prohibit Commerce: A Crucial Constitutional Issue*, 18 CORNELL L.Q. 477, 481 (1933); Edward S. Corwin, THE COMMERCE POWER VERSUS STATES RIGHTS: BACK TO THE CONSTITUTION (Princeton, NJ: Princeton Univ. Press, 1936).
86. *Hammer*, 247 U.S. at 279–81.
87. Carter v. Carter Coal Co., 298 U.S. 238 (1936).
88. United States v. Darby, 312 U.S. 100, 115–16, 124 (1941).
89. Wickard v. Filburn, 317 U.S. 111 (1942).

90. United States v. Aluminum Co. of Am., 148 F.2d 416, 444–45 (1945).
91. United States v. Women's Sportswear Mfg. Ass'n, 336 U.S. 460, 464 (1949).
92. Parker v. Brown, 317 U.S. 341 (1943).
93. *See* Victoria Saker Woeste, THE FARMER'S BENEVOLENT TRUST: LAW AND AGRICULTURAL COOPERATION IN INDUSTRIAL AMERICA, 1865–1945, at 230 (Chapel Hill: Univ. North Carolina Press, 1998).
94. *See* 1A PHILLIP E. AREEDA & HERBERT HOVENKAMP, ANTITRUST LAW ¶¶221–226 (4th ed. 2013).
95. United States v. South-Eastern Underwriters Ass'n, 322 U.S. 533 (1944).
96. Paul v. Virginia, 75 U.S. 168, 183–84 (1868).
97. *South-Eastern Underwriters*, 322 U.S. 533.
98. 59 Stat. 33 (1945), codified at 15 U.S.C. §§ 1101–1102 (1945); *and see* Note, *The Trend of Insurance Regulation*, 35 GEO. L.J. 102 (1946).
99. Irwin M. Stelzer, *The Insurance Industry and the Antitrust Laws: A Decade of Experience*, 1955 INS. L.J. 137 (1955).

EPILOGUE

1. Grant Gilmore, *Book Review*, 60 Yale L.J. 1251–52 (1951) (reviewing Karl N. Llewellyn, THE BRAMBLE BUSH (New York: Oceana, 1951)).
2. Jerome Frank, LAW AND THE MODERN MIND (New York: Brentano's, 1930).
3. Will Herberg, PROTESTANT, CATHOLIC, JEW: AN ESSAY IN AMERICAN RELIGIOUS SOCIOLOGY (Garden City, NJ: Doubleday, 1955); Oscar Handlin, THE UPROOTED: THE EPIC STORY OF THE GREAT MIGRATIONS THAT MADE THE AMERICAN PEOPLE (Boston: Little, Brown, 1951).
4. Brown v. Board of Education, 347 U.S. 483 (1954). *See* Taylor Branch, PARTING THE WATERS: AMERICA IN THE KING YEARS, 1954–1963, at 112–25, 283–84, 585–94, 767 (New York: Simon and Schuster, 1989).
5. For different views of McCarthyism, *see* Richard M. Fried, NIGHTMARE IN RED: THE MCCARTHY ERA IN PERSPECTIVE (New York: Oxford Univ. Press, 1990); M. Stanton Evans, BLACKLISTED BY HISTORY: THE UNTOLD STORY OF SENATOR JOE MCCARTHY AND HIS FIGHT AGAINST AMERICA'S ENEMIES (New York: Crown Forum, 2007).
6. *See* Walker Lewis, *The Birth of the American Bar Association*, 64 A.B.A. J. 996 (1978); Lawrence M. Friedman, A HISTORY OF AMERICAN LAW 305, 541 (New York: Simon & Schuster, 3d ed. 2005).
7. *See* William W. Marvin, WEST PUBLISHING COMPANY: ORIGIN, GROWTH, LEADERSHIP 24 (St. Paul, MN: West, 1969). *See also* Robert M. Jarvis, *John B. West: Founder of the West Publishing Company*, 50 Am. J. Legal Hist. 1 (2010).
8. On the relationship between the organization of the regional reporter system and interstate judicial citation, *see* Peter Harris, *Ecology and Culture in the Communication of Precedent among State Supreme Courts, 1870–1970*, 19 L. & Soc'y Rev. 449 (1985).

9. *Report of the Committee on the Establishment of a Permanent Organization for the Improvement of the Law Proposing the Establishment of an American Law Institute*, 1 A.L.I. Proc. 1 (1923).
10. *See* N.E.H. Hull, *Restatement and Reform: A New Perspective on the Origins of the American Law Institute*, 8 LAW & HIST. REV. 55, 70–74 (1990); and the symposium in 32 S. ILL. UNIV. L.J. 1 (2007).
11. On Beale, *see* Chapter 7; *and* Symeon C. Symeonides, *The First Conflicts Restatement through the Eyes of Old: As Bad as Its Reputation?*, 32 S. ILL. UNIV. L.J. 39 (2007).
12. On this impulse in the first Restatement, *see* G. Edward White, THE CONSTITUTION AND THE NEW DEAL 170–74 (Cambridge, MA: Harvard Univ. Press, 2000).
13. Leon Green, *The Torts Restatement*, 29 Ill. L. Rev. 582 (1935).
14. Charles E. Clark, *The Restatement of the Law of Contracts*, 42 YALE L.J. 643, 647 (1933). For the reactions of other Legal Realists at Yale, *see* LAURA KALMAN, LEGAL REALISM AT YALE, 1927–1960, at 26–28 (Chapel Hill: Univ. of North Carolina Press, 1986).
15. Percy Bordwell, unpublished review, quoted in Clark, *supra* note 14, at 646–47 n.6; Percy Bordwell, *Restatement of the Law of Property*, 51 HARV. L. REV. 565, 569 (1938).
16. Myres S. McDougal, *Book Review*, 32 ILL. L. REV. 509 (1937) (reviewing first Restatement of Property).
17. Mitchell Franklin, *The Historical Function of the American Law Institute: Restatement as Transitional to Codification*, 47 HARV. L. REV. 1367 (1934).
18. Samuel Williston, *Written and Unwritten Law*, 17 A.B.A. J. 39, 41 (1931). On the Legal Realists' treatment of Williston, *see* Mark L. Movsesian, *Williston as Conservative-Pragmatist*, 32 S. ILL. U. L.J. 135, 137, 138 (2007).
19. *See* Grant Gilmore, THE DEATH OF CONTRACT 55–68 (Columbus: Ohio State Univ. Press, 1974); and Grant Gilmore, *Legal Realism: Its Cause and Cure*, 70 YALE L.J. 1037 (1961).
20. RESTATEMENT OF TORTS § 826 (1939).
21. Smith v. Staso Milling Co., 18 F.2d 736 (2d Cir. 1927).
22. Heppenstall Co. v. Berkshire Chem. Co., 11 Conn. Supp. 82 (Conn. Super. 1942), citing RESTATEMENT OF TORTS § 826 and Comment, *Injunction—Nuisance—Balance of Convenience*, 37 YALE L.J. 96 (1927).
23. *See* Walter P. Armstrong, JR., A CENTURY OF SERVICE: A CENTENNIAL HISTORY OF THE NATIONAL CONFERENCE OF COMMISSIONERS ON UNIFORM STATE LAWS (St. Paul, MN: West, 1991).
24. Swift v. Tyson, 41 U.S. (16 Pet.) 1, 18 (1842).
25. *See* William Schofield, *Uniformity of Law in the Several States as an American Ideal*, 21 HARV. L. REV. 510 (1908).
26. Robert Braucher, *The Legislative History of the Uniform Commercial Code*, 58 COLUM. L. REV. 798, 799 (1958).

27. William Twining, KARL LLEWELLYN, AND THE REALIST MOVEMENT 270–73, 313, 316 (London: Weidenfeld and Nicolson, 1973) (quotation on 316).
28. GILMORE, THE DEATH OF CONTRACT, *supra* note 19, at 94–95.
29. United States v. Carolene Prods., 304 U.S. 144, 152 & n.4 (1938).
30. Samuel D. Warren & Louis D. Brandeis, *The Right to Privacy*, 4 HARV. L. REV. 193 (1890).
31. Buchanan v. Warley, 245 U.S. 60 (1917).
32. Meyer v. Nebraska, 262 U.S. 390, 399 (1923).
33. Pierce v. Soc'y of Sisters, 268 U.S. 510 (1925).
34. Skinner v. Oklahoma, 316 U.S. 535 (1942).
35. 388 U.S. 1 (1967).
36. 381 U.S. 479 (1965).
37. Roe v. Wade, 410 U.S. 113 (1973).
38. Lawrence v. Texas, 539 U.S. 558 (2003), overruling Bowers v. Hardwick, 478 U.S. 186 (1986).
39. *See* Geoffrey P. Miller, *The True Story of Carolene Products*, 1987 SUP. CT. REV. 397.
40. Shelley v. Kraemer, 334 U.S. 1 (1948).
41. Black v. Cutter Labs., 351 U.S. 292 (1956). Chief Justice Warren and Justices Douglas and Black dissented.
42. Leon Green, *Tort Law Public Law in Disguise*, 38 TEX. L. REV. 1 (1959).
43. 3 J.L. & ECON. 1 (1960) (actually published in 1961). *See* the discussion *infra*.
44. HENRY M. HART, JR. & ALBERT M. SACKS, THE LEGAL PROCESS: BASIC PROBLEMS IN THE MAKING AND APPLICATION OF LAW (tent. ed., 1958).
45. Henry M. Hart, Jr., Albert M. Sacks, William N. Eskridge, Jr. & Philip P. Frickey, THE LEGAL PROCESS: BASIC PROBLEMS IN THE MAKING AND APPLICATION OF LAW (Westbury, NY: Foundation Press, 1994). *See* William N. Eskridge, Jr. & Philip P. Frickey, *The Making of the Legal Process*, 107 HARV. L. REV. 2031 (1994).
46. Herbert Wechsler, *Toward Neutral Principles of Constitutional Law*, 73 HARV. L. REV. 1 (1959). Hart and Wechsler's classic law school casebook is Henry M. Hart, Jr. & Herbert Wechsler, THE FEDERAL COURTS AND THE FEDERAL SYSTEM (Brooklyn, NY: Foundation Press, 1st ed., 1953).
47. Mayor & City Council v. Dawson, 350 U.S. 877 (1955) (per curiam) (beaches and bath houses); Muir v. Louisville Park Theatrical Ass'n, 347 U.S. 971 (1954) (per curiam) (city-sponsored operas).
48. Two forceful critiques, a generation apart, are Arthur S. Miller & Ronald F. Howell, *The Myth of Neutrality in Constitutional Adjudication*, 27 U. CHI. L. REV. 661 (1960); Mark V. Tushnet, *Following the Rules Laid Down: A Critique of Interpretivism and Neutral Principles*, 96 HARV. L. REV. 781 (1983).
49. *See* Alexander M. Bickel, *The Original Understanding and the Segregation Decision*, 69 HARV. L. REV. 1 (1955).
50. Alexander M. Bickel, THE LEAST DANGEROUS BRANCH: THE SUPREME COURT AT THE BAR OF POLITICS (Indianapolis, IN: Bobbs-Merrill, 1962).

51. James M. Landis, THE ADMINISTRATIVE PROCESS (New Haven, CT: Yale Univ. Press, 1938); JAMES M. LANDIS, REPORT ON REGULATORY AGENCIES TO THE PRESIDENT-ELECT (U.S.G.P.O, 1960). *See* Thomas McCraw, PROPHETS OF REGULATION: CHARLES FRANCIS ADAMS, LOUIS D. BRANDEIS, JAMES M. LANDIS, ALFRED E. KAHN (Cambridge, MA: Harvard Univ. Press, 1984).
52. *See* Walter Gellhorn, *The Administrative Procedure Act: The Beginnings*, 72 VA. L. REV. 219 (1986); Reuel E. Schiller, *Reining in the Administrative State: World War II and the Decline of Expert Administration*, *in* TOTAL WAR AND THE LAW: THE AMERICAN HOME FRONT IN WORLD WAR II 185, 186 (Daniel R. Ernst & Victor Jew eds., Westport, CT: Praeger, 2002).
53. *See Report* of The President's Committee on Administrative Management in the Government of the United States (U.S.G.P.O., 1937); and Donald R. Brand, *The President as Chief Administrator: James Landis and the Brownlow Report*, 123 POL. SCI. Q. 69 (2008); Elena Kagan, *Presidential Administration*, 114 HARV. L. REV. 2245 (2001).
54. Jones v. Sec. & Exchange Comm'n, 298 U.S. 1, 28 (1936).
55. LANDIS, REPORT ON REGULATORY AGENCIES, *supra* note 51, at 19, 50.
56. *The Federalist*, No. 10 (Nov. 22, 1787) (Madison).
57. Lincoln Steffens, THE STRUGGLE FOR SELF-GOVERNMENT: BEING AN ATTEMPT TO TRACE AMERICAN POLITICAL CORRUPTION TO ITS SOURCES IN SIX STATES OF THE UNITED STATES (New York: McClure, Phillips, 1906); Lincoln Steffens, THE SHAME OF THE CITIES (New York: McClure, Phillips, 1904).
58. Woodrow Wilson, *The Law and the Facts*, 5 AM. POL. SCI. REV. 1, 2 (1911).
59. *See* Shelton Stromquist, REINVENTING "THE PEOPLE": THE PROGRESSIVE MOVEMENT, THE CLASS PROBLEM, AND THE ORIGINS OF MODERN LIBERALISM (Urbana: Univ. of Illinois Press, 2006).
60. *See* Akhil Reed Amar, *The Bill of Rights as a Constitution*, 100 YALE L.J. 1131, 1164 n.152 (1991).
61. Arthur F. Bentley, THE PROCESS OF GOVERNMENT: A STUDY OF SOCIAL PRESSURES (Chicago: Univ. of Chicago Press, 1908). *See* Daniel T. Rodgers, CONTESTED TRUTHS: KEYWORDS IN AMERICAN POLITICS SINCE INDEPENDENCE 176–211 (New York: Basic, 1987).
62. Charles A. Beard, AN ECONOMIC INTERPRETATION OF THE CONSTITUTION OF THE UNITED STATES (New York: Macmillan, 1913).
63. Adolf A. Berle & Gardiner C. Means, THE MODERN CORPORATION AND PRIVATE PROPERTY (New York: Macmillan, 1933); *see* Chapter 9.
64. John R. Commons, THE ECONOMICS OF COLLECTIVE ACTION, esp. at 25–35 (New York: Macmillan, 1950).
65. *See, e.g.*, R.E. Dowling, *Pressure Group Theory: Its Methodological Range*, 54 AM. POL. SCI. REV. 944 (1960).
66. C. Wright Mills, THE POWER ELITE (New York: Oxford Univ. Press, 1956); Anthony Downs, AN ECONOMIC THEORY OF DEMOCRACY (New York: Harper

& Row, 1957); Robert Dahl, WHO GOVERNS? DEMOCRACY AND POWER IN AN AMERICAN CITY (New Haven, CT: Yale, 1961); and Robert A. Dahl & Charles E. Lindblom, POLITICS, ECONOMICS AND WELFARE: PLANNING AND POLITICO-ECONOMIC SYSTEMS RESOLVED INTO BASIC SOCIAL PROCESSES (New York: Harper, 1953).

67. A good survey is William C. Mitchell, *Political Science and Public Choice: 1950–70*, 98 PUB. CHOICE 237 (1999). A more technical study of the mathematical and economic approaches is Dennis C. Mueller, Public Choice III (New York: Cambridge Univ. Press, 3d ed., 2003). An excellent although now somewhat dated study is Daniel A. Farber & Philip P. Frickey, LAW AND PUBLIC CHOICE: A CRITICAL INTRODUCTION (Chicago: Univ. of Chicago Press, 1991).

68. Kenneth Arrow, SOCIAL CHOICE AND INDIVIDUAL VALUES (New York: Wiley, 1951; 2d ed. 1963); Mancur Olson, Jr., THE LOGIC OF COLLECTIVE ACTION: PUBLIC GOODS AND THE THEORY OF GROUPS (Cambridge, MA: Harvard Univ. Press, 1965); James M. Buchanan & Gordon Tullock, THE CALCULUS OF CONSENT: LOGICAL FOUNDATIONS OF CONSTITUTIONAL DEMOCRACY (Ann Arbor: Univ. of Michigan Press, 1962).

69. *See* Herbert Hovenkamp, *Arrow's Theorem: Ordinalism and Republican Government*, 75 IOWA L. REV. 949 (1990).

70. BUCHANAN & TULLOCK, THE CALCULUS OF CONSENT, *supra* note 68, at 15, 92, 95, 154–58.

71. Richard A. Epstein, TAKINGS: PRIVATE PROPERTY AND THE POWER OF EMINENT DOMAIN (Cambridge, MA: Harvard Univ. Press, 1985).

72. *See* OLSON, THE LOGIC OF COLLECTIVE ACTION, *supra* note 68, at 9–24, relying on Edward Chamberlin, THEORY OF MONOPOLISTIC COMPETITION (Cambridge, MA: Harvard Univ. Press, 1933). *See* the excellent treatment by Richard Tuck, FREE RIDING (Cambridge, MA: Harvard Univ. Press, 2008); and William C. Mitchell, *The Calculus of Consent: Enduring Contributions to Public Choice and Political Science*, 60 PUB. CHOICE 201 (1989). Much of the theory was developed in Richard A. Musgrave, THE THEORY OF PUBLIC FINANCE: A STUDY IN POLITICAL ECONOMY (New York: McGraw-Hill, 1957).

73. OLSON, THE LOGIC OF COLLECTIVE ACTION, *supra* note 68, at 24–28. *Cf.* BUCHANAN & TULLOCK, THE CALCULUS OF CONSENT, *supra* note 68, at 136.

74. *See* Lonnie K. Stevans, *The Effect of Endogenous Right-to-Work Laws on Business and Economic Conditions in the United States: A Multivariate Approach*, 5 REV. L. & ECON. 595 (2009).

75. *E.g.*, Romer v. Evans, 517 U.S. 620, 636 (1996) (Scalia, J., dissenting); Mertens v. Hewitt Assocs., 508 U.S. 248, 261–63 (1993); AT&T Corp. v. Iowa Utilities Bd., 525 U.S. 366 (1999); Pennell v. City of San Jose, 485 U.S. 1, 15 (1988) (Scalia, J., dissenting).

76. Chevron, U.S.A., Inc. v. Natural Resources Defense Council, Inc., 467 U.S. 837, 840–43 (1984).

77. Richard A. Posner, *The Chicago School of Antitrust Analysis*, 127 U. PA. L. REV. 925, 931 (1979).
78. Mark J. Green, THE CLOSED ENTERPRISE SYSTEM: RALPH NADER'S STUDY GROUP REPORT ON ANTITRUST ENFORCEMENT (New York: Grossman, 1972). Senator Hart's proposal is in S. 3832, 92d Cong., 2d Sess. (1972).
79. *E.g.*, Robert H. Bork & Ward S. Bowman, Jr., *The Crisis in Antitrust*, 65 COLUM. L. REV. 363 (1965); Robert H. Bork, *The Rule of Reason and the Per Se Concept: Price Fixing and Market Division* (pts. 1 & 2), 74 YALE L.J. 775 (1965), 75 YALE L.J. 373 (1966); Richard A. Posner, *Oligopoly and the Antitrust Laws: A Suggested Approach*, 21 STAN. L. REV. 1562 (1969).
80. On the Chicago School revolution, *see* THE MAKING OF COMPETITION POLICY: LEGAL AND ECONOMIC SOURCES 390–442 (Daniel Crane & Herbert Hovenkamp eds., New York: Oxford Univ. Press, 2013). Macroeconomics went through a similar revolution, recounted in Daniel T. Rodgers, AGE OF FRACTURE 47–78 (Cambridge, MA: Harvard Univ. Press, 2011).
81. INDUSTRIAL CONCENTRATION: THE NEW LEARNING (Harvey J. Goldschmid, H. Michael Mann & J. Fred Weston eds., Boston: Little, Brown, 1974).
82. *See* William H. Beveridge, THE LONDON SCHOOL OF ECONOMICS AND ITS PROBLEMS, 1919–1937 (London: Allen & Unwin, 1960); and Herbert Hovenkamp, *Coase, Institutionalism, and the Origins of Law and Economics*, 86 IND. L.J. 499 (2011).
83. 4 ECONOMICA 386 (1937); *see* Chapter 12.
84. RONALD COASE, *The Problem of Social Cost, supra*, note 43.
85. Lochner v. New York, 198 U.S. 45, 62 (1905).
86. Arthur C. Pigou, THE ECONOMICS OF WELFARE 296–99, 334 (London: Macmillan, 1st ed. 1920; 4th ed. 1932). On whether Coase characterized Pigou correctly, *see* A.W. Brian Simpson, *Coase v. Pigou Reexamined*, 25 J. LEGAL STUD. 53 (1996); Herbert Hovenkamp, *The Coase Theorem and Arthur Cecil Pigou*, 51 ARIZ. L. REV. 633 (2009).
87. Sturges v. Bridgman, 11 Ch.D. 852 (1877). The facts are detailed in Simpson, *Coase v. Pigou, supra* note 86.
88. *See* Oliver E. Williamson, MARKETS AND HIERARCHIES: ANALYSIS AND ANTITRUST IMPLICATIONS (New York: Free Press, 1975); Oliver E. Williamson, THE ECONOMIC INSTITUTIONS OF CAPITALISM (New York: Free Press, 1985). *See* Herbert Hovenkamp, *Harvard, Chicago and Transaction Cost Economics in Antitrust Analysis*, 55 ANTITRUST BULL. 613 (2010).
89. For an admiring history by a participant, *see* Edmund W. Kitch, *The Fire of Truth: A Remembrance of Law and Economics at Chicago, 1932–1970*, 26 J.L. & ECON. 163 (1983).
90. James M. Buchanan, *Politics, Policy, and the Pigovian Margins*, 29 ECONOMICA 17 (1962); James M. Buchanan, *The Relevance of Pareto Optimality*, 6 J. CONFLICT

RESOL. 341 (1962); Harold Demsetz, *Information and Efficiency: Another Viewpoint*, 12 J.L. & ECON. 1 (1969).

91. Guido Calabresi & A. Douglas Melamed, *Property Rules, Liability Rules, and Inalienability: One View of the Cathedral*, 85 HARV. L. REV. 1089 (1971).
92. *E.g.*, Robert C. Ellickson, *Alternatives to Zoning: Covenants, Nuisance Rules, and Fines as Land Use Controls*, 40 U. CHI. L. REV. 681 (1973); Edward Rabin, *Nuisance Law: Rethinking Fundamental Assumptions*, 63 VA. L. REV. 1299 (1977).
93. Allen V. Kneese, THE ECONOMICS OF REGIONAL WATER QUALITY MANAGEMENT (Baltimore: Johns Hopkins Press, 1964). *See* Steven G. Medema, THE CURIOUS TREATMENT OF THE COASE THEOREM IN ENVIRONMENTAL ECONOMICS, 1960–1979 (Working Paper, Dept. of Economics, Univ. of Colorado Denver, 2012); Ezra J. Mishan, *The Postwar Literature on Externalities: An Interpretive Essay*, 9 J. ECON. LITERATURE 1 (1971). *See also Coase Theorem Symposium* (pts. 1 & 2), 13 NAT. RESOURCES J. 557 (1973), 14 NAT. RESOURCES J. 1 (1974).
94. *E.g.*, Clean Air Act Amendments of 1990, Pub. L. No. 101-549, § 106, 104 Stat. 2399 (1990). An earlier example is exchangeable rights to include lead in gasoline, approved in 1982. *See* 47 Fed. Reg. 49,331 (1982). *See* Thomas H. Tietenberg, EMISSIONS TRADING: AN EXERCISE IN REFORMING POLLUTION POLICY (Washington, DC: Resources for the Future, 1985).
95. Guido Calabresi, THE COSTS OF ACCIDENTS: A LEGAL AND ECONOMIC ANALYSIS 26–31 (New Haven, CT: Yale, 1970); *see also* Richard A. Posner, ECONOMIC ANALYSIS OF LAW 78 (Boston: Little, Brown, 1972). *See* RESTATEMENT (SECOND) OF TORTS, particularly § 402a (1977).
96. POSNER, ECONOMIC ANALYSIS OF LAW, *supra* note 95, at 78.
97. *E.g.*, A. Mitchell Polinsky, *Economic Analysis as a Potentially Defective Product: A Buyer's Guide to Posner's Economic Analysis of Law*, 87 HARV. L. REV. 1655, 1680–81 (1974).
98. *E.g.*, George J. Stigler, *The Theory of Economic Regulation*, 2 BELL J. ECON. & MGMT. SCI. 3 (1971); Richard A. Posner, *Theories of Economic Regulation*, 5 BELL J. ECON. & MGMT. SCI. 335 (1974).
99. Stephen G. Breyer, REGULATION AND ITS REFORM (Cambridge, MA: Harvard Univ. Press, 1982). For a more critical history of deregulation, but focused more on environmental deregulation and less on transportation and telecommunications, *see* Thomas O. McGarity, FREEDOM TO HARM: THE LASTING LEGACY OF THE LAISSEZ FAIRE REVIVAL (New Haven, CT: Yale, 2013).
100. Bruce A. Ackerman & William T. Hassler, CLEAN COAL/DIRTY AIR, OR HOW THE CLEAN AIR ACT BECAME A MULTIBILLION-DOLLAR BAIL-OUT FOR HIGH-SULFUR COAL PRODUCERS AND WHAT SHOULD BE DONE ABOUT IT (New Haven, CT: Yale, 1981), reviewed by Jack L. Landau, 12 ENVTL. L. 271 (1981).
101. The history of banking and other financial deregulation is not discussed here. *See* Lawrence G. Goldberg & Lawrence J. White, THE DEREGULATION OF THE

BANKING AND SECURITIES INDUSTRIES (Frederick: MD: Beard Books, 2003); Charles W. Calomiris, U.S. BANK DEREGULATION IN HISTORICAL PERSPECTIVE (New York: Cambridge Univ. Press, 2000). For good writing on the link between the recent (at this writing) financial crisis and financial deregulation, *see* WHAT CAUSED THE FINANCIAL CRISIS (Jeffrey Friedman ed., Philadelphia: Univ. of Pennsylvania Press, 2011).

102. Motor Carrier Act of 1980; Motor Carrier Act of 1980, Pub. L. No. 96-296, 94 Stat. 793; Staggers Rail Act of 1980, Pub. L. No. 96-448, 94 Stat. 1895.
103. ALOHA AIRLINES, Inc. v. CAB, 598 F.2d 250, 254 (D.C. Cir. 1979).
104. Quoted in MCCRAW, PROPHETS OF REGULATION, *supra* note 51; *see* Alfred E. Kahn, THE ECONOMICS OF REGULATION: PRINCIPLES AND INSTITUTIONS (New York: Wiley, 1970).
105. Airline Deregulation Act of 1978, Pub. L. No. 95-504, 92 Stat. 1705. *See* Steven A. Morrison & Clifford Winston, THE EVOLUTION OF THE AIRLINE INDUSTRY (Washington, DC: Brookings, 1995).
106. CAB Sunset Act of 1984, Pub. L. No. 98-443, 98 Stat. 1703 (1984).
107. Hush-A-Phone v. United States, 238 F.2d 266 (D.C. Cir. 1956).
108. *In re* Carterfone, Inc., 13 F.C.C.2d 420 (1968).
109. MCI Commc'ns. Corp. v. AT&T, 708 F.2d 1081 (7th Cir.), *cert. denied*, 464 U.S. 891 (1983).
110. United States v. AT&T, 552 F. Supp. 131 (D.D.C. 1982). For an excellent history of deregulation in telecommunications and media, *see* Tim Wu, THE MASTER SWITCH: THE RISE AND FALL OF INFORMATION EMPIRES (New York: Vintage, 2011).
111. Village of Euclid v. Ambler Realty Co., 272 U.S. 365 (1926). For a brief history, *see* Stuart Banner, AMERICAN PROPERTY: A HISTORY OF HOW, WHY, AND WHAT WE OWN 183–92 (Cambridge, MA: Harvard Univ. Press, 2011).
112. The leading case is Southern Burlington County NAACP v. Mount Laurel Twp., 67 N.J. 151 (N.J. 1975).
113. Eves v. Zoning Bd. of Adjustment, 401 Pa. 211, 217 (1960).
114. *See* Fred W. Tuemmler, *Zoning for the Planned Community*, URB. LAND 3 (Apr. 1954).
115. Robert W. Burchell & James W. Hughes, PLANNED UNIT DEVELOPMENT: NEW COMMUNITIES AMERICAN STYLE 6–13, 41–43 (New Brunswick, NJ: Rutgers Univ. Press, 1972).
116. *See* Evan McKenzie, PRIVATOPIA: HOMEOWNER ASSOCIATIONS AND THE RISE OF RESIDENTIAL PRIVATE GOVERNMENT 8–11 (New Haven, CT: Yale, 1994); *and see* the contemporary essay by the chief land planner for the Department of Housing and Urban Development. Byron R. Hanke, *Planned Unit Development and Land Use Intensity*, 114 U. PA. L. REV. 15 (1965).
117. Buchanan v. Warley, 245 U.S. 60 (1917).
118. Corrigan v. Buckley, 271 U.S. 323 (1926).

119. Shelley v. Kraemer, 334 U.S. 1 (1948).
120. Neponsit Property Owners' Ass'n v. Emigrant Indus. Sav. Bank, 15 N.E.2d 793 (N.Y. 1938).
121. MCKENZIE, PRIVATOPIA, *supra* note 116, at 11.
122. Harvey Averch & Leland Johnson, *Behavior of the Firm under Regulatory Constraint*, 52 AM. ECON. REV. 1052 (1962).
123. Robert B. Reich, *Secession of the Successful*, N.Y. Times, Jan. 20, 1991, section 6 at 16.
124. Matthews v. Bay Head Improvement Ass'n, 95 N.J. 306, 471 A.2d 355 (N.J. 1984).

Index

www.ingramcontent.com/pod-product-compliance
Lightning Source LLC
LaVergne TN
LVHW091534200926
848483LV00002B/394
* 9 7 8 0 1 9 9 3 3 1 3 0 7 *